THE POWER
OF THE
MAYOR

To Hakeem Jeffries,

Best wishes,

Chris McNickle

THE POWER

OF THE

MAYOR

David
Dinkins
1990-1993

Chris McNickle

Transaction Publishers

New Brunswick (U.S.A.) and London (U.K.)

Library of Congress Catalog Number: 2012014738
ISBN: 978-1-4128-4959-3
Printed in the United States of America

Library of Congress Cataloging-in-Publication Data

McNickle, Chris.
The power of the mayor : David Dinkins, 1990-1993 / Christopher J. McNickle.
    p. cm.
  Includes bibliographical references.
  ISBN 978-1-4128-4959-3
    1.   Dinkins, David N. 2.   New York (N.Y.)--Politics and government--
  1951- 3.   Mayors--New York (State)--New York--History. I. Title.
F128.57.D56M36 2012
974.7'043092--dc23
[B]
                                                        2012014738

For Mom and for Mike

Contents

Acknowledgments

Mark Gallogly proved a loyal friend while I worked on this book. He read the manuscript cover to cover and offered detailed edits. Buddy Stein did the same with an earlier version at a time when I sorely needed an outside reader, and Sam Roberts also reviewed a draft of the manuscript and shared questions, suggestions, and insights.

Ken Jackson, Philip Leventhal, and Lisa Keller gave crucial encouragement at an early stage of this project. Ken Cobb's encyclopedic knowledge of the materials held in New York City's municipal archives and library served as a critical source of support. His colleague, David Ment, also located buried archival treasure. Fernando Ferrer, Stanley Litow, Lee Miringoff, John Mollenkopf, Joel Seigel, Alex Turetsky, and Rabbi Avraham Weiss shared with me materials or recollections not available in the public domain. I am grateful to them all.

The members of the Dinkins administration who allowed me to interview them were generous with their time. Police commissioner Raymond Kelly, deputy mayors Bill Lynch and Milton Mollen, budget director Philip Michael, director of operations Harvey Robins, and press secretary Albert Scardino provided firsthand information and insight. First deputy mayor Normal Steisel was especially helpful. Mr. Steisel and some others do not agree with my conclusions; they bear no responsibility for them. I alone own the interpretations.

Writing is a solitary endeavor. When so much time is spent alone, the company of family and friends becomes more important than ever. Litna, Danny, Cecily, Katie, Becky, and my brother Nick all cheered me on, as did Joe Lynch and Sheila Walters, and Alex Grimes, and Philip and Sarah Reyman during summer vacations. Fred Walters was my constant companion, as always. I am lucky to have them all in my life.

Introduction

Mayor David Dinkins

David Dinkins failed as mayor. His Tammany clubhouse heritage and his liberal political philosophy made him the wrong man for the times. His overly deliberate approach to decision making left the government he led lacking direction. His courtly demeanor and highly formal personal style, often a great strength, at crucial moments left the people he led feeling detached from their leader. An African American chief executive in a city nearly half of whose population was white, he never won the trust of more than a sliver of the race he displaced atop the city's totem pole of power, and that trust diminished over time. When David Dinkins governed, many New Yorkers felt adrift. They lacked confidence in their mayor's ability to wield the authority of his office with the skill required to run the city.

Fiscal solvency, public safety, and public education are three essential tasks of the mayor. David Dinkins balanced four budgets during a period of severe and prolonged economic distress, and he avoided a fiscal takeover, a threat that loomed during his entire term in office, by the unelected New York State Financial Control Board. Major crime dropped 14 percent from his first year to his last, and murders fell by more than 12 percent. He left the ungovernable school system he inherited no worse off than when he got it, and some of the policies initiated on his watch arguably set the stage for future successes. He had other achievements as well.[1]

Yet David Dinkins's administration managed its accomplishments in ways that diminished confidence in the mayor's ability to govern. Balanced budgets emerged from chaotic fiscal management, alienating Wall Street bankers and municipal union leaders alike. Policing policies left much of the city believing the mayor was too soft on crime and unsupportive of the cops who enforced the law. Even more distressing, many believed the mayor treated blacks and Latinos who broke the law one way and whites another. Mayor Dinkins participated actively in decisions that mired the Board of Education in a series of intractable cultural battles that distracted from its central task of promoting policies to educate the city's children. He lost control of the board, which declined to renew the contract of the chancellor he thought best qualified for the job.

When New Yorkers elected David Dinkins mayor in November 1989, a series of high-profile, racially charged events had rubbed city nerves raw. The worst crime wave in New York City history and the racial crosscurrents that accompanied it added to the tensions. A mounting fiscal crisis compounded a rising sense of despair. A school system responsible for teaching reading, writing, and arithmetic to nearly one million children—a scale unmatched anywhere in the nation—suffered from a fractured central Board of Education that overlapped with thirty-two substantially dysfunctional and often corrupt local school boards. The unworkable governance structure sat atop a mind-bogglingly broken bureaucracy that had been failing its students—two-thirds children of color, disproportionately poor, and disadvantaged—for years. Streets filled with overwhelming numbers of homeless, hospices filled with disheartening numbers of dying AIDS victims, inadequate health care for the poor, and an infrastructure in desperate need of repair added to New York City's woes and a sense that its social order risked complete collapse. "I wouldn't want the job for a billion dollars," David Dinkins's father told a journalist at the *Trenton Times* the year the city's voters elected his son mayor.[2]

David Dinkins's victory created hope. As borough president of Manhattan, he was the city's highest-ranking elected African American official. In a career that spanned more than a quarter of a century, he had built a reputation as a politician able to reach across New York's growing racial divide with unusual skill. His campaign pledge to restore harmony to the city provided the premise for his triumph over Edward Koch in the Democratic primary and over Rudolph Giuliani in the general election. African Americans and many other people of color believed one of their own—a man who understood them, their sometimes bitter legacy, and their compelling needs—would look after them. Whites who voted for him, and many who did not, shared a fervent desire that his ascent to power would calm racial crosscurrents, restore civility to the city, and help manage down the murder and mayhem afflicting New York. This is the historical moment when David Dinkins governed—a time when the people of a city torn by racial strife sought a leader who would unite them and command their government's resources fairly and wisely in response to the awesome challenges that lay before them.

Dinkins's election had national implications too. President George H. W. Bush sat in the White House, heir to the Reagan Revolution, which included a pledge to reduce the role of the federal government. Republicans launched policies to unravel Lyndon Johnson's Great Society programs, which above all intended to help people of color and other disadvantaged citizens to gain full access to the American Dream. George Bush's 1988 campaign for president included the infamous Willie Horton ad, featuring a black convict who raped a white woman during a weekend leave from a Massachusetts prison while Michael Dukakis, Bush's Democratic adversary, had been governor. The Republican candidate's transparent effort to scare whites into voting against his opponent dismayed many Americans who sought better from their leaders. The ad also reflected the racially polarized, national political climate of the times.[3]

In the midst of an environment that seemed increasingly hostile toward African Americans, the election of a black mayor for the first time in the country's premier metropolis—its most cosmopolitan and diverse city, a key arbiter of national tastes and television trends—took on special significance. David Dinkins's unusual stature as a politician who could credibly aspire to lead a multiracial coalition provided hope that the nation could produce leaders capable of guiding the country toward harmony instead of hostility. The contrast with Ed Koch was stark. By his third term, the outgoing mayor had become highly combative, loud, and obnoxious even by New York standards. His egregious comments on matters pertaining to race had alienated blacks, Latinos, and many whites as well. In tone, Dinkins struck people as the anti-Koch.[4]

For the first six months of his term, David Dinkins seemed poised to deliver on his promise. By temperament, he was a conciliator. When the city he led required a voice of reason to calm rising anger that threatened violence, his instincts served him well. The new mayor's unfailingly courteous public demeanor, his obvious, heartfelt compassion for people, his keen knowledge of city government, and his highly rational if excessively cautious approach to decision making for a time put New Yorkers at ease. He set about assembling his team and began to tend to municipal affairs in a competent, workmanlike fashion. To be sure, doubters existed from the start. Some thought their city simply ungovernable—too complex and too broken for anyone to manage. Others believed Dinkins lacked the right experience and temperament for the job. Some, sadly, saw the world through the dirty lens of racism and did not trust a black man with the power city voters gave him. Yet polls suggest that during his first months in office, more New Yorkers than elected him approved of the way Mayor Dinkins handled his job. The confidence would not last.[5]

A product of the Harlem outpost of Tammany Hall, the Manhattan Democratic political machine that rewarded patient loyalty with jobs and contracts, David Dinkins believed in the clubhouse rules that had helped make him mayor, and he sought to follow them. He tried to deliver generous wages and benefits to municipal unions that helped to elect him, at a time when a rolling budget crisis made the politically appealing action irresponsible. An urban liberal, he wanted to provide government social programs to the poor to compensate for the inherent inequalities of a market-based, capitalist society. The financial controls built after the fiscal crisis of the 1970s would render Dinkins's efforts to follow his political heritage and his philosophical instincts untenable. His clumsy management of the high-profile conflict that emerged between his administration, municipal unions, and the city's fiscal monitors damaged his credibility with power brokers and the city's financial elite, with its taxpayers, and with its social service advocates.

As a classic urban liberal, an African American one at that, Dinkins harbored reservations about the police powers of government. In his lifetime, law enforcement agencies had been used many times to support racially and politically suspect agendas. Bull Connor's Birmingham, Richard J. Daley's Chicago in 1968, and FBI wiretaps of Martin Luther King Jr. were all part of David Dinkins's political education. Closer to home, the controversial use of force by the NYPD against black New Yorkers like Michael Stewart and Eleanor Bumpers in the 1980s intensified feelings of distrust toward the police. With a horrific crime wave creating an unusual degree of fear among New Yorkers in the early 1990s, Dinkins's ambivalence toward aggressive police tactics damaged his credibility. Delays in hiring cops and a series of actions perceived as limiting the police in their ability to do their job—unsupportive and unappreciative of the daily risks they ran—gutted Dinkins's ability to convince people he was serious when he vowed to take back the city's streets by day and by night.

During his first month in office, African American protestors launched a boycott against two Korean groceries in Brooklyn and used intimidation tactics to scare shoppers away from the businesses. For months the police department, commanded by the mayor, refused to enforce a legal injunction ordering the demonstrators to stay fifty feet or more away from the stores. By the time the mayor and the police department acted, many Asians and whites had come to doubt that the city's black mayor would defend them fairly. In August 1991, riots broke out in the polarized neighborhood of Crown Heights, long a place of intense friction between Hasidic Jews and blacks. For several terrifying days the mayor and the police failed to react with the urgency the situation demanded, irreparably damaging public confidence in David Dinkins's ability to maintain order. In July 1992, an undercover officer killed a suspected drug dealer in the Dominican neighborhood of Washington Heights. Witnesses declared the shooting a cold-blooded murder, and protests escalated into civil unrest. Dinkins sought to keep the peace by showing compassion for the family of the slain man, but an investigation revealed the suspect had indeed been a dangerous criminal who had threatened the cop's life. The mayor meant to signal to the city's Latinos that his government would protect them from police abuse. In the mind of the cops, he demonstrated that he would not support them if they used force against people of color, no matter how justified. A police riot laced with racism followed a few weeks later on the steps of City Hall. The scene created the image of a civilian leader who had lost control over the law enforcement agency he relied on to maintain social order.

David Dinkins was capable of decisive action, but more typically he hesitated. He demonstrated an inherent caution and a highly dispassionate and unemotional approach to decision making that served him well in his Harlem clubhouse but not in City Hall. Historian Arthur Mann, describing Tammany's greatest leader, Charles F. Murphy, and his cronies for a generation who did not know them, called them a "dour" crew, "cold, distant, reticent men." Fifty years later, *New York Times* journalist Sam Roberts would describe David Dinkins as "taciturn, almost dour." The common description is telling. Seven decades separate Murphy in his prime from David Dinkins's election as mayor, but the two were of a type. Tammany trained its leaders to deliver tangible benefits to voters in return for the power to reward themselves and loyal followers with jobs and contracts. They kept their own counsel and avoided making decisions that could alienate followers until forced to act.[6]

The leader of a government, however, must provide direction. He must set priorities and communicate them, anticipate events and react to them at the pace they demand. Again and again observers would criticize Mayor Dinkins for taking too long to decide important matters. His commissioners and deputies complained they could not get the guidance they needed to run their departments properly. Dinkins "won't make decisions until he absolutely has to," and "often won't tell his commissioners or the public what he really thinks, and then complains that people don't understand him or do what he wants," journalist Todd Purdum wrote of the mayor in 1993. Mayor Dinkins's unwillingness at times to commit left competing views and priorities inside his administration in a halting stalemate. Unresolved feuds among deputy mayors caused a sense of "complete disarray and disorganization . . . a sense that nobody was controlling anything," one city commissioner complained.[7]

Tammany leaders could be emotionless. But the mayor of New York is the human point where the collective consciousness of the city's millions of people comes together in a single person. He must read the public mood and respond to it to give expression to citywide emotions. When a series of dispiriting acts of violence caused a surge of fear and anxiety throughout the city, David Dinkins issued dispassionate pleas for patience and perspective while his police department analyzed their needs and developed a comprehensive plan. His urge for calm backfired. New York's tabloids—reflecting the will of an enraged public—erupted in an agonized, collective cry for action. Journalists of nearly all stripes attacked the mayor for not acting more swiftly and forcefully to repel the intolerable levels of crime, and they scolded him for not expressing the city's outrage. Dinkins proved unwilling or unable to absorb the city's anger and then dissolve it with rapid and powerful symbolic and substantive action. Many people felt detached from their mayor.[8]

While Dinkins governed, the central school board became the stage for cultural collision between liberal and conservative visions of New York. A proposed curriculum that promoted tolerance for gay lifestyles and a plan for school health officials to distribute condoms to protect teenagers from contracting AIDS drew protests from Catholics and other conservative groups. Attitudes toward homosexuality dominated the debate, and the seven adults charged with the responsibility for overseeing the schooling of young New Yorkers, instead of making education policy, traded recriminations and public insults. The battle further polarized an already divided city, and the mayor lost control of the board.

Mayor Dinkins's strong stands at the school board were at odds with his innate caution but consistent with his liberal convictions. He adopted his positions with uncompromising intensity before establishing consensus in support of them, even though confronting issues so heavily charged with religious emotion was sure to generate intense resistance among a large enough group to divide the city. The mayor allowed the dispassionate logic of protecting teenagers from AIDS to steer him, without allowance for the danger public emotions can create for implementation of a policy. An admirer once described President Franklin Roosevelt as leading the country by letting it get out in front of him. The most successful politicians possess the preternatural instinct to know when the critical point has been reached that public opinion will drive their policies forward with sustained momentum.

New York City government does much more than provide fiscal solvency, public safety, and public education. David Dinkins modified and followed through on a far-reaching program Mayor Koch launched to provide affordable housing for the city. He recast the way government thought about helping its neediest citizens—the homeless—by restructuring and refocusing the office responsible for providing them with services. Health care for the poor underwent a substantial renovation on his watch, which caused improved access to medical treatment for impoverished New Yorkers and created a smarter financial structure as well. More managerial efficiencies occurred during his administration with more effective oversight of city resources than people realized. With exceptional skill, Dinkins defused potentially violent emotions surrounding the trials of eight white youths for the racially motivated murder of a young black man named Yusuf Hawkins in Brooklyn. When riots broke out in Los Angeles and elsewhere in the country after a jury acquitted a group of white cops videotaped beating a black man named Rodney King, David Dinkins kept the peace in New York. Mayor Dinkins has received less credit for these things than he should because they live in the shadows of the way he led the city on the essential tasks that matter most and because he failed to fulfill his promise of guiding the city to racial harmony.

Notes

1. *Statistical Report, Complaints and Arrests,* New York City Police Department, Office of Management Analysis and Planning, Crime Analysis Unit, 1990–1993.

2. John T. McQuiston, "William Dinkins, Mayor's Father and Real Estate Agent, Dies at 85," *New York Times,* October 19, 1991.

3. Lou Cannon, *President Reagan: The Role of a Lifetime* (New York: Public Affairs, 2000), 66–69; Timothy Naftali, *George H. W. Bush* (New York: Holt & Company, Times Books, 2007), 61–62.

4. Jeffrey S. Adler, "Running for Office: African American Mayors from 1967 to 1996," in David R. Colburn and Jeffrey S. Adler, eds., *African-American Mayors* (Urbana and Chicago: University of Illinois Press, 2005), 1–22.

5. The Marist Institute for Public Opinion, "Dinkins Approval Rating." March 1990, in possession of the author courtesy of the Marist Institute and Lee Miringoff; "Remarks by Mayor David N. Dinkins, Annual Dinner of the Reveille Club, Holiday Inn Grand Plaza West 49th Street and Broadway, Manhattan," June 16, 1990, in New York City Municipal Archives, Office of the Mayor, David N. Dinkins, Speeches, Microfilm Roll #10; Joe Klein, "The Real Deficit: Leadership." *New York,* July 22, 1991, 20–25.

6. William L. Riordan, *Plunkitt of Tammany Hall* (New York: E. P. Dutton, 1963), Introduction by Arthur Mann, ix; Sam Roberts, e-mail communication with the author, March 30, 2011.

7. Todd S. Purdum, "Buttoned Up," *New York Times Sunday Magazine,* September 12, 1993, online version.

8. David Siefman, "City's Latest Crime Shocker Fails to Stir Mayor's Anger," *New York Post,* September 5, 1990; Editorial, "Where Are the Voices of Outrage?" *New York Post,* September 6, 1990; Front Page, "Dave, Do Something," *New York Post,* September 7, 1990; Jerry Nachman, "Do-Nothing Dave Dinkins," *New York Post,* September 7, 1990; Sam Roberts, "Metro Matters; Dinkins Style and the Pressure to Sound Tough," *New York Times* (hereafter, *NYT*), September 10, 1990; Ed Koch, "It's Time to Take off the White Gloves," *New York Post,* September 7, 1990; Ray Kerrison, "Do Nothing Dave Dinkins: His Approach to Crime Crisis Is Alarming," *New York Post,* September 7, 1990.

1

Scandal, Race, and the Seeds of Victory[1]

Mayor Edward I. Koch never wore an overcoat, but in January 1989, winter winds chilled him colder than ever before. Private polls revealed the popularity rating of New York's most powerful politician for over a decade had sunk to 17 percent—lower than even John Lindsay's at his worst.[2] Elected mayor in 1977—his lifelong political ambition—through hard work, tough decisions, and force of personality, Koch rescued New York from the brink of bankruptcy, where it teetered at the time of his inauguration on January 1, 1978. That day, he declared New York had "been shaken by troubles that would have destroyed any other city. But we are not any other city. We are the City of New York, and New York in adversity towers above any other city in the world."[3]

Municipal coffers sat nearly empty the day Koch took office, drained by a fiscal crisis so severe that the state forced the city to surrender budget control to a special board of unelected officials controlled by the governor. The impact of several years of layoffs and budget cuts, service reductions, and protests had left their mark. New Yorkers found themselves dispirited, lacking energy, and suffering from unaccustomed fatigue. Koch responded. He extolled New York's nightlife, its culture, the excitement of its streets, and the remarkable diversity of its people. He made a show of eating in restaurants around town, praising his favorites publicly. He emphasized how much more New York did for its citizens than most other municipalities, even as he insisted on fiscal austerity. He rode the subways and asked the passengers, "How'm I doing?" with an energy that sparked the riders.

Koch spoke to the public in terms so informal they bordered on the vulgar. He dismissed his detractors as kooks, nuts, wackos, and crazies. When asked why he did not support one program or another, he offered his favorite reply: "Because I'm not a schmuck." So successful was Koch's first term, so grateful were New Yorkers to the man who led them from financial darkness, that the light of renewed hope dispersed all opposition. In an unprecedented display of political muscle, Koch sought and won both the Democratic and Republican nominations for mayor in 1981. Never before had anyone dared. Koch coasted to victory by a wider margin than any candidate in history. Four years later, with the economy in recovery and the city that had flirted with bankruptcy displaying a $500 million budget surplus, Koch ran for reelection again. The outcome seemed never in doubt. In 1985, he won his third term by a margin as lopsided as the victory for his second.[4]

The trouble began almost instantly afterward.

Within weeks of Mayor Koch's triumphant third inauguration, a highway patrol unit discovered Queens borough president Donald Manes weaving his car dangerously across the Grand Central Parkway. The powerful politician and ally of the mayor had slit his wrists. At first, Manes concocted a story about a mugging, but then confessed from his hospital bed that he had tried to end his own life. Soon afterwards the distraught man plunged a knife into his own chest in the kitchen of his home. He died as his horrified wife and daughter tried bravely but helplessly to revive him. The politician was corrupt, and he had fallen despondent from the unbearable burden of the discovery of his guilt by US Attorney Rudolph Giuliani. Manes's fatal decision ended the investigation into his actions. For dozens of politicians and city government workers, it was just the beginning.

In the months that followed, a remarkable series of revelations left the city numb. Donald Manes, Bronx Democratic County leader Stanley Friedman, Bronx congressman Mario Biaggi, Bronx borough president Stanley Simon, Brooklyn's recently retired boss Meade Esposito, and a host of less well-known city government officials found themselves indicted, tried, and convicted of bribery, extortion, thievery, influence peddling, and other crimes. The arrogance of the men stunned New Yorkers. In his law office, Stanley Friedman proudly hung a sign that read, "Crime does not pay . . . as well as politics." The city's atrophied Democratic machine could still muster enough power to enrich dozens of petty local politicians.[5]

Koch felt betrayed by his cronies, but the city felt betrayed by the mayor. No one doubted that Koch had never stolen from city coffers, but few found interesting the mayor's defense that the villains were independent of him. To be sure, the main culprits held elected public or party offices that they won on their own accounts. But the mayor had maintained close relationships with the county leaders and many of the others caught up in the scandals. He had been personal friends with Donald Manes and Stanley Friedman for nearly twenty years. Koch had praised them publicly, endorsed them and their candidates, and helped them to raise money for their campaigns. He had appointed their political workers to responsible government jobs, jobs they used to loot the city.

The mayor fell from grace particularly hard because of the image he had brought with him when first elected. He had declared himself the outsider, the radical reformer, the man who had battled and defeated Tammany's Carmine DeSapio when the boss staged his political comebacks in 1963 and 1965. As a candidate, Koch had vowed to throw out his predecessor's clubhouse politics. As mayor, he had attacked corruption in poverty programs with a vengeance, and he had established himself as Mr. Clean. New Yorkers close to city politics knew that Koch worked shrewdly with the boroughs' Democratic organizations. But to the average citizen, the intimacy of the ties and the ultimate consequences shocked and offended.

The scandals damaged the mayor's public standing, and they weakened him personally too. Joe DeVincenzo, a longtime aide and Koch's chief patronage distributor, shredded documents that he thought might embarrass his boss. The cover-up did more harm to the mayor than the evidence it sought to conceal—that the administration took job recommendations from the county leaders. The revelations went on and on, shattering the mayor's confidence in some of his closest colleagues and friends. At times the beleaguered chief executive had no recourse but to sit by himself in Gracie Mansion and cry. He even contemplated suicide. In the summer of 1985, the mayor suffered a "tiny, trivial" stroke. Many thought the unrelenting pressures of his job compounded by the weight of the scandals were proving too much for the sixty-two-year-old man.[6]

Other things soured as well. A series of scandals surfaced in New York's financial industry as startling as the revelations crippling New York's politicians. Prosecutor Giuliani's office found case upon case of insider trading and organized cheating at the most successful houses on Wall Street. Ivan Boesky, a man with a reputation as a remarkably shrewd investor, turned out to be a crook. He went to trial and jail, as did Michael Milken, the celebrated creator of the junk bond market. Enough Wall Street bankers at enough firms turned out to have engaged in illegal activities that New Yorkers began to wonder if all of the rich and powerful men in the city were corrupt.[7]

In October 1987, the stock market crashed. The relentless upward motion of share prices that had helped carry the profits of Wall Street to dizzying heights finally broke, and a profound reassessment of the strength and direction of the city's financial industry occurred. The future looked hard in comparison to the easy money of the past. Fragile firms collapsed while stronger ones began to lay off staff. Bonuses and salaries dropped as precipitously as market indices. Cooperative apartments and condominiums bought when salaries pushed endlessly upward suddenly became unaffordable. The luxury residences under construction no longer had eager potential owners waiting in line to buy them. The need for office space declined, and the city had an enormous and overpriced glut. Building construction stopped, construction workers lost their jobs, and real estate developers sweated as they assessed their finances. New York's upbeat mood faded, and Koch's triumphant return of the city to fiscal health began to appear ephemeral.

In the winter of 1986, three black New Yorkers suffered car trouble in the Howard Beach section of Queens, a white middle-class neighborhood. They left their automobile to seek help. A group of local teenagers crossed paths with the three men. Without provocation the youths beat the black men with bats and fists, and chased one, Michael Griffiths, onto a parkway where a passing motorist struck and killed him. Racial bigotry and the vicious fear it creates appeared to be the sole motivation for the conflict that led to the death of an innocent black man and the brutal beatings of two others. Mayor Koch, likening the event to a modern day lynching, vowed that it would be punished. Police arrested the attackers, but black militants Al Sharpton, C. Vernon Mason, and Alton H. Maddox Jr. saw a chance to use the tragedy for their own purposes.

Professional provocateurs, Sharpton, Mason, and Maddox made their careers by fanning racial flames in an effort to create heat so intense it would melt the rules of a society they believed institutionally racist. The three militants got themselves appointed advisers to the victims' families and convinced the survivors not to cooperate with Queens district attorney John Santucci. Blacks claimed they could never expect a fair trial from the "system," and they demanded that the governor appoint a special prosecutor to try the case. Their rhetoric was inflammatory and divisive, their legal tactics obstructionist. Ultimately, Governor Mario Cuomo negotiated the appointment of Charles J. Hynes as special prosecutor. An Irish Catholic New Yorker whose background included a stint as a state special prosecutor, Hynes rapidly and competently brought the assailants to justice, winning convictions and substantial prison sentences. Sharpton claimed the protests he led forced the outcome—without the pressure he and his collaborators applied, the assailants would have walked free, he declared. Others thought the militants simply escalated and exacerbated destructive racial tensions.[8]

The hot racial embers of the Howard Beach trial had not quite cooled by November 1987, when a young black teenager named Tawana Brawley from Dutchess County, New York, declared that a gang of white men, including law enforcement officials, had abducted her and raped her repeatedly over the span of four days. It had nothing to do with New York City, but the accusations generated publicity, and Sharpton, Mason and Maddox drove to the girl's home. Once again, they succeeded in having themselves appointed advisers to the family. Mason and Maddox publicly accused the Dutchess County assistant district attorney of raping Brawley. They likened New York State attorney general Robert Abrams to Adolph Hitler, and Mason declared that the mild-mannered, balding Abrams had masturbated over photographs of the young girl. They went on and on with their wild, unsubstantiated accusations. They once again convinced the family not to cooperate. When officials subpoenaed Tawana Brawley's mother, Glenda, the three men brought her into New York City and offered her sanctuary in a Queens church, creating a media extravaganza. The militants issued demands, held press conferences, and refused to cooperate with any formal agents of justice.

It was all a hoax. Tawana Brawley was a troubled teenager whose stepfather frightened her. She had played hooky from school to visit her boyfriend in prison and feared her stepfather would punish her severely if he found out. She had stayed away from home to avoid confronting what she had done and to escape her stepfather's wrath, and she invented a story upon her return to hide the truth. The advisers had known it almost from the start, but to them it did not matter. They played on and exacerbated the racial tension of the city because it suited them temperamentally and philosophically—and because they made their living at it.[9]

By 1988, race relations in New York were as bad as any time in memory when presidential politics brought the Democratic contenders to town. The field of significant candidates had narrowed to three by April when New York State Democrats went to the polls to vote for Michael Dukakis, Jesse Jackson, or Albert Gore. By then, Dukakis led the national contest for his party's nomination, but Jesse Jackson's campaign sparked the hopes of the country's racial minorities as it had four years before. In 1984, a number of New York's black leaders had backed Walter Mondale over Jackson. By 1988, Jackson's candidacy had become a litmus test of racial loyalty among African American politicians. All of New York's senior black political spokesmen, and most of the Puerto Ricans as well, strongly supported Jackson. Many of the city's largest labor unions, heavily populated by blacks and Latinos, also endorsed Jackson and mobilized their members on his behalf.

The shadow of Jesse Jackson's links to anti-Semites followed the black man as he campaigned around the city that was home to more Jews than any other in the nation. At one point, a journalist asked Koch about Jackson's support among Jewish voters. "Jews and other supporters of Israel would have to be crazy to vote for Jackson," the mayor responded in his typical blunt style. The comment enraged blacks and offended Jews. Most New Yorkers found the comment egregiously antagonistic in a city already struggling to maintain racial harmony.[10]

Koch endorsed Tennessee senator Al Gore, who on primary day won only 11 percent of the vote in New York City. Jackson won a stunning 45 percent of the vote within the five boroughs, a razor-thin plurality over Dukakis, who ran much stronger upstate and won the primary. City politicians found the results telling. An African American candidate, supported by a solid coalition of black and Latino politicians, with strong help from organized labor, had won a citywide vote. More than nine blacks out of ten voted for Jackson, more than 60 percent of Latino voters cast ballots for him, and a small but crucial number of white liberals completed his coalition. If the vote could be duplicated in a race for mayor, Koch could be defeated.[11]

Notes

1. This chapter is excerpted from Chris McNickle, *To Be Mayor of New York: Ethnic Politics in the City* (New York: Columbia University Press, 1993).
2. Andy Logan, "Around City Hall," *The New Yorker*, January 2, February 13, 1989.
3. Lee Dembart, "Koch in Inaugural, Asks that 'Pioneers' 'Come East' to City," *NYT*, January 2, 1978.
4. Arthur Browne, Dan Collins, and Michael Goodwin, *I, Koch: A Decidedly Unauthorized Biography of the Mayor of New York City, Edward I. Koch* (New York: Dodd, Mead & Company, 1985), 162–67; Edward I. Koch, *Mayor: An Autobiography* (New York: Warner Books, 1985), 63.

5. Jack Newfield and Wayne Barrett, *City for Sale: Ed Koch and the Betrayal of New York* (New York: Harper, 1988), *passim.*

6. Koch, "How'd I Do?" *New York Times Sunday Magazine*, December 31, 1989; "New York and Region: The Jurors Judge: How Sukhreet Gabel Hurt the Prosecution," December 22, 1988.

7. James B. Stewart, *Den of Thieves* (New York: Simon & Schuster, 1991), *passim.*

8. Jim Sleeper, *The Closest of Strangers: Liberalism and the Politics of Race in New York* (New York: Norton, 1990), 138–40, 184–88; Al Sharpton and Anthony Walton, *Go and Tell Pharaoh: The Autobiography of the Reverend Al Sharpton* (New York: Doubleday), 119, 133.

9. Robert D. McFadden, et al., *Outrage: The Story Behind the Tawana Brawley Hoax* (New York: Bantam Books, 1990), *passim;* Al Sharpton wrote in his autobiography: "As far as I'm personally concerned, the Brawley case comes down to this: some believe, some disbelieve, and I don't know if the definitive truth will ever be known. I examined this case, and in my best judgment, I believe I came to the right conclusion." Sharpton and Walton, *Go and Tell Pharoah*, 138, 140.

10. Joyce Purnick, "Koch Says Jackson Lied About Actions After Dr. King Was Slain," *NYT,* April 18, 1988.

11. Jeffrey Schmalz, "New York: 'Melting Pot' Yielding to 'Boiling Pot,'" *NYT,* April 21, 1988.

2

A City in Search of Harmony[1]

Not long after Jesse Jackson left town, New York politicians began talking about David Dinkins. As the borough president of Manhattan, he was New York's senior black elected official, and he possessed three attributes that made him particularly attractive to a disparate group of politicians looking for an African American candidate to back for mayor in 1989. As the product of a political clubhouse, he could be counted on to reward his supporters. In a city searching for harmony, he had a low-key and courteous style that contrasted sharply with Koch's confrontational bluster. And while he had an unblemished record of supporting minority causes, he did not practice the kind of protest politics that scared white voters away from candidates of color. To the contrary, throughout his career Dinkins had been a steady supporter of Israel and had been one of the few black politicians to condemn anti-Semitic remarks emanating from the likes of Nation of Islam leader Louis Farrakhan. Dinkins could appeal to Jewish liberals in a way few other black politicians in New York could and therefore had the potential to hold together a coalition to defeat Koch.[2]

I. David Dinkins Rising

David Norman Dinkins's career was a study in the slow, predictable rise a competent soldier of a political machine could achieve. He was born in Trenton, New Jersey, on July 10, 1927. His father, William, had come north a year earlier from Newport News, Virginia, and took on odd jobs before opening a barber shop. Later he developed success-ful real estate and insurance businesses. When David was in the first grade his mother, Sally, also from Newport News, left her husband and took her son and his younger sister, Joyce, to live in Harlem with their grandmother. "It was one of those things," William Dinkins once told an interviewer, the only public explanation of the split that ended formally some years later with a divorce. William Dinkins eventually remarried, wedding a school teacher named Lottie. "I didn't want that to happen," David Dinkins remembered. "I thought I would die." Like so many children of divorce, he hoped his parents would reconcile and restore family harmony. At the age of fourteen, David returned to Trenton with his sister. Their mother found working as a maid in a Manhattan hotel and raising two children at the same time too great a challenge, and the well-established father, who lived in a comfortable house, had more resources to offer the children. David developed loving relationships with his stepmother and father as well as with his mother.[3]

David Dinkins had pluck from the start. As a child in Harlem, he bought shopping bags two for a nickel and sold them for three cents apiece. Back in Trenton, he took on a paper route, boosting profits by selling peanuts to his subscribers. When he and friends sent a softball through the window of a home on the street where they played, the others ran. David rang the doorbell to apologize and tell the owner his father would pay for the repair. "[T]hat's how he was," the elder Dinkins said of his son. "He was always the kind of kid that, as a parent, you could look up to."[4]

The separation of Dinkins's parents had an impact on his upbringing. So did the separation of America. The public high school David attended, 95 percent white, did not allow blacks to use the pool. Such was the cruel custom in segregated America. Other teams would have declined to compete with a school that violated this policy. In 1945, while World War II raged, Dinkins graduated with a series of honors, one of the top ten students in his class. Several times he sought to enlist in the marines on the theory that "the best way to survive is to be well trained," but the quota for "Negro" recruits was filled. Finally, an opening occurred. By the time he finished boot camp, the war had ended. Still, the experience had a lasting impact. Stationed at Camp Lejeune, North Carolina, from July 1945 to August 1946, Dinkins tasted the Jim Crow South, and it left its bitter flavor in his mouth. "They weren't making white and black bullets," he said of the indiscriminate risk of death all marines faced, while second-class status seemed to define other aspects of his service. The fierce bigotry directed toward him and other African Americans who volunteered to protect the nation's freedom made him angry.[5]

When he left the marines, Dinkins took advantage of the GI bill and enrolled in Howard University in Washington, DC, his stepmother's alma mater. The school was the citadel of the country's all-black colleges. Living and studying in the nation's capital—the seat of American government created to protect the country's liberties—Dinkins found himself sent with other African Americans to the back of the bus, directed to different water fountains from the ones reserved for whites, and allowed to sit only in the balcony of theaters. Once he donned a turban and claimed to be a foreign diplomat to gain access to the main seats at the movies. The experiences made a lasting impression.[6]

At Howard, Dinkins majored in mathematics, joined Alpha Phi Alpha fraternity, and took up tennis, which became a lifelong passion. After receiving his diploma with honors in 1950, he entered a graduate program in math at Rutgers but soon dropped it. "I didn't love mathematics the way you have to nor have the sheer genius you need," he realized, so he took a job selling insurance instead, at which he excelled. At Howard, he also met Joyce Burrows. "He was carrying a calculus book," his future wife remembered of their first encounter. "I was very impressed." In 1953, they wed. The announcement in the *Amsterdam News* makes it clear David Dinkins married into Harlem royalty. It described their wedding event as "one of the most elaborate . . . of the Summer Season," attended by eight hundred guests, including Mayor Vincent Impelleteri and his wife, "at fashionable St. Martin's Episcopal Church," with a reception at the Renaissance Ballroom in Harlem. "The radiant bride . . . entered the chapel . . . attired in a Gladys I. David creation of white silk satin and imported Alencon lace, reembroidered with silver thread," the notice reported. "On the eve of the wedding the bride and her wedding party were dinner guests at Las Sabados Club at the Hotel Theresa," and a wedding shower took place aboard a yacht called *The Phantom*.[7]

The couple moved to Harlem, where Dinkins's father-in-law, a successful local businessman, had been a New York State assemblyman. That same year Dinkins entered Brooklyn Law School, attending classes by day and working at his father-in-law's liquor store at night to pay the bills. He earned his degree in 1956 and became an attorney.[8]

Dinkins had married into a political family, and like many young lawyers he realized that political activity could help his professional practice. With his law career the primary motivation at first, he joined the Carver Democratic Club run by legendary leader J. Raymond Jones, the Harlem Fox. Dinkins became a loyal worker, particularly active in voter registration campaigns, and eventually became a captain in the local machine Jones managed with such skill that in 1964 Mayor

Robert Wagner made him head of the Manhattan Democratic Party, Tammany Hall. Jones was the first black to hold the post in the organization whose roots dated back to 1789.[9]

Black New Yorkers, like African Americans in other regions of the country, had once been loyal to the Republican Party. Effectively disfranchised between 1821 and 1870 in New York, blacks cast their ballots solidly for Republicans after Lincoln's slave-freeing party passed the Fifteenth Amendment to the Constitution and secured them the right to vote. Even before they developed an attachment to the Grand Old Party (GOP), the group felt little love for the Irish-dominated Democratic organization that had administered the denial of black political rights for nearly half a century. Moreover, blacks and Irish often competed for manual labor during the nineteenth century, creating antagonism between the outsiders seeking recognition and the people who ruled the city's dominant party. [10]

Coldly calculating politicians saw little reason to pay much attention to the sixty thousand blacks scattered throughout the five boroughs at the turn of the century. Just a few drops in a sea of nearly three and half million people and without a neighborhood of great concentration to focus the mind of a local candidate, African Americans counted for little in the ethnic arithmetic of city politics. In 1897, a group of ambitious black men decided that the Republicans took their people's vote for granted and established the United Colored Democracy (UCD), a citywide unit intended to give blacks some political clout. Boss Richard Croker recognized the organization according to Tammany's unwritten rules: "We can treat the colored people in proportion to their work, and give them patronage in accordance with their merit and representation," he informed the UCD. He kept his word, but with so few blacks in New York, and most remaining loyal to Tammany's opposition, the group did not go far.[11]

Blacks began migrating north in large numbers after 1890, when a postslave generation fleeing the brutality of Jim Crow and the poverty of the South looked for work in America's major economic centers. The process accelerated during World War I, which generated a great demand for labor. The influx of black men and women into New York coincided with a real estate bust in Harlem, at the time a decidedly upper-crust quarter, but one with a noticeable minority of blacks living on its periphery. Unrented apartments built for the city's elite became homes for the migrants, who could afford to live in them only by piling an extraordinary number of paying tenants into each. More and more, Harlem became a black neighborhood, and as waves of African Americans continued to arrive, its size grew.[12]

Harlem gave blacks an identifiable political base, and during the first three decades of the twentieth century, party professionals begrudgingly made room for a few of their numbers in elected and appointed offices. But the clubhouses stayed segregated, in keeping with the bigotry of the times, and Democratic machine workers did little to attract blacks to their organization. As late as 1932, when the nation rejected the party of the Great Depression in favor of Franklin D. Roosevelt, blacks still voted overwhelmingly for the Republican candidate. Then came the New Deal with its alphabet soup of job programs, relief assistance, and other tangible benefits. Starving worse than their neighbors as a consequence of the nation's economic catastrophe, blacks developed an unshakeable loyalty to the man in the White House who offered them work, food, and hope. First Lady Eleanor Roosevelt's tireless and uncompromising commitment to civil rights strongly reinforced the devotion of the black community to the president. In 1936, there occurred a political migration of profound import as blacks, for six decades solidly Republican voters, moved into the Democratic Party with the force of an earthquake. They remain there to this day.[13]

In New York City, blacks perceived Mayor Fiorello LaGuardia as the voice of the New Deal and their protector. They continued to cast their ballots for him even as they developed an allegiance to the party that opposed him. When LaGuardia passed from the scene, black votes landed on the Democratic line in local as well as national elections. In 1930, 327,000 blacks lived in New York, less than 5 percent of the population. By 1950, three-quarters of a million African Americans lived within the five boroughs, representing nearly one in every ten inhabitants. Black communities existed in Brooklyn and were developing in the Bronx, but one-fifth of the people who lived in Manhattan, Harlem's home, were black. Almost all voted Democrat by the time David Dinkins joined J. Raymond Jones's political club. There, Dinkins met Basil Paterson with whom he would forge a lifelong political alliance. He would meet Percy Sutton and Charles Rangel as well. In time, Dinkins and his three friends would dominate Harlem's politics. They became known as the Gang of Four.[14]

In its late nineteenth- and early twentieth-century heyday, Tammany controlled up to twelve thousand municipal jobs. It served as the employment agency of the working class, providing immigrants, laborers, and most anyone able to deliver a few votes on Election Day with a job. Political philosophy, fancy oratory, and other trappings of high-minded public service mattered little to machine politicians. They were in the business of winning votes to secure jobs and contracts for themselves and their allies.[15]

LaGuardia tamed the Tammany Tiger with good government policies and civil service tests, but he did not kill it. Carmine DeSapio reengineered the machine in the 1950s, disarming a rising generation of political activists with process reforms while retaining the power to select candidates for office. He distributed a diminished number of jobs still accessible to a boss in good standing with the mayor, influenced the selection of judges, and directed city and state government contracts to allies wherever possible. In 1958, DeSapio ran afoul of important Democratic Party leaders, and in 1961, in a dramatic showdown that split the Democratic Party, Mayor Robert Wagner broke with the Tammany boss who had been his ally. When Wagner delivered the Manhattan Democratic county leadership role to J. Raymond Jones in 1964—the formal position of Tammany's boss—the organization held a fraction of its once-formidable power. Still, through the mayor Jones controlled more jobs and wielded more influence than any other politician in the city. And Tammany rules—attractive government jobs and contracts dispensed to lawyers and others in return for loyal work and for delivering votes—still applied. David Dinkins's political education took place in that school.[16]

In 1965, Jones tapped Dinkins to run for the New York State Assembly, but a year later reapportionment eliminated his district. His career almost ended prematurely in 1966 when the car he was in on his way to the assembly from Harlem had a blowout. Percy Sutton, at the wheel, found himself about to head into oncoming traffic at sixty miles per hour. He turned hard and rolled the car onto its roof rather than crash into the southbound lane. Dinkins, Sutton, Charlie Rangel, and another passenger, Alphonso Jenkins, escaped with modest injuries. In 1967, Dinkins won a party primary for Democratic district leader, a post he held for the next twenty years. "A district leader should be in the vanguard of efforts in his or her community to solve its problems of education, housing, narcotics addiction, economic development, health and transportation. Whatever the thrust at a given moment, the district leader should be involved," he wrote.[17]

Also in 1967, Dinkins served as a delegate at the New York State Constitutional Convention, which is when his attitude toward politics changed from a means to support his law practice to a pursuit in its own right. "I saw history being made and how power could be used for good or evil." After that "I was convinced for public service," he remembered. In 1970, he became counsel to the Board of Elections, a part-time position that allowed him to continue to practice law. In 1972, he received a seat on that board, the first black to hold one. The other members named him president, also a first.[18]

Over the years, Dinkins took his various responsibilities seriously and acquitted himself well. In the assembly, he helped pass legislation to improve minority access to public colleges. As a district leader, he attracted attention to the needs of local schools and organized elected officials to protest budget cuts. He joined the election board less than a decade after Congress passed the 1965 Voting Rights Act. Expanding African American political participation remained a priority for black leaders. Dinkins, who later described it as his mission in politics "to empower those who have been underserved," sought to make voting easier for people intimidated by cumbersome administrative procedures. He launched an initiative to allow voter registration by mail that the legislature eventually passed into law. His tenure at the election board turned out to be short. In June 1973, the state legislature doubled the size of the Board of Elections in response to a court ruling that declared the existing structure unconstitutional. Dinkins resigned, saying he believed the decision would make his job more tedious, make the board less efficient, and weaken voter access to the polls.[19]

Dinkins work during the 1960s and 1970s established him as a dedicated Democratic Party worker with a liberal political philosophy. For black politicians in Harlem during that time—a period when Lyndon Johnson pursued the Great Society at the national level and John Lindsay sought to implement similar programs in New York City—liberalism dominated the political landscape. When conservative Democrat Mario Proccacino won his party's nomination for mayor in 1969 and John Lindsay lost the Republican nomination to John Marchi, Dinkins showed his progressive teeth. "The swing to the right is now complete. The reactionary forces in our city have triumphed," a statement he issued said. "As a Democratic district leader, I have a responsibility to my party, but there is no doubt at all in my mind that my primary allegiance is to myself and to my community. I cannot support Mr. Proccacino." After securing political commitments, Dinkins and other Harlem Democrats endorsed Lindsay, who won reelection on the Liberal Party line.[20]

Dinkins took predictable stands on the two New York City liberal litmus tests of the 1960s. He supported John Lindsay's proposed police civilian complaint review board that went down to crushing defeat in a racially polarizing referendum. And he endorsed the school decentralization movement that embittered relations between blacks and Jews, with lasting consequences. He also established himself as firmly committed to liberal causes such as protection against residential discrimination, expanded civil rights for minorities, affirmative action jobs programs, and other progressive ideas. In 1973, Dinkins was named a member of the board of the newly created Rehabilitation Mortgage Insurance Corporation, a Lindsay-created public authority to encourage private financing for neighborhood preservation and housing rehabilitation. At the time, he issued a statement that identified what he believed to be the major issues of the day. "If the problems of the inner city are to be satisfactorily resolved, in addition to solving the problems of education, unemployment and underemployment, drug abuse and health, we must transcend all barriers to the problem of decent housing for all." The chairmen of Chemical Bank and of the Metropolitan Life Insurance Company were fellow board members. Dinkins climb up the Tammany ladder had connected him to the city's white financial and business elite.[21]

By then, Percy Sutton had become the most powerful politician in Harlem. Born in Texas, the youngest of fifteen children, Sutton possessed grace and style, a penetrating intellect, and a commanding voice that radiated a rare charisma. In 1966, President Lyndon Johnson named Manhattan borough president Constance Motley a federal court judge, and Ray Jones had Sutton named as her replacement. When Jones retired in 1969, his mantle as Harlem's leader passed to Sutton, whom his allies had taken to calling "The Chairman," a term of deep respect. Detractors, suspicious of his smooth-talking style, called him the "wizard of ooze." In 1973, with an election for mayor approaching, Sutton detected a "mood of Jewishness" to the city's politics, and he wanted to be on the winning team. So Sutton threw Harlem's support to Abe Beame, a clubhouse politician of the Brooklyn persuasion. Then sixty-seven, Beame claimed he would serve only one term and promised to support Sutton for mayor in 1977.

Beame won. Soon after his election, he offered Dinkins a post as deputy mayor—repayment to Harlem's political establishment for their support during his successful campaign. A routine investigation into the nominee's background revealed Dinkins had failed to file federal, state, and city income taxes for four years. In a tearful press conference, Dinkins apologized to his family, his law partners, and his many friends and supporters for the embarrassing lapse. Even though he had already paid the $15,000 due in back taxes, formal dispensation of the matter would take some time. He and Mayor Beame had agreed the job could not remain vacant for a number of months, so Dinkins decided to withdraw his name from consideration. When asked why he had not filed his taxes, he could only say, "It was one of those things I was always going to take care of but sometimes I did not have all the funds available or I did not have all the documents and other material I needed." Two years later, with his tax issues cleared up, Beame appointed the Harlemite to the office of city clerk, a plum patronage position responsible principally for processing marriage licenses. Dinkins held the job for the next decade, pursuing elected office all the while.[22]

In 1977, Beame decided to stand for reelection. Feeling double-crossed, Sutton challenged Beame in that year's seven-way Democratic primary, opening up the contest for the Manhattan borough president office Sutton held.

Every Manhattan borough president since 1953 had been black. That year, mayoral candidate Robert Wagner and Tammany boss Carmine DeSapio, who backed him, recognized the rising importance of African Americans in city politics. They determined that a candidate from Harlem on a ticket with Wagner would strengthen their coalition. They secured the Democratic nomination for Manhattan borough president for Hulan Jack, a black city councilman, who went on to win. In the years that followed, an often unspoken but unchallenged political logic prevailed. A city with a substantial and growing black population—by then about one-third people of color—should have some minority representation on the Board of Estimate, at the time the city's most important governing council. When Tammany ruled, it enforced the practice. Even after the Democratic Party split in 1961 and Tammany's influence diminished, the custom endured. All of the black politicians who held the job moved out or on to higher office midterm, leaving the vacancy to be filled by the borough's city council members, who generally abided by traditional party practices. Sutton's decision to run for mayor in 1977 created a vacancy in a city election year. He and his Harlem political allies chose David Dinkins as their candidate. Manhattan assemblyman Andrew Stein and Manhattan city councilman at large Robert Wagner, Jr., son of the former mayor, also entered the race, along with Ronnie Eldridge, a politically active liberal who had worked in the Lindsay administration, and the only woman in the contest.

With Sutton running for mayor, Harlem's attention focused on him rather than on the race for borough president. Stein had a well-financed campaign and had earned a reputation as a crusader by exposing maltreatment of the elderly in the city's nursing homes. Bobby Wagner also raised a substantial campaign fund and had his father's name and considerable influence working to his advantage. The *Amsterdam News* described Dinkins chief opponents as "two men who tower over him only in family name and fortune." Dinkins described himself as "the only candidate for the office who is able to relate to people of diverse ethnic backgrounds. I can function equally well in the boardrooms of Wall Street, the chambers of City Hall or the corner of 117th and Lenox Avenue. No other candidate for the office has that ability." That year it was not enough. Stein defeated Wagner by a small margin, and Dinkins ran a distant third in his inaugural effort to win Manhattan's top elective office.[23]

Sutton fared poorly in his quest for the mayoralty in 1977, winning votes only from blacks. The contest embittered him, leaving him feeling the citywide media, controlled by whites, refused to take his campaign seriously. They rendered him invisible in his view, causing backers outside of Harlem to stay away. "I shall not return to elective politics," Sutton announced a few months later. "The whole thing . . . really took a toll on him," one man close to him said. Sutton's and Dinkins's defeats had an impact on blacks in Harlem and across the city. Had both won, African Americans would have held real clout in City Hall and on the Board of Estimate. The double loss meant the one seat normally reserved for blacks on the board had disappeared. Basil Paterson called it "the worst thing that could happen."[24]

The 1977 mayoral contest included a pivotal moment in late July when the lights went out in New York. A citywide blackout led to widespread looting in African American neighborhoods around the city. The *Amsterdam News* interviewed more than one hundred black leaders and ordinary citizens and found their reactions to the awful event bitterly divided. Opinions of the looters ranged from those who viewed them as "animals" and the "scum of the earth" to those who perceived them as victims of joblessness and discrimination "who saw a chance to strike back at their oppressors." David Dinkins demanded that Mayor Beame establish a blue-ribbon panel to "seek funds immediately for a year-round emergency youth jobs program."[25]

In 1981, Dinkins challenged Stein again. The other contests for city office generated little drama that year, so the battle for the top post in Manhattan attracted a lot of attention. During the campaign Dinkins raised the issue of minority representation on the Board of Estimate. He lost the Democratic primary by just a few percentage points, and Manhattan's voters returned Stein to office easily in the general election against a Republican and against Dinkins running on the Liberal Party line. But black turnout for Dinkins in both contests had been unusually high and the edge to the battle sharp. "Fifty percent of the city will no longer let the label 'minority' condemn them to silence and political impotence," Dinkins declared on election night. Minority political leaders made clear their dissatisfaction with a system that denied so significant a proportion of the population representation on the city's most important governing body. Some threatened to create a separate African American political party.[26]

In 1985, city council president Carol Bellamy challenged Ed Koch for mayor, and Andrew Stein decided to run for the office she vacated. He endorsed Dinkins for the post he left behind to secure support from Harlem for his citywide contest. So in his third bid for Manhattan borough president, Dinkins had the backing of the exiting incumbent. Governor Cuomo, many of the city's top Democrats, and virtually all the major newspapers, which expressed sympathy for the argument that the Board of Estimate should have a black voice, endorsed him as well. Dinkins easily defeated Assemblyman Jerrold Nadler in the Democratic primary and went on to victory in the general election in November. "I have to be a borough president of all the people and not just the minority community," Dinkins said the night he won the Democratic nomination, "but I have a special concern for the minority community because I am one." He was the first black in twenty-four years to win the office in a contest.[27]

By the time he held Manhattan's top elected spot, Dinkins had developed a distinctive style. He dressed in custom-made eight hundred dollar suits and always looked meticulously groomed—some said it came from growing up the son of a barber. Those who knew him well learned he would shower several times a day and change clothes between appearances so he always looked fresh. Dinkins attributed his fetish for cleanliness to a school gym teacher who checked the boys' wrists every day to make sure they had washed. One man who knew him detected the influence of the mayor's heritage in his personal habits and also in his use of language. His grandmother had grown up in late nineteenth-century Tidewater, Virginia, in a time and place where successful blacks adopted courtly manners, formal dress, and highly proper speech to put the lie to nasty white caricatures of their race as inherently inferior, dirty, and uncivilized. Dinkins's grandmother played an important role in some of the early formative years of his life and appears to have had a lasting impact on his public style.[28]

Dinkins often attended three events an evening, mingling with local politicos and, especially, Manhattan's elite. He relished contact with the city's powerful financiers, celebrities, media moguls, and real estate titans. The social nature of the ceremonial aspects of his job appealed to him greatly, as did the status he enjoyed during ribbon cuttings, groundbreakings, and other public events. He behaved with unfailing courtesy in public settings and projected a highly formal politeness. Here again his upbringing showed through. Once in his youth, while walking with his mother on a Harlem street, he addressed one of her friends by her first name. His usually gentle mother slapped him square across the face for what she deemed disrespectful behavior, unbecoming a young man. The lesson stayed with him.[29]

Dinkins weighed his words carefully and learned to speak with ponderous caution, often relying on labored syntax to make points by indirection rather than blunt statements. "Be careful of your choice of language," Dinkins admonished less temperate colleagues. "[W]hat do I say to a young black or Puerto Rican kid on Seventh Avenue when I want him to put down a brick? How can I say, go out and vote, if he can come back at me with my own words and say, 'Well elections are stolen anyway?'" An innate caution guided the man. He believed, "We should be very careful. We have an *obligation* to be careful. The rhetoric of advocacy, so frequently extreme, can do more harm than good."[30]

The caution David Dinkins displayed when speaking applied equally to his approach to decision making. He believed his training in mathematics and the law gave him "an orderly mind." Carefully and thoroughly, some would say tediously and painstakingly, he would gather facts, listen to all sides, consider opposing arguments, and reserve his own judgment for as long as possible. When colleagues criticized him for taking a "maddeningly long" time to make up his mind, he responded with pedantic logic. "You know, it seems to me that wisdom dictates that you gather in intelligence and weigh it carefully before you arrive at a judgment on things. If you're about to affect people's lives, you have a certain responsibility." He allowed that the approach he described could sound stuffy and pompous, but he did not mind. David Dinkins deliberated at his own pace. Politicians who grew up in Tammany clubhouses often did.[31]

Although Dinkins was unfailingly kind and polite in public—and quite charming as well—his staff knew he could be exacting, impatient, and more than a little sharp when they did not meet his standards. He could fuss over small details, typographical errors, or minor matters. He insisted analysts prove their points with careful logic, and he could put them through their paces on the topics that mattered to him. He could be high-handed as well. As mayor, members of his cabinet would remember meetings in which a gloved server brought him a three-course meal on fine china set upon a lace doily while they watched or ate sandwiches. *New York* magazine political editor Joe Klein described the style of his administration as "neo-monarchy." Another journalist started a long profile of the publicly charming man with a short, arresting sentence. "He is not so nice," Todd Purdum wrote in the *New York Times.* "It is the first thing that anyone who knows him comes to realize and the last thing that most New Yorkers would imagine."[32]

On the personal front, borough president Dinkins indulged his passion for tennis whenever he could, with standing court time reserved at Stadium Tennis in the Bronx—an hour and a half on Saturdays and two hours on Sundays most weekends. Other than politics and tennis, only family occupied his time. He lived with his wife, who preferred to avoid the public limelight, and, until they were grown, his son David Jr. and daughter Donna. They made their home in a three-bedroom city-subsidized cooperative residence on One Hundred Fifty-Seventh Street and Riverside Drive that they moved into in 1963. Their eleventh-floor apartment overlooked the Hudson River. By the time he became Manhattan borough president, David Dinkins had slowly and steadily built a life that suited him. He did not want to risk what he had labored for decades to achieve in a race for mayor unless he believed he would win.[33]

II. A Path to Winning

As early as May 1988, political analysts saw Dinkins as the favorite to challenge and defeat Koch. With typical caution, the potential candidate kept his own counsel, but in October 1988 his key political advisor, Bill Lynch, commissioned a poll.

Bill Lynch grew up the son of a potato farmer in Mattatuck, toward the eastern tip of Long Island. In high school, he was more jock than student, gravitating toward basketball courts, baseball diamonds, and soccer fields rather than books, classrooms, and libraries. He served a tour of duty in the air force as a material control airman and then sought to continue his education at Virginia Union, at the time an all-black college. On his way there, Lynch spent some time in the "bright lights, big city of New York" and said to himself, "I'm coming back here."[34]

After two years in Virginia, Lynch decided academic life did not suit him, and he returned to Long Island, where he spent three years working for a federally sponsored program as a community organizer. When the director of the program moved to New York City, he invited Lynch to come work with him, and the young man made good on his promise to himself to make it to the big city. Community organizing led seamlessly to union organizing, and eventually Lynch became the political director for Local 1707 of the Association of Federal, State, County, and Municipal Employees (AFSCME), representing home health care workers. In 1975, he managed the successful Democratic district leader campaign of Diane Lacey Winley across neighborhoods spanning the Upper West Side and Central Harlem. Later he managed her unsuccessful campaign for the assembly, but she had been a heavy underdog and placed second in a field of seven. Local politicians took note of her campaign manager's effectiveness.

In 1980, Lynch volunteered for Senator Edward Kennedy's campaign for president, and in 1984, he worked for Jesse Jackson, collaborating closely with the candidate's Manhattan coordinator, David Dinkins. Dinkins asked Lynch to manage his campaign for borough president the next year. Lynch declined, opting instead to manage the state senate race of Basil Paterson's son David, with the hope of providing Harlem a new generation of leadership. Paterson and Dinkins both won. During the course of the campaign, Lynch worked so closely with the Dinkins team that for all intents and purposes he felt he had managed the borough president's successful race as well. Lynch agreed to manage Dinkins's transition team and then stayed on as chief of staff. Observers thought them something of an odd-couple—the newly elected borough president physically fit, perfectly groomed, and fastidiously attired, his new top advisor heavyset, bearded, and unkempt, projecting the demeanor and aura of a "rumpled genius." Yet the two men had a natural affinity for each other, and they fell easily into a relationship of mutual respect and trust.[35]

In 1988, Dinkins and Lynch both worked hard for Jesse Jackson during the Democratic primary. To ensure the candidate's inspirational rhetoric resulted in a surge of support, Lynch helped organize voter registration drives among African Americans and other people of color traditionally underrepresented at the polls. When Jackson won a plurality over his two rivals, Lynch took note of the coalition that supported him: African Americans and Latinos, plus progressive white voters, mostly Jewish liberals, pulled to the polls on Election Day by union workers and community organizers. The same coalition supported David Dinkins. As a mayoral election year approached, Lynch contemplated the political landscape. With his boss's acquiescence more than his encouragement, in October 1988, Lynch commissioned a citywide poll testing support for Dinkins for mayor. "The numbers showed a path to winning," Lynch concluded.[36]

Lynch and pollster Peter Hart brought the results to Dinkins in his Harlem apartment. At first, the cautious politician dismissed his advisors' assessment. "You guys cooked those books," he declared, fearing his team's loyalty and ambition caused them to read into the numbers what they wanted to believe. "No, this could happen," Lynch assured the skeptical man. As word got out and the notion of a Dinkins run for mayor gained currency, African American and Latino leaders across the city, intent on ousting Koch, quietly traveled to Dinkins's office in Manhattan to pledge their help. Rivalries between Harlem's political establishment rooted in Tammany's ways and Brooklyn's more militant African American politicians who had grown up during the battles of the 1960s were set aside in the face of a common enemy. To add credibility to the nascent effort, Lynch organized a high-profile fund-raiser at Tavern on the Green to demonstrate that a Dinkins candidacy could attract enough money to mount a viable campaign. Working with the teamsters union, he conducted a second poll in January 1989 that reconfirmed the October findings. By then Dinkins had attracted nearly unanimous support among black and Latino politicians.[37]

Finally, the cautious candidate asked himself: Did he want to be mayor? And did he have a chance of winning? Enough of a chance to sacrifice what he already had? He decided he wanted the job and that it was within his grasp. On February 15, 1989, Dinkins announced his intentions. "I am running [for mayor] because our city has become sharply polarized. We need a mayor who can transcend differences so we can work together to solve our problems," he said. He referred to New York as a "gorgeous mosaic" of peoples, each one contributing something unique to the quality and character of the city, each one worthy of respect.[38]

Dinkins's announcement knocked out several potential challengers. Others threw their hats into the ring.[39]

Harrison J. Goldin decided he would run for mayor. For sixteen years the city's comptroller, he viewed himself as exceptionally well-qualified to manage the municipal government, and in 1989, he saw a chance to replace Koch as the Jewish candidate of the white middle class. These voters still wanted someone who shared their priorities, Goldin reasoned, but one who spoke to the city's people in gentler tones than the three-term incumbent.[40]

New York businessman Richard Ravitch also decided to run for mayor. A native New York City Jew who grew up in East Harlem, Ravitch graduated from Columbia University and then Yale Law School. He made a fortune building housing in New York City and participated in a variety of civic organizations where he often crossed paths with politicians and government officials. In 1978, Governor Hugh Carey called on him to rescue the New York State Urban Development Corporation from failure. Ravitch accepted the challenge and succeeded at the task. The governor then named him to head the Metropolitan Transportation Authority (MTA). Once again Ravitch successfully oversaw the renewal of a struggling public agency. Ravitch impressed Mayor Koch enough as head of the MTA that in 1986 he asked him to head a commission to update and revise the City Charter. Labor leaders who had worked with Ravitch, politicians who had relied on him to solve complicated problems, and public-minded peers who respected his ability all urged him to run for mayor because they thought him an exceptional manager of public agencies. Many agreed that he would make the best mayor, but just as many doubted that he would be a viable candidate against a group of seasoned political professionals.[41]

III. Rudy the Challenger

The Republicans too had a Jewish businessman candidate but one far less familiar with city government than Dick Ravitch. Ronald Lauder, scion of the Estée Lauder cosmetics fortune and a Republican party stalwart who served briefly under Ronald Reagan as ambassador to

Austria, decided to run for mayor. He had no qualifications at all for the job. His candidacy grew out of a political battle between federal prosecutor Rudolph Giuliani and US senator Alfonse D'Amato.[42]

D'Amato was New York State's senior Republican official, a status he guarded jealously. A machine politician who built his career through loyal service to the powerful Nassau County GOP, D'Amato practiced his trade like the gruff local party hack he was rather than as a high-minded US senator. Credible if unproven accusations of corruption cast shadows over his reputation. Giuliani, who had converted to the GOP in 1980 after a youthful infatuation with President John F. Kennedy and the Democratic Party, harbored political ambitions of his own. Almost inevitably the two men ended up at odds.

Rudolph William Louis Giuliani was born in Brooklyn on May 28, 1944, an only child and the grandson of Italian immigrants. A few years later the family moved to Long Island, where the boy attended Catholic grade school. He returned to Brooklyn as an adolescent to attend Bishop Loughlin Memorial High School. His mother, Helen C. D'Avanzo, believed in the strength of tradition and discipline, and she instilled these values in her son. Giuliani's father, Harold, was a work-ing man—a plumber's assistant and a maintenance man and at times a tavern operator. But there was another side to him.

Unable to make a living during the Great Depression, Harold Giuliani and a partner in crime assaulted and robbed a milkman mak-ing the rounds in a Manhattan building. A cop caught Harold Giuliani at the scene, and the man arrested in the act ended up serving time in Sing Sing prison, where a Department of Hospitals psychiatrist wrote this report: "A study of this individual's make-up reveals that he is a personality of the deviate aggressive, egocentric type. This aggressivity [sic] is pathological in nature and has shown itself from time to time as far back as his childhood. He is egocentric to an extent where he has failed to consider the feelings and rights of others." The man had an explosive temper.[43]

When Harold Giuliani got out of prison, he went to work for his brother-in-law, Leo D'Avanzo, who owned a restaurant in Brooklyn. In addition to keeping bar, Harold served as enforcer for a loan-sharking and gambling racket that D'Avanzo and a partner linked to organized crime ran out of the restaurant. When borrowers failed to pay their debts on time, Harold beat them with a baseball bat. He tried to hide his background from his son, but relatives made clear to Rudy that he should be wary of the uncle who employed his father. "Don't be like

Leo," they told him. He was "Mafia, bad, bad, bad." The elder Giuliani hoped his son would have a more respectable life than his own.[44]

Rudy won an academic scholarship to Manhattan College, at the time an all-male Catholic institution run by the Christian Brothers in the Bronx. He contemplated joining the priesthood, but at the age of twenty decided against a vocation that required celibacy. He graduated in 1965—the first in his family to earn a college diploma—and then attended New York University Law School, graduating with honors in 1968. Later that year he married Regina Peruggi, a second cousin who had been his date at his high school senior prom.

For two years, the new attorney clerked for federal district court judge Lloyd MacMahon and then joined the office of US attorney Whitney North Seymour as a prosecutor in New York's prestigious southern district. He became chief of the anticorruption unit and established a reputation as an ambitious, hardworking, and capable lawyer. He garnered some fame when he put Brooklyn congressman Bertram Podell in jail for influence peddling. After Jimmy Carter's election, Giuliani spent a few years in private practice at a Manhattan firm, Patterson, Belknap, Webb, and Tyler. In 1981, Attorney General William French Smith offered him the job of associate deputy attorney general, the third-highest-ranking job in the Justice Department in Washington, responsible for, among other things, the nation's ninety-four US attorneys. Two years later, endorsed by both Al D'Amato and New York's Democratic senator Daniel Patrick Moynihan, Smith recommended Giuliani to President Ronald Reagan for appointment as the US attorney for the Southern District of New York. The office gave Giuliani the power and autonomy to pursue the cases he chose.

In some respects, the new job constituted a demotion, but the independence it offered appealed to Giuliani. In addition, he wanted to return to New York City for two reasons. Giuliani had separated from his wife by then, and he had developed a serious relationship with Donna Hanover, a television anchorwoman who had been work-ing in Miami when they met. Hanover wanted to move to New York, the nation's television news capital, rather than to Washington, DC. And according to Giuliani's high school friend and lifelong confidant, Peter Powers, "[I]t was natural to think that with Rudy's interest in politics, the US Attorney's Office would lead to a run for public of-fice." Shortly after returning to New York, Giuliani arranged to have his first marriage formally annulled on the dubious grounds that he had not known Regina Peruggia was his second cousin when they wed. That cleared the way for him to marry Donna Hanover in the Catholic Church.[45]

The political corruption trials that Giuliani pursued, the Wall Street scandals his office uncovered, and his hard-hitting investigations into organized crime made Giuliani a media star. A constant barrage of publicity attended the arrests, indictments, and convictions of some of New York City's most powerful men. The public perceived Giuliani as a bold and relentless champion of justice who took on anyone who broke the law without fear or favor. Journalists and politicians noticed that the prosecutor sought out and enjoyed the attention he received. Some said he chose his high-profile targets with the potential for publicity foremost in mind, with little regard for the damage he might do to innocent people caught in the mix. They speculated that he planned to seek elective office and a broader forum for his crusading zeal.[46]

Initially, Giuliani and Senator D'Amato made common cause in New York. One night, in search of headlines, the two Republicans accompanied drug enforcement agents on an undercover bust. D'Amato wore the brown uniform of a United Parcel Service worker and Giuliani dressed like a Hell's Angels bike rider. They claimed unconvincingly that their quest for photo opportunities was meant to dramatize the ease with which drugs could be bought on city streets. One indignant FBI agent commented off the record that the next time the two wanted attention they should dress in Bozo the Clown outfits, but celebrity status and a law-and-order image suited both men.[47]

In 1988, D'Amato wanted Giuliani to challenge Daniel Moynihan for his Senate seat. The Republicans were unlikely to defeat the twelve-year incumbent whose reputation as one of Washington's brainiest politicians made him a formidable opponent. Still, as his party's leader, D'Amato wanted the Republicans to wage a respectable race, and Giuliani was the strongest potential contender. With several important investigations at critical stages, and the prospects for victory slim, Giuliani declined to leave the US Attorney's Office. The timing of Giuliani's decision left D'Amato without a serious candidate and feeling burned. More important, the discussions between D'Amato and Giuliani revealed a brewing conflict.

As a senator belonging to the president's party, tradition gave D'Amato a strong say in the selection of a US attorney in New York. Had Giuliani run for Moynihan's seat, D'Amato would have played a role in choosing his successor. Rumors circulated that he planned to propose someone who would not pursue the cases against Wall Street's bankers because the firms involved raised large sums of money for D'Amato's political campaigns. Giuliani wanted to be certain that his successor would follow through on investigations underway. As 1989 arrived and Giuliani contemplated a race for mayor, the conflict over his replacement became severe.[48]

Giuliani was popular, and in a climate of corruption and rising crime who better to run against a tainted mayor than a prosecutor? He was clearly the most attractive Republican candidate, and he hoped to win the Liberal Party endorsement as well. Neither Dinkins nor Koch had close ties to Liberal Party leader Ray Harding, and neither Goldin nor Ravitch could match Giuliani's standing in the polls. Harding was a political pragmatist who consolidated his control as party boss after a bitter fight with the remnants of the philosophically motivated core of the organization. He delivered the party's backing to whichever candidate had the best chance to win and to give the Liberals the best political reward. Giuliani appeared to fit the criteria, and the federal prosecutor also thought he had a good chance to win the backing of the Conservative party. That would give him three lines on the ballot.

Giuliani's posture threatened D'Amato. If the prosecutor succeeded in naming his own replacement, it would be a blow to the senator's prestige, and if he won election as mayor, he would have an independent base of support with far more patronage power than D'Amato. Giuliani would become New York's top Republican. To throw nails in his rival's path, D'Amato convinced Ronald Lauder to run for the Republican nomination for mayor. The candidacy would ensure a GOP primary and a chance to damage the prosecutor's image. Why Lauder did it is hard to discern. He had no background in urban affairs or elected office, and he was not even from New York City. To the amusement of political professionals, on January 4, 1989, he announced his candidacy for the New York City mayoralty standing on the steps of the state legislature in Albany. "At least, the announcement wasn't made in Vienna," Ray Harding commented. Lauder clearly was no match for Rudolph Giuliani, but he had personal assets in excess of $300 million with which to wage a campaign designed to expose Giuliani's weaknesses.[49]

Within days after Lauder's announcement, Giuliani declared that he was leaving his post as US attorney. His interim replacement, Benito Romano, was an experienced and competent prosecutor who had worked for Giuliani and who intended to pursue vigorously the corruption cases in progress. When asked if he would run for mayor,

Giuliani replied, "I have not ruled out that option." He took a position with a private law firm and soon began campaigning.[50]

IV. Koch the Underdog

By January 1989, Ed Koch's private polls showed that only a loyal core of about 17 percent wanted him to be mayor again. Public polls revealed that barely one New Yorker in three approved of the way he was handling his job, compared with nearly three-quarters of the city's residents at the height of his popularity. Worse, more than half of the city now disapproved of Koch, compared with barely one New Yorker in five in January of 1985 when his last reelection campaign had begun. Several close friends thought he should not seek reelection at all and instead exit gracefully from City Hall.[51]

Koch never really considered not running. "I was too proud to put my tail between my legs and get driven from office," he would later say. "And I knew that things were going to get very bad, and I didn't want whoever took over to be able to say that I made a mess and left. [By going] to the mat to hold onto power myself, they could never say that by the time they got it, it wasn't worth anything." For Koch, this last point was especially important if the city elected a black mayor. He was determined not to be the scapegoat of minority politicians.

A formal announcement would not come for months, but Koch made it clear he would run and he adopted a strategy. With the city headed for a new round of fiscal crises, the mayor reasoned, New Yorkers would want the most capable man available in City Hall. With a dozen years of experience, having rescued the city from financial trauma once before, Koch obviously fit that description. He would emphasize the point in his daily activities as mayor.[52]

Koch was clearly the underdog against Dinkins in the Democratic primary and against Giuliani in the general election as well. Despite the powers of incumbency, the mayor's ability to mount a field operation had diminished since his last campaign in 1985. The Democratic Party in Staten Island, the smallest county organization in the city, agreed to support him. The corruption scandals had created a fissure between Koch and the Democrats in Queens, where the new county leader, Congressman Thomas Manton, was just consolidating his power. The Queens organization endorsed Dick Ravitch in May. In Brooklyn, borough president Howard Golden had replaced Meade Esposito as county leader. Golden and Koch had feuded publicly over Board of Estimate decisions and become bitter enemies. Golden threw his support to Comptroller Harrison Goldin, while many of his borough's district leaders, particularly those representing minority neighborhoods, backed Dinkins. Bronx County leader George Friedman added up the number of minority voters in his borough and decided prudence and survival required he support Dinkins. The Manhattan borough president's home base rallied to his cause as well.[53]

Municipal unions offered a second important source of potential campaign workers. Koch had battled most of them from the very start of his administration, and the shifts that had taken place in New York's population during his twelve years in office created a city workforce with more minorities than ever before. The membership of the municipal unions reflected the change. By 1989, the heads of some of the most important labor organizations were minorities loyal to the city's most senior African American elected official. Stanley Hill, a black man who succeeded Victor Gotbaum as president of District Council 37 of AFSCME, the largest city union, announced his organization's support for Dinkins. Dennis Rivera, the Puerto Rican–raised son of an Irish American father and a Puerto Rican mother, had just consolidated his position in the spring of 1989 as president of Local 1199 of the Drug, Hospital, and Health Care Workers. Rivera guided his heavily black and Latino union of private and public workers into Dinkins's camp during the Democratic primary. In gratitude, Dinkins joined a hospital workers' picket line. Some found so strong a show of support for labor from a man campaigning for the right to negotiate contracts with unions on the city's behalf disconcerting.[54]

Other unions had white leaders at serious odds with Koch over policies and tactics and the tone of the mayor's administration. And with so many blacks and Latinos among their rank and file, the leaders could not prudently back a politician who had developed a reputation among minorities as a bigot. Teamster leader Barry Feinstein had endorsed Jesse Jackson in 1988 and answered back to Koch's dictum to Jews not to vote for the man, saying, "I'm as Jewish as anyone who ever lived, and I'm supporting Jackson." In 1989, he supported Dinkins. Sandra Feldman, president of the United Federation of Teachers, with more than one hundred thousand well-organized active and retired members, endorsed Dinkins early. The action broke with the union's traditional posture of remaining neutral in Democratic primaries. But Feldman felt philosophically comfortable with Dinkins and thought he could win. It helped that Feldman's husband, Arthur Barnes, head of the New York Urban Coalition, had been friends with Dinkins since their boyhood days together in Harlem. After a dozen years out in the cold while Ed Koch ruled, municipal labor leaders saw David Dinkins as a chance to restore their influence over city policies that affected their wages and working conditions. The support of the largest municipal unions and the better part of the regular Democrats gave Dinkins the best field organization by far among the candidates.[55]

The Democratic primary turned into a contest between two coalitions. Dinkins was the candidate of the city's minorities and most liberal voters. Koch, Goldin, and Ravitch were Jewish candidates running on the claim of competence, with their greatest appeal among the white middle class. By July, when the candidates filed sufficient nominating petitions to secure ballot lines, it had already become clear that comptroller Jay Goldin's campaign lacked momentum. Similarly, Dick Ravitch could claim just a sliver of support. Each man registered only single digits when newspapers took polls to gauge their standing. The battle for the Democratic nomination would be between Dinkins and Koch, whose ratings, while low, had stabilized and begun to turn. Because his field operation was weak, Koch's campaign resorted to television ads earlier than usual. They emphasized that competence mattered more than style. "You don't like how he says it, but you like what he says," was Koch's description of the theme.[56]

The mayor knew blacks would not vote for him over Dinkins, so he sought instead the backing of Jews, Catholics, and Latinos. Among Jews, Koch campaigned as one of their own. He traveled to synagogues and Jewish community centers around the city and sought support from rabbis. A group of seventy Orthodox organizations brought together in a Unity Coalition endorsed the mayor after he spoke to them at a candidates' forum in Borough Park, Brooklyn. Wealthier Jews from Manhattan, Riverdale, and Forest Hills—areas partially isolated from the poorer neighborhoods that often served as crucibles of racial fears—supported the mayor more tepidly. Koch campaigned actively in those areas in an effort to regain the confidence of the voters who lived there.

The mayor had fence-mending to do with the Irish. In the past they had supported him strongly, but in one of the many political gaffes of his third term, he praised the policies of British prime minister Margaret Thatcher in Ireland. In response to the criticism that followed, he retracted the statement and throughout the campaign emphasized his past support for the Irish people and their causes, as well as the personal values he shared with them. He pitched his conservative attitude and sense of fiscal responsibility to Italian voters as well.[57]

Koch also sought favor among Latino voters who had backed him in past elections. Yet competing visions of what Latinos wanted from a candidate gave Dinkins a means to compete for their loyalty. Many felt oppressed and believed they lived in a society that discriminated against them. These voters reasoned that a black man who could sympathize with their plight was more likely to give them a fair hearing than a white man who did not share their experience. Puerto Ricans in particular, the largest segment of the Latino population and its poorest, held this view strongly. On the other hand, traditional Catholic values and respect for the established order played an important role in the lives of many Latinos, particularly Central American and South American immigrants. Koch appealed to these sentiments more strongly than Dinkins, and he emphasized it in his Spanish-language communications.[58]

Not surprisingly, Dinkins's campaign reflected the mirror image of Koch's. Bill Lynch built an extensive field operation of ten thousand volunteers drawn from the city's political clubs and labor unions. Their role was to bring out the vote in black and Puerto Rican districts. In an effort to attract white liberals, particularly Jews, to their coalition, Dinkins's team aired television commercials that reinforced their candidate's image as a man who would bring harmony to the racially divided city. For the most part, the campaign accepted the votes of white Catholics as lost.[59]

The Republican primary was on the one hand high farce and on the other serious drama. Ronald Lauder spent millions of dollars to hire an all-star team of Republican political consultants who then tripped over each other to tell him what to do—and who charged him a lot of money for the privilege. No message emerged; no image developed. The man became a laughingstock. To some it looked like Alfonse D'Amato using Lauder's checkbook to enrich his favorite advisers, with the candidate's interests of secondary concern. D'Amato did deliver the Conservative Party ballot line to his candidate in what would be Lauder's only success.[60]

Giuliani won Liberal Party chief Ray Harding's endorsement, assuring him the Liberal Party line. His victory in the Republican primary was never in doubt, but even so he paid a political price. Lauder's staff revealed that one of the law firms Giuliani joined after leaving his post as US attorney had represented a Panamanian government agency during the regime of General Manuel Noriega. Associating the former prosecutor with a drug-running dictator, whom the United States would later oust from power by force, hit at the center of Giuliani's reputation. It was a cheap shot to be sure, but typical of political campaigns. Giuliani, while media-wise, had no experience with the rough-and-tumble side of politics. He simply proved unable to silence the charge.

Then the Supreme Court dented the *Roe vs. Wade* abortion decision by expanding the power of state governments to forbid women to terminate pregnancies. The other candidates immediately declared their support for a woman's right to choose. Giuliani, however, waffled. He said he opposed abortion but would obey the law. That did not answer the question of whether he favored a change in the state's statutes now that the court allowed it. Finally, he declared he did not. The press made much of Giuliani's lack of conviction.[61]

Shortly after the controversy over abortion, a *Daily News* poll asked voters how they would cast their ballots if Giuliani faced Dinkins in a November general election. It revealed that the former prosecutor's position among Jews had dropped 17 percent compared to six months before, and his overall standing had softened a little among almost all groups. Giuliani remained formidable to be sure, but as a prosecutor he had developed an aura of invincibility. The primaries shattered that. He had become a candidate like all the rest.[62]

V. The Politics of Racial Murder

During the primaries, the candidates' skirted delicately around the issue of race. None wanted to exacerbate the tensions in the city, and none wanted to bear the political burden of running a nasty campaign against the first black with a serious chance of becoming mayor. Besides, Dinkins's political strength rested in part on his call for harmony. His opponents understood that hostile rhetoric would make him stronger. Two episodes that under other circumstances might have hurt Dinkins instead helped him.

On an April night, with the campaign still in its early stages, a young white woman jogging alone in Central Park was attacked, raped repeatedly, and beaten within a breath of her life with fists and a pipe. Almost miraculously, the strong-willed woman, a vice president at a prominent investment bank, survived. The police rounded up a band of youths who had been on a "wilding spree" in the park, harassing passersby just for "kicks." They fit the general description of the woman's attackers, so detectives charged them with the crime. At the local precinct where officers booked them, in the presence of reporters, the young men joked uncaringly about the crime in apparent public confessions that sounded like bragging. Newspaper accounts of the event horrified the city. It was as if the youths did not understand that a human being had been shattered. The event boiled fear and rage into voters' blood. Many years later, evidence turned up that exonerated the group arrested, making the terrible event even worse. The court reversed the verdicts, but in 1989, the public did not doubt the guilt of the suspects, and nothing tempered the intensity of the outrage the episode caused.

David Dinkins responded rapidly to news of the attack by denouncing the band as "urban terrorists" and by talking with obvious sincerity about his concern for his own daughter's safety. His posture boosted his reputation as a man who would be able to respond to the deeply felt resentments that fueled minority hostility but who also understood the importance of enforcing the law. "I'll be the toughest mayor on crime this city ever had," he declared in the neighborhoods where he campaigned. His staff and volunteers distributed pamphlets that called for enactment of an "antiwilding" law. Dinkins offered a combination of social programs and police that appealed to many New Yorkers more than the blunt call for punishment that the other candidates mustered.[63]

The second event occurred in late August, just a few weeks before the primary, in what Koch would consider the turning point of that election. A sixteen-year-old black Brooklyn youth named Yusuf Hawkins traveled a few miles from his home in East New York to Bensonhurst to look at a used car advertised in that day's newspaper. He crossed the path of some white teenagers who mistook him for a black man who had dated a white woman in their neighborhood. Without provocation, the white men shot him to death. In the days that followed, Al Sharpton and other militants marched in protest in Bensonhurst, provoking vicious hostility from local residents captured live on television. The name calling and spitting and the vulgarity and offensive gestures once again brought the potential for racial calamity to the fore. Governor Mario Cuomo, who declared himself neutral in his party's primary, responded to the emotions the event evoked by saying the city should select as its next mayor the man who said to its people, "I will bring you together." It was a virtual endorsement of Dinkins and a repudiation of Koch. The image of the Hawkins murder burned sharply in people's minds as they went to the polls on September 12, 1989, to vote for candidates for mayor.[64]

In an unequivocal victory David Dinkins won 51 percent of the vote in the Democratic primary. Ed Koch took 42 percent, Richard Ravitch just 4 percent, and Jay Goldin 3 percent. For the first time in history, the Democratic Party in New York had chosen a black candidate for mayor. Dinkins's support from the city's blacks was virtually complete. About 93 percent cast their ballots for him. He won nearly 70 percent of Latino votes and 30 percent of white votes. New York's few white Protestants split their ballots equally between Koch and Dinkins. Three white Catholics in ten voted for Dinkins, and just under a quarter of the city's Jews voted for him as well.

Koch won more than 60 percent of white votes, with Ravitch and Goldin splitting about 10 percent between them. Catholics cast 63 percent of their ballots and Jews 68 percent for the three-term incumbent. The decline in support these groups gave Koch in comparison to his previous bids for reelection was significant. In 1981 and 1985, Koch had won more than three-quarters of Catholic and Jewish votes. But the defections went to Ravitch and Goldin, not Dinkins. When the few percentage points won by those two candidates are added to Koch's totals, the decline in the white vote going to Jewish candidates campaigning on a claim of competence was modest indeed. The white voters who cast ballots for Dinkins in the Democratic primary were a loyal core of liberals who almost certainly had voted against Koch in the past. The decline in support for Koch among Latinos constituted the more important shift by far. Fewer than 30 percent of this group cast their ballots for the mayor, compared with 70 percent four years earlier. Koch ran somewhat better in non–Puerto Rican neighborhoods than in Puerto Rican ones but suffered a precipitous decline overall.[65]

Dinkins's success with Latino voters and the changed composition of the city's population were at the root of his victory. The year after Koch's 1977 election, a census bureau survey identified nearly 55 percent of New Yorkers as white, 23 percent as black, and fewer than 16 percent as Latino. By 1987, a similar survey showed the proportion of whites had dropped to 46 percent, the number of blacks had risen modestly to 24 percent, and the number of Latinos had grown to more than 23 percent. Asians and others made up the difference. In short, the number of people of color exceeded the number of whites.

Virtually all blacks and Latinos who registered to vote in New York City did so as members of the Democratic Party. Whites split their affiliations between the Democratic and Republican organizations. Almost all of New York's Liberal and Conservative Party members were white as well. This diluted the strength of white voters in a Democratic primary. A Democrat who could keep together a minority coalition was bound to beat a white candidate in a primary election. With the black vote firmly in his camp on the basis of ethnic pride, the key to Dinkins's Democratic primary success was the strong support he had received from Latinos. When asked by pollsters why they cast ballots for David Dinkins, fully a third of Latinos replied "because he cares about people like me." Koch, a white candidate appealing to Latino respect for tradition and authority, could not maintain his strength with the group against Dinkins, a black candidate who spoke for the city's disfranchised, endorsed by almost all of the city's leading Spanish-speaking politicians.[66]

VI. The Jewish Vote and Victory

Dinkins appeared poised for an easy victory. He held the Democratic nomination in a city where five voters out of six registered with his party. His standing among blacks and Latinos was solid. And despite a tough primary against three Jewish opponents, when asked on primary day whom they would favor in the general election, Jewish voters who responded chose Dinkins over Giuliani by a margin of five to three. The Italian former prosecutor had won the Republican primary in a landslide, and he held the confidence of a strong majority of white Catholic voters. Typically, more Catholics voted in the general election than in the primary, so he could expect a boost from their increased numbers. But even so, one analyst determined that if the Republican/Liberal won the votes of every Democrat who cast a ballot for Koch, when added to the total number of votes cast in the Republican primary, Giuliani would still lose a general election to Dinkins by a small margin. Polls taken in the weeks following Dinkins's impressive primary victory showed the Democrat headed for City Hall in a landslide.[67]

Dinkins's victory caught Giuliani's inexperienced team by surprise. Among his advisors, only Ray Harding was a New York City pro. Republican media strategist Roger Ailes had joined Giuliani's campaign team, but the man's experience at the national level did not always translate well to the political streets of New York. Giuliani's friend,

Peter Powers, and Denny Young, his key aide from the US Attorney's Office, whose relationship dated back to the 1970s when they both worked for Whitney North Seymour, were his closest counselors. Both were capable and above all loyal, but neither was experienced in electoral politics. The campaign team had thought Koch would win, and that an anticorruption candidate would be a natural alternative to the discredited incumbent. They had built a campaign strategy to target him.

One of the more tawdry efforts to gather ammunition against Koch occurred while Giuliani was still a US prosecutor. An IRS investigator Giuliani had assigned to his office launched an investigation of a $12,000 city contract awarded without a competitive bid for a health care consulting project. The probe had scant legal merit, but, according to various reports, years before the consultant involved had had a homosexual relationship with Ed Koch. The investigator sought to intimidate the purported lover into outing Koch to damage the mayor's political standing. The consultant declined to conspire with the IRS investigator, and the dubious case went away. Giuliani denied any involvement in the episode, denouncing the reports as "totally untrue," "baseless," and "disgusting."[68]

Shortly after he won the Democratic primary, Giuliani's team displayed a similar lack of class in an effort to discredit Dinkins on a personal basis. A former secretary in the Manhattan borough president's office, unhappy that she had not received the jobs she thought she deserved, delivered to a Giuliani aide a box of personal letters stolen from Dinkins's office. They had nothing to do with Dinkins's performance as a public servant but promised to embarrass the man and potentially hurt him at the polls if published. Giuliani's team wanted the material aired but not attributed to them since they feared that would make their candidate look nasty. Besides, the former prosecutors working in the campaign understood the potential consequences of trafficking in stolen property, so they leaked the material anonymously to the press. When editors declined to print it, Giuliani's men called various newspapers saying they had heard about the letters and thought them newsworthy. To provoke publication, they tried to convince each newspaper that a rival was about to scoop them. Dinkins learned of the episode and became furious. He had a letter hand delivered to Giuliani's campaign headquarters. "If you persist in your present course, you will learn something I learned in the Marine Corps. Marines aren't very good at picking fights, but they certainly know how to end them," the outraged candidate wrote. The cryptic reference and events that followed suggest Dinkins would have revealed embarrassing aspects of Giuliani's life from a time when he was married to his first wife. The purloined letters remained unpublished, and the dirt duel never happened.[69]

On a more fundamental level, with Dinkins's victory, Giuliani's advisors had to rethink their approach. They had expected to attract black voters hostile toward Koch. But they understood the hopelessness of trying to win black votes away from the first African American Democratic candidate for mayor, so they had to try to cut into his support among whites and Latinos. It would not be easy. To gain maximum advantage from his supporters and maintain the momentum of his campaign, Giuliani played to his strengths. The Police Department's Columbia Association of Italian officers endorsed him, reemphasizing his law-and-order image. The candidate marched in the Columbus Day parade, giving his fellow Italians a chance to cheer him heavily before TV cameras. President George Bush announced his support for the Republican candidate and implied Washington would work with New York City more effectively with a GOP mayor in office. Senator D'Amato ostensibly buried the hatchet with his rival, creating an aura of party unity; in practice, however, the senator did little to help the campaign.[70]

Giuliani's team gave special attention to Jewish voters. On the one hand, New York's Jews traditionally voted for Democrats. On the other, they were white and subject to the same racial fears as other whites in the city, although the relationship between blacks and Jews was more complicated and subtle than the relationship between blacks and other whites. The mutual resentment between the two groups offered levers that a skillful politician could use to try and pry Jewish voters away from a black candidate.[71]

In one effort to appeal to Jews, Giuliani's advisers invited Jackie Mason, New York's quintessential Jewish comedian, to join the campaign as an unofficial ambassador to the Jewish community. At the time the entertainer enjoyed tremendous popularity with a one-man show on Broadway in which he poked fun at the ethnic differences of all of the city's people. The routine left his audiences in stitches. At first the celebrity attracted attention in a way that helped Giuliani. Then, in a long interview published in the *Village Voice*, Mason seemed to take his schtick seriously. "There is a sick Jewish problem of voting for a black man no matter how unfit he is for the job," the comedian philosophized. "They feel guilty for the black predicament as if the Jews caused it. . . . The Jews are constantly giving millions to the black people. Have you ever heard of a black person giving a quarter to a Jew?" He went on to declare Dinkins incompetent and insulted him personally. A loud uproar ensued the day the weekly newspaper appeared on the stands. Mason resigned from Giuliani's campaign while the candidate announced that "the remarks do not reflect my views."[72]

Next Giuliani tried to scare Jewish voters away from his adversary by linking Dinkins to Jesse Jackson. He ran ads in the *Algemeiner Journal*, a Yiddish weekly newspaper, showing a picture of the two black men with their hands clasped together. Dinkins, the advertisement read, is a "Jesse Jackson Democrat." This appeal backfired too. A *Newsday* editorial intoned that Giuliani had made "a sly appeal that exploits Jewish fears" and urged him to steer his campaign clear of "ugly low-road pitches." The *Jewish Daily Forward*, the city's largest Yiddish newspaper, responded by endorsing Dinkins. Their editorial pointed out that Dinkins had been "among the first to criticize his friend, the Rev. Jesse Jackson, when the latter characterized New York City as 'Hymie-town,' and he has consistently condemned Minister Louis Farrakhan for his anti-Semitic utterances." Democrats around the city denounced what one called Giuliani's "desperation game to get Jewish votes."[73]

Dinkins's campaign staff understood their candidate's potential vulnerability among Jewish Democrats and sought to anchor their support. Dinkins asked Koch and the other former Democratic contenders to campaign for him in Jewish communities. New York's senior Democratic politicians, prominent Jews among them, announced their support for Dinkins, as did most of the city's Jewish organizations. On just one well-orchestrated day, Dinkins received "a double portion" of good luck from Rabbi Menachem Mendel Schneerson, leader of Brooklyn's Lubavitcher Hasidic sect, and the endorsement of more than three dozen rabbis and Jewish lay leaders in the Pelham Parkway section of the Bronx.[74]

The Dinkins campaign hosted a kosher breakfast for 1,300 Jewish leaders to allow them to see the candidate for themselves. Aides passed out Hebrew "Dinkins for Mayor" buttons. The black candidate reaffirmed his unswerving support for Israel, reminded the crowd assembled that he had opposed the "Zionism is racism" resolution the United Nations had passed, and announced to the strongest applause of the day that "I am proud that in 1985, I denounced the anti-Semitic remarks of Louis Farrakhan." Ed Koch rose to the podium to praise Dinkins for having denounced anti-Semitism his entire adult life. Abe Beame, New York's first Jewish mayor, also spoke for Dinkins. "You know, when I first ran, there were people who worried I'd be a mayor for the Jews instead of a mayor for all the people. Now there are people who say Dave Dinkins will be mayor for black people. But I think I was a mayor for everybody, and Dave Dinkins will be a mayor for everyone too."[75]

In early October, with just a month to go before the election, Dinkins's standing with Jews remained strong. Almost half planned to vote for him, compared with a little over a third for Giuliani. The rest remained undecided. Dinkins held a comfortable lead, but a few days before the breakfast with Jewish leaders took place, the momentum began to change.[76]

Jitu Weusi served as an unpaid adviser to Dinkins's campaign staff. Although his name had changed from Leslie Cambell, he was the man who in 1968, while the Ocean Hill-Brownsville crisis over community control of New York's public schools was unfolding, read over the radio a viciously anti-Semitic poem scornfully dedicated to United Federation of Teachers president Albert Shanker. During the primary Weusi had helped to bring voters in Brooklyn neighborhoods to the polls, and he continued to work on behalf of Dinkins as the general election approached. The Giuliani campaign denounced the association, and newspapers printed reminders of how nasty the verse he once broadcast had been.

> Hey Jew boy, with that yarmulke on your head
> You pale faced Jew boy—I wish you were dead;
> I can see you Jew boy—no you can't hide
> I got a scoop on you, yeh, you gonna die.

"How can you be sure who will work in a Dinkins's administration?" Giuliani's aides asked reporters in a question meant to raise fears in Jewish minds. Weusi denied he was an anti-Semite, but he resigned from Dinkins's team. The candidate distanced himself from the unhelpful connection but found himself forced to meet with Jewish leaders to explain the relationship.[77]

Then *Newsday* reporter Lenny Levitt, reviewing Dinkins's election finance filings, discovered that in August campaign chairman Bill Lynch had ordered almost $10,000 worth of payments to Sonny Carson, a black militant from Brooklyn. Like Weusi, Carson had a fierce reputation for anti-Semitism dating back over twenty years to the Ocean Hill-Brownsville school crisis. The man was also a convicted kidnapper and had been accused of attempted murderer. As details of the payments emerged, it became apparent that after Yusuf Hawkins's killing in August, Carson had led hostile street protests in Bensonhurst. Dinkins's campaign staff had feared that an eruption of racial violence would scare white voters away from their candidate. The checks constituted "hush money" paid to buy peace. In an effort to hide the purpose, the campaign channeled the funds quietly through a phony organization called the Committee to Honor Black Heroes.[78]

The Giuliani team ran a campaign commercial that pointed out that the same David Dinkins who had failed to file income taxes "has paid a convicted kidnapper through a phony organization with no members, no receipts, and no office" to work on his campaign. It was not lost on listeners that the man whose election staff had done that was asking for the power to control the city's finances. It was not lost on Jewish voters that the convicted kidnapper hated Jews. Carson did little to defuse the issue when he called a press conference to declare that he did not hate Jews in particular but rather despised all whites. "Don't limit my anti-ing to just being one little group of people. I think you'd insult me if you tried to do that," the militant with enough hatred to go around told reporters.

Dinkins released a statement condemning the man. "Sonny Carson's comments represent the kind of bigotry and intolerance I utterly reject and have fought against my whole life. Had such comments come to my attention he would never have played any role in my campaign," the candidate declared. But the man had played a role—and a well-paid one at that. And the same day that Giuliani's ads condemning Dinkins's connections to Carson began to appear, the former prosecutor's election team broke the stock sale scandal.[79]

In 1985, Dinkins bought a number of shares in Percy Sutton's Inner City Broadcasting Company. The corporation held lucrative cable TV franchises that astute New Yorkers knew the city typically awarded on the basis of political connections. Dinkins initially reported that before assuming his position on the Board of Estimate as Manhattan borough president, he had given the stock to his son as a gift to avoid the potential for conflict of interest. But the candidate had filed no gift tax form as required. Dinkins then changed the story. He had not given the stock to his son, he now said, but had sold it to him for $58,000, so no gift tax filing was needed. Later it would become evident that the transaction he described required another tax form, but that had not been filed either.

Dinkins released a handwritten letter dated October 30, 1985, addressed to "Dear Daddy," in which his son agreed to purchase the stock, but with no payments called for until January 1, 1991, when the entire principal amount was due, plus 8 percent interest. The letter in turn implied a loan, which did not appear on Dinkins's city financial disclosure forms as required. Because a close family member still owned the stock, the city's ethics rules made it inappropriate for Dinkins to vote on matters affecting the company, including an affiliate that held a cable TV franchise in Queens. Dinkins's staff, acting on behalf of the borough president, cast votes twice on such matters, through a lack of managerial oversight according to the candidate.

Then information surfaced that showed three years before the $58,000 transaction with his son, Dinkins had valued the stock in excess of a million dollars on a New York State financial disclosure form. He explained the huge discrepancy as the consequence of the difficulty inherent in valuing the price of shares of a closely held corporation. Percy Sutton refused to release any documents that would clarify the matter, and Dinkins's son took an extended vacation and could not be reached. Their actions created the appearance that the candidate's friend and relative were stonewalling to protect him. Dinkins held a press conference, accompanied by an accountant, and answered at great length under hot press lights the many detailed questions about the arcane transaction. Supporters felt he put the matter to rest, but for many New Yorkers the episode had caused doubts.[80]

Faced with evidence of anti-Semites in his midst and with a financial scandal that made the man appear both incompetent and dishonest, voters recoiled, especially Jews. One poll showed that Dinkins's position among Jews had deteriorated from a substantial lead over Giuliani to an eighteen-point deficit. Others showed that the number of Jews undecided how to vote had risen. While Jewish voters reacted strongest, other whites too began to doubt they could trust the Democratic Party's first black nominee for mayor. Dinkins's lead over Giuliani, once as high as 24 percent, plummeted to four points in one survey. The momentum of the campaign had changed entirely. Dinkins's once-inevitable victory was slipping away, with the changing attitude of Jewish voters the key factor in his decline.[81]

Dinkins stepped up his campaigning in Orthodox Jewish communities where his support was least certain, but he found the response to his efforts mixed. On his way into a meeting with the Council of Jewish Organizations of Borough Park in Brooklyn, hecklers called him an anti-Semite. Inside, in response to tough questioning, Dinkins felt compelled to declare that his friend Jesse Jackson would have no influence in his administration if he were elected mayor. The group endorsed Dinkins, but on the same day, elsewhere in Brooklyn, a group of opponents hurled eggs at his podium.[82]

The Dinkins campaign put Ed Koch on the air to ask voters to cast ballots for the Democrat because "he will fight for the people of this city." Dinkins paraded a succession of prominent rabbis before the news media to announce their endorsements. The candidate reminded Jewish voters at every opportunity that his opponent belonged to the Republican Party while he, like them, was a Democrat. "My opponent campaigned with a man who was the only governor in America who refused to condemn the vile idea that Zionism is racism—White House Chief of Staff John Sununu," Dinkins told one heavily Jewish breakfast gathering.[83]

In the final weeks of the election, the *New York Times*, the *Daily News*, and *Newsday* all endorsed Dinkins, citing the need for racial comity. A poll taken a week before the final balloting showed that Dinkins's appeal to Jews was working. He had pulled even with Giuliani among Jewish voters with an opinion, although 16 percent remained undecided. His support among Latinos, solid until the damaging news appeared about his ethical practices and about the militants in his campaign, had eroded modestly, while Giuliani had picked up support among the group. Still, a majority of Latino voters favored Dinkins compared with less than 40 percent for Giuliani. The Republican's support among white Catholics remained solid, but overall, Dinkins appeared to be regaining his lost ground.[84]

Giuliani's campaign aired commercials that hit hard at Dinkins's tax troubles and made the man appear dishonest. And they also made much of his association with self-declared antiwhites in a ploy sure to raise racial fears. During the last days of the campaign, while accepting the endorsement of the conservative United Jewish Coalition, Giuliani declared that the "naked truth is that David Dinkins will be the trusted servant of Jesse [Jackson] in City Hall." In the last two days of the campaign Giuliani shook hands in predominantly Jewish neighborhoods in Brooklyn and Queens "pleading with Democrats to abandon their party." According to a journalist who accompanied him on these last forays, "Jews . . . would be Giuliani's Little Big Horn." Dinkins, on the other hand, when asked on the Sunday before the election how Jews would vote, declared, "I am confident that the members of the Jewish community will be supportive of my candidacy." Polls showed his lead expanding.[85]

On November 7, 1989, almost 1.75 million New Yorkers went to the polls. They elected David Dinkins mayor by the smallest margin of victory in a New York City contest for mayor since 1905. Fewer than fifty thousand votes separated the winner, who took just over half the ballots, from the loser, who took 48 percent. While the closeness of the race surprised political analysts, it did nothing to dampen the euphoria among Dinkins's followers and all black New Yorkers. As midnight approached and the outcome became clear, the beaming mayor-elect stood before an ecstatic crowd accompanied by his elegant wife. First he pledged to be mayor of all the people. Next, with his eighty-three-year-old father by his side, he declared that his election "forged a new link in the chain of memory" marking "another milestone on freedom's road." For the descendants of slaves, the event evoked powerful emotions. Then Dinkins, a three-decade veteran of New York City politics, who had studied the election returns district by district as reported to his campaign headquarters, offered "a special word" to New York's Jews. "That community is a light unto the nation tonight," he said. He owed his victory to them.

Nearly 40 percent of the city's Jews voted for Dinkins. It was less than a majority to be sure, and far less than most polls had predicted, but dramatically higher than the 23 percent of white Catholics who voted for the black Democrat. If Dinkins had won no more support from white Jews than he did from white Catholics, Rudolph Giuliani would have been elected mayor. Dinkins's total support among whites was just over 30 percent. The rest of the balloting was unsurprising. Dinkins won 97 percent of the votes cast by blacks, and 70 percent of Latino votes. These results essentially mirrored the outcome of the Democratic primary. Giuliani won three-quarters of the votes of white Catholics, 60 percent of Jewish ballots, and just 30 percent of the city's Latino votes. It was an impressive display for a non-Democrat in New York City, but by the slimmest of margins, it was insufficient to elect him. Dinkins had kept his coalition together, and New York City, for the first time in its history, would have a black mayor.[86]

VII. A New City Government

On Election Day 1989, New Yorkers also approved a new city charter that changed the structure of municipal government. Late in 1981, the New York Civil Liberties Union had filed a federal suit on behalf of three Brooklyn residents claiming that the Board of Estimate acted as a de facto legislative body and that its borough-wide basis of representation violated the constitutional norm of "one person, one vote." Brooklyn, with more than two million inhabitants, had just a single vote on the Board of Estimate, the same as Staten Island, where only three hundred fifty thousand New Yorkers lived. After a series of suits, in 1986, a federal appeals court ruled against the city. In response, Mayor Koch established a Charter Revision Commission, but the city continued to pursue the legal battle and the Supreme Court agreed to hear the case, so the commission's work lost its drama for a time.

On March 22, 1989, the highest court in the nation ruled that the structure New York City had used to govern itself for nearly a century violated the Constitution of the United States. The Charter Revision Commission went back to work and ultimately developed a plan that abolished the Board of Estimate and reduced the role of the borough presidents and the city council president to little more than ceremonial status. The new charter expanded the number of seats on the city council from thirty-five to fifty-one, with an express intent to draw district lines that would increase the number of minority representatives. As a result, this gave the city council some legislative and budgetary authority for the first time. At the same time, the power of the mayor and the operating agencies he controlled increased. In short, the city council and the mayor divided between them the powers once held by the Board of Estimate, with the larger portion going to the mayor. The proposal promised the most dramatic change in the structure of city government since consolidation in 1898. A ballot referendum allowed New Yorkers to declare their approval of the new charter, which they did by a margin of five to four.[87]

Another structural change received much attention during the 1989 campaign. It was the first conducted under a new law governing the size of contributions allowed in city elections. In return for limiting donations from a single source to $3,000, candidates received matching public funds. Participation was voluntary, but if one candidate did not join in, that candidate's opponent benefited from an even higher allotment of public money. Good government groups hailed it as a great advance while throughout the race candidates complained that the new law limited their ability to raise funds.

For two reasons, the new law had little impact on election results in 1989. First, the chance to elect the city's first black mayor gave the campaign an exceptionally high profile, and the unusual circumstance of a colorful incumbent like Koch at risk of dethronement attracted enormous media attention. Serious candidates had little trouble getting heard. Second, the four major Democrats and two Republicans all spent large sums of money, certainly sufficient to send a message. There is no correlation between the money the candidates spent and the votes they won, nor any reason to believe that if any of the candidates had raised more money, it would have changed the outcome. In each primary the richest candidate lost.[88]

Notes

1. This chapter originally appeared in Chris McNickle, *To Be Mayor of New York: Ethnic Politics in the City* (New York: Columbia University Press, 1993). It has been updated and revised for this book.

2. Kevin Flynn and Ellis Henican, "The Steady Rise of David Dinkins: Lessons from Harlem's Politics," *New York Newsday*, October 29, 1989; Joe Klein "The Friends of David Dinkins," *New York*, October 30, 1989, 14; Jim Sleeper, *The Closest of Strangers*, 269–73.

3. Judith Michaelson, "Man in the News: Deputy Mayor David Dinkins, All Lines Open," *The New York Post*, December 8, 1973; Celestine Bohlen, "Groundbreaker Bound by Tradition: David Norman Dinkins," *The New York Post*, November 8, 1989.

4. Pamela Newkirk, "Honest Kid Named 'Dink.'" *The New York Post*, September 17, 1989; Carole Argus, "Youthful Years of Segregation Hardened Victor's Will to Win," *New York Newsday*, November 8, 1989.

5. Dennis Duggan, "Dinkins Day of Decision," *New York Newsday*, February 14, 1989; Pamela Newkirk, "Honest Kid Named 'Dink,'" *New York Post*, September 17, 1989.

6. Carole Argus, "Youthful Years of Segregation Hardened Victor's Will to Win," *New York Newsday*, November 8, 1989.

7. *New York Amsterdam News*, September 5, 1953; Ronald Smothers, *NYT*, November 29, 1973.

8. Ronald Smothers, *NYT*, November 29, 1973.

9. "Both Parties, NAACP, In Registration Drives," *New York Amsterdam News*, October 6, 1962. The discussion of the evolution of African American politics is adapted from McNickle, *To Be Mayor of New York*, 99–101.

10. John Albert Morsell, "The Political Behavior of Negroes in New York City." PhD diss., Columbia University, 1950, 8–11; Gilbert Osofsky, *Harlem: The Making of a Ghetto*, 2nd ed. (New York: Harper & Row, 1971), 45.

11. John Albert Morsell, "The Political Behavior of Negroes," 26–31; Edwin R. Lewinson, *Black Politics in New York City* (New York: Twayne Publishers, Inc., 1974), 44.

12. Osofsky, *Harlem*, 18–28, 89–91.

13. Lewinson, *Black Politics*, 144; Nancy J. Weiss, *Farewell to the Party of Lincoln: Black Politics in the Age of FDR* (Princeton: Princeton University Press, 1983), 209 and *passim*.

14. William Spinrad, "New Yorkers Cast Their Ballots." PhD diss., Columbia University, 1955, 50–51; US Census Office, *Census of the Population*, Vol. I, 85.

15. McNickle, *To Be Mayor of New York*, 8–11.

16. McNickle, *To Be Mayor of New York*, 124–48; 182–84.

17. "Looking Like a Winner," *New York Amsterdam News*, September 11, 1965; "Sutton, Dinkins in Crash," *New York Amsterdam News*, June 25, 1966; "Dinkins To Take Over from Jones," *New York Amsterdam News*, March 18, 1967; David Dinkins, "What Is A District Leader," *New York Amsterdam News*, September 11, 1971.

18. Ronald Smothers, *NYT*, November 29, 1973; "A Good Appointment," *New York Amsterdam News*, July 1, 1972.

19. Gertrude Wilson, "White-On-White: What's Wrong With Black Power," *New York Amsterdam News*, July 9, 1966; "Bd of Ed Prez Looks At a Rotted School," *New York Amsterdam News*, May 3, 1969; Chuck Andrews & Co., "Politics in Black," *New York Amsterdam News*, February 12, 1972; "Black Politicians Oppose Election Board Changes," *New York Amsterdam News*, June 16, 1973; Andy Cooper, "One Man's Opinion," *New York Amsterdam News*, June 18, 1975.

20. Jesse H. Walker and Cathy Aldridge, "Primaries Shock NY Blacks," *New York Amsterdam News*, June 21, 1969.

21. James Booker, "Uptown Lowdown: Next Right March," *New York Amsterdam News*, August 28, 1965; Dinkins Bundy Report Forum Set To Further Understanding," *New York Amsterdam News*, January 6, 1968; Jesse H. Walker and Cathy Aldridge, "Primaries Shock NY Blacks," *New York Amsterdam News*, June 21, 1969; "Dinkins Named," *New York Amsterdam News*, August 18, 1973.

22. "Paul Gibson Jr., To Be Deputy Mayor: Dinkins Bows Out Of Job," *New York Amsterdam News*, January 5, 1974.

23. Editorial, "We Are For Dinkins," *New York Amsterdam News*, June 11, 1977; McNickle, *To Be Mayor of New York*, 246, 278–79.

24. Bryant Rollins, "Paterson Accepts the Challenge," *New York Amsterdam News*, December 3, 1977; "It's Not a Manhattan Problem," *New York Amsterdam News*, December 24, 1977; "No More Politics—Percy Sutton," *New York Amsterdam News*, March 4, 1978.

25. AM News Editorial Staff, "Black Opinion Mixed On Looting; Merchants, Politicians Outraged," *New York Amsterdam News*, July 23, 1977.

26. Andrew Cooper, "Dinkins Fails to Win Borough Presidency," *New York Amsterdam News*, November 7, 1981; McNickle, *To Be Mayor of New York*, 279.

27. Kevin Flynn and Ellis Henican, "The Steady Rise of David Dinkins: Lessons from Harlem's Politics," *New York Newsday*, October 29, 1989; Joe Klein, "Mr. Softy," *New York*, January 16, 1989; Sleeper, *The Closest of Strangers*, 272–74; Josh Barbanel, "Dinkins Is Victorious, Setting Stage to Return a Black to Estimate Board," *NYT*, September 11, 1985.

28. Author's interview, Albert Scardino, December 10, 2010; Joe Klein, "Is He Up To It," *New York*, November 5, 1991, 39; Marie Brenner, "Being There," *Vanity Fair*, January 1991, 93; Michaelson, "Man in the News," *The New York Post*, December 8, 1973; Todd S. Purdum, "Buttoned Up," *NYT*, September 12, 1993.

29. Todd S. Purdum, "Buttoned Up," *NYT*, September 12, 1993.

30. Michaelson, "Man in the News," *The New York Post*, December 8, 1973.

31. Elizabeth Kolbert, "Two Views of Dinkins: Conciliator or Hesitator," *NYT*, August 14, 1989.

32. Todd S. Purdum, "Buttoned Up," *NYT*, September 12, 1993; Author's interview, off the record.

33. Dennis Duggan, "Dinkins Day of Decision," *New York Newsday*, February 14, 1989.

34. Author's interview, Bill Lynch, October 29, 2010.

35. Author's interview, Bill Lynch, October 29, 2010; Don Terry, "The 1989 Elections: Dinkins Strategist; 'Rumpled Genius' Who Guided Mayor-Elect's Race Savors Its End," *NYT*, November 9, 1989.

36. Author's interview, Bill Lynch, October 29, 2010.

37. Author's interview, Bill Lynch, October 29, 2010; Frank Lynn, "Political Notes; Dinkins and His Advisors Consider Campaign Costs," *NYT*, December 18, 1988; Frank Lynn, "Many Say It's All But Certain: Dinkins Will Run," *NYT*, January 29, 1989; Scott McConnell, "The Making of the Mayor 1989," *Commentary*, February 1990.

38. Joe Klein, "Mr. Softy," 20; Peter Wilkinson, "Who'll Stop the Reign?" *7 Days*, 14; *NYT*, December 8, 1988; January 29, February 15, September 17, 1989; Duggan, "Dinkins Day of Decision," *New York Newsday*, February 14, 1989.

39. Joe Klein, "Koch's Last Stand?," *New York*, December 5, 1988, 54ff.

40. Ibid.

41. Klein, "Koch's Last Stand?" 54–55; Author's interview with Richard Ravitch, New York City, September 9, 1991.

42. Joe Klein, "Great Man Theory," *New York*, February 13, 1989, 16; *NYT*, January 5, 1989.

43. Wayne Barrett, "Thug Life: The Shocking Secret History of Harold Giuliani, the Mayor's Ex-Convict Dad," *Village Voice*, July 4, 2000; Wayne Barrett assisted by Adam Fifield, *Rudy! An Investigative Biography of Rudolph Giuliani* (New York: Basic Books, 2000), 17, 25–26.

44. Wayne Barrett, "Thug Life: The Shocking Secret History of Harold Giuliani, the Mayor's Ex-Convict Dad," *Village Voice*, July 4, 2000; Barrett assisted by Fifield, *Rudy!*, 17, 25–26.

45. Barrett assisted by Fifield, "Rudy!," 54, 57, 135, 143–45.

46. Joe Klein, "Ready for Rudy," *New York*, March 6, 1989, 31; Jack Newfield and Wayne Barrett, *City for Sale* (New York: Harper and Row, 1988), 18.

47. *NYT*, August 12, 1986; Author's interview with FBI official, name withheld, 1986.

48. Klein, "Great-Man Theory," 19; *NYT*, January 5, 1989.

49. Klein, "Great-Man Theory," 16; Klein, "Ready for Rudy," 31; *NYT*, January 5, 1989.

50. *NYT*, January 11, 1989.

51. Andy Logan, "Around City Hall," *The New Yorker*, January 2, February 13, 1989; *Newsday*, July 14, 1989; Koch interview, September 24, 1991; Wagner, Jr. interview, September 9, 1991.

52. Joe Klein, "Been Down So Long It Looks Like Up To Me," *New York*, February 20, 1989, 35; Koch interview, September 24, 1991; Wagner, Jr. interview, September 9, 1991.

53. Andy Logan, "Around City Hall," *The New Yorker*, April 17, 1989, 123. Just days before the Democratic primary the Queens Democratic organization realized that Ravitch had no chance to win and switched their endorsement to Koch.

54. Joshua Freeman, *Working Class New York* (New York: The New Press, 2000), 295, 317; Nick Ravo, "Hospital Union Elects Leader," *NYT*, May 1, 1989; Sam Roberts, "As Hospital Agreement is Reached, A Strong Union and Leader Emerge," *NYT*, October 5, 1989.

55. Klein, "The Friends of David Dinkins," October 30, 1989, 14; Neil A. Lewis, "Teachers' Leader Ready to Reap Gratitude," *NYT*, November 13, 1989; Blanche Blank, "Bureaucracy: Power in Details," 124–25, in Bellush and Netzer, eds. *Urban Politics New York Style.*

56. *Newsday*, July 7, 19, 1989.

57. *Newsday*, July 8, 21, 1989.

58. *NYT*, May 2, 1989.

59. *Newsday*, July 21, 23, 24, 1989; Joe Klein, "Can Dinkins Do It?," *New York*, July 31, 1989, 31ff.

60. *Newsday*, July 8, 9, 1989.

61. Linda Greenhouse, "The Supreme Court; Supreme Court, 5–4, Narrowing Roe V. Wade, Upholds Sharp State Limits on Abortions," *NYT*, July 4, 1989.

62. *Daily News*, July 14, 1989; Joe Klein, "Rudy's Fall from Grace," *New York*, August 21, 1989.

63. *NYT*, April 21–29, November 4, 1989; Campaign paraphernalia paid for by the Committee for David Dinkins, in the possession of the author; Susan Saulny, "Convictions and Charges Voided In '89 Central Park Jogger Attack," *NYT*, December 20, 2002.

64. *NYT*, August 23–29, September 1, 1989; Roger Biles, "Mayor Dinkins and the Politics of Race in New York City," 136, in David R. Colburn and Jeffrey S. Adler, *African-American Mayors: Race Politics and the American City* (Urbana and Chicago: University of Illinois Press, 2001); Jonathan Soffer, *Ed Koch and the Rebuilding of New York City* (New York: Columbia University

Press, 2010), 385. Joe Klein, "Brotherhood Week," *New York*, September 11, 1989, 36ff.; Sleeper, *The Closest of Strangers*, 193.

65. *Newsday*, September 14, 1989; *NYT*, September 14, 1989.

66. *Newsday*, September 13, 14, 1989; *NYT*, September 14, 1989. Both newspapers report the election results broken down by ethnic group and other demographic characteristics according to information gathered in exit polls on primary day. The two sets of data are consistent except for how the Hispanic vote split. *Newsday*, relying on a poll commissioned in conjunction with WNBC-TV, reports the breakdown of the Hispanic vote as 68 percent in favor of Dinkins and 27 percent for Koch. In this poll, Hispanics are presented as an independent category separate from whites and blacks. *The New York Times*, relying on a poll commissioned in conjunction with CBS-TV News, did not offer Hispanic as a separate category, but makes the following statement in a footnote: "Not shown are 160 respondents who indicated they were Hispanic and 35 who indicated other races. Of Hispanics, 41 percent said they voted for Koch; 54 percent said they voted for Dinkins." I have cited the *Newsday* figure in the text because it appeared to gather the information in a more direct and therefore more reliable manner. The figures are sufficiently different that the nuance of the analysis would change, but the basic point still holds even with the more even split reported in *The New York Times*.

67. *Newsday*, September 13, 14, 1989; *NYT*, October 9, 1989.

68. Barrett assisted by Fifield, *Rudy!*, pp. 175–81; Jonathan Soffer, *Ed Koch*, 367.

69. Barrett assisted by Fifield, *Rudy!*, pp. 231–35.

70. *Newsday*, October 7, 1989.

71. Jonathan Rieder, *Canarsie: The Jews and Italians of Brooklyn Against Liberalism* (Cambridge: Harvard University Press, 1985) offers an insightful analysis of the ways that Jewish attitudes toward race compare and differ with the attitudes of Italians even when the two groups live in the same neighborhood and are therefore faced with the same environmental circumstances. Sleeper, *The Closest of Strangers*, examines the peculiar relationship between New York's white liberals, predominantly Jews, and blacks.

72. *Village Voice* September 27, 1989; *Newsday*, September 28, 1989; Jeanie Kasindorf, "Jackie Mason Tries to Talk Himself Out of Trouble," *New York*, October 16, 1989, 36ff.

73. *Newsday*, September 29, October 2, 3, 10, 1989.

74. *Newsday*, September 28, October 10, 1989.

75. *Newsday*, October 13, 1989.

76. *Newsday*, October 8, 1989.

77. *Newsday*, October 13, 1989.

78. *Newsday*, October 12, 1989.

79. *Newsday*, October 13, 20, 1989.

80. *Newsday*, October 12, 13, 14, 15, 16, 17, 18, 19, 20, 21, 1989. Andy Logan, "Around City Hall: Inexakte," *The New Yorker*, November 6, 1989, 138–52.

81. *Newsday*, October 24, 1989.

82. *Newsday*, October 30, 1989.

83. *Newsday*, October 30, November 1, 1989.
84. *Newsday*, November 2, 1989.
85. *Newsday*, November 3, 5, 6, 1989.
86. *NYT*, November 9, 1989; *Newsday*, November 9, 1989.
87. *NYT*, March 23, November 8, 1989.
88. *NYT*, September 9, 1989.

3

Credibility Gap, Budget Gap

David Dinkins launched his administration with soaring rhetoric on New Year's Day 1990. "I stand here before you today as the elected leader of the greatest city of a great nation to which my ancestors were brought, chained, and whipped in the hold of a slave ship," he told a crowd gathered outside City Hall as he took the public oath of office. "We have not finished the journey towards liberty and justice," he declared. "But surely we have come a long way. This day is not a tribute to me; it is a tribute to you, the people of New York."[1]

The new mayor reaffirmed his commitment to seek social justice in all its forms for every group in New York's "gorgeous mosaic," in keeping with the identity politics of the day. He promised to "set our priorities to strengthen the weak, to help those who have been hurt and to keep the middle class in New York City." His administration would support "community-based efforts to provide prenatal care, lead screening, child care, after-school programs, and centers of culture and companionship for seniors," and he explicitly dedicated his administration to the children of New York—"voices of hope," he called them. He also renewed his campaign pledge to be "the toughest mayor on crime this city has ever seen."[2]

South African archbishop Desmond Tutu, winner of the Nobel Peace Prize for his efforts to end his country's sinister apartheid policies, blessed the proceedings. His presence added international luster to the swearing-in ceremony of New York's first black mayor and a human connection to the continent of David Dinkins's heritage. It added controversy as well. Tutu had expressed support for Palestinian causes, and he had likened some of Israel's practices on the West Bank to those of South Africa. Riverdale rabbi Avi Weiss, a champion of Jewish justice to some, a religious rabble-rouser to others, led a demonstration against Tutu's involvement. Weiss kept the event deliberately small to limit the hostility he knew a Jewish protest at the inauguration of New York's first African American mayor would cause. Dinkins still scolded the rabbi for "raining on my parade." Even on a day dominated by joyous celebration, racial and ethnic tension followed New York's first African American mayor into City Hall.[3]

The lofty and expansive goals of David Dinkins's inaugural speech ignored the unsettling truth that he entered office with his authority already diminished. A 2 percent victory over his Republican opponent, despite a five-to-one advantage in registration for Democrats, gave him a weak mandate. Bill Lynch blamed racism for the narrow outcome. "It was because he was a candidate of color," the mayor's chief political advisor concluded. Surely, there were white New Yorkers disinclined to vote for a black man for mayor. The stark racial voting pattern supports the claim. Just as surely, continuing questions surrounding the Inner City Broadcasting transaction created a cloud of suspicion around the mayor. Exit polls revealed that one-fourth of the voters who cast ballots for Giuliani and nearly four in ten of those who made up their mind late cited the troubling reports about Dinkins's financial affairs as the reason for their decision. If the man was not honest or competent handling his own business, how could he be expected to handle the city's? Ominously, before the polls even closed on Election Day, the Brooklyn federal prosecutor's office alerted Dinkins's attorney that it had opened an inquiry into the transaction, already under scrutiny by the city's Department of Investigation. For months, articles appeared with headlines such as "Dinkins Stock: The Questions That Persist." The columns contained damning quotes from attorneys and other experts. "[There] must be at least some suspicion of a violation of a law other than . . . taxes" for the investigations to continue was typical of comments on the topic.[4]

Late in July, nearly seven months after Dinkins became mayor, Brooklyn federal prosecutor Andrew J. Maloney announced that his office had decided not to file criminal charges. The issue went away for a while, but resurfaced several months later. The city's commissioner of investigation had appointed Elkan Abramowitz, a former prosecutor in Manhattan district attorney Robert Morgenthau's office, to examine the mayor's role in the stock scandal. In January 1991, he released his report. "There is troubling circumstantial evidence indicating that the . . . letter [documenting the mayor's transfer of the stock to his son] might have been written at a much later date" than claimed, Abramowitz wrote. US Secret Service analysis and other facts suggested the younger Dinkins wrote the "Dear Daddy" note during the election campaign and backdated it. The piece of paper on which the letter had been written had come from a pad. It included impressions of phone numbers written on sheets of paper above it of people the mayor's son met years after the date on the letter. But David junior had moved to Las Vegas and refused to return to New York to testify about the matter, "rendering us unable to resolve this factual issue with certainty," the investigators concluded. "We have not cleared [the mayor]," Abramowitz told reporters. "We have simply concluded that the evidence is legally insufficient to warrant a criminal prosecution." Dinkins declared the matter closed, but, when asked about the evidence in the fifty-two-page report, he had to respond defensively. "I don't think there is a cloud hanging over me. If [Abramowitz] feels that way, he and I are not in concert," the mayor said.[5]

Despite Dinkins's assertion, the scandal left many New Yorkers of goodwill with a lingering sense that the man responsible for making decisions that affected their lives daily had escaped criminal charges by a margin as narrow as his electoral victory. The episode called into question his judgment and his integrity. Moral authority is one source of a mayor's power. The Inner City Broadcasting stock affair left David Dinkins weakened.

I. The Rhythm of a City, the Pace of a Mayor

In the days leading up to his inauguration, the mayor's deliberate management style began to cause concern. After the election, a palpable sense of excitement surged through Dinkins's supporters, anticipating change after twelve years of a hostile incumbent. The mayor-elect named Nathan Leventhal, president of Lincoln Center and a former housing commissioner and deputy mayor, head of his transition committee. On November 14, 1989, Dinkins announced its members, an all-star cast. The committee included the former congresswoman and Democratic vice presidential candidate Geraldine Ferraro, former city council president Carol Bellamy, president of the New York Conference of the NAACP, Hazel Dukes, Lazard Freres investment banker and Municipal Assistance Corporation chairman Felix Rohatyn, and sixteen other similarly prominent New Yorkers. Former mayors Beame, Lindsay, and Wagner would serve as special advisors. Some saw in the committee representatives of the diverse coalition that elected the new chief executive. To politically astute historian Richard Wade, it was a "message of David's caution that he wants to reassure people who were afraid of a black mayor that he would do nothing different from what they were accustomed to."[6]

The transition team then named five search committees to seek candidates to fill the most important posts in city government. Each panel included fifteen or more members—more than eighty people in total when all had been chosen. Before long, the broad, consensus-based approach to nominating talent for jobs turned unwieldy. The process created the impression that including everyone and offending no one in his selections mattered most to the mayor, and that he lacked the decisiveness required of the chief executive of America's largest city. By December 1, reporters compared the pace of his appointments to his predecessors' unfavorably. The mayor-elect dismissed the criticisms, declaring it more important to act wisely than quickly.[7]

During the second week of December, Dinkins elevated three members of his borough president staff to deputy mayor. Bill Lynch took on intergovernmental relations. Barbara Fife, chief of staff of his borough president's office, became responsible for planning and development. Former deputy borough president Sally Hernandez-Pinero became deputy mayor for finance and economic development. Dinkins appointed Victor Kovner, a longtime reform political figure as his corporation counsel, and Albert Scardino, a *New York Times* journalist became press secretary. Before year-end the mayor-elect named a career firefighter, Carlos Rivera, fire commissioner—a nod toward the Latino element of his coalition. Harvey Robins, deputy chancellor of the Board of Education for finance and operations and former first deputy commissioner of the Human Resources Administration became the mayor's director of operations.

For first deputy mayor, the man who would run the city's affairs day-to-day and who would oversee the government when the mayor traveled out of town, Dinkins chose Norman Steisel. The two men had met years earlier as members of a group of tennis-playing city government officials organized by Lindsay "Whiz Kid" Sid Davidoff. The group traveled to Florida resorts twice a year, where they would spend a week at a clinic improving their game. Steisel and Dinkins bonded on the court and off, developing a friendship and a relationship of mutual trust.[8]

Steisel was the Brooklyn-born son of a Jewish baker who had fled Poland with his wife and young daughter just months before the 1939 Nazi invasion. He had attended Brooklyn Technical High School—one of the city's best—and earned a chemical engineering degree from Pratt

Institute, followed by a master's degree in the same subject from Yale. He joined city government during the Lindsay years, serving for four years as a budget analyst and budget liaison aide. Later he became the head of planning and policy for the police department, followed by two years as the deputy budget director during the worst of Abe Beame's fiscal crisis. After Ed Koch's election, Steisel was among those who schooled the new mayor in the complex intricacies of the budget he would have to defend before Congress to secure federal guarantees critical to the city's financial future. The budget expert impressed the third mayor he worked for sufficiently to earn an appointment as commissioner of sanitation. "He inherited a department in chaos," Robert McFadden would write in the *New York Times*. "Half the equipment was out of service, the work force was demoralized, there were no long-range plans to cope with a looming garbage crisis, and city streets from Riverdale to Far Rockaway were filthy." Eight years later, Steisel had completely turned things around. He had also negotiated two-person staffing levels on garbage collection trucks, down from three, an efficiency move that saved the city millions of dollars.

In 1986, Steisel left city government to join Lazard Freres investment bank as a senior partner. When the city created the School Construction Authority to streamline the school-building process, Koch named the banker with extensive city government experience its first board chairman. The role kept Steisel in direct contact with senior city officials, including Manhattan borough president Dinkins, as he searched for administrative talent to staff the new agency. A solid personal relationship with the mayor-elect, years of senior municipal management expertise, and credibility with business people made Steisel a logical candidate for first deputy mayor. Finance professionals in particular thought the man a smart choice. The new mayor had no particular financial background, and Steisel could help Dinkins manage through the tough budget gaps that already loomed. Widespread praise greeted the selection. Koch called the man "an exceptional individual . . . a first rate budget director . . . [and] the best Sanitation Commissioner this city ever had." Nathan Leventhal, citing the new first deputy's "encyclopedic knowledge of city government," called the selection "purely a merit appointment."[9]

A first deputy with Steisel's budget expertise lent confidence to the new team. Still, the heaviest lifting on the fiscal front would inevitably fall to the budget director. To fill that spot, Dinkins chose Philip R. Michael, a University of California at Berkeley–trained lawyer and former federal prosecutor who came to New York from San Francisco during the Lindsay administration to serve as the police department's trial commissioner, the official responsible for hearing disciplinary complaints against cops. Some years later, Koch named Michael finance commissioner in the hope that a man with enforcement expertise would take aggressive steps to increase the city's revenue collections. Michael did exactly that. He fired city employees who had become comfortable and lazy in their jobs and hired Internal Revenue Service investigators to audit sales tax receipts. Working with the police, his department seized the books of Cartier, Tiffany's, and Van Cleef and Arpels to lay bare the open secret that high-end Fifth Avenue stores conspired with rich New Yorkers to evade sales tax. They mailed empty boxes to New Jersey addresses to create phony documentation for out-of-town purchases that cost the city millions in lost tax revenue until the finance department exposed them. Investigators reviewed the taxes paid by the major clearinghouse banks and secured a check for $100 million. Cross-checking audits on real estate firms revealed tax evasion there as well.[10]

Michael worked briefly in Merrill Lynch's municipal finance group and as general counsel for a medical insurance company after serving as finance commissioner. Then he became the director of the New York State Financial Control Board, the special agency created to ensure fiscal discipline for New York City's budget. When Dinkins won election, Michael called Norman Steisel and expressed interest in the budget director's job. He also called Peter Goldmark, another Lindsay-era official involved in Dinkins's transition. "You haven't got a chance," Goldmark told him. The transition team had offered the spot to Frank Raines, a Lazard Freres banker who had worked in the federal Office of Management and Budget under Jimmy Carter, among other roles. But Raines declined the job. So Steisel introduced Michael to the mayor-elect, who appointed him budget director. When he announced the decision, Dinkins declared it "should send a strong signal to the business community, to the city's bondholders and to the taxpayers that we will not relax our vigilance over the bottom line, even in difficult times."[11]

The appointment did not please everyone. Stanley Hill of District Council 37 called his friend the mayor to complain. The unions had found Michael's personnel management of the finance department way too aggressive. Dinkins assured Hill his union would have "effective communications" with the new budget director.[12]

The team in formation included a healthy balance of longtime Dinkins loyalists and experienced municipal executives who could manage city government as well as anyone. Its members' ethnic and gender diversity matched the city's better than governments past. Die-hard anti-Koch elements protested the inclusion of senior members of the old regime in the new, but Koch had reigned for twelve years. It should have surprised no one that a search for competent city government managers found professionals who had served him. And many members of the team, including some who had worked for Koch, actually began their city government careers as part of the best and the brightest John Lindsay attracted to New York in the 1960s and 1970s. Those officials had been part of an administration with a philosophy more in tune with Dinkins's.

Crime remained public enemy number-one, making selection of a police commissioner the mayor-elect's highest profile appointment. By mid-November, a screening panel had a search underway, and within just a few weeks it provided the mayor with three names for him to consider. A fourth candidate, Houston's chief of police Lee Brown, had canceled a meeting with the panel on short notice when a Houston police officer got shot. Reports suggested the panel still wanted to meet with him.[13]

Lee Brown had been among the names considered from the start. Born in a small town in Oklahoma during the Depression, his family migrated to California in search of work, like thousands of others John Steinbeck made famous in the *Grapes of Wrath*. Brown's father picked grapes in the San Joaquin Valley, and his mother worked as a cook. Brown grew up poor. According to one longtime friend, "[H]e learned to keep a lot of things inside so he could be strong on the outside." A football scholarship took him to California State University at Fresno, where he stumbled into criminology as a major. After graduation, he joined the San Jose Police Department—the second African American on the force—and he made the rounds. "I did about everything you do as a police officer," Brown recalled of his time there. "They had me working undercover in narcotics. I worked undercover in vice. Then I walked a beat. I worked patrol cars and traffic. Juvenile. You name it. I've done it as a cop," he told a reporter. He rose steadily up the ranks for the next dozen years or so and completed a doctorate in criminology at the University of California at Berkeley, adding impressive academic credentials to his field experience. After a few years teaching law enforcement as a professor, he returned to the job as a county sheriff in Oregon and achieved a position of national stature when he became the head of the public safety department in Atlanta. There, and later as the head of the police department in Houston, he established himself as one of the most prominent law enforcement officials in the country. And he was African American. After several other black candidates faded from consideration, Brown became increasingly attractive to Dinkins and the mayor's closest advisors.[14]

The Houston department had been considered one of the worst in the country when Brown took charge of it. Its officers had earned a reputation as a band of "psychotic cowboys," according to one journalist who wrote about them. Observers generally gave Lee Brown credit for slowly and steadily making it a more professional organization, despite powerful cultural resistance. Yet, as the seriousness of Brown's candidacy grew, press scrutiny of his career mounted, and some troubling findings surfaced. One reporter doing homework on the potential pick for New York's top cop took note that, despite claims Brown had cleaned up the Houston department, "In the last six weeks, two Houston police officers have shot and killed motorists after traffic stops. Two other officers were found guilty in rape cases. One more was arrested for heroin possession, one was charged with coercing sex from a prostitute, one was reassigned amid charges of police harassment and two officers' houses were searched as part of a drug investigation." The article went on to state the obvious—the events risked damaging the department's image and Brown's. Most observers blamed the spate of embarrassing events on bad luck and bad timing, not on Houston's police chief. Mayor Kathryn J. Witmire, in response to rising speculation about the career plans of her city's top law enforcement official, said, "I believe that Lee Brown is the best police chief in the country. I hope the Mayor of New York finds a good police chief—as long as he's not mine."[15]

Unsurprisingly, actions to reform a police department overrun with renegades earned Brown some enemies. One Houston police union boss called Brown "a phony and inept chief of police." His main agenda was the "Lee Brown promotion agenda," the unhappy man told a journalist. Critics took to calling him "Out-of-Town Brown" because of his frequent travels to conferences, particularly those organized by the International Association of Chiefs of Police, which Brown had agreed to lead as its president beginning late in 1990. Many of the cops on Houston's streets would not miss him. When they heard the news their boss had agreed to head for the Big Apple, they sang, "I Love New York," into their patrol car radios.[16]

On December 18, 1989, a little more than six weeks after winning the election, Dinkins named Brown police commissioner. The reason is that Brown is "the best," singling out his skill managing the "relationship between the community and the police . . . he's just excellent at it," the mayor-elect said. For the first time in more than a quarter century a non–New Yorker would head the NYPD, and for the second time a black man would lead the force. Dinkins said race had nothing to do with his decision. Others challenged the dubious denial. "[S]everal people involved in the search process said that by picking Chief Brown, Mr. Dinkins had sent a strong signal to his core constituency that he was sensitive to their concerns about justice from a police force that remains more than 75 percent white in a city that is now estimated to be more than half black, Hispanic and Asian," the *New York Times'* Todd Purdum reported.[17]

When David Dinkins took office on January 1, 1990, he had not yet selected a housing commissioner or a head of the Human Resources Administration that oversees the city's sprawling social services system. Many other posts of near comparable importance for finance, transportation, and other areas remained unfilled as well. The city should not have been surprised. The man they elected had a well-established reputation for moving at a steady pace of his own choosing. Nearly two months after the mayor took office, a February 20, 1990, *New York Times* editorial entitled "The City's Empty Chairs," criticized the mayor for "vacancies that are beginning to do damage, and not just in theory." Concern mounted that the city's problems would not wait for the new mayor. *New York* magazine political editor Joe Klein perceived the staffing delays as part of a broader issue of indecisiveness. Dinkins "hasn't had much to say about programs, priorities, initiatives," Klein wrote. "Dinkins hasn't said, '*This* is what's going to be important over the next few years. *This* is how I'm going to differ from the last guy. *This* is where the city is going.'" As early as his first month in office, observers of city politics worried about a growing sense of drift.[18]

II. Our Dreams Are Bigger than Our Budget

David Dinkins came to office in the midst of a falling economy and a rising fiscal crisis. He governed during what would be one of the worst periods in New York's economic history since the 1930s. Officially, the country experienced a mild recession—an actual decline in gross domestic product—from August 1990 to March 1991. The recovery proved tepid, and the national economy remained "almost comatose," in the words of one economist, as late as September 1992. "The current slump already ranks as the longest period of sustained weakness since the Great Depression," he wrote. New York City suffered "from an intensified case of the same economic malaise that [gripped] the national economy—runaway deficits, an overbuilt real-estate market, and shaky financial institutions," along with "neglect of its manufacturing base," another analyst observed.[19]

New York lost nearly 14 percent of its jobs between January 1989 and December 1992, whereas the country as a whole lost fewer than 2 percent. Unemployment in the city peaked above 13 percent early in 1993, roughly double national rates. New York's welfare rolls would rise to over 1 million people out of a total population of 7.4 million. The crippled local economy left Dinkins confronting dire budget choices throughout his entire term.[20]

A decade-long restructuring of New York City's manufacturing industry was still in process in 1989, causing local economic trauma to exceed national pain by some measure. When World War II ended, nearly a million people worked in manufacturing jobs within the five boroughs. By the time of Dinkins's election, just over one-third of those jobs remained. They provided work for only 360,000 residents, the continuously shrinking remnants of a once-vibrant army of garment workers and printers, builders of ships and specialized machinery, makers of chewing gum and pencils, and other manufacturing jobs. The city had never really served as home to extensive heavy industry, such as automobile assembly plants or steel production. Its geography did not lend itself to expansive spaces for large factory floors. But light manufacturing, particularly tasks that required specialized skills, had once made the working class the heart and soul of New York. Over time, that changed.[21]

Innovations in transportation and technology, particularly a continuous drive to automate tasks requiring special skills, transformed how things got made, and where. Factories that produced by machine what once required human talent could be built more cheaply where land cost less than in New York's densely populated neighborhoods. Unskilled labor in other parts of the country, often unorganized by unions, could be paid lower wages than city workers. The success of the civil rights movement in the 1950s and 1960s allowed millions of African Americans across the South to seek employment previously denied to them. This raised the supply of workers, depressed pay, and attracted businesses seeking cheap labor. Air-conditioning made production more efficient in the hottest regions of the country. Jobs followed Americans west as migration toward the Pacific coast remained a part of the national romance. Trade with Asia surpassed trade with Europe, denying the port of New York a three-centuries-long natural advantage in overseas commerce. Europe and Japan recovered from the devastation World War II wrought on their productive capacity. They rose up to manufacture their own goods and to compete around the world with US businesses. In Asia, Latin America, and Africa, backwater economies slowly went mainstream as global trading patterns steadily displaced regional ones.[22]

National policies intensified the market trends that so devastated New York City's manufacturing economy. Free trade agreements promoted overseas production. Federal subsidies for highways expanded access to cheap land and made moving raw materials and goods to and from remote locations easy. Federal subsidies for oil development kept gasoline prices and transport costs low. Tax deductions for interest paid on home mortgages supported construction of houses and made apartment living, so typical of New York, a less attractive option by comparison. Some workers moved to the suburbs, depleting the city's tax base. Some moved away all together. As people moved their homes elsewhere and reoriented their lives around new communities, the businesses they worked in followed. Between 1958 and 1993, 130 Fortune-listed headquarters left New York City.[23]

Many economists believed city and state officials intensified New York's multi-decade job loss with damaging government policies. In the 1950s and early 1960s, Mayor Robert Wagner allowed public workers to organize into unions and engage in collective bargaining with the city. About the same time, New York City and New York State expanded meaningfully the social contract with citizens, providing a broader range of welfare support services. Benefits were more generous and access easier than elsewhere. The combination caused public sector employment to rise from under 10 percent of total city jobs in the 1950s to 17 percent by the early 1990s. To support the growth of the municipal workforce and the increased social services benefits, local taxes rose from about the same as in other cities in the 1950s to nearly double by the time David Dinkins became mayor. New Yorkers surrendered almost 18 percent of the city's economic production in the early 1990s to state and local taxes versus less than 10 percent on average around the United States. The added cost placed an economic brake on private companies and the jobs they created, mainstream and conservative economists asserted. In the minds of these analysts, a reassessment of services the city could afford to provide and a cut in the size of the municipal workforce was necessary to restore private-sector competitiveness and economic growth.[24]

During his first term in office, in response to the severe fiscal crisis, Ed Koch did cut employment and services. Once the worst was behind the city, and with a buoyant economy for support between 1981 and 1987, he rehired laid-off workers and restored the workforce to its earlier level. His administration seemed less concerned with the size of the municipal government he ran than with the uncomfortable reality that federal policy, in conjunction with national and global market trends, overwhelmed city government's ability to control economic events. "If we try, we will be fighting against forces that are so profound we will be doomed to fail," Bobby Wagner, then Koch's deputy mayor for policy, believed. Instead of resisting changes that harmed the city, they embraced the ones they thought would replace lost jobs with new ones, even if they came in different industries requiring different skills and higher levels of education.[25]

Since companies required less labor to create the products that had become the norm for middle-class life in America, it made economic sense for people to dedicate more of their time to providing services that required trained human talent. Finance, insurance, and real estate, FIRE for short, replaced light manufacturing as the city's center of economic gravity. The legal, accounting, and other services FIRE industries required also grew, and the media and advertising businesses continued to prosper as well. The new market in which the city operated was global, and New York, along with London and Tokyo, had become a critical metropolis in a worldwide network that connected service industries across the Americas, Europe, and Asia.[26]

The change had profound implications. For generations, basic literacy and knowledge of arithmetic had been sufficient to allow New Yorkers to find a job, develop specialized skills, and earn a living wage. In the emerging information economy, high school at a minimum, with college and graduate school more the norm, was the price of admission. Those who had these credentials became the new workforce. Those who lacked them flipped burgers at fast food outlets or settled for other options that promised a life hovering near the poverty line. Young urban professionals—yuppies—displaced working-class New Yorkers as the city's new face.[27]

Businesses did not need warehouses to store goods they no longer produced. Young professionals converted vacant lofts into spacious, if somewhat austere apartments while fledgling service companies found the archaic spaces cheaper than midtown offices. Some curious social events followed. One twenty-something banker lived on the second floor of a converted warehouse that provided offices for a media company on the third. The industrial elevators opened right into the rooms that once stored only goods. Inevitably, someone on the media company staff would hit the button for two instead of three and make an unanticipated stop in the banker's living quarters, finding him many mornings fixing breakfast clad only in Fruit of the Loom briefs. Typically, he waved good naturedly to the amusement of the crowd.[28]

The Koch administration sought to speed the transition of tired remnants of the city's light industry infrastructure into a vibrant source of gentrified living quarters and service office space. New zoning policies and aggressive promotion of tax abatement programs helped real estate developers to convert lofts into luxury apartments and to build new housing on vacant or underused land. His administration negotiated tax incentives individually with companies to encourage construction of new office buildings.[29]

Critics on the left hated Koch's programs. They wanted the city to protect manufacturing space in the wistful belief that working-class jobs could be kept in New York. They found surrender to the forces denuding the city of gainful employment for laborers dispiriting. Many objected to projects that replaced decrepit living spaces with upscale alternatives because they replaced affordable options with more expensive ones, often changing the complexion and character of neighborhoods in the process. Tax relief for companies making billions of dollars of profit offended many. They denounced the approach as ill-considered, unnecessary corporate welfare. In the minds of the conspiratorial among them, real estate interests were the reason New York's working-class kept diminishing, not inexorable market forces.[30]

During Koch's first term, his programs had little impact. Federal Reserve chairman Paul Volker responded to rising inflation between 1979 and 1981 by driving interest rates to record heights. The national economy stalled, and New York City suffered along with the rest of the country. Less than one million square feet of new office space emerged in New York City during that time. But after Volker broke the inflationary cycle, a period of declining interest rates powered a real estate surge. Between 1981 and 1990 developers built fifty-three million square feet of offices. Inevitably, bust followed boom, this time exacerbated by national policies affecting savings and loan banks.[31]

Federal regulations fixed the interest rates paid by banking institutions from the days of the Great Depression until the 1970s. When inflation and interest rates soared, the system fell apart. Depositors withdrew money from traditional accounts and put them in money market funds not subject to interest rate limits. Regulators loosened rules on deposit rates to allow savings and loan banks and other closely regulated entities to compete and broadened their lending authority too. Savings and loan bankers could suddenly engage in a range of activities for which they had no training or experience. An orgy of foolishness followed. It ended badly, as such episodes always do. Commercial real estate firms and others defaulted on hundreds of billions of dollars of obligations. Olympia and York, the city's largest real estate organization and its largest taxpayer, went into receivership, delivering a severe blow to city revenues. Donald Trump assessed the worth of his real estate empire at minus $900 million. Construction projects and the jobs they generated gave way to debt renegotiations. Many savings and loans collapsed. Public taxpayers got stuck with the bill for saving the system from private mistakes.[32]

New York City felt the impact more than elsewhere because its savings and loans were among the nation's largest. Two of its most prominent, the Anchor Savings Bank and the Dime suffered real estate losses so severe that they cut thousands of staff and shuttered dozens of branches in the early 1990s. They would finally merge out of their misery in 1994 with the promise to eliminate hundreds more management jobs from the city forever. The commercial banking industry, one of New York's largest private sector employers, felt the fallout as well. Chemical Bank and Manufacturers Hanover Trust, two of the city's and the nation's largest banks, merged in 1991, heralding the disappearance of six thousand white-collar jobs. Others would follow in a wave of employment-eliminating consolidations. Along the way Salomon Brothers, one of the city's largest investment banks, tried to gain control of the US Treasury debt market in an illegal bid-rigging scheme. John Gutfreund, the chairman, resigned in disgrace and fled the country in 1991. Warren Buffet had to take control of the company to rescue it from its flirtation with disaster.[33]

So Dinkins arrived in office with the city's manufacturing sector still suffering from a long, slow bleed exacerbated by a recession and weak recovery. The crippled national economy and failed savings and loan banking policies forced a period of consolidation on the financial industry the city hoped would replace vanishing working-class employment. The real estate market—and the construction industry that depends on it—was a mess. In the three years prior to David Dinkins's election, the jobs of over one hundred thousand New Yorkers vanished. In the three years following his inauguration, the miserable downward trajectory continued. More than three hundred thousand additional workers lost their jobs before the economy finally stabilized and turned up.[34]

Dinkins, like Koch, believed the impact of global and national economic forces overwhelmed a mayor's ability to control the local economy. As a consequence, he followed similar policies. His administration would negotiate tax concessions case by case, with companies deemed at risk of leaving New York. And the city continued to promote the creation of space that would ease the transition to new industries with tax abatements and zoning rules. Dinkins, like Koch and Wagner, believed that federal government policies had a profound impact on the city's economy and that decisions made in Washington, DC during the 1970s and 1980s were awful for New York and other large cities. He sought to use his stature as mayor of America's premier metropolis to draw attention to the issue and to persuade the nation to correct what he thought an unwise, highly damaging course. In this, he was fighting against the times.[35]

In his inaugural address, tucked between the commitments to provide more services of almost every kind, the mayor had acknowledged the bleak reality. "I recognize we cannot do everything we should, that our finances may get worse before they get better, that for now our dreams are bigger than our budget." By the time he was sworn in, he inherited a financial gap estimated at $715 million for the remainder of the fiscal year that would end June 30, 1990. The outlook for the following year, more stark still, included initial estimates that projected a shortfall of at least $395 million and potentially as much as $1.8 billion.

At a breakfast for a thousand business and civic leaders sponsored by the Association for a Better New York, Dinkins found himself forced to declare, "Government simply cannot afford to do all that needs to be done." He went on to say that "[w]e have run smack into a wall," and the ability to invest in social services and crumbling infrastructure would be constrained as a result. The tone of his talk was at odds with the election campaign he had just run, during which he suggested he would do more for the city's disadvantaged than his predecessor.

Felix Rohatyn publicly urged additional austerity, including no wage increases for municipal workers, hiring freezes, and reductions in the workforce through attrition.[36]

The call for fiscal restraint clashed with the cry to respond to social needs perceived as contributing to the intolerable level of violent crime. The case to continue rebuilding the city's long-suffering infrastructure sounded just as compelling. Of the city's schools, 83 percent stood in disrepair and 40 percent of the city's 846 bridges needed renovating. Fourteen sat partially or completely closed, too dangerous to cross. Only two landfills remained open to absorb the mountains of trash—twenty-two thousand tons daily—that more than seven million people created. Unless the city moved forward with a plan to build five incinerators, the Fresh Kills garbage dump on Staten Island would reach an astonishing fifty stories high by the turn of the century. The city also needed to upgrade tunnels to ensure a clean water supply and to create holding tanks or adopt some other solution to avoid dumping untreated sludge into rivers and bays, and on and on. During the last ten years of the Koch Administration, the city spent some $19 billion on infrastructure projects, a meaningful down payment on the cost of restoring the city's physical plant to acceptable levels. The next ten years would require $57 billion more to finish the job. A professor of urban studies at Rutgers University, George Sternlieb summarized the challenge facing the new mayor simply. "There just ain't no dough. . . . There is no significant money coming from Washington and Albany, and I think the immediate human problems of the city are going to preclude putting more money into bricks and mortar."[37]

A change in federal policies compounded the financial challenges the new mayor faced. Dinkins assumed office at a time when the administration of President George H. W. Bush continued to promote the Reagan Revolution. Among other things, the federal government sought to reduce spending on many of the programs developed to help cities and states achieve national social goals. Proponents of the Reagan Revolution described the philosophical argument in simple terms: The federal government should remain as limited as possible and keep federal taxes as low as possible. If local politicians wanted to support initiatives they and their constituents deemed important, they could raise the money required from local taxes. As a tangible matter, the approach diminished the revenue sent by the federal government to cities and states. The program had a huge negative budget impact on large urban centers like New York, where disproportionate numbers of poor Americans lived. Dinkins sought to use his position as mayor of the nation's most important city to rally municipal leaders across the country to challenge Republican policies. But his efforts to restore federal support for urban priorities had little impact while Republicans ruled in Washington.[38]

By February 1, 1990, the new mayor had to present a preliminary budget to the city council with projections for the next four fiscal years. This was the process defined by the city charter that voters approved in 1989. Members of the administration, including budget officials and agency heads, were then expected to meet with city council committees. This new procedure gave the legislative body a meaningful role it had lacked for the near century the Board of Estimate dominated the city's budget decisions. The process also provided for the mayor and his staff to confer with state legislators and other officials about the many aspects of the city's finances dependent on decisions made in Albany. The New York State Legislature was supposed to approve the state budget by the end of March, although it rarely met that deadline. In April or May, in theory armed with knowledge about state fiscal actions, the mayor was to submit a spending plan called the executive budget. After council committees reviewed this version, the mayor's office would negotiate with the council speaker to create a final plan. The council had to vote and adopt a budget by June 5, but in any event, as a practical matter, before the new fiscal year began on July 1.[39]

In addition to the process defined by the city charter, as a legacy of New York's near bankruptcy in the 1970s, a second set of institutions exercised substantial power over city money decisions. In June 1975 the state created the Municipal Assistance Corporation (MAC) to issue long-term bonds on behalf of the city, backed by a pledge of revenues from local sales and stock transfer taxes. At the time, the city teetered on the brink of financial collapse, and the legislation that created MAC gave the corporation additional authority over city finances to ensure bondholders got paid. Consequently, budgets had to satisfy its requirements.

Also in 1975, in response to another imminent credit default, the state created the Emergency Financial Control Board to supervise city finances. The board consisted of the governor, the mayor, the New York State and New York City comptrollers, and three private citizens named by the governor. It had the power to review—and reject—the city's financial plan, its expense and capital budget, the contracts negotiated with municipal unions, and all municipal borrowing. If the board believed city officials were not complying with the approved financial plan, it had authority to take control of the city's bank accounts and to give direct orders to city officials. It could remove from office city officials who violated its directives and press criminal charges against them. One observer described the relationship between the city's chief executive and the board in colorful terms. "The mayor was left with as much power as the mayor of Paris during the Nazis' occupation." Originally chartered for three years, in 1978 the state dropped the word *emergency* from its title and extended its existence for three decades.[40]

By 1986, under Mayor Koch, the city fulfilled the requirements of a sunset provision that rescinded most of the board's formal powers. However, the law required the board to continue to monitor the city's finances. And under certain circumstances, including a budget deficit of $100 million or more, its powers returned automatically. The threat of reverting to what one academic called "political receivership" held little appeal for the mayor of New York.[41]

How a mayor manages the city's budget is a telling indicator of priorities and competence. The allocation of public resources reveals what the mayor thinks is important, and successful adoption of a budget demonstrates a mayor's ability to negotiate, build consensus, and promote his agenda. When David Dinkins submitted his first preliminary budget to the council on February 1, 1990, analysts observed how similar it looked to the ones his predecessor had offered. Hyman C. Grossman, managing director of the bond-rating agency Standard & Poor's Corporation, told reporters, "I don't think this budget document would have been much different if Mayor Koch had been here." Budget Director Philip Michael explained to reporters, "There aren't a whole lot of brand-new, unthought-of solutions," for city money woes.[42]

With just a month to prepare a budget as complex as New York's, perhaps the continuity is unsurprising. Experts considered 70 percent of the city's spending hard to change—determined by federal mandates like Medicaid or by legal and commonsense requirements, like making debt service payments, staffing prisons, or fixing bridges in dangerous disrepair. At the margins, Mayor Dinkins's first budget did include modest new spending on health, education, and social service programs, consistent with his promises to the city. As council speaker Peter Vallone remembered it, "Dinkins's top priority was to rebuild the city's social services, a legitimate concern, but a difficult priority to stick to during the hard financial times we were enduring." The budget proposal added $550 million in new taxes, including higher property taxes and a surcharge on the personal income tax to respond to the dire fiscal shortfall. The mayor's team portrayed the surcharge as a temporary increase until the economy improved. The plan proposed postponing anticipated cuts in energy taxes and extending New York City's mortgage recording tax to sales of cooperative apartments, a decision requiring action by the state legislature.[43]

Perhaps most distressing to many citizens, the mayor planned to delay hiring more police officers. A proposal to increase the size of the New York Police Department to more than twenty-eight thousand uniformed officers from under twenty-six thousand had great symbolic significance in a city besieged by lawlessness. To accomplish the increase and account for attrition, the city needed five thousand more police. The decision not to add cops put Dinkins at odds with his own pledge to be the toughest mayor on crime the city had ever seen. In years past he had criticized Mayor Koch for creating "phantom cops"—adding police officers to the city budget but never actually hiring them when fiscal constraints developed. Dinkins's own approach in his first budget seemed little different.[44]

Months of negotiations in New York City and discussions in Albany framed the stakes, but little progress could occur until the state passed its budget. The mayor's proposal counted on approval of state-determined revenue sources totaling $540 million. Seven weeks later than required by law, the dysfunctional legislature reached an agreement with New York's prickly governor, Mario Cuomo. The state authorized only $427 million of the city's requests. The action added more than $100 million to the task facing the mayor and the council, while leaving them only a few days to complete their work and meet their own statutory deadline. The outcome emerged—mostly from two final days of intense negotiation—a few weeks later than required by law. The mayor's budget team, led by First Deputy Norman Steisel and Budget Director Philip Michael, reached agreement with the city council, led by Speaker Peter Vallone, just a day before the new fiscal year started.[45]

The final budget called for more than $800 million in new taxes and charges, including $263 million in higher property taxes. This total exceeded the initial tax proposals by a quarter of a billion dollars. The city needed the extra money because the budget gap had widened, and in the end property taxes and personal income tax surcharges seemed among the few options available for raising the funds needed. Other expected sources of revenues had not materialized.[46]

The council insisted on restoring $40 million of services the mayor had marked for cuts, including funding for 500 more police officers for a total of 3,200. This exceeded modestly the number needed to keep the size of the force stable after attrition, allowing council members to present themselves to their districts as champions of the law. Council members also secured additional money for favored programs, and the mayor's team added back money for certain social services consistent with Dinkins's pledge to care for the needy. But when all was said and done, the five months of negotiations that occurred following the mayor's preliminary budget involved much less than 1 percent of expenses and under 3 percent of revenues. [47]

Since this budget negotiation was the first between the mayor and the city council under the new charter rules, each side sought to emphasize the importance of its impact. As in years past, the mayor's proposal dominated the deliberations, and maneuvering took place within very narrow bands. The newly cast council had not yet found the levers of power. Yet in his first budget the mayor did little to demonstrate how his leadership of the city would differ from his predecessor's, save a few gestures at the margin. His proposals signaled no major shifts in priorities and no structural changes in how the city ran or financed its activities. The budget lines traced no emerging picture of a new direction for the metropolis. As an opening statement of the mayor's intentions for his administration, the budget constituted a declaration of business as usual in a time of fiscal constraint—a responsible effort, but not an inspiring one. His team did a competent job managing the process, and, along with the city council, his administration passed a budget in time for the start of the new fiscal year—a basic tenet of public housekeeping that consistently eluded the governor and the state legislature in New York. Indeed, in March 1990 Standard & Poor's lowered its rating on New York State bonds two notches, remarking at the time that the city, in contrast to the feckless state government, had plans to bridge its budget gaps.[48]

Politically, the budget was a loser. In return for dirtier streets, less maintenance for their parks, and cutbacks in other, more vital services, New Yorkers would pay more than $800 million in additional taxes. Budget Director Michael acknowledged that "[w]e've had to forget about what the mayor's program was, forget about what his promises were as far as the campaign was concerned." Analysts also criticized the administration for raising taxes during an economic downturn, contending it would deepen and lengthen the recession. The mayor might have taken some consolation that the crisis came early in his term, leaving time to recover political lost ground later.[49]

Just a few weeks before passing the budget, the mayor had occasion to reflect on his administration's first six months of progress when he addressed a friendly crowd at the Reveille Club, a society of successful black men. "[T]his year . . . I bring you the official greetings of the people of the city of New York. It took a longtime for me to be able to say that," he said to his fellow African Americans, who had waited with him for their turn in power. He described himself as cherishing "every piece of this gorgeous mosaic—even as I take special pride that my group has now seen one of its own elected to the highest office in this city. And . . . it happened to be me." He described his efforts to build an open and representative administration that would allow the city's people to see in it a "reflection of themselves," and he dismissed critics of the pace with which he assembled his team. "They say we took time. I say it takes time to do this right . . . [to ensure that] the politics of inclusion and civility, unity and respect are here to stay," he declared. He also took pride that "if certain polls are to be believed, my approval ratings are going up—particularly among those communities that were most apprehensive about this city having its first African American mayor."[50]

"I will not be denied by a tight budget," he vowed with determination, although he acknowledged that he had been forced to spend enormous amounts of "time, energy and concern" on financial matters that he would have preferred to devote to improving the quality of life in the city. He felt he owed the successful African Americans sitting in front of him an explanation for the painful sacrifices he had imposed on them and the rest of the city after he campaigned on a program of "greater hope and higher aspiration."[51]

Without a solid fiscal foundation, he explained, "[W]e won't have the base from which we can build toward our goals." He blamed the situation on recession-induced revenue shortfalls and on "Republicans . . . in Washington who have deliberately destroyed the fiscal integrity of our nation's government to prevent any future attempts to enact a progressive political agenda." He reminded listeners that the Financial Control Board "remains in existence . . . and retains the power to reassert control over the City's finances. . . . I am determined that our people did not scrape and struggle for political power, only to have it seized by an unelected committee. . . . And I did not campaign long and hard as I did . . . only to have somebody say that I couldn't handle the responsibility."[52]

So after six months in office, having made the decision to enforce budget discipline as a matter of necessity, the mayor looked forward to the day he could invest in the social programs dear to his heart. And while serious problems confronted the city, the man still had the confidence of the coalition that elected him plus a little bit more, according to the polls he referred to in his speech.[53]

III. The Price of Police

Over the next few months, things changed rapidly for the worse. Public outrage over crime, already severe when Dinkins took office, surged as one high-profile attack after another shocked the city throughout the summer and into the fall of 1990. Brutal violence permeated New York's streets so pervasively that it began to call into question the mayor's credibility as the city's leader. On October 2, 1990, just three months into the fiscal year, Dinkins responded with a budget-busting set of programs called "Safe Streets, Safe City: Cops and Kids," initially projected to cost $1.8 billion over four years. To finance it, he suggested another increase in property taxes, a new city payroll tax for workers and employers, and a twenty-five-cent surcharge on state lottery tickets. The first tax required city council approval, the other two a vote by the state legislature.

City council speaker Peter Vallone supported the proposal and worked with the mayor to issue the home rule message required to set in motion negotiations with the state. The governor and assembly speaker Mel Miller from Brooklyn both indicated support for the plan, but the Republican-dominated state senate refused to pass the payroll tax. After several weeks, the mayor and the council agreed to extend an income tax surcharge as the best available option. Convincing senate majority leader Ralph Marino, who controlled the state's upper chamber, to support the program would prove problematic. Marino told the deputy mayor for public safety, Milton Mollen, he would allow the financing package out of committee for a vote when all six Republican senators from New York City endorsed it. Several signed on readily. Others, from white middle-and upper-class areas where crime rates remained lower than in other parts of the city, resisted. They feared their neighborhoods would receive little visible benefit in return for higher taxes if the police deployed the additional forces only in high crime areas. They insisted the mayor guarantee their districts more police, which in turn caused other legislators to demand the same.[54]

Dinkins resisted the ill-considered interference in police decision making. Negotiations dragged on, and in December, despite intense lobbying by the mayor's team and city council speaker Vallone, the state legislature adjourned without passing the financing package. In the weeks that followed, state budget analysts discovered the proposed tax plan would actually raise over $500 million more than the anti-crime package required. The facts contradicted statements the mayor made implying the incremental taxes would be directed exclusively to programs to combat lawlessness. Legislators feared a ploy to raise revenue for general purposes buried deep within a police-hiring plan. They demanded an iron-clad commitment that tax money meant for the politically acceptable purpose of new cops would be used for them. Vallone found the negotiations offensive, the actions of "a multitude of condescending state assemblymen and senators who insisted on having their petty parochial demands met before agreeing to allow us to tax ourselves."[55]

As a consequence of all the maneuvering, the mayor missed an important window of opportunity. An effort to deliver a bold plan to respond to high anxiety about crime ended up bogged down in tedious budget talks. Support for the policing program became wrapped up with the general budget discussion for the next year. The surplus built into the tax plan, which surfaced publicly only after legislative analysts discovered it, damaged Dinkins's credibility. It looked like the mayor had not leveled with the legislature or the people. "I did not do the arithmetic myself," the college math major found himself forced to declare in a *de facto* apology for the apparent deception. The lead negotiator for the senate Republicans assessed the situation this way: "[T]he city's team up in Albany seems competent, [but] they are constantly undercut by conflicting signals from City Hall." The state legislature finally passed the anti-crime package in February 1991 while the budget outlook for the year ahead caused tensions to mount.[56]

IV. Labor Leaders and Bond Markets

The day before the mayor announced his expensive policing program, his administration agreed to a budget-busting 5.5 percent salary increase for teachers—a little more including benefits. That same week, without prior consultation with city unions, Dinkins announced his budget director had recommended a job freeze and fifteen thousand layoffs to keep city finances in balance. The confusing combination of decisions raised doubts about the city's fiscal stewardship. The

New York Times spoke for many in an October 10, 1990, editorial headlined: "New York's Fears Won't Wait." They wrote: "Conscientious citizens are still reeling from Mayor David Dinkins's mercurial performance last week, which started with his giving the teachers' union a 5.5 percent raise and ended with his suggesting he might have to lay-off 15,000 city workers." They went on to call the school contract "unaffordable when he announced it nine days ago," and "ominous now." The editorial stated the obvious. "Mr. Dinkins did not create the sharp drop in revenues; the city would be short of cash whoever was mayor now," but it went on to conclude that the "lack of a coherent program . . . creates the rising sense of alarm. Who's in charge here? What's the plan? New Yorkers . . . need a better answer than 'Stay tuned.'"[57]

New Yorker columnist Andy Logan entitled her November 1990 "Around City Hall" article, "Lurching." The longtime observer of city chief executives wrote that the October announcements caused Dinkins's mayoralty "to seem to be in a state of disarray." She quoted Felix Rohatyn as saying the decisions "seem to be hanging off a Calder mobile in the air with their own motion and their own life, and they don't relate to the past or the future." Labor leaders liked the decisions no more than Wall Street bankers. The Teamsters' Barry Feinstein called the announcement regarding potential layoffs—which would be the first city job cuts since the 1970s fiscal crisis—"a declaration of war." DC 37's Stanley Hill declared, "To say the left hand doesn't know what the right hand is doing is an understatement. It's not a matter of left or right hands, but the head of David Dinkins." Citizens Budget Commission president Ray Horton called the sequence of events the most chaotic in memory. Standard & Poor's put the city on credit watch.[58]

The contradictory announcements reflected a fundamental conflict that plagued the Dinkins administration. The mayor had strong working-class sympathies, and he had long-standing friendships and political ties to the many labor leaders who helped elect him. It suited the Tammany-trained mayor to treat municipal unions who supported him generously. But the city's dire fiscal condition and the looming power of the Financial Control Board to seize New York City's government demanded discipline and restraint. The mayor never successfully resolved the tensions the predicament caused. His commissioner of labor, Eric Schmertz, a nationally respected arbitrator, like the mayor had friendships and long-standing professional relationships with union leaders. He crafted the deal with the United Federation of Teachers and convinced the mayor to support it, even though it provided more than three times the 1.5 percent budgeted for salary increases.[59]

Deputy Mayor Steisel and Budget Director Philip Michael objected to the proposal in the most strenuous terms, as did others involved in the decision. On its own, the agreement would cost the city hundreds of millions of dollars it did not have. More importantly, it would frame the terms for all the labor negotiations that would follow and put the administration back on its heels for every one of them when other union leaders demanded parity. One government official reacted to the decision with a sinking feeling that he was witnessing the beginning of the unraveling of David Dinkins's mayoralty.[60]

Fiscal watchdogs reacted harshly and expressed a lack of confidence in Schmertz. The city's chief labor negotiator approached his job like a mediator seeking common ground between the mayor's budget office and the unions, they said, rather than as management's representative in an adversarial relationship with the goal of securing the best outcome for the city. Schmertz unapologetically acknowledged as much. "I believe in working with the unions as problem-solving partners. I don't believe in confrontational . . . bargaining," he once said of his own style. For that reason, in 1982, Mayor Koch had refused to reappoint Schmertz to the city's bargaining board as one of three impartial members, a post he had held for fifteen years. Koch found the man's decisions too favorable to labor.[61]

Journalists reported Bill Lynch played a key role in the decision to grant the teachers the unaffordable package. Lynch himself downplayed his influence. "My heart was with giving teachers more," Lynch acknowledged. And he remembered "wrangling in Gracie Mansion" with others about what to do. But the decision to grant a raise depended on financial constraints as well as union sympathies, putting it "above my pay grade," he contended. A budget hawk present for the discussion of the teachers' contract remembered Lynch approaching such issues with savvy calculus. "Mr. Mayor," Dinkins's top political advisor would say, "Wall Street is not our friend. If we have problems with our friends, they'll give us a chance to win them back. If we lose Wall Street, we'll never win them back." Still, none in the room at the time the mayor approved the teachers' contract doubted Lynch, the mayor's key political advisor, supported it.[62]

Dinkins's budget director, Philip Michael, feared bond markets more than labor leaders. He took it as a simple matter of fact that if the administration decided to give more money to one priority it would have to cut somewhere else to compensate, or lose the confidence of investors. First Deputy Mayor Norman Steisel, a former deputy budget director and Lazard Freres investment banker, shared the concern. Announcement of the budget-busting teachers' contract the same week that the mayor unveiled his hugely expensive policing program risked spreading negative sentiment across Wall Street. So the two men convinced the mayor to announce a hiring freeze and potential layoffs in an effort to inoculate investment markets against fear of irresponsible budget management. No one, it seems, anticipated the fierce reaction the confusing combination of decisions would cause in the press. The administration had no communications strategy.[63]

Just after the uproar over potential layoffs caused Barry Feinstein to declare a state of war with the administration he helped elect, un-identified carpenters from the city's Human Resources Administration provided *Newsweek* with details and documentation of a request they had received from the mayor's office. They had been asked to hand carve a handsome, Federal-style headboard for a bed out of cherry wood. They delivered the $11,500 ornament to Gracie Mansion on October 5, 1990—the same week as the worrisome budget announcements. The reason for the unusual work order did little to assure city taxpayers or city workers at risk of losing their jobs that the mayor looked out for them. Ed Koch, it seems, had brought his bed with him to Gracie Mansion and took it when he left. The new mayor and his wife found themselves without a headboard that matched their bedroom furniture, so they had the city make them one. While silly, the incident further diminished the mayor's credibility. The leak of the details to *Newsweek* suggested that the mayor's union friends would respond to layoffs with guerrilla tactics.[64]

The chaotic announcements caused alarm among business leaders. Real estate mogul Lewis Rudin thought the city needed a public-private partnership like the one that helped save the city when bankruptcy threatened in the mid-1970s. He convened a private breakfast meeting of the city's most important movers and shakers. Citibank CEO Walter Wriston, Goldman Sachs co-CEO Robert Rubin, and Preston Robert Tisch, president of the New York City Partnership among other things, attended along with other corporate leaders. UFT head Sandra Feldman, DC 37 boss Stanley Hill, the president of New York City's Central Labor Council, Tom Van Arsdale, and other labor leaders were there—twenty-five to thirty people in total. Tellingly, Felix Rohatyn, whose strong objections to the size of the teacher's contract angered union leaders, did not receive an invitation, nor did any administration officials.[65]

During the ninety-minute session, the business leaders stressed the importance of retaining investor confidence for the city to be able to finance its operations. They were shocked by how angry the union leaders were with Dinkins. "They thought we were on the inside," one told a journalist. "No one is on the inside. It's really scary. David and his people don't even know how to talk to us," he went on. "They come to a meeting and say, 'Tell us what you can do.' Union leaders can't deal with that. What we need is for them to say, 'This is what we want from you.' Even if they want something ridiculous, at least we can begin negotiating." The union bosses used the session as an opportunity to call for business pressure on Dinkins to maintain labor peace. The two monologues never really turned into a dialogue. Labor remembered the 1970s pact as costing them dearly in wage givebacks, hiring freezes, and layoffs, while the bankers got paid every nickel of principal and interest the city owed. The business leaders viewed the unions as irresponsibly and selfishly opposed to productivity improvements at a time of desperate fiscal straits. And as precarious as the city's financial position appeared, it had not reached the hours-from-bankruptcy point that had forced the cooperation the last time. Moreover, the leadership Governor Hugh Carey had provided that helped bridge mistrust and misunderstanding a decade and a half earlier was absent. Nothing more came from the meeting.[66]

The controversial teachers' contract required the approval of the state legislature and the governor's signature. About 2.5 percent of the money would come from raising earnings estimates on state-controlled pension benefits and channeling the savings to the teachers. Another 1.5 percent would come from other sources funded mostly by the state. Albany budget officials were vexed by the city's decision to use state money for salary increases rather than to maintain services despite crisis budget conditions. They responded by announcing cuts in aid for the city by just about the same amount the Dinkins administration expected the state to contribute to the teachers' salary increase.[67]

For months, Governor Cuomo resisted the agreement. When he finally signed the enabling legislation in December 1990, he did so because he feared a veto at that point "would only make the existing confusion and the city's position worse." He took the occasion to issue a fierce warning. " [U]nless [the city] corrects its illusory reliance on unavailable state resources and makes a convincing case for how it can accommodate all its new commitments and existing needs, it will be risking the independence and control we all wish to maintain." The man the Financial Control Board made the city's fiscal sheriff was placing his hand on his gun in plain sight for all to see. The statement "Doesn't please me," was all Dinkins said. Others in his administration responded with greater trepidation. "The city is in very perilous circumstances," one acknowledged.[68]

V. A Mayor without a Plan

On January 3, 1991, after protracted negotiations, the city announced contract agreements with Stanley Hill's District Council 37 and Barry Feinstein's Teamsters. The settlement covered the majority of the municipal workforce. Over a fifteen-month period, the city would pay the workers covered 5 percent more in wages and benefits. The agreements, like the teachers pact, seemed unaffordable. The announcement came just a few weeks in advance of the date the mayor would submit a preliminary budget that all knew would be horrendous. It gave the impression of a mayor without a plan—or perhaps a Tammany-trained mayor more committed to his labor union allies than to the citizens who elected him. State and private fiscal watchdogs asked why the money the mayor found to grant the raises—by changing the calculations for pension fund contributions for these unions, just as he had for the teachers—should not be used to prevent reductions in service. Others questioned the strategy of so short a contract, setting the stage for new negotiations and additional uncertainty in just another year and a quarter.[69]

Press leaks describing budget discussions in conflicting and often negative terms exacerbated the perception that the mayor's team lacked direction and cohesion. "There was this collection of about eight people," who had come with Dinkins from the borough president's office, First Deputy Steisel recalled. "They were [social services] advocates . . . they just didn't accept that the money questions and the right financial balance had to be struck . . . they did not understand that the mayor's success to even get what *they* wanted . . . would depend on his fiscal stewardship. What was particularly upsetting," he continued, "was that they would leave these meetings and leak to the press. It made the administration look disorganized." It also created the impression among social service advocacy groups that the administration was not living up to its promises as a matter of choice rather than fiscal necessity. "This young staff did not appreciate they were contributing to the impression the mayor was weak," Steisel lamented. And since the mayor displayed the stubborn loyalty clubhouse politicians are known for to his supporters, his first deputy found it hard to discipline them. In at least one case, he eventually fired an offender.[70]

About the same time the administration faced criticism for the way it handled agreements with workers, its handling of city contracts came under more general scrutiny. Sid Davidoff had been a highly influential patronage dispenser and a top City Hall aide for eight years when John Lindsay was mayor. He had an unequalled instinct for getting things done and a well-honed network of city and state government contacts. He had teamed up with another former city official, Robert J. Malito, to create a law firm that specialized in helping clients win contracts and settle matters with government agencies.[71]

Davidoff played tennis with Mayor Dinkins regularly and raised money for his campaigns. At the end of the mayor's first year in office, Davidoff and Malito reported over $1.5 million in fees from clients doing business with the city. Influence-peddling charges abounded. Despite the optics the relationship caused and editorial critiques, the mayor seemed not to mind. At the 1991 Inner Circle Show—an annual charity event sponsored by City Hall reporters—the mayor invited Davidoff to join his skit. The decision surprised people concerned with integrity in government. It also offended other lobbyists, who resented the highly public acknowledgment of their rival's clout. Only a few weeks earlier Deputy Mayor Steisel had found himself forced to ask the city's Conflict of Interest Board to rule whether a vacation he spent at Davidoff's Florida condominium violated ethics rules. It did not, but the appearance of impropriety lingered. In response to a reporter's question, Davidoff admitted, "[I]t shouldn't look like I'm being bought because I can lead them into City Hall, but," he could not resist adding, "the fact is, I can."[72]

Scandals followed, but Davidoff always managed to finesse his way through them. One firm he represented, BI Monitoring Corporation of Colorado, won a contract worth nearly $2 million to provide electronic security bracelets for a prison-release program. An attorney formerly with Davidoff's law firm was then the top legal officer at the Department of Correction. Accusations emerged that she had intervened on behalf of her former colleague's client and allowed it to modify its bid, an opportunity not offered to others. The Dinkins's administration canceled the contract, and the city Department of Investigation launched an inquiry. The "magnitude and seriousness" of the findings caused them to refer the issue to the Manhattan district attorney's office and to federal prosecutors. Eventually, the correction department lawyer involved resigned. The episode did nothing to increase confidence in the mayor's management of the city's contracts. Yet it also did nothing to diminish Davidoff's influence with the mayor's administration, which continued without pause.[73]

VI. Worst-of-Both-Worlds Budget

On January 16, 1991, two weeks after granting hundreds of thousands of city workers 5 percent raises, Mayor Dinkins released his preliminary budget for fiscal year 1992 that would begin in July. The local economy remained deeply mired in recession. "The city and state of New York are near collapse," one veteran political journalist wrote at the time. The mayor's budget team projected a $2.2 billion gap. The plan called for a billion dollars in service cuts, including elimination of twenty-five thousand jobs through layoffs or attrition while proposing $580 million in higher taxes, principally on property and income. Some called the commitment to raise taxes and to cut services the mayor's "worst-of-both-worlds" budget. Council members and state legislators expressed little enthusiasm for the cuts and taxes the mayor proposed they support. Knowledgeable observers questioned whether even this dismal proposal would allow the city to meet its legal obligation to balance its budget, and they criticized the mayor's approach. Instead of more taxes and fewer services, they demanded "structural changes" to the way the city worked.[74]

Governor Cuomo, faced with a mounting state budget gap expected to approach $5 billion, announced a plan that would reduce city aid by $400 to $600 million. Dinkins responded that the governor's program would "cripple our ability to provide even the most basic of services." Thus began a duel between the mayor and the governor as each sought to blame the other for budget blues.[75]

The New York City Board of Education would feel the pain of staff cuts disproportionately in the mayor's preliminary plan—elimination of some ten thousand full- and part-time employees. The devastation such a program would inflict on the city's schools made it appear a ploy to negotiate more education aid from the state. The plan also proposed cuts in many of the types of social programs the mayor had pledged to champion when elected. Contracts for family-planning services would be reduced 70 percent, caseloads for social workers assigned to AIDS patients would rise, drug treatment programs would remain too scarce to meet demand. Sanitation, parks, bridge maintenance, and hospitals would all suffer as well. Streetlight wattage would be reduced, the Children's Zoo in Central Park would close, and so on.[76]

So severe did the cuts appear, that to the surprise and consternation of many, Felix Rohatyn raised the possibility that New York consider "postponing" balancing its 1992 budget and increase borrowing to pay for necessary services. "At some point the tradeoff between balancing the budget and the long-term social and economic harm may not make sense," he said at a Municipal Assistance Corporation board meeting. New York's budget hawks reacted as if the Pope had counseled heresy, wrote one *New York Times* reporter. City comptroller Elizabeth Holtzman responded unequivocally: "The city has to balance its budget," she said. "Deficit financing is not the answer." Citizens Budget Commission president Raymond Horton saw it the same way. "We should have the courage to deal with our problems today instead of foisting them off on our children," he declared.[77]

At first, the Dinkins administration dismissed the idea. Deputy Mayor Hernandez-Pinero said flatly, "The Mayor clearly disagrees." But two days later, even while restating his commitment to balance the budget as required by law, the mayor waxed more equivocal, saying, "[I]t is very difficult to take horrendous cuts and handle it in a short period of time, as opposed to stretching it out." He seemed to be testing the possibility of following Rohatyn's lead.[78]

Within days, Moody's downgraded New York City's bond rating.[79]

A few weeks later, one business leader told a journalist, "I've never seen so many people ready to leave town. This is far more serious than the last fiscal crisis," he said. "There's a general feeling—unfair, but clearly there—that Dinkins isn't capable of doing the job."[80]

The mayor's inability to assert convincing control over the city's finances, along with the many other serious matters that challenged his administration, created the impression that the man elected to lead could not. In the inevitable way that success creates greater confidence and authority, the perception of failure diminishes it. As early as the end of his first year, pictures appeared in newspapers and on magazine covers of Dinkins perspiring profusely and wiping his brow, a man unable to handle the pressure. The headlines read: "Is He up to It?" The articles called his administration "terminally amateurish."[81]

Mayor Dinkins's dapper dress—elegant tuxedos for a seemingly endless array of black-tie events, handsome double-breasted suits that framed his athletic body, a wardrobe full of freshly dry-cleaned warm-up jackets he donned when working at his desk or in informal settings—and his habit of showering several times a day created an image of a mayor perhaps too concerned with appearance and not so much with substance. The formality of his speech reinforced the perception. Some thought the man took more stock of how to say things rather than what to say. His obvious enjoyment of the ceremonial aspects of his job contributed to the impression that he lacked the gravitas for the things that really mattered. Detractors derided him as "borough president of New York City" rather than mayor. His well-known love of tennis, a game he played most mornings, allowed critics to cast him as someone who could be found on the court when work needed to be done. The *New York Daily News* reported it had audited Dinkins's first eighty-nine days in office and found he spent only three hours a day on city business, a claim the mayor derided. Some suggested he was a lady's man, his attention diverted from his job by pretty women. Dinkins found the commentary petty and a little nasty. In private, he wondered if reporters and others would subject a white mayor faced with so severe a budget crisis and other exceptional challenges to the same harsh personal scrutiny.[82]

First Deputy Mayor Norman Steisel wondered as well. "When the US Open came to New York, that was his vacation," Steisel said of the mayor's highly publicized visits to the nation's preeminent tennis match that brought millions of tourist dollars to the city. "He never took vacation except for that," yet the press criticized him for it. "And here's this guy in his sixties . . . he'd get up at . . . five o'clock in the morning to play an hour-and-a-half of tennis . . . he would run his ass around the court. . . . Any other chief executive, people would have said this guy has his stuff together . . . but they always criticized him. I always thought that was . . . a racial thing," Steisel said. He believed that for many people, "[T]his black guy playing tennis," a sport with an elite heritage, "there's something screwy about that." So a 1990s echo of white displeasure with "uppity Negroes," followed the mayor in Steisel's view.[83]

Dinkins's longtime Harlem friend, Basil Paterson, would find it "hard to believe [the mayor] wouldn't assume some of the criticism is racist." Percy Sutton also thought the press unfair. "In previous administrations, I haven't seen the kind of criticism I see of David Dinkins," he told a reporter after his longtime ally's first year in office. "Why can't David Dinkins wear a tuxedo, or play tennis? If he dressed like a ragamuffin, people would say we expected that of a person who comes from Harlem." The last comment suggested aspects of Dinkins's behavior may have developed over the years out of a desire to overcompensate for nasty stereotypes.[84]

Press secretary Albert Scardino interpreted the media's attitude toward Dinkins more charitably if more cynically. He believed it was a journalist's ambition to "inform and entertain," not necessarily to be fair. Reporters treated the mayor the same as they treated other politicians in Scardino's mind—open game for critique and ridicule. Unfortunately, Dinkins had character traits that made lampooning him easy. And he happened to govern at a time when the city's three tabloids, the *New York Daily News*, the *New York Post*, and *New York Newsday*, engaged in mortal combat since the city lacked the capacity to support all three. *Daily News* City Hall reporter and later bureau chief Joel Siegel remembered management and editors applying intense pressure on journalists to create fetching headlines that would attract television coverage and boost sales. So Dinkins governed at a time when any politician risked serving as fodder for journalists' ink-loaded canons.[85]

Siegel did perceive a double standard on one dimension of press coverage. "Every time some black guy popped off on any topic, we asked Dinkins to comment. We didn't ask Mario Cuomo about every Italian or Ed Koch about every Jewish guy." The mayor clearly resented being asked to explain and judge every dopey or nasty quip spewing forth from an African American. But another City Hall reporter saw it differently. Dinkins, among the many roles he played as mayor, served as the senior leader of the city's African Americans, so when others purported to speak for the race, it seemed appropriate to ask him his view. If it appeared reporters did not question Ed Koch with the same intensity about Jewish commentary, it may have been because Dinkins's brash predecessor issued his opinions so fast and furious they never needed to ask.[86]

By the time Dinkins's second year in office began, the mayor and top members of his team had become disillusioned with the news media. They believed the rising perception that they fumbled their way through most decisions resulted from inadequate communication and unfair coverage—not from the wisdom of their policies or a lack of management discipline. In an effort to deliver his message directly to citizens without the filter of editorial boards or New York's City Hall reporters, the mayor began a series of town hall meetings in neighborhoods throughout the five boroughs. He also dismissed his press secretary, an event *New York Times* reporter Todd Purdum described as the culmination of "a tempestuous 14-month tenure in which Mr. Scardino's attempts to be the chief executive's main fire extinguisher just as often produced flames that burned them both." He had a point. Scardino's appointment had been problematic from the start.[87]

Scardino was raised in Savannah, Georgia, the privileged son of a doctor in the days when Jim Crow strode the South without fear. As a teen, from time to time he would drive the two women who tended to the Scardino family from his home to theirs—two-room shanties in the black part of town that had open fire pits for cooking and out-houses without plumbing. When it rained hard, floods floated human feces out of the latrines and into the streets where children played. The brutal inequality of their lives made an impression on the youngster. When civil rights organizers came to Savannah, Scardino signed up at the age of sixteen to register voters. He got beat up twice for his troubles—once by whites and once by blacks.[88]

Scardino attended Columbia University where he wrote for the college newspaper during the 1960s. He worked for the Associated Press, freelanced, and completed a master's degree in journalism at the University of California at Berkeley before returning with his wife, Marjorie, to Savannah where in 1978 they established a weekly news-paper, the *Georgia Gazette.* Their crusading journalism helped convict thirty-eight corrupt local officials, earning Scardino a Pulitzer Prize for editorial writing in 1984. Not long afterward, the city of Savannah dropped the *Gazette* from its roster of newspapers used for advertising legal notices, and it went bust.[89]

New York Times editor Jimmy Greenfield arranged for the young Pulitzer winner to join the nation's newspaper of record as a metro editor for the week in review. Scardino found the transition to the staid daily a struggle. As the editor and publisher of his own newspaper, he had been his own man—in charge of himself and of every aspect of his small-town weekly. He found the rules and culture at the *Times* stultifying, pompous, and at odds with his personal views of what con-stituted first-rate, professional journalism. He cycled through a series of positions, never quite finding a comfortable fit for any length of time.[90]

Scardino and his wife, who had landed the job of president of the North American edition of the *Economist,* lived with their three children on the Upper West Side of Manhattan, where they blended easily into Democratic reform circles. They became friends with Victor Kovner and his wife, and with politically active attorney Harold Ickes, son of one of President Franklin Roosevelt's closest advisors and a confidant of David Dinkins. As Dinkins geared up to challenge Ed Koch in 1989, Ickes asked Scardino to sign on as campaign press secretary. He demurred, but, at the request of his friends, he met with Bill Lynch and the candidate and shared some of his thoughts on policy issues. After Dinkins won election, the transition team approached Scardino again. This time, he agreed to serve.[91]

Scardino was traveling in Paris when the call came confirming the mayor's decision to appoint him press secretary, so he boarded a plane for an overnight flight. By the time he landed, the *New York Post* had published a front-page story stating that Scardino had given policy advice to Dinkins as a candidate while serving as a *New York Times* reporter. They portrayed the matter as a serious breach of journalistic ethics. Max Frankel, executive editor of the *Times*, issued a memo and posted it on bulletin boards around the newspaper's office that declared, "[I]t is a conflict of interest for a reporter to give advice to a major political candidate. . . . Such action clearly compromises the *Times's* independence and reputation." It went on to say that Scardino's departure to take the press secretary job rendered the matter moot, but that there should be no doubt that "such a clear violation of our policy would have provoked disciplinary action." Frankel also published the statement in the newspaper that day.[92]

Scardino found it all rather shocking. The *Post* had a well-deserved reputation for tabloid sensationalism, so it surprised him Max Frankel would take it seriously as an accurate source of information. The decision to distribute an accusatory memo to the staff of the *Times* and to publish it without giving its subject an opportunity to share his side of the story struck Scardino as highly unprofessional. It conflicted with the most basic source-checking rules of journalism. Since Scardino had not covered the Dinkins campaign, he did not view a conversation with the candidate as a conflict of any kind. The two strong personalities discussed the matter, but each stood his ground. According to Scardino, after he spoke with Arthur Sulzberger, scion of the publishing family that owned the *Times*, Frankel sent him a handwritten, carefully worded, partial apology.

Some press room veterans shrugged off the controversy. Conversations between reporters and candidates often bled into news analysis, with journalists offering their interpretations of what it would take for the subject of an article to win a campaign. To them, Frankel's behavior seemed a hypersensitive overreaction to being called to task by a competitor he no doubt viewed as unworthy to judge his elite newspaper's ethics. But the *New Yorker's* Andy Logan, already dean of the City Hall press corps by then, took offense to Scardino's behavior just as Frankel had. She published a story dripping with sarcasm, declaring Scardino's appointment, "[N]ot a helpful development for an officeholder who, like Dinkins, was already being charged with ethical lapses," referencing the Inner City Broadcasting stock scandal, then still under investigation.

Logan pointed out that Frankel's rebuke was not the first the *Times'* editors leveled at Scardino. They had distanced themselves from an article published earlier in the year in which the press secretary designee wrote: "Most reporters do not feel themselves bound by ordinary rules of social behavior. Given their financial and social status, few of them would ever be invited to participate in the counsels of government or big business; but because they operate the spotlights, they are invited to the big events." Since Scardino had been a reporter, "[I]t seemed that he didn't care to be a member of a club that would have him," Logan surmised wryly. "If Dinkins's press secretary is to succeed in getting out the word about the new mayor's visions for the city, he will have to learn to put up with the socially and financially inferior types who will be writing about them," she wrote.

The whipping continued. "[Scardino] had never covered New York politics and does not know the reporters who do," she pointed out. When he arrived at City Hall for the announcement of his appointment, "[H]e did not know where anything was—not even the pressroom." When asked why he selected a man with Scardino's apparently low opinion of reporters to represent him before the press, "Dinkins, looking a bit bewildered, said that he hadn't known about the episode: nobody had told him."[93]

Like Frankel, Logan had not talked with Scardino before launching her broadside. The longtime City Hall columnist and newly named press secretary had a testy exchange over the article, with no resolution. So the mayor's senior spokesman, by the time he began his job, found himself at odds with the editors of the city's most influential newspaper and with City Hall's most tenured columnist. Things did not improve. Within six months, the *Times* editors sent Dinkins a note accusing Scardino of saying different things to different journalists, destroying his credibility in their view.[94]

The final event that caused the mayor to dismiss his press secretary occurred after a long, unfavorable article about Dinkins appeared in *Vanity Fair*. "New York has become the impossible metropolis," it began, "and its Mayor David Dinkins has been charged with an impossible mandate: to save the city from social and fiscal devastation, and to carry the black dream for real political enfranchisement. And being there is not enough." The article all but called the mayor an empty suit destined to fail. It also described Scardino. Calling him a man "known for his bow ties and his disdain for most City Hall reporters," it quoted him as saying, "Most white people in this city . . . think that black men are felons and black women are maids." He went on to inform the reporter that "City Hall is no longer run by tired old Jewish men." The comments seemed to offend Dinkins as much as those referenced in the gratuitous remarks.[95]

For several months, the mayor sought a replacement who could craft a different type of communication strategy, one who would bring more coherence to public perception of his policies and decisions. He tried to recruit Randy Daniels, a former CBS News television correspondent and media executive who had once worked for Dinkins's old nemesis, city council president Andrew Stein. But the man declined, citing contractual commitments he felt obligated to fulfill. So Dinkins elevated Leland T. Jones, who had been Scardino's top assistant and who had worked for Ed Koch as well, to be his senior spokesman. Jones, a competent, known quantity and better liked by the City Hall press corps than his predecessor, had a more cordial relationship with the reporters covering the mayor. But the administration would never manage to develop a communication program that successfully presented a coherent story of the mayor's vision and accomplishments.[96]

VII. A Meaner City, a Shrewder Council

Meanwhile, news of the city's ongoing financial crisis persisted. In March 1991 the skirmishing between the Dinkins administration's two budget factions—fiscal conservatives and friends of labor—broke into a public war. In a futile effort to persuade the bond-rating agencies not to downgrade the city, Budget Director Philip Michael crafted a memo to Moody's Investors Service outlining the administration's fiscal plan. He asserted the city had entered into negotiations with municipal unions to defer the wage increases they had only recently won. The revelation humiliated union leaders, who reacted angrily. "The head stinks," Stanley Hill said of Dinkins. "This administration is going into the toilet," Barry Feinstein declared. Labor commissioner Eric Schmertz announced that only informal talks had begun and threatened to resign to protest the way the news leaked out. He all but called Michael a liar, suggesting the budget director deliberately sought to mislead Wall Street about the status of negotiations.[97]

The battle created a public relations crisis. Dinkins rejected Schmertz's threat to resign and criticized Michael's memo as "inartful." He called both men to a Saturday morning showdown at Gracie Mansion along with First Deputy Steisel and Deputy Mayor Lynch. None knew what action the mayor would take, but it was clear that he had to put a stop to a public feud in which two of his cabinet members accused each other of duplicity. Steisel and Lynch rode to the tense session together from City Hall. "Before we got there Lynch told me the union guys were practically gleeful that they were finally going to get rid of Phil Michael," Steisel remembered. But when the budget director met with the mayor, he produced a note Schmertz had sent him that read, "[D]eferrals are and will be part of our negotiations," although it pointed out that unions would not be prepared to discuss the topic until later.[98]

With that revelation, Dinkins decided Schmertz had to go. "I think your usefulness is at an end," the mayor told his labor commissioner, insisting the man step down. "It ought never appear that this administration is dishonest on this kind of thing," Dinkins said of the matter. "[T]here is a vindication of Phil Michael and this administration with respect to the question of whether we misled the rating agencies," he declared. Schmertz insisted in a handwritten letter to the mayor that Michael had "misconstrued my memo and miscast it in a way to suit . . . predetermined ends." He also wrote, "[M]y integrity for over 30 years in the labor relations field speaks for itself. I will not be a scapegoat and choose not to be so victimized."[99]

Many involved hoped the change in personalities and the mayor's implicit decision to side with fiscal austerity over labor generosity would end the confusion surrounding this critical aspect of budget management. At least one labor leader, however, had his doubts. To him, the episode suggested not that one liar had been cast out and those remaining exonerated, but rather that there may have been three liars. "The Mayor was clearly desperate for a spin that would protect him in the market," the union man told a reporter, off the record. The episode made all involved, the mayor included, look bad.[100]

Over the next few months, New York's recession deepened, revenue estimates spiraled down, and the budget gap widened until it reached a daunting $3.5 billion. Political brinksmanship followed. Additional revenue could come from the federal government, the state government, the Municipal Assistance Corporation, or higher city taxes. Cuts in city jobs or services or voluntary concessions from municipal unions could reduce expenses. The possibilities were limited, and the power brokers, each controlling a part of the city's financial future, refused to act. Each hoped the others would have their hands forced, believing whoever acted first would lose out and whoever held out longest would end up with the least burden to bear.

On May 4, 1991, Mayor Dinkins outlined his executive budget in a daylong series of meetings with Governor Cuomo, legislative leaders, union representatives, and city council officials. Dinkins described his proposal as promising "a meaner city." It leaned heavily on the one area the mayor could control—service cuts—while seeking help from all other sources. It upped the proposed layoffs to more than twenty-seven thousand full-time and part-time employees beginning July 1. Many immediately detected a time-honored ploy—a plan that contained cuts so crippling they would prove politically intolerable and force negotiation of a better budget. Still, the severity of the cuts, which came paired with nearly $1 billion in higher taxes requiring city council or state legislature approval, shocked the political system. The city actually began laying off workers, underlining the seriousness of the stakes. Four hundred forty-seven sanitation workers lost their jobs. Their union staged a work slowdown in response. The tough negotiations had begun.[101]

As the extent of the crisis became increasingly evident, a specter loomed over the mayor. If he missed the budget deadline or presented a plan that did not satisfy the Financial Control Board, it could seize responsibility for managing the municipal budget. Mayor Dinkins viewed the prospect of losing control over the city's finances as an outrageous affront to him and to the people who had elected him in a democratic process. He was determined to avoid it at all costs. When he formally unveiled his $28.7 billion budget on May 10, 1991, at City Hall, Mayor Dinkins made his case passionately. "The nearly eight million people who are privileged to call this great city home must decide whether we shall make our own destiny or have another destiny forced upon us," he said. "If we lose control of our finances, we lose control of our government—and—that is something we cannot allow," he declared, casting the issue as a fundamental matter of democracy.[102]

When the governor left his meeting with the mayor a week before the public unveiling, he called Dinkins's budget proposal "candid and courageous." He offered words of support but then proved incapable of negotiating his own budget with the state legislature. *New York* magazine political editor Joe Klein had once described Cuomo's annual budget announcements as "vault[ing] beyond mere revenues and disbursements into some higher realm of accounting . . . it compares to other such presentations . . . as Richard Wagner does to Barry Manilow." But after state budget meetings, journalists present found themselves wondering, "Yeah, but what are the numbers?" Other governors had been "[b]oring, but you found out what was what." Cuomo impressed with words but not with deeds. Stalemate in so crucial a component of the city's plan left municipal unions free to sit on the sidelines and observe, waiting to see how the state's commitment would unfold before making any concessions to the mayor.[103]

Fiscal monitors and journalists roundly criticized Dinkins and his financial plan. It "reflected two essential Dinkinisian qualities: paralysis and denial," one wrote. Allen Proctor, executive director of the Financial Control Board, found the document lacking in a fundamental way. "You ought to have an idea of what you want to achieve with your administration," he told a reporter. "What's needed is a budget review that is program rather than dollar-driven. This requires a decisiveness, an overall view, that we haven't seen so far. I don't know where [Dinkins] wants to take us."[104]

The city council dissented from the mayor's budget from the start. It objected to the many cuts in high-profile services and to another round of tax increases, especially on small-home owners. The typical New Yorker already paid roughly twice the proportion of local taxes levied on other Americans, and the idea of raising taxes during an economic downturn struck many as wrongheaded, likely to intensify and prolong the city's economic misery. City council speaker Peter Vallone worked with outside experts and newly hired professional budget staff—something the council did not enjoy prior to charter revision in 1989—to develop alternatives. The legislators proposed deeper cuts in administrative and managerial jobs to protect money for programs constituents benefited from daily and to reduce the tax burden on them. The mayor's staff resisted the changes. They feared the council's plan would damage the city's ability to manage its essential affairs and that aspects of the proposal would be counterproductive. Cutting tax examiners, for example, would cost more in uncollected revenue than it would save in expenses.[105]

With the mayor and council in a standoff just three days before the deadline for the city to pass a balanced budget, with the threat of Financial Control Board intervention present, the city council flexed its new political muscles. Speaker Vallone released an alternative financial plan. He announced that he hoped to reach an agreement with the mayor but that, if he could not, the council would pass its own budget on time to comply with the law. The city charter gave the council the authority to do so, although it lacked the means to actually implement a plan.[106]

Negotiations continued right up until the deadline when at the last minute the mayor's team and speaker Vallone reached an agreement. It took two days to draft the details and to organize a vote, so the budget actually passed a few days after the fiscal year began on July 1, 1991. It included a $335 million income tax increase that required state legislative approval and a $400 million property tax increase that required a city council vote. This raised the rates on homeowners by nearly 11 percent and on cooperative owners by about 8 percent. The mayor's original property tax proposal had requested double the increase actually approved.[107]

The council accepted most of the cuts the mayor proposed, but it restored $117 million worth of high-profile services—roughly half of the $220 million they had hoped to protect. The money for the restorations came from cuts in the number of managers at city agencies, cuts in supplies, a delay in hiring civilians at the police department to free officers from administrative duties so they could combat crime, and savings from refinancing bonds and modest increases in expected tax receipts. "The budget contains a lot more pain, and a lot less gain than any of us would like," the mayor said. Speaker Vallone called the agreement, "[W]hat we can do in the worst of times."[108]

The council emerged from the talks with its prestige enhanced. Its threat to pass its own budget established it as a serious participant in the negotiations and gave it the leverage to modify the mayor's plan. It had insisted on lower taxes and fewer service cuts than the mayor, a winning political position. In the end, the council compromised, avoiding accusations of obstructionism. The episode made it clear Peter Vallone understood the power charter reform had given to the city council, and he knew how to use it to achieve his goals.

The budget agreement contemplated some contingencies. If municipal unions agreed to cost-saving concessions, the city could reduce layoffs and cutbacks. The Municipal Assistance Corporation stood ready to make additional money available to the city—$1 billion—if its negotiations with labor leaders promised permanent savings. It was left to the mayor to pursue these options. They seemed unlikely to happen. The mayor did not appear committed to serious negotiations that would go beyond business as usual. "The essential sloppiness and ineptitude of the Dinkins administration, plus some basic miscalculations," turned "a crisis into a disaster," according to one union leader, whose confidence and support would be needed to make lasting changes. The budget also contained its share of one-time sources of money and debt issues for operations that fiscal monitors frown upon as unhealthy practices, like a $20 million bond to raise funds for bridge painting and maintenance. By the end of fiscal year 1991, city general obligation debt had reached nearly $17 billion, up nearly 50 percent from $11.5 billion at the start of fiscal year 1990, adding to the level of concern over the state of city finances. MAC bonds outstanding actually declined modestly to $6.7 billion, down from about $7.5 billion during the same period.[109]

The fiscal crisis Mayor Dinkins faced prevented the Tammany-trained politician from rewarding his union friends the way he wanted. The raises he granted had to be renegotiated down almost as soon as they had been approved. His failure embarrassed the man and diminished his credibility as a manager of the municipal treasury. The same overriding economic reality prevented Dinkins from pursuing his liberal political philosophy that called for expansive government services to help the poor and disadvantaged. With somewhat cruel irony, the antipoverty agenda of New York's first African American mayor fell victim during his first two budget cycles to the city's recession-induced poverty. And the mayor paid a price for the "disastrous budget." The press published stories about the eighty-year-old wheelchair-bound widow who lost her daily lunch, about the young, pregnant woman who would no longer have access to a caseworker helping her secure prenatal care, about the psychologist with no programs to offer drug addicts seeking help, and on and on. Streets would be swept and park trees pruned less often. Cultural institutions would reduce their hours, suffer layoffs, and cancel days of operations. Mayor Dinkins did not have it easy. Many of the people who relied on city social services and voted for him with enthusiasm felt let down, even betrayed. And soon Governor Cuomo would make things worse for him.[110]

Notes

1. "Text of David Dinkins Inaugural Address," *NYT*, January 2, 1990.
2. "Text of David Dinkins Inaugural Address," *NYT*, January 2, 1990.
3. Avraham Weiss, "Confronting David Dinkins," 5–6, unpublished manuscript in possession of the author, courtesy of Rabbi Avraham Weiss; Don Terry, "Mayor Dinkins: An Era Begins with a Little Fun; A Mosaic of Humanity Gathers near City Hall," *NYT*, January 2, 1990.
4. Author's interview, Bill Lynch, October 29, 2010; Sam Roberts, "The 1989 Elections: The New York Vote; Almost Lost at the Wire," *NYT*, November 9, 1989; William L. Glaberson, "Campaign Questions Reverberate in Inquiry on Dinkins's Stock," *NYT*, December 5, 1989; Sam Roberts, "Metro Matters: Dinkins Stock: The Questions That Persist," *NYT*, December 7, 1989; Scott McConnell, "The Making of the Mayor, 1989," *Commentary*, February 1990,online version, www.commentarymagazine.com, accessed 2011.
5. Josh Barbanel, "Inquiry on Dinkins Stock Raises Possibility He Lied under Oath," *NYT*, January 11, 1991; "Report of the Special Deputy Commissioner Concerning the Transfer of Inner City Broadcasting Corporation Stock by David Dinkins," January 10, 1991, Transmitted by Elkan Abramowitz, Special Deputy Commissioner to Susan E. Shepard, Esq., Commissioner, Department of Investigation.
6. Alan Finder, "The Region: Nathan Leventhal; One Who's Been Everywhere Leads Dinkins's Transition," *NYT*, November 19, 1989.
7. Sam Roberts, "Dinkins Still Has Many Jobs to Fill and Many Groups to Placate," *NYT*, December 3, 1989; Todd S. Purdum, "Dinkins Asks for Time in Filling City Hall Jobs," *NYT*, November 30, 1989.
8. Robert D. McFadden, "Man in the News: A Savvy and Efficient Manager," *NYT*, December 9, 1989; Author's interview, Norman Steisel, October 28, 2010.
9. Robert D. McFadden, "Man in the News: A Savvy and Efficient Manager," *NYT*, December 9, 1989; Peter Blauner, "The Big Squeeze: How Bad Will the Budget Crisis Get?" *New York*, April 2, 1990, 53; Author's interview, Norman Steisel, October 28, 2010.
10. Author's interview, Philip Michael, November 6, 2010.
11. Todd Purdum, "Fire Director, Budget Chief Are Selected," *NYT*, December 23, 1989; Richard Levine, "As Deficit Threatens, City Hall Budget Watchdog Becomes Master," *NYT*, December 23, 1989; Author's interview, Philip Michael, November 6, 2010.
12. Todd Purdum, "Fire Director, Budget Chief Are Selected," *NYT*, December 23, 1989; Richard Levine, "As Deficit Threatens, City Hall Budget Watchdog Becomes Master," *NYT*, December 23, 1989; Author's interview, Philip Michael, November 6, 2010.
13. M.A. Farber, "Ward Resigns, Citing Problems with Asthma," *NYT*, September 26, 1989; Ralph Blumenthal, "Dinkins Gets Candidate List for Top Police and Fire Posts," *NYT*, December 12, 1989; Peter Blauner, "The Rap Sheet on Lee Brown," *New York*, January 22, 1990, 34–38; Lisa Belkin, "For New Police Commissioner, Towering Challenges: Rampant Drug Abuse and Record Murder Toll Compete with 911 Calls and Budget Freezes," *NYT*, December 21, 1989; Todd S. Purdum, "Dinkins Names Houston's Chief to Be His Police Commissioner," *NYT*, December 19, 1989.

14. Blauner, "The Rap Sheet on Lee Brown," *New York*, January 22, 1990, 34–38.
15. Lisa Belkin, "New Turmoil over Police in Houston," *NYT*, December 19, 1989.
16. Lisa Belkin, "New Turmoil over Police in Houston," *NYT*, December 19, 1989; Blauner, "The Rap Sheet on Lee Brown," *New York*, January 22, 1990, 34–38.
17. Purdum, "Dinkins Names Houston's Chief to Be His Police Commissioner," *NYT*, December 19, 1989.
18. Todd S. Purdum, "Dinkins Names Eight Appointees, Including Four Deputy Mayors," *NYT*, December 9, 1989; Joe Klein, "The City Politic: What Dinkins Must Do," *New York*, January 29, 1990, 12–13.
19. Caroline Baum, "Opening Remarks: The Good Old Bad Days," *Business Week*, September 6–12, 2010; Alton Slagle, "City, State and Nation Whacked," *New York Daily News*, July 3, 1992; Richard Levine "Economic Pulse: The New York Region—A Special Report: New York Region Faces Slowdown of the Economy," *NYT*, February 25, 1990; Richard Levine, "Middle-Class Flight Feared by New York City Experts," *NYT*, April 1, 1991; Michael Stone, "Hard Times," *New York*, November 19, 1990, 36–44; Christopher Byron, "Down the Down Staircase," *New York*, May 27, 1991, 10.
20. Joshua B. Freeman, *Working Class New York*, 332.
21. Joshua B. Freeman, *Working Class New York*, 6–11, 293; Matthew P. Drennan, "The Decline and Rise of the New York Economy," 25–42 in John H. Mollenkopf and Manuel Castells, eds., *Dual City: Restructuring New York* (New York: Russell Sage Foundation, 1991).
22. Joshua B. Freeman, *Working Class New York*, 103–104, 273; Walter Thabit, *How East New York Became a Ghetto* (New York: New York University Press, 2003), 23–25; John Steele Gordon, *An Empire of Wealth: The Epic History of American Economic* Power (New York: Harper Collins, 2004), 373–75; Richard Harris, "The Geography of Employment and Residence in New York Since 1950," 129–52 in Mollenkopf and Castells, eds., *Dual City*.
23. John Steele Gordon, *An Empire of Wealth*, 378; Stephen Kagann, "New York City's Vanishing Supply Side," *City Journal*, Autumn 1992, online version, www.city-journal.org, accessed 2011; Richard Harris, "The Geography of Employment and Residence in New York Since 1950," 129–52 in Mollenkopf and Castells, eds., *Dual City*.
24. Stephen Kagann, "New York's Vanishing Supply Side," *City Journal*, Autumn 1992, online version, www.city-journal.org, accessed 2011; Fred Seigel, *The Future Once Happened Here: New York, D.C., L.A. and the Fate of America's Big Cities* (New York: The Free Press, 1997), 46–61; Vincent J. Cannato, *The Ungovernable City: John Lindsay and His Struggle to Save New York* (New York: Basic Books, 2001), 539–45.
25. Soffer, *Ed Koch*, 256.
26. Soffer, *Ed Koch*, 256–59; John Steele Gordon, *An Empire of Wealth*, 373, 387–88; Joshua Freeman, *Working Class New York*, 293.
27. Soffer, *Ed Koch*, 258.
28. Richard Harris, "The Geography of Employment and Resdience in New York Since 1950," 129–52 in Mollenkopf and Castells, eds., *Dual City*; Author's personal recollection.

29. Soffer, *Ed Koch*, 260.

30. Robert Fitch, *The Assassination of New York* (New York: Verso), xii–xiv, 3–30; Soffer, *Ed Koch*, 258–60.

31. John Steele Gordon, *An Empire of Wealth*, 396; Soffer, *Ed Koch*, 259.

32. John Steele Gordon, *An Empire of Wealth*, 398–401; Julie Baumgold, "Fighting Back: Trump Scrambles off the Canvas," *New York*, November 9, 1992, 40.

33. Saul Hansell, "Company News; Dime and Anchor Plan a Merger to Form No. 4 U.S. Savings Bank," *NYT*, July 7, 1994; Michael Quint, "The Bank Merger; Big Bank Merger to Join Chemical, Manufacturers," *NYT*, July 16, 1991; Christopher Byron, "Winners and Sinners, 1991: Wall Street," *New York*, December 23–30, 1991, 26–27.

34. New York State Department of Labor Employment Statistics, reported Total Non-farm Employees for New York City as 3.553 million in January 1991 and 3.229 million in January 1993. By December 1993, the figure rose to 3.359 million. *NYT*, January 2, 1990.

35. Fitch, *The Assassination of New York*, 256; Fred Siegel, *The Prince of the City*, 15–17.

36. "Text of David Dinkins Inaugural Address," *NYT*, January 2 1990; Richard Levine "Economic Pulse: The New York Region—A Special Report: New York Region Faces Slowdown of the Economy," *NYT*, February 25, 1990; Todd S. Purdum, "Rohatyn Urges Dinkins to Hold Spending Line," *NYT*, December 1, 1989.

37. Alan Finder, "Fixing New York City: Needs Are Awesome," *NYT*, December 28, 1989.

38. Lou Cannon, *President Reagan: The Role of a Lifetime*, 67–68; 197–98; Timothy Naftali, *George H. W. Bush*, 42, 52–55; Siegel, *The Prince of the City*, 16–17; Jeannette Walls, "League of Cities Seeks Solutions," *New York*, October 8, 1990.

39. Don Terry, "Dinkins Proposes 'Painful' Budget of $27.8 billion," *NYT*, February 2, 1990; New York City Charter, 84–95.

40. Martin Shefter, *Political Crisis/Fiscal Crisis: The Collapse and Revival of New York City* (New York: Basic Books, Inc., 1985), 133–34; Lynne A. Weikart, *Follow the Money: Who Controls New York City Mayors?* (Albany: State University of New York Press, 2009), 42–44; Seymour P. Lachman and Robert Polner, *The Man Who Saved New York: Hugh Carey and the Great Fiscal Crisis of 1975* (Albany: State University of New York Press, 2010), 123–45.

41. Alan Finder, "Financial Control Board Loses Most of Its Control," *NYT*, June 30, 1986; John Hull Mollenkopf, *A Phoenix in the Ashes: The Rise and Fall of the Koch Coalition in New York City Politics* (Princeton: Princeton University Press, 1992), 14.

42. Todd S. Purdum, "A Familiar Budget: Much of Spending Plan from Dinkins Is Reminiscent of the Koch Approach," *NYT*, February 2, 1990.

43. Purdum, "A Familiar Budget," *NYT*, February 2, 1990; Peter Vallone, *Learning to Govern: My Life in New York Politics from Hell Gate to City Hall* (New York: Chaucer Press, 2005), 178.

44. Todd S. Purdum, "Dinkins to Delay Most Police Hiring Till '91, Aides Say," *NYT*, February 1, 1990; Purdum, "A Familiar Budget," *NYT*, February 2, 1990.

45. Kevin Sack, "Albany Lurches Toward Adjournment," *NYT*, July 1, 1990; Editorial, "The City Council Passes a Tax Test," *NYT*, July 5, 1990.
46. Don Terry, "Council Gains Budget Pact with Dinkins," *NYT*, June 30, 1990.
47. Don Terry, "Council Gains Budget Pact with Dinkins," *NYT*, June 30, 1990.
48. Todd S. Purdum, "Reporter's Notebook: Bumpy Road Ends at Budget for New York City," *NYT*, July 1, 1990; Elizabeth Kolbert, "New York Is Given Cut in Bond Rating by Credit Agency," *NYT*, March 27, 1990.
49. Peter Blauner, "The Big Squeeze: How Bad Will the Budget Crisis Get?" *New York*, April 2, 1990, 50–55.
50. "Remarks by Mayor David N. Dinkins, Annual Dinner of the Reveille Club, Holiday Inn Grand Plaza West 49th Street and Broadway, Manhattan," June 16, 1990 in New York City Municipal Archives, Office of the Mayor, David N. Dinkins, Speeches, Microfilm Roll #10.
51. "Remarks by Mayor David N. Dinkins, Annual Dinner of the Reveille Club, Holiday Inn Grand Plaza West 49th Street and Broadway, Manhattan," June 16, 1990 in New York City Municipal Archives, Office of the Mayor, David N. Dinkins, Speeches, Microfilm Roll #10.
52. "Remarks by Mayor David N. Dinkins, Annual Dinner of the Reveille Club, Holiday Inn Grand Plaza West 49th Street and Broadway, Manhattan," June 16, 1990 in New York City Municipal Archives, Office of the Mayor, David N. Dinkins, Speeches, Microfilm Roll #10.
53. "Remarks by Mayor David N. Dinkins, Annual Dinner of the Reveille Club, Holiday Inn Grand Plaza West 49th Street and Broadway, Manhattan," June 16, 1990 in New York City Municipal Archives, Office of the Mayor, David N. Dinkins, Speeches, Microfilm Roll #10. The Marist Institute reported Dinkins had a 56 percent approval rating in March 1990, the Marist Institute for Public Opinion, "Dinkins Approval Rating," March 1990, in the possession of the author, courtesy of the Marist Institute and Lee Miringoff.
54. Author's interview, Milton Mollen, November 10, 2010.
55. Author's interview, Norman Steisel, October 28, 2010; Author's interview, Milton Mollen, November 5, 2010; Peter Vallone, *Learning to Govern*, 180.
56. Kevin Sack, "Dinkins Plan for More Police Mired in Mistrust in Albany," *NYT*, January 22, 1990; Josh Barbanel, "Dinkins Says Tax for Police Hides Surplus," *NYT*, January 23, 1990.
57. Editorial, "New York's Fears Won't Wait," *NYT*, October 10, 1990.
58. Andy Logan, "Around City Hall: Lurching," *The New Yorker*, November 5, 1990, 131–37; Joe Klein, "The Real Deficit: Leadership," *New York*, July 22, 1991, 20–25.
59. Joe Klein, "The City Politic: The Pinochle Club, Dinkins and the Dinosaurs," *New York*, October 29, 1990, 9–10; Josh Barbanel, "Negotiator's Quiet Style Elicits Loud Protest,"*NYT*, October 23, 1990; Dennis Hevesi, "Eric Schmertz Dies at 84; Settled Many Labor Disputes," *NYT*, December 22, 2010.
60. Joe Klein, "The City Politic: The Pinochle Club, Dinkins and the Dinosaurs," *New York*, October 29, 1990, 9–10; Josh Barbanel, "Negotiator's Quiet Style Elicits Loud Protest," *NYT*, October 23, 1990; Author's interview, Norman Steisel, October 28, 2010; Author's interview, off the record; Dennis Hevesi, "Eric Schmertz Dies at 84; Settled Many Labor Disputes," *NYT*, December 22, 2010.

61. Joe Klein, "The City Politic: The Pinochle Club, Dinkins and the Dinosaurs," *New York*, October 29, 1990, 9–10; Author's interview, Norman Steisel, October 28, 2010; Author's interview, off the record.

62. Author's interview, Bill Lynch, October 29, 2010; Author's interview, off the record.

63. Author's interview, Bill Lynch, October 29, 2010; Author's interview, Normal Steisel, October 28, 2010; Joe Klein, "Is He up to It?" *New York*, November 5, 1990, 39.

64. "Bed Adds to Dinkins Woes," *NYT*, October 8, 1990.

65. Josh Barbanel, "Using 1975 Tool, Business and Labor Leaders Form Fiscal Council," *NYT*, October 25, 1990.

66. Josh Barbanel, "Using 1975 Tool, Business and Labor Leaders Form Fiscal Council," *NYT*, October 25, 1990; Joe Klein, "The City Politic: The Mother-in-Law of All Parades," *New York*, June 24, 1991, 9; Joe Klein, "The Real Deficit: Leadership," *New York*, July 22, 1991, 9–10.

67. Elizabeth Kolbert, "Criticizing Dinkins, Cuomo Warns of Possible Takeover of Finances," *NYT*, December 27, 1990.

68. Elizabeth Kolbert, "Criticizing Dinkins, Cuomo Warns of Possible Takeover of Finances," *NYT*, December 27, 1990.

69. Richard Levine, "Mayor and Unions Agree on 5% Raise in New York Pact: Cost Is $233 Million," *NYT*, January 3, 1991; Richard Levine, "The Region: Layoffs and Cutbacks and 5 Percent Raises," *NYT*, January 6, 1991.

70. Author's interview, Norman Steisel, October 28, 2010.

71. Sam Roberts, "Metro Matters: A Lindsay Aide Turned Lobbyist Keeps Growing," *NYT*, December 10, 1990; Susan Heller Anderson, "Chronicle," *NYT*, May 19, 1990.

72. "Topics of the Times; The Inner Inner Circle," *NYT*, March 17, 1990; Author's interview, Norman Steisel, October 28, 2010.

73. Selwyn Raab, "New York City Prison Chief Quits After Rebuke on Contract Bidding," *NYT*, December 24, 1991; Selwyn Raab, "2 Accused of Favoritism in Bid Process," *NYT*, May 6, 1992; Martin Gottlieb, Dean Baquest and Eric N. Berg, "Money and Meters: One Firm, Many Companies—A Special Report; Winning New Contracts: Hard Questions for a Supplier," *NYT*, March 19, 1991; Calvin Sims, "Adviser to Dinkins Again Tops List of City Lobbyists," *NYT*, April 3, 1992.

74. Editorial, "Earning the Right to Borrow," *NYT*, February 12, 1991; Joe Klein, "The City Politic: The Red Sea," *New York*, January 21, 1991, 14.

75. Todd S. Purdum, "The Dinkins Budget: Dinkins Offers $29 Billion Budget with Cutbacks and Layoffs," *NYT*, January 17, 1991; Sam Roberts, "Metro Matters: Shaving Nickels from the Budget at City Hall," *NYT*, January 17, 1991.

76. Todd S. Purdum, "The Dinkins Budget: Dinkins Offers $29 Billion Budget with Cutbacks and Layoffs," *NYT*, January 17, 1991; Sam Roberts, "Metro Matters: Shaving Nickels from the Budget at City Hall," *NYT*, January 17, 1991; Editorial, "Mr. Dinkins Does His Painful Duty," *NYT*, January 17, 1991.

77. Josh Barbanel, "New York City Given Warning by Rohatyn on the 1992 Budget," *NYT*, February 7, 1991; Todd S. Purdum, "Dinkins Budget Stand," *NYT*, February 9, 1991.

78. Todd S. Purdum, "Dinkins Budget Stand," *NYT*, February 9, 1991.

79. Josh Barbanel, "Dinkins Effort Set Back by Cut in Bond Rating," *NYT*, February 12, 1991; Joe Klein, "Less Than Zero," *New York*, February 25, 1991, 35–37.

80. Joe Klein, "The City Politic: Root-Canal Work," *New York*, April 8, 1991, 14.

81. Joe Klein, "Is He up to It?," *New York*, November 5, 1990, 57.

82. Felicia Lee, "Dinkins Aims at the Critics of His Tennis," *NYT*, April 30, 1991; Alessandra Stanley, "After First Year a More Relaxed Dinkins," *NYT*, January 1, 1991.

83. Author's interview, Norman Steisel, October 28, 2010.

84. Alessandra Stanley, "After First Year a More Relaxed Dinkins," *NYT*, January 18, 1991.

85. Author's interview, Albert Scardino, December 10, 2010; Author's interview, Joel Siegel, December 20, 2010; Joe Klein, "Race: The Mess. A City on the Verge of a Nervous Breakdown," *New York*, May 28, 1990, 35.

86. Author's interview, Joel Siegel, December 20, 2010; Author's interview, off the record.

87. Todd S. Purdum, "Press Secretary Resigns as Dinkins Reaches out to Public," *NYT*, February 14, 1991.

88. Author's interview, Albert Scardino, December 10, 2010.

89. Frank J. Prial, "New Administration: Profiles of Dinkins's Eight Appointees; Albert Scardino: Press Secretary," *NYT*, December 9, 1989; Author's interview, Albert Scardino, December 10, 2010.

90. Author's interview, Albert Scardino, December 10, 2010.

91. Author's interview, Albert Scardino, December 10, 2010.

92. "Accounts Say Reporter Gave Advice to Dinkins," *NYT*, December 9, 1989.

93. Andy Logan, "Around City Hall: That's Life," *The New Yorker*, December 25, 1989, 96–103.

94. Author's interview, Albert Scardino, December 10, 2010.

95. Author's interview, Albert Scardino, December 10, 2010; Todd S. Purdum, "Press Secretary Resigns as Dinkins Reaches out to Public," *NYT*, February 14, 1991; Marie Brenner, "Being There," *Vanity Fair*, January 1991, 90.

96. Elizabeth Kolbert, "Political Talk," *NYT*, April 14, 1991; Susan Heller Anderson, "Chronicle," *NYT*, July 18, 1991.

97. Todd S. Purdum, "Team Unity for Dinkins; Fiscal Message Sent as Labor Chief Quits," *NYT*, March 11, 1991.

98. Todd S. Purdum, "Labor Chief Resigns in Dispute with Dinkins and Budget Head," *NYT*, March 10, 1991; Todd S. Purdum, "Team Unity for Dinkins; Fiscal Message Sent as Labor Chief Quits," *NYT*, March 11, 1991; Author's interview, Norman Steisel, October 28, 2010; Author's interview, off the record.

99. Todd S. Purdum, "Labor Chief Resigns in Dispute with Dinkins and Budget Head," *NYT*, March 10, 1991; Todd S. Purdum, "Team Unity for Dinkins; Fiscal Message Sent as Labor Chief Quits," *NYT*, March 11, 1991; Author's interview, Norman Steisel, October 28, 2010; Author's interview, off the record.

100. Sam Roberts, "Mayor Dinkins: Every Day a Test," *NYT*, April 7, 1991.

101. Allan R. Gold, "Sanitation Workers Begin Slowdown," *NYT*, June 21, 1991; Joe Klein, "The City Politic: Where's the Pea?" *New York*, May 13, 1991, 21–22.

102. Josh Barbanel, "Dinkins Presents a Dire New Plan to Meet Budget," *NYT*, May 5, 1991; Josh Barbanel, "Dinkins Presents '92 Budget Vowing to Bar Takeover," *NYT*, May 11, 1991; Christopher Byron, "The Bottom Line: Wrong-Way Dinkins," *New York*, May 20, 1991, 14–15.

103. Barbanel, "Dinkins Presents a Dire New Plan," *NYT*, May 5, 1991; Joe Klein, "Mario the Magician," *New York*, February 5, 1990, 33–34.

104. Joe Klein, "The City Politic: New York to Dave: Get Real," *New York*, May 27, 1991, 12.

105. Christopher Byron, "The Bottom Line: Wrong-Way Dinkins," *New York*, May 20, 1991, 14; Josh Barbanel, "Council Speaker Vows to Avert Steep Cuts by Dinkins," *NYT*, May 10, 1991; Josh Barbanel, "City Council Budget Plan Resists Dinkins Cuts," *NYT*, June 28, 1991; Eric Pooley, "The City Politic: Heaven Sent," *New York*, August 9, 1993, 22.

106. Josh Barbanel, "Council Speaker Vows to Avert Steep Cuts by Dinkins," *NYT*, May 10, 1991; Josh Barbanel, "City Council Budget Plan Resists Dinkins Cuts," *NYT*, June 28, 1991.

107. Josh Barbanel, "At the Budget Wall: Accord Reached for Grim Budget in New York City," *NYT*, July 1, 1991.

108. Josh Barbanel, "At the Budget Wall: Accord Reached for Grim Budget in New York City," *NYT*, July 1, 1991.

109. Todd S. Purdum, "The Budget Battles: New York City Budget Hardly Final," *NYT*, July 3, 1991; Josh Barbanel, "Critics Fear Time Bombs in Dinkins Budget Tactics," *NYT*, July 9, 1991; Joe Klein, "The City Politic: The Never Ending Story," *New York*, July 15, 1991, 9–10; Independent Budget Office, "Debt Affordability Ratio Analysis," 1980–2006, spreadsheet in the possession of author, courtesy of Independent Budget Office and Douglas Turetsky.

110. Celia W. Dugger, "New York Losing Weapons against Poverty," *NYT*, July 10, 1991; Allan R. Gold, "Outlook Grim and Dirty for New York Ecology," *NYT*, July 16, 1991.

4

Policies for a Penniless City

Just hours after the mayor and council passed a budget that they claimed would allow the city to operate in balance during fiscal year 1992, the state Financial Control Board announced it would institute extraordinary monitoring procedures. Rather than convene annually to review the city's finances, the board decided to meet monthly throughout the summer and quarterly throughout the year to ensure the proposed cuts totaling $1.6 billion occurred. Experts viewed the mayor's budget as achieving its goals with a fragile mix of policies that events could cause to unravel. "I don't think anyone would claim it represents structural balance. It represents hanging on by your teeth," said Elinor B. Bachrach, deputy state comptroller for New York City.[1]

"It will be at least as difficult to implement this budget as it was to design and pass it," Governor Cuomo announced in his capacity as chairman of the Financial Control Board. "The cuts in service are easy to write into a budget; they are more difficult to achieve," he said. He implied that, without additional oversight, the mayor could not be trusted to produce the savings contemplated. Rumors circulated that the governor wanted to activate the Financial Control Board formally but backed off when Dinkins threatened to make it "a black-white thing" if he did. At least one anonymous civic leader close to city budgets agreed with the governor's assessment of the integrity of the mayor's plan. "Utter bullshit. The budget is bullshit," he said. "Disgusting, embarrassing, and dangerous bullshit," bound to be $500 million out of balance by September. "It can't work. It's nonsense," he declared. Pundits took the mayor to task as well. "It seems almost unfair to pile on at this point," Joe Klein wrote in *New York* magazine, "but some plain truths need to be told about David Dinkins and his administration: It has been a failure, and perhaps a disaster for the city." In the *New York Observer*, even Jack Newfield, a Dinkins supporter, criticized the mayor. He called David Dinkins "too passive. . . . He thinks he is a victim of bad luck, racism, and unfair media. He doesn't see his own power and his own choices. He doesn't take responsibility."[2]

The board's decision dealt the mayor a severe public blow. He found the governor's position particularly infuriating, since Cuomo had been no more successful negotiating a sound budget at the state level than Dinkins had been at the municipal one. In a lengthy statement before the Financial Control Board in July 1991, Mayor Dinkins told the members that the city had a sophisticated reporting system to ensure its expenditures matched budget targets, and he asserted his commitment to reducing city costs permanently. He had a sharp-edged message for the governor. "Without casting aspersions on neighboring governments, I will not be bashful in pointing out . . . [f]or more than a decade, the City has completed every budget on time and in balance, without carrying hundreds of millions of dollars in deficits from one year to the next." The state could not make the same claim. "With this latest budget, New York City has proved its fiscal mettle," he declared. And he reminded people that "the Governor has said many times, we need cooperation, not control."[3]

One city government official involved in budget deliberations found the battle between the governor and the mayor ferocious. "Cuomo devoured Dinkins," the man said. He believed the governor, with "Machiavellian" intent, deliberately directed attention to city money problems to distract from his own at the state level. The governor could portray himself as fiscally responsible by "holding the mayor's feet to the fire," even if he failed to balance and pass his own budget on time. Yet, for all the unfairness, senior city officials also believed the Financial Control Board served a purpose. In Deputy Mayor Steisel's opinion, it was part "fig leaf" and part "bat." The threat of Financial Control Board action gave Steisel and Budget Director Philip Michael more authority when negotiating with city agency heads. Without the discipline the board imposed, analysts feared the city would have done no better than the irresponsible state when it came time to make tough choices.[4]

Whatever the actual merits of the position, the Financial Control Board's stance left David Dinkins looking inept—unwilling or unable to enact the structural reforms required to make city government operate more efficiently at a time when circumstances demanded it. The board challenged his control over the city's money, which in no small measure meant his power over the government itself. The governor had boxed the mayor into a corner. The mayor punched back. Two days before the August 1991 Financial Control Board meeting, Dinkins took to the airwaves in an effort to reassert his authority. He hoped to communicate that he was "on top of things," he told a reporter, "and that's important, because sometimes some have the impression that's not the case."[5]

Dinkins addressed New Yorkers directly in an eighteen-minute speech delivered from behind his desk at City Hall. He told the people who elected him their leader, "This city cannot and should not endure one more late-night budget negotiation, one more race to a budget deadline, where the price to be paid for failure is the existence of our city itself," he said with some hyperbole. "A patchwork approach to the challenges we face promises only failure, augurs only broken promises and portends only unfulfilled dreams for you and your children," he continued. He took credit for having "done more with less in the most difficult time our city has ever faced." And he lamented that the Depression-era partnership between Mayor Fiorello LaGuardia and President Franklin Roosevelt risked becoming a "sad remembrance of the past because our federal government and the Bush administration have turned their back on us—saying in effect 'New Yorkers need not apply,'" for assistance of a kind that urban America needed and had received for decades under more enlightened leadership. Declaring it his responsibility as mayor, despite the challenging circumstances, "to ensure that New York not only survives but that it be renewed, that it be reinvented before the dawn of the twenty-first century," he announced a plan "for the reform of New York City government . . . [and] for the renaissance of New York City . . . no single program has ever been as important to the future of New York City," he asserted boldly.[6]

The Reform and Renaissance program, somewhat grandly named by a member of the mayor's press office, packaged together thirty-six different ideas and initiatives underway to improve the efficiency and quality of municipal services. They ranged from the complex to the mundane—from restructuring health and hospital care for the poor and revising Medicaid-reimbursement formulas to reduced staff for public affairs offices in city agencies. It promised better management of supplies, the consolidation of technology systems, and smarter maintenance of city vehicles along with better control of fuel depots. The program included a proposal to create new public authorities to finance garbage collection and bridge maintenance with fees and tolls, while outsourcing certain government functions to private agencies, like the tasks of the parking violations bureau. The mayor pledged to seek new work rules from municipal unions to achieve higher productivity, while announcing a series of symbolic costs savings, including a salary freeze for himself and the elimination of drivers for all city commissioners, save police and fire. He tempered the commitment to austerity and efficiency by restoring some of the most obnoxious service cuts from the recently passed budget, such as the planned closing of city pools in August, and he called for the right to appoint a majority of the members on the central school board to begin the process of turning around New York City's failing education system.[7]

"Tomorrow," the mayor told New Yorkers, "we will begin the implementation of a new citywide program to reduce costs and improve service delivery. The changes we begin to institute as a city, will over time, be the most dramatic ever conceived or executed in any American city, and will serve as the blueprint for success elsewhere."[8]

David Dinkins had established a reputation over more than a quarter of a century as a clubhouse politician—a Harlem product of the Tammany machine—who understood the need for political leaders to reward their friends. That meant more jobs and higher wages in return for the backing he received from municipal unions, who cared nothing about efficiency. He also had a well-defined image as an urban liberal whose instincts were to expand city government to do more for the neediest. The bold statement of purpose in the Reform and Renaissance program—that the mayor's administration would reinvent the government to make it more efficient—was driven by the need to reinvent the mayor's image. He sought to present himself as committed to the type of structural change fiscal monitors demanded to preempt any effort by the Financial Control Board to deny his authority over the city's resources. The initiatives identified were real enough, and members of Dinkins's staff, committed to improved delivery of government services, pursued them with energy. Yet the notion that David Dinkins had suddenly developed a passion for government efficiency nineteen months into his mayoralty strained credulity. Politics, not policy, motivated the announcement.

The origins of the program stretched back to the end of the Koch administration. A grant and support from eighty of the city's largest companies allowed development of the "Mayor's Private-Sector Survey," a project designed to identify ways to make municipal operations more effective and less costly. The study identified some $1.6 billion of potential savings over five years, with annual benefits afterward of about $500 million. It covered only 10 percent of the city's total activities. The project's executive director wrote to Felix Rohatyn in December 1989, "The potential . . . application of the same principles throughout City government would, I am sure, astound us all." The project's most basic recommendation, "[M]easur[e] the cost of work performed and manage it against targets," was a practice followed by well-run businesses as a matter of course. Rohatyn referred a summary report to mayor-elect Dinkins. "I believe these numbers are large enough and compelling enough in light of the problems we are going to have before us [to be] well worth following up on," he wrote. Responsibility for the program ended up with First Deputy Mayor Steisel, who instructed Harvey Robins, the mayor's director of operations, to assess the recommendations and to develop a plan.[9]

Harvey Robins was born in Brooklyn, the second of two children and the only son of a boiler equipment manufacturer. Raised in the suburbs just over the Nassau County line, the day of his bar mitzvah was his last in a synagogue for all intents and purposes. Yet the Jewish concept of *zedakah*—the obligation to give something back to the world—made an impression on him. He would describe himself to others as a product of the sixties. As a student at George Washington University in the nation's capital, Robins studied sociology and English, but he "majored in the Mall." Not a day went by, or so it seemed, without a protest on the park that sat between the Capitol building and the Lincoln Memorial about social injustice, civil rights, the war in Vietnam, or some other issue. Robins participated in most all of them. After college, Robins completed a master's program in public policy at the University of Pittsburgh and then a PhD, analyzing everything from deplorable conditions in the city's notorious jailhouse, the Tombs, to patterns of garbage collection in Boston, Denver, and Cincinnati on a National Science Foundation project.[10]

Robins entered city government formally after Ed Koch became mayor, rising from budget analyst to first deputy and acting commissioner of the Human Resources Administration (HRA). The role put him in charge of the sprawling social services agency responsible for the programs designed to help New York's neediest citizens. When the AIDS crisis surged, caseworkers realized that the victims suffering from the debilitating disease lacked the stamina to navigate through a range of city agencies, each one charged with providing a different aspect of the care they needed. Some city workers refused to process forms completed by AIDS clients because they feared touching the paper would infect them with the deadly disease. In response to pleas from caring workers witnessing misery on the front lines daily, Robins sought money to create a specialized unit. The budget office turned him down. "Harvey," one senior bureaucrat told him, "these people will be dead in a couple of months. How can we spend money on them?"[11]

Robins went back to his staff and told them to proceed with the project anyway, violating city budget protocol. But he insisted the caseworkers create detailed, professional records, something the organization did not always do diligently. A few months later, armed with more than six hundred reports that assessed the human benefits of the work that had been done, he secured a private meeting with Mayor Koch in which he laid out the facts and the need for additional resources. Moved, Koch came from behind his desk and put his arm around Robins. "I understand why you did what you did, but why didn't you come to me sooner?" he asked his acting commissioner, who had broken budget rules. "Mayor," Robins responded, "I didn't have the data. Now I have the data." Toward the end of Koch's last term in office, school board president Bobby Wagner lured Robins to the central Board of Education to serve as deputy chancellor for finance and operations. At a send-off party, Mayor Koch proclaimed: "After my job, every job at HRA is the hardest job in city government." And of Robins he said: "As mayor, seventy percent of what people tell me is bullshit. When dealing with experts, thirty percent is bullshit. When I talk with Harvey, I know I am getting one hundred percent accurate facts."[12]

When Joseph Fernandez became schools chancellor, he asked Robins to stay on. But it had become clear that Stanley Litow would serve as the new leader's key assistant, a role Robins had enjoyed when Richard Green led the education system. Norman Steisel had known and respected Robins for years and had contact with him while serving as chairman of the School Construction Authority. Bill Lynch also knew and respected the man from work done years earlier when Robins, then a budget analyst, wound down a federal works program being discontinued in a way that helped qualified workers transition to full-time employment where possible. With recommendations from his two key advisors, the mayor-elect met with the experienced and passionate city government official and asked him to serve as his director of operations. Ensuring implementation of policies that required coordination across agencies was the principal responsibility of the job, along with publishing the *Mayor's Management Report* twice a year—a document that emerged out of the financial crisis that provided exceptional detail about city government activity so fiscal monitors could track the use of municipal resources. Robins signed on.[13]

Working with Steisel, other deputy mayors, and agency heads, Robins took on the projects identified in the Mayor's Private-Sector Survey. He developed implementation plans for those they agreed made sense and reported progress to Steisel monthly for action. The focus and discipline created momentum behind the initiatives fairly early on in the administration. When the demand for structural reform of city government became an issue affecting the mayor's credibility, packaging the disparate measures together and giving them a name made sense.[14]

The program fit the times. A growing number of academics, politicians, and state and city managers had come to recognize that American governments no longer kept pace with the economy, the society, and the people they intended to serve. Structures set in place during the first half of the century caused municipalities to struggle mightily, often ineffectively, to fulfill their purpose in the second half. Governments typically offered citizens a choice between service cuts and higher taxes—two bad options. People wanted better management of city and state services that would deliver more of what they needed for less money, which meant adopting new approaches.

At the time Mayor Dinkins launched his program to reform New York City's bureaucracy, David Osborne and Ted Gaebler were finishing their book, *Reinventing Government: How the Entrepreneurial Spirit Is Transforming the Public Sector.* The two authors catalogued examples of innovative programs from around the country designed to make government work better. They hoped the book would serve as a "map: a simple, clear outline of a new way of conducting the public's business." It became a national best seller, and across America local governments seized on the work's basic idea that they needed to change the way they did things to remain relevant and to retain the confidence of the people who paid their salaries. Vice President Al Gore would champion the ideas at the federal level after the 1992 national election. Shortly after the book appeared, Robins adopted the ten categories of change its authors identified to organize and report on New York City's efforts. Public documents on the initiative dropped the grandiose, Reform and Renaissance title, replacing it with the trendier, "Entrepreneurial Government: New York City's Approach." Insiders continued to call the program by its original name, and every major efficiency project became subject to the discipline of its monthly status reports.[15]

Eventually, the document relied upon to track progress grew to nearly four hundred pages, cataloguing 138 initiatives. It listed 88 projects—some quite modest in scope, others major—as having been completed during the mayor's tenure. Good government groups cited the remarkably transparent tracking system and management approach Robins's team developed as one of the best in the country.[16]

By the time they launched the Reform and Renaissance initiative, the mayor and his staff had realized that they would need to fund any new programs through reallocations and greater efficiencies, not new money, since there was none. "Save a dollar, spend a nickel," Robins called it. Among many other matters, Robins's review caused him to focus on libraries. He thought budget savings achieved by limiting the hours libraries stayed open foolish. The considerable capital invested in the buildings and their contents represented a substantial sunk cost that modest operating funds could leverage. And it perplexed him that parents around the city had to post schedules on their refrigerators to know when their children could gain access to books. Fiorello LaGuardia had kept the city's libraries open seven days a week in the depths of the Depression, so Robins found the city's fiscal plight an inadequate excuse for what he considered a bad policy decision. He combed city agency line-item budget reports until he found the savings needed to keep every public library in New York open for five days a week by the summer of the second year. And he developed plans to extend hours to six days later on.[17]

When Robins presented the proposal in a meeting with the mayor and his senior staff, Bill Lynch immediately endorsed it. The other deputies and officials, however, could imagine better uses in the departments they controlled for the money Robins found. After hearing everyone out, Dinkins spoke. "I am invoking the rules of Lincoln's cabinet," he said. "I vote yes, and the ayes have it." So library doors opened for extended hours with Dinkins announcing the city's libraries are "precious jewels," and that "like schools and churches," they are "part of the heart and soul of a neighborhood and a city. . . . Keeping them open five days a week is one way of making sure our city continues to shine."[18]

Robins was particularly proud of his success consolidating a chaotic array of six different economic development offices into just two, and of the decision to move the HRA's senior citizen programs to the

Department of Aging so seniors could access most all the relevant city resources from a single place. The city also adopted an ambitious contracting-out policy for senior services, relying on local community agencies rather than government employees in an initiative intended to improve the quality and efficiency of the programs.[19]

Of the many initiatives undertaken, restructuring Medicaid reimbursement policies offered the greatest opportunity for providing the city with fiscal relief. First Deputy Mayor Steisel led an extensive review of the city's municipal health-care systems, and, a little more than a year after the Reform and Renaissance speech, the administration launched a managed-care pilot program for Medicaid recipients. Deputy Mayor Cesar Perales sponsored the plan. It sought to save the city money, but, equally important to Mayor Dinkins, it aimed to improve the quality of medical care available to the poorest New Yorkers. Its goal was to ensure timely, ongoing treatment for patients who might otherwise wait until their illnesses became serious enough to land them in a city hospital emergency room, the most expensive and least effective way to maintain their health.[20]

Recognizing smarter financing would have limited value without easier access for the poor to medical services, the city simultaneously launched the Communicare program. Its first phase privatized twenty Medicaid clinics in thirteen underserved neighborhoods and expanded services by staffing them with more than one hundred doctors. The city estimated sixty-five thousand patients benefited. In a second phase, it established programs to help nonprofit agencies secure state loans to establish more medical facilities in low-income neighborhoods. Steisel thought the Medicaid managed-care initiative one of the most important of Dinkins's term in office. Assessing the mayor's performance in 1993, the *New York Times* acknowledged, "Mr. Dinkins has launched innovative programs to improve the health care of the city's poorest families. The health effort may be his strongest program."[21]

About the same time the city launched its Medicaid managed-care pilot, in a decision that paralleled a nationwide movement, the city agreed to allow municipal medical facilities to manage their own budgets rather than rely on a central system controlled by the Health and Hospital Corporation (HHC). The new plan, championed by HHC president Dr. Billy E. Jones, applied to eleven city hospitals, five long-term care centers, and a network of neighborhood clinics. The total budget of the system exceeded $3 billion. Like the Medicaid managed-care pilot, administrators hoped the plan would improve the quality of medical service as well as create greater financial accountability and reduce the pace of increase in the cost of city-sponsored medical care.[22]

I. The Bad News Keeps on Coming

The political theater of Dinkins as an efficiency-minded reformer did nothing to change the drama caused by persistent budget gaps. Over the next few months, revenues lagged forecasts and costs rose because the weak economy caused welfare rolls and Medicaid payments to surge and because the mayor had restored some services designated for cuts. Within city departments, promised workforce reductions did not happen. In late June, the mayor's budget office had reported that 6,000 workers would be laid off in the first wave of job cutbacks. By August, it turned out that only three thousand layoffs had actually occurred, out of the total city payroll of some 225,000 workers. Staffing shifts from departments facing cuts to those with openings and other creative efforts by city bureaucrats had limited the actual number of employees let go. The most striking case occurred at the Board of Education, where at one time administrators feared ten thousand layoffs. By August, the board expected to hire more teachers rather than reduce the number employed.[23]

The Financial Control Board required the mayor to submit a five-year fiscal plan in November. Dinkins expected to include $1 billion of support from the Municipal Assistance Corporation (MAC), which could refinance bonds, extend the repayment period, and free up sales tax revenues for the city. Felix Rohatyn adopted an aggressive posture. He warned the mayor that any help from MAC would depend on a two-year city tax freeze and cuts in the city workforce of thirty to thirty-five thousand employees through attrition while negotiating productivity improvements. Rohatyn had taken to heart loud protests from real estate owners about the impact two years of property tax hikes had on them at a time of general economic weakness. Rohatyn also feared the city would use the one-time funds released in a refinancing for operating expenses rather than to secure a permanent change in the size of the city workforce. He encouraged the mayor to provide bonuses to unions willing to agree to work-rule changes to promote efficiencies and to freeze wages for unions who would not. He also called on the mayor to defer his expensive police-hiring program. "The mayor remains unwilling to face the basic problem: how to make the city's government more efficient, flexible and accountable, and responsive to changing conditions," one columnist wrote.[24]

The staff at the Financial Control Board and municipal bond-rating agencies found the plan the mayor submitted unconvincing. It failed to cut the workforce enough and lacked details about the job reductions proposed. It also depended on highly uncertain labor concessions and many special fees. New York State Comptroller Edward Regan, a statutory member of the control board, accused City Hall of suffering from a leadership "vacuum." He called for a formal board resolution threatening a state takeover to force a more serious response. Despite the mayor's effort to present his Reform and Renaissance program as the kind of profound change fiscal monitors demanded, Rohatyn roundly criticized the mayor for not addressing structural change in a serious way. "There comes a time when you have to say the emperor has no clothes," he told reporters. After tense negotiations he and the mayor agreed to abide by the judgment of the control board on the ability of a new plan to achieve long-term structural change. The mayor then instructed his budget director to work with the heads of city agencies to develop a proposal that would win approval.[25]

As the stalemate among the city, the Financial Control Board, and the Municipal Assistance Corporation continued, Barry Feinstein, head of the Teamsters union, worried about mounting pressure for municipal unions to deliver concessions. He described the situation this way: "The nongovernment government," referring to the Financial Control Board and the Municipal Assistance Corporation, "has decided that the . . . plan that the government government gave did not meet the nongovernment government's needs." He suggested that the mayor consider allowing the Financial Control Board to assume responsibility for the city's finances. The board had the power to relieve the city of the need to balance its budget annually, which in the midst of a deep recession created unusual hardship. Were the stricture removed, the drive to squeeze givebacks from unions would ease. But if the control board took over, then effectively the governor would end up responsible for politically unappealing labor negotiations, while the mayor would lose face—his credibility as the city's leader further diminished. Neither politician found the prospect appealing.[26]

For Dinkins, the bad news kept on coming. On December 13, 1991, Financial Control Board executive director Allen Proctor announced that new forecasts indicated an additional city budget gap of $333 million that would require more measures on top of other steps already contemplated. Proctor also recommended the city develop contingencies for potential income tax shortfalls of $200–300 million the following spring. He did praise the city's cost-cutting efforts, saying that the mayor's administration had established the means to monitor the progress of the budget decisions it had made. But he also reported that twenty of the initiatives were delivering less relief than anticipated, so another $106 million would have to be found. The story had become so repetitive that New Yorkers appeared increasingly numb to the never-ending tale of fiscal woe and to the continuous challenge the mayor faced as he struggled to balance fiscal prudence with the delivery of services New Yorkers expected.[27]

II. Homeless for a Reason

More than any other issue perhaps, the care of New York's homeless epitomized the simultaneous challenges David Dinkins faced as he sought to pursue liberal social policies in a time of retrenchment. As Manhattan borough president, he had often criticized the city's shelter system as inadequate and ill-conceived. Yet, in his early days as mayor, Dinkins struggled to develop a coherent policy of his own. His commitment to the indigents charged to his care clashed badly with the economic realities he faced and with the fear and hostility the intractable troubles of the homeless provoked in many New Yorkers.[28]

The problem first surged when Ed Koch ruled. Slowly at first, then with mounting intensity, dozens of seemingly broken men and women, often with vacant stares, pitiable visages, and alarming demeanors, began to haunt New York's streets. They congregated en masse in public spaces like Grand Central Terminal, Pennsylvania Railway Station, and the Port Authority Bus Terminal. They slept and lived on benches in comfortable neighborhoods as well as poor ones. The dozens turned into hundreds, and then into thousands. Ultimately, more than ten thousand homeless single men would sleep in city-run shelters on any given night. Social workers claimed that at least that many, perhaps more, rode the subways and roamed the streets.

The number of homeless single men had the greatest effect on the city's physical space, but the number of homeless families laid a greater claim to the city's heart. Typically a young and husbandless mother with more than a single child, the families generated pity in a way that men without homes did not. The obvious victims—young children, in no way responsible for their plight—painfully reminded New Yorkers of poverty's unfair cruelty. Each and every night, up to twenty thousand family members, in addition to ten thousand single men and women, needed room and board. New York City became ward to a population of more than thirty thousand some nights, the size of a substantial city itself.

In large measure, the unintended consequences of a series of city and state policies caused the surge. Single-room occupancy buildings, the cheapest form of housing that traditionally catered to individual men and women living at the margins of life, were disappearing from the lower Manhattan neighborhoods where they long had stood. City tax programs designed to encourage renovation of the often-decrepit, vermin-invested structures led to refurbishments, but the rent of apartments in the renovated buildings moved up, out of the reach of the city's near destitute. A sharp decline in federal support for construction of subsidized housing meant that as the stock of cheap apartments declined over time, nothing replaced them. Public assistance payments in fiscally strapped New York fell far behind inflation and diminished the ability of the poorest New Yorkers suffering from a range of increasingly common antisocial maladies to negotiate life in a tough city. Decades earlier, New York State had decided to stop placing mentally ill residents not overtly dangerous to themselves or others in institutions where they received the care they required but lost their freedom. The policy put a generation of people unable to fend for themselves on the streets without the support they needed to function at even a minimal level. Over time, the constellation of policies left more people homeless than ever before.[29]

Compassionate people urged Mayor Koch to build sufficient public housing to provide the suffering city of homeless with permanent residences. Koch rejected the simplistic proposal as a prescription for bankruptcy. If the government offered a free or cheap apartment to every person or family that asked, Koch reasoned logically, then the number of people asking would skyrocket. The city therefore provided dormitory-style shelters, or placed families in hotels, or sought other short-term solutions. The numbers were overwhelming, the daily task of caring for the homeless daunting. The quality of some of the facilities, particularly the later ones, was humane and impressive. The conditions at others, particularly the open-floor armories with up to nine hundred cots littered across them, were deplorable, beneath any standard of decency or dignity. Mayor Koch's critics condemned his policy harshly. And they looked at the composition of the homeless population, overwhelmingly African American and Puerto Rican, and accused the mayor of racism. If New York's homeless were white, they implied, Ed Koch would find them someplace to live.[30]

So the controversial shelter system Dinkins had inherited represented a special problem for New York's first African American mayor. Dinkins understood the issues in great detail, and he felt passionately that the homeless deserved better. When a group of homeless raised fifty dollars to contribute to the cost of the mayor's inauguration, Dinkins responded by sending them two hundred tickets to the event. He made it clear he would be proud, not embarrassed, to have them at his celebration. In 1987, while still Manhattan borough president, his office wrote a study entitled *A Shelter Is Not a Home* that catalogued the complexity of the challenge and laid out a series of recommendations for addressing them. After he became mayor, his staff developed a plan to build twenty-four high-quality shelters of modest size at an estimated cost of $200 million and to place them in residential communities around the city. But the intimidating concentration of urban ills from which the homeless suffered—drug and alcohol abuse, mental illness, and damaged psyches from abusive childhoods and substantial prison terms—made them scary neighbors. Violence, along with loud and frightening psychotic musings, public urination and defecation, communicable diseases like tuberculosis and frightening ones like AIDS, and the smells of humans no longer possessed of the self-respect or wherewithal to keep themselves clean or to change their clothes traveled with the vagrants. New Yorkers understood the homeless needed help, but they wanted them kept out of their neighborhoods and away from their families.[31]

The antagonistic attitude toward the homeless came not just from middle-class and affluent residents. Early on in Dinkins's administration, fifty demonstrators showed up at City Hall from public housing projects to protest a highly successful city policy designed to move homeless families out of welfare hotels and into permanent apartments. "We have our own homeless inside the developments—families that are doubled or tripled up in one apartment," a protestor complained, "and some have been waiting twelve years. It's not fair that these outsiders from the shelters should get in first." The protestors also feared the homeless families would bring more vandalism and drugs into the projects. The resistance to Dinkins's proposal in communities all around the city left it "dead-on-arrival" in the words of Queens borough president Claire Shulman. "It's almost as if you're saying we have a serious disease and we'll spread it so everybody will suffer from it," city council speaker Peter Vallone said of the plan, offending Dinkins with his metaphor that likened homeless people to an illness.[32]

Dinkins anticipated rejection of his plan and in this instance faced the challenge head-on with the courage of his convictions. "Of the many difficulties that urban America must confront, few are more tragic and discouraging than homelessness," he said at one point as debate around the topic continued. "I have a commitment to fashion a shelter system that works better, a system that uses smaller facilities with targeted social services, a system that will really begin to solve the problem of homelessness." With those objectives in mind, in September 1991 Dinkins appointed Andrew Cuomo, the governor's son, to head a nineteen-person commission to study the city's homeless programs and to recommend improvements.[33]

The younger Cuomo had appeared on the New York political scene in 1982 when, at the age of twenty-four, he helped to run his father's successful campaign for governor. As the homeless problem mounted, the young, ambitious man focused his energy on the issue and created an organization called Housing Enterprise for the Less Privileged (HELP), designed to bring together government and private developers to build nonprofit housing for the homeless. In 1988 he dedicated himself to the effort full-time, and its success earned him a reputation as an expert on the subject and as a man who could make things happen and get things done.[34]

In February 1992 the Cuomo Commission reported back to the mayor. It proposed a "wholesale restructuring with new, radically different policies, priorities, and programs." The commission, relying on objective data gathered systematically by the John F. Kennedy School of Government at Harvard, the Center for Social Research of the City University of New York and the Brookdale Medical Center, demonstrated that people became homeless for reasons more profound than the absence of affordable housing. The quality of the analysis contrasted with many reports prepared by advocacy groups that sought to portray the homeless as people simply down on their luck. For any program to provide meaningful help, the commission concluded, the underlying reasons for homelessness had to be addressed directly. Severe mental illness, medical conditions, and alcohol and substance abuse, along with inadequate work skills and an absence of elementary social skills topped the list. Each homeless person or family needed social service support to compensate for the specific problems that left them without a place to live. The commission proposed that when a person or family entered the emergency shelter system, the city allow up to twenty-one days to assess them and to develop a program tailored to their circumstances. It also recommended that a network of not-for-profit agencies deliver the needed social services, not the city itself, and that the city create a department independent of the sprawling, sclerotic HRA to implement and run the new structure. Finally, in a bold departure from the established practice of providing temporary shelter, the commission advised the city to issue the homeless with rent vouchers to help them afford permanent housing so the city would not have to serve as landlord of last resort for so many thousands of people.[35]

The call for a radical policy overhaul ran into instant opposition at the bureaucracies that would lose authority, HRA in particular. In keeping with his deliberate style, Dinkins appointed a panel to study the commission's recommendations. The panel then authorized six work groups to examine different parts of the findings. Some thought the approach was a classic effort to stall the proposal to death, or at least until after the 1993 mayoral election. A more discerning assessment reveals something different—a cautious yet determined effort to develop an implementation plan for a radical departure on an enormously complex and emotional public policy matter. Eventually, Dinkins's administration adopted most key elements of the plan. Yet the decision came so late in his tenure that throughout his term in office the mayor's budgets and policies wavered back and forth between proposals to build more permanent housing targeted expressly for the homeless and commitments to provide richer social services to help the homeless fend for themselves more effectively. The flip-flops left people confused.[36]

Dinkins policy toward creating more permanent housing had been set in no small measure by Mayor Koch, who in 1986 launched a ten-year plan to create more than 250,000 apartments. Rehabilitation of abandoned, city-owned buildings were expected to account for nearly fifty thousand units. The ambitious program proposed to convert urban wastelands into vibrant neighborhoods with rentals priced at levels that New Yorkers making as little as $19,000 could afford. The city also committed to construct thirty-five thousand new apartments for middle-income residents earning between $32,000 and $53,000 a year as part of the program. The cost of the initiative would total over $5 billion. It dwarfed by far any other local program in the nation. Koch deemed the plan necessary to compensate for the substantial reduction in federal support for urban renewal, which left New York without a crucial source of financing that had helped maintain the densely populated city's housing stock since the 1930s.[37]

In his first months in office, Dinkins made it clear the program—already well underway with real momentum—would continue during his administration. "Especially in this day and age, local dollars are precious, making it doubly important that the plan that has been launched is completed within budget and on time," he said when he appointed Felice Michetti commissioner of the Department of Housing, Preservation, and Development. She had served as first deputy for the prior four years, making her a natural choice to maintain continuity. Critics of the original plan thought it favored middle-class New Yorkers too much over the poor. In keeping with his politics and priorities, Dinkins put his own stamp on the program, targeting more units for the neediest, including the homeless. "In housing," Dinkins declared when announcing the changes, "this city is the leader, and that's where we will stay." By the time he left office, Dinkins could lay claim to the creation of twenty-two thousand apartments in formerly vacant buildings—many of them providing permanent housing for the homeless—rehabilitation of twenty-one thousand units in privately owned buildings and five thousand new homes for low- and moderate-income residents.[38]

III. In Search of Heritage

In October 1991 David Dinkins's father died at the age of eighty-five. The death of his immediate ancestor occurred shortly before the mayor undertook a bold voyage to honor his African heritage.[39]

Just weeks after Dinkins's inauguration, in February 1990, South African President F. W. de Klerk released African National Congress leader Nelson Mandela from his prison on Robben Island after twenty-seven years. Challenging his countrymen to "adapt-or-die," de Klerk made clear that he had planned to end the brutal apartheid regime that South Africa endured for decades and establish multiracial democratic rule in his beleaguered land. The chance to accomplish this long-sought-after change without violent upheaval and blood in the streets seemed nearly miraculous. It contained enormous personal meaning for African American leaders in the United States, including Dinkins, who for years passionately supported policies intended to bring about just such a transformation. Among other things, the event set the stage for the eventual repeal of a 1986 federal law that prevented US institutions, including New York City, from conducting business with South Africa.

In June 1990, Mandela, whose stature as a moral leader had reached unmatched heights over the years, traveled to the United States as part of a world tour to secure support for the final stages of the quest to bring democracy to South Africa. His visit included a reception by President Bush in the White House, a meeting with Secretary of State James Baker, and an address to a joint session of Congress—honors more typical of heads of state than former prisoners. But Bill Lynch had seen to it that Mandela's trip to the United States began in New York, with a hero's welcome. It included a ticker tape parade on Wall Street and a formal luncheon in Mandela's honor at City Hall. Police estimated that the day he arrived—in various motorcades, parades, and events—seven hundred fifty-thousand people saw the man who for decades had been hidden from view in a prison cell.

The next day, South Africa's most famous freedom fighter addressed fifty thousand New Yorkers in Yankee Stadium. There Dinkins placed a Yankee jacket on Mandela's shoulders and a cap on his head. With regal grace worthy of a man descended from tribal chiefs, Mandela stepped back from the podium so the fans could see him, then returned to the microphone and said, "You now know who I am. I am a Yankee," to the delighted roar of the crowd. Earlier in the day he told an ecstatic gathering of eighty thousand people in Harlem at 125th Street, at the intersection where Martin Luther King Jr. and Adam Clayton Powell Boulevards meet, that "[t]here is an umbilical cord that ties us together."[40]

Dinkins basked "in the reflected glory" of Mandela, wrote *New York Times* reporter Martin Gottlieb. "Whatever its international implications, the Mandela visit locally has become perhaps the largest and most vivid symbol of the fact that after years on the edges of New York City power and politics, the black community has arrived." It had other benefits as well. "It was a celebration that could take minds away from thinking about crime, drugs, the homeless, and all the pain we have," Deputy Mayor Barbara Fife believed. For many of Dinkins's closest supporters, the event played to deep emotions. As Mandela praised Mayor Dinkins on the steps of City Hall, Bill Lynch sat one row behind them with tears in his eyes. Years afterward, Lynch considered his role as the "architect" of that visit one of the greatest contributions he made to the Dinkins administration.[41]

In years past, New York mayors had traveled to the three I's of Ireland, Israel, and Italy, paying respect to the ancestral lands of the three ethnic groups that had dominated the city's politics for decades.

For Dinkins, a trip to South Africa applied the same tradition to contemporary circumstances, with great symbolic significance. He envisioned what he described to a *New York Times* reporter in pompous if sincere language, a "mission of succor to a struggling brethren" and an effort to forge business links that he called an investment that would yield dividends "to every New Yorker" in a postapartheid world. He announced he would travel to South Africa and invited an elaborate entourage—several dozen business leaders and city finance, health, welfare, housing, and other officials—to join him in September 1991.[42]

But the mayor and his team failed to organize the trip as scheduled. Dinkins had designated the task of raising half a million dollars from private sources to fund the trip to Deputy Mayor Bill Lynch, who had not been able to get it done in time for the departure. A diabetic with severe vision problems, Lynch had literally worked himself sick in the aftermath of race riots in Crown Heights, Brooklyn, and the fundraising had gotten lost in the crisis atmosphere that followed. At the last minute, the trip collapsed.

"It's a comment both on how tough times are, and on the way [Dinkins] dreams and doesn't plan things," one of the mayor's oldest political allies told Todd Purdum of the *New York Times*. "I think it is a reflection that they don't have a designated chain of command and responsibility, but they expect Bill Lynch to be superhuman at the expense of his own health. Why the trip had to be planned in a way that made it so expensive and hard to pull off, I don't understand." To Purdum, the fiasco "epitomized something much bigger."

> With a government of a quarter-million workers, and his own top staff of five deputy mayors, Mr. Dinkins still has a hard time getting things done. . . . [H]e has fostered a system in which Mr. Lynch, nominally in charge of politics, is his First Deputy in many other fields. First Deputy Mayor Norman Steisel has the full powers of his title in other areas, with the rest of the staff left in some shifting and ill-defined terrain in between.[43]

The trip took place after all in November 1991. Dinkins described it as "one of the most profound experiences I've ever had," and the mission launched a broad range of training programs for South Africans sponsored by businesses and New York City government agencies. But the tone of the trip had been set by the chaos surrounding its planning. The mayor could not help projecting his bitterness over the controversy, convinced that it stemmed at least in part from racist journalists who held him to a different standard than other mayors who had visited ancestral homelands without similar criticism.[44]

Not long after he returned from South Africa, while his administration grappled yet again with budget challenges, Dinkins's public image suffered another blemish. In a show of solidarity with New Yorkers facing service cuts, the mayor had agreed to a 5 percent reduction in pay for himself and eight hundred senior city officials. When an analyst pointed out that the lower salaries would also have a significant long-term effect on the pension benefits of the people involved, the mayor decided the cost to the hardworking senior managers he relied on to run the city exceeded the threshold of fairness. He reversed the decision, which had already been announced to the public. That made it seem like the mayor took better care of the city's employees than of the citizens who paid their salaries and his own, and it appeared he had not done his homework.[45]

A minor but embarrassing scandal at the New York City Housing Authority added to his woes. Laura D. Blackburne, whom Dinkins had appointed to head the agency, accompanied the mayor to South Africa. Dinkins had been explicit that all members of the entourage needed to pay their own way or to secure appropriate private-sector sponsorship. Yet Blackburne had relied on a Housing Authority foundation to pay her bill, against the explicit advice of the mayor's personal counsel, George Daniels. She had funded an overly elaborate inaugural party for herself the same way. The *New York Daily News* surfaced the details about the trip in February 1992 and also reported that Blackburne spent $345,000 to refurbish the Housing Authority's executive suite, laying out more than $3,000 for a pink leather sofa for her office to match pink venetian blinds that cost more than $5,000 to install. Dinkins had Bill Lynch fire her and appointed Sally Hernandez-Pinero to her post, which opened up the possibility of bringing into the administration a business person of stature in the economic development role.[46]

Hernandez-Pinero had been considered diligent and hardworking in the job, but without the standing and credibility a successful private-sector executive would bring. Dinkins's relationships with business leaders suffered as a consequence of the persistent fiscal crisis and his reactions to it. The mayor found himself hiking taxes while presiding over high crime, poor schools, and generally inadequate services. Inconsistent budget decision making did not help. The combination caused any number of large corporations—the New York Mercantile

Exchange, Morgan Stanley, and Prudential-Bache Securities, among others—to consider leaving the city, or at least to threaten they would. The postures forced tense negotiations, and in some instances expensive tax concessions, to keep jobs in the city at a time when organic job departures measured in the hundreds of thousands. In this respect, Dinkins's policies differed little from the ones followed by the Koch administration. Among Dinkins's senior staff, Norman Steisel had a few years of private-sector experience, but no more. No one else in the administration had any standing in business. The absence caused both a communication and a credibility gap.[47]

At the strong suggestion of Chase Manhattan Chairman David Rockefeller, Dinkins named Barry Sullivan, a former senior Chase banker who had spent several years as chief executive of First Chicago Corporation, as his new deputy mayor for finance and economic development. A sixty-one-year-old Bronx native with a mind for public service, Sullivan had advised Chicago's first black mayor, Harold Washington, on business issues while leading that city's largest bank. In New York, he saw it as his role to ensure the mayor understood the impact his policies would have on private business, the key to the city's economic success. In an unusual but not unprecedented arrangement, Sullivan would retain a $780,000 consultancy role with First Chicago while serving as deputy mayor. He agreed to donate his $112,000 city salary to charity. "We're frankly all a little scared of him," one senior mayoral aide told a reporter when asked about Sullivan. His new colleagues seemed intimidated by a man who would earn more than the other five deputy mayors combined and who was accustomed to the deference shown to a large-bank CEO.[48]

When Sullivan arrived, the mayor had yet to respond to an invitation from the New York City Chamber of Commerce and Industry to lead a trade delegation to Western Europe. The mayor smarted from criticisms of his handling of the budget from some of the chamber's members, and he was planning a mission of his own. In 1991, the German promoter of the Compaq Grand Slam Cup in Munich had invited the mayor to come watch its tennis tournament as a guest. When Dinkins sought to organize a trade mission around the invitation, the press portrayed the trip as a boondoggle with a fig leaf. The date of the tournament in Munich happened to follow Dinkins's planned trip to South Africa by a month, causing images of an absentee mayor. It did not help that the sponsor had loose ties to the United States Tennis Association, then negotiating terms for ongoing use of the city-owned

Forest Hills Tennis Club for its celebrated national open. The mayor canceled the proposed trip to Germany under pressure but remained resentful of the way the press treated the topic. His desire to undertake it belatedly represented an act of defiance on his part.[49]

Sullivan rapidly convinced the mayor to combine his plan to visit Germany with the invitation from the Chamber of Commerce. A few months after he joined the administration, the one-time bank CEO escorted the mayor and a dozen of New York's senior businessmen through a whirlwind three-nation tour of England, France, and Germany. As the mayor had hoped, Sullivan's presence convinced important business leaders that his administration took economic development seriously. In London and Paris the entourage met with senior executives considering investing in New York. With classic British understatement, one executive said the contacts made on the trip "couldn't but be helpful." Attracting foreign investment into financial services, entertainment, fashion, and other New York industries constituted part of Sullivan's thinking for reviving New York's economy, along with programs to promote high-tech companies and small businesses.[50]

IV. A Government Not Bigger than Its Checkbook

Meanwhile, Dinkins unveiled his third preliminary budget in January 1992. When he did, he announced that the challenge the city faced was "to make sure our government is not bigger than its checkbook, but maintains and in some cases even expands the core services that make this city a livable, humane place for the eight million people who have the privilege to call it home." The budget included serious cuts in capital expenditures, less money for jails, road and sewer repairs, and park maintenance and larger school class sizes. It also proposed workforce reductions of twenty thousand employees over the next four years through attrition. But it did not reduce hospital or health services, police, or libraries. Respect for the mayor's campaign commitments to provide essential services to the poor, to police the streets aggressively, and to provide the average New Yorker access to the cultural richness of the city defined the document. After three years, the mayor seemed to have found his voice.[51]

One social work advocate begrudgingly took note of the priorities implicit in the proposal. "Progressive social agenda, hardly. But it does seem to try to carry out his commitment to services for low-income New Yorkers, at least in community-based organizations and health," she commented. Manhattan borough president Ruth Messinger echoed the sentiment. "There's a clear statement that he will take some steps that are very hard to take … But he's also saying, 'I stand for something. I'm going to protect against infant mortality, and keep health and library services for children, because they're things I believe in and part of the reason I'm Mayor.'"[52]

The response Dinkins's third budget received differed markedly from the prior two. Unlike the previous preliminary budgets sent to the council, this one included no real estate and no income tax increases on New Yorkers. This welcome aspect of the plan caused city council speaker Vallone to declare that the council and the mayor were starting budget negotiations from common ground for the first time. In many respects, it was a new council led by Vallone. Charter revision had increased the number of council seats to fifty-one from thirty-five to ensure the newly empowered legislative body adequately represented the city's diverse population. The expanded class of legislators, elected in 1991, took office in January 1992, just a few weeks before the mayor submitted his preliminary fiscal year 1993 budget.[53]

The mayor's plan did call for specific taxes and fees on gasoline, automobiles, and out-of-state commuters that required approval by the state legislature. His proposal also included a creative bond-refinancing scheme and expectations of improved revenue collections, as well as a series of productivity improvements to close a projected $1.8 billion gap. Felix Rohatyn, often the mayor's toughest fiscal critic, called the budget, "[A] serious plan put forward by serious people." The mayor appeared to achieve fiscal prudence while managing to pursue at least some of his most important social service priorities.[54]

The mayor's budget team acknowledged that their objective included a goal seemingly absent in past years' efforts. "We want to protect the Mayor," Philip Michael said. The proposed budget would take the city halfway through 1993, a mayoralty election year. The chance for David Dinkins to hold on to his office and for his team to continue to run the city depended in no small measure on their ability to deliver a fiscally sound and politically smart financial plan.[55]

A few weeks before the mayor submitted his executive budget to the city council, he rode a horse through a hotel ballroom as part of his skit at the annual Inner Circle charity event sponsored by the press. He also performed rope tricks with the cast of *The Will Rogers Follies,* a popular Broadway show at the time. In their own skit, the press lampooned the mayor, portraying him as a monarch followed by police attendants who rolled out a red carpet for him while ironing his clothes. The mayor responded with some good-natured, satirical barbs of his own and then joined in the post-skit dancing until 1:30 a.m. Attentive spectators noticed the mayor sweating profusely. He had not been feeling well, but, with a show-must-go-on attitude and fearing misinterpretation of his motives if he declined to appear, he fulfilled his public obligations. Early the next morning, he checked into the hospital with what turned out to be diverticulitis, an abscess on the wall of the colon. Strong antibiotics and a few days rest put the generally healthy, sixty-four-year-old man back to work. The public also learned that their mayor had suffered a minor heart attack years earlier in 1985 but had no recurring symptoms from the event.[56]

A fully recovered mayor submitted a $29.5 billion executive budget to the council in late April 1992. By the time he did, revised tax and other revenue forecasts exceeded the city's initial estimates for the first time in years. In part, the welcome news resulted from a modest improvement in the economy. But in greater measure, more conservative revenue estimates after years of surprises in the other direction caused the welcome evolution. The higher income figures and the cumulative impact of all of the measures Dinkins's team had taken over two years created a surplus of $450 million while eliminating the need to refinance MAC debt and absorbing $200 million of federal aid the city anticipated losing. The plan, however, still included commuter and other taxes requiring state legislative action deemed unlikely. The city insisted on pursuing the doubtful tax package, mainly for the political optics it created. Failure by the state legislature to act would allow the mayor to blame some of the negative aspects of the budget on others.[57]

As the good news emerged, Dinkins traveled to Brooklyn and the Bronx to draw attention to programs he intended to restore. Some local officials detected more political art than fiscal science. "Yes, Dave, I do believe in the Easter Bunny," Bronx borough president Fernando Ferrer commented drily when the mayor traveled to 161st Street and Brook Avenue to announce capital spending for a new police academy and hundreds of apartments for middle-income residents. "It was raining just a little while ago, but the sun now shines on the Bronx," Ferrer mused, disbelieving the mayor would make good on his promises. Ferrer's instincts on the police academy proved accurate. It would never get built.[58]

Despite the general positive tenor of the mayor's numbers, or perhaps because of them, new concerns emerged. Dinkins had pledged to offer municipal workers no wage increases without productivity gains. Union leaders smelled a surplus larger than the one the mayor announced and demanded a share. They felt deceived—suspicious of City Hall's discovery of additional money so soon after laying off employees. At the time of the announcement, two hundred thousand city employees were working under expired contracts and had not had raises in over a year. Dinkins understood the political reality he faced. "[I]f we do see some relief from a long and painful recession, I fully expect that our work force—as well as all residents and businesses in our city—will benefit," he told reporters.[59]

Fiscal monitors reacted to the proposed budget positively since it contained few gimmicks and rested on reasonable if somewhat optimistic judgments about the persistently fragile economy. Yet they feared the more favorable environment would reduce the pressure on New York City to reform the way it delivered services. For example, the April plan promised to reduce the city payroll by 16,500 jobs over the next four years through attrition, down from 20,000 included in the January plan. The proposal included $235 million of streamlining savings, meaning reductions in administrative and office staff. It provided for $129 million in restructuring, such as consolidation of scofflaw towing and privatization of some city-owned housing. The numbers amounted to little more than 1 percent of the total budget. Fiscal hawks deemed a 25 percent reduction necessary for the city to achieve structural balance—the point where stable levels of revenue and annual operating costs aligned.[60]

The criticisms went generally unheeded. The city council, relieved not to be asked again to raise taxes on businesses, workers, and homeowners while enacting voter-alienating service cuts rapidly reached agreement with the mayor. The accord came a month earlier than in the past and for the first time before the June 5 deadline called for in the city charter. The final budget added $88 million for schools, police, parks, highway cleaning, cultural institutions, and city colleges. The anticipated surplus exceeded $500 million, even though the state legislature had not approved the commuter and other taxes once included in the plan. One City Hall reporter, accustomed to prolonged negotiations into the wee hours of the morning on the day the new fiscal year started, described the development as nothing short of startling.[61]

When the Municipal Assistance Corporation met in August, Chairman Felix Rohatyn declared that the mayor had made commendable progress. He credited Dinkins with having stabilized

New York's finances to an extent that would have been hard to anticipate six months earlier. More progress remained with respect to improved workforce productivity, but overall the corporation praised the mayor's management of the city's finances. When a reporter asked Rohatyn, who endorsed Dinkins in 1989 if he planned to do so again in 1993, he demurred but added, "I am fully alive to the fact that this meeting may be beneficial to the Mayor."[62]

Dinkins's potential challengers reacted ungraciously to the ease with which he negotiated his budget that year. Assuming a confrontational posture, city council president Andrew Stein declared the plan "a disaster. There's been no fundamental change in the culture of the way we deliver services and the way we do things in the city." Dinkins's former and future Republican rival, Rudolph Giuliani, took similar aim. "The real problem with this budget is that it doesn't address any of the fundamental problems that make New York one of the largest spending engines in the United States," Giuliani declared at a news conference held on the steps of City Hall. Had he been mayor, the prosecutor-cum-politician declared, he would have saved $800 million and returned it to taxpayers while reducing the workforce by 10 percent through attrition over the next twelve months.[63]

The Financial Control Board and the Citizens Budget Commission provided support for the mayor's critics. Both organizations published reports in July 1992 that said the city would continue to face budget gaps and service reductions unless it substantially reorganized the government. While crediting Dinkins with doing more to recognize New York's long-term fiscal problems than any mayor in two decades, the control board found the efforts fell short of the need. The city still had no restructuring plan sufficient to achieve a stable relationship between the size of local government and the size of the local economy. "What this plan . . . makes patently clear," the staff of the control board wrote, "is that the city has neither the economy nor the revenues to do everything its citizens have become accustomed to expect." In an earlier report, the control board staff urged the city to integrate its multiyear plan more closely with its annual budget to facilitate structural balance in its financing. In letters to Mayor Dinkins and speaker Vallone, Citizens Budget Commission president Raymond D. Horton told the men, "[Y]our actions belie your words," with respect to overhauling the government. He accused the two leaders of missing opportunities to consolidate agencies, to improve tax policies, and to change unproductive work rules, among other things.[64]

Budget Director Philip Michael thought the critics unrealistic. "Our view is that we have structural balance and inherent in that is that we do have to make midcourse adjustments, through good times and bad," he argued. At one level, he had a point. The typical American municipality financed three-quarters of its expenses from real estate taxes—a fairly stable source. New York City raised only 44 percent of revenue from real estate. It generated nearly 30 percent of revenue from income taxes, which experienced particularly wide swings in a city whose wealthiest residents tended to work on Wall Street. The typical city raised just 5 percent of revenues from income taxes. Heavy reliance on income taxes meant New York City revenues would always rise and fall with the economy, requiring the adjustments Michael described. Sales and consumption taxes accounted for the remainder of municipal money, some 27 percent in New York and 20 percent elsewhere. Still, the reality of volatile revenues aside, the strong impression endured that the city bureaucracy remained too big to afford and too cumbersome to work efficiently. In important ways, fiscal balance continued to elude New York City.[65]

V. Election Year Relapse

Even as his team wrestled with budgets they brought into balance, the mayor's credibility as a responsible manager of financial affairs continued to come under assault. In January 1992 accountants prepared a routine financial disclosure filing with the city Board of Election for Dinkins campaign committee. They discovered the mayor's campaign finance chairman, Arnold I. Biegen, had written himself $158,000 of unauthorized checks.[66]

The episode caught Dinkins completely unaware. "I am shocked and saddened by the startling events which caused the resignation of my finance chair," the mayor said at a Gracie Mansion press conference. "I don't think I did anything wrong," Biegen protested to reporters. Still he wrote the campaign committee a check for the amount owed. Before it cleared, the Internal Revenue Service put a lien on it against some $300,000 in back taxes and interest. Biegen owed the government hundreds of thousands of dollars more, resulting from a 1987 loan default related to a failed bank with reputed organized crime connections. He eventually pled guilty to state charges of stealing the campaign money and also to embezzling some $850,000 from an elderly Brooklyn widow. The corrupt man received a sentence of thirty-five months in prison.[67]

The ink had barely dried on the 1993 fiscal year budget when planning for fiscal year 1994 began. It would include the second half of 1993 with the election race for mayor in full sprint. The concerns New York's financial watchdogs raised, despite the relative ease with which the mayor and council adopted the 1993 budget, rapidly proved well-founded. In his preliminary estimates, Budget Director Michael projected the city would face an anticipated $1.6 billion shortfall, which soon grew to over $2 billion. The success of the prior year was not a structural breakthrough but a one-time event. Michael asked city agencies to identify $500 million of cuts as a starting point.[68]

In January 1993, the city reached a three-year agreement with municipal unions representing 180,000 employees that allowed for raises totaling 8.25 percent through March 1995. The agreement also created a three-member panel, consisting of management, labor, and an independent arbitrator to negotiate money-saving changes in work rules. The mayor's labor commissioner, James Hanley, who had replaced Eric Schmertz, called the new panel a breakthrough that would lead to meaningful change. James Butler, president of Local 420 of the hospital workers' union dismissed the panel as "window dressing" to allow the mayor "to save face." He vowed to reject efforts designed to get more work from fewer workers. The agreement raised city expenses while leaving productivity gains Dinkins promised to the uncertainty of tough negotiations.[69]

On January 30, 1993, the mayor presented a preliminary budget totaling over $31 billion. The document anticipated maximum aid from the state and federal governments, even more than in past years. An electoral analysis had entered into the budget calculations. With New York's first black mayor up for reelection in 1993, the Dinkins team expected their fellow Democrat in the statehouse—Governor Cuomo, who would be up for reelection himself the following year—to make an extra effort to deliver support. And with Bill Clinton's election as president in November 1992, they now had a Democrat as an ally in the White House for the first time during Dinkins's term in City Hall. So the Dinkins team expected more help than usual from the federal government as well. In addition to $600 million from those sources, the mayor proposed $300 million in tax increases the state legislature would have to approve. The plan also called for loans against yet-to-be-collected delinquent property taxes, which struck some as a gimmick. Others pointed out many municipalities engaged in such borrowing as a matter of course.[70]

With the prior year's recent history in mind, some observers suspected the mayor and his budget director of deliberately portraying things as desperate to apply maximum pressure on others to provide support. The real budget would appear in May, they surmised, with revenue estimates sufficiently higher to avoid forcing the mayor to lay off workers and to cut programs in an election year. But in actuality the budget had tilted as out of balance as it appeared.[71]

In March the Financial Control Board issued a seventy-nine-page report that acknowledged the Dinkins administration continued to find ways to balance its budget but condemned it sharply for not confronting structural challenges. "The critical problems causing persistent billion-dollar gaps remain largely unaddressed or unabated by this financial plan," the report declared. "Indeed, the gaps to be closed over the next four years are larger than they were in the financial plan one year ago." Budget Director Michael took exception to the report, calling it unrealistic and simplistic. "We have shown an ability to deal with each and every one" of the problems cited in the report, "and there is no reason to question our resolve or ability to deal with them in the future," he insisted.[72]

By May 1993, with the following year's budget still under negotiation, it became apparent that the Dinkins administration would spend more in the current year than originally anticipated—even as it warned of a severe shortfall to come. The city claimed forces beyond its control caused the awkward posture. Among other things, welfare rolls had continued to rise until they tallied more than one million recipients, and two severe winter storms plus a terrorist bombing of the World Trade Towers on February 28, 1993, created higher overtime payments for sanitation and public safety workers. The AIDS epidemic caused a rise in city-funded health care, and the number of students enrolling in public schools went up. State and federal government-mandated programs also had risen more than expected.

Critics contended the city's practices perpetuated its fiscal problems. "Their approach is that you reduce the government if you have to and when the resources appear, you say you don't have to anymore," Charles Brecher, director of research for the Citizens Budget Commission said. One analyst perceived little mystery. "Part of the answer to the puzzle is they had more money to spend, and they spent it," he said. In an election year, the perceived lack of fiscal discipline drew the self-interested fire of political opponents. "Had the Mayor managed the budget and kept spending roughly within the budget that had been agreed upon last year, the Mayor would not be sitting there with a budget deficit [for next year]," Rudy Giuliani said. "That creeping up of the budget is really a failure of management at the highest level," he continued, making it clear where he wanted voters to put the blame. "The city spends whatever it can confiscate," he concluded, driving his point home.[73]

By the end of May, the state and federal governments had returned disappointing news with respect to the city's revenue requests. Every level of government, it seemed, had its own fiscal troubles. The Dinkins administration acknowledged it would have little choice but to cut programs. Among the items on the contingency list that Budget Director Michael said would have to be pared back: summer classes for high school students, day care for nearly five thousand children, money for AIDS patients, and drop-in centers designed to keep the homeless off the streets. He denied it was a doomsday list designed to create political heat, but rather the least offensive of bad options to get the budget in balance as required by law. A *New York Newsday* editorial gave Dinkins some credit for stamina even as it chastised him. "If there were an Olympic medal for treading water in tough fiscal straits, Mayor David Dinkins would take home the gold," the editors wrote. Yet they called on him "to persuade city unions to go for real productivity deals and gainsharing. . . . Whether it's sanitation workers, cops or teachers, reconfiguring basic services is crucial to stabilizing and improving everyone's quality of life."[74]

The city sought to blame its partners in government for failing to come through with needed funds, but the three private citizens the governor had appointed to the Financial Control Board assessed the situation differently. For the first time in eleven years, they issued a statement harshly critical of a mayoral budget. In addition to accusing the mayor of relying on more than $1 billion of one-time revenue sources and of continued—even if diminished—expectations of doubtful state and federal aid, they faulted Dinkins for failing to shrink the municipal workforce. As a consequence, they accused him of creating a "permanent deficit" that would rise above $2 billion. The statement went on to declare that the city continued to harbor unrealistic expectations of the range of services it could afford to provide. "They have got to set priorities, do those services which they place a high priority on as efficiently as possible and be prepared to eliminate low-priority services," one board member told reporters.[75]

The *New York Times* editorial board added its criticism to the mix. The mayor should have known better than to think the city would get the aid he requested from the state and federal governments, they wrote, and they accused him of offering a list of contingency cuts to compensate that were "so harsh that it is hard to take him seriously." They feared the mayor and the city council, all up for reelection, would postpone needed reductions until after November's vote. Cuts would have to be more severe as a consequence because they would come four months into the next fiscal year. The editorial concluded with the mantra fiscal watchdogs kept repeating. "In the long run, if the city does not do more to bring spending into line with foreseeable revenues, it will simply have to grapple with gaps like this year's again and again."[76]

On the defensive, the city conceded that it had not developed a plan for responding to its long-range fiscal needs. The mayor resorted to a time-honored approach for dealing with intractable issues with serious political repercussions: he appointed a committee to study the problem. It included William H. Gray, III, then the president of the United Negro College Fund and a former Pennsylvania congressman and House Budget Committee chairman; Donald H. Kummerfeld, a former New York City budget director; and Dall Forsythe, a former New York State budget director. They agreed to serve on an ad hoc team to deliver a report to the mayor after the election.[77]

The relationship between the mayor and the governor became badly frayed as budget negotiations wore on. In January, the mayor had traveled to Albany to testify before the Assembly Ways and Means Committee. "Time and again the state has asked local governments to carry a heavy fiscal load. And after we have done so, we have been asked to carry even more," he said at the time. He went on to assert that the state had shifted $1.1 billion of expenses to the city since 1990, a claim the governor's office disputed. Mario Cuomo thought David Dinkins had no one to blame but himself for the city's predicament. The mayor had failed to make the tough decisions required, and now he hoped the governor and the state would rescue him. The total number of staff reductions Dinkins had made—13,000 out of a workforce of about 225,000 when he assumed office—was half as large as those the governor had implemented. "You can't ask us to damage ourselves in order to provide assistance that you can do within your own budget," one Cuomo aide offered by way of explanation of the standoff. And the governor understood he would need every dollar he could find to stabilize his own election year budget in 1994.[78]

The Dinkins team felt all but betrayed. When the mayor asked the governor about the public statement made by his three appointees to the Financial Control Board, Cuomo feigned ignorance. When handed a copy of the press release, the governor read it slowly. Then he removed his glasses, clasped his hands behind his head, and uttered the single word "fascinating," according to those present. The mayor was not amused. Dinkins's aides thought the governor had laid it on a "little too thick, even for him." Back in 1989, in the weeks between Dinkins's election and his assumption of office, one high-ranking Democrat had said, "David should understand a basic fact of life. Mario Cuomo is not his ally." The comment proved prescient.[79]

VI. The Last of the Dinosaur Budgets

In June, a week later than required by charter and after intense negotiations, the mayor and the city council reached an agreement. The $31.2 billion accord restored a few programs the mayor's office proposed to cut. It totaled $1.8 billion more than the budget adopted the prior year. The 5 percent election-year increase exceeded the 3 percent rise the year before and the 2 percent increases each of the two years prior to that. Mayor Dinkins and city council speaker Peter Vallone recognized the budget did little to solve long-range fiscal problems. "This is the last of the dinosaur budgets," Vallone said, paying lip service to the demand for structural reform. "The administration and the council now recognize that we really have to make some permanent changes." Dinkins described himself as very concerned about the deficits forecast for the future and reminded reporters he had appointed a committee to report back to him with recommendations in December.[80]

Events would not wait for the committee's report. Within weeks, Standard and Poor's threatened to lower the city's bond rating again. Budget Director Philip Michael took the call from the rating agency while playing golf with state legislative counterparts. He asked for a delay so the city could present a revised plan. The company seemed disinclined to wait, but someone high up on Dinkins's team "played the race card," according to a senior official involved in the talks. The administration threatened to accuse the company of mistreating the mayor because he was black if the agency did not give the city a chance to respond.[81]

On July 3, 1993, just two days into the new fiscal year, Dinkins announced additional cuts that had been promised to Standard and Poor's in return for no downgrade. Citizen Budget Commission president Ray Horton interpreted the unusual announcement "as the city starting early the process of cleaning up the mess everybody recognized was the 1994 budget." Before long, Dinkins would seek to undo the promised cuts to prevent damage to constituents more important to him than the rating agencies.[82]

David Dinkins had the bad luck to enter office during a seemingly relentless economic slowdown that squeezed local revenues during most of his four years in office. His term corresponded with a push by national leaders to diminish the stream of money flowing from the federal government to states and cities. The combination meant David Dinkins governed during an era of forced austerity that would have challenged any mayor. The times called for an aggressive and creative reformer who would lead the city in an effort to restructure its government to work more efficiently. As a matter of political philosophy and training, David Dinkins was ill-equipped to respond. An urban liberal who believed government had an obligation to help the city's poorest and most disadvantaged citizens, his instincts were to channel city resources into generous social service programs. A Tammany-trained politician, he sought to use the city budget to reward his allies.

Institutions with extraordinary power that embodied the legacy of the city's near bankruptcy in the 1970s limited David Dinkins's ability to pursue the policies he wanted. The Financial Control Board and the Municipal Assistance Corporation sought to force Dinkins to fire municipal workers and to restructure the government to operate more efficiently. In many respects, they championed the classic agenda of good government groups and municipal reform movements from across the decades. These were not the policies that Dinkins wanted to pursue, so conflict followed. Dinkins tried, with his Reform and Renaissance program, to project the image of a mayor committed to efficiency, but the ploy lacked credibility. Fiscally aware New Yorkers understood that Dinkins sought to maintain as much of the municipal workforce as he could, to give unions the largest raises possible, and to expand government programs designed to help the needy. Whether the efforts were admirable or wrongheaded is a matter of political philosophy. But the clumsiness and ineffectiveness of David Dinkins's efforts to pursue expansion during a time of severe budget limitations constituted a failure of political skill and leadership.

Mayor Dinkins found himself caught in a well-built trap designed to constrain New York City mayors from engaging in deficit financing to fund operations. He pursued his preferred policies with additional debt to the degree that he could. The city's general obligations exceeded $20 billion for the first time at the end of fiscal year 1993, and total debt, including MAC obligations, exceeded $26 billion—$7 billion more than in fiscal year 1989. The rise, over 35 percent, added up to $3,500 of debt for every man, woman, and child in the city—just about $1,000 more per person than in 1989. As a percent of the city's total economic output, total municipal debt rose to over 13 percent, up from less than 11.5 percent when Dinkins won the office. The increase, while noticeable, did not reach alarming levels. The enforced discipline of external constraints had worked.[83]

Only once in four years did the mayor and his team seize the budget initiative. In January 1992 when they announced their plans for fiscal year 1993, they framed the debate in terms that suited the mayor and his agenda while accommodating the many constituencies with a stake in the city's fiscal fortunes. Yet the next year the mayor again found himself reacting to events rather than guiding them, with election-year politics driving him to spend money the city did not have, damaging his reputation for fiscal stewardship as he sought a mandate from voters to continue in office.

The Dinkins administration did launch one important effort to create structural change of a sort through a court action. New York State had long applied a complicated system of fifteen formulas to determine how much state money each local school district received. The complexity masked political decisions and systematically short-changed New York City in favor of suburban and rural counties. The city educated 37 percent of the state's students but received only 34 percent of education funds—an annual shortfall of hundreds of millions of dollars, billions over time. The formulas discriminated against poorer neighborhoods and created racist outcomes by favoring white middle-class districts at the expense of those that contained largely African Americans, Latinos, and Asians. Three state commissions that reviewed the issue over two decades recommended changing and simplifying the formulas. But the state legislature did not act for fear of political fallout in the areas that lost revenue. One out-of-town school-financing consultant described the situation in colorful terms: "Attempting to change [school aid] formulas is like a Russian novel: it's long, boring and in the end everybody gets killed."[84]

The dire budget outlook, election-year politics, and decades of pent-up frustration at the unwillingness of the legislature to respond to the compelling reality that the state education budget systematically shortchanged New York City spurred Dinkins on. On March 15, 1993, New York City and the New York City Board of Education sued Governor Cuomo and other New York State officials over school-funding formulas. Announcing the legal action, Mayor Dinkins declared that for years the city "had to endure a state aid allocation system that has been grossly unfair to its children. With the filing of today's lawsuit, our city loudly and strongly notifies the State Legislature of its intent not to put up with this inequity any longer." Joseph Fernandez, chancellor of the New York City Board of Education, added his voice to the charge. "We have exhausted all of the political remedies to get our fair share of aid, with very little progress being made. Our city's children have no choice but to seek the protection of the courts." The city accurately recognized that the judicial branch offered the only hope for redress of the long-standing, unfair budget matter. Resolution would take years, offering no short-term budget relief.[85]

Notes

1. Sam Roberts, "The Region: The Budget Balances, but Now Reality," *NYT*, July 14, 1991.
2. Joe Klein, "The Real Deficit: Leadership," *New York*, July 22, 1991, 20–25. The Newfield quote appears in this article.
3. "Statement by Mayor David N. Dinkins: Meeting of the State Financial Control Board," July 2, 1991; Josh Barbanel, "The Budget Battles: Wary State Control Board Tightens Monitoring of New York City Budget," *NYT*, July 3, 1991; Joe Klein, "The Real Deficit: Leadership," *New York*, July 22, 1991, 20–25.
4. Author's interview, Norman Steisel, October 28, 2010; Author's interview, off the record.
5. Todd S. Purdum, "Dinkins Outlines Plans to Remedy Fiscal Problems," *NYT*, July 31, 1991.
6. "Remarks by Mayor David N. Dinkins: The Reform and Renaissance of New York City Government—Making the Future Work for Us," July 30, 1991, Office of the Mayor, David N. Dinkins, Speeches, Microfilm Roll #10.
7. "Supporting Document for the Mayor's Speech," July 30, 1991, attached to "Remarks by Mayor David N. Dinkins: The Reform and Renaissance of New York City Government—Making the Future Work for Us" July 30, 1991, Office of the Mayor, David N. Dinkins, Speeches, Microfilm Roll #10.
8. "Supporting Document for the Mayor's Speech," July 30, 1991, attached to "Remarks by Mayor David N. Dinkins: The Reform and Renaissance of New York City Government—Making the Future Work for Us," July 30, 1991, Office of the Mayor, David N. Dinkins, Speeches, Microfilm Roll #10.

9.   Letter from Felix Rohatyn to the Honorable David Dinkins, December 13, 1989, in New York City Municipal Archives, Office of the Mayor, David N. Dinkins, D.M. Norman Steisel, Correspondence, Microfilm Roll # 128.

10.   Author's interview, Harvey Robins, December 17, 2010.

11.   Author's interview, Harvey Robins, December 17, 2010.

12.   Mayor Edward I. Koch, informal remarks at a celebration of Harvey Robins's tenure as first deputy commissioner of the New York City Human Resources Administration, 1989, author in attendance.

13.   Author's interview, Norman Steisel, October 28, 2010; Author's interview, Harvey Robins, December 1, 2010.

14.   Memorandum to: Norman Steisel, from: Harvey Robins, Date: January 7, 1993, Subject: Update on Structural Initiative for an example of the monthly action report Robins provided to first deputy mayor Norman Steisel; Memorandum to: Norman Steisel, from: Harvey Robins, Date: May 12, 1993, Subject: NYC Partnership Task Force on Privatization with draft report and the city's response attached, in New York City Municipal Archives, Office of the Mayor, David N. Dinkins, D.M. Norman Steisel, Correspondence, Microfilm Roll # 128.

15.   David Osborne and Ted Gaebler, *Reinventing Government: How the Entrepreneurial Spirit Is Transforming the Public Sector* (Addison-Wesley Publishing Company Inc: Reading, MA, 1992), xvii; Author's interview, Harvey Robins, December 1, 2010.

16.   *The Reform and Renaissance of New York City Government: Monthly Milestone Report,* November 1993, David N. Dinkins, Mayor; Norman Steisel, First Deputy Mayor; Harvey Robins, Director, Mayor's Office of Operations is the last monthly report on the program prepared during the Dinkins administration, in the possession of Harvey Robins; Katherine Barrett and Richard Greene, "The State of the Cities Managing for Results: Direct Accountability: New York City," *Financial World*, February 1, 1994, 45.

17.   Author's interview, Harvey Robins, December 1, 2010.

18.   Author's interview, Harvey Robins, December 1, 2010; Paul Schwartzman, "Make Book on City Library Comeback," *New York Post*, April 20, 1992.

19.   Author's interview, Harvey Robins, December 1, 2010.

20.   Kevin Sack, "Cuomo Details His Medicaid Plan, and Reviews Are Less Than Raves," *NYT*, October 10, 1991; "Supporting Document for the Mayor's Speech," July 30, 1991, attached to "Remarks by Mayor David N. Dinkins: The Reform and Renaissance of New York City Government—Making the Future Work for Us," July 30, 1991, Office of the Mayor, David N. Dinkins, Speeches, Microfilm Roll #10; Mary B.W. Tabor, "New York's Poor Trying Alternative to Medicaid," February 1, 1993; "Maximizing Resources: Managing in a Time of Retrenchment, Commitment to Neighborhood Services, 1990–1993," City of New York, David N. Dinkins, Mayor; Mayor's Office of Operations, Harvey Robins Director, August 1993 in the possession of the author.

21.   "The Mayoral Campaign—At Issue: Health Care; New York's Health Challenge," *NYT*, October 21, 1993; "Supporting Document for the Mayor's Speech," July 30, 1991, attached to "Remarks by Mayor David N. Dinkins: The Reform and Renaissance of New York City Government—Making the

Future Work for Us," July 30, 1991, Office of the Mayor, David N. Dinkins, Speeches, Microfilm Roll #10; Mary B.W. Tabor, "New York's Poor Trying Alternative to Medicaid," February 1, 1993; "Maximizing Resources: Managing in a Time of Retrenchment, Commitment to Neighborhood Services, 1990–1993," City of New York, David N. Dinkins, Mayor; Mayor's Office of Operations, Harvey Robins, Director, August 1993 in the possession of the author.

22. "Supporting Document for the Mayor's Speech," July 30, 1991, attached to "Remarks by Mayor David N. Dinkins: The Reform and Renaissance of New York City Government—Making the Future Work for Us," July 30, 1991, Office of the Mayor, David N. Dinkins, Speeches, Microfilm Roll #10; Josh Barbanel, "Dinkins Is Backing Budget Autonomy at City Hospitals," *NYT*, July 18, 1992.

23. Josh Barbanel, "Labor Cuts by New York City Are Fewer Than Anticipated," *NYT*, August 12, 1991.

24. Todd S. Purdum, "New York City Budget Has Big Gap," *NYT*, October 31, 1991; Joe Klein, "The City Politic: Cuomo's Hologram," *New York*, October 7, 1991, 16–17.

25. Sam Roberts, "Rohatyn Pushes Dinkins to Drop Fiscal Proposal," *NYT*, November 10, 1991; Todd S. Purdum, "City Hall Tells Agencies to Cut as Deficit Rises," *NYT*, November 23, 1991; James C. McKinley, "Comptroller Urges Control Board to Press Dinkins on Fiscal Goals," *NYT*, December 6, 1991.

26. Todd S. Purdum, "Feinstein Says Use of Control Board Deserves Study," *NYT*, December 8, 1991.

27. James C. McKinley Jr., "Deficit Grows $333 Million in New York," *NYT*, December 14, 1991.

28. *A Shelter Is Not a Home*, Report of the Manhattan Borough President's Task Force on Housing for Homeless Families, Dr. James R. Dumpson, Chairman, March 1987.

29. Soffer, *Ed Koch*, 276–90.

30. McNickle, *To Be Mayor of New York*, 282–83.

31. Don Terry, "Mayor Dinkins: An Era Begins with a Little Fun; A Mosaic of Humanity Gathers Near City Hall," *NYT*, January 2, 1990; *A Shelter Is Not a Home*, Report of the Manhattan Borough President's Task Force on Housing for Homeless Families, Dr. James R. Dumpson, Chairman, March 1987. Senior city government officials attribute much of the work on this report to Nancy Wackstein, who continued to work on homeless issues after David Dinkins became mayor; Guy Trebay, "Street News," *Village Voice*, May 11, 1993; Pete Hamill, "How to Save the Homeless and Ourselves," *New York*, September 20, 1993, 35–39.

32. *New York City Five-Year Plan For Housing and Assisting Homeless Adults*, Felice Michetti, Commissioner HPD, Barbara Sobol, Commissioner HRA, Nancy Wackstein, Director, Mayor's Office on Homelessness and SRO Housing, October 1991. Todd S. Purdum, "Dinkins Lists Possible Shelter Sites to Irate Protests on Many Fronts," *NYT*, October 11, 1991; John Tierney, "Using Housing Projects for Welfare Angers Tenants," *NYT*, June 28, 1990.

33. *The Way Home: A New Direction in Social Policy*, Report of the New York City Commission on the Homeless, Andrew M. Cuomo, Chairman, February 1992, Preface.

34. Frank Lynn, "Andrew Cuomo to Shift to Full-Time Housing Work," *NYT*, October 18, 1988; Joe Klein, "The National Interest: Now for the Good News," *New York*, January 7, 1991, 10–11.

35. Celia W. Dugger, "Report to Dinkins Urges Overhaul in Shelter System for the Homeless," *NYT*, January 31, 1992; *The Way Home: A New Direction in Social Policy*, Report of the New York City Commission on the Homeless, Andrew M. Cuomo, Chairman, February 1992.

36. Author's interview, Norman Steisel, October 28, 2010; Celia W. Dugger, "Panel's Report on Homeless Is Criticized by Dinkins Staff," *NYT*, February 1, 1992; Editorial, "Too Slow for the Homeless," *NYT*, May 23, 1992. Memo from: David N. Dinkins to: Deputy Mayor Norman Steisel, Deputy Mayor Cesar A. Perales, Deputy Mayor Bill Lynch, Date May 15, 1992, Subject: Plan for Implementation of Commission Recommendations; *Reshaping New York City's Policies and Programs for Homeless Individuals and Families: A Comprehensive Strategy for Implementing the Recommendations of the New York City Commission on Homelessness*," Marsha A. Martin, DSW, Director Mayor's Office on Homelessness and SRO Housing; Sally Hernandez-Pinero, Chairwoman, NYCHA; Luis R. Marcos, MD, Commissioner Department of Mental Health, Mental Retardation, and Alcoholism Services; Felice Michetti, Commissioner, Housing Preservation and Development; Charles V. Raymond, Director, Mayor's Office for Homeless Facilities and Service Development; Barbara Sabol, Commissioner, Human Resources Administration, May 1992; *New York City Revised and Updated Plan for Housing and Assisting Homeless Single Adults and Families*, March 1993.

37. Soffer, *Ed Koch*, 290–91.

38. Alan Finder, "Dinkins Appoints New Housing Chief," *NYT*, March 17, 1990; Alan Finder, "The Region; Should the Poor Get the Housing That Koch Built?" *NYT*," March 18, 1990; Don Terry, "Dinkins Expands Housing Plan to Assist the Poor," *NYT*, May 17, 1990; Shawn G. Kennedy, "The 1993 Campaign: Housing—The Agenda; Housing's Waiting List Includes Policy for Growth," *NYT*, October 31, 1993.

39. John T. McQuiston, "William Dinkins, Mayor's Father and Real Estate Agent, Dies at 85," *NYT*, October 20, 1991; Author's interview, Harvey Robins, December 1, 2010.

40. Author's interview, Bill Lynch, October 29, 2010; John Kifner, "The Mandela Visit; Mandela Takes His Message to Rally in Yankee Stadium," *NYT*, June 22, 1990; John Kifner, "The Mandela Visit; Mandela Gets an Emotional New York City Welcome," *NYT*, June 21, 1990.

41. Martin Gottlieb, "Mandela's Visit, New York's Pride," *NYT*, June 24, 1990; Author's interview, Bill Lynch, October 29, 2010.

42. Todd S. Purdum, "Failed Trip Shows Dinkins's Weak Spots," *NYT*, September 12, 1991.

43. Todd S. Purdum, "Failed Trip Shows Dinkins's Weak Spots," *NYT*, September 12, 1991.

44. "Mayor David N. Dinkins Radio Station WINS Commentary: South Africa," November 22, 1991; Todd S. Purdum, "Dinkins in South Africa, Widens Economic Efforts," *NYT*, November 18, 1991; Sam Roberts, "Political Memo: Dinkins Lets His Bitterness Show," *NYT*, November 25, 1991.

45. Calvin Sims, "Dinkins Rescinds Pay Cuts for Himself and 800 Others," *NYT*, December 18, 1991; Editorial, "Wrong Symbolism on Mayoral Pay," *NYT*, December 21, 1991.

46. "New Housing Authority Chief," *NYT*, September 28, 1990; Jacques Steinberg, "Housing Agency Expenses Questioned," *NYT*, February 15, 1992; Calvin Sims, "Housing Chief Gets Rebuke from Dinkins," *NYT*, February 19, 1992; Calvin Sims, "Housing Chief Quits Her Post under Pressure," *NYT*, February 23, 1992.

47. Calvin Sims, "Former Chase Manhattan Official Named Deputy Mayor by Dinkins," *NYT*, March 24, 1992; Editorial, "Two Sound Choices: A Business Pro at City Hall," *NYT*, March 25, 1992; Richard Levine, "New York Fears Exodus of Jobs on Wall Street," *NYT*, November 3, 1990; Richard Levine, "Middle-Class Flight Feared by New York City Experts," NYT, April 1, 1991; James C. McKinley, "Dinkins Pledges 4-Year Corporate Tax Freeze," *NYT*, October 20, 1992.

48. Calvin Sims, "Former Chase Manhattan Official Named Deputy Mayor by Dinkins," *NYT*, March 24, 1992; Editorial, "Two Sound Choices: A Business Pro at City Hall," *NYT*, March 25, 1992; "The Region: Q&A: Barry F. Sullivan; New Deputy Mayor, a Banker, Outlines His Business Plan," *NYT*, March 29, 1992.

49. James C. McKinley, "Dinkins's New Economic Chief Finding Life in the Spotlight a Bit Unsettling," *NYT*, June 5, 1992; Calvin Sims, "Mayor Said to Plan 5-Day Trip," *NYT*, April 30, 1992; Jacques Steinberg, "Dinkins Plans Munich Trip, Expenses Paid," *NYT*, October 28, 1991; Editorial: "The Flights from City Hall," *NYT*, October 29, 1991.

50. James C. McKinley, "Dinkins's New Economic Chief Finding Life in the Spotlight a Bit Unsettling," *NYT*, June 5, 1992; Steven Prokesch, "Dinkins's Europe Trip Polishes City's Image," *NYT*, June 15, 1992.

51. Todd S. Purdum, "Fiscal Balancing Act: Dinkins Is Seeking to Keep City Livable and Still Hold Line on Budget Cuts," *NYT*, January 31, 1992.

52. Todd S. Purdum, "Fiscal Balancing Act: Dinkins Is Seeking to Keep City Livable and Still Hold Line on Budget Cuts," *NYT*, January 31, 1992.

53. Peter Vallone, *Learning to Govern*, 195.

54. Purdum, "Fiscal Balancing Act," *NYT*, January 31, 1992.

55. Purdum, "Fiscal Balancing Act," *NYT*, January 31, 1992.

56. Todd S. Purdum, "Colon Abscess Is Diagnosis for Dinkins," *NYT*, March 11, 1992.

57. Calvin Sims, "Surplus in Budget Expected for Year by New York City," *NYT*, April 22, 1992; Calvin Sims, "Dinkins Proposes a Modest Growth in His Budget Plan," *NYT*, April 28, 1992.

58. Calvin Sims, "Surplus in Budget Expected for Year by New York City," *NYT*, April 22, 1992; Calvin Sims, "Dinkins Proposes a Modest Growth in His Budget Plan," *NYT*, April 28, 1992.

59. Todd S. Purdum, "Not Yet Out of the Woods: For Dinkins, a Projected Budget Surplus Means Good News and New Challenges," *NYT*, April 23, 1992; Calvin Sims, "New York City Begins Talks with Its Unions," *NYT*, June 4, 1992.

60. Purdum, "Not Yet Out of the Woods," *NYT*, April 23, 1992; Sims, "Dinkins Proposes a Modest Growth," *NYT*, April 28, 1992.

61. Calvin Sims, "Dinkins and Council Reach Accord on $29 Billion Budget," *NYT*, May 31, 1992.

62. Alan Finder, "Rohatyn, a Dinkins Critic on Budgets, Praises the Mayor," *NYT*, August 27, 1992.

63. Purdum, "Not Yet Out of the Woods," *NYT*, April 23, 1992; Alan Finder, "Giuliani Says New Budget Fails to Cut Spending," *NYT*, June 5, 1992.

64. Alan Finder, "Political Memo: Dinkins Is Mastering the Art of the Mayor," *NYT*, July 5, 1992; Alan Finder, "Board Urges Fiscal Shifts in New York," *NYT*, July 30, 1992; New York State Financial Control Board, *The Structure of the FYs 1993–1996 Financial Plan*, July 29, 1992, 1; New York State Financial Control Board, *Financial Planning in the Nineties: Building on New York's Pioneering Efforts in the Seventies*, June 1992, ii.

65. Alan Finder, "Board Urges Fiscal Shifts," *NYT*, July 30, 1992.

66. Jacques Steinberg, "Dinkins Adviser Resigns over Bank Withdrawals," *NYT*, January 19, 1992.

67. Jacques Steinberg, "Dinkins Adviser Resigns," *NYT*, January 19, 1992; Ralph Blumenthal, "Inquiries Unearth Pieces of Biegen's Secret Life," *NYT*, February 16, 1992; Alessandra Stanley, "Man of No Prominence, Biegen Received Trust," *NYT*, February 1, 1992; Todd S. Purdum, "Dinkins Denounces Ex-Treasurer as Inquiries on Campaign Widen," *NYT*, February 15, 1992; Blumenthal, "Inquiries Unearth Pieces of Biegen's Secret Life, *NYT*, February 16, 1992; Ralph Blumenthal, "A True-Crime Adventure with a City Hall Backdrop; Beyond Campaign Embezzling Case, Uncertainties Cloud Inquiries into Stock and Other Deals," *NYT*, February 18, 1992; Ralph Blumenthal, "Biegen's Sentencing Delayed as Lawyers Continue Talks," *NYT*, March 14, 1992; Ronald Sullivan, "Prison Term Completes Political Fall from Grace," *NYT*, October 30, 1992; Ronald Sullivan, "Dinkins's Former Aide Is Sentenced for Embezzlement," *NYT*, November 5, 1992.

68. Robert D. McFadden, "New York's Budget Chief Asks Reduced Requests," *NYT*, September 13, 1992.

69. Robert D. McFadden, "New York's Budget Chief Asks Reduced Requests," *NYT*, September 13, 1992; James C. McKinley, "Municipal Labor Accord Is Seen as Budget Hurdle," *NYT*, January 13, 1993; James C. McKinley, "Contract Talks Did Not Stress Productivity," *NYT*, January 16, 1993.

70. Alan Finder, "The Fiscal Fictions of Winter," *NYT*, January 31, 1993.

71. Alan Finder, "The Fiscal Fictions of Winter," *NYT*, January 31, 1993; Jonathan Hicks, "Property Values Fall in New York City," *NYT*, January 16, 1993.

72. Robert D. McFadden, "Unit Says Budget Balanced, but It Faults Dinkins," *NYT*, March 26, 1993.

73. James C. McKinley, "Puzzle of New York City's Growing Budget," *NYT,* May 17, 1993.

74. Editorial, "Staying Alive," *New York Newsday* May 4, 1993; James C. McKinley, "Dinkins Administration Acknowledges Need for Cuts," *NYT,* May 26, 1993.

75. James C. McKinley, "Dinkins Administration Acknowledges Need for Cuts," *NYT,* May 26, 1993.

76. Editorial, "New York City's Teetering Budget," *NYT,* May 4, 1993; James C. McKinley, "Dinkins Administration Acknowledges Need for Cuts," *NYT,* May 26, 1993.

77. James C. McKinley, "Puzzle of New York City's Growing Budget," *NYT,* May 17, 1993.

78. Kevin Sack, "Dinkins Tells Legislators of Burdens," *NYT,* January 27, 1993.

79. Todd S. Purdum, "New York's Budget Maze: Dinkins and Cuomo Jousting over a Plan Wrapped in a Series of Conflicting Motives," *NYT,* June 5, 1993; Joe Klein, "The New Mayor and the Crisis of New York," *New York,* November 20, 1989.

80. James C. McKinley, "Mayor and Council Make Budget Pact for New York City," *NYT,* June 13, 1993.

81. Author's interview, off the record.

82. Author's interview, off the record; Clifford J. Levy, "Dinkins Orders Sharp Budget Cuts to Save New York's Bond Rating," *NYT,* July 3, 1993.

83. Independent Budget Office, "Debt affordability ratio analysis," 1980–2006, spreadsheet in the possession of author, courtesy of Independent Budget Office and Douglas Turetsky.

84. Sam Dillon, "School Board Challenges Aid Formula," *NYT,* March 16, 1993; James Dao, "Politics Complicates Formulas for Aid to Schools," *NYT,* February 16, 1993.

85. Sam Dillon, "School Board Challenges Aid Formula," *NYT,* March 16, 1993; James Dao, "Politics Complicates Formulas for Aid to Schools," *NYT,* February 16, 1993.

5

Sexual Dysfunction at the School Board

Savvy New Yorkers knew that no one smart enough to do the job of schools chancellor was dumb enough to accept the position. The New York City Board of Education consisted of seven members appointed by six different elected officials, virtually ensuring incoherence. In theory, the board—one member chosen by each of the five borough presidents and two by the mayor—selected the chancellor, who served as chief executive of the system. In practice, board members and thirty-two local school districts, the teachers' and administrators' unions, school custodians, central office bureaucrats, education advocates, parents, local politicians, the governor, the mayor and their deputies, and others with a stake in the system clawed the chancellor to pieces.

In May 1989, as David Dinkins headed for his primary showdown with Ed Koch and his slim victory over Rudy Giuliani, New York schools' chancellor Richard Green died of an asthma-induced heart attack. Few doubted the stress of his job caused it. He was the sixth leader the system had discarded in twelve years. Green had been in the role only fourteen months. His short term followed a five-month search during which an acting administrator oversaw New York's schools, so the vast, decrepit educational bureaucracy had been drifting, even more directionless than usual, when it killed its leader.[1]

At one point, Mayor Koch had sought to appoint his all-purpose advisor, Bobby Wagner, chancellor. New York State commissioner of education Thomas Sobol derailed the appointment by refusing to exempt the gifted public servant from required educational certifications. Race considerations drove the seemingly petty decision. African American and Latino politicians and educators protested the selection of a white man to head a school system whose students were overwhelmingly children of color. Koch ended up appointing Wagner to the school board, whose members in turn elected him president.

So it fell on Wagner to lead the search that named Green the city's first African American chancellor, and then to find Green's successor in the politically charged atmosphere leading up to the election of a new mayor. Working with education advocate Stanley Litow and the search committee that recruited Green, Wagner found Joseph Fernandez.[2]

The son of Puerto Rican parents, Fernandez grew up in Harlem and dropped out of high school as a teen to join the air force. Armed with an equivalency diploma, he enrolled in college, and after graduating became a math teacher in Miami. Over the years, he worked his way up through the Dade County Public School System until he led it. Fernandez and others believed his personal experience helped him understand the challenges of educating young, disadvantaged minorities.

The two thousand-square-mile Dade County district ranked as the nation's fourth largest with 273 schools and some three hundred thousand students as mixed in their racial and ethnic composition as New York's. In two years as superintendent, Fernandez introduced innovative schools-based management programs and earned a national reputation as a skillful educational administrator. His approach drew private businesses, parents, teachers, and principals into a partnership to support learning in Miami's classrooms. He understood politics as well, successfully spearheading a $980 million bond issue for the construction of new schools at a time when voters elsewhere rejected similar proposals. He seemed the right man for the New York job. Once the board made its choice, Wagner made sure Fernandez met with David Dinkins, Rudolph Giuliani, and even the fringe candidates for mayor to be sure whoever became the city's next chief executive would support the new chancellor. The search committee had included people who had Dinkins's confidence, and, when he met with Fernandez, the man who would soon be mayor felt comfortable with the choice.[3]

I. A Mind-Bogglingly Broken Bureaucracy

It would be hard to exaggerate the enormity of the challenge the new chancellor inherited or the structural obstacles to managing New York's schools in 1990.

The Board of Education employed almost 120,000 people, managed close to one thousand buildings, and spent over $6 billion a year in its efforts to educate nearly one million students—children and teens, many suffering from the ills that afflict poor people of color in urban America. About 38 percent of the children were African American and 34 percent Latino. Nearly 60 percent came from families eligible for food stamps, and the same proportion came from single-parent households. More than one hundred thousand spoke no English. About one-third came from families receiving welfare payments. Over four thousand lived in homeless shelters or welfare hotels. Half read below their grade level, and 60 percent of high school students failed at least one class every semester. Nearly one-third dropped out and never completed high school, and a quarter took five years to graduate.[4]

The school buildings reflected a state of disrepair comparable to the deficiencies in the educational programs. School construction suffered from all the ills of major public works in New York, including bid rigging and labor racketeering by organized crime factions, according to state and federal prosecutors. Approximately eight hundred of the nearly one thousand schools needed substantial capital improvements at an estimated cost of $4.2 billion. In the decades before the 1975 fiscal crisis, the city built an average of ten schools each year. In the entire decade after 1975, the city built just one. Inadequate physical plant coupled with administrative incompetence led to debilitating overcrowding, use of bathrooms replete with urinals for classroom instruction, students taught in supply closets and makeshift annexes, and lessons conducted in hallways. Bushwick High School in Brooklyn, with 2,200 students, operated at 158 percent of capacity. The Board of Education had not rezoned its schools for fifteen years, fearful of the political fallout such a decision would cause. Its cowardice left some schools underutilized, despite the critical need for space.[5]

Constraints on the chancellor's authority over the system's physical resources compounded the challenge of maintaining the city's educational infrastructure. For nearly a century, New York's school custodians operated simultaneously as unionized employees receiving a salary and contractors who received budget allotments to hire staff and buy supplies. The peculiar arrangement, along with agreements negotiated by Union Local 891, gave custodians—paid $20,000 per year more than teachers—extraordinary power. Principals had virtually no authority over the people responsible for maintaining the schools they administered. Classrooms used daily were cleaned every other day, and cafeteria floors used by thousands of students were mopped once a week because the contract required no more. Custodians painted the outside walls of a school up to ten feet off the ground and no higher. Equipment of all kinds that custodians purchased with school funds became theirs after three to five years. At one point, 164 janitors owned jeeps paid for virtually in their entirety by the Board of Education.

One ended up owning a lawn mower at board expense, even though the school he tended had no lawn. His home, of course, did. All manner of relatives and paramours cluttered custodians' payrolls. Janitors received high additional payments for any use of a school building after standard hours, and so on.[6]

At its best, the structure of the city's contract for physical maintenance ensured ineffective results unless a custodian took personal pride in his school. Many did. Others saw the peculiar arrangement as a license to steal. In November 1992, Edward F. Stancik, special commissioner for investigation for New York City schools, released a report, *A System Like No Other: Fraud and Misconduct by New York City School Custodians.* The astonishing 108-page document revealed custodians operating as charter jet pilots on school time, managing law and real estate practices while neglecting the buildings citizens paid them to keep clean, and hiring convicted criminals who established shooting ranges in the basements of the schools where children attended classes. One maintained his private yacht with Board of Education cleaning supplies, spending school days on his boat, miles away from the city, captured on film happily shirtless under the Long Island sun. Some custodians commingled public and private funds, submitted fraudulent receipts to cover personal debts with school money, and undertook all manner of abuse of their positions, petty and grand, disregarding any sense of propriety and the ultimate impact on the environment in which children were meant to learn.[7]

New York City bused 136,000 riders to school every day. Contracts awarded to busing companies totaled more than $225 million per year. When the Board of Education eliminated competitive bidding in 1979 with the intention of streamlining its decision process, the mob moved in. Some students were chauffeured by drivers working for companies that employed Colombo crime family soldiers as consultants. Others traveled on vehicles controlled by the Genovese or Gambino families, including one boss whose company received over $8 million from school transportation contracts until he was slain. Some physically challenged children in Brooklyn rode to school in transportation provided by a professional killer. It cost New York more to bus its students than any other district in the United States, nearly twice what it cost nearby suburbs to provide comparable service.[8]

Stanley Litow, whom Fernandez appointed deputy schools chancellor for operations, acknowledged the situation was "obviously disturbing." He recalled one conversation with a contractor responsible for transporting prekindergarten children. The agreement was set to expire at midnight on December 31. As the hour approached, tense negotiations continued with no sign of resolution. "Are you really going to leave three- and four-year-olds standing on the street with no way to get to school in the middle of the winter?" the dedicated educator asked. "What the fuck do I care about a three-year-old? I'm here to get my money," came the response.[9]

Two epidemics infecting the city—AIDS and crack—attended school more reliably than the students did, it seemed. New York City housed 3 percent of the nation's teens, but 20 percent of teenage victims of AIDS at a time when the disease allowed no effective treatment. Crack—the highly addictive cocaine derivative—surged in use in the mid-1980s. By 1990, babies exposed to the drug during pregnancy entered the school system, an estimated three thousand of them suffering from short attention spans, violent outbursts of temper, poor speech, and hyperactivity, their cruel inheritance from addict mothers.[10]

Rising violence throughout the city during the late 1980s afflicted the schools with disheartening impact. The United Federation of Teachers (UFT) released statistics in April 1990 revealing more than 1,500 physical assaults on teachers during the school term the prior fall, a year-on-year rise of 25 percent. Grade school students beat a Bronx teacher so badly he lost partial hearing in both ears. An elementary school teacher was hit with a desk when she tried to break up a fight. Another teacher was cut with a razor. Yet another teacher was beaten by a twelve-year-old and his mother after the teacher disciplined the student for disrupting an assembly meeting called to address the issue of violence in the classroom. On occasion, students were gunned down in the halls of the schools meant to secure them a bright future. While most schools operated safely every day, the headlines generated from about forty of the toughest high schools caused many New Yorkers to view the education system as uncontrollable.[11]

II. Fernandez the Fighter

Fernandez understood the issues. Even before he began his new job, he started to confront the constraints on the chancellor's power that had doomed his predecessors. Every weekend between the time he agreed to serve and the moment he actually took control of the Board of Education, he traveled to New York to meet with important stakeholders—twenty to thirty most weekends. He used meetings with influential political figures to signal he would seek legislation to increase his authority. Three topics particularly perplexed him: the practice of building tenure for principals, the role of the Board of Examiners, and the relationship between the central Board of Education and New York's thirty-two local school districts.[12]

Building tenure for principals crippled a chancellor's effectiveness. In 1975 the New York State Legislature passed a law forbidding the transfer of principals from school buildings they had worked in for five years or more. Supporters claimed the rule shielded administrators from crony-based reassignment. In reality, Governor Hugh Carey had pushed the measure through the legislature in the rush before adjournment out of gratitude to the Council of Supervisors and Administrators (CSA). The union, which represented the city's principals, had supported his election the year before. The provision meant the Board of Education did not control the most important human resources in the school system. Chancellors had complained since its inception that the rule protected incompetents.[13]

The CSA had long kept favor with the state legislature by distributing generous campaign contributions and election support to the Republicans who controlled the senate and to the Democrats who dominated the assembly. They had endorsed Dinkins for mayor in 1989 as well, even though as a candidate Dinkins supported elimination of the special protection the politically potent administrators enjoyed. Despite the CSA's power politicking, popular sentiment demanded action. In response to a public request from Fernandez, Governor Cuomo expressed his support for elimination of building tenure. Mayor Dinkins, important labor leaders like Barry Feinstein, and legislative leaders encouraged CSA president Don Singer to reach an agreement with Fernandez, who aggressively pushed the issue during his first week on the job by reassigning an ineffective administrator. Doing so directly defied the practice of building tenure for principals and the cumbersome procedures it required to remove one from a school. The decision challenged the CSA's power.[14]

At first Singer protested and resisted surrendering the unseemly but long-held privilege. Then political pressure mounted, and he opted for strategic retreat. After several months of negotiations, the union chief agreed to a formula that allowed the chancellor to reassign principals who did not meet performance standards. Their agreement also made provisions for better training for principals to help them improve. The accord prevented arbitrary action but gave Fernandez the authority he sought and substantial momentum in increasing the power of the chancellor to manage the schools. Dinkins's support helped make the change happen.[15]

The archaic Board of Examiners, established in 1898, had long outlived its usefulness. At the end of the nineteenth century, reformers created it to separate the assessment of teachers' qualifications and licensing standards from hiring decisions in an effort to keep politics out of the schools. Ironically, the Board of Examiners had become a source of patronage, and the institution had earned a reputation for exceptional inefficiency and ineptitude. Teachers seeking certification found themselves victims of bureaucratic rules that left even the most patient of souls bewildered and resentful. Those familiar with the details believed the Board of Examiners seriously hindered the ability of the schools to attract and retain talent.[16]

Beginning in 1984, New York State required all teachers to pass a privately administered qualifying test, the National Teacher Examination. The test had emerged as a standard for educators across the country. This change and other state licensing procedures rendered the Board of Examiners redundant. Yet it continued to exist and to frustrate all forced to depend on it. In January 1990 nearly 20 percent of the city's 64,895 teachers lacked a Board of Examiners' certification, leaving them with reduced benefits and no job security. In some fields, no certification exam had been offered for five years. The teachers affected were "made to feel like second-class citizens," United Federation of Teachers president Sandra Feldman said. She strongly supported the abolition of the institution. So did almost all of New York City's leading political figures, including Governor Cuomo and Mayor Dinkins.[17]

Fernandez's initial effort to eliminate the Board of Examiners ran into the peculiar opposition of Utica Republican James Donovan, the chairman of the New York State Senate Education Committee. The man had long protected the school-funding formula that advantaged upstate counties like his at the expense of the five boroughs. In more general terms, he seemed hostile to the city and to its diverse population, according to school officials who negotiated with him. Despite evidence that the Board of Examiners served as a patronage nest, Donovan claimed to believe it played a role in keeping "shenanigans" out of teacher hiring. He insisted on receiving a plan that included "a detailed alternative to the present Board of Examiners," before agreeing to close it. In March 1990 Fernandez responded with a proposal to create the Office of Personnel Assessment and Licensing under his control that would rely on the state and national exams already required and conduct interviews and background investigations as necessary. He expected the plan to establish a "more accountable, efficient and responsive personnel assessment system" while saving over $3 million annually. Still, Donovan seemed reluctant to act, and others tread carefully around the prerogatives of the committee chair to determine what legislation to bring to a vote.[18]

As the issue dragged, editorial boards, union leaders, and others interested in the schools pressured New York City's six Republican state senators to act. Manhattan's Roy Goodman in particular took up the cause. Meanwhile, Donovan had fallen ill, and in June, as the legislative session headed for its usual final flurry of activity, his ability to control his committee fell victim to his health as he underwent chemotherapy. The illness created a vacuum that Senate Majority Leader Ralph Marino of Long Island stepped in to give the chancellor what he wanted. "[Fernandez] is trying to make effective changes in the overall system, and he indicated to me that this is a major part of his overall effort to improve the schools," Marino said the day he informed his colleagues that he supported the bill and would bring it forward for a vote. Soon afterward the measure became law, and the chancellor scored another coup in his efforts to exercise authority commensurate with his responsibility. The Dinkins administration had again provided the chancellor with support.[19]

So during his first school term, Fernandez accomplished two things others had dismissed as nearly impossible. Along the way, the chancellor made other organizational changes that did not require legislative approval. Board of Education headquarters at 110 Livingston Street in Brooklyn, with its thousands of anonymous staffers, had come to symbolize the bloated, ineffective nature of the system—a monument to inefficiency. Board president Bobby Wagner found the office so dysfunctional he once threatened to clean house by pulling the fire alarm and locking the doors once everyone left as the only tactic to cure the place of bureaucratic sclerosis. By the end of his first week, Fernandez announced the consolidation of fourteen bureaus and the elimination of more than two hundred jobs. The number hardly impressed in comparison to the more than five thousand who worked in the building, but the swift action signaled the new chancellor's intention "to reduce central administration and bring decision making down closer to where the action is [to] make things better for people in schools—for teachers, administrators and most of all for children."[20]

In another initiative, Fernandez appointed six panels to study changes needed to improve the schools. The topics included the math curriculum, arts and culture, high school overcrowding, expanded use of school buildings, community service, and the management information needed to run the system. He ended a ten-year practice of holding back students automatically after the fourth and seventh grades if their reading test scores did not measure up. The policy, called Promotional Gates, seemed to disillusion students and cause them to dropout. Fernandez replaced the plan with special summer sessions and after-school programs.[21]

Perhaps most important in his own mind, Fernandez set the stage for school-based management to begin in the fall. In March 1990 he invited all 984 city schools to submit proposals outlining how they would create a committee of ten or twelve teachers, parents, and administrators to assume a broad range of responsibilities for decisions normally dictated by the central board or the local school district. Despite many concerns over authority and compensation, and the ever-present resistance to change, 151 schools responded by June. By September 1990, 82 began operating under the system, and eventually 240 would participate in the bold reform experiment during Fernandez's term as chancellor.[22]

An initiative to create thirty-seven theme-based high schools, launched in 1993, served almost as a bookend to the experiment in school-based management Fernandez launched early in his tenure. The program recognized that part of the reason many students failed was a numbing anonymity that pervaded the vast, hulking buildings that housed high school students and the factory-like approach to education developed for another population in another era. Identifying schools with specific concepts, tangible and relevant to New York's children, and organizing them into smaller units would allow a greater sense of identity and purpose for students and teachers, Fernandez and other reformers argued. Specialization would make it harder for the system's teens to disengage from their lessons and disappear from their classes without a trace. The schools would be set up inside the Board of Education's existing buildings, but each would have its own principal and staff; each would have its own reason for being. The School for the Physical City would rely on New York's bridges, tunnels, and infrastructure to provide the context for its lessons. At the High School for Economics and Finance, classrooms would be organized like a corporate office. El Puente Academy in Brooklyn would organize science classes around a community-based measles vaccination program. Others would feature global citizenship, or music, and so on. "This is the most extensive reform of secondary schools going on anywhere in the nation," Deputy Chancellor Litow claimed. Educators around the nation agreed. "What's unique is that they're opening so many new schools as a way of decentralizing the bureaucracy and offering more personal attention to students. One would think it was an act of genius if it weren't so obvious," the executive director of the Council on Great City Schools concluded.[23]

III. Bleak Budget Battles

Since he arrived in the middle of the school year in January 1990, Fernandez inherited a budget set by others. The chancellor negotiated for money with the mayor and his fiscal team much the same as heads of other city agencies, but with a few advantages the others lacked. He had the support of a separate board and a large, high-profile budget that gave him more media clout than most department heads commanded. During Fernandez's first months running the schools, the city's dire and deteriorating financial position led the mayor's finance team to reassess spending at all city agencies, including the Board of Education. Initially, Fernandez sought to cooperate. Reflecting on streamlining of the administrative staff at central board headquarters, which promised to save the city millions of dollars, he told a reporter, "I want to be a player. I don't want to put my head in the sand when it comes to cuts." A few weeks later, he submitted a preliminary budget for the next fiscal year beginning July 1, 1990. It totaled nearly $6.9 billion, an increase of almost $500 million and greatly at odds with the direction of city spending. Yet, even as he unveiled the plan that made his priorities clear, his staff acknowledged the numbers represented little more than the opening steps in the three-way dollar dance among the Board of Education, the city, and the state for school funding.[24]

By April 1990 the city signaled the board would need to find an additional $190 million in savings. Board president Bobby Wagner ritualistically warned cuts that size would be "very bleak for the system and for the children." Fernandez echoed the concerns but largely kept a low profile. When the budget went final on July 1, it totaled $6.5 billion, about the same as the year before. The board accepted just over $60 million in reductions, less than 1 percent and much smaller than cuts to many other agencies.[25]

The city's financial position continued its downward spiral. By the fall, under pressure from fiscal monitors and at risk of a bond-rating downgrade, the mayor's budget office insisted on $94 million of additional reductions from the Board of Education. The request came just weeks after the city agreed to raise teachers' salaries by 5.5 percent. Fernandez and others believed the Dinkins administration's decision to trim the school budget so severely constituted a ploy to force the teachers' union into accepting wage givebacks to avoid layoffs. "The cut was a clear attack on the teachers' contract. It was something that was meant to put fear in the hearts of teachers," Barry Feinstein said. "They agreed to it," one school official said of the highly controversial settlement. "Now their plan is to run away from the contract as far as they can go." In his view, the cuts amounted to an effort to "force [UFT president Sandra] Feldman to crawl up the steps of City Hall saying, 'Don't lay off teachers. We'll take back 2 percent.'" More important to Fernandez, he feared that cuts of the magnitude demanded risked eliminating the discretionary funds needed to pursue the reforms he had launched, including schools-based management. Accepting the cuts meant failure for his programs, so he fought back.[26]

The day before the mayor announced publicly his plan for filling the budget gap, Fernandez issued a statement saying the school provisions were "riddled with inaccuracies and terribly misleading to the public." He called the proposed cuts "a tragedy for our schools . . . unfair and a cruel message to our city's children." With the unanimous backing of his board, Fernandez submitted a proposal to City Hall showing a way to achieve nearly $60 million in savings with minimal impact on children, while asserting that any additional reductions would result in massive teacher layoffs with a "disastrous and devastating" impact. In the worst-case scenario, black and Latino neighborhoods—Dinkins's political base—suffered most. It had the look of a transparent ploy to force the mayor to compromise or bear the blame for unacceptable hardship. The *New York Times* scolded Fernandez for it. In an editorial titled, "Yes, Defend the Schools, but Credibly," the newspaper accused him of making his case against cuts "melodramatically" and "taking obstinacy to the point of incredibility." The piece encouraged him to work with the beleaguered mayor and to look for savings in the district school boards where surely some could be found.[27]

Dinkins responded with a statement regretting Fernandez's "intemperate comments" and urged him to use his "proven management and leadership skills" to keep layoffs to a minimum. The mayor's plan, which Fernandez dismissed, aimed to achieve the full savings, mostly through attrition. In the end, the mayor prevailed. Fernandez toned down his complaints and adopted plans for the cuts demanded amid high anxiety on the part of school administrators across the city. A wage-deferral program reached with the teachers union prevented almost all layoffs. The giveback left UFT leader Sandra Feldman, one of the mayor's most powerful allies, more than a little bitter toward the administration.[28]

In December 1990 the mayor's office offered more bad news as it released its ten-year capital-spending program. The plan called on the Board of Education to reduce by 20 percent its ambitions for construction of fifty new schools, thirty annexes, and seventy renovations over the next three and a half years. Fernandez declared the proposed cuts illegal.[29]

In December 1988, in an effort to remove obstacles that hindered building new schools in the city, the New York State Legislature created the School Construction Authority. Among other things, the authority could operate without adhering to the Wicks Law that prevented the city from relying on general contractors to manage construction projects. The restriction contributed greatly to the high costs and long delays typical of New York City building programs. Felix Rohatyn had forced the action by refusing to release money held by the Municipal Assistance Corporation until the authority had been created. The $4.3 billion capital budget established for school construction at the time included a provision that forbade any reduction unless the city reduced capital spending for all agencies. Since the mayor's revised plan exempted police, fire, corrections, and sanitation department projects, the chancellor believed the mayor's proposal violated the law. After negotiations and some recriminations, the mayor, who ultimately controlled the city's budget, prevailed. Fernandez had once again opposed the mayor in a high-profile disagreement and once again had been forced to defer to him.[30]

By the time the next fiscal year approached, Fernandez had come to realize that the city faced real constraints. Foot stomping and chest thumping gained him little. Money for the schools fell by over $400 million in the budget for July 1, 1991, to June 30, 1992. It reflected a dismal economy and reductions by the state and the city in response. Deeper cuts would have occurred, except for a fifteen-year-old state mandate called the Stavisky-Goodman Law that required the city to spend as large a proportion of its budget on schools in any fiscal year as the average over the previous three years. The United Federation of Teachers, usually reliable supporters of incumbent city council members, found the budget so distasteful that it declined to provide any endorsements in that fall's council primary elections. "This is the first time we've done something this severe," UFT president Sandra Feldman said. "But we felt very strongly that the schools were really hurt, and there was nobody out there fighting for the education budget."[31]

To avoid laying off more than three thousand teachers and a total of seven thousand staff to meet budget goals, Fernandez launched an early retirement program. More than four thousand experienced educators and six hundred administrators took the package, meaning some of the most seasoned professionals left the schools, saving younger teachers in the process. Meanwhile, enrollment grew, so the average class size rose. Money for textbooks and libraries fell, after-school programs were cut, truancy initiatives stopped, guidance counselor support declined, and equipment purchases were deferred. "It would be the gravest mistake to understate the results of this budget," Stanley Litow warned. "If this . . . doesn't spell devastation, it's hard to imagine what does."[32]

The negative impact of the budget cuts could not be denied. Veteran teachers felt the stresses of inadequate resources to a degree they had not experienced since the worst days of the fiscal crisis of the mid-1970s. Still, most education officials deemed the management of the challenge about as good as it could have been, given the severity of the constraints. "It is difficult to predict how schools will be affected by the city's troubles," the *New York Times* editorialized. "But the best way to spare the children is to focus remaining resources on classroom services—as Mr. Fernandez has wisely done," it concluded.[33]

In his budget for the fiscal year July 1, 1992, to June 30, 1993, Fernandez began by requesting an increase of over $500 million, while the mayor had asked him to reduce it by $100 million. To the irritation of City Hall, Fernandez also maneuvered to secure for the schools any money that might result from refinancing Municipal Assistance Corporation bonds. Yet the budget battle turned out to be less acrimonious that year than in others. The mayor and city council passed a budget with relative ease a month before the fiscal year ended in 1992. The mayor and the chancellor found a creative use of state money to issue construction bonds and restore the School Construction Authority capital accounts to the levels agreed upon before the cuts of the prior year. Moreover, the overall education budget of over $7 billion allowed restoration of many programs also reduced the year before. All things considered, the chancellor and his team proved competent managers of a complex budget under very tough circumstances.[34]

The chancellor broke new ground in the spring of 1992 by publishing the budgets of all thirty-two local school districts. They showed a wide range of practices, with some allocating far more money to classrooms, whereas others spent disproportionately on administration and overhead. Fernandez distributed ten thousand copies of the three thousand-page document to parent leaders and encouraged them to explore the uses of education money with the local boards responsible for teaching their children. It was an unusual commitment to transparency consistent with Fernandez's efforts to establish greater accountability for the decentralized elements of the school system.

IV. The Evil of Local School Boards

Securing control over New York City's thirty-two local school districts proved troublesome. Each one had its own elected nine-person board. The boards exercised substantial authority over all elementary and junior high schools in their designated neighborhoods—subject to the many rules protecting teachers and administrators negotiated by the United Federation of Teachers and the CSA. In total, the local boards controlled some $2.6 billion of the school budget.[35]

The central board retained direct control over 124 high schools and over special education programs serving 125,000 children. The central board also retained residual power over the local districts. A catchall provision of the law establishing the decentralized structure authorized a chancellor to supersede a local board for failing "to comply with any applicable provision of law, bylaws, rules or regulations, directives and agreements." In practice, the battle over decentralization that played out between 1968 and 1970 had been so emotionally charged that over the years, except in extreme circumstances, chancellors typically avoided interfering with local hiring decisions. In particular, they left the selection of superintendents who ran the districts to the local boards. They feared interference would attract accusations of racism and elitism, or simply create the risk of running afoul of local power brokers with unpredictable consequences. As a result, the central board had just enough authority over local districts that a chancellor could not deny a measure of responsibility for them. This unworkable hybrid caused Fernandez to call the system he had agreed to run a "two-headed monster."[36]

It would be hard to exaggerate the bitterness that surrounded the decision to decentralize New York City's school system. In theory, competing views of how best to educate inner-city schoolchildren created the conflict. In reality, African American activists wanted to control the resources of the communities where they lived, and a substantially Jewish union wanted to maintain control over the workplace of its members. Maximum feasible misunderstanding characterized the event. In the words of historian Jerald Podair: "At Ocean Hill-Brownsville, blacks punished white New Yorkers for assuming they both believed in the same things, and for attempting to do their thinking for them. . . . The anger with which whites reacted to this discovery had far-reaching consequences for race and class relations in the city." Cooperation between blacks and whites—blacks and Jews in particular—would be far more difficult after the crisis than it had ever been before.[37]

Some twenty years passed between the Ocean Hill–Brownsville crisis and David Dinkins's election as mayor, but the generation who lived through it had its fault lines chiseled into their minds. To community-control advocates, the aggressive posture of the UFT in opposition to decentralization was the work of a self-serving union cruelly placing their petty interests before the urgent need to educate disadvantaged school children. They viewed the UFT's leader, Albert Shanker, as a monster. In the futuristic movie *Sleeper,* released some years later, the plot unfolds when the leading character is transported to a postapocalyptic world destroyed when "a man by the name of Albert Shanker got hold of a nuclear warhead."[38]

The wounds on the other side remained just as raw. Anti-Semitic-rhetoric militant-decentralization advocates spat at Jewish teachers, and the thuggery that accompanied it created rancid memories. The ugly hatred distracted attention from complex, legitimate issues of race and class. It prevented a contest among different groups for control over public resources from evolving in a civilized manner. Nonacrimonious discussion over school curricula and the values implicit in lesson plans became impossible. These issues remained as relevant as ever when David Dinkins governed, and the tensions around them remained taught.[39]

The 1970 state legislation that authorized decentralization in the context of a dual system created ambiguous lines of authority that added unwelcome complexity to an already complicated system. Worse still, soon after lawmakers defined the electoral process for choosing school board members, neighborhood politicians, community activists, union representatives, and others more intent on securing power than improving education applied their organizing skills to the local contests. Self-interested parties turned many of the local boards into cesspools of personal privilege. Citizen confidence in them diminished until typically just 7 percent or so of eligible voters bothered to cast ballots. At the time the central board approached Fernandez about the chancellor's job, eleven local school districts—more than one-third—were under criminal investigation, never mind any consideration of managerial competence. Seven school board members had been indicted in the prior year or so. The charges, petty and vulgar, added to the disgust of anyone intent on educating children.[40]

Insiders long understood the degree to which the romanticized experiment in community control had degenerated into an orgy of abusive politics. For many New Yorkers outside the system, the epiphany came on November 9, 1988, when police arrested Matthew Barnwell for buying ten dollars' worth of crack from undercover police. It was the first such arrest on record for a New York City school principal.

As Barnwell's woeful tale unfolded on the front pages of Gotham's newspapers, the city's privileged classes learned just how bad things had become in the classes the underprivileged depended upon to educate their children. The fifty-five-year-old veteran of the New York City school system had been responsible for Public School 53 for sixteen years, during which time he had amassed a history of drinking, absenteeism, lateness, and serious lapses in professional performance. In the school year prior to his arrest, Barnwell missed work or arrived late 142 of 184 days. His example created an environment in which 25 percent of teachers typically came to work late or not at all. Unsurprisingly, the school's reading levels ranked among the lowest in New York.

Central school board president Bobby Wagner declared himself shocked that a "local board would tolerate a principal so clearly bad as Mr. Barnwell for such a long period of time." The board president Reverend Jerome A. Greene and his assemblywoman wife, Aurelia, who also served on the board, were longtime friends of Barnwell. Both were under investigation for stealing school property at the time of the principal's arrest. Rumors circulated that the power couple of dubious integrity had protected the drug-abusing administrator. Chancellor Green, after initially infuriating the city and damaging his credibility by calling for compassion for a man as obviously troubled as Barnwell, suspended the board.[41]

In response to the uproar caused by the Barnwell affair, Mayor Koch and the Board of Education created the Joint Commission on Integrity in the Public Schools. They asked New York attorney James F. Gill to chair the panel and charged it with investigating corruption in local school districts. Gill's commission delivered its report in April 1990, after Dinkins had assumed office. The superintendent of District 27 in Queens, Coleman Genn, provided the highlights. He had taped conversations with the treasurer of his board, James C. Sullivan, and with the president, Samuel Granirer, and others. The recordings left little to the imagination. "Honestly, at the end of the day, I'm a political leader, that's why I'm here," Sullivan told Genn in one conversation, unaware the man he spoke with recorded the conversation. "And I make sure my people get fucking jobs." Sullivan's eloquence led to his indictment and to guilty pleas for mail fraud and coercion. Granirer suffered the same fate. Eventually, the Board of Education dismissed fifty paraprofessionals, one principal, and one assistant principal for complicity in the illegal activities of District 27 board members.[42]

A venal miasma hovered over the entire system. An investigative report by Ralph Blumenthal and Sam Howe Verhovek of the *New York Times* had identified the board members of Bronx District 12 as the city's most skilled at converting a school system into "an enterprise for patronage and profit by trading jobs for political favors, seeking payoffs, putting relatives on the payroll and allowing school supplies to be looted." The two journalists chronicled forged letters justifying politically motivated hiring; a drug-addicted and homeless board member who provided crucial swing votes on jobs and policy while incoherent; rampant nepotism; "application fees" for job candidates that board members pocketed; "borrowed" school supplies; trips to Las Vegas, Honolulu, and San Juan paid for by public funds; and on and on. The district ranked last in the city on reading and math scores.[43]

The widespread abuse practiced by the local boards, so pervasive and so entrenched, caused a "corrosive effect" on the school system in the words of Bobby Wagner. For many, it called into question the benefits of decentralization. Mayor Koch had asked for control of the schools, expressing a desire to eliminate local boards all together and return the system to central administration. In December 1987 Governor Cuomo endorsed the concept and called a summit meeting of key legislative leaders to consider the idea. Yet the lawmakers who decided the fate of New York City's education system included many politicians with an interest in perpetuating the decentralized structure. Disingenuously, they dismissed the importance of accountability out of hand. "If the Mayor were to name seven wise persons tomorrow—tomorrow—to the Board of Education, what have you done in terms of improving the basic . . . services at the school?" asked assembly speaker Mel Miller, a Brooklyn Democrat. "[S]imply shifting responsibility to one person and then having that one person to beat on, that isn't the way I'd like to see this thing develop," state senate majority leader Warren Anderson told a reporter. Some viewed Koch's proposal as a pure power grab by a confrontational mayor. Black and Latino legislators feared Koch would not appoint minorities to important roles in a school system he controlled. The legislature simply never considered the request seriously.[44]

Still, public outcry about the sorry state of New York City's schools and the boards who ran local districts for personal gain required a response. Politicians in the state legislature did what they often do when facing an uncomfortable problem: they created a commission. With Governor Cuomo's approval, state senator John Marchi established a panel to review the consequences of two decades of decentralization. And the legislature passed conflict of interest laws that forbid school employees or elected officials to serve on local boards and limited their ability to hire their own relatives. The law proved ineffective. Politicians and others swiftly adapted their abuses to the new terms of trade. They barely missed a beat as they put beholden surrogates into jobs they could no longer take themselves and swapped positions in one district for those in another to sidestep the spirit of the new rules.[45]

As Manhattan borough president, Dinkins had issued a report in December 1987, *Improving the Odds: Making Decentralization Work for Children, for Schools and for Communities.* It condemned the cronyism rampant in the local boards but also expressed a strong commitment to the concept of decentralization. The report accused the central Board of Education of behaving like "an isolated fortress," providing inadequate oversight of the local districts. He urged that seats be set aside on all local boards for parents with children in the public schools and called for the type of conflict of interest legislation that eventually became law to prevent the self-interested few from crowding out those with a legitimate stake. The report also bemoaned the inadequate representation on boards of blacks, Latinos,

Asians, and residents of low-income neighborhoods. Mayor Dinkins's philosophical belief in community involvement in government and city affairs showed no signs of diminishment, despite the evidence that the approach had failed in the context of New York's local school boards. He viewed decentralization as something that needed to be fixed, not discarded.[46]

Fernandez wanted parents and communities actively involved in the education of their children, but he thought the local school board system structurally flawed as well as ineptly run. New York City's local districts in many cases exceeded the size of central school boards in cities and towns around the country, making them too big to work in the way supporters imagined, even if they had not been undercut by corruption and incompetence. He believed his school-based management program had a far better chance of creating a collaborative environment for learning than the complex, overlapping system that had evolved so sadly. But so long as the local school boards existed, he wanted them to have competent leaders, which the system in place failed to provide. In response, he asked the state legislature to grant him explicit authority over the selection of the superintendents in the local districts. He proposed a process that would require the boards to provide him with three candidates for a district's top post, from which he would choose, as long as he found them qualified. The proposal respected the right of local boards to put forward their choices but introduced an independent assessment that would limit political influence. Importantly, it would allow the chancellor to insist on capable appointments and not wait for evidence of serious abuse and the damage it caused before acting.[47]

Fernandez did not wait for validation of his authority over local superintendents to assert his position. On January 18, 1990, just weeks after he arrived in New York, he rejected the politically motivated choice of a superintendent chosen by Community School Board 19 in the East New York section of Brooklyn. Citing the chancellor's authority to supersede local decisions, Fernandez invited the board to submit three choices to him and announced he planned to formalize his proposed superintendent-selection process soon in a circular. Predictably, the people seeking personal benefit from the system denounced Fernandez's move. They suggested racism motivated the action, along with a desire to kill decentralization.[48]

A few weeks later, Fernandez applied his new policy to the selection of a superintendent in District 29 in Queens. The local board took him to court, contending the chancellor's interference violated decentralization laws. Ten boards joined the suit, hoping to repel Fernandez's power play. They succeeded in part. On July 6, 1990, Judge Herbert A. Posner of the state supreme court in Queens ruled the chancellor could not tell a board how to screen superintendent applicants, nor could he require boards to submit names for him to review and possibly veto. The judge recognized the right of the central board to set minimum standards of "experience and education background" and to bar candidates deficient on those dimensions from serving. But in his decision he declared the "law is bigger than any man and as praiseworthy as Circular 37 may be in its stated purpose . . . the Chancellor has exceeded his statutory authority, [so] the circular must be declared invalid." The judge invited Fernandez to "persuade the Legislature to change the law." The next day the chancellor announced he would do just that while appealing the ruling. He had little success.[49]

In October 1990, Fernandez presented his case to the Marchi Commission, still in the process of assessing the impact of decentralization on the school system. He appealed to the panel, which included three influential state legislators, to support his request for a legal mandate to control the selection of district superintendents. The commission rejected his plea. Instead, the politicians reaffirmed their commitment to local control and, remarkably, called for an expansion of the number of local boards to around fifty. Disingenuously, they cited a desire for smaller, neighborhood-based districts to foster greater parent and community involvement in the schools. They also recommended giving the mayor two additional appointments on the central board so the city's chief executive would name four of nine members and exercise greater control over the body. Dinkins proposed the mayor receive six appointments out of eleven, ensuring mayoral control, and otherwise endorsed the commission's findings.[50]

The recommendations produced mild controversy and little more. Different stakeholders objected to one aspect or another of the proposals, and, despite strong legislative participation on the panel, nothing came of its suggestions. The "two-headed monster" that devoured schoolchildren continued to challenge Fernandez in his quest to improve education throughout his tenure.[51]

The failure to secure control over the local school boards slowed Fernandez's momentum. "For six months as chancellor, he enjoyed a string of triumphs," Joseph Berger, a *New York Times* journalist covering the education beat wrote shortly after the court decision. "Tall and burly, he seemed invincible: the brash, single-minded Harlem-raised kid punching his way through a comparatively anemic education establishment. But in the last month, Mr. Fernandez has suffered a few knockdowns," the reporter concluded. By force of personality, and with meaningful authority to intervene when incompetence emerged, Fernandez continued to wage war with the districts. But he lacked the authority to appoint superintendents on the merits. Handing out shopping bags bearing the name of the right school board candidate remained the most important credential for securing a job as principal. The system damaged the morale of the professionals working in it, and as a consequence the quality of instruction making its way to the students in the city's classrooms. Mayor Dinkins, stubbornly committed to school decentralization despite the overwhelming evidence the experiment had failed, did nothing to help Fernandez secure a different outcome.[52]

V. The Landscape Changes

Still, during his first six months, Fernandez made a good start at redirecting the vast system charged with educating a million New York City children. In a *New York Times Magazine* article published shortly before Judge Posner's decision, James Traub wrote: "As his first school year ends, New York's impatient chancellor has achieved more than anyone thought possible." Most important, perhaps, "[H]e has given cynical, beleaguered New Yorkers hope that change in the school system is actually possible."[53]

Yet the article also noted that Fernandez's hard-charging style risked creating enemies who could undermine his efforts. One administrator suggested he was winning all the battles, but so alienating his constituents that he risked losing the war. Many teachers, parents, and administrators felt the chancellor—"a tough guy . . . a big, tough guy," as his first deputy, Stanley Litow, described him—did not listen to them or show them the deference they thought their due because of their stake in the system. "If you act first and consult later, that is going to catch up with you," one district superintendent said. "Part of being successful is working with all these groups," he pointed out, referring to the many constituencies Fernandez had confronted. About the same time, the Public Education Association, a nonprofit educational advocacy group, graded the chancellor a B in his first six months, but a C on efforts to involve parents in schools. And they criticized him for advancing "his own ideas without consulting the seasoned professionals and school board members who could help him refine those ideas."[54]

As the summer school break began, Fernandez set his sights on the impending launch of school-based management that fall. While he did, the landscape around him shifted. On June 30, 1990, the four-year terms expired for all of the members of the school board who had hired him and who had given him strong support. When the politicians who chose the replacements completed their selections, the composition and complexion of the board had changed dramatically. Just two of seven members remained.

Dinkins reappointed Dr. Gwendolyn C. Baker, national executive director of the YWCA He had originally named her to the board when he was Manhattan borough president. A black woman described by one journalist as "a gracious, decorous woman," she was a sometime Ann Arbor, Michigan, schoolteacher with a reputation for championing multicultural education. Baker had once been excluded from a high school trip to Washington, DC because she and her white classmates could not stay in the same hotel. As a professional, she had dedicated much of her life to helping people understand and appreciate the meaning of diversity. Brooklyn borough president Howard Golden reappointed Dr. Irene Impellizzeri, a white woman and veteran board member, then on leave as dean for teacher education at the City University of New York. The rest of the board changed.

Upon recommendation of a search committee, Dinkins chose Dr. Westina L. Matthews as his second appointment. Matthews, a black woman who was vice president for corporate contributions and community affairs at Merrill Lynch had once been a teacher in Ohio. Ruth Messinger, Manhattan borough president, appointed Dr. Luis Reyes, a Latino who served as deputy director of Aspira, an advocacy group for Puerto Rican and other Latino students. Bronx borough president Fernando Ferrer appointed Ninfa Segarra, a Latina lawyer who was executive director of the city's Voter Assistance Commission with a child in the public schools. Queens borough president Claire Shulman appointed Carol A. Gresser, a white woman who was a teacher and former parents' association leader. Staten Island borough president Guy Molinari appointed Dr. Michael J. Petrides, a dean at the College of Staten Island and the board's only non-Hispanic white man, who had served for a time as president of Staten Island's lone community school board and whose children had attended public school.[55]

Dinkins flexed his mayoral muscles and saw to it that the new board chose Gwen Baker as its president. With five women on the board, including its president, the reconstituted body respected the traditional role of women in primary and secondary education to a degree that prior boards had not. And with three white, two black, and two Latino members, the board came closer to mirroring the population it represented than the one that chose Fernandez as the city's first Latino chancellor, which had included five whites. "New School Board Reflects Mosaic of New York City," read a *New York Times* headline featuring the mayor's favorite metaphor for the city's diversity. More significant, perhaps, the article pointed out other changes. "In contrast to the departing board, the new board will have stronger advocates for the role of parents in school decisions and for the authority of the 32 community school boards. Mr. Fernandez has been criticized by some groups for not including parents in the selection of school superintendents and principals and in his blueprints for more autonomous school government."[56]

Bobby Wagner was out. United Federation of Teachers leader Sandra Feldman credited him as the man who "started building back a system that for a decade had been left to rot." Under his guidance teacher salaries rose and class sizes shrunk, two critical improvements. Wagner's clear vision of a different, more effective school system coupled with his political skill had created unaccustomed consensus on the board—a body that always carried within it the seeds of disunity, since six different officials appointed its seven members. "I fear that we will go back if not to a Balkanized [board], then to a provincialized [one] that will look at issues from a narrow geographic and special-interest perspective," Wagner said when asked about the new body as its shape emerged. He was not the only one concerned. In a July 14, 1990, editorial, the *New York Times* wrote, "[I]t's an open question whether [Baker] has the political skills needed to build consensus, keep the focus on citywide concerns and wage budgetary and legislative battles with city and state officials." Wagner had also helped ensure that the board that sought out a chancellor with a national reputation for reform supported the efforts he launched. Fernandez would soon miss Wagner's wisdom and consensus-building skill as the board descended into paralyzing conflict.[57]

VI. The Perils of Prophylactics

Sex ruined school board harmony. For a brief period in 1986, school health clinics made condoms available to students, but strong resistance to the program, particularly from the Catholic Church, caused the board to end the practice. In September 1990, President Baker, with the backing of four of the five new members and strong support from Chancellor Fernandez and Mayor Dinkins, announced she would ask the board to reinstate condom distribution. Advocates of the change cited startling statistics that moved the debate from pregnancy prevention to saving lives. New York City accounted for 20 percent of the nation's teenage AIDS cases, even though only 3 percent of the teen population lived there. Children as young as eleven had contracted the disease, which at the time allowed no effective treatment. The Alan Guttmacher Institute for family planning had reported a few years before that 80 percent of 261,000 New York City high school students engaged in sexual intercourse by the time they were nineteen. The figure made clear the daunting extent the threat AIDS posed to teenage health in the five boroughs.[58]

The debate on the controversial proposal rapidly assumed an irreconcilable air. "Our children are sick, our children are dying," Dr. Matthews declared in announcing her support for the program. "The issue is not should we distribute condoms, but how," Dr. Baker announced, casting her view in a way that allowed no room for opposition. Dr. Impellizzeri, while reserving final judgment until a formal plan appeared, made her very different outlook clear. "It sends a message that we expect that young people will engage in sexual activity," she said, adding that she did not feel that the "problems young people face will be alleviated by the distribution of condoms." Michael Petrides also objected. "Will the next step be the distribution of hypodermic needles" because drug-abusing students risked contracting AIDS? he asked rhetorically.

The Catholic Church weighed in, instantly and loudly. Bishop Thomas V. Daily of the Diocese of Brooklyn called the plan "an affront to parents.... It says that the universal value that places sexual activity as acceptable only within the context of marriage can neither be taught by our schools nor accepted by our students." Chancellor Fernandez responded with a pragmatic argument. "I'm a Catholic," he said. "But . . . we have preached safe sex and no sex, and 80 percent of the kids are sexually active. Then we have to do something else."

John Cardinal O'Connor would have none of it. His spokesman replied for the New York Archdiocese. "I don't see how they can say the policy has failed, because I don't think the policy has ever been tried to challenge our young people, our students, to some higher goal. If we continually demand of them only the least they have to give, that's all we're going to get from them." Deep religious conviction confronted passionate belief in a moral imperative to save young lives.[59]

Over the next few months, it only got worse. In early December, Fernandez circulated a plan even more aggressive than anticipated. All high schools would make condoms available to students of any age with no requirement for counseling. The proposal caused even his supporters to pause. Dr. Impellizzeri cited reports, erroneously as it turned out, that distributing condoms increased sexual activity, with disease transmission from the increased incidence of sex offsetting the lower rate of infection. In short, she argued, the chancellor's program would not reduce AIDS and not save lives, while encouraging teenage sex.[60]

When the board convened later that month, Impellizzeri escalated the battle further. She asked her colleagues to end Board of Education relationships with the gay advocacy group ACT-UP and with the Hetrick-Martin Institute for Gay and Lesbian Youth. Both organizations were on a list of seventeen approved to help schools planning classes or assemblies on AIDS. She quoted from a booklet the Hetrick-Martin Institute published advising readers how to use lubricants for anal intercourse and encouraging withdrawal before ejaculation to limit the risk of spreading AIDS. The section concluded: "Do it! (Have fun)." In language remarkable to think of in the context of a school board meeting, her proposed rule began: "RESOLVED, that this Board hereby takes note that anal intercourse is an extremely dangerous form of sexual activity . . . [and] hereby prohibits all schools . . . from offering students any form of instruction that would encourage them to engage in anal intercourse or facilitate their doing so."[61]

Dr. Luis Reyes responded to Impellizzeri's call for a ban on classroom instruction in anal intercourse—which was never contemplated—by attacking her. He called her comments "at best trivial and at worst an act of gay bashing and McCarthyite witch hunting." Fernandez pointed out that the brochure Impellizzeri read from was not part of the approved curriculum the institute used in city classrooms, and the board declined to take any action. The issue dominated the year-end meeting, which also reported that the city's students had improved in math but lost ground in reading over the past year. It was hard not to conclude the condom issue, whatever its merits as a public health concern, distracted from the board's principal mission of educating children.[62]

The issue created a racial divide. The board's four African American and Latino members voiced the strongest support for condom distribution, along with Mayor Dinkins and Chancellor Fernandez. Although the African American and Latino members were successful and middle class, their sensibilities lived closer than their white colleagues' did to poor neighborhoods suffering daily assaults from AIDS. Indeed, Ninfa Segarra lost three of her cousins to the disease. Impellizzeri, a lay leader in the Roman Catholic Diocese of Brooklyn objected in part on religious grounds, and she, and Michael Petrides from Staten Island, had white middle-class roots and lived in communities where the impact of AIDS remained more remote. Carol Gresser from Queens also came from such a place. Observers described her support for the condom plan as lukewarm. Around the city, principals and politicians came down on both sides of the issue.[63]

Fernandez rejected efforts at compromise. He declined to force counseling on students seeking condoms for fear it would turn them away from the program. Similarly, he opposed requiring parental consent or allowing parents to exclude their children from the program because "children don't tell their parents when they're sexually active." He stood by his original proposal, the most far-reaching in the nation.[64]

The drama intensified. Carol Gresser announced she would not back a program that denied parents "responsibility for their children's welfare." Westina Matthews also expressed doubts about the absence of an opt-out provision for parents, putting the plan at risk. Two days before the crucial vote, Mayor Dinkins intervened. He announced unequivocal support for the chancellor's proposal without amendment, even as discussions surrounding a possible compromise program continued. Dr. Matthews was "free to exercise" her own judgment, a top aide to the mayor assured the press, but Dinkins invited her and Dr. Baker to City Hall for a private conference the next day. At the board vote on February 27, 1991, Dr. Matthews voiced her decision to vote for the plan, ensuring its passage. "On behalf of a child's right not to lose his or her life, I vote yes," she declared. She also indicated a desire to amend it later to include an opt-out provision, something the mayor's other appointee, board president Baker, also expressed a willingness to consider. Fernandez pronounced himself thrilled with the outcome and hoped that in time those who cast ballots against the plan would see it as a good decision. Michael Petrides lamented that in such a close vote on such a sensitive issue, "[N]o one wins."[65]

The condom controversy created a confrontational tone at the board. In a dispute over hiring a general counsel, four members overruled the president's choice, an unusual event. Dinkins intervened on behalf of Baker, convening a meeting of the five borough presidents to try to convince them to force their board appointees to allow her to have her way. He failed, and the next day Dinkins announced that he would pursue his desire for authority to name a majority of the board. "Although I previously did not believe the mayor should have complete control, in the year that I have been mayor it has become crystal clear that if there is one thing for which New Yorkers hold their mayor responsible, it is the education of the children of our city," he declared.[66]

To other board members, Baker was the issue, not their independence. Some complained the president shared information with the black and Latino board members only, creating an unwelcome and unnecessary de facto minority caucus. Others, even those favorably disposed to Baker, felt she had shown no real leadership on instructional issues. Questions arose about her ability to dedicate the time required to do the job properly while contending with her demanding full-time position at the YWCA. She changed her mind on public issues in ways that confused her colleagues, and doubts emerged about her ability to get the board to work as a team. A sense of drift settled in. Members requesting anonymity told journalists they might not vote for her to continue as president when her term expired in June. In challenging the mayor's selection as school board president, they challenged the mayor. Some said as much, calling Baker too deferential to Dinkins on policy. Ninfa Segarra displayed ambitions of her own and sought the support of her colleagues for the board's top spot.[67]

Dinkins responded forcefully. On June 12, 1991, he announced he had accepted Baker's resignation and that H. Carl McCall, a prominent African American and a longtime Dinkins friend and ally, would replace her as a member of the board. He called on the others to name McCall president. The mayor made it clear he intended to maintain as strong a position of authority over the school system as he could since the public held him responsible for it despite the limits on his control. Interestingly, Baker's resignation was dated May 1. Dinkins had kept the matter quiet until he had persuaded McCall to take the job.[68]

A Citibank vice president for government relations, McCall was also a former state senator and an ordained minister who had served as New York State commissioner of the Division of Human Rights and as a member of the US Mission to the United Nations. He had political experience, connections, and clout that Baker lacked. He declared his goal would be to persuade the board to support the chancellor. Bronx borough president Fernando Ferrer called the decision "a first-rate appointment," and soon afterward Ninfa Segarra announced she would support McCall.[69]

At first glance, Dinkins appeared to have converted the risk of diminished influence over the board into a position of strength. But McCall found forging consensus on the board and getting it to focus on educating children no easier than his predecessor. His formal election included one vote against him, cast by Michael Petrides, and one abstention from Ninfa Segarra, despite an earlier commitment of support. They both implied McCall would not challenge the mayor at a time when budget constraints and other issues required independent support for the schools. Carol Gresser, while voting for McCall, voiced the same concern.[70]

Within weeks of McCall's appointment, the condom issue returned. Board members, as promised, presented an "opt-out amendment" to allow parents who disapproved of the program to exclude their children from it. The action infuriated Fernandez. McCall opposed the idea but could not prevent his board from proposing it. Right up until the day of the decision, Dr. Matthews supported the amendment, despite clear signals Mayor Dinkins did not. The night the board met to decide, it appeared the provision would pass. Then, during the board meeting itself, Matthews took a call from Mayor Dinkins. He told her "what my wishes were," he reported to journalists when asked about the conversation. The heavy-handed intervention caused the woman to cast her ballot against the measure amid protests of mayoral interference. The best she could do to defend herself was to declare, "I am an educator. I leave politics to the politicians." Bronx borough president Fernando Ferrer had a similar phone conversation with his appointee, Ninfa Segarra.[71]

Critics accused Dinkins of caving to pressure from AIDS activists to shore up support with his liberal political base while ignoring parents' rights and responsibilities. Whatever the motivation, the mayor managed to get his way, demonstrating he could still control the board. Yet the need to throw his weight around as transparently as he did suggested his authority had its limits, that his control of the school board had become fragile. And many New Yorkers found it disconcerting that the body charged with setting educational policy kept arguing about sex while the school system's deficiencies demanded urgent attention.[72]

Eventually, Fernandez oversaw implementation of a fully developed HIV/AIDS curriculum as a supplement to the school system's health program. Its supporters designed it to teach dangerously precocious children how to avoid the deadly disease at a young enough age to make a difference. In a minority report, members of the advisory board who wrote the curriculum objected to lessons—beginning with third graders as young as eight—that were "unnecessarily sexually explicit, elaborating on body parts, body fluids, various kinds of sexual intercourse, details about condoms and their usage." The dissenters feared the developmental impact on prepubescent children. They also objected to the lack of emphasis on abstinence and to the implication that a range of choices—from abstinence to intercourse with condoms—had equal merit. In their protest, they asserted: "Marriage and the traditional role of the family must be recognized as the foundation of society and the basic framework for sex education. The curriculum fails to affirm the value of the traditional two-parent heterosexual family."[73]

Four board members, Impellizzeri, Gresser, Petrides, and Segarra, sympathized with the minority view and in May 1992 passed a resolution declaring that lessons on AIDS prevention had to place more emphasis on abstinence than condom use. They interpreted state law as requiring the approach. The action caused the New York Civil Liberties Union to file a lawsuit. McCall, Matthews, and Reyes did not want the board to defend its position in court. Acrimonious public debate followed. "The HIV/AIDS curriculum will once again become the overriding issue before the Board," the president and his allies declared, "and we will not be able to focus on the critical issues of education funding, academic standards, and the physical conditions of our schools. In short," it continued, "we will be distracted from fulfilling our fundamental mission and responsibility to provide our children with a first-rate quality education."[74]

The other side would not be outdone. They suggested McCall abused his authority as president by not respecting the will of the majority of the board, and they accused him of cynical posturing, incendiary behavior, and "cheap political theater." They threw in "outright distortion and deception" for good measure. So the school board remained mired in the most fundamental and unresolvable disagreements about the city's mores and values.[75]

VII. Rainbow Revolt

The same week as the vote on parental opt-out, the Board of Education released a new, 443-page multicultural curriculum for first graders called *Children of the Rainbow*. The teacher's manual covered the subjects normally associated with grade school—mathematics and reading, science, and social studies—and it sought to encourage instruction on these topics in an environment that would "build respect and understanding among students of various ethnic and cultural backgrounds." It advised educators to use examples and illustrations of many different types of people in their lessons to avoid "contextual invisibility," the absence of certain groups that risked causing children to conclude the groups did not really exist or were not valued. It suggested that classes sing folk songs, share poems, and enjoy dances from a broad range of countries, encouraging teachers to look for similarities in these universal traditions that spanned diverse groups of people. Conceived in 1989, before Fernandez arrived in New York, as a way to teach tolerance to youngsters in a city teeming with ethnic violence, few objected to its purpose. Moreover, such documents generally had advisory status. Local districts could adapt or modify curricula created by the central board. Initial reaction to the work was muted. One wonders how many administrators or teachers read the weighty tome.[76]

Mary Cummins, president of District 24 in Queens, did, and she did not like what it said. "Classes should include references to lesbian/gay people in all curricular areas," the guide advised. "According to statistics, at least 10 percent of each class will grow up to be homosexual," the document declared, without providing supporting evidence for the claim. "Children need actual experiences, via creative play, books, visitors, etc., in order for them to view lesbians/gays as real people to be respected and appreciated," it continued as part of two pages of notes on how to introduce six-year-olds to same-sex relationships. The bibliography included *Heather Has Two Mommies, Jennifer Has Two Daddies,* and *Gloria Goes to Gay Pride,* encouraging teachers to confront the reality that some of the students in their classes lived with parents in nontraditional relationships and should not be embarrassed by it.[77]

Cummins, described by supporters as a devoutly religious Catholic, viewed the guide as gay propaganda that threatened traditional values. Indeed, she saw it as an affront to her way of life. Attacking "Sodom on the Hudson," as she termed New York City, Cummins launched a crusade to reject the curriculum. Her board, all Catholics, including a priest, backed her unanimously.[78]

Fernandez invited Cummins and her board, and any others with objections, to propose a different approach to addressing the topic of same-sex relationships. Eventually, eighteen districts would modify *Children of the Rainbow*, in many cases deferring the controversial subject until fifth or sixth grade. Eight districts adopted the curriculum in its entirety. Four pointedly rejected the pages dealing with gays and lesbians. Only Cummins's district steadfastly refused to meet with Fernandez to discuss the issue.[79]

In a letter of protest mailed to twenty-two thousand parents, Cummins described the curriculum as "shot through with dangerously misleading homosexual/lesbian propaganda." In another letter informing parents of a planned protest in front of Board of Education headquarters at 110 Livingston Street to oppose the HIV/AIDS health curriculum, she declared, "We will not accept two people of the same sex engaged in deviant sexual practices as family." Fernandez and his staff accused the board members of District 24 of a malicious campaign to distort the curriculum and alarm parents.[80]

For months, provocative charges continued in both directions. Finally, on December 1, 1992, Fernandez suspended the entire board when it failed to meet with him as required, and he appointed three trustees to oversee its affairs. It marked the first time in twenty-two years of decentralization that a chancellor had suspended a district school board over a curriculum issue. It was the first time Fernandez suspended an entire district board. Cummins appealed to the central Board of Education to overturn the decision.[81]

In Fernandez's mind, what began as a curriculum dispute had turned into a challenge to the chancellor's authority. It had also escalated into a battle for the soul of the city. For years, white, middle-class Catholics in New York suffered from a sense of displacement. They could see it visually as the number of African American and Latino New Yorkers grew, and they experienced it as racial minorities expanded their exercise of political power and secured important jobs. When the city elected an African American mayor and selected a Puerto Rican schools chancellor, it delivered two potent, symbolic reminders to Mary Cummins and others like her of how far they had fallen in New York's totem pole of power. Now they were being told to accept sexual behavior they found deviant and to allow instruction they viewed as offensively wrong and in violation of their religious beliefs to be imposed on their children, beginning at the age of six. It is no exaggeration to say that the most vocal opponents of *Children of the Rainbow* felt they were defending civilization as they knew it. At one point, Cummins accused Fernandez of creating "as big a lie as any ever concocted by Hitler or Stalin," and she declared that "[w]e are not going to teach our children to treat all types of human behavior as equally safe, wholesome or acceptable."[82]

Letters written to Chancellor Fernandez reinforce the point in dramatic terms. One, handwritten in Spanish, began, "May God bless and enlighten you. With all the respect you deserve, my wife and I want to protest the book, Children of the Rainbow." It went on to say: "Based on the sacred scripture—it is said in Corinthian 6–9, 10 the fornicators, the unjust and homosexuals will not enter the Kingdom of God. This means we cannot teach things like this to our children." Anyone who does, the letter warned, will "be accountable to God, and God will treat these people accordingly if they do not repent." Another New Yorker begged Fernandez to "OPPOSE homosexual education," enjoining him to "[r]emember that 99% of homosexuals are child abusers." A female ex-addict who wrote she had "done all the things that most drug abusers have done—sell myself, participate in all types of deviant sex, steal, lie, etc." who had "many friends . . . now dying from AIDS including my husband," wrote the chancellor that his endorsement of the Rainbow curriculum upset her deeply because "the word of God . . . declares homosexuality is an abomination." She went on to say, "As a black woman, I am very grateful for the strides that my race have [*sic*] made in the last three decades, but I would pick cotton on a plantation before I let a child of mine be exposed to this curriculum."[83]

While the controversy raged, McCall, other members of the Board of Education, and the press tried to make sense of the intense conflict. The multicultural curriculum generally featured things like Mexican dances, Irish ballads, and African games that offended no one. It turned out that gay and lesbian activists, working through the mayor's office, won representation on the group drafting the guide. The professionals overseeing program development failed to realize that featuring gay and lesbian life in it had different ramifications than the other topics covered. The passages that created the storm had been written by a lesbian teacher and promoted by gay rights activists with insufficient scrutiny to the emotional nature of the subject. The posture Fernandez adopted placed the central board in the position of choosing between competing visions of the future of New York, including one that could be interpreted as hostile to the teachings of the Catholic Church. The confrontation had escalated beyond David Dinkins's political comfort level.

In what McCall called "an attempt to bring all parties together," the central board—including the mayor's two appointments—overruled Fernandez's decision to suspend Cummins's board. McCall instructed the chancellor to work with the district to develop a tolerance program acceptable to all, perhaps with the help of a mediator. Fernandez felt undercut and micromanaged. He chafed at the decision and criticized his bosses. "By failing to enforce adherence to their policy promoting tolerance," he said, "the members of the central board have left themselves open to serious challenges to their policymaking roles." Under pressure, he fired one of the administrators responsible for the curriculum, even as he declared he would again use his authority to supersede the Queens board if it did not mediate the issue. At the same time, at McCall's urging, he agreed to revise the curriculum, deleting the controversial books about gay parents from the bibliography and dropping language detractors perceived as endorsing gays in favor of a more anodyne goal. The objective was "not to support or promote any particular belief system or lifestyle, but to protect the rights of all." The posture resembled the school system's approach to religious tolerance. The specific dispute with District 24, however, dragged on and remained a standoff that never really came to a resolution.[84]

VIII. Fernandez Falls

The brash style Fernandez brought to his job served him well at first. A city fed up with the bureaucratic inertia of a failing school system applauded the early successes of the new chancellor's take-no-prisoners campaign for reform. Yet one by one his victories made clear to the bureaucracy's stakeholders that the man's drive for change threatened them all. District boards, parents, teachers, principals, community leaders, and local politicians had all discovered Fernandez cared less about their long-held prerogatives than he did about implementing a vision for the school system that would ensure it educated children. As a consequence, his opponents became allies.

Diplomacy and compromise, tact and grace seemed absent from the chancellor's portfolio of skills. Just about the time the central board overturned his decision to suspend the leaders of District 24, Fernandez published *Tales Out of School*, a book written with John Underwood recounting his career in Miami and New York. To the astonishment and dismay of the board members who supervised him, in it the chancellor described his testy relationship with them name by name in catty, gossip-filled language bound to offend. Deputy Chancellor Litow and Fernandez's chief press spokesperson, James Vlasto, saw the manuscript in galley proofs. The comments about the board members stunned them, and they told Fernandez he could not publish them. When the book came out, complete with the offending passages, they were shocked again. The publisher apparently had convinced Fernandez to retain the paragraphs bound to produce sales-generating headlines. Many viewed publication of the work an indication Fernandez had decided to leave New York when his contract expired. Actually, Fernandez hoped to stay, but he was as careless about his relationship with the people who could fire him as he was with the other constituents he had alienated.[85]

Two months later, in a raucous central Board of Education meeting during which one man shouted, "Mr. Fernandez is a devil!" while outside the building supporters chanted "We want Joe!" the board voted not to renew Fernandez's contract when it expired June 30, 1993. Security guards had to intervene several times to restore order, forcibly escorting several demonstrators from the room. Michael Petrides, Irene Impellizzeri, Carol Gresser, and Ninfa Segarra formed a bare majority in opposition to extending the chancellor's term, ensuring another leadership change for the struggling school system.[86]

The mayor's appointments to the board, Carl McCall and Westina Matthews, tried desperately but unsuccessfully to delay a vote while Dinkins and many other Fernandez supporters from outside the system tried to save him. Just days before the vote, Felix Rohatyn, traveling abroad, sent Queens borough president Claire Shulman a note urging her to support renewal of the chancellor's contract. The highly influential banker and head of the Municipal Assistance Corporation called Fernandez "by far and away the best" person for the job and declared plaintively that a search for a new leader for the school system "would be very destructive and counterproductive." But Rohatyn's effort and similar appeals from other business leaders failed. It was too late. Only Luis Reyes sided with McCall and Matthews. Gresser expressed ambivalence, but her Queens constituents, including Shulman, who had appointed Gresser to the board, had lost confidence in Fernandez. The man had devoted too much of his time to a controversial social agenda rather than improving the schools, Gresser said. Ninfa Segarra cited an accumulation of differences with Fernandez and his harsh criticism of her in his book as the final factor in her decision.[87]

The vote revealed the mayor had lost control over the Board of Education. Dinkins denounced the decision as not in "the best interests of the children." He vowed to seek more formal power in a ritualistic statement designed to remind people he did not really have the authority to run the $7 billion system the city relied on to educate its children. It implied he should not be blamed for the mess the schools were in as his reelection campaign took form. But the comment did not hide the mayor's failure to manage the city's school agenda effectively and his defeat in a power struggle over the system's leadership. United Federation of Teachers president Sandra Feldman feared the change would destabilize the fragile system and accused some board members of "putting their personal and political agendas before what's best for children." City council speaker Peter Vallone from Queens drew a different conclusion. "The next chancellor must concentrate on the basics and involve parents in the education of their children," he concluded. Both had a point. Nastiness continued to reign at the board with the majority denouncing comments McCall made, decrying Fernandez's ouster as "disgraceful."[88]

The board's conservative majority moved to create a screening panel to select a new chancellor. Dinkins feared his opponents would select an extremist. With the support of three borough presidents—Ruth Messinger, Fernando Ferrer, and Howard Golden—the latter two seeming to have lost their influence with their own appointees to the board, he submitted a list of recommendations to serve on the panel. The board ignored him. Meanwhile, the mayor's man, McCall, who as president continued to try to maintain some decorum among the board's combative members, became a candidate for appointment to New York State comptroller when the incumbent, Edward Regan, left to become president of Bard College. In May 1993 the state legislature elevated McCall to the statewide post, creating a leadership vacuum at the already troubled Board of Education. About the same time the mayor's other board appointee, Westina Matthews, also resigned. She cited health reasons but gave the general impression the querulous group had left her fed up. The mayor rushed to name Dennis Walcott, president of the New York Urban League, to one of the openings. But he had just one vote in place on the board when the six sitting members chose Carol Gresser from Queens as their new president. Gresser had opposed the mayor's positions more often than not. The board ignored the mayor's desire to delay a vote until he could fill the last vacancy. Eventually, he named Victor Gotbaum, the retired labor leader, to the spot.[89]

In August, after a national search, the board selected former San Francisco schools superintendent Ramon Cortines as its new chancellor in a four-to-three vote. Dinkins had not supported the choice, but his view seemed no longer to matter. For the first time in seven years, the mayor did not choose the president of the city's Board of Education, nor had his wishes been respected when the board chose its new chancellor. Dinkins declared once again that he favored a change that would allow him to appoint a majority of the board's members and to exercise real control over the school system, but nothing close to consensus existed on the proposal that required a state legislature vote.[90]

About the same time the board named Cortines chancellor, investigators made an alarming discovery. Asbestos tests performed over the past decade to certify the safety of school buildings had been grossly mismanaged and were so unreliable as to be meaningless. Evidence suggested fraud and conflict of interest directed the contract to a firm unqualified for the work. The mayor immediately cancelled more than forty-five contracts awarded to the firm involved, tragicomically named Enviro-Safe. At a press conference at City Hall, the mayor urged parents not to panic, and acting health commissioner Benjamin Chu advised there "is really no basis for alarm now," although the commotion surrounding the issue was sure to cause anxiety. Dinkins ordered new inspections immediately for all 1,069 city schools and declared none would reopen in September without a new test. The decision caused a several-week delay in the start of the academic year, creating a modicum of chaos in the lives of the students, parents, and teachers involved.[91]

The contracts predated Dinkins's term. Still the scandal emerged on his watch. It fell to the "outraged" mayor, by then in the homestretch of his reelection campaign, to explain why such negligence had endured undetected during his three and a half years in office. United Federation of Teachers president Sandra Feldman called the situation "a major, major nightmare." For weeks alarming headlines and disheartening revelations continued as First Deputy Mayor Steisel, who described the scope of the negligence as "breathtaking," led a special committee to respond to a decade of spectacular ineptitude, a shining example of the dysfunctional quality of the governance of New York City's school system.[92]

IX. The Report Card

An assessment of how the school system fared while David Dinkins served as mayor is decidedly mixed.

Fernandez, who served as chancellor for three and a half years of Dinkins's term with the mayor's approval from the start, implemented important structural changes. Elimination of the Board of Examiners and the end of building tenure for school principals rid the system of two obstacles to success. On their own the changes mattered, and, as indications that the dysfunctional system could be bent to the will of a determined leader who would not allow special interests to rule, they mattered all the more. Mayor Dinkins provided solid support for these victories.

The chancellor's confrontations with local districts, while far less successful, also sent a message that school administrators and professionals would be held to higher standards of rectitude and competence than in the past. The mayor offered tepid support for the chancellor in this crucial area. David Dinkins, the local politician, had supported the notion of local control of schools for more than twenty years. He kept faith with a romantic, liberal vision of what community involvement in education meant. His belief in community control over local schools blinded him to the awful unintended consequences of decentralization. Consequently, he did little to purify the harshly corrosive environment that educators lived in daily while it endured. Fixing New York City's dysfunctional school governance called for a radical solution, and David Dinkins was no radical.

The chancellor and his team managed skillfully through a tough fiscal environment. Fernandez established priorities and provided clear direction for spending money, seeking to protect classroom instruction while streamlining bureaucracy. He also proved himself an able combatant in the continuous budget battles the role and the times imposed on him. He skillfully tread the line between cooperating with the mayor and his staff facing citywide constraints, while defending school turf with the toughness required of the leader responsible for a critical function suffering severely from inadequate resources. The mayor and his money men, while at times exasperated with the forcefulness of Fernandez's style, gave the schools more than equal treatment with other agencies when directing scarce dollars. Stanley Litow considered the chancellor's successful management of the budget and his ability to avoid widespread layoffs and massive disruption despite the sometimes dire budget constraints a great achievement. It contrasted sharply with the chaos that prevailed at the Board of Education during the 1970s fiscal crisis. Late in the tenure of the mayor and the chancellor, the city and Board of Education filed suit against the governor and New York State to adjust the unfair allocation of resources the state legislature inflicted annually on the city's children. Dinkins and Fernandez deserve credit for acting and setting in motion a long overdue process to undo an obvious and consequential injustice.[93]

With respect to physical plant, some progress occurred. The chancellor initiated an outsourcing program for custodial services at roughly one hundred of the system's nearly one thousand schools. The approach led to budget savings and improved quality where implemented, and it created pressure on custodians across the entire system to do their jobs diligently. The capital program to refurbish dilapidated schools and to build some new ones gained slow traction. The School Construction Authority presented some evidence in 1993 that its projects cost meaningfully less and took significantly less time to complete than comparable government building, despite operating for roughly half the time of Fernandez's tenure with only an interim chief.[94]

Violence in the school system declined modestly on Fernandez's watch according to the board's official statistics, but incidents of robbery and assaults increased according to a report from the mayor's director of operations. More metal detectors appeared at high schools, programs were initiated to maintain discipline during the rush of teenage humanity that descended upon city streets and subways during afternoon recess, and conflict-resolution training took place. Still, the number of serious crimes—assault, robbery, drug use, weapons possession, and sex offenses—that occurred annually measured in the thousands. The board and the teachers union agreed that the majority of schools operated safely, but they disagreed about events at some thirty to forty high schools around the city where a disproportionate share of the most violent incidents happened. The board refused to release school-by-school information for fear it would stigmatize the offending ones. Neither educators nor administrators found the situation acceptable, and neither indicated that any fundamental improvement occurred during Dinkins's term in office.[95]

School-based management, in place for more than two years when Fernandez departed, showed promise. Early reviews suggested the greater sense of ownership the approach instilled in its participants helped schools to make good decisions for their students. The theme—high school initiative Fernandez launched in his final year was still in the conception phase when he left. Implementation would begin in the fall after his departure, so its effectiveness would be judged by future observers based on how new stewards managed it. The idea held great appeal and at the very least had captured the imagination of a committed core of educators.

What did all this mean for the education of one million New York City schoolchildren? By the time Mayor Dinkins lost control of the school board, not much. A surge in math and reading scores after Fernandez's first year as chancellor buoyed hopes and expectations. But then they slipped back significantly, notching up just a little his final year. The sharp movements in both directions caused many to believe the changes occurred because of inconsistencies in the tests, not improvements or declines in the quality of education. Attendance rates improved and dropout rates fell some, but the number of students graduating within four years also declined. On balance, there is little evidence to support any claim that educational initiatives launched while David Dinkins was mayor had a meaningful impact on what children learned. Chancellor Fernandez's supporters—and he had many—claimed he set the Board of Education on a path toward reform that would renovate the system over time. His detractors feared his confrontational style and personal arrogance prevented him from securing broad-based commitment for his agenda, so it would not outlive him.[96]

None questioned Fernandez's commitment to improving education for schoolchildren and his willingness to work long hours and to take on the most formidable challenges in pursuit of his noble goal. Dinkins was right to endorse his appointment and to support the man's serious effort to revamp a broken system. To the degree Fernandez's incomplete success resulted from his short tenure, the clumsy and arrogant way he managed his board stands out as a serious failing. He fought with members stubbornly and obtusely over highly emotional matters pertaining to sex, criticized them personally in a book published while he served at their pleasure, and lost the support of a majority.

He seemed not to understand that battles involving religious beliefs and moral convictions could create unwinnable confrontations and that personal insults result in animosity and retribution.

Fighting over condom distribution, AIDS education, and attitudes toward gays caused an enormous distraction from the school system's primary mission of educating children. It also caused Fernandez to self-destruct. In his defense, the condom-distribution plan in all likelihood reduced the incidence of AIDS among the city's teens, and therefore saved young lives. In that context, much stubbornness can be forgiven, although the unhelpful tone of the conversation remains cause for criticism. It is hard to blame Mayor Dinkins for the counterproductive behavior of so strong-willed a personality as Joseph Fernandez, but the outcome did not suit the mayor, and it unfolded before him, ending badly. With hindsight, a more engaged mayor might have managed toward a different outcome.

Mayor Dinkins, true to his liberal political beliefs, advocated strongly in favor of the provocative condom-distribution and multicultural education programs, intervening personally with his appointees to ensure their votes. He did not appreciate the damage he caused to his authority with the board or the political dangers he ran until too late. New Yorkers hold their mayor responsible for the quality of education in the public schools. Given the structure of the Board of Education at the time—seven members appointed by six different elected officials—the mayor's role was to ensure his appointees and the chancellor maintained a citywide perspective for the system and to prevent the politics of the board from interfering with the imperatives of instruction. Easier said than done with the governance model and personalities then in place, but that was the job. Mayor Dinkins failed at it, losing control of the board and losing the chancellor he thought best fit for the job.

Notes

1. Neil A. Lewis, "Schools Chancellor Green Is Dead: New York System Faces Disarray," *NYT*, May 11, 1989.
2. Joseph Fernandez with John Underwood, *Tales Out of School: Joseph Fernandez's Crusade to Rescue American Education* (Boston: Little Brown, 1993), 187–95; Author's interview, Stanley Litow, September 30, 2010.
3. Author's interview, Stanley Litow, September 30, 2010; Fernandez with Underwood, *Tales Out of School, passim.*
4. Joseph Berger, "New York Schools Open, Facing Test: Do More with Less," *NYT*, September 10, 1990;. Fernandez with Underwood, *Tales Out of School, passim.*

5. Selwyn Raab, "52 Companies Banned from School Construction Bids," *NYT*, August 27, 1991; Fernandez with Underwood, *Tales Out of School, passim;* Joseph Berger, "School Construction Money to Shrink in City Hall Plan," *NYT*, December 18, 1990; Jane Perlez, "New York School Buildings Scarred by Years of Neglect," *NYT*, May 13, 1987.

6. *A System Like No Other: Fraud and Misconduct by New York City School Custodians*, November 1992, Edward F. Stancik, Special Commissioner for Investigation for New York City Schools; Joseph Berger, "Report Details School Fraud by Custodians," *NYT*, November 13, 1992.

7. *A System Like No Other: Fraud and Misconduct by New York City School Custodians*, November 1992; Edward F. Stancik, Special Commissioner for Investigation for New York City Schools; Joseph Berger, "Report Details School Fraud by Custodians," *NYT*, November 13, 1992.

8. Selwyn Raab, "School Buses, Unions and the Mob: A Special Report; School Bus Pacts Go to Companies with Ties to Mob," *NYT*, December 26, 1990.

9. Selwyn Raab, "School Buses, Unions and the Mob: A Special Report; School Bus Pacts Go to Companies with Ties to Mob," *NYT*, December 26, 1990; Author's interview, Stanley Litow, September 30, 2010.

10. Joseph Berger, "New York Schools Open, Facing Test: Do More with Less," *NYT*, September 10, 1990.

11. Douglas Martin, "About New York; Teacher Learns All about Cruelty; All Except Why," *NYT*, December 5, 1990; Felicia R. Lee, "New York City's Schools See Crime Rising in Lower Grades," *NYT*, April 24, 1990.

12. Joseph Berger, "Fernandez Meets Leader of Principals," *NYT*, October 16, 1989; Joseph Berger, "New York's School Chief Visits City and Faults System," *NYT*, October 14, 1989.

13. Joseph Berger, "New York Schools Chief Challenges Board's Power," *NYT*, January 19, 1990.

14. Joseph Berger, "Chancellor Vows to Take Charge of Failing Schools," *NYT*, January 5, 1990; Joseph Berger, "New York Schools Chief Challenges Board's Power," *NYT*, January 19, 1990.

15. Joseph Berger, "Principals Union and Fernandez in Accord to Shift Incompetents," *NYT*, March 9, 1990.

16. Fernandez with Underwood, *Tales Out of School*, 224–30; "Metro Datelines: Donovan Opposes Licensing Board Plan," *NYT*, February 15, 1990.

17. "Metro Datelines: Donovan Opposes Licensing Board Plan," *NYT*, February 15, 1990; Author's interview, Stanley Litow, September 30, 2010.

18. "Metro Datelines: Donovan Opposes Licensing Board Plan," *NYT*, February 15, 1990.

19. Sam Howe Verhovek, "Accord to End License Board for New York City Teachers," *NYT*, June 20, 1990.

20. Joseph Berger, "Fernandez Reorganization Will Cut Jobs and Bureaus," *NYT*, January 7, 1990.

21. Joseph Berger, "Fernandez to End a Policy on Holding Pupils Back," *NYT*, May 3, 1990; Donatella Lorch, "Tougher Math to Be Sought by Fernandez," *NYT*, June 25, 1990; Joseph Berger, "High School: Sometimes 7 Years to Diploma," *NYT*, June 27, 1990.

22. Joseph Berger, "80 Schools Chosen for New York Test of Power Sharing," *NYT*, July 19, 20, 1990.

23. Sam Dillon, "New York City Readies 37 Specialized Schools," *NYT*, April 5, 1993; Fernandez with Underwood, *Tales Out of School, passim.*

24. Joseph Berger, "Schools Chief Seeks Rise in Spending," *NYT*, January 25, 1990.

25. Joseph Berger, "New York City Schools Face $62.3 Million Budget Cut," *NYT*, July 28, 1990.

26. Andrew Yarrow, "Chief of Schools Sees Furloughs as Way to Save," *NYT*, November 20, 1990.

27. Editorial, "Yes, Defend the Schools, but Credibly," *NYT*, November 19, 1990.

28. Joseph Berger, "Schools to Cut Hundreds of Jobs to Save New York $94 Million," *NYT*, October 24, 1990; Joseph Berger, "Budget Jockeying Is Fight for Survival," *NYT*, November 9, 1990; Joseph Berger, "Fernandez Warns of Impact of Cuts," *NYT*, March 7, 1991.

29. Joseph Berger, "School Construction Money to Shrink in City Hall Plan," *NYT*, December 18, 1990.

30. Joseph Berger, "School Construction Money to Shrink in City Hall Plan," *NYT*, December 18, 1990.

31. Gwen Fill, "City Teachers Won't Support Council Races," *NYT*, August 14, 1991.

32. Joseph Berger, "School's Budget Cuts: Looking for Magic," *NYT*, July 11, 1991; Joseph Berger, "New York City to Start School with Fiscal Ills and Hope," *NYT*, September 9, 1991; Joseph Berger, "Less Money, More Pupils Spell Trouble for Schools," *NYT*, October 17, 1991.

33. Joseph Berger, "New York City to Start School with Fiscal Ills and Hope," *NYT*, September 9, 1991; Joseph Berger, "Less Money, More Pupils Spell Trouble for Schools," *NYT*, October 17, 1991; Editorial, "School Bells Ring, Nervously," *NYT*, September 13, 1991.

34. Jacques Steinberg, "Asked to Cut Back, Fernandez Seeks $517 Million More," *NYT*, April 2, 1992; Joseph Berger, "Funds Pact Would Avoid More Cutbacks in Schools," *NYT*, July 9, 1992; Memorandum to: Philip Michael, from: Stanley Litow, Date: December 7, 1992, Re: MAC Funding Proposal for Early Childhood Interventions in New York City Municipal Archives, Office of the Mayor 1990–1993, D.M. Steisel, Roll #128.

35. Diane Ravitch, *The Great School Wars: A History of the New York City Public Schools* (New York: Basic Books, Paperback Edition, 1988), Introduction xi–xxv; Fernandez with Underwood, *Tales Out of School*, 188.

36. Ravitch, *The Great School Wars*, Introduction xi–xxv; Fernandez with Underwood, *Tales Out of School*, 188.

37. Podair, *The Strike That Changed New York*, 5–6, 183–205.

38. Freeman, *Working Class New York*, 227.

39. Podair, *The Strike That Changed New York*, 5, 202; Naomi Levine, *Ocean Hill-Brownsville: A Case History of Schools in Crisis* (New York: Popular Library, 1969); Martin Mayer, *The Teachers Strike: New York 1968* (New York: Harper, 1998).

40. Russ W. Baker, "An Election Marred by Chaos and Corruption," *Village Voice*, June 1, 1993.

41. Robert D. McFadden, "Jury Acquits 3 in The Removal of School Piano," *NYT*, March 16, 1990; Joseph Berger, Neil A. Lewis, Sarah Lyall, "Inert System Let Shaky Principal Go On," *NYT*, December 27, 1988.

42. Andrew L. Yarrow, "Stress Forces Whistleblower to Retire from the Schools," *NYT*, November 13, 1990; Joseph Berger and Elizabeth Kolbert, "Schools and Politics: Channels of Power—A Special Report: New York Schools and Patronage: Experience Teaches Hard Lessons," *NYT*, December 11, 1989; *Findings and Recommendations of the Joint Commission on Integrity in the Public Schools*, April 1990, James F. Gill, Chairman, 9.

43. Ralph Blumental, Sam Howe Verhovek, "Patronage and Profit in Schools: A Tale of a Bronx District Board," *NYT*, December 16, 1988.

44. Jane Perlez, "Cuomo Calls Meeting on Proposal to Give Koch Control of Schools," *NYT*, December 3, 1987; Andrew Stein, "Too Much Political Interference in New York City's Schools," *NYT*, December 3, 1987; Jeffrey Schmalz, "Leaders in Albany Cool to Koch Bid on School Board," *NYT*, December 10, 1987; Jane Perlez, "Cuomo Meeting Fails to Agree on Restructuring School Board," *NYT*, December 11, 1987.

45. "Topics of the Times; A Bargain for the Schools," *NYT*, April 16, 1990.

46. *Improving the Odds: Making Decentralization Work for Children, for Schools and for Communities*, December 1987, Report to Manhattan Borough President, David N. Dinkins; Associated Press, "Dinkins Assails School Board for Cronyism," *NYT*, December 24, 1987; Josh Barbanel, "New York's Mayoral Rivals Support School Innovations," *NYT*, October 29, 1989.

47. Felicia Lee, "As Scores Drop, Schools Look for Lessons," *NYT*, March 24, 1990; Special to the *New York Times*, "Sobol Reverses Self on Chancellor," *NYT*, March 24, 1990; Author's interview, Stanley Litow, September 30, 2010.

48. Joseph Berger, "New York Schools Chief Challenges Boards' Power," *NYT*, January 19, 1990; Leonard Buder, "Little Criticism of Chancellor, for Now," *NYT*, January 20, 1990; Dennis Hevisi, "A Bronx School Superintendent Is Indicted," February 1, 1990.

49. Joseph Berger, "Judge Limits Fernandez Role in Hiring of Superintendents," *NYT*, July 6, 1990; Joseph Berger, "Fernandez Takes Charge," *NYT*, July 8, 1990.

50. *Temporary State Commission on New York City School Governance: Draft Recommendations for Public Comment*, January 22, 1991, John Marchi, Chairman.

51. Evelyn Nieves, "Fernandez Rebuffed in Bid for Veto of Superintendents,"*NYT*, January 23, 1991; Evelyn Nieves, "Schools Panel Urges Addition of New Districts," April 5, 1991.

52. Joseph Berger, "Fernandez Takes Greater Control in Local Districts," *NYT*, March 31, 1990; Joseph Berger, "Fernandez Pushes an End to Patronage," *NYT*, May 11, 1990; Joseph Berger, "Fernandez at 6 Months," July 31, 1990.

53. James Traub, "Fernandez Takes Charge," *New York Times Magazine*, June 17, 1990; Joseph Berger, "Fernandez at 6 Months," *NYT*, July 31, 1990.

54. Joseph Berger, "Education Group's Report Card for Fernandez: 'B Average,'" *NYT*, July 10, 1990; Joseph Berger, "Fernandez at 6 Months," *NYT*, July 31, 1990.

55. Joseph Berger, "Woman in the News; New Chief for School Board: Gwendolyn Calvert Baker," *NYT*, July 4, 1990.

56. Joseph Berger, "New School Board Reflects Mosaic of New York City," *NYT*, July 3, 1990.

57.   Editorial "The Right Role for the School Board," *NYT*, July 14, 1990; Joseph Berger, "Wagner's Schools Legacy: Varied Grades and a Major Impact," *NYT*, June 13, 1990. Joseph Berger, "The Region: It Isn't Easy to Design a Board of Education," *NYT*, June 17, 1990.

58.   Joseph Berger, "5 of Board's 7 for Condoms in the Schools," *NYT*, September 27, 1990.

59.   Joseph Berger, "5 of Board's 7 for Condoms in the Schools," *NYT*, September 27, 1990.

60.   In a December 17, 1990 Letter to the Editor of the *New York Times*, Jeannie I. Rosoff, President of the Alan Guttmacher Institute, said Board Member Impellizzeri was mistaken in her comments. The letter declared Impellizzeri misunderstood the study she cited and quotes a National Research Council study, "Risking the Future," described as a "landmark 1986 study on adolescent sexuality, pregnancy and childbearing, [which] stated categorically after having reviewed all known evidence, 'there is no available evidence to indicate that availability and access to contraceptive services influence adolescents' decisions to become sexually active.'" Impellizzeri accused Rosoff and authors of some of the studies cited of denying facts in their own research papers to defend their political points of view. Letters between Impellizzerri and Rosoff and others are in New York City Municipal Archives, Board of Education, Members of the Board, Irene Impellizzeri files, Series 345, Box 19.

61.   Resolutions proposed by Irene Impellizzeri, Vice President of New York City Board of Education for the December 19, 1990, meeting, in Impellizzeri files, Series 345, Box 19.

62.   Joseph Berger, "New York School Chief to Offer Plan for Distributing Condoms," *NYT*, December 4, 1990; Joseph Berger, "New York City School Board Members Clash on Condom Proposal," *NYT*, December 20, 1990.

63.   Joseph Berger, "Opposition to Condom Plan by Some Principals Is Seen," *NYT*, December 5, 1990; Joseph Berger, "Condom Plan for Schools Draws Criticism," *NYT*, December 6, 1990; Joseph Berger, "Condoms in Schools," *NYT*, December 22, 1990.

64.   Joseph Berger, "Compromise Still Uncertain on Condoms," *NYT*, February 27, 1991; Joseph Berger "School Board Approves Plan for Condoms," *NYT*, February 28, 1991.

65.   Joseph Berger, "Compromise Still Uncertain on Condoms," *NYT*, February 27, 1991; Joseph Berger "School Board Approves Plan for Condoms," *NYT*, February 28, 1991.

66.   Joseph Berger "Dinkins Seeks to Control School Board," *NYT*, February 8, 1991.

67.   Joseph Berger "Unity Eludes School Panel; After Discord, Focus Is on Board President," *NYT*, February 13, 1991; Joseph Berger "Dinkins Seeks to Control School Board," *NYT*, February 8, 1991.

68.   Joseph Berger, "McCall Says He Will Push for More Minority Teachers," *NYT*, June 28, 1991.

69.   Joseph Berger, "New Diversity Old Hat in Some Schools," *NYT*, June 22, 1991; Joseph Berger, "McCall Says He Will Push for More Minority Teachers," *NYT*, June 28, 1991.

70. Joseph Berger, "School Board Rebukes, but Elects, a Chief," *NYT*, July 3, 1991.

71. Joseph Berger, "School Board Renews Debate over Condoms," *NYT*, July 18, 1991; Joseph Berger, "Dinkins Shores Up Power in Condom Vote," *NYT*, September 13, 1991.

72. Joseph Berger, "School Board Renews Debate over Condoms," *NYT*, July 18, 1991; Joseph Berger, "Dinkins Shores Up Power in Condom Vote," *NYT*, September 13, 1991.

73. "HIV/AIDS Curriculum, A Supplement to a Comprehensive Health Curriculum, Grades K-6, A Minority Report, April 1992," New York City Municipal Archives, Mayor's Office for the Lesbian and Gay Community, Files of Deputy Director Jan Carl Park, Box 10; DM Norman Steisel Files, Roll #112.

74. New York City Municipal Archives, Mayor's Office for the Lesbian and Gay Community, Files of Deputy Director Jan Carl Park, Box 10; Joseph Berger, "School Panel Assails Chief on AIDS Issue," *NYT*, July 18, 1992; Press Release, "Board Members Object to Response to NYCLU Suit," July 16, 1992.

75. New York City Municipal Archives, Mayor's Office for the Lesbian and Gay Community, Files of Deputy Director Jan Carl Park, Box 10; Joseph Berger, "School Panel Assails Chief on AIDS Issue," *NYT*, July 18, 1992; Press Release, "Board Members Object to Response to NYCLU Suit," July 16, 1992 and "Statement by Board of Education Members Gresser, Impellizzeri, Petrides, Segarra," July 17, 1992 in DM Norman Steisel Files, Roll #112.

76. *Children of the Rainbow, First Grade*, New York City Public Schools. The quote is from the forward by Nilda Soto Ruiz, Chief Executive for Instruction. A copy of the book is in New York City Municipal Archives, Mayor's Office for the Lesbian and Gay Community, Files of Deputy Director Jan Carl Park, Box 10.

77. *Children of the Rainbow*, 158, 371–72.

78. Joseph Berger, "Queens Board Bars Curriculum on Gay People for 1st Graders," *NYT*, April 24, 1992; Steven Lee Meyers, "In Curriculum Fight, an Unlikely Catalyst," *NYT*, November 27, 1992.

79. Josh Barbanel, "Under 'Rainbow' a War: When Politics, Morals and Learning Mix," *NYT*, December 27, 1992; New York City Municipal Archives, Mayor's Office for the Lesbian and Gay Community, Files of Deputy Director Jan Carl Park, Box 10; DM Normal Steisel Files, Roll #112.

80. Josh Barbanel, "Under 'Rainbow' a War: When Politics, Morals and Learning Mix," *NYT*, December 27, 1992; New York City Municipal Archives, Mayor's Office for the Lesbian and Gay Community, Files of Deputy Director Jan Carl Park, Box 10; DM Normal Steisel Files, Roll #112.

81. Steven Lee Myers "Queens School Board Suspended in Fight on Gay-Life Curriculum," *NYT*, December 2, 1992; Josh Barbanel, "Under 'Rainbow' a War: When Politics, Morals and Learning Mix," *NYT*, December 27, 1992.

82. Steven Lee Myers "Queens School Board Suspended in Fight on Gay-Life Curriculum," *NYT*, December 2, 1992.

83. Municipal Archives, City of New York, Board of Education Records, Series 1140, Chancellor Joseph Fernandez, Box 65.

84. Joseph Berger, "Board of Education Reinstates Rebels in Queens District," *NYT*, December 10, 1992; Letter from Board of Education President H. Carl McCall to Mayor David N. Dinkins, January 26, 1993, in New York City Archives, Office of the Mayor, DM Norman Steisel Department Correspondence, Roll #112.

85. Author's interview, Stanley Litow, September 30, 2010; Memorandum to: Mayor David N. Dinkins from: Lee Blake Re: *Tales Out of School* by Joe Fernandez. Date: January 6, 1993 in DM Norman Steisel Files, Roll #112.

86. Sam Dillon, "Board Removes Fernandez as New York Schools Chief after Stormy 3-Year Term," *NYT*, February 11, 1993.

87. Sam Dillon, "Board Removes Fernandez as New York Schools Chief after Stormy 3-Year Term," *NYT*, February 11, 1993; Telecopy Cover Sheet Date: February 4, 1993 Name of Company: President of the Borough of Queens, Name of Individual: The Honorable Claire Shulman, From: Felix and Elizabeth Rohatyn, Letter from Preston Robert Tisch and Reuben Mark, New York City Partnership to Honorable H. Carl McCall, in New York City Municipal Archives, Office of the Mayor, 1990–1993, D.M. Norman Steisel, Roll #112.

88. Sam Dillon, "Board Removes Fernandez as New York Schools Chief after Stormy 3-Year Term," *NYT*, February 11, 1993; Statement by New York City Board of Education Members: Carol Gresser, Irene Impellizzeri, Ninfa Segarra, February 19, 1993 in DM Norman Steisel Files, Roll #112.

89. Josh Barbanel, "Mayor Offers Panel to Select a Chancellor," *NYT*, March 6, 1993; Catherine S. Manegold, "Woman in the News: 'A Full-Time Volunteer': Carol Ann Gresser," *NYT*, May 13, 1993; Sam Dillon, "Dinkins Concedes a Setback on Board of Education Post," *NYT*, May 12, 1993; James Bennett, "Gotbaum Is Dinkins's Pick for a School Board Seat," *NYT*, May 19, 1993.

90. Josh Barbanel, "Mayor Offers Panel to Select a Chancellor," *NYT*, March 6, 1993; Catherine S. Manegold, "Woman in the News: 'A Full-Time Volunteer': Carol Ann Gresser," *NYT*, May 13, 1993; Sam Dillon, "Dinkins Concedes a Setback on Board of Education Post," *NYT*, May 12, 1993.

91. Sam Dillon, "New York Asbestos Tests Are Voided," *NYT*, August 7, 1993; Josh Barbanel, "Earliest Date for Opening of School Year Is September 20," *NYT*, 1993.

92. Sam Dillon, "New York Asbestos Tests Are Voided," *NYT*, August 7, 1993; Christopher Byron, "The Bottom Line: The Phony Asbestos Scare," *New York*, September 13, 1993, 24–26.

93. Author's interview, Stanley Litow, September 30, 2010.

94. Sarah Lyall, "Union Rule Faces a Rare Fight; Dear to Labor, Wicks Contracting Law Is Debated in Albany," *NYT*, April 15, 1993.

95. Fernandez with Underwood, *Tales Out of School*, 254; Robert McFadden, "In Debate over Security in Schools, System's Diversity Keeps Solutions Elusive," *NYT*, March 2, 1992; Memorandum to: Norman Steisel, from: Harvey Robins, Date: February 16, 1993, Subject: Increased School Security: A Proposal for Inclusion in the FY94 Executive Budget in New York City Municipal Archives, Office of the Mayor 1990–1993, D.M. Norman Steisel Files, Roll #112.

96. Josh Barbanel, "Legacy of a Schools Chancellor; Fernandez's Changes May Not Live on after His Departure," *NYT*, June 30, 1993.

6

A City Living in Fear

New Yorkers lived in fear the year they threw Ed Koch from office and elected David Dinkins mayor. During 1989, 1,905 murders left blood on the streets and sidewalks of every neighborhood in the city. More Americans died violent deaths within the confines of the five boroughs in those twelve months than would die in the worst twelve months of combat in Iraq following the US invasion in 2003. Fear hovered over every aspect of people's lives in a town grown more deadly than a war zone. Daily reports of shootings, stabbings, assaults, and attacks intimidated all but the toughest residents. They combined with a series of horrific events and confusing decisions during David Dinkins's first months as mayor to create a severe crisis of confidence. By October 1990, Dinkins's credibility as the city's leader risked becoming another chalk silhouette drawn on a city sidewalk, the ultimate victim of the crime wave.

Twelve homicides took place on the day David Dinkins declared in his inaugural address he would be the "toughest mayor on crime the city has ever seen." Two days later, he announced he would delay the hiring of the next class of police recruits due to budget pressure. A *New York Times* editorial called the move "Blunt, but Brave." None called it smart politics. During his first month in office, grim year-end statistics emerged, reporting at least thirty victims died from stray bullets in 1989, with dozens more wounded. "If there was ever any comfort in the knowledge that most murder victims know their attackers, even that has fallen prey to the random violence inflicted on New Yorkers.... Death by bad luck . . . has a powerful effect," one journalist wrote.[1]

A few weeks after Dinkins's inauguration, a Manhattan resident beat a homeless man to death on the Columbus Circle subway platform. A six-foot-tall, two hundred-pound derelict—known to harass people regularly at the station—spat on, punched, and chased a subway rider traveling home from a movie with his three-year-old son. The father fought back to protect his child and himself, crashing the head of the homeless man into the concrete floor of the station so forcefully he died. The Manhattan district attorney's office leveled manslaughter charges, but a grand jury declined to indict. The public mood surged ugly.[2]

In March, at the cruelly misnamed Happy Land Social Club in the Bronx, eighty-seven people burned to death or died from asphyxiation in a fire set deliberately by a thirty-six-year-old man angry with a former girlfriend in the building. After a bouncer ejected him, the arsonist bought a dollar's worth of gasoline, poured a trail of it through the single entrance to the building, and lit it, extinguishing the lives of all inside save three. In a grim irony, the ex-girlfriend survived. The scorned lover watched the club burn before going home to sleep, where police arrested him twelve hours later, his shoes still reeking of gas. The blaze caused the worst loss of life in a New York fire since the Triangle Shirtwaist Company burned in 1911. Sixteen months earlier, the city had ordered the club closed due to hazardous conditions, but it had continued to operate illegally. Who could blame New Yorkers for feeling their city had spun out of control?[3]

David Dinkins arrived at the gruesome scene with several of his senior advisors. He looked at the faces of the dead for a long time. And then the mayor went back and looked at each one again. Many of the asphyxiation victims had taken their final breaths with their eyes wide open, their faces stuck in macabre, lifeless stares. "I don't ever want to forget what it looks like when the city does not enforce the building code," the mayor said. Perhaps his gut felt painfully what in his mind he must already have known. As mayor, he would bear a measure of responsibility for any number of awful tragedies of a kind that could happen on any day.[4]

I. Tinderbox City

In the first few months of David Dinkins's administration, the case of Yusuf Hawkins came to trial. Brooklyn district attorney Charles J. Hynes charged eight white youths in the killing of the sixteen-year-old African American, shot to death in Bensonhurst without provocation in August 1989. The most notorious among them, eighteen-year-old baby-faced Joseph Fama stood accused of pulling the trigger. Keith Mondello, the same age, faced charges of second-degree murder and other crimes. Their proceedings began in April with separate juries.

John S. Vento, twenty-one, also faced second-degree murder. At first, he agreed to testify against the others in return for reduced charges. Then he changed his mind. Reports circulated that the Fama family had threatened him. In January 1990 he fled, only to surrender to police in Dayton, Ohio, in March. His trial would follow in June. Trials for the others on lesser charges would come later. Reverend Al Sharpton mobilized his masses shortly after the murder. He led a series of marches in Bensonhurst, weekend after weekend, to insist that violent racists could declare no street in New York City off-limits to African Americans. Hostile crowds greeted the demonstrators with cries of "Niggers go home!" When marchers chanted: "We want the killer!" bands of local residents responded: "We want to kill *you!*" The city's muscles tensed, waiting for the verdicts. Sharpton declared that acquittals would mean, "[Y]ou are . . . telling us to burn the town down."[5]

At the same time, a seemingly trivial matter elsewhere in Brooklyn had developed a racial head of steam. Around 6:00 p.m. on January 18, 1990, a Haitian American woman named Ghislaine Felissaint had been shopping at the Family Red Apple Market, a Korean-owned grocery store on Church Avenue in Flatbush. Felissaint claimed that as she sought to leave the store without buying anything because the line was too long, an employee stopped her and asked her to open her bag, presumably to make sure she had not stolen anything. When she refused, the store worker grabbed her by the neck, slapped her, and knocked her down, she claimed. Then another employee kicked her. Later she would report a cashier said, "I'm tired of the fucking black people." The original police report of the incident did not include the comment, and the woman accused knew little English and usually spoke only Korean.[6]

The store employees' version differed. They claimed Ms. Felissaint had three dollars' worth of produce but gave the cashier only two dollars. While the shopper looked for more money, the cashier began to wait on the next customer in line. Felissaint took offense, began yelling racial slurs, and threw a pepper at the cashier, who threw one back. Felissaint then knocked down some boxes of peppers and spit at the cashier, the employees claimed. The storeowner tried to end the altercation. He told the woman to forget about the dollar, and he asked her to leave, placing his hands on her shoulders, at which point Felissaint lay down on the floor in protest, with shoppers taking sides as the dispute escalated. The police arrived. They called an ambulance for Felissaint, who went to the hospital with some scratches on her face. The police arrested the storeowner, Bong Jae Jang, for assault—charges a judge would later dismiss. The employees closed the store as a gathering crowd began to get violent, throwing rocks and bottles at the Koreans.[7]

The next day African American protestors appeared in front of the store, denouncing Korean disrespect for black patrons. They called for a boycott of the shop and of another Korean-owned grocery store across the street. Before long, militant activist Sonny Carson showed up on the scene, supporting the boycotters' call to shut the groceries down. For months a few dozen demonstrators paced the sidewalk outside the stores, verbally harassing and threatening would-be patrons, with devastating impact on the businesses.[8]

Korean merchants operating in various African American neighborhoods around the city had been subjected to intimidation tactics before, forcing some shops to close. Angry black militants harboring racist sentiments resented the presence of Asians in their midst, operating stores they believed African Americans should own themselves to provide jobs and income for local residents. Their hearts burdened by centuries of injustice and infected by the venom of bigotry that poisoned their outlook on the economic system they lived in, the activists could not admit an uncomfortable truth. The Korean family-run businesses succeeded while local initiatives remained inadequate to serve poorer African American neighborhoods.[9]

Cultural collision exacerbated the tensions. Koreans had little understanding of the troubled racial history they had entered, and they had a history of their own. One Korean man explained the circumstances that created conflict by analogy. "I don't like expressing it this way," he told a reporter, "but we Koreans are like the Jews—a small country located between hostile countries, always under threat of invasions. We had to protect to survive . . . that's been our history." Small wonder, the man implied, that Koreans reacted with an intensity that struck shoppers as rude and disrespectful when misunderstandings occurred. They were responding to two thousand years of Russian, Mongol, and Chinese invasions and, within the span of memory, decades of Japanese occupation. In Brooklyn the grocery boycott became the line in the sand in reaction to African American–Korean tensions. "This must stop and it will stop here," one storeowner said. "They cannot close," said another, referring to the two shops. "We could be next," he feared. Koreans and others sympathetic to the grocers' plight raised thousands of dollars a month to keep the stores in operation.[10]

Behind the scenes, Deputy Mayor Bill Lynch sought to negotiate an end to the boycott. He also tried to insulate the mayor from the controversy. "[A community] organizing tactic is not to bring the principal in unless you can close the deal, and we didn't have the deal," he recounted years later. So the boycott dragged on. The police, fearing confrontation would escalate tensions, attract publicity, and encourage the demonstrators, refused to enforce a court injunction that required protestors to stand back at least fifty feet from the stores to prevent physical intimidation. Many believed the mayor's office instructed the police to adopt this approach. "Not true," Lynch asserted when challenged on the subject. "The police [were] never ordered not to enforce the law. It was their decision about how to deal with it. I believe [from] discussions we had they did not want to exacerbate [the situation] by coming down on the protestors."[11]

The police and the mayor's advisors believed that the activists and their supporters would tire and that the issue would simply fade over time if confrontation could be avoided. They underestimated the militants' determination to keep hate alive. And the hands-off posture fed the view that the mayor was a man of inaction, unable to respond forcefully to the city's problems. Worse still, some concluded that the city's first African American mayor lacked the courage and integrity to confront people of his own race, even when they sought to achieve their goals through intimidation and threats of violence. A dollar's worth of vegetables had created a symbol of racial strife that would not die.[12]

As the Fama and Mondello cases approached a verdict in May, Al Sharpton, advisor to the Yusuf Hawkins family, and C. Vernon Mason, advisor to the grocery boycotters, planned a joint day of protests in Bensonhurst and Flatbush. With two of the city's most skillful provocateurs of racial animosity poised to seize center stage, the risk of violence, particularly in Bensonhurst, seemed real. Suddenly Mayor Dinkins faced a battle in Brooklyn that put his pledge to heal the city's race-inflicted wounds at risk. Black activists threatened to eclipse the city's first African American mayor, cast him as irrelevant, not in control even of his own political base much less able to lead the entire city. "You've got to come out strong," Bill Lynch advised the mayor. "We need to calm the town down, or else there might be an explosion."[13]

Dinkins understood the threat to his credibility to govern, and he moved to preempt it. The evening before the protests, he invited one thousand public, business, church, labor, and community leaders to City Hall to hear a citywide appeal for tolerance. He requested television coverage for the twenty-five minute talk. Four stations broadcast live, while others showed parts live or aired the entire speech later in the evening.[14]

The mayor told his audience and the city, "Together, we've tasted a tiny piece of the sweet substance called hope, yet again and again, we're confronted by the bitterness of hate." He pledged to do "whatever is necessary and whatever is right to maintain public order and public safety," and then he addressed the impending trial on everyone's mind. He called it "a painful passage for our city," and said, "[O]ne thing is for sure: No verdict can undo the damage that was done on that devastating night last August. The hate that was unleashed on Yusuf Hawkins can never be called back. The pain that ripped through his body, his family, and this city can never be fully healed. And his sacrifices must never be forgotten."

The mayor went on to stress that "this was a crime committed by individuals. All of Bensonhurst did not commit this crime; rather, a few people committed this crime in Bensonhurst. We must absolutely, categorically reject the notion of group guilt. We abhor those who preach it, and we must be mindful that predictions of violence and anger tend to be self-fulfilling." He left no doubt that he hoped the "individuals responsible for the death of Yusuf Hawkins will feel the strong arm of the law," and he affirmed his view that the legal system and trial by jury remains "the fairest and best method of judging our fellow citizens that anyone has ever come up with in the history of humanity." But whatever the outcome, he continued, "[W]e must repress our rage, channel our energies and come together to make this tragedy transforming."

The mayor inspired a standing ovation when he challenged the city's media, insisting they "must join in too—with public service announcements and programming that fights bigotry by teaching tolerance." The strong reaction reflected a broadly shared view that television stations and newspapers craved the emotional heat of racial animosity and stoked it with provocative reports and irresponsible headlines designed to attract viewers and sell newspapers. Their cynical competition created what one observer called a "ceaseless cacophony" that amounted to the "hijacking of the city" by journalistic carnival barkers promoting their shows without regard to the damage their provocative language caused. The mayor also challenged his audience and the citizens who elected him. "Right now, each of you must look into your own hearts, in your own families," he said. "Look honestly at yourselves—and your own communities—and ask whether you can be swayed by prejudice, and what you're going to do about it. Because no matter how much government can do, government cannot substitute for the content of our character."[15]

Addressing the Korean grocers boycott, Dinkins condemned the harassment taking place in no uncertain terms. He described the circumstances of the newest immigrants from Asia in the context of the city's long history as a gateway for refugees seeking a better life, often greeted at first by discrimination from those who preceded them. The mayor allowed that "[b]oycotts can be an appropriate and effective response" to injustice. The tactic had played a vital role in the civil rights movement that was so important to Dinkins's political base and to the mayor himself. But he continued, "[T]his one is not and the vast majority of the people in that community know it. Whatever happened in the actual incident, did not warrant this sort of ongoing intimidation. . . . We will never allow any group or any person to turn to violence or the threat of violence to intimidate others, no matter how legitimate their anger or frustration may be." He called upon all involved "to set aside their intransigence, to come in, to sit down, to settle this, and to settle it now. My personal commitment is absolute." He outlined a series of initiatives to help foster tolerance, and he called on all leaders to go back to their communities and appeal for harmony.[16]

The speech inspired many in the audience, and the leaders present pledged to support the mayor's effort to restore the city's civility—a quality his personal demeanor seemed to embody at a time when New York sorely needed such a symbol. Some also offered implicit criticisms. "It was exactly the kind of strong message that should have been delivered months ago. I just hope it wasn't just a speech," Reverend Calvin O. Butts, III, pastor of the Abyssinian Baptist Church told a journalist. Floyd H. Flake, also a pastor and a black congressman from Queens, suggested the mayor had to speak out because he "realized he has a city that sits on a tinderbox."[17]

And Vernon Mason was just the sort to strike a match. The next day as marchers gathered at the Slave Theater on Fulton Avenue in preparation for protests in Flatbush and Bensonhurst, the antiestablishment firebrand hurled disrespect at the mayor. "I could not believe what this Negro said last night. It was all I could do to prevent myself from breaking the TV," he told the crowd, who responded with chants of "Judas, Judas!" Mason went on to call the mayor "a traitor" and "a lover of white people and the system. And last night he bashed black people. He ain't got no African left in him. He's got too many yarmulkes on his head," Mason continued, adding a dose of anti-Semitism to his nasty invective. Sharpton, displaying an uncanny ability to rile and inflame while claiming to be justice's responsible conscience, offered this advice to the marchers. "When we go out to Bensonhurst, we're going to see the zoo," he said. "And when you go to the zoo, if animals bark at you and lash out at you, you don't strike back." He then told the young people in the group very pointedly that if they did not intend to be peaceful they should not join the protest. With that as backdrop, five hundred people climbed aboard ten buses and drove to Bensonhurst, while two hundred others walked to the Korean grocery on Church Avenue and joined one hundred boycotters already present.[18]

In Bensonhurst, two hundred fifty police officers, including fifty riding motorcycles and others stationed on rooftops, kept the peace. When local youths tried to step in the way of the marchers, a blue wall kept them in their place. Some jeers and offensive gestures slipped past the protective screen, but nothing more. A similar air of controlled tension prevailed at the Korean grocery protest. No violence marred the day.[19]

On Thursday, May 17, 1990, a jury convicted Joseph Fama, and a judge would soon sentence him to thirty-two years to life in prison. The next day, Keith Mondello's jury convicted him of rioting, unlawful imprisonment, menacing, discrimination, and weapons charges, but acquitted him of murder and manslaughter. William Glaberson, writing for the *New York Times,* captured the atmosphere at the moment the jury announced its decision. "In the end, the hate was there in the courtroom, just as it was there on 69th Street in Bensonhurst on the August night when Yusuf K. Hawkins was shot to death." Momentarily, everyone seemed stunned when the jury foreman, an African American woman named Mimi Snowden, read the not guilty verdict on the murder charge. "But then, rage was coming from the group on the Hawkins side so fast, in a blast of angry voices, that it was often impossible to pick out words from the chorus of fury." Reporters heard Sharpton threaten the woman fulfilling her civic duty. "You are finished!" he screamed. Mondello was sentenced to five years and four months up to a maximum of sixteen years.[20]

Dinkins continued his tolerance offensive. He spoke out frequently in the weeks surrounding the high-profile cases. At a church in Harlem, he told parishioners that all New Yorkers had immigrant roots. That all had come "to escape prejudice and persecution, hunger and deprivation . . . [so] the children of the oppressed must now turn to each other as allies and neighbors instead of turning on each other as enemies." He acknowledged "everyone feels threatened and . . . on edge from the daily pounding of the prospect of crime," but collective blame of other groups for it would only "plunge" the city "into a cycle of fear and frustration that could spin out of control." He urged his listeners to consider and respect the special values and the different symbols that mattered in different ways to New York's many ethnic groups.[21]

"Violence is no way to express our displeasure," he said to reporters as he stepped to the front of a parade honoring Dr. Martin Luther King Jr. on May 22. Later that evening, he hosted a two-hour town meeting at the Cathedral of St. John the Divine where Governor Cuomo, John Cardinal O'Connor, schools chancellor Joseph Fernandez, and other leaders came and spoke. The mayor introduced the evening as "the time to come together to create a wave of energy and unity so powerful that it could wash away the hate and the hurt." At Chancellor Fernandez's urging, many in attendance and around the city began sporting small blue ribbons as an emblem of support for the search for harmony. Joe Klein wrote in *New York* magazine, "David Dinkins had done about all that could be asked of a politician for the moment: He had set a moral tone and helped cool out a tough situation. He had done another thing, too—through his relentless civility, he had offered an alternative method of doing business to a fevered, frothing city." In an implicit criticism of the tone Ed Koch set from City Hall, Klein found it "nice to have a mayor selling sedatives, rather than amphetamines for a change."[22]

Dinkins's efforts seemed to have some effect. In July, when a jury convicted John Vento of unlawful imprisonment while unable to agree on the charges of murder and rioting, the verdict's announcement unleashed none of the courthouse rage that accompanied the earlier decisions. Vento received two years and eight months to eight years in prison for his role in Hawkins's murder. As time passed the rest of Yusuf Hawkins attackers met their fates, some acquitted and some convicted of the various charges filed against them, with an absence of public drama. Reverend Sharpton would declare the outcome a "mixed victory." Some involved in the murder got off easy, he believed, and others in the crowd when Fama shot Hawkins were never even arrested. But the city's emotions on the issue were largely spent. Only for the family of Yusuf Hawkins and the families of those implicated in his murder would the pain of the incident continue undiminished.[23]

Meanwhile, the boycott of the Korean grocers continued. At the end of August, a nine-person committee the mayor had appointed to investigate the incident published its report. It only added to the controversy. The document seemed intended to appease the protestors. It criticized the district attorney and the police department for not acting swiftly enough to investigate Ghislaine Felissaint's charges and for not assigning more resources to the case. It also endorsed the police department's decision not to enforce the court order to keep protestors fifty feet from the stores. Even more surprisingly, the committee found the event "incident based and not race based" even though protestors handed out fliers that read "Boycott all Korean stores," and "Don't shop with people who don't look like us." One protestor held a sign that said, "God is love, Koreans are the devil," while others called the grocers "yellow monkeys." The city council issued its own report in response, questioning the impartiality of at least three members of the mayor's committee while coming to very different conclusions on the substance of the matter. *The New York Post* described the report of the mayor's commission as "rewarding the racists." Ultimately, all efforts to mediate an end to the dispute failed because the boycotters refused to entertain discussions. In September, ten to fifteen thousand Asian New Yorkers showed up on the steps of City Hall in what was billed as an "Asian Rally for Racial Unity." The euphemistic label provided a fig leaf to hide Asian anger at the boycott and the city's feckless response.[24]

Finally, months after many people of good faith had urged him to and days after a unanimous appeals court decision denied the city's plea to exempt it from enforcing the court order to protect the grocers' businesses from intimidating protests, David Dinkins rode out to the store and bought ten dollars' worth of fruit and potatoes from the shop. He accused "some of those involved as . . . wishing only to beat these store owners into submission and force them out of business.... It is time for those who stubbornly maintain that Korean merchants should go away to welcome them as full partners in the great enterprise of our democracy." The action cast the prestige of the mayor's office on the side of the Asian victims and in opposition to the black militants. Many thought it the right thing but very long overdue. The police pushed the protestors back fifty feet, shopping at the store resumed, and eventually the boycott withered. Still, the damage had been done. Some months later, the owner of the Red Apple Grocery sold the store.[25]

In February 1992 the United States Commission on Civil Rights published a report entitled *Civil Rights Issues Facing Asian Americans in the 1990s.* In the section on the Flatbush Korean grocers boycott, it concluded:

> [The] incident illustrates what can happen when racial tensions are unchecked and racial incidents mishandled by local governments. An incident that might have been managed in such a way as to improve racial relations in New York City instead ended up worsening racial relations and disillusioning many Korean Americans about the American political process.[26]

Year's afterward Bill Lynch would cite the episode as one of his greatest disappointments. He wished he had not advised the mayor to stay away from the store for as long as he did. With admirable humility and loyalty, Lynch took the blame on himself. But ultimately the decision to wait so long had been the mayor's.[27]

II. Metropolis of Murder

If the threat of race riots retreated, the unrelenting reality of violence persisted without pause. In April, *New York* magazine ran an article headlined: "Victims: The Stories of Seven New Yorkers Caught in the War Zone." It catalogued the intimate impact attacks caused on people's lives. "I don't think there's any law in New York anymore," a twenty-year-old college student—who had his back slashed while walking along East 79th Street on a sunny Sunday afternoon—told the article's author. He did not plan to return to Manhattan after graduation.[28]

On June 16, 1990, *New York Times* reporter Donatella Lorch filed a story headlined, "Nine Hours, Nine Killings, No Answers." It began very matter of fact:

> At 3 P.M., 14-year-old Shawn Chapman saw two friends being harassed by another teen-ager on a Bronx street. He tried to intercede. Without a word, the teen-ager pulled out a revolver and shot him.
>
> At 6:10 P.M., Jacqueline Lewis hurried to pull a child away from her apartment door in Harlem. She knew that her roommate's boyfriend was outside and angry. A single shotgun blast tore through the door and killed her.
>
> At 7:10 P.M., Kevin Nimmons was sitting in his parked Cadillac in Brooklyn. The windows were rolled up and it was raining gently.

In a matter of moments, a small group of men had walked up, pulled out their semiautomatic pistols and riddled him with at least 15 bullets.

The three deaths were among nine killings in the city in a nine-hour period beginning Thursday afternoon.[29]

By summer, the ever-rising death count promised a new murder record would be set in 1990. A gunman who shot three people and killed a fourth left notes with his victims and sent messages to news organizations creating the scary specter of a New York Zodiac killer. Police feared the shooter sought to mimic a San Francisco serial murderer, never caught, who killed thirty-seven people between 1966 and 1974. Dinkins offered a $10,000 reward for information leading to the killer's capture. In Greenwich Village, a young advertising executive, John Reisenbach, "a thin, wiry . . . man, with a happy-go-lucky, mischievous grin . . . as if a joke was inside his head just waiting to get out," stepped out of his apartment to use a pay phone. A homeless man, who "lived in the neighborhood parks among the disordered lives of the transvestite prostitutes and pimps and hustlers and homeless," accosted him and shot him three times. Reisenbach staggered twenty feet and fell into the gutter. There his college sweetheart and bride, Vicki, found an emergency medical services team hovering over him in a brave but futile effort to save his life when she came to find out why his call was taking so long. That was how she learned she had become a widow. The city's professional class reacted with horror. It could have been any one of them. During nine days in July, four children—one less than a year old—died from gunshots meant for others. One Brooklyn mother expressed her most profound fear. "We tell our children: Good morning; pay attention in school; be good. We don't say what is in our hearts: Come back alive; come back to me this afternoon."[30]

New York magazine reporter Eric Pooley would write an article entitled, "Kids with Guns." A fourteen-year-old Harlem boy explained why he carried a weapon. "Where I'm from," he said, "guns are about common as water.... It's just like a part of life. Bein' strapped . . . that gives you the feeling of power.... I don't want to shoot nobody. But if they bully on me, disrespect my mother, or mess with any one of my family, they're just going to have to get it. That's what it's about." Having a gun had become a "symbol of power and prestige, a charged, mystical icon in the urban rite of passage from childhood to manhood . . . another consumer item, a status symbol to be showed off like a set of gold chains," Pooley wrote. But once a teenager had a weapon, he wanted to use it. "The gun want to get blood on itself. It want to get a body on it," a youth explained. And the kids coined an expression to describe life in their neighborhoods that were filled with child-men who had both fathered and killed. "Make a life, and take a life," they said.[31]

The relentless violence frightened and sickened the city, yet the mayor seemed helpless to respond. An obnoxious journalist asked Dinkins if he considered himself "the toughest mayor on crime the city has ever seen," as he had promised. "I will be," he answered. Other reporters in earshot laughed at the vow, so at odds with the daily headlines. The reaction angered the mayor. "The rest of them had at least four years, some have had eight years, some had 12 years. I've had seven months. So I say again, I will be," he shot back. But the incident told a story. Fairly or not, public patience had run out. Every bullet the city's faceless army of thugs fired wounded David Dinkins's authority. Under pressure, the mayor reversed his position from just a few weeks earlier during budget negotiations when he declined to increase the number of new officers planned for the next year. He announced he would cut other services to hire 1,058 additional police and put them on the street by April 1991. But he delayed any actual hiring until the police department completed a full analysis.[32]

In August 1990, for nearly two days, hundreds of correction officers blocked all access to Rikers Island, the city's largest prison. The protest came in response to a vicious attack by inmates on one of the guards. The Bronx district attorney charged the assailants with robbery, assault, and other crimes but not attempted murder. The decision angered the corrections officers, who also fumed that Mayor Dinkins visited an injured police officer in the hospital on the day of the attack but not the badly battered correction officer. And they complained that budget cuts made their jobs unsafe.

The unruly guards disrupted meal deliveries, causing inmates to riot and to take over one of their dormitories. A melee followed involving 250 officers for more than two hours before tear gas canisters brought order to the chaos. Many of the officers had been stuck on duty for more than forty-eight hours because of the bridge blockade. The angry, exhausted guards lined up some of the rioters and systematically beat them with nightsticks in retaliation for the attack on their colleague and the disturbance that followed. Investigators found bloodstained corridors littered with blood-soaked clothes when they inspected the site where the riot happened. Seventy-seven inmates went to local hospitals, and another forty-three required treatment at the prison—all with head injuries. The official report said all the prisoners had hurt themselves when they tripped over furniture while evacuating their cells. Twenty-one correction officers also required medical care. The justice system—a cornerstone of the structures that maintained social order among New York's nearly 7.5 million inhabitants—appeared ready to crack.[33]

A few weeks after the Rikers Island riots, the US Open tennis tournament came to Queens. New York's number-one tennis fan traveled to Flushing Meadows by police helicopter, lampooned in the *New York Post* as an ill-considered display of the perquisites of the mayor's office. Twenty-two-year-old Brian Watkins, a tourist from Utah, traveled to the matches by subway. After spending a day enjoying the event with his mother and father, brother, and sister-in-law, the family headed out to a late supper at Tavern on the Green. While they stood on the subway platform at 53rd Street and 7th Avenue in Manhattan waiting to head uptown, eight youths entered the station. They slashed open the pocket to the father's pants to grab his wallet and threw the mother to the ground and kicked her in the head. Brian and his twenty-five-year-old brother, Todd, fought back. One of the attackers stabbed Brian in the chest. Wounded, Brian chased the muggers down the platform, trailing blood as he ran. Less than an hour later, doctors at St. Vincent's Hospital pronounced him dead—the eighteenth corpse to exit the city's subway system that year. The boys who killed him needed the money to pay for an evening at Roseland Ballroom, a popular discotheque on West 52nd Street. Police found five of the hoodlums there later that night, seemingly unconcerned about the murder they had committed. Detectives arrested them on the spot and the others shortly afterward. Some belonged to a gang that required a mugging as an initiation rite. Perplexingly, some came from middle-class families not typically associated with the type of lethal violence they perpetrated, adding another layer of anxiety to the city's psyche.[34]

The innocence of the victims—out-of-towners enjoying a sporting event—the universal empathy for a son protecting a mother viciously assaulted—the pain of a mother, father, and brother witnessing the final, sudden gasps of life of a son and brother—the descriptions of Brian from his Utah hometown as a good and caring person—the location of the murder in the heart of midtown Manhattan, far from the city's most violent streets—an attack on five people traveling together, three of them men—the triviality of the motive, a night of dancing—combined to create a public reaction of despondent horror. Some wondered why anyone would visit New York, indeed, why anyone would live there.

Dinkins offered the family condolences and expressed sadness at the tragic event. In an effort to limit the damage publicity about the murder would cause to the city's reputation, Dinkins urged reporters to keep the ugly event in perspective. Other large cities suffered from worse crime than New York, he reminded them. The city found the reaction unacceptable. It hungered for outrage. The attempt to spin down the tabloid headlines backfired. It ignited "a press riot, which just destroyed everything in sight, burned down everything it saw," in the words of press secretary Albert Scardino.[35]

The *New York Post* editorialized on September 6, 1990: "When thugs commit murder, not to eat, but to go dancing at Roseland—and actually carry out the killing after they've already secured the money—someone in a leadership post (the mayor, the governor, someone) has to step forward and articulate the moral outrage all of us feel." And the next day the newspaper captured the city's disgust and sense of helplessness with a front-page headline that read pointedly in big, bold letters: "Dave, Do Something." Inside the paper, editor Jerry Nachman, referring to past mayors LaGuardia, Lindsay, and Koch, wrote, "[E]ach man knew he was the embodiment of the city's spirit. Each man knew that, during crises, the people of New York wanted action and, if not action, the symbolic gestures of action that galvanize change." He suggested the mayor show New Yorkers "the private David Dinkins insiders know very well: a man with strong opinions, a sharp temper capable of angry words and much more than the courtly figure we see on television. It's time for a new style," the columnist declared.[36]

The mayor responded to the plea to show his temper by telling reporters, "I've seen styles that I don't wish to emulate. I've seen styles that, frankly, I don't think were so great, albeit popular at the moment." It was a thinly veiled reference to Ed Koch, who criticized Dinkins in his column in the same edition of the *Post*. So did columnist Ray Kerrison. "As the city plunges deeper into its life-and-death crisis, as small children, ordinary citizens, law-enforcement officers, visitors, and cab drivers are shot down, stabbed, mugged, robbed, and raped with increasing ferocity, the mayor fiddles and muddles and contemplates what he might do," the journalist wrote. Frustrated, Dinkins rejected what he deemed impossible standards and unfair criticisms in his trademark formal language. "How, pray tell, can people simply say, 'Oh, well, you're not doing anything and Rome's burning and we saw you playing tennis someplace,'" when he and his staff were working seven days a week on the city's intractable problems.[37]

Despite his protests, the mayor knew he had to take action to restore confidence. The day after the dispiriting "Dave, Do Something" headline, Dinkins and police commissioner Lee Brown appeared at the New York headquarters of the federal Drug Enforcement Agency. They posed with senior law-enforcement officials in front of $5 million in cash and a machine gun seized from heroin traffickers. The posturing generated a front-page photograph of the event and the headline, "Dave Comes Out Swinging." Cardinal O'Connor invited the mayor to address the congregation at St. Patrick's Cathedral the following Sunday. "I come to you . . . to ask for your help in defending the public order of our neighborhoods against an onslaught by antisocial forces that threaten to tear our city apart," the mayor said grimly. While pledging a stronger police response, he told his fellow New Yorkers we must "come out from behind the locks on our doors and the bars on our windows," and "recognize crime is our problem . . . and that it is up to us to create the solutions," he said. "Come out and put your eyes and ears on the streets; come out to help stop the violence," he pleaded from the pulpit. The cardinal called on priests to support a new initiative the mayor had launched called a "Night Out Against Crime." The idea was to encourage a critical mass of law-abiding citizens one night a week to walk the streets together and reclaim them from the city's thugs.[38]

At a rally a few days later in East Harlem, the mayor again pledged more police, as well as more social programs to provide young people with better options than drugs and violence. And he told the gathering a personal story. "Some years back, in the 1950s, a young man was putting himself through law school, managing a liquor store in Harlem," the tale began. "One day, someone walked into the shop while the young store manager had his back to the counter. When he turned to help the customer, he faced a gun that appeared, to his fear-struck eyes, the size of a cannon." The young man, of course, was David Dinkins, who assured the crowd their mayor, sometimes accused of being detached and aloof, understood "the horror and injustice of facing a criminal head on, who threatens your life, who takes away your last bit of control." The gun barrel remained "permanently etched" in his mind, he said.[39]

A few weeks later, *Time* magazine ran a lengthy story headlined, "The Decline of New York." The cover featured a drawing of a magnificent skyline beneath which all manner of muggings and crime unfolded. They labeled it, "The Rotting of the Big Apple." The article acknowledged the obvious: "New York's plunge into chaos cannot be blamed on Dinkins, who has been in office for only nine months. In fact, he has inherited the whirlwind sown by decades of benign neglect, misplaced priorities and outright incompetence at every level of government." But it went on to note, "[S]o far, Dinkins' lackluster performance has strengthened the unsettling sense that he is simply not up to his job." And the article offered an ominous conclusion. "Unchecked violence has already dulled the luster of the Big Apple. The daunting task before its leaders is to prevent it from rotting to the core."[40]

New York magazine political editor Joe Klein faulted the mayor for inspiring the media feeding frenzy. "The art of politics . . . is to build public confidence through the illusion of mastery—to seem on top of things. . . . [O]ver the past few months, Dinkins has given the opposite impression. . . . Dinkins hasn't seemed vaguely in control, or even in the general neighborhood, as the city has careened into despair," he concluded. He returned to the theme with cutting wit in a year-end wrap-up article. "David Dinkins spent his first year in office behaving as if he were still city clerk. . . . Too often he seemed a visiting celebrity politician when the city needed a pro." In November the magazine Klein wrote for ran a special report titled, "How to Save New York." The city's problems "seem insurmountable now, because its leaders and common folk alike can see no path through today's intractable tangle of recession, crime, race, AIDS, and other woes," editor and publisher Edward Kosner wrote. It asked more than forty New Yorkers for ideas. They had some good ones, but implementing any would require leadership many feared the city lacked.[41]

III. Caution in a City Crying for Action

Dinkins's criminal justice team had been grappling with the relentless violence tearing at New York with the kind of dispassionate analysis that leads to carefully considered policy rather than with the sense of urgency an intolerable situation demanded. Lee Brown, the mayor's handpicked choice for police commissioner, an out-of-towner who needed to meet the department he would command and learn how it operated, had a low-key, thoughtful style consistent with the academic credentials he brought to the job. He had inherited a mess.

One journalist described the police force Brown agreed to run as "embattled, demoralized, and desperately in need of rejuvenation." A former Bronx borough commander who had become Minneapolis police chief, Anthony Bouza summarized its situation succinctly. "The department is really screwed up. It's been adrift for sixteen years. They're bloated and superannuated at the top, and they're not doing well on street crime at the bottom."[42]

Mayor Koch had talked tough on crime but did little to help control it. All departments, police included, bowed before budgets during his first term in office. He allowed the NYPD to decline by attrition until it bottomed out at fewer than 22,000 officers in 1981, compared with 31,700 cops before the city's fiscal crisis. The department clawed its way back to nearly 26,000 by 1989, still well shy of the size needed to police nearly 7.5 million people. The department's physical plant, vehicles, communication equipment, and resources had suffered similar fates. Koch's first police commissioner, Bob McGuire, described his job as crime management by "smoke and mirrors." He remembered learning one night that in the entire borough of Queens not one radio car was operating during the late tour, "a petrifying thought for a police commissioner."[43]

When McGuire stepped down, Koch appointed Ben Ward the city's first black police commissioner. Ward had walked a beat for the NYPD for seven years, earned a college diploma and law degree, and then served in senior police administrative posts. John Lindsay named him the city's traffic commissioner, and later Hugh Carey named him corrections commissioner for New York State, where Ward earned praise for cleaning up a troubled system. Koch named him head of the city housing police, and then head of the New York City corrections system before appointing him police commissioner. But the man had a reputation as a drinker and for erratic habits. He entertained lady friends in his city offices and at times lost contact with the departments he ran. His involvement in a controversial event during the Lindsay years—when black Muslims in Harlem shot two police officers and the department backed away from the scene fearing riots—caused the Patrolman's Benevolent Association to distrust him.[44]

Yet the man met Koch's needs. "He's black. There's no question about that," Koch said, patting Ward on the shoulder when he announced his selection to the press. "If that is helpful, isn't that nice," he told reporters, his ever tactless tongue in cheek. Koch needed an African American police commissioner to defuse a rising chorus of accusations by 1984 that he and the police force he oversaw were racist. Ward qualified as the highest-ranking and most experienced African American insider available for the job. While some credit Ward for launching important internal reforms as commissioner, departmental corruption and serious crime both surged on his watch. The police force he left behind remained troubled and ineffective. Under Koch crime rose sharply between 1978 and 1981, dropped sharply between 1981 and 1985, and surged again between 1985 and 1989, when crack-related violence hit the streets. Lee Brown and Mayor Dinkins inherited a rising tide of lawlessness. As a matter of objective fact, they took office during the worst crime wave in the history of New York City.[45]

The New York Police Department had nearly 26,000 officers when Brown became commissioner. For historic, anachronistic reasons separate departments policed the city's subways and public-housing units. The extra officers helped, some 3,600 for the Metropolitan Transportation Authority (MTA) and 2,100 for the Housing Authority, but the surge of crime throughout the city overwhelmed its law-enforcement machinery. None doubted it needed an overhaul and more resources. Changing a bureaucracy that size and finding the money to do it presented formidable challenges.

Key decisions confronted Commissioner Brown. New York continued to assign two officers to every patrol car, while in many major cities police cruised solo, effectively doubling their presence. New York cops feared single-officer cars raised safety risks at a time when drug traffickers wielded ever more powerful weapons with growing impunity. Drug-intervention forces—tactical narcotics teams—that flooded specific areas for three months at a time to shut dealers down had grown from four hundred to almost two thousand officers. That cut into the resources needed to police city streets, leaving the department beneath the minimum levels required according to the chief of patrol. Taking into account days off, vacations, sick leave, court appearances, administrative tasks, and special units, no more than three thousand officers cruised the city at any one time. And emergency 911 calls—nearly four million a year—absorbed 90 percent of patrol-car resources. One criminologist saw breaking this pattern as fundamental. "It really becomes a question of who runs the police department. Do you want the department to set the priorities, or [whoever] picks up the phone?" The structure in place left almost no officers on the beat to act as visible deterrents to violence and illegal activity. It reduced cops to the justice system equivalent of sanitation workers, picking up human debris only after crimes littered the streets.[46]

Relations between the police and New Yorkers in black and Latino neighborhoods remained strained. The force the city's second African American commissioner commanded remained over 70 percent white. The mismatch created tension inside the department and out. The rise in violent crime led predictably to more police shootings, most easily justified. But the split-second decisions required of armed officers, some experienced and some not, inevitably led to a number of contentious cases of white cops shooting suspects of color. Law-abiding dark-skinned New Yorkers found the chance a cop would shoot them by accident unsettlingly high.[47]

Brown's signature program idea, community-based policing, seemed designed to address many of the problems crippling the NYPD. It proposed to put patrolmen on the street to learn the neighborhoods they needed to protect, to prevent crimes before they occurred, and to create a relationship of trust and mutual support between police and residents. An outsider himself, Brown reached for a consummate insider to help him implement change.

The department had sent Raymond W. Kelly, the head of the NYPD Office of Management, Analysis, and Planning, to Texas to brief the incoming commissioner soon after the Houston chief agreed to accept the job. Kelly's first words of advice were, "[A]lways remember it's HOUSEton Street, not HEWSton Street." The story is more than just cute. Kelly likened the NYPD to the Vatican—a complex institution with its own traditions, culture, and rituals often difficult for outsiders to fathom. In addition to laying out facts and figures, Kelly began Brown's education in the ways of New York and its cops.[48]

Kelly had grown up on the city streets, the youngest of five children. His father worked as a milkman when deliveries still took place by horse and cart and later as a shipbuilder and an Internal Revenue Service clerk. His mother worked as a fitting-room checker at Macy's. While Kelly was still a youth, the family moved from 91st Street and Columbus Avenue to Queens, where Kelly attended Catholic high school. He would earn an undergraduate degree from Manhattan College in the Bronx, and over the years, law degrees from St. John's and New York University, and a master's degree in public administration from Harvard.[49]

In 1963 Kelly graduated first in his class from the New York Police Academy. By the time Brown met him, he had accumulated more than twenty-six years of experience inside the department. He had also served in the United States Marine Corps, including twelve months of combat duty in Vietnam. He remained in the reserves for years afterward, reaching the rank of colonel. In a number of sensitive NYPD assignments, both in the field and in headquarters, Kelly demonstrated skill and judgment. More than once, commissioners reached to him for the booby-trapped task of cleaning up dirty precincts. He got the jobs done without losing any limbs. As the head of the planning office he had developed a keen awareness of virtually all areas of the organization's activities. "Kelly knows every button, lever and switch" of the department, one deputy chief said of the man. When Brown asked former commissioner Ben Ward who could help him negotiate his way through the land mine–littered corridors of New York's Police Department, he responded, "[T]here was one guy, Colonel Kelly." So in February the new commissioner named the forty-eight-year-old two-star commander his first deputy. The move made Kelly responsible for key management functions, including budgeting, personnel, and disciplinary actions. It leapfrogged him over several of higher rank.[50]

Robert J. Johnston, Jr., chief of department and the highest-ranking uniformed official on the force, remained in his role, reporting directly to the commissioner. Kelly previously had reported to Johnston and was considerably his junior. The chief, whom some described as a man with a "larger than life ego," reinforced his understanding of his role with the commissioner. He made it clear that he would answer only to the department's top official and that police operations and tactics rested outside the bounds of the first deputy's authority. Only in the absence or disability of the commissioner, or at the commissioner's explicit direction, or under certain circumstances at the scene of a large-scale incident, was the first deputy allowed to assume responsibility for the department's activities. Kelly, a consummate professional with a marine's respect for chain of command, honored the strictly cast lines of authority.[51]

Also in February Dinkins named Milton Mollen deputy mayor for public safety. The newly created post signaled the importance the mayor placed on combating crime. Born in Brooklyn the son of Russian immigrants, Mollen was part of what Tom Brokaw would enshrine as the "Greatest Generation." The day after the attack on Pearl Harbor in 1941, Mollen enlisted and became a navigator in the US Army Air Corps. When the war ended, the Brooklyn boy went to college and law school at St. John's under the GI bill. He ended up working with a politically connected lawyer named Dennis Hurley. In 1951 Hurley and his team, working for Queens County Democratic leader James Roe, got an upstart challenging the organization's candidate for a judge-ship disqualified from the ballot. A short time later, Roe arranged for Mayor Vincent Impelliterri to name Hurley as corporation counsel. Mollen went with him.[52]

Mollen remained at the corporation counsel when Robert F. Wagner became mayor in 1954, and in time became a trusted advisor. When Robert Moses ran afoul of neighborhood activists with heavy-handed slum-clearance tactics, Wagner reached to Mollen to create the Hous-ing and Redevelopment Board, an agency charged with overseeing the sensitive process of forcing people out of substandard housing to allow construction of new apartments. Mollen became the general counsel and then chairman, traveling to all of the city's neighborhoods to meet with local elected officials, community leaders, city administrators, and state and federal authorities. In Harlem he met Basil Patterson, Percy Sutton, Charles Rangel, and David Dinkins. In 1965, John Lindsay's mayoral campaign manager, Robert Price, tapped Mollen to run for city comptroller on the Republican and Liberal lines to add a Jewish Democrat to the ticket for ethnic and political balance. Mollen lost but went on to become a highly respected judge and the presiding justice of the Appellate Division of the state's Second Judicial Department in Brooklyn by the time Dinkins took office.[53]

By then Mollen had reached the mandatory retirement age of sev-enty, and he was planning to enter private practice when the mayor asked him to serve as his coordinator of criminal justice. Mollen had worked with others who held that role in the past, including some highly competent people. They never proved effective. In his judg-ment the position lacked the clout to get things done. "If you leave it in its current form, not only do I not want the job, but my advice to you is abolish it," he told the mayor. Dinkins, convinced that the city's sprawling criminal justice system needed better coordination, asked Mollen how the role could be improved. Make it a deputy mayor, Mollen advised, so people will know that when your man speaks, he speaks with authority. Dinkins agreed, and a few days later Mollen accepted the job he had upgraded for himself with responsibility for coordinating activities across the city's many law-enforcement agencies—police, corrections, probation, and juvenile justice de-partments—as well as the district attorneys operating across the five boroughs.[54]

In April the Metropolitan Transportation Authority attracted William Bratton to head up the transit police department. Bratton had earned a reputation as a charismatic and innovative head of the Boston transit police, leadership qualities the New York system sought to import. His arrival added more competent talent to the city's pool of senior police officials.[55]

The team in place appeared strong, yet results did not follow rapidly. Police commissioner Brown had begun assessing the department's situation almost as soon as he arrived. By May the conflict between the need to add more police to protect the besieged city and the financial reality of a budget crisis came to a head. The mayor instructed Brown to provide a comprehensive report on police manpower and strategy by October 1, 1990, including an assessment of what it would cost to police the city properly and a plan for financing it.[56]

Four months was not a long time to assess a department as complex as the NYPD, something that had not been done for two decades. But it was a very long time to wait for New Yorkers, who felt their lives threatened daily. "Six months after taking office with a mandate from the Mayor to 'take back our streets and our parks, by night as well as by day,' Police Commissioner Lee P. Brown, while well regarded, has yet to show that he can make a difference," *New York Times* reporter Ralph Blumenthal wrote in August 1990. "Even some supporters say that in the process of analyzing the department and formulating his plans . . . [Brown] has shed little of the stranger's aura of mystery that clings to him and his program, to the detriment of public confidence." One former department official had "no question he knows exactly what he's doing—he just hasn't shared it." He found the man an enigma.[57]

Communication challenges emerged. After one press conference, a reporter present wrote, "Brown spoke like a college professor with tenure, his words a dense fog engulfing the journalists." Without clearer messages and a more forceful presence, some feared the commissioner would lose public confidence and his program would fail. Insiders wondered if his inexperience in New York's rough-and-tumble politics and budget battles left the NYPD disadvantaged at a time of exceptionally high stakes for the department and the city. It did not help that Brown accepted the role of president of the International Association of Police Chiefs, which often caused him to travel away from the city. Just as in Houston, New York critics dubbed him, "Out-of-Town Brown."[58]

A few weeks before Brian Watkins's murder, Brown could point to a number of steps he had already taken to protect New Yorkers more effectively. A ten-member Community Patrol Officer Program had been established in all seventy-five precincts around the city to put additional cops on the beat, with more to come. The department established overtime commitments for seven high-crime districts. All desk-duty detectives and officers spent one day a week on patrol, and low-priority 911 calls were being redirected to telephone units to take reports rather than dispatching radio cars. Officers were scheduled to change to steady shifts rather than rotate through three different eight-hour shifts—the wheel—that disrupted their lives and made them less effective. Special training and new procedures had been established for police shootings. Still Brown acknowledged what the city knew. These steps did not measure up to the task. The department needed a more substantial renovation and more resources to confront the crime epidemic terrorizing New York. "I think we've pulled our rabbits out of the hat. We have to face the fact that we are understaffed," First Deputy Kelly told a reporter. Meanwhile, the analysis, and the killings, continued.[59]

After Brian Watkins's murder, public outrage caused politicians of all stripes to call for more cops. "The time for exquisite analysis is passed," Governor Cuomo said. City council speaker Peter Vallone determined to wait no longer for a comprehensive initiative. He proposed the city hire five thousand more police over three years and pay for it with hiring freezes, service cuts, increased property taxes, and other sources. The *New York Times* responded to Vallone's initiative by excoriating the mayor and his studious police commissioner. While pointing out some meaningful flaws in the speaker's proposal, the paper called it a plausible reaction to an intolerable situation, while declaring

> Mayor Dinkins has yet to do even that much. In response to rising public concern he promised earlier this summer to add 1,058 cops, then assigned Police Commissioner Lee Brown to conduct an exhaustive study of the Police Department's needs. Now the mayor hesitates, pending the release of Mr. Brown's report in October. . . . In terms of perceptions and public confidence, Mr. Dinkins's call for patience seems weak and aloof. If he and Mr. Brown don't know and can't explain the basic points of an anticrime program by now, they can't expect to retain the public's trust.[60]

Around the same time, stray bullets killed a thirty-year-old Bronx assistant district attorney, Sean Healey, who had been buying doughnuts at a grocery store near the borough's courthouses.[61]

The mayor and his police commissioner stubbornly resisted the bullying by the city's tabloids and editorial pages. Dinkins remained steadfastly committed to a comprehensive program that placed the need to police the streets in the broader context of a far-flung and complex criminal justice system. He insisted the plan take into account the predictable fallout more police would have on the rest of the city's law-enforcement machinery—five district attorneys, civil and criminal courts, jails, probation officers, drug treatment centers, and so on—without which the additional cops could not be effective. He also wanted prevention programs directed toward young, disadvantaged youths who tended to commit the most violent crimes. Offered better options and responsible supervision, the mayor believed many young men could be convinced to follow a smarter path than the downward spiral of violence and prison followed by a vastly reduced chance for a productive life. In the tough budget environment the city faced, the mayor feared if he separated the demand for more cops from the rest of the services a comprehensive program required, he would never secure the votes he needed from the city council and the state legislature to finance them. "There was going to be only one bite at the apple," First Deputy Mayor Norman Steisel remembered. "We had to get it right."[62]

Commissioner Brown delivered his report as planned, and on October 2, 1990, Dinkins released the details of his administration's "Safe Streets, Safe City: Cops and Kids" program in an eloquent speech. "Fear is the ugliest of emotions," he declared. "It is the child of ignorance and the father of hatred. It can spawn intolerance, greed and disorder. Unchecked, it may become the greatest criminal of all, robbing us of every freedom, crushing our birthright and burning our future before us. . . . Well, we are here tonight to present our battle plan against fear." The proposal, developed by First Deputy Kelly and a team of seventy city and police department analysts and officers, called for expanding the city's effective patrol presence by more than nine thousand cops through a number of measures. In addition to hiring six thousand more police for the NYPD, the transit, and the housing police, the plan called for reassignment of many tasks performed by uniformed officers to civilians or other agencies, notably the traffic and corrections departments, freeing up three thousand more officers. Kelly and Brown knew that to secure financing for the expansive initiative, their analysis had to be thorough and defensible. The team developed the staffing numbers through systematic analysis of the tasks required to protect the city, the time each one took, and the optimum level of expertise and training each one needed. They built the assessment position by position, precinct by precinct. The plan would put cops on the street in numbers not seen in New York for many years with a clear commitment to community policing. The program's subtheme, "Cops and Kids," resonated powerfully with the mayor. Teens with access to gyms or involved in organized activities and after-school programs with competent adult supervision would not find themselves walking the streets at night, creating deadly mischief as a source of entertainment, he reasoned.[63]

The cost of the initiative—the uniformed officers and the civilians plus additional youth services—amounted to nearly $650 million a year as originally conceived. It was money the city did not have that the mayor would have to find in his own bare coffers or in the emaciated budget of the state. Even after various revisions scaled back some aspects of the program and extended the timing of others, the incremental cost totaled an estimated $1.8 billion over six years.[64]

For a time, the thoughtful and forceful plan to take back the streets restored the mayor's credibility. Some weeks after he announced it, he spoke at the Citizens Crime Commission. "While some may argue with my timing, quibble with the way I communicate, or quarrel with specific program or funding choices," the mayor said, "no one can dispute that my priorities—adding more cops and protecting and educating our kids—reflect the prevailing sentiments of an overwhelming majority of New Yorkers." Yet before long negotiations regarding the financing for the initiative began to drag. Recalcitrant Republicans in the state senate tried to force the city to commit to specific numbers of police in their districts. Then inconsistencies in budget reports created the specter of the city using the program as an excuse to raise taxes without a clear commitment to hire the cops promised. The negotiations dragged on into the next year before the fiscal provisions passed and the plan could move forward. The state senate–induced delay diminished the sense that the city's chief executive had seized control of the public safety issue.[65]

Then the mayor's office slowed down the bold hiring plans even after they had been approved and financing for them secured because of the relentless budget crisis. Replacement hiring of police continued, and previously planned increases in the levels of cops occurred. The number of uniformed officers grew to nearly twenty-nine thousand from twenty-six thousand. But the first cadets actually hired under

"Safe Streets, Safe City" would not enter the academy for training until August 1993. They would not hit the streets of New York until February 1994. The people footing the extra tax bill and suffering the consequences of crime without the benefit of the additional police took note of the delay. The president of the Real Estate Board of New York, Stephen Spinola, wrote to Deputy Mayor Barry Sullivan on March 23, 1993, following a lunch meeting. "We have analyzed the implementation of the [Safe Streets, Safe City] program in the numerous budget documents and SSSC reports. . . . Our concern about the implementation of the program has been very simple. The additional officers have not been hired. . . . We have paid too much and waited too long for the hiring of these additional officers," he wrote. Spinola accused the administration of "pure sophistry" when budget officials pointed to classes of recruits hired in accordance with historic commitments and in response to attrition as if those cadets represented the additional forces some $432 million in incremental taxes already paid were meant to fund. A month after Spinola wrote his letter, the state comptroller's office launched an audit "to measure the extent to which the funding obtained by the Safe Streets/Safe City legislation has resulted in an increase in the presence of the police on the streets of the City." So the comprehensive, thoughtful plan helped the administration briefly, but budget-constrained, disingenuous implementation hurt it.[66]

Shortly before Christmas 1990 the new transit police chief, William Bratton, asked the MTA board to allow his officers to carry nine-millimeter semiautomatic weapons instead of thirty-eight-caliber revolvers. The new weapons carried more bullets and could be fired and reloaded faster than the old ones. Bratton claimed his officers needed them to match the arms drug dealers used. At the urging of the NYPD, Mayor Dinkins opposed the change, fearing the additional firepower would cause an increase in accidental shootings, and he tried to convince the MTA to vote down the proposal. Bratton disarmed the mayor's effort to block the weapons upgrade by announcing he would order his officers to use lower-power, hollow-point ammunition to reduce the likelihood of strays ricocheting or bullets piercing targets and causing unintended damage. The board approved the proposal. The event made the mayor look like a soft-on-crime political weakling. As 1990 wound to a close, police tabulated 2,245 murders—the most killings in any single year on record.[67]

IV. A Brief Respite

In April 1991 more than two thousand cadets finished training and prepared for active duty. The new officers constituted replacements for the normal levels of attrition the department experienced. The mayor, presenting them as tangible evidence of the city's commitment to combat crime, declared them "the finest as far as the people of New York are concerned; the finest as far as their Mayor is concerned." The event took place in the backlash of the brutal March 3, 1991, beating of an African American motorist named Rodney King by Los Angeles police. A bystander had captured the event on videotape, and news stations had aired it repeatedly all across the country. To loud applause Dinkins declared that the L.A. cops caught on film "are not good cops.... They are not your friends. They have crossed the line from being protectors to being avengers and have themselves become a public menace." He urged the new recruits to avoid becoming "burned-out bullies with billy clubs."[68]

The line between necessary force and abuse of police power remained as faint as it had ever been in New York. Unlike his predecessor, who engaged in endless rhetorical executions of criminals and sided with the police in the absence of compelling evidence otherwise, Dinkins expressed concern for the consequences of aggressive police actions. For many, weary of living in an unsafe city, the mayor's emphasis seemed misplaced. Others, however, shared the mayor's anxieties about police misconduct. Some months before the graduation ceremony, the Manhattan district attorney's office "had quietly created a special unit to handle police misconduct cases, including accusations of brutality and corruption, which the unit's chief said are rising sharply," according to the *New York Times*.[69]

Some signs of progress emerged through the despair that surrounded the battle against violence and crime in the early part of the Dinkins administration. At year-end 1990, the New York State Department of Substance Abuse reported that the surging crack epidemic, perceived as a central factor in the crime wave, had peaked. While still an enormous problem, it had stopped growing, and evidence suggested the use of the cocaine derivative had declined along with the destructive activity associated with it. In April 1991, when the police published figures for the prior year, they confirmed the city suffered a record level of murders, as well as robbery and car thefts, but reports of assaults, burglary, and larceny all dropped by modest amounts from the prior year. The numbers offered hope that the wave of illegal activity had begun to crest. During the first three months of 1991, major crimes fell by more than 7 percent. The actual levels of violence continued to intimidate, but the relentless increases had stopped—and reversed. During intense budget negotiations through the spring and into early summer, Dinkins made his commitment to restore public safety clear, virtually exempting the police department while other city agencies endured severe cuts. The mayor and his public safety team seemed to be less often on the defensive and instead appeared focused on implementing their comprehensive program to confront the violence so damaging to the fabric of the city.[70]

In May 1991 at Tompkins Square Park in a fringe neighborhood on the Lower East Side, police tried to prevent a group carrying open beer bottles from entering the park during a rock concert. A melee followed, with people throwing bottles, lighting fires, and looting a pharmacy. The conflict brought with it reminders of a 1988 incident in the same place that left fifty people hurt and thirty-one arrested and generated more than 120 complaints of police brutality. Over the years, the park had attracted a gathering of homeless who lived there and also a group of young radicals sporting punk rock haircuts, body piercings, and anarchist tendencies. They asserted squatters' rights in abandoned buildings nearby and looked for opportunities to challenge authority for the sake of it. They organized demonstrations on behalf of the homeless that had little meaning for those they purported to represent. "We don't have time for protests," one of the men living in the park told a reporter. "We're not the purple-hair homeless. We're not let's pretend homeless. We're the authentic homeless." A local officer confirmed the situation. "The homeless were never the problem. It's those young people who are calling us names," he told a reporter. The Koch administration had given up trying to restore order to the park and allowed an uneasy truce to prevail among homeless, anarchists, and residents. A few weeks after the May 1991 melee, Dinkins ordered the bulk of the park closed for renovations, forcing the homeless and others to move out. Local residents split on the decision. Some found it harsh and inconvenient, while others welcomed it, but most New Yorkers took it as a sign the city intended to reclaim its public space and applauded. The city also removed the homeless from Columbus Circle at 59th Street, where an outdoor café was scheduled to open. The two locations "were symbols of a city out of control," Deputy

Mayor Barbara Fife told a reporter, and the mayor wanted order reestablished.[71]

Around the same time Bryant Park, the backyard of the New York Public Library, partially reopened. It had closed for renovations under Mayor Koch, at a time when homeless men and drug pushers had commandeered it. "Splendiferously" restored about a year later, in the words of one reporter, New Yorkers marveled at the transformation. Subtle but important architectural changes opened the space directly to the sidewalks and streets around it. The openness drew good people in and exposed the bad ones to the eyes of private security workers. "The social transformation of Bryant Park is as astonishing as its architectural evolution," Paul Goldberger would write in the *New York Times*. "Where once the park was the home of derelicts, drug dealers and drug users, it is now awash with office workers, shoppers, strollers and readers from the New York Public Library next door." At the same time, he noted, the space had "not been gentrified beyond all reason . . . the poor do not appear to have been driven out of the park, but merely to have begun to share it." So a sense of order returned to another prime patch of city land.[72]

Mayor Dinkins and his team had a feel-good moment in June 1991 when the city hosted an enormous celebration for the servicemen and women who fought in the Gulf War. *New York Times* reporter Robert D. McFadden described the event as "a magnificent blizzard of ticker tape, patriotism and affection in a homecoming parade up lower Broadway's Canyon of Heroes." Crowds chanted "USA! USA! USA!" in an outpouring of national emotion and pride. "It's a great day to be back home in New York," Harlem-born and Bronx-raised General Colin L. Powell, chairman of the Joint Chiefs of Staff, told a reporter. Incredibly, the police estimated nearly five million people lined the route that stretched from Battery Park to Worth Street. They called it the largest crowd for a single event in city history. Dinkins called it "the mother of all parades" and spent the day reveling in the attention. The event ended late in the evening with fireworks lighting the night over the East River and dazzling displays of color exploding over the skylines of Manhattan and Brooklyn. "I've never experienced anything like this," one private told a reporter. "The City of New York has spoiled us," he gushed.[73]

Journalist Joe Klein detected deeper meaning in "New York's big, sloppy wet kiss to the returning heroes." He found them "a source of pride, a reminder . . . of what America *hoped* it would be all about."

In his view, "The contrast between that spirit and the despair gnawing away at the vitals of the city was part of what made the parade so moving, so much of a surprise. The hunger for heroes, for leaders—for an aggressive attack on our toughest problems—seems manifest and profound. But sadly, the mayor mopes and dithers."[74]

V. A Collision of Religion and Race

A few weeks after the spectacular parade on July 16, 1991, someone firebombed the Fillmore Real Estate Office in the Canarsie section of Brooklyn, a solidly middle-class Jewish and Italian neighborhood. Successful African Americans seeking the comfort and safety Carnarsie offered had been slowly moving in for some time. Most residents took the arrival of black newcomers in stride. The attitude seemed to be that anyone who could afford to buy a home there—they sold for $200,000 or so—would probably be okay as neighbors. But a violent minority of locals felt otherwise. They adopted intimidation tactics, hoping to scare whites from selling homes to blacks and to terrorize African Americans into staying away. More than a dozen bias incidents occurred between the beginning of July and the first weeks of August, including a second firebomb at the Fillmore Real Estate Firm on July 27. The pattern made clear the violence came from an organized group, not the spontaneous actions of individuals. Reverend Al Sharpton rallied his marchers and, protected by four hundred police, walked Canarsie's streets chanting, "No justice! No peace!" Three dozen white youths paced alongside yelling, "White Power!" "Go Back to Africa!" and other insults. Some held up watermelons. One precociously malicious eleven-year-old boy told a reporter, "Everybody here hates Al Sharpton. We'd like to kill him." Mayor Dinkins met with local leaders a few days before the march to try to defuse the situation, while city community workers distributed anti-bias literature. Tensions continued to simmer. A third bomb would hit Fillmore in September.[75]

The violence in Canarsie coincided with a rising sense of crisis in the relationship between blacks and Jews across the country, nowhere with greater intensity than in New York City. The special bond that connected the two minorities during the height of the civil rights movement—much romanticized, exaggerated, and simplified later on, but real enough at the time—had become badly worn. The morally pure crusade against racial oppression enforced by the rule of law solidified the connection between the two groups in the 1950s and early 1960s. During the 1970s and 1980s, the civil rights movement evolved into a far more ambiguous and controversial quest for social and political justice. The relationship between blacks and Jews evolved as well, and not in a good way.[76]

Natural resentments born of the very different stations in society the two groups enjoyed had receded during the shared experiences of freedom rides, sit-ins, and marches. As those moments became memories, the resentments resurfaced. Nowhere were the differences more apparent than in New York City, with its huge and enormously successful Jewish population. The teachers who determined if African American students passed or failed and the landlords who collected the rent and evicted black tenants who could not pay were often Jews. The small business owners who fixed the salaries of black workers, the supervisors who decided which African Americans advanced and which did not, the social workers who controlled the flow of government resources as often as not in New York were Jews. The black writer James Baldwin once explained the situation in arresting language. "[J]ust as a society must have a scapegoat, so hatred must have a symbol. Georgia has the Negro and Harlem has the Jew." A certain level of black bitterness seemed the inevitable result of the asymmetric relationship. That in turn caused Jews to feel unappreciated for the commitment they had shown to civil rights' battles, including dangerous ones in which lives were risked.[77]

Black militancy that emerged out of the 1960s intensified the distrust. Aggressive African American demands for fundamental change threatened anyone benefitting from the status quo, including Jews. Tangible issues, like the battle for local control of schools in New York, or more general ones, like broad-based demands for greater economic and social justice, challenged an established order. An evolving sense of identity traced African American roots back to Africa and its liberation movements. For some black leaders that led to a sense of solidarity with Palestinian aspirations for a homeland. They felt a symbolic connection to a group perceived as forcibly oppressed by Israelis, a European people like the ones who dominated blacks in the United States for centuries. Tensions with Jews inevitably followed.[78]

The general tone of race relations, and between Jews and blacks in particular, deteriorated in New York City during Mayor Koch's twelve years in office. He engaged in aggravated public dialogue with the city's African American elected officials, as well as with more militant leaders. Many of them responded in unconstructive kind. The flow of violence streaming through New York with its racial crosscurrents exacerbated tensions. Periodic anti-Semitic rants from black leaders added considerably to the hostile atmosphere. Nation of Islam leader Louis Farrakhan's description of Judaism as a gutter religion and of Adolf Hitler as a great man topped the list of nasty statements. Jesse Jackson's less vicious but still highly offensive reference to New York as "Hymietown" came from a man who presented himself as a serious candidate for president of the United States. That raised the stakes of the damage.[79]

"Black anti-Semitism and Jewish antiblack racism are real, and both are as profoundly American as cherry pie," Princeton scholar of race in America, Cornel West, would write. By the early 1990s, the relationship between the two groups, once characterized by an appreciation of "common histories of oppression and degradation" that "served as a springboard for genuine empathy and alliances," had reached a "nadir," he concluded. It was in the midst of this troubled atmosphere that African American City College professor Leonard Jeffries launched a battery of verbal missiles at New York City's Jews.[80]

Jeffries belonged to a group of scholars who studied African American history as an expression of black nationalism. After earning his PhD in political science from Columbia University, he produced few scholarly publications. He established his reputation instead on the basis of a dynamic and provocative lecturing style. When City College created a department of African American studies, he became chairman with an immediate grant of tenure. Along the way Jeffries articulated a fantastic theory about the races. Blacks were the "sun people," possessed of an abundance of melanin that gave them intellectual, creative, and physical advantages over whites. Caucasians were the "ice people," a materialistic, warlike, and greedy race representing the "cold rigid element in world history."[81]

Despite the dubious quality of his scholarship, Jeffries ended up a consultant to a New York State Department of Education curricula committee in 1990. Concerns that the state's social studies program lacked sufficient attention to the role of racial minorities in American history caused education commissioner Thomas Sobol to appoint a task force to develop a more inclusive one. Jeffries offered a scathing indictment of what the state's schools taught, saying, "[T]he spillover of racism into the American education system has been so profound that it has produced the 'Miseducation of America.'" He presented his conclusions in harsh, accusatory tones that generated controversy, backlash, and publicity that the man clearly enjoyed.[82]

In a rambling lecture at the Empire State Black Arts and Cultural Festival in Albany on July 20, 1991, Jeffries indicted the state's history curriculum. Some "very nice white folks . . . who go to church and the synagogue . . . didn't hesitate to distort history in what I call a racial pathology," he said. Education in America, he declared, was "designed to support the system of white supremacy," making it "the sacred mission [of] . . . black folks" to change it. The complete "denigration" of African Americans in the movies, he announced, "was a conspiracy planned and plotted and programmed out of Hollywood, where people called Greenberg and Weisberg and Trigliani and whatnot . . . put together a system of destruction of black people." "We went to the movies every Saturday and saw native Americans being wiped out and Africans being denigrated. . . . It was by design. It was calculated," he asserted accusatorily, by "Russian Jewry [who] had a particular control over the movies and their financial partners, the Mafia." Together, he insisted, they "put together a system of destruction of black people."[83]

Jeffries denounced as "slick and devilish" three members of the curricula committee, Pulitzer Prize–winning historian Arthur Schlesinger, Harvard scholar of ethnicity Nathan Glazer, and Columbia University urban historian Kenneth T. Jackson, who dissented from the committee's conclusions. They thought some of the recommendations had been based on inaccurate representations of American life and were unconstructively divisive to teach to youngsters. Jeffries also denounced US assistant education secretary Diane Ravitch, who had advised the commission. A renowned Texas-born scholar of education in America, and New York City's schools in particular, Ravitch had objected to history that branded everyone as "either a descendant of victims or oppressors," fearing the practice fanned "ancient hatreds" and recreated them in each new generation. Jeffries responded by calling her "the new standard" for cultural oppression of African Americans. "The old standard," he explained, "was a Bible Belt Texas rural family. . . . Now the standard is . . . a sophisticated Texas Jew." Jeffries managed to work denunciations of Albert Shanker and Ed Koch into his speech as well, and he reported that the "head Jew at City College, Dr. Bernard Somer," had confirmed to him that "everybody knows rich Jews helped finance the slave trade" as his justification for teaching the subject in his classes.[84]

Unsurprisingly, the provocative, fantastic speech generated a powerful response. Many called for City College to dismiss the man. Others denounced his ideas but believed academic freedom of speech so important it trumped even Jeffries's foul classroom diatribes. Some dismissed the man's significance. "If you talk about the scholarly community as represented by the academy, Len probably isn't taken that seriously," one black professor who declined to be identified told a journalist. "Many people would think of him as a polemicist rather than a scholar." The presence at City College of another professor, Michal Levin, who promoted white-superiority doctrines, only made matters worse. Eventually, City College administrators reappointed Jeffries to his department chairmanship for a limited eight-month term instead of the standard three years. When it expired, they forced him to step down from his departmental role while maintaining his position as a tenured professor. Jeffries filed a suit in federal court claiming the action violated his civil rights. A jury found in his favor.[85]

Black-Jewish tensions weighed heavily in the sweltering New York City summer air on August 19, 1991, when *New York News-day* ran a front-page article under the title, "Blacks and Jews: What Went Wrong." African American columnist Sheryl McCarthy wrote, "[T]he recent furor over the Leonard Jeffries affair has shed light on the growing mistrust, even contempt, with which some members of these groups view each other." In her article, McCarthy recounted the many decades of collaboration and partnership between blacks and Jews in opposition to discrimination. She catalogued the many sources of mutual resentment as well. In conclusion, she wrote, "[T]he biggest point of contention . . . the one that cuts the deepest, is the unspoken competition of which group has suffered more," the Jews who survived centuries of anti-Semitism and the holocaust, or blacks who endured hundreds of years of brutal slavery. The sad result was that "two groups that should be working together, find themselves increasingly polarized."[86]

Such was the state of relations between blacks and Jews in New York City on Monday, August 19, 1991, captured in the headline that filled the front page of the tabloid sitting on newsstands in Brooklyn, when a Grand Marquis station wagon collided with a Chevrolet Malibu and caused Crown Heights to erupt.

Every Monday evening for many years, Grand Rebbe Menachem M. Schneerson, world leader of Lubavitch Judaism, visited the graves of his wife and of his father-in-law, who had been his predecessor. A three-vehicle motorcade, led by an NYPD cruiser from the 71st Precinct in Crown Heights, Brooklyn, escorted him to the cemetery and home again. Yosef Lifsch, a young Hasidic man driving the chase car with three additional passengers on August 19, 1991, accelerated through the intersection of President Street and Utica Avenue, trying to keep up with the two lead vehicles. He claimed the traffic light had just turned yellow from green. Others said it shone red. As he sped up, a car entering the intersection from another direction struck his station wagon, causing him to careen onto the sidewalk. His car struck and killed Gavin Cato, a seven-year-old black boy kneeling on the sidewalk, repairing the chain on his bicycle. The car injured the boy's seven-year-old cousin, Angela, too.

Police, a Hasidic-sponsored Hatzoloh volunteer ambulance, and several city emergency vehicles arrived on the tense scene within minutes. A crowd of African Americans had already gathered, menacing the hapless driver involved in the accident and his passengers. The police ordered the Jewish ambulance to remove the Hasidic men from the area to protect them and to defuse the tensions their presence caused. "Get your people out of here or they'll all be killed," a cop told the Hatzoloh driver, according to one report. City EMS officers along with another Hatzoloh volunteer tended to the victims. But the image of Jewish men leaving the scene in a Jewish ambulance while the black children they struck lay dead or injured infuriated the crowd. Rumors began to circulate that no one provided any help to the two youngsters. Decades-long embers of resentment flamed into violence. The accident occurred at 8:20 p.m. Not long after nine o'clock, callers began inundating the police department's 911 switchboard with reports of a riot. The calls continued for four days.[87]

Crown Heights had been home to African Americans since freed slaves moved there to farm early in the nineteenth century. Over time, successive waves of Irish, Jewish, Italian, and other immigrants moved into the area, which became home to moderately well-to-do newcomers for several decades after World War I. Beginning in the 1950s and 1960s, white working-class New Yorkers began moving to the suburbs. The neighborhood became predominantly African American and heavily Caribbean as well. Large numbers of West Indians immigrated there, bringing with them immigrant discipline and ambition, along with social structures and cultural values specific to the various islands. The Orthodox Jews in the area belonged to Chabad Lubavitch, an East European Hasidic sect that fled the Nazi holocaust in the 1940s. They brought their traditions and their belief in a rabbinical dynasty with them to Brooklyn, where they established their worldwide headquarters at 777 Eastern Parkway. Since their religion strictly forbids use of motor vehicles on the Sabbath, its members clustered near headquarters. When other white New Yorkers left the area, the Lubavitch stayed. They numbered ten to fifteen thousand or more of the two hundred thousand who lived in the community, but the impact of the group's presence far exceeded its numbers.

The Lubavitch believed themselves the leaders of a historic, divinely mandated mission on behalf of all Jews. Their distinctive dress—black suits, white shirts, wide-brimmed, black fedora hats, curled side burns, and long beards for the men, and wigs and dark full-length dresses for the women—followed nineteenth-century East European customs. Such anachronistic traditions, coupled with extreme devotion to the Torah and Jewish law, made the group highly insular. They discouraged their children from contact with people outside the sect and built a fully developed social infrastructure to manage their affairs with minimum reliance on others. The grand rebbe at one point forbid the Lubavitch to move from the neighborhood and strongly discouraged followers from selling property to outsiders. Indeed, tensions arose surrounding high-pressure tactics by the Lubavitch to expand their real estate holdings in the community. The Lubavitch, in their own minds, constituted a small minority surrounded by a sea of often hostile others. They felt constantly at risk of attack because of their distinctive appearance and practices and the ever-present reality of anti-Semitism in the minds of a people who fled the Nazis. To survive, they needed to band together and to use the strength of their ties to their community to compensate for their limited numbers.

The police escort for the grand rebbe's visits to the cemetery had emerged initially during the Lindsay administration when a competing group of Hasidim threatened the Lubavitch leader's life. Over time, the privilege had taken on great symbolic importance. The sect's members did not view the police protection as an act of special consideration but rather recognition befitting the leader of a worldwide religious movement, much the same way the police escort the Pope. Black residents who observed the weekly demonstration of influence saw it as a double standard made all the more offensive by the generally intolerable level of crime they experienced and the inadequate police protection they received themselves.

Mayor Abe Beame, himself a Brooklyn Jew of East European heritage, keenly understood the intense cohesion of the Lubavitch and the political significance of ten thousand or more committed followers. He extended additional privileges to the group. The city closed certain roads on the Jewish Sabbath, ignoring the inconvenience it caused others, and Beame agreed to reorganize the structure of the area's advisory boards to create Community Board Nine, generally perceived as a move to provide the Lubavitch with a district over which they could exert influence. Whether the decision actually accomplished much is unclear. But it created the distinct impression the city treated the Hasidic in Crown Heights one way and other citizens lacking the same degree of cohesion and access another. Mayor Koch tempered the relationship between the Lubavitch and the government some, but the suspicions and resentments surrounding the group in Crown Heights remained intense.

Activities unrelated to government exacerbated the problem. Hasidic neighborhood-watch groups designed to protect their community in an unacceptably lawless New York struck some blacks as vigilante committees aimed at them. Brooklyn reverend Herbert Daughtry accused the Lubavitch groups of cowardly violence against blacks—assaulting women and children, but "seldom . . . men," and then "only in droves." He organized African American patrols in response, announcing provocatively that when "men meet men, we will see what the people in the long black coats will do." The Hasidic volunteer ambulance corps, Hatzoloh, appeared to some a statement that the Lubavitch valued the lives of their own but not others. And the particular tension between the Lubavitch and African Americans took place in the context of general feelings of unfair treatment from the city and by the police common among black New Yorkers. A 1984 Carnegie Corporation report described Crown Heights as "awash in a sea of ethnocentrism, prejudice, and violent conflict." In 1987 some five hundred blacks marched on Eastern Parkway and compared the Lubavitch to South Africa's ruling Afrikaners. In 1988, after the slashing of a Hasidic man and an attack by blacks on a group of Yeshiva students, two hundred Lubavitch stormed the 71st Precinct to demand more protection.[88]

When the grand rebbe's motorcade struck Gavin and Angela Cato and the Hatzoloh ambulance spirited the men responsible away from the scene of the killing amid rumors that the medical technicians had refused to treat the injured children, leaving one to die, the long-standing resentments exploded. At the site of the accident, blacks and Hasidim argued fiercely, and rocks and bottles flew back and forth accompanied by racist and anti-Semitic insults. Bricks plummeted down from rooftops, and several shots rang out. By eleven o'clock, roving bands of black youths had begun hurling stones through windows and assaulting people. They overturned cars, lit them on fire, and attacked police. One group of marauders shouting, "[T]here's the Jew. Get the Jew!" stabbed Yankel Rosenbaum, a twenty-nine-year-old Hasidic graduate student from Australia, in the lungs. Police arrested sixteen-year-old Lemrick Nelson for the stabbing. From his ambulance gurney Rosenbaum identified the teenager as his attacker. Later that night Rosenbaum died, and police charged Nelson with murder.[89]

The spontaneous violence caught the police by surprise. The commander of the 71st Precinct, Captain Vincent Kennedy—his first day in that job—mobilized several task forces and rallied 350 officers in response, drawing from police assigned to a nearby B.B. King concert after it ended. He assigned officers to protect Lubavitch headquarters and shops on Utica Avenue and President Street and deployed the remainder in a fixed-post formation across thirty square blocks around the location where the riots began. The commanding officer of the Brooklyn South Patrol Borough, Assistant Chief Thomas Gallagher, supported the strategy. He hoped that the visible presence of several hundred cops on the street coupled with "restraint and non-confrontation . . . [would] limit violence, and prevent the police from becoming the focus of the crowd's hostility." But the angry youths turned into a roving mob. The law-enforcement tactics adopted, more appropriate for a large group of peaceful demonstrators, allowed the mob to engulf the neighborhood in chaos until about 4:00 a.m., when it simply ran out of steam. Morning brought an uneasy calm. Some observers praised police restraint. Hasidic residents condemned the NYPD for failing to protect them and their property.[90]

Senior police officials received reports of the riots Monday night or early Tuesday morning, yet none took clear command of the situation. The top brass of the department seemed caught off-balance. Robert Johnston had retired as chief of department just a few days before. His successor, David Scott, happened to be on vacation on August 19. The chief of detectives, Joseph Borelli, served as acting chief of department, and Mario Selvaggi, a former Manhattan borough commander, had been appointed chief of patrol on the very day the riots occurred. First Deputy Commissioner Ray Kelly sat outside the formal chain of command, authorized to give orders to uniformed officers only if the commissioner became incapacitated or asked him to take charge. In theory, the first deputy could assume control of a major incident. But doing so without explicit instructions from the commissioner would constitute a serious violation of police protocol. The local commanders, many themselves new to their roles as a consequence of the shuffle of the chiefs above them, lacked clear guidance.[91]

Commissioner Brown and Mayor Dinkins, along with Deputy Mayor Mollen, met at Kings County Hospital in Brooklyn about 12:30 a.m. as Monday night bled into Tuesday morning. The mayor spoke with Gavin and Angela Cato's fathers, and, along with Brown and Mollen, met with Yankel Rosenbaum at his hospital bed. The mayor talked to the young scholar, held his hands, and sought to comfort him. At the time, the attending physicians told the mayor they expected the man to recover. Tragically and inexcusably, the doctors identified only some of Rosenbaum's wounds, allowing him to bleed to death hours later. At the hospital, the mayor also met with Rabbi Joseph Spielman, chairman of the Crown Heights Jewish Community Council. Spielman expressed fear of renewed violence and demanded the city provide adequate protection. Later, the mayor went to the 71st Precinct, where he met with the local commanders and several elected officials to discuss the situation and the police response.[92]

The next morning Deputy Mayor Mollen telephoned police commissioner Brown to ask about his plans that day for Crown Heights. The weather forecast called for rain, Brown reported. He assured Mollen bad weather invariably discouraged protesters and that his department had the situation under control. The two men left it at that. They did not have a particularly good working relationship, and communication between them was often terse and strained. Mollen had tried to clear the air when he detected a certain coolness toward him from Brown early on. The commissioner paid lip service to the need for cooperation, but the relationship never evolved. Over time, the deputy mayor concluded it had more to do with Brown's natural reserve than anything personal. Still the ability of the two men to work together effectively remained limited as a consequence.[93]

The same morning, the mayor convened a meeting and named Deputy Mayor Bill Lynch the point person to coordinate the city's response. The experienced community organizer assembled a team that included representatives from various city agencies—the mayor's Community Assistance Unit, the Human Rights Commission, and the Department of Juvenile Justice—to focus on community outreach. Lynch hoped to dispel the rumors that ignited the riot, and more generally to ease the ferocious tension between the neighborhood's blacks and Jews by getting them to talk to each other.[94]

The city set up a communications command center at Public School 167, right in Crown Heights. Tuesday morning and afternoon Lynch and other city and local officials met there for four hours with community leaders. Dinkins's staff, Lynch in particular, felt it best that the mayor not attend the talks as that would draw attention to the situation rather than de-escalate it. During the meetings blacks insisted that the city arrest the driver of the car that hit Gavin and Angela Cato. They complained bitterly about the failure to hold him accountable, accusing the city of a double standard. Deputy Mayor Mollen, an experienced judge, had discussed the issue with the police the night before. He had told them to follow normal procedure without regard to the politics of the situation and not to do anything different because the driver happened to be white and the child killed black. The city rarely prosecuted drivers in traffic accidents unless egregious negligence occurred. Of 351 fatal crashes the prior year, only eleven indictments followed. The police typically defined negligence as a violation of at least two rules of the road. The driver of the car that killed Gavin Cato stood accused of running a red light and speeding, but eye witnesses contested both charges. Ultimately, the police made the judgment that the accident was just that. Jewish leaders who participated in the meetings left no happier than the blacks. They criticized Lynch's handling of the session, saying he never responded to the rumors as originally intended and that he ignored anti-Semitic comments, accusations Lynch denied.[95]

Meanwhile, hundreds of angry black youths gathered in the streets again, determined to secure justice for the injured children with their own hands. Local politicians and city officials would later report the crowd included relatively few Caribbean youths, despite the large proportion of the local black population they represented. "I doubt many of those children [the rioters] were Caribbean," one local minister told a reporter. "The parents tend to be very strict. They'd never allow such behavior." Differences between the two segments of the black population meant little to the Lubavitch. Hundreds of angry Hasidim took to the streets, determined to defend their turf. Violent clashes had already occurred when Sonny Carson appealed to teenage demonstrators in front of the 71st Precinct to take action. "Somebody's got to pay!" he yelled. "You know, we do a lot of talk. We ain't talking no more." With that, the crowd marched to President Street and Utica Avenue, clashing violently with Hasidim along the way. "Bricks were coming out of the sky like raindrops," Al Sharpton told a reporter for the *Amsterdam News* about the fusillades of dangerous objects that flew in all directions. A splinter group broke off from the crowd, yelling, "Death to the Jews!" as they roamed down a side street. When the rioters reached the intersection where the accident occurred, they accosted the police so violently with rocks and bottles that the commander ordered the officers to retreat to safety. The mob routed the NYPD.[96]

Jews, overwhelmed with fear, placed panicked 911 emergency calls—ultimately, nearly eight hundred of them—to report attacks. One woman called three times within three minutes. "They're headin' down to my house. They're breaking the windows. Utica and President, please come! . . . Where are the police. . . . What are you doing to us?" she lamented desperately. "It's a pogrom! You know what that means?" another distraught woman shouted at a dispatcher as a mob surged outside her apartment house hurling rocks and bottles at it. The police seemed unwilling or unable to restore order. The mob smashed and overturned police cars, lit fires, and looted shops. With too few officers deployed to respond to the outrages safely, police stood by while the rioters broke the law. Orders to "hold the line" and "stand fast" were issued, and officers were told "not to take independent action" that would isolate them and put them at risk. The restrained posture left the cops feeling like sitting ducks. *Channel 11* news reporter Tim Malloy told New Yorkers watching that night: "This is as ugly as it gets. . . . It's escalating. There's no sign it will cool off." Another reporter left the neighborhood around midnight "horrified . . . that civilians and police could be injured, windows broken, and patrol cars burned in the streets with almost no police response." The violence continued until midnight when the heavy rain Commissioner Brown had been counting on finally dispersed the crowd.[97]

Wednesday morning the mayor met with senior advisors and agreed to go to Crown Heights that afternoon to meet with community leaders. Meanwhile, the Lubavitch complained bitterly to Herbert Block, the mayor's liaison to the Jewish community, and to Dinkins and Milton Mollen as well, that the police were not arresting people flagrantly violating the law and that the danger was mounting, not subsiding. One rabbi told Mollen, "Jews, because they were Jews, were being physically attacked." During the course of the day on the steps of City Hall, Reverend Al Sharpton and Alton Maddox held a press conference. They gave the city seventy-two hours to arrest Yosef Lifsch or else they would "mobilize their forces to make a citizens' arrest." Lifsch, fearing for his safety, fled to Israel. Sharpton and Maddox would eventually follow him there in an effort to serve him with notice of a civil suit through the United States Consulate in Tel Aviv.[98]

Marchers took to the streets in Crown Heights again Wednesday afternoon. Four hundred African Americans arrived at Lubavitch headquarters, where they hurled rocks and bottles at the building. They burned an Israeli flag and yelled, "Heil, Hitler!" Richard Green, an African American community activist who had created a black and Lubavitch basketball team in Crown Heights, would later tell an interviewer that many of the youths yelling the deeply offensive words did not actually know who Hitler was, so removed were they from any grounding in the history of the world or their neighbors. One hundred Hasidim retaliated against their attackers with stones and bottles. Police in riot gear kept the two groups apart, but once again the mob outnumbered the officers. Commissioner Brown appeared near the scene in advance of the mayor's arrival at the local school serving as a communications center. As he did, a group of rioters converged on his car, pelting it with rocks and bottles. The situation became intense, beyond the capacity of his security detail to control, as the violent mob surrounded them.[99]

Ray Kelly learned of the disturbances in Crown Heights on Monday night, but in his first deputy role he had no authority or responsibility for police operations or tactics. So on Tuesday and Wednesday Kelly went to his office and tended to his management duties. He had watched television reports of the riots those days with concern, but he knew the responsible members of the department were focused on the crisis. Then, late Wednesday afternoon, a call came in over the police radio—"ten-thirteen Car One." *Ten-thirteen* is the police code for "officer needs assistance." It is, to policemen, the most urgent signal. It means one of their own is in distress. *Car One* was the department's designation for the commissioner's vehicle. Neither Kelly nor anyone else at headquarters ever remembered a New York City police commissioner issuing a ten-thirteen. Ray Kelly left his office, got into his car, and drove to Crown Heights.[100]

The distress signal Brown's security detail issued brought reinforcements to protect him. At least nine officers suffered injuries helping him to maneuver through the attacking crowd to get into the school. When the mayor's car approached, police made him wait until the mob passed. The best they could do was to redirect the rampage. They seemed helpless to stop it. Kelly saw the mob of youths throwing rocks and bottles as he drove down Eastern Parkway. By the time he arrived at the communications center, he found a visibly upset Mayor Dinkins in conversation with an unusually animated Lee Brown. "These are kids, these are kids," Kelly recalled Brown telling the mayor, in disbelief that the police force he commanded—the largest in the nation—could not suppress the roaming bands of teenagers subjecting the mayor, his police commissioner, and everyone in Crown Heights to senseless, dangerous violence. Kelly approached Brown. "Would you like me to get involved?" he asked. Brown said yes, giving Kelly the authority he needed to take charge. He left the mayor and the commissioner and headed for the 71st Precinct, which he had once commanded. Years later, Deputy Mayor Mollen could not "fathom" why Brown had not called upon Kelly sooner.[101]

After meeting with his senior staff and talking to a group of fifty youths inside the school building, the mayor tried to address a crowd on the street through a bullhorn. "Will you listen to me?" the city's chief executive pleaded. "No," came the mob's reply. When he said, "We will have justice, but we will not get it through violence," people booed and threw bottles at him. His security detail discouraged him from walking four blocks to the Cato residence to meet with the family of the slain boy and injured girl. "He was told by the police brass not to walk over there . . . and the thing that really got me to back up was that they believed there were six guns in the crowd," Bill Lynch said. "I don't believe anyone would have shot him, but I wasn't going to take that chance." Mollen also remembered rumors of a gun in the crowd. So they went by motorcade, the wrong way down a one-way street, adding to the general confusion. The police cordoned off the two ends of the street, but not before a crowd had already gathered in front of the Catos' apartment building. When Dinkins and Mollen got out of the car together to walk about fifty feet to the building, someone threw a bottle at them. "It whizzed right by my head," Mollen, seventy-one at the time, remembered.[102]

About the same time the mayor arrived at the Cato residence, populist journalist Jimmy Breslin was traveling to Crown Heights by taxi to cover the mayor's efforts to restore calm. "A group of youths blocked his cab, demanded money, smashed out the windshield with a baseball bat, piled into the back seat punching him, then pulled him from the car, ripped off his clothes and beat him until two passersby, one wielding a large knife, rescued him," *Newsday* reported. "And somewhere up in the higher echelons of journalism some moron starts talking about balanced coverage," the indignant writer, who had been left stranded in his underwear, lamented. Also that night, Patrolmen Benevolent Association president Phil Caruso accused police brass of using tactics that jeopardized officers' lives. In a statement posted the next day in precinct houses around the city, Caruso wrote with disdain, "[I]n Crown Heights, mob rule now prevails. Over the last three nights, New York's Finest have been transformed into New York's lamest." He went on to say cops "need not cower in fear . . . if police officers are placed under life-threatening attack, they should use their nightsticks or firearms" in self-defense.[103]

When Dinkins and his entourage left the Cato residence, the mayor again tried to address a crowd of angry youths. Again he met intransigent hostility, and in a tense moment the mob surged toward the mayor, but he left unharmed to meet with the Crown Heights Emergency Committee. There, rabbis declared the situation out of control and demanded Dinkins call for the National Guard. They accused the mayor of instructing the police not to make arrests, an accusation Dinkins denied. The meeting ended with the mayor's commitment to ensure safety. Back at Gracie Mansion, the mayor spoke live with *Channel 4* news reporter Mary Civiello. "[T]his administration will not tolerate lawlessness and violence, under any circumstances," he told the city. "We are not going to permit thugs to take over this city," he told reporters at a news conference that same night. A short time later, word arrived that a sniper with a shotgun wounded eight police officers as the violence escalated. The mayor, Commissioner Brown, First Deputy Mayor Steisel, Bill Lynch, and Milton Mollen headed for Kings County Hospital where they learned the officers' wounds were superficial. En route, Mollen had called ahead and requested the hospital set aside a room where the mayor and his top advisors could meet. In no uncertain terms, the group agreed the time had come for the police to put an end to the chaos on the streets with whatever force necessary. Some remembered reading the riot act to Commissioner Brown, but by then the man needed no great convincing.[104]

Earlier in the evening, after the meeting with the Crown Heights Emergency Committee, Commissioner Brown had gone to the 71st Precinct, where he found Ray Kelly and other top officers. Kelly had already made his rounds. He had gone to borough headquarters at the 67th Precinct, where he had talked with the deputy chief in charge. The man's answers to Kelly's questions left the first deputy unimpressed. "He wasn't particularly well organized, he did not know what was going on, it bothered me," Kelly recalled. The commanders on the scene, he realized, "were not being as proactive and aggressive as, in my judgment, they should be. . . . In reality, they were reluctant to make arrests." Kelly could only speculate why—no one articulated a reason to him. "Maybe they read in the tea leaves that an African American mayor and police commissioner" would not want them to adopt an aggressive posture against black youths. But as far as Kelly was concerned, the constraint "was self-imposed," and, whatever the reason, it led to "a lack of aggressiveness when aggressiveness was needed." Kelly, Brown, and Chief Selvaggi agreed to implement new tactics under Kelly's leadership. At 7:00 a.m. the next morning, the first deputy laid out a plan to deploy some 1,800 officers organized into four sectors, each with appropriate command structures, each saturated with foot patrols supported by mobile response units and reserves. Police were instructed to escort any gangs that emerged and disperse them. If they resisted, fifty mounted police and special teams in vans were available to close off streets, pin rioters in place, and allow the police to sweep in and lock them up. Instructions were clear. If "anyone does anything, arrest them," the chiefs told the cops. They were not to wait for assaults, destruction of property, or other violence before acting. Police posted on roofs would prevent a recurrence of sniper fire, and a searchlight-equipped helicopter would provide aerial intelligence.

A large group formed Thursday at the emotionally charged intersection of President Street and Utica Avenue, but the police presence maintained the peace. Gangs broke off from the crowd and began to roam, but the police followed and reacted at the first sign of trouble. They arrested sixty-one people that night, more than the combined total of the prior three days of riots. Someone fired six shots at two cops. The bullets struck their cruiser three times but missed the officers. Other serious acts of violence occurred, but far fewer than before. Each one elicited a more forceful response. The mob got the message. Scattered episodes continued for a few days, but the riot ended. A tense truce took hold on the streets of Crown Heights.[105]

Earlier that day, Bill Lynch called Al Sharpton to ask for his help restoring order. Sharpton met with the mayor, along with several of his top advisors and senior police officials. Parents of some of the black children who had been arrested attended as well. Sharpton complained that the police had detained only African Americans while Jews had also played a role in the disturbance. He insisted that the mayor release the black youths being held in jail. During the meeting, the parents lit into Dinkins and called him an Uncle Tom. The insults provoked an angry response from the beleaguered mayor. The tense meeting accomplished little. Deputy Mayor Lynch remembered Sharpton as "not playing the role of an honest broker" at a time when he might have helped defuse violent tensions.[106]

The rioters injured at least 38 civilians and 152 police officers. Twenty-seven police vehicles suffered damage or total destruction. At least six local businesses reported looting, arson, or property damage. Yankel Rosenbaum lay murdered. And one woman, a holocaust survivor, killed herself. Neighbors attributed her suicide to a mob-induced revival of the terror she had experienced decades before at the hands of the Nazis.[107]

Dinkins spoke at Gavin Cato's wake. He described the event to a crowd of over two thousand people as "[t]wo tragedies—one a tragedy because it *was* an accident, the other a tragedy because it was *not*. Two precious lives lost, senseless and for no reason. And yet, brothers and sisters, in the tragic deaths of these two young people, also lie the seeds of our redemption. We have an opportunity now to right old wrongs—to heal old wounds—and to make our city a better, more just place." He also promised to continue his efforts to "rid our city of the scourge of racial hatred and violence."[108]

The next day Dinkins attended Gavin's funeral. As the congregation entered the building, the "keening shrieks" of the young boy's mother "penetrated every corner of the church, and every soul in it," Joe Klein would write. The mayor spoke briefly, urging all to "increase the peace." Yet speeches by Reverend Al Sharpton and Reverend Herbert Daughtry overshadowed the mayor's. "I heard the word peace, but they don't want peace," Sharpton declared. "They want quiet." And Reverend Daughtry warned that, unless the city ended its favoritism toward the Hasidic community, "we will be back here very soon and it may be fire next time." Neither criticized the violent rioters. Sonny Carson, C. Vernon Mason, Colin Moore, and other activists also attended, turning Gavin Cato's funeral bier into something of a political stage. When the service ended, Sharpton, who movingly told the congregation that "we are ready to say goodbye to a young man who we should be saying good morning to," led the funeral cortege that walked for three miles behind the little boy's coffin from the church to his grave.[109]

The Rosenbaum family had requested that Yankel's body be flown to Australia for burial earlier in the week. Arrangements called for the hearse to slow as it passed by Lubavitch headquarters in symbolic respect for the man's connection to his coreligionists and faith and then to continue to the airport. Yet the community needed to grieve, and, by the time the hearse arrived at 8:00 a.m. Wednesday morning, a thousand people or more had gathered. The hearse stopped, and a group of men lifted the casket and carried it down Eastern Parkway while speakers offered eulogies and prayers.

The mayor's liaison to the Jewish community, Herbert Block, happened to be present. He had been told there would be no service, and so he had made no arrangements for the mayor to be there. In the charged atmosphere, Dinkins's absence at the memorial for the slain Jew seemed a glaring slight to any unaware of the sequence of events. When reporters questioned him about it, implying he lacked compassion for the Jewish victim, Dinkins became visibly angry. Pounding his fist on a podium, his voice rising, the mayor lashed out at the press. "Nobody has asked me. . . . Did you talk to [Rosenbaum]? What did he say to you? Did you touch him? Did you hold his hand? But I did. I held his hand. He held mine. He looked into my eyes. I looked into his. We talked to one another. He is dead now. So now I am being obliquely criticized for not having attended the funeral?" the exasperated mayor spat out in disgust. He insisted that he had demonstrated compassion and concern for Yankel Rosenbaum when it mattered most. Yet, however unfair, the symbolism of the mayor attending the memorial service of the black victim, but not the Jewish one, made matters worse.[110]

And inexplicably, Rebbe Menachem Schneerson, whose motorcade killed Gavin Cato, never expressed condolences to the family. He made no statement, public or private, of sorrow or remorse about the event. The driver, Yosef Lifsch, and other Lubavitch did, but not their leader, whose personal involvement in the event that ignited the riots made his silence deeply troubling. His posture angered African Americans. Through intermediaries, Deputy Mayor Lynch sought some expression of concern. Nothing. The rebbe's supporters offered excuses. Some remembered a few cryptic remarks that may have referred to the violence that had erupted around him, which they said was the rebbe's way of addressing all such matters. One suggested Schneerson was too important to be decent. "The Rebbe is an international figure," the man said, dismissing the issue. "If there is an incident in Washington, D.C. should the President get involved with white and black leaders to settle the insurrection?" The explanations rang loudly hollow. Some speculated that the man had reached a stage where he no longer had his full faculties. Aloof to the point of arrogance, seemingly indifferent to the deadly consequences of his convoy for a seven-year-old boy, silent when his people and those who lived with them needed a compassionate voice of reason to help restore calm, on this occasion, whatever the reason, the grand rebbe failed as a leader.[111]

A few weeks later, a journalist named Arnold Fine published an interview with Governor Cuomo in the *Jewish Press*. Fine reported that Cuomo told him he spoke with Dinkins the day after the riots started and quoted the governor as saying, "[T]he Mayor said that the night before had been sort of a day of grace to the mob, and that wouldn't happen a second day because it was abused and because there were crimes perpetrated that were not prevented." Dinkins adamantly denied ever saying such a thing, and the governor denied having told Fine he did. No one else remembered the mayor using the phrase "day of grace." Some speculated the governor made the statement to disassociate himself from Dinkins's handling of the riot. Others believed that the *Jewish Press*, a conservative publication, fabricated the charge to embarrass the mayor.[112]

The rumor persisted, unsubstantiated in any way, that the Dinkins administration had handcuffed the NYPD. In the minds of many, as soon as the mayor allowed the police force to mobilize itself, it shut the rioters down. Indeed, many thought cops among the victims of the violence, subjected by a black politician to excessive restraint against a black mob that left more police injured than anyone else. Little awareness emerged about the dysfunctional response of the senior command during the first days of chaos until much later, long after people had made up their minds about what had happened. The mayor found himself in an impossible situation. If he berated the police, he berated his own administration and his own choice of commissioner. If he kept his own counsel, he received all the blame for the tragic events.

Eventually, Governor Cuomo would ask Richard H. Girgenti, New York State director of criminal justice, to issue a report on the riots and the city's response. It laid out the facts in great detail and leveled plenty of criticism at Lee Brown and the police department's top brass. "A collective failure by top-ranking NYPD officials delayed the implementation of appropriate tactics to control [the] disorder," the report stated. It even criticized Ray Kelly: "Given the seriousness of the disturbances, it is unfortunate that the First Deputy did not assume a role in coordinating the development and implementation of a different strategy sooner," it said of the man who provided the experienced leadership it took to end the violence. "It is regrettable . . . Kelly did not seek an active role prior to late Wednesday," it repeated elsewhere. When asked about the report years later, Kelly said matter-of-factly: "It was politics. No one who understood the culture of the department, no one who understood the organization structure . . . the role of the first deputy, would have written that."[113]

Norman Steisel, distracted by tense budget negotiations during the first days of conflict at Crown Heights, felt he let the mayor down. His role included oversight of major disasters that required a response from multiple city agencies. In his own mind, he should have involved himself and played a greater role helping to marshal the resources needed to deal with the disturbances sooner and more effectively than happened.[114]

Bill Lynch would remember the events at Crown Heights as one of his greatest disappointments. With admirable humility and loyalty, he blamed himself for the tragic sequence of events since he had been the administration's point person. In some ways, he seemed the perfect man for the job. He had long experience as a community organizer. He was a leader who at other times in his career had managed to defuse the anger so often present in young black men raised amid broken homes and street violence, limited job opportunities and racial discrimination. Yet Lynch's very experience blinded him in Crown Heights. He saw the rioting teens as "misdirected" children of promise who had veered down a wrong path and needed to be guided back to a better one for their own good. "We've got to get a program together to work with these young people, to get them something to do and to diffuse this whole thing," he told a reporter after the riots subsided. But while the rampage raged, he seemed unable to understand the youths were attackers—victimizers rather than victims—who had gone beyond mobilization to mob, who sang no civil rights anthem but screamed anti-Semitic slurs. Their march created terror, not justice. Intent on violence, only force could stop them.[115]

Lynch would forever remember Crown Heights as overblown in the press. The night eight police officers suffered shotgun wounds was the night Lynch did not believe a hostile crowd would really shoot David Dinkins. He wondered suspiciously how the police concluded there were "six" guns in the mob they warned the mayor not to walk through. He remembered people throwing objects at Dinkins and acknowledged someone could have been hurt, but "they weren't 'mad[ly]' throwing rocks," he would say, playing down the severity of the action. Lynch's background, training, and instincts did not allow him to appreciate the seriousness of the violence until two additional nights of avoidable rage had terrorized the Jews of Crown Heights—something neither he nor Mayor David Dinkins would ever have wished upon them.[116]

For David Dinkins, the Crown Heights riots constituted an unmitigated disaster. The man who promised to heal racial tensions had presided over the city's worst race riots in twenty years. The man who had built a lifelong record of support for Jewish causes appeared unwilling to get tough with black mobs engaged in the worst outbreak of anti-Semitic violence in American history. The man who vowed to be the toughest mayor on crime the city had ever seen stood accused of ordering the police not to arrest people committing serious unlawful acts. At the intersection of President Street and Utica Avenue in Crown Heights, Brooklyn, confidence in David Dinkins's ability to lead the city lay mortally wounded.

In the immediate aftermath of the crisis, some members of the media rallied to the mayor's defense. "One has to have sympathy for David Dinkins and his aides, neck-deep in this ugly tide of anger and misunderstanding," Joe Klein wrote in *New York* magazine. And he praised the mayor's "stubborn persistence in returning to the area, even after he had been pelted with rocks and bottles and called a traitor," as an act of real courage. The editors of the *New York Post*, often the mayor's harshest critics, praised him. The day after the massive show of police force put the mob down, they wrote that "the mayor's actions throughout the crisis have been right on target—and we have every reason to hope that in coming days and nights he will do whatever is required to restore calm to Crown Heights." The mayor would later quote the editorial in his defense. Yet in the very same issue of the *New York Post* columnist Mike McAlary came to a different conclusion. "It has already taken David Dinkins one day longer to reclaim a dozen blocks in Brooklyn than it took Boris Yeltsin to reclaim the Soviet Union [after a coup attempt]. . . . Indeed, blacks and Jews are said to agree on only one thing in Crown Heights today, and that is our mayor's inability to lead." In stark, simple terms McAlary concluded: "David Dinkins has failed his city." The mayor's political future, he declared morbidly, "lies dead" with Yankel Rosenbaum.[117]

Notes

1.   Robert D. McFadden, "Eight Hours of Bloodshed: New York Records 13 Slain," *NYT*, January 2, 1990; Editorial, "The Mayor's Signal: Blunt, but Brave," *NYT*, January 6, 1990; Suzanne Daley with Michael Freitag, "Wrong Place at the Wrong Time: Stray Bullets Kill More Bystanders," *NYT*, January 14, 1990; Richard L. Madden, "Increasingly, Stray Shots Find a Mark," *NYT*, March 18, 1990.

2. Ronald Sullivan, "Self-Defense Claim in Subway Death," *NYT*, January 24, 1990; Editorial Jan 28, 1990; Editorial, "The Subway Killing's Lesson," *NYT*, January 28, 1990; Ronald Sullivan, "No Indictment in a Killing at IND Stop," *NYT*, March 24, 1990.

3. Ralph Blumenthal, "Fire in the Bronx; 87 Die in Blaze at Illegal Club; Police Arrest Ejected Patron; Worst New York Fire since 1911," *NYT*, March 26, 1990; Ralph Blumenthal, "Fire in the Bronx; Portrait Emerges of Suspect in Social Club Blaze," *NYT*, March 27, 1990.

4. Author's interview, Albert Scardino, December 10, 2010; Author's interview, Milton Mollen, November 10, 2010.

5. "The Bensonhust Case; Bensonhurst: Key Events," *NYT*, May 18, 1990; Robert D. McFadden, "Vital Witness Won't Testify in Bensonhurst Slaying," *NYT*, March 13, 1990; Joe Klein, "Race: The Mess; A City on the Verge of a Nervous Breakdown," *New York*, May 28, 1990, 33; Sharpton and Walton, *Go and Tell Pharaoh*, 162–64.

6. *Civil Rights Issues Facing Asian Americans in the 1990s*, A Report of the United States Commission on Civil Rights, February 1992, 34–35.

7. *Civil Rights Issues Facing Asian Americans in the 1990s*, 34–35.

8. *Civil Rights Issues Facing Asian Americans in the 1990s*, 34–35; Eric Pooley, "The Koreans: Caught in the Furor," *New York*, May 28, 1990.

9. *Civil Rights Issues Facing Asian Americans in the 1990s*, 34–35; Ari L. Goldman, "Other Korean Grocers Give to Those in Brooklyn Boycott," *NYT*, May 14, 1990.

10. Ari L. Goldman, "Other Korean Grocers Give to Those in Brooklyn Boycott," *NYT*, May 14, 1990; Eric Pooley, "The Koreans: Caught in the Furor," *New York*, May 28, 1990.

11. Author's interview, Bill Lynch, October 29, 2010.

12. Chris Hedges, "Brooklyn Judge Drops Charge against Grocer," *NYT*, June 7, 1990; Sam Roberts, "Turning Boycott of Greengrocer into Green Power," *NYT*, June 7, 1990; Mireya Navarro, "Black Customers, Korean Grocers: Need and Mistrust; For a Store Owner, Boycott Raises Fears of Misunderstandings," *NYT*, May 17, 1990; "Judge Orders Ruling Enforced on Picketing," *NYT*, June 28, 1990.

13. Joe Klein, "Race: The Mess; A City on the Verge of a Nervous Breakdown," *New York*, May 28, 1990, 33.

14. Todd Purdum, "Dinkins Asks for Racial Unity and Offers to Mediate Boycott," *NYT*, May 12, 1990.

15. Todd Purdum, "Dinkins Asks for Racial Unity and Offers to Mediate Boycott," *NYT*, May 12, 1990; Joe Klein, "Race: The Mess; A City on the Verge of a Nervous Breakdown," *New York*, May 28, 1990, 33–35.

16. "Remarks by Mayor David N. Dinkins: An Affirmation of Tolerance and Respect. Board of Estimate Chambers," May 11, 1990 in Municipal Archives, Office of the Mayor, David N. Dinkins, Speeches, Roll #10.

17. Todd Purdum, "Dinkins Asks for Racial Unity and Offers to Mediate Boycott," *NYT*, May 12, 1990; Joe Klein, "Race: The Mess; A City on the Verge of a Nervous Breakdown," *New York*, May 28, 1990, 34.

18. Dennis Hevesi, "Black Protesters March in Brooklyn Communities," *NYT*, May 13, 1990.

19. Dennis Hevesi, "Black Protesters March in Brooklyn Communities," *NYT*, May 13, 1990.

20. William Glaberson, "Bensonhurst Aftermath: Reporter's Notebook: Hate Quickly Overflows a Courtroom Fishbowl," *NYT*, May 20, 1990.

21. "Remarks by Mayor David N. Dinkins: What Hurts and What Heals: Community Relations at a Crossroads, Salem United Methodist Church, May 20, 1990 in New York City Municipal Archives, Office of the Mayor, David N. Dinkins, Speeches, Microfilm Roll #10; "Topics of the Times; Ribbons for Racial Harmony, *NYT*, May 23, 1990.

22. James Barron, "Dinkins Calls for Racial Unity at 'Town Meeting,'"*NYT*, May 23, 1990; Joe Klein, "Race: The Mess; A City on the Verge of a Nervous Breakdown," *New York*, May 28, 1990, 37.

23. Marvin Howe, "3d Defendant in Bensonhurst Case Gets Maximum Sentence," *NYT*, August 23, 1990; Sharpton and Walton, *Go and Tell Pharaoh*, 165.

24. "Report of the Mayor's Committee Investigating the Protest against Two Korean-Owned Groceries on Church Avenue in Brooklyn," Laura Blackburne, Co-Chair; Reverend S. Michael Hahm, Co-Chair, August 30, 1990; "An Analysis of the Report of the Mayor's Committee Investigating the Protest against Two Korean-Owned Groceries on Church Avenue in Brooklyn," December 1990, The Committee on General Welfare, Hon. Morton Povman, Acting Chairperson. Hon. Noach Dear, Ronnie M. Eldridge, Abraham Gerges, Jose Rivera, Walter Ward; Editorial, "The Mayor's Boycott Report: Rewarding the Racists," *New York Post*, September 5, 1990.

25. Todd Purdum, "Dinkins Supports Shunned Grocers," *NYT*, September 22, 1990.

26. *Civil Rights Issues Facing Asian Americans in the 1990s*, 40.

27. Author's interview, Bill Lynch, October 29, 2010.

28. Jeanie Kasindorf, "Victims: The Stories of Seven New Yorkers Caught in the War Zone," *New York*, April 9, 1990, 36–46.

29. Donatella Lorch, "Nine Hours, Nine Killings, No Answers." *NYT*, June 16, 1990.

30. Jack Curry, "Police Sketch the Man Who May Be the Zodiac Killer," *NYT*, June 26, 1990; James C. McKinley, "In the Zodiac Case, Still More Riddles Than Clues," *NYT*, July 9, 1990; Jeanie Kasindorf, "A Random Murder Shakes the West Village, "*New York*, September 17, 1990; "The Region: New York's Deadly Season," *NYT*, August 5, 1990; Andrew Stein, "In NYC Streets of Terror," *NYT*, May 21, 1990.

31. Eric Pooley, "Kids with Guns," *New York*, August 5, 1991, 20–29.

32. Ralph Blumenthal, "Crime and the Commissioner: Pressure Mounts for Results," *NYT*, August 3, 1990; Todd Purdum, "The Perpetual Crime Wave Crests, and a City Shudders," *NYT*, August 1, 1990.

33. Jack Curry, "47 Are Injured as Inmates Rebel Just as Impasse Ends at Rikers I.," *NYT*, August 15, 1990; James Barron, "After Uprising at Rikers, Guards Are Said to Have Beaten Inmates," *NYT*, August 16, 1990; "The Disturbance at the Rikers Island Otis Bantum Correctional Center, August 14, 1990: Its Causes and the Department of Correction Response," Office of the Inspector General Department of Correction, Michael Caruso Inspector General.

34. Sam Roberts, "Metro Matters; Dinkins Style and the Pressure to Sound Tough," *NYT*, September 10, 1990.

35. David Siefman, "City's Latest Crime Shocker Fails to Stir Mayor's Anger," *New York Post*, September 5, 1990; Author's interview, Albert Scardino, December 10, 2010.

36. Editorial, "Where Are the Voices of Outrage," *New York Post*, September 6, 1990; Front Page, "Dave, Do Something," *New York Post*, September 7, 1990; Jerry Nachman, "Do-Nothing Dave Dinkins," *New York Post*, September 7, 1990.

37. Ed Koch, "It's Time to Take off the White Gloves," *New York Post*, September 7, 1990; Ray Kerrison, "Do-Nothing Dave Dinkins: His Approach to Crime Crisis Is Alarming," *New York Post*, September 7, 1990; David Siefman, "Dave Fights Back," *New York Post*, September 8, 1990.

38. Front page, "Dave Comes out Swinging: Insists He's on Top of War on Crime," *New York Post*, September 8, 1990; "Remarks by David N. Dinkins, St. Patrick's Cathedral: A Call to Community: A New Order for New York," September 9, 1990, in New York City Municipal Archives, Office of the Mayor, David N. Dinkins, Speeches, Microfilm Roll #10; Mark Mooney, "O'Connor: Priests to Fight Crime," *New York Post*, September 10, 1990.

39. "Remarks by Mayor David N. Dinkins, "Keeping the Faith in NYC" Rally, September 16, 1990 in New York City Municipal Archives, Office of the Mayor, David N. Dinkins, Speeches, Microfilm, Roll #10.

40. James Barron, "Tourist-Slaying Suspects Are Tied to a Gang of Ritualistic Muggers," *NYT*, September 5, 1990; *Time Magazine*, September 17, 1990.

41. Joe Klein, "The Panic of 1990: Dinkins and the Vision Thing," *New York*, October 1, 1990, 28–31; Joe Klein, "1990 Winners and Sinners: Politics, *New York*, December 24–31, 1990, 18; Special Report, "How to Save New York," *New York*, November 26, 1990, 14–65.

42. Blauner, "The Rap on Lee Brown," *New York*, January 22, 1990.

43. Soffer, *Ed Koch*, 317–21.

44. Soffer, *Ed Koch*, 334–39.

45. Soffer, *Ed Koch*, 322, 334–39.

46. James C. McKinley Jr., "New Police Chief Facing a Familiar Task of Building Bridges," *NYT*, January 21, 1990; Herman Goldstein, "Does Community Policing Work; Efficient, Cooperative," *NYT*, December 30, 1990.

47. James C. McKinley Jr., "New Police Chief Facing a Familiar Task of Building Bridges," *NYT*, January 21, 1990; James C. McKinley Jr., "Toll Is Rising in Shootings by the Police in New York," *NYT*, January 5, 1991; Herman Goldstein, "Does Community Policing Work; Efficient, Cooperative," *NYT*, December 30, 1990.

48. Author's interview, Raymond W. Kelly, October 7, 2010.

49. Eric Pooley, "Bulldog," *New York*, February 22, 1993, 33–40.

50. Leonard Buder, "Brown Chooses Top Police Assistant," *NYT*, February 10, 1990; Eric Pooley, "Bulldog," *New York*, February 22, 1993, 33–40.

51. Author's interview with Raymond W. Kelly, October 7, 2010.

52. Don Terry, "Dinkins Appoints a Judge to New Deputy Mayor Job," *NYT*, February 1, 1990; Author's interview, Milton Mollen, November 5, 2010.

53. Author's interview, Milton Mollen, November 5, 2010; McNickle, *To Be Mayor of New York*, 200.

54. Author's interview, Milton Mollen, November 5, 2010.

55. Calvin Sims, "With Subway Crime up, Transit Police Get a New Chief," *NYT*, April 12, 1990.

56. Ralph Blumenthal, "Crime and the Commissioner: Pressure Mounts for Results," *NYT*, August 3, 1990.

57. Blumenthal, "Crime and the Commissioner," *NYT*, August 3, 1990.

58. Blauner, "The Rap Sheet on Lee Brown," *New York*, January 22, 1990, 34; Blumenthal, "Crime and the Commissioner," *NYT*, August 3, 1990.

59. Blumenthal, "Crime and the Commissioner," *NYT*, August 3, 1990.

60. Frederic Dicker and Richard Steier, "Cuomo and Morgy Call for More Cops 'Now!'" *New York Post*, September 11, 1990; Editorial, "A Subway Tragedy's Aftermath: Mr. Vallone Stands up to Crime," *NYT*, September 8, 1990: Peter Vallone, *Learning to Govern*, 179–80.

61. "The Decline of New York," *Time*, September 17, 1990; Miguel Garcia and Don Broderick, "2 Charged in Slaying of Bronx Asst. DA," *New York Post*, September 1, 1990.

62. Author's interview, Norman Steisel, October 28, 2010; Author's interview, Raymond Kelly, October 7, 2010.

63. Ralph Blumenthal, "New York Police Seek 9,000 Officers," *NYT*, October 2, 1990; Author's interview, Raymond W. Kelly, October 7, 2010.

64. "Safe Streets, Safe City: An Omnibus Criminal Justice Program for the City of New York: Cops & Kids," New York City Office of the Mayor, October 1990; "Dinkins on Crime; Excerpts from Dinkins's Address: Mobilizing to Fight Crime," *NYT*, October 3, 1990.

65. Sam Roberts, "Metro Matters; Test for Dinkins: Can He Deliver on Police Plan," *NYT*, November 29, 1990; Author's interview, Milton Mollen, December 10, 2010.

66. Author's interview with Raymond W. Kelly, October 7, 2010; Letter dated March 23, 1993 To Honorable Barry Sullivan From Steven Spinola, and "Police Department's Monthly Report for May 1993," in New York City Municipal Archives, Office of the Mayor 1990–1993, D.M. Norman Steisel, Roll #112.

67. Andrew Karmen, *New York Murder Mystery: The True Story behind the Crime Crash of the 1990s*" (New York: New York University Press, 2000) 26; Joseph B. Treaster, "New York State Reports a Drop in Crack Traffic," *NYT*, December 27 1990; James C. McKinley Jr., "Subway Police to Get New Pistols," *NYT*, December 21, 1990.

68. James C. McKinley, "Dinkins Has Tough Talk with Police Graduates," *NYT*, April 10, 1991.

69. Joseph P. Fried, "5 Officers Charged with Murder in Slaying of a Suspect in Queens," *NYT*, March 21, 1991; Ronald Sullivan, "Investigating Police: A Flood of New Cases," *NYT*, April 4, 1991.

70. "Crime Fell 7.1% in First Three Months of 1991," *NYT*, June 20, 1991; George James, "New York Killings Set a Record, While Other Crimes Fell in 1990," *NYT*, April 23, 1991.

71. Evelyn Nieves, "Tensions Remain at Closed Tompkins Square Park," *NYT*, June 17, 1991; Editorial, "Make Tompkins Square a Park Again," *NYT*, May 31, 1991; Sam Roberts, "Evicting the Homeless: All Sides Show an Increasing Frustration as New York City Uses Harsher Measures," *NYT*, June 22, 1991.

72. Nick Ravo, "Bryant Park Journal; After 3 Years, a Park Awaits a Wary Public," *NYT*, June 13, 1991; Bruce Weber, "After Years under Wraps, A Midtown Park Is Back," *NYT*, April 22, 1992; Paul Goldberger, "Architecture View; Bryant Park, an Out-of-Town Experience," *NYT*, May 3, 1992.

73. Robert D. McFadden, "New York Salutes; In a Ticker-Tape Blizzard, New York Honors the Troops," *NYT*, June 11, 1991.

74. Joe Klein, "The City Politic: The Mother-in-Law of All Parades," *New York*, June 24, 1991, 9–10.

75. Sara Rimer, "Block's First Blacks: Ashes to an Open House," *NYT*, February 17, 1991; Robert D. McFadden, "Taunts and Outrage Greet Protest March in Canarsie," *NYT*, August 11, 1991; James C. McKinley Jr., Dinkins Tries to Ease Tension from Canarsie Bias Incidents," *NYT*, August 8, 1991.

76. Andrew Hacker, *Two Nations: Black and White, Separate, Hostile, Unequal* (New York: Charles Scribner's Sons, 1992), 18; Jim Sleeper, *The Closest of Strangers: Liberalism and the Politics of Race in New York* (New York: W.W. Norton & Company, 1990), *passim*; Matthew Frye Jacobson, *Whiteness of a Different Color: European Immigrants and the Alchemy of Race* (Cambridge, MA: Harvard University Press, 1998), 274–83.

77. Jim Sleeper, *The Closest of Strangers: Liberalism and the Politics of Race in New York* (New York: W.W. Norton & Company, 1990), *passim*; Jonathan Rieder, *Canarsie*, passim; Nathan Glazer, *Ethnic Dilemmas 1964–1982* (Cambridge, MA: Harvard University Press, 1983), 30 for James Baldwin quote. Stephen D. Isaacs, *Jews and American Politics* (Garden City, NY: Doubleday & Company, 1974), 160–82.

78. McNickle, *To Be Mayor of New York, passim;* Hacker, *Two Nations,* 18; Podair, *The Strike That Changed New York, passim;* Cornel West, *Race Matters* (Boston: Beacon Press), 74.

79. McNickle, *To Be Mayor of New York, passim;* Stephen D. Isaacs, *Jews and American Politics,* 160–82; Sharpton and Walton, *Go and Tell Pharaoh,* 203–207.

80. Cornel West, *Race Matters* (Boston: Beacon Press), 71.

81. Eric Pooley, "Doctor J: The Rise of Afrocentric Conspiracy Theorist Leonard Jeffries and His Odd Ideas about Blacks and Whites," *New York*, September 2, 1991, 32–37.

82. Nick Chiles, "Suspicion on Racism Rift: Is State Curriculum Plan Real Target of Jeffries Foes?" *New York Newsday*, August 19, 1991; Jacques Steinberg, "Jeffries Misses Brooklyn Rally on Racial Issues," *NYT*, August 16, 1991; Eric Pooley, "Doctor J: The Rise of Afrocentric Conspiracy Theorist Leonard Jeffries and His Odd Ideas about Blacks and Whites," *New York*, September 2, 1991, 32–37.

83. "Text of Jeffries' July Speech," *New York Newsday*, August 19, 1991.

84. "Text of Jeffries' July Speech," *New York Newsday*, August 19, 1991; John Taylor, "Are You Politically Correct?" *New York,* January 21, 1991, 33–40.

85. Alan Finder, "Faculty Senate Assails Jeffries but Resists Censure," *NYT*, September 20, 1991; Samuel Weiss, "Jeffries Aides Warns CUNY on Sanctions," *NYT*, October 28, 1991; Joseph Berger, "CUNY Board Votes to Keep Jeffries in Post," *NYT*, October 29, 1991; Mervyn Rothstein, "CUNY Vote on Jeffries Pleases Few, *NYT*, October, 30, 1991; Nick Chiles, "Suspicion on Racism Rift: Is State Curriculum Plan Real Target of Jeffries Foes,"

New York Newsday, August 19, 1991; Samuel Weiss, "City College Chief to Seek Removal of Jeffries as Department Head," *NYT*, January 29, 1992; Andrew L. Yarrow, "Jeffries's Replacement Hope to Be Agent of Calm," *NYT*, March 25, 1992; Eric Pooley, "Doctor J: The Rise of Afrocentric Conspiracy Theorist Leonard Jeffries and His Odd Ideas about Blacks and Whites," *New York*, September 2, 1991, 32–37; John Taylor, "The National Interest: He's Back!" *New York*, May 24, 1993, 10–11.

86. Sheryl McCarthy, "Blacks and Jews: What Went Wrong," *New York Newsday*, August 19, 1991.

87. Joseph A. Gambardello and Curtis Rist, "Car Jumps Curb, Kills Child," *New York Newsday*, August 20, 1991.

88. *A Report to the Governor on the Disturbances in Crown Heights: Volume I: An Assessment of the City's Preparedness and Response to Civil Disorder,* 1993; Richard H. Girgenti, Director of Criminal Justice, 4, 39–50; Edward S. Schapiro, *Crown Heights: Blacks, Jews and the 1991 Brooklyn Riot* (Waltham, MA: Brandeis University Press, 2006), 70–102; Herbert D. Daughtry, Sr., *No Monopoly on Suffering: Blacks and Jews in Crown Heights (and Elsewhere)* Trenton, NJ: Africa World Press, Inc.), 48–62, 169–220, 195 for the "men in the long black coats" quote; Sharpton and Walton, *Go and Tell Pharaoh*, 193–200: Edward S. Shapiro, "Interpretations of the Crown Heights Riot," American Jewish History, Vol. 90, 2002; Edward S. Shapiro, *Crown Heights, passim;* Thomas Kessner and Betty Boyd Caroli, *Today's Immigrants: Their Stories* (New York: Oxford University Press, 1982) 185–204; Linda Basch, "The Vicentians and Grenadians," 182–85; and Nancy Foner, "The Jamaicans: Race and Ethnicity among Migrants in New York City," in Nancy Foner, ed. *New Immigrants in New York* (New York: Columbia University Press, 1987), 195–214.

89. Russell Ben-Ali, Virginia Breen, Mitch Gelman, Wendell Jamieson, Jennifer Preston, and Vivienne Walt, "Hasidic Jew Slain after Fatal Crash," *New York Newsday,* August 21, 1991; Mitch Gelman, "Rabbi: Victim No Match for Hateful City," *New York Newsday*, August 22, 1991.

90. Richard H. Girgenti, *The Disturbances in Crown Heights,* 60, 206; Shapiro, *Crown Heights*, 36–42; Daughtry, *No Monopoly on Suffering*, 170–80.

91. Richard H. Girgenti, *The Disturbances in Crown Heights*, 58–59; Shapiro, *Crown Heights*, 36–42; Daughtry, *No Monopoly on Suffering*, 170–80.

92. Richard H. Girgenti, *The Disturbances in Crown Heights*, 61; Shapiro, *Crown Heights*, 36–42; Daughtry, *No Monopoly on Suffering*, 170–80; Author's interview, Milton Mollen, November 5, 2010.

93. Author's interview, Milton Mollen, November 5, 2010.

94. Richard H. Girgenti, *The Disturbances in Crown Heights*, 68; Author's interview, Bill Lynch, October 29, 2010.

95. Wendell Jamieson and Scott Ladd, "Jews Seek More Protection," *New York Newsday, August 22, 1991;* Patricia Hurtado, "Few Drivers Face Charges in Deaths," *New York Newsday*, August 27, 1991; Author's interview, Milton Mollen, November 5, 2010.

96. Richard H. Girgenti, *The Disturbances in Crown Heights*, 5–6, 66–70; Shapiro, *Crown Heights*, 38; Joe Klein, "Deadly Metaphors," *New York*, September 9, 1991, 26–29; Kessner and Caroli, *Today's Immigrants*, 185–204; Linda Basch, "The Vicentians and Grenadians," 182–85; and Nancy

Foner, "The Jamaicans: Race and Ethnicity among Migrants in New York City," 195–214 in Foner, ed. *New Immigrants in New York*.

97. Richard H. Girgenti, *The Disturbances in Crown Heights*, 73–88; Shapiro, *Crown Heights*, 40–1; Daughtry, *No Monopoly on Suffering*, 170–80.

98. Richard H. Girgenti, *The Disturbances in Crown Heights*, 89–91; Author's interview with Milton Mollen, November 5, 2010; Mike McAlary, "Dave Lets City's Wounds Fester," *New York Post*, August 23, 1991; Sharpton and Walton, *Go and Tell Pharaoh*, 199–200; Shapiro, *Crown Heights*, 39.

99. Richard H. Girgenti, *The Disturbances in Crown Heights*, 91–93; Shapiro, *Crown Heights*, 40; Frank Rich, "Diversities of America in One-Person Shows," *NYT*, May 15, 1992.

100. Author's interview, Raymond W. Kelly, October 7, 2010; Richard H. Girgenti, *The Disturbances in Crown Heights*, 93.

101. Author's interview, Raymond W. Kelly, October 7, 2010; Author's interview, Milton Mollen, November 5, 2010; Shapiro, *Crown Heights*, 40.

102. Author's interview, Bill Lynch, October 29, 2010; Joseph A. Gambardello et al., "Third Night of Violence in Torn Neighborhood," *New York Newsday*, August 22, 1991; "Blacks Boo Dinkins," *New York Newsday*, August 22, 1991; Shapiro, *Crown Heights*, 40.

103. Jimmy Breslin, "Stripped and Beaten in My Furious City," *New York Newsday*, August 22, 1991; James Barron, "Tension in Brooklyn: Reporters Notebook; Fear, Loss and Rage Tear Area," *NYT*, August 22, 1991; "Fourth Night Brings More Violence," *New York Newsday*, August 23, 1991; Author's interview, Bill Lynch, October 29, 2010.

104. Author's interview, Raymond W. Kelly, October 7, 2010; Richard H. Girgenti, *The Disturbances in Crown Heights*; Joseph A. Gambardello, "Third Night of Violence in Torn Neighborhood," *New York Newsday*, August 22, 1991; Rose Marie Arce et al. "Dinkins Won't Let Thugs Take City," *New York Newsday*, August 23, 1991; Mitch Gelman, "Moving to the Next Level," *New York Newsday*, August 23, 1991; Shapiro, *Crown Heights*, 40–42.

105. Author's interview, Raymond W. Kelly, October 7, 2010; Richard H. Girgenti, *The Disturbances in Crown Heights*, 102–05; Shapiro, *Crown Heights*, 41–42.

106. Sharpton and Walton, *Go and Tell Pharaoh*, 197–98; Daughtry, *No Monopoly on Suffering*, 170–80; *Newsday*, August 23, 1991; Author's interview, Bill Lynch, October 29, 2010.

107. Richard H. Girgenti, *The Disturbances in Crown Heights*, 125–31; Shapiro, *Crown Heights*, 52–53; James Barron, "Tension in Brooklyn: Reporter's Notebook; Fear, Loss and Rage Tear Area," *NYT*, August 22, 1991; James McKinley, "Dinkins Describes Killing of Jew in Crown Heights as a 'Lynching,'" *NYT*, September 10, 1991; Felicia Lee, "Mayor Strongly Attacks Race Hatred," *NYT*, September 26, 1991.

108. Jennifer Preston, "Dinkins Tells Churchgoers Tragedy Can Be Catalyst," *New York Newsday*, August 26, 1991; Joe Klein, "Deadly Metaphors," *New York*, September 9, 1991.

109. Dennis Dugan, "A Platform, Not a Resting Place," *New York Newsday*, August 27, 1991; Dinkins' Staff Finds Its Legwork Paying Off," *New York Newsday*, August 24, 1991; Sharpton and Walton, *Go and Tell Pharaoh*, 198; Shapiro, *Crown Heights*, 15; Daughtry, *No Monopoly on Suffering*, 184.

110. Richard H. Girgenti, *The Disturbances in Crown Heights*, 89–90; Shapiro, *Crown Heights*, 47–48; Michael H. Cottman and Jennifer Preston, "Dinkins Walks through Racial Fire," *New York Newsday*, August 22, 1991.

111. Shapiro, *Crown Heights*, 9–10.

112. Arnold Fine, *The Jewish Press*, September 6, 1991; Shapiro, *Crown Heights*, 48.

113. Richard H. Girgenti, *The Disturbances in Crown Heights*, 351; Author's interview, Raymond W. Kelly, October 7, 2010.

114. Author's interview, Norman Steisel, October 28, 2010. Steisel viewed Ray Kelly as the instrument of implementation of the police plan but believed any of the top brass would have done the same at that stage.

115. Author's interview, Bill Lynch, October 29, 2010; Joe Klein, "Deadly Metaphor," *New York*, September 9, 1991, 26–29.

116. Author's interview, Bill Lynch, October 29, 2010.

117. Joe Klein, "Deadly Metaphors," *New York*, September 9, 1991, 29; Editorial, "Dinkins in Crown Heights," *New York Post*, August 23, 1991; Mike McAlary, "Dave Lets City's Wounds Fester," *New York Post*, August 23, 1991.

7

Policing the Police

Crown Heights added to a sense of despair permeating New York. A little over a year earlier a *Time*/Cable News survey showed that more New Yorkers than ever wanted to leave the city and more than ever before thought the city would be worse off in ten or fifteen years. Perceptions had only deteriorated since. A few weeks after the Brooklyn riots, *New York* political columnist Joe Klein wrote:

> Add to [the conflict in Crown Heights] an atmosphere of racial antagonism nearing the point of hysteria in the city, the frothing and bubbling of conspiracy theories, the rise of an almost casual anti-Semitism, the endemic street crime, the family disintegration and hopelessness in the black community, the constant tattoo of minority youths shot dead by police under questionable circumstances, the daily tide of bile fantasies and paranoia on talk radio (white and black), the sagging municipal finances and waning civic presences in the poorest neighborhoods, the spiritual depression caused by the lack of leadership, the sense of a steady stream of families and businesses heading for the exits—given all that, the senseless caprice of Gavin Cato's death and the murderous fury of the anti-Jewish riot that followed seemed to push New York toward yet another spiritual crossroads.[1]

By year-end Klein would surmise, "Crown Heights may have been the last straw for both the public and Dinkins himself. Afterwards, his administration seemed to disintegrate."[2]

Discouraging events continued to damage the collective psyche. Less than a week after the police put a stop to the Brooklyn riots, a drunken subway motorman ran his train off the tracks at 14th Street, killing five riders and injuring more than two hundred passengers in the worst accident of its kind since 1918. The front car leapt into a support pillar that sheared it in half. Four of the nine cars behind derailed and

251

ran into each other, creating a tangled metal mess. Rescue workers and the mayor expressed astonishment that more people did not die. The tragedy suspended service on the IRT line from 86th Street on the Upper East Side to Bowling Green at the tip of Manhattan for six days, disrupting life for more than four hundred thousand riders every hour during peak periods. Two hundred Metropolitan Transportation Authority (MTA) employees worked round the clock in twelve-hour shifts to restore service. "We rallied to get the job done because we wanted to show the public that not all transit workers are drunks, and that most of us work damn hard to keep this system safe and running smoothly," a track worker said, obviously appalled by the deadly irresponsibility of his coworker.[3]

In October 1991 the *New York Times* also sensed the dispirited public mood:

> New Yorkers are losing heart. And it is no wonder that many fear their city is disintegrating. A huge budget deficit means dirtier streets, unkempt parks and shorter library hours. Almost a million New Yorkers are on welfare, supported by an ever-thinner base of taxpayers. Homeless mental cases huddle in corners everywhere, or beg aggressively. Drugs so ravage neighborhoods that desperate parents in the Bronx are driven to chain their daughter to a bed to save her from the streets. And every macho teen-ager seems to be packing a gun.
>
> Who can feel safe in an era of random shootings? Who does not fear the flare-up of race hatred when vicious whites in Queens club a black athlete senseless in Atlantic Beach and vicious blacks stab a young Jew to death in Crown Heights?
>
> At a time when we crave strong leadership, Mayor David Dinkins has been dishearteningly passive and Gov. Mario Cuomo has been irresponsibly remote.

Yet they concluded, "New York has emerged from worse crises, over and over again, and been stronger than ever.... Great cities don't die; they adapt."[4]

As the mayor and his team fielded the political fallout from Crown Heights and tried to contend with the public mood of despair, Commissioner Brown and the police department pursued the "Safe Streets, Safe City," blueprint for transforming New York from chaos to order. The budget pressure that delayed the rise of the department to full force dealt a blow to a key element of the program, but other aspects proceeded despite ongoing money woes. The department launched a pilot plan for single-officer patrol cars and redeployed civilians. It launched Operation All Out to reduce the number of cops locked in headquarters and sent them into the streets. In the months and years that followed, the operation added a quarter of a million tours of foot patrol duty. Implementation of the community-policing strategy caused the number of officers assigned to neighborhood beats to rise fourfold.[5]

A public relations campaign responded to people's need to know that the city had launched a program to restore safety. Posters appeared around the city of an elderly couple walking on a city street with the reassuring figure of a policeman in full view atop a caption that read: "The beat cop is back." When analysts tabulated year-end 1991 figures, they announced crime fell in every major category for the first time in thirty-six years—albeit modestly. During the first three months of 1992, the pattern continued. Chief Bratton's efforts in the subways also began to take hold. Major crime under New York's streets declined 15 percent in 1991 to the lowest it had been in four years.[6]

The mayor should have benefited from the positive momentum building behind anticrime initiatives, but he continued to adopt positions that undermined his law-and-order credentials. The NYPD launched a controlled pilot program with police supervisors to determine the impact of issuing semiautomatic weapons. The state legislature deemed the program inadequate and threatened legislation—supported by the Patrolman's Benevolent Association— to require the city to issue the more powerful pistols to all cops. Commissioner Brown and senior NYPD officials feared the impact the greater firepower could have in New York's concrete canyons. At their urging, the mayor opposed the measure loudly, just as he had when the transit police sought a weapons upgrade. Dinkins deeply resented the legislature's interference in management of the city's affairs, yet he found he had to compromise and expand the experiment by one thousand more weapons to beat back the push by lawmakers. So for a second time on the issue of new police firearms, the mayor looked like a soft-on-crime political weakling. His posture did nothing to improve his standing with the rank and file on the police force.[7]

From the first of the year through March 15, 1992, New York registered 149 bias incidents. The figure represented a dramatic increase from 68 during the same period the prior year, despite accelerating declines in most other categories of serious crime. Gay bashing was on the rise, and racial and ethnic tension kept the city on edge. Then, on Wednesday, April 29, 1992, a jury acquitted the white police officers videotaped beating Rodney King. A stunned nation gasped as Los Angeles erupted in riots, which African Americans in some other cities joined in sympathetic outrage. In Harlem, Councilman Adam Clayton Powell, IV, captured the fury of his constituents. "It makes you hate this country," he told a reporter. "It makes you hate the flag. It makes you hate cops. It makes you hate all white people who can even think to begin to excuse this verdict." Thursday night, riots erupted in other cities, and a soft blanket of fear fell on New York. Friday, unfounded or grossly exaggerated rumors of race-related attacks began to spread. That afternoon, shops spontaneously closed. Without a word spoken, Wall Street bankers evacuated the financial district.[8]

Dinkins reacted to the dangerous verdict with unaccustomed speed and effectiveness. As soon as he learned of it, he reached to community leaders across the city to encourage peaceful marches and protests. He put the police on alert and publicly condemned the decision while declaring violence off-limits. He walked the streets of Harlem, thanking people for controlling their anger. He made common cause with blacks, bitter about the injustice inflicted on one of their own, a transcontinental reminder of the type of humiliation any African American could suffer at any time. The heat of the anger caused the City of Angels to burn and riots ignited in several other urban areas—San Francisco, Seattle, Atlanta, and Las Vegas. In New York, David Dinkins kept the peace. "Dave, Take a Bow," read the front page of the May 4, 1992, *New York Post*.[9]

A few weeks after the riots that never happened, the mayor traveled to Queens, where people treated him like a conquering hero. Sometime before, his team had initiated a series of local City Hall events during which the mayor would conduct his business from one of the boroughs outside Manhattan for five days. They were part of the administration's effort to take the mayor's message directly to the people and a symbolic statement of his commitment to represent all New Yorkers. "I expected big trouble after the King verdict," one resident, washing a large plate glass store window, told a reporter. "This window could be gone. This *store* could be gone. I give him credit," the man said of the mayor. The week coincided with the announcement of an unexpected budget surplus, play-off victories by the Rangers and the Knicks, sunshine, and blossoming trees.[10]

Realtor Donald Zucker described a change in the city's mood toward Dinkins. "We voted for David because we thought he could ease racial tensions. He has; we're appreciative. But the economy fell off a cliff. That wasn't his fault, but he wasn't *handling* it. People wrote him off, but now he's pulling it back together. His budget looks good. Crime is down. Real estate taxes have been frozen. He hit his stride." Morale among his staff reflected the change. "There's a sense of having been underwater for two years, and now finally coming up and getting a gasp of air. It's nice not to be drowning for a change," one aide said. A little while later another reporter took up the same theme. "Political Memo: Dinkins Is Mastering the Art of the Mayor," a *New York Times* headline read. "I think we're beginning to find ourselves," a senior aide said. "When John Lindsay came in, people said, 'These people can't even find the lights.' I think we're beginning to find the light switches, and things are working a lot better."[11]

A more cynical political insider reacted differently. "The good news is just a blip. A happy little blip that will soon be forgotten." The mayor himself feared as much. "You're on a roll, aren't you?" a reporter said to him. "It'll end," Mayor Dinkins replied with an old pol's sage smile the reporter wrote. The comment proved prescient.[12]

On Friday, July 3, 1992, in the lobby of 505 West 162nd Street, in the heavily Dominican neighborhood of Washington Heights, Officer Michael O'Keefe and two plainclothes partners sought to arrest a suspected drug dealer thought to be carrying a gun. The target, a Dominican named Jose Garcia, known to friends as Kiko, resisted. In the struggle that followed, O'Keefe shot and killed him. Two women who claimed to witness the event reported the police beat Garcia senseless and that, while he lay helpless on the ground, pleading for his life, O'Keefe shot him in cold blood.[13]

The next day, reporters found the words, "Kiko, we love you," written in the dead man's blood on the wall near where he died. Neighbors described him as a decent man. Rumors circulated that O'Keefe was a dirty cop, and the killing an assassination by a policeman dealing drugs in the neighborhood he had sworn to protect. The charge had currency because the local precinct, the 34th, had come under federal investigation for providing drug dealers in the community with protection in return for bribes. The story caused sporadic protests to break out on Saturday, with local residents lighting trash cans and a car on fire and throwing debris into the streets in demonstrations of disgust. Police responded by closing off the street where the dead man lived, and sanitation trucks cleared away the burning refuse.[14]

Monday, simmering tensions continued to boil. Anticipating trouble, Dinkins sought to contain potential violence by visiting Garcia's family and assuring them a full investigation would take place. Family members expressed appreciation for the mayor's sympathy and concern. Newspapers published photos of the mayor consoling them.[15]

A demonstration organized by Councilman Guillermo Linares, the city's first Dominican elected official, began peacefully later that evening outside the building where the shooting occurred. Then the crowd marched to West 181st Street and approached the 34th Precinct, O'Keefe's assigned station. There, sixty officers in riot gear confronted the crowd. Spanish chants of "killer cop" and demands for justice punctuated the night. Things turned ugly. Someone hurled a powerful M-80 firecracker at the police, and then a bottle. Pockets of protesters—bands of fifty to one hundred people—threw garbage cans into the street, overturned dumpsters, smashed car windows, and set other cars on fire. A police helicopter hovered overhead, shining a spotlight on the mob until someone fired a shot at it and hit it, forcing the helicopter to retreat. A man who hurled a bottle at cops fled across a rooftop on 172nd Street and fell five stories to his death when the officers gave chase. The chaos engulfed some forty square blocks. Four police reported injuries, none serious, and eleven arrests occurred on charges ranging from arson to disorderly conduct. Reports surfaced later that drug dealers provoked some of the violence, seeking to use the emotions hovering on the streets where they plied their illegal trade to turn the people against the police. The outbreak deflated the prestige the mayor won just weeks earlier when he led the city's response to the Los Angeles riots. It occurred the week before the Democratic National Convention would come to town, raising the stakes of the disruption.[16]

The mayor urged calm the next day over Spanish television and English, and he returned to the neighborhood to address local residents personally. Cardinal O'Connor joined him, assuring people that the Catholic Church—an institution with more credibility than government in the neighborhood—would insist on a full and fair investigation of the shooting. Having learned the lessons of Crown Heights, police responded with sufficient force and discipline to prevent the violence from spreading, while local elected officials and community-outreach experts initiated contacts between protesters and police. Dinkins invited Garcia's relatives to meet with him at Gracie Mansion, and he arranged for the city to pay to transport Garcia's body to the Dominican Republic for burial. He walked the streets with local officials, Dominican celebrities, Commissioner Brown, and others, promising justice and calling for calm. Latino leaders gave him high marks for his handling of the crisis.[17]

Yet the investigation into the killing revealed something very different than what many imagined. Garcia had indeed been armed with a loaded thirty-eight-caliber revolver. Investigators confirmed his association with a drug gang and that he often carried a concealed weapon. Testimony of the witnesses who reported the incident as a police-sponsored murder did not stand up to scrutiny. Forensic experts determined it unlikely the accusers could have seen what they reported from where they said they stood when it happened. Pathologists who examined the body refuted the charge the man had been beaten, and they found cocaine in his system at the time of his death. For the police rank and file, Dinkins's behavior smacked of betrayal. He had offered comfort and condolences to the armed drug dealer's relatives at a time when a courageous officer who put his life on the line stood falsely accused of vicious crimes.[18]

I. A Police Department at War with the Mayor

The Washington Heights riot coincided with rising tension between the mayor and the department he relied on to protect the city. Distant rumblings of an insidious wave of corruption in the NYPD, first heard several months earlier, had become a steady beat. Rampant drug dealing and the battle to contain it had put more cops in greater contact with huge amounts of money than ever before. A half-dozen years earlier John Guido, who oversaw the division responsible for investigating police corruption from 1972 to 1986, retired. Feared and hated by dishonest cops, Guido helped keep the department honest. When he left, the office he ran lost stature, power, and institutional memory. On May 7, 1992, Suffolk County detectives arrested five New York City police officers and dozens of others across Long Island for running a cocaine ring. The cops were all thirty or younger. The episode, disturbing enough on its own merits, suggested the torch of corruption had been passed to a new generation.[19]

As supervisors reviewed wire-tap transcripts, it became apparent the dishonest officers had developed routines to avoid detection. The department's internal procedures to prevent corruption seemed wanting. Questions had emerged about the cops involved, particularly one, Officer Michael Dowd. Yet, despite serious suspicions, the NYPD had not managed to make a case against him until Suffolk police busted his gang. Commissioner Brown asked Robert J. Beatty, chief of Inspectional Services, which included the internal affairs division responsible for investigating allegations of police misconduct, to assess what went wrong. Then on June 15, 1992, the *New York Post* reported that over a period of four years during which an internal affairs field unit sergeant suspected Dowd of crimes, senior police officials refused to allocate the resources necessary to pursue a serious investigation. The reason seemed to be that such a scandal in a captain or commander's jurisdiction hurt careers. Brown, uncomfortable leaving the investigation in the hands of the division now accused of conscious neglect, asked First Deputy Kelly to lead a second, independent review.[20]

Before long the United States attorney for the Southern District of New York launched a federal probe of the department. The arrest of the Brooklyn drug gang had caused a number of police officers to acknowledge a widespread problem. Honest cops still found themselves surrounded by a culture that discouraged reporting the misdeeds of another officer—even serious ones. Credible reports of cops taking bribes to ignore drug trafficking and acting as guardians for dealers made their way to the prosecutor's office. In one case, informants alleged a group of officers cordoned off a block that served as a hub of illegal activity to prevent other officers from combating the dealers. Another report suggested that the same Michael Dowd arrested in Brooklyn had been hired by a gang in the 34th Precinct to protect them. "If they are looking for other Dowds," an officer in the 34th Precinct told a journalist, "then they have come to the right place." The cop insisted on anonymity.[21]

The mayor determined he could not let the police department investigate itself. He appointed a five-member independent panel chaired by Milton Mollen to investigate police corruption. Mollen had retired from the administration a few months earlier, at the age of seventy-two, but the former deputy felt he could not turn down the mayor's request. He agreed to lead the highest-powered look at NYPD corruption since the Knapp Commission twenty years earlier. "To me it's crystal clear," Dinkins said. "It is absolutely essential that the people have confidence in the Police Department. I believe they will not have that confidence unless there is this kind of independent inquiry." The mayor named his one-time law partner and New York

State Court of Appeals Judge, Fritz Alexander, his new deputy mayor for public safety.[22]

At the same time that he created the Mollen Commission, Dinkins renewed his support for an all-civilian complaint review board to replace the police-dominated structure that investigated accusations of abuse. This long-standing controversial idea had divided the city for decades. In May 1966, Mayor John Lindsay had signed an executive order creating a civilian review board. The decision infuriated the police. They perceived it as an implicit indictment of their integrity. They feared a witch hunt and resented the outside control. The president of the Patrolmen's Benevolent Association announced that the city's police officers did not accept the mayor's decision and launched a campaign to place a referendum on the ballot that would allow the citizens of New York to decide if they wanted the board or not.[23]

Two of every three New Yorkers voted to abolish the board, leaving Mayor Lindsay's prestige badly damaged. Blacks and Puerto Ricans overwhelmingly favored the civilian review board, and Catholics of every European descent opposed it vigorously. There was slight softening of Catholic opposition among wealthier, better-educated members of the faith, but nearly 90 percent of all Irish and Italian Catholics and more than 80 percent of non-Hispanic Catholics of other heritages rejected the board. The pattern among Jewish New Yorkers was more nuanced. Working-class Jews at the lower end of the economic and educational spectrum, many of whom lived in neighborhoods that bordered black ghettos, voted against the board in large numbers. Upper-income, well-educated Jewish professionals who lived in the city's safest neighborhoods voted fairly strongly in favor of the plan. The daily threat of crime and violence was more distant to them. The outcome reaffirmed that, as a group, Jews were more liberal than the city's Catholic voters. It also revealed limits to Jewish liberalism. Strong support for civil rights did not overpower a desire to live in safety.[24]

A quarter of a century later, little had changed but the demographics of the city. Proponents of law and order continued to see a civilian board as an unnecessary means of second-guessing the cops who had to deal with dangerous criminals on the street. Critics feared naïve citizens who lacked investigative training and who had little experience with the real stresses police face would punish officers for using the level of force sometimes required to be effective. Supporters of a civilian board perceived it as a necessary check on a powerful paramilitary organization whose culture prevented effective self-discipline.

The racial divide the issue created persisted. African Americans and Latinos tended to support the idea while whites tended to oppose it. People of color had an easier time imagining themselves the victims of police abuse. Whites feared the cops less than they feared the consequences of making it harder for the police to enforce the law.

Dinkins's two initiatives—the commission to investigate police corruption and a renewed push for a civilian review board—put the mayor and his police commissioner at odds. Brown saw the moves as mayoral meddling in his department's affairs, an expression of lack of confidence in him and the NYPD and damaging to morale. When the mayor announced his positions, Brown did not join him and declared he would lobby against the civilian review board proposal at the city council. "In his 36 years of policing, he has never seen an external board that works," his spokesperson told the press. Just over a month later, Brown resigned. His wife, Yvonne, had cancer and wanted to return to Houston for treatment near her family. "My priorities are quite clear," the commissioner said. "My family comes first." Yvonne Brown's life ended before the year did. The mayor appointed Ray Kelly acting commissioner and praised Brown's work. So did Philip Caruso, head of the Patrolmen's Benevolent Association (PBA). Caruso had less kind things to say about the mayor and his recent decisions.[25]

Seeking to channel patrolman anger at Dinkins into opposition for the civilian review board, Caruso organized a protest at City Hall on September 16, 1992. Ten thousand angry cops showed up, some wearing T-shirts saying, "Dinkins Must Go!" Others carried signs that said, "Dear Mayor, have you hugged a drug dealer today?" When First Deputy Mayor Steisel caught sight of a sign that referred to the often-tuxedo-clad black mayor as a "washroom attendant," he knew things would get bad. Una Clarke, an African American politician, sought to enter the building the cops had blockaded. An off-duty policeman standing in her path turned to another and said, "[T]his nigger says she's a council member," before letting her pass.[26]

Rudolph Giuliani, gearing up to challenge Dinkins for the mayor's office in 1993, joined the protest. From the podium, he described the mayor's policies as "bullshit" and he led the crowd in anti-Dinkins chants. Caruso and Officer Michael O'Keefe also delivered impassioned criticisms of the mayor. After their leaders finished their vulgar speeches, the men and women responsible for maintaining public order responded like the mobs the city normally expected them to control. They swarmed over barricades, surrounded City Hall, stopped traffic

on the Brooklyn Bridge for nearly an hour, roughed up several reporters, and trampled automobiles while their on-duty colleagues stood
by. Some hurled racial insults at the mayor's office. "He never supports
us on anything," Officer Tara Fanning of the Midtown South Precinct
told a reporter, summing up the crowd's anger with the mayor. "A cop
shoots someone with a gun who's a drug dealer and [Dinkins] goes
and visits the family," she said with obvious disgust.[27]

Furious at the off-duty officers' behavior, Dinkins denounced the
event as hooliganism and held Caruso responsible. He accused Giuliani
of crass opportunism, seizing "upon a fragile circumstance in our city
for his own political gain." Acting commissioner Kelly oversaw a swift
investigation. Within a week, he ordered forty-two officers disciplined
and issued a thirteen-page interim report that condemned the actions
as "unruly, mean-spirited and perhaps criminal." Reports that racial
epithets punctuated the near riot led him to declare that such language
would be grounds for immediate dismissal. Ironically, a year earlier,
Commissioner Brown had circulated a "Message from the Police
Commissioner" to the department that began: "Police Officers' use of
ethnic slurs or other abusive language demeans our profession, and
undermines the public's confidence in our ability to do an increasingly
difficult job." At the time no one would have imagined such slurs would
be directed toward the mayor.[28]

Kelly declared the behavior of the protesters "an embarrassment to
a department widely respected for its professionalism." He acknowledged that "[p]ublic confidence in the Department has been shaken"
and would need to be restored. Not long afterward, Dinkins officially
appointed Kelly to the commissioner's post. Before the year ended,
the mayor and the city council created a thirteen-member all-civilian
review board, with many council members citing the ugly demonstration as the turning point that solidified their support. The mayor won
a political victory, but it came at a cost. "The thing that every mayor
tries to avoid is exactly what Dinkins has," urban historian Richard
Wade noted. The city's chief executive and the city's police department were at war.[29]

The mayor had no illusions about the depth of deterioration in his
relationship with the NYPD. A few weeks after the offensive protests,
he called every precinct commander in the city to Gracie Mansion
on a Saturday morning "[b]ecause it is important . . . after all that has
happened in the last few weeks that we . . . meet. We need to talk. . . .
We need to get things back on track. And we need to start right away."[30]

He praised the senior police professionals for their work that had helped cause crime to drop "across the board for the first time since nineteen fifty six, and for all but one month in the past two years." Together, he said, they had "at least captured the upper hand against the forces of social disintegration," a proud achievement. He went on to say that he envisioned "a New York where police officers are held in more respect than they have ever, ever been." Accomplishing that goal in "an era in which African Americans and Latinos—people of color, long commonly thought of as 'minorities'—have become the majority . . . with a police department whose demographics are more like the demographics of this city thirty or forty years ago," presented special challenges, he told the group. And "as the first African American Mayor of New York," Dinkins believed he was "in a unique position to understand why there has sometimes been alienation between cops and the communities they serve." He thought that put him in a unique position to help achieve the objective of a police department respected and welcomed in every neighborhood.[31]

Then he got to the heart of the matter. "I accept the fact that most officers do not agree with the way I handled the situation in Washington Heights last July," he said. And "I accept that, when a crowd of thousands of police officers gathered outside City Hall on September sixteenth, they had a perfect right to be there—and a constitutional right to express their views. Actually, I had a pretty good idea of what those views were before September sixteenth, but never mind." Yet he asserted the officers "who engaged in . . . illegal and unacceptable conduct . . . were an embarrassment to this city, [and] to the shield." He asked the commanders to recognize "[t]hat whatever I have done, I have done in what I honestly believe was the long-term interest of promoting and securing . . . respect and admiration" for each member of the department. He also asked them to recognize that his own respect and admiration for the police was genuine and that they take that message down through the ranks. The mayor also met with all of the police department's chaplains and rabbis. "[T]o continue the sound and the fury of the past few weeks will accomplish nothing," he told the people responsible for the spiritual well-being of the city's police officers. With the help of God, the mayor hoped all would find a way to put the bitter moment behind and move on.[32]

II. Religion and Race Redux

Within days of the disgraceful police action, Lemrick Nelson's trial for the murder of Yankel Rosenbaum began. Prosecutors presented their opening statement to a courtroom packed with Hasidic Jews and the defendant's family and friends. They accused the teenager of killing the Australian scholar "in the frenzy of the moment," while the mob screamed, "Kill the Jew!" Police had arrested him nearby shortly after the attack and found a knife in his pocket with Rosenbaum's blood on it. Before an ambulance took him to the hospital, Rosenbaum had identified Nelson as the one who stabbed him. The lawyer of the accused teenager countered that the arresting officers framed his client to distract attention from the "police riot" that the NYPD launched against Crown Heights residents. He also insisted Rosenbaum would have lived except for medical negligence at Kings County Hospital.[33]

The case appeared open-and-shut when it started. But the prosecution's story contained contradictions. Confusion emerged surrounding details of Rosenbaum's identification of Nelson when police brought him back to the scene of the stabbing. Sloppy treatment of evidence damaged the credibility of key witnesses. In the end, inconsistencies in police testimony deftly managed by Nelson's attorney led the jurors to acquit the accused murderer on all charges. "The police were not honest," one juror told a reporter. And in an act of supreme insensitivity and poor judgment, the day after the trial ended, the jurors joined Nelson and his attorney for a dinner to celebrate their shared experience.[34]

The Hasidim and many other New Yorkers reacted with stunned disbelief and outrage. Jews gathered outside Lubavitch headquarters on Eastern Parkway shortly before 9:00 p.m. on the evening of the verdict, where some speakers talked of revenge. Isolated incidents of bottle throwing, shoving, and fights between Hasidim and blacks occurred. Heavy police presence in fully equipped riot gear and a general lack of violent intent kept the situation from spiraling out of control. Yet the verdict left many with a dispiriting sense that the racially divided city they lived in could not deliver justice. Outside the courthouse, after Nelson's acquittal, Hasidim adopted the battle cry of black militants, chanting, "No justice, no peace!" In the circumstances, it seemed less like a defiant call to action than an objective observation about life in New York.[35]

The next day Dinkins announced the reassignment of fifty detectives to the Rosenbaum investigation, and the city offered a $10,000 reward for the capture of Rosenbaum's killer. The act had a surreal quality. At face value, the jury's decision meant they did not believe Nelson committed the murder, so launching a renewed investigation to search for the murderer seemed necessary. Except in the minds of many Lemrick Nelson was indeed guilty, and he could not be tried on the same charges again. So an elaborate, renewed investigation appeared a cynical charade. Dinkins provoked more anger when he refused to condemn the Lemrick verdict as he had when a jury acquitted the Los Angeles police who beat Rodney King. Saying the videotape in the King case created a difference as clear as "night and day," Dinkins dismissed the critics of his seemingly contradictory positions. Governor Cuomo launched a special inquiry to determine what happened, and so did Commissioner Kelly.[36]

None of the official actions lessened the outrage among Jews in Crown Heights and elsewhere around New York. "It was not just Yankel," the murder victim's brother, Norman, told a crowd of protestors who gathered at Lubavitch headquarters. "What we had in this neighborhood was a pogrom." Jewish leaders denounced the verdict, and with reinvigorated, vicious emotion, many once again condemned David Dinkins's handling of the Crown Heights riots. The charge that he had deliberately prevented the police from responding more forcefully in the first days of rioting recurred persistently. Riverdale rabbi Avi Weiss organized a demonstration in front of Gracie Mansion. "If New York's finest were allowed to do their job," he declared with bombast, "Yankel Rosenbaum would be alive today." The protesters he led brought with them a coffin, a symbolic reminder of Rosenbaum's death. Some, including Weiss, carried posters that read, "Wanted for Murder," under a photograph of the mayor. Weiss would later regret hoisting the sign. Yet it revealed the emotions the dubious verdict unleashed.[37]

Dinkins felt compelled to confront the accusation that he held back the police. He spoke to 125 rabbis at Jewish Theological Seminary a few weeks after the Lemrick Nelson verdict. With Rabbi Weiss seated prominently in the front row of the audience, Dinkins talked of "the lynching" of Yankel Rosenbaum and all that had followed. "Some people look at this large and very complicated picture and see only two things: the Mayor is African American and the rioters are African American and they conclude that therefore, the Mayor must have held the police back. But," he continued, "there is not a single shred of evidence that I held the N.Y.P.D. back and there never will be.

And every time this utterly false charge is repeated, the social fabric of our city tears just a little bit more." Reminding his audience of his lifelong opposition to anti-Semitism, he told them, "I know that all decent, fair-minded New Yorkers share my sorrow, and my desire to bring to justice the bigots who committed this unspeakable crime. At the same time, I note with shame that some people no longer even seem interested in finding Yankel Rosenbaum's killers—they are more interested in my political scalp."[38]

The Nelson acquittal coincided with a troubling rise in anti-Semitic episodes around the city. The police registered nineteen criminal acts against Jews during the high holidays in 1992. "The quality of the attacks has clearly changed," New York City human rights commissioner Dennis de Leon, noted. "In the past, there were more anti-Semitic incidents of property damage than any other kind. Now there seem to be more one-on-one personal assaults." The American Jewish Committee polled New Yorkers and made the disquieting discovery that nearly half believed Jews had too much power and influence in the life and politics of the city. Two-thirds of Latinos and nearly as high a percentage of blacks supported the view. Well over one-third of Jews declared anti-Semitism a major problem, and nearly 60 percent said the problem had gotten worse during the past year. "There is a sense among Jews that they are no longer welcome in the city," city councilman Herbert Berman declared. "What frightens me is I don't think City Hall understands. The mayor's inability to make people feel he is truly sensitive to these issues has exacerbated the issue."[39]

Two weeks after his address at Jewish Theological Seminary, the day before Thanksgiving, the mayor addressed the entire city on the topic of Lemrick Nelson's acquittal and the broader issues Crown Heights had come to symbolize. Most stations carried the sixteen-minute speech live. "In the past weeks our nightly news shows and morning newspapers have been filled with charges and countercharges.... A few members of the clergy have forsaken the prayer book for the press release.... Round and round the spinning wheel of accusation goes and where it stops nobody knows," Dinkins began, obviously fed up. He recounted the events that had taken place in Crown Heights the prior August and in highly personal terms his meetings with the Cato family and with Yankel Rosenbaum before his death. "Yankel Rosenbaum, here in New York to study the Holocaust, was stabbed for one reason and one reason only—because he was a Jew," Dinkins said, making sure all knew that he had not missed that essential point.[40]

"By their own accounts . . . the Police Department did make tactical errors in judgment and deployment of police officers in the early hours of the disturbance which may have delayed a return to normalcy. I know and accept that when a mistake is made that it is the Mayor who is called to account," Dinkins told the city. But he called the claims that he had instructed the police to temper their response "false, reprehensible and despicable." And he could not, he declared, "allow a quiet riot of words and epithets to poison our citizenry."[41]

"Race baiters and rabble-rousers do not understand our lives," the mayor said to the citizens who elected him. "Because every day and every night, on subways and buses, at work stations and in offices, at lunch counters and in libraries, in our parks, and in our movie houses, New Yorkers live and work and learn and play, side by side and shoulder to shoulder. . . . I was elected to be the Mayor of all our people. And I am Mayor of all our people," he declared. His comments refuted any suggestion that the city he led could not live in harmony and any notion that he favored one group over others. Of the posters bearing his picture that said "Wanted for Murder," the deeply offended mayor asked the city, "In burying a seven year old boy and a quiet bible scholar, did we bury decency too?"[42]

Over the next several months, the mayor "tried to talk the problem away, appearing before countless Jewish groups, but no matter how good his intentions, the strategy wasn't working," Craig Horowitz wrote in *New York* magazine in an article headlined, "The New Anti-Semitism." One rabbi pointed out the obvious. "Mayor Dinkins knows he's very, very vulnerable politically," he said. "[A]nd he's gonna become more vulnerable as time goes on," the man surmised. The mayor met with Crown Heights leaders of every persuasion, searching for ways the city could restore the community's confidence in government. As a matter of decency and responsibility, he wanted to. As a political matter, he had to. *New York Times* reporter Todd Purdum, in an article headlined, "Crown Hts. Drives Contest for Mayor," summed up the situation. "The scalding racial tensions of Crown Heights have unfolded against the backdrop of next year's New York city mayoral race, and while none of the three announced candidates would put it this way, all are trying to turn the undercurrents of anger and recrimination to their political advantage."[43]

Yankel Rosenbaum's ghost haunted David Dinkins and New York for years. The dead scholar's brother, Norman, refused to let his sibling's death pass into history without justice. He had attended Lemrick

Nelson's state trial every day, and when that jury acquitted he sought federal prosecution on civil rights charges. With strong pressure from senators Alfonse D'Amato, Daniel Moynihan, and others, a reluctant Justice Department indicted Lemrick Nelson shortly before the statute of limitations expired. It brought him to trial in 1997, along with Charles Price, a drug addict and petty criminal accused of helping incite the riot that raged around the stabbing. A federal jury convicted both men, and the judge in the case sentenced Nelson to the maximum penalty of nineteen-and-a-half years.[44]

Still the matter did not rest. After a lengthy appeal, in 2002 a federal court ruled the judge in the first civil rights case mishandled jury selection and ordered a new trial. By the time it took place, the Rosenbaums had filed a civil suit against Kings County Hospital in Brooklyn where Yankel had been treated for his stab wounds. A New York State Health Department report found the hospital negligent and determined that with proper care Yankel Rosenbaum would have lived. On the basis of that information, Nelson's lawyers adopted a new strategy. Now the man confessed to the stabbing but claimed he had not intended to kill Rosenbaum. He also denied that he had attacked him because he was Jewish or to prevent him from using a public street, the accusations that justified the federal civil rights action. The jury convicted anew, but on charges with a maximum penalty of ten years, which Nelson had virtually served by then. On June 2, 2004, Lemrick Nelson left his federal prison in Beaumont, Texas, for a halfway house in New Jersey. In 2005, fourteen years after Yankel's death, the Rosenbaum family finally settled the hospital suit for $1,250,000.[45]

Along the way Dinkins's successor, Rudolph Giuliani, settled a civil suit on the matter. New York City paid eighty Crown Heights residents and institutions and the Rosenbaum family a total of $1,100,000. Announcing the settlement, Giuliani apologized "to the citizens of Crown Heights, to the Rosenbaum family and to all of the people that were affected by [what was] probably one of the saddest chapters in the history of the city." The decision and statement infuriated Dinkins and former police commissioner Lee Brown. "It is obvious to any fair-minded person that within the first few hours of the rioting when he was stabbed, no police action, no matter who the Mayor was, could have protected [Yankel Rosenbaum]," Dinkins told a reporter. Holding him responsible for the tragic death, in Dinkins view, meant every mayor was to blame for "everybody who has been mugged or shot or stabbed" during their term. And the city also settled a civil suit with the family of Gavin Cato for $400,000 in response to claims the city's emergency medical service delayed treating the young boy after the tragic accident.[46]

III. Kelly Takes Command

While the mayor dealt with the racial politics of the city, Ray Kelly dealt with the racial politics of the department he now ran. The rude racial slurs directed toward the mayor by white police officers during the riot at City Hall and the image of a white police force battling African Americans in Crown Heights had raised the sensitivity of the city and its police commissioner to the need to recruit more African American cops. A survey of the nation's fifty largest cities ranked New York worst in terms of the racial alignment of its police department and its people despite the fact that its last two commissioners had been African Americans.[47]

A department veteran of nearly three decades by the time Dinkins named him commissioner, Kelly, with his Irish Catholic heritage, reflected the organization's ethnic past. Over the years he had worked inside six precinct houses across three boroughs and had developed a knowledge of the department's affairs few could match. In his first six months on the job, he worked seven days a week, often ten to fourteen hours a day, sending an unmistakable message that he was in command. Kelly's background, experience, and drive gave him strong credibility with the rank and file and the PBA, something the mayor desperately needed in his new commissioner. As he pursued meaningful change, none could claim Kelly did not understand how the policies he promoted affected cops on the street or the sensitivities of the department's overwhelmingly white, working-class officers.[48]

The man's very strengths made him suspect to African American and Latino leaders. Abyssinian Baptist Church leader Calvin Butts, III, suggested that had Kelly been younger he would have been one of the cops protesting at City Hall. Kelly understood the problem. "I knew I'd better hit the ground running because I bring so much baggage into this job," he acknowledged. "I'm stuck with this face"—the chiseled look of the marine he was, set in unmistakably Irish features. "I'm a cop for 29 years—part of this system, but I think that's my strength. I'm reaching out—it's the Nixon-to-China approach," he said. Even as acting commissioner, he had taken to visiting black churches on Sundays and meeting with prominent African Americans and Latinos to hear their concerns. The need to add more of their own to the police force featured prominently in these talks, which in turn required a review of the department's selection process. In particular, African Americans did poorly when faced with psychological screening. Tests that identified normal behavior for white working-class candidates miscategorized responses offered by blacks who grew up in tough inner-city neighborhoods where distrust of the police was common. The mismatch sometimes eliminated as many as nine black applicants out of ten who passed the written exam.[49]

In a bold move shortly after his appointment, Kelly postponed the next round of cadet recruiting to allow for a comprehensive review of the hiring process. He intended to eliminate the cultural biases that froze in time the ethnic makeup of the force. Unlike the two African American commissioners who preceded him, because he was white, he could pursue an aggressive policy for hiring blacks without fearing accusations of favoritism. His first official day on the job, Kelly declared recruiting more black officers his "most vital" priority. He promised an "all out" marketing plan to overcome the reluctance of many young African Americans and Latinos to apply to the NYPD since they grew up distrusting cops. Without more black and Latino representation on the force, Kelly feared "increased tension between the communities and the police. Tension leads to hostilities and that will lead to more cries of racism in the department," a charge Kelly claimed not to believe, but one he knew needed to be defused.[50]

True to his word, Kelly expanded the outreach drive. Instead of 16 recruiters, he put to work 109, 86 of them black or Latino. He visited dozens of black churches to get out the word. His sales pitch was simple and direct. "Our department does not now reflect the community it serves," he told parishioners. "To put it bluntly, it is disproportionately white. We have to change the composition of our department, and that's why I'm here. That's why I'm turning to you for help," he would say. "We need the kind of talent that is right here in this community, the kind of talent that is too often overlooked." The pool of African Americans signing up for the exam ballooned to over 14,000 from just 1,800, and more than 13,000 Latinos applied as well. Kelly also secured approval to award city residents a five-point bonus on the qualifying exam, which improved the chances for city-bound people of color over suburban whites. The policy had the added advantage of increasing the number of officers who actually lived in the city that employed them and that relied on them for protection.[51]

Within six months, Kelly had reversed his reputation among black and Latino critics. Calvin Butts declared he had changed his mind about the man. "I was against Kelly from the start," Reverend Charles Mixon of the Baptist Ministers' Fellowship in Queens confessed. "I told the mayor I did not think this man could deal with the situation of African Americans. But he came out to see us, sat in our churches, made it clear he was trying to make a difference. I've changed my mind about him. A lot of people have," he concluded of Kelly.[52]

On corruption, Kelly struggled. He knew he had to act to maintain public confidence, yet he feared the impact on morale of holding his senior officers accountable for illegal police activity when the culture they lived in made it all but impossible for them to punish corrupt cops and continue to function in the department. Cops "ratting" on other cops remained for most a forbidden act, a violation of the code imposed by the "blue wall of silence."[53]

In November 1992 Kelly released a 160-page report prepared under his direct supervision: *An Investigation into the Police Department's Conduct of the Dowd Case and an Assessment of the Police Department's Internal Investigation Capabilities.* It described an internal affairs division that had become a "bunglers bureaucracy of inexperienced, poorly trained detectives using inferior equipment and ineffective techniques, and closing out cases with sloppy, misleading reports." It took seventy pages to document twenty separate internal affairs investigations of Michael Dowd over the years. Offenses ranged from harassing his girlfriend to sex with prostitutes at a Brooklyn bar. He had been accused of drinking alcohol on duty and of smoking marijuana. Reports said he stole money from prisoners, drug dealers, and corpses. Fellow officers said he trafficked in narcotics and protected kingpins in return for bribes of thousands of dollars a week. They said he had reported a stab wound received when a drug transaction went bad as an injury in the line of duty, and on and on. Yet until Suffolk County detectives busted Dowd, he faced no serious charges. The NYPD disciplined him three times for departmental infractions, never for crimes.[54]

Kelly claimed to find no evidence that senior department officials interfered with any investigation of Dowd, and he punished no one. His report did not contemplate the possibility that the department's investigations did not catch the brazenly dishonest and decadent cop once in twenty tries because officials who feared their careers would suffer saw to it he never got caught in their command. "There's no heroes in this report," but "I don't think it's clear who is accountable here," Kelly said. In his mind, the episode revealed a "systems problem." He did not believe it would "do much good to take out somebody who was in the middle of the system.... In order to have accountability, you have to have a reasonable shot at being aware of what happened." He believed the "overlapping responsibility and bifurcated authority" that had developed between the internal affairs division and the field units made it too hard for commanders to exercise real control over investigations. Singling out a handful of senior cops for "ritual blood-letting" struck Kelly as arbitrary and ultimately damaging. "Negative discipline only works so far; you need loyalty and trust" to make the police department work seven days a week and twenty-four hours a day, Kelly told a reporter. Cleaning up dirty precincts, Kelly had learned that punishing supervisors for corruption that occurred on their watch created a dysfunctional response. It motivated otherwise good cops to look the other way, to deny incidents rather than confront them. So his message seemed to be stricter discipline in the future, but no accountability for the past—a pragmatic cop out.[55]

Not everyone found Kelly's logic convincing. "It's easy to find culprits just by reading Kelly's report," one said. "It wasn't just that the system stank. Some people inside the system did too." Kelly knew his position risked damaging his personal credibility, but he made his decision and moved on. He elevated the internal affairs division to full bureau status, equal in standing to the department's patrol forces and detectives. It would report directly to the commissioner, and it would receive more resources and better surveillance equipment. It would operate with a more tightly controlled central unit to improve its effectiveness. Kelly, as commissioner, made a point of meeting with the head of internal affairs every day. Before the year ended, he named John S. Pritchard, III, his first deputy. A former NYPD detective and FBI agent, Pritchard had been the inspector general at the MTA, where he earned a reputation as an aggressive corruption fighter. His appointment reinforced the message that Kelly would root out bad cops going forward, even if he declined to punish senior commanders for past transgressions. And since Pritchard was African American, his presence in so high profile a position furthered Kelly's goal of creating a department that could attract more black cops as well.[56]

A year later, the Mollen Commission would issue a twenty-page interim report on its investigation into police corruption. It would deliver its final report in July 1994. It concluded no individuals could be held accountable for the extent of corruption in the NYPD. Yet it accused the department in stinging language of fostering a culture that tolerated even gross and violent misconduct by police officers. It did not find the type of wide-scale graft the Knapp Commission had found permeated the department in the 1970s. Instead it asserted that small gangs of rogue cops thrived because senior officials feared their careers would suffer if they exposed the misdeeds in their units and because officers themselves feared the social and personal consequences of reporting their peers' illegal activities. "We find . . . shocking the incompetence and the inadequacies of the department to police itself," the interim report stated. It declared the department's unwillingness to confront corruption a system-wide, institutional flaw. The need to police the police required an authority outside of the department, the panel concluded. They proposed that a commission like theirs become a standing body to investigate accusations of wrongdoing. The return of a special state prosecutor charged with the responsibility, a post created after the Knapp Commission that had existed until 1990, when Governor Cuomo shut the office in a cost-saving move, seemed another logical solution to a problem sure to persist.[57]

At first, police commissioner Kelly objected to the language and recommendations of Mollen's panel. But as detailed revelations emerged during public hearings, Kelly declared himself "revolted" by the behavior described. He accepted the wisdom of an outside body authorized to scrutinize accusations of police corruption as long as it did not impede the power of the commissioner to punish cops when the department found them wanting.[58]

Meanwhile, beneath the dramatic headlines and extraordinary tensions surrounding the police department, the city actually became a little safer. In 1992 the overall level of crime fell nearly 8 percent, the second consecutive year of decline. That had not happened since Robert Wagner served as mayor in the 1950s. The number of incidents reported, well over six hundred thousand, remained alarmingly high but constituted a reversal to a level last reached in 1985. Murders fell below two thousand again—still intolerable by any reasonable standard, but at least a welcome shift in direction. Mayor Dinkins cited the numbers as evidence the "Safe Streets, Safe City" program his administration launched had begun to accomplish its goals as he set his sights on reelection. His opponents, of course, would present things differently.[59]

Notes

1. Esther Pessin, "Poll Says Most New Yorkers Want to Move," *New York Post*, September 10, 1990; *Time*, September 17, 1990; Joe Klein, "Deadly Metaphors," *New York*, September 9, 1991, 26–29.

2. Joe Klein, "Winners and Sinners, 1991: Politics," *New York*, December 23–30, 1991, 22.

3. John T. McQuiston, "At Least 5 Dead and 150 Hurt as Subway Derails," *NYT*, August 28, 1991; Alan Finder, "The Subway Crash; IRT Driver Charged in 5 Deaths; Crash Shuts Line and Ties up City," *NYT*, August 29, 1991; Alan Finder, "The Subway Crash; Crash Prompts MTA to Impose Random Drug and Alcohol Testing," *NYT*, August 30, 1991; Calvin Sims, "The Subway Crash; Newest Safety Equipment Lacking at Union Square Switching Point," *NYT*, August 30, 1991; "Topics of the Times; After Tragedy, Teamwork," *NYT*, September 6, 1991.

4. Esther Pessin, "Poll Says Most New Yorkers Want to Move," *New York Post*, September 10, 1990; John T. McQuiston, "Girl Chained by Parents Says She Wants to Stay at Home," *NYT*, September 17, 1991; Sarah Lyall, "Atlantic Beach Struggles to Explain Assault on Black Youth," *NYT*, June 7, 1991; Jeanie Kasindorf, "Blood Sport," *New York*, August 26, 1991, 38–45; Editorial, "New York's First Hurdle: Defeatism," *NYT*, October 13, 1991. The Bronx reference was to fifteen-year-old Linda Marrero whose parents took the drastic action of chaining her to a bed in a bizarre effort to prevent their drug-abusing child from harming herself. The Bronx district attorney arrested them. The reference to an event in Queens that the editors saw as a counterpoint to Yankel Rosenbaum's stabbing occurred in June 1991 at a graduation party. A seventeen-year-old African American student, Alfred Jermaine Ewell, and a white girl he was friends with sat together on a beach. A white student who knew them both was angered by the scene and with a group of friends beat Ewell with a baseball bat.

5. "Police Department's Monthly Report for May 1993," in New York City Municipal Archives, Office of the Mayor, 1990–1993, D.M. Steisel, Roll #128; George James, "Police to Put Lone Officers in Patrol Cars," *NYT*, September 19, 1991; George James, "Patrol Officers in New York to Test Semiautomatic Guns," *NYT*, September 25, 1991.

6. George James, "On Foot and Twirling a Nightstick, Via Madison Ave.," *NYT*, October 9, 1991; Jacques Steinberg, "Subway Crime Fell in 1991, Officials Say," *NYT*, February 21, 1991; George James, "In Every Category, Crime Reports Fell Last Year in New York City," *NYT*, March 25, 1992.

7. George James, "With Nine New Attacks, Bias Crimes Far Outpace Last Year," *NYT*, March 16, 1992; Jane Fritsch, "Gun of Choice for Police Officers Runs into Fierce Opposition," *NYT*, May 31, 1992.

8. Eric Pooley, "With Extreme Prejudice: A Murder in Queens Exposes the Frightening Rise of Gay-Bashing," *New York*, April 8, 1991, 36–43; Calvin Sims, "How Dinkins Strove to Keep the Peace," *NYT*, May 3, 1992; Edwin Diamond, "Media: Riot Act," *New York*, May 18, 1992, 10–11.

9. Calvin Sims, "How Dinkins Strove to Keep the Peace," *NYT*, May 3, 1992; Ralph Blumenthal, "Seeing Challenges Instead of Problems," *NYT*, May 17, 1992; Sam Roberts, "Metro Matters; Black Rage, White Fear, and a Call for Remedies," *NYT*, May 4, 1992; B. Drummond Ayers Jr. "Riots in Los Angeles;

A Cautious, Hopeful Quiet Prevails in Other Cities," *NYT*, May 3, 1992; "New York's Riots That Didn't Happen," *New York Post*, May 5, 1992.

10. Eric Pooley, "Air Dinkins: Avoiding an L.A. Meltdown, the Mayor Catches a Break," *New York*, May 25, 1992, 32–35.

11. Eric Pooley, "Air Dinkins: Avoiding an L.A. Meltdown, the Mayor Catches a Break," *New York*, May 25, 1992, 32–35; Alan Finder, "Political Memo: Dinkins Is Mastering the Art of the Mayor," *NYT*, July 5, 1992.

12. Eric Pooley, "Air Dinkins: Avoiding an L.A. Meltdown, the Mayor Catches a Break," *New York*, May 25, 1992, 32–35.

13. Helen Peterson and Patrice O'Shaughnessy, "Rage as Cop Kills Suspect," *New York Newsday*, July 5, 1992; Sonia Reyes et al., "Don't Let Him Kill Me," *New York Newsday*, July 6, 1992; Jere Hester, "Anger and Mistrust Stalk Uneasy Streets," *New York Newsday*, July 6, 1992; Peter Hellman, "The Cop and the Riot: Michael O'Keefe's Story of the Storm in Washington Heights," *New York*, November 2, 1992, 41–46.

14. Helen Peterson and Patrice O'Shaughnessy, "Rage as Cop Kills Suspect," *New York Newsday*, July 5, 1992; Sonia Reyes et al., "Don't Let Him Kill Me," *New York Newsday*, July 6, 1992; Jere Hester, "Anger and Mistrust Stalk Uneasy Streets," *New York Newsday*, July 6, 1992; Peter Hellman, "The Cop and the Riot: Michael O'Keefe's Story of the Storm in Washington Heights," *New York*, November 2, 1992, 41–46.

15. Serge F. Kovaleski and Joel Siegel, "Dave Visits a Troubled Nabe," *New York Newsday*, July 7, 1992; Peter Hellman, "The Cop and the Riot: Michael O'Keefe's Story of the Storm in Washington Heights," *New York*, November 2, 1992, 41–46.

16. Jere Hester et al., "Protesters in Rage over Police Shoot," *New York Newsday*, July 7, 1992; Juan Gonzalez, "Grim Specter of L.A. Nears," *New York Newsday*, July 7, 1992; James Dao, "Angered by Police Killing, a Neighborhood Erupts," *NYT*, July 7, 1992; Peter Hellman, "The Cop and the Riot: Michael O'Keefe's Story of the Storm in Washington Heights," *New York*, November 2, 1992, 41–46.

17. Sonia Reyes, "Chats and Congrats: Mayor Tours the Nabe, Wins Praise," *New York Newsday*, July 9, 1992; Joel Seigel, "Dave Gets New Chance with Latino Community," *New York Newsday*, July 9, 1992.

18. Editorial, "The Lesson of Washington Heights," *NYT*, September 13, 1992.

19. Joseph Treaster, "New York City Officers Charged with Running L.I. Cocaine Ring," *NYT*, May 8, 1992; Selwyn Raab, "A Corruption Fighter Says Fear Is the Best Deterrent," *NYT*, June 21, 1992.

20. George James, "2d Police Inquiry Begins into Drug-Dealing Charge," *NYT*, June 16, 1992.

21. Craig Wolff, "US Is Investigating Reports of Corrupt New York Police," *NYT*, June 19, 1992.

22. James C. McKinley, "Dinkins Names Police Corruption Panel and Urges Civilian Police Review," *NYT*, June 26, 1992.

23. McNickle, *To Be Mayor of New York*, 214–15.

24. David W. Abott, Louis H. Gold, and Edward T. Rogowsky, *Police, Politics and Race: The New York City Referendum on Civilian Review* (New York: American Jewish Committee and The Joint Center for Urban Studies of the Massachusetts Institute of Technology and Harvard University, 1969), *passim*.

25. George James, "Brown's Gospel: Community Policing," *NYT*, August 14, 1991; Calvin Sims, "Brown's Resignation; Brown Abruptly Resigns His Police Post," *NYT*, August 4, 1992.

26. James C. McKinley, "Officers Rally and Dinkins Is Their Target," *NYT*, September 17, 1992.

27. James C. McKinley, "Officers Rally and Dinkins Is Their Target," *NYT*, September 17, 1992.

28. Craig Wolf, "Kelly Lashes out at 'Police Bashing' in New York City," *NYT*, October 31, 1992; "Message from the Police Commissioner," Lee P. Brown, Police Commissioner, July 1991, No. 6 in New York City Municipal Archives, Office of the Mayor, 1990–1993, D.M. Steisel, Roll #128.

29. Craig Wolf, "Kelly Lashes out at 'Police Bashing' in New York City," *NYT*, October 31, 1992; James C. McKinley, "Council Backs New Board to Review Police Conduct," *NYT*, December 18, 1992.

30. "Remarks by Mayor David N. Dinkins, Breakfast with N.Y.P.D. Precinct Commanders, Gracie Mansion, East End Avenue at 88th Street, Manhattan," October 3, 1992 in New York City Municipal Archives, Office of the Mayor, 1990–1993, Mayor David N. Dinkins, Speeches, Roll #1.

31. "Remarks by Mayor David N. Dinkins, Breakfast with NYPD Precinct Commanders," October 3, 1992.

32. "Remarks by Mayor David N. Dinkins, Breakfast with NYPD Precinct Commanders," October 3, 1992; "Memorandum to: Mayor David N. Dinkins from: Maria Laurino Date: October 1, 1992 Re: Meeting with Police Chaplains and Rabbis," in New York City Municipal Archives, Office of the Mayor, 1990–1993, Mayor David N. Dinkins, Speeches, Roll #1.

33. *A Report to the Governor on the Disturbances in Crown Heights: Volume II: A Review of the Circumstances Surrounding the Death of Yankel Rosenbaum and the Resulting Prosecution,* 1993, Richard H. Girgenti, Director of Criminal Justice, 21–54; Shapiro, *Crown Heights*, 172–76.

34. Girgenti, *A Review of the Circumstances Surrounding the Death of Yankel Rosenbaum and the Resulting Prosecution,* 21–54; Shapiro, *Crown Heights*, 172–76.

35. Robert D. McFadden, "Teen-Ager Acquitted in Slaying During '91 Crown Heights Melee," *NYT*, October 30, 1992.

36. Donatella Lorch, "Inquiries Set in '91 Slaying in Crown Hts.," *NYT*, October 31, 1992; John Taylor, "The City Politic: The Politics of Grievance," *New York*, December 7, 1992, 18–19.

37. Donatella Lorch, "Inquiries Set in '91 Slaying in Crown Hts.," *NYT*, October 31, 1992; Editorial, "No Way to Honor Yankel Rosenbaum," *NYT*, November 10, 1992; Avraham Weiss, "Confronting David Dinkins," 42, unpublished manuscript in possession of the author, courtesy of Rabbi Avraham Weiss.

38. "Remarks by Mayor David N. Dinkins, Jewish Theological Seminary, Institute for Religious and Social Studies, Broadway & 122nd Street, New York," November 17, 1992 in New York City Municipal Archives, Office of the Mayor, David N. Dinkins, Speeches, Microfilm Roll #10; Martin Gottlieb, "Emotions Rise on US Inquiry in Crown Heights," *NYT*, November 9, 1992; Sam Roberts, "Passionately, Dinkins Reviews Crown Heights," *NYT*, November 12, 1992; Sam Roberts, "Metro Matters; Is Mayor Held to Different Standard?" *NYT*, November 16, 1992; James C. McKinley,

"Dinkins Says Critics Distort Facts of His Response to Crown Heights," *NYT*, November 18, 1992.

39. Craig Horowitz, "The New Anti-Semitism," *New York*, January 11, 1993, 23–24.

40. "Remarks, Mayor David N. Dinkins Delivers a Thanksgiving Eve Address on 'Reason, Respect and Reconciliation in New York City,'" Wednesday, November 25, 1992—12:01 PM, The Mayor's Office—City Hall," in New York City Municipal Archives, Office of the Mayor, David N. Dinkins, Speeches, Microfilm Roll #10; Robert D. McFadden, "Dinkins Plans Major Appeal for Harmony," *NYT*, November 23, 1992; Excerpts from Mayor Dinkins's Speech on Crown Heights and Race," *NYT*, November 26, 1992; James C. McKinley, "Dinkins, in TV Speech, Defends Handling of Crown Hts. Tension," *NYT*, November 26, 1992.

41. "Remarks, Mayor David N. Dinkins Delivers a Thanksgiving Eve Address on 'Reason, Respect and Reconciliation in New York City,'" Wednesday, November 25, 1992—12:01 PM, The Mayor's Office—City Hall," in New York City Municipal Archives, Office of the Mayor, David N. Dinkins, Speeches, Microfilm Roll #10; Robert D. McFadden, "Dinkins Plans Major Appeal for Harmony," *NYT*, November 23, 1992; "Excerpts from Mayor Dinkins's Speech on Crown Heights and Race," *NYT*, November 26, 1992; James C. McKinley, "Dinkins, in TV Speech, Defends Handling of Crown Hts. Tension," *NYT*, November 26, 1992.

42. "Remarks, Mayor David N. Dinkins Delivers a Thanksgiving Eve Address on 'Reason, Respect and Reconciliation in New York City,'" Wednesday, November 25, 1992—12:01 PM, The Mayor's Office—City Hall," in New York City Municipal Archives, Office of the Mayor, David N. Dinkins, Speeches, Microfilm Roll #10; Robert D. McFadden, "Dinkins Plans Major Appeal for Harmony," *NYT*, November 23, 1992; Excerpts from Mayor Dinkins's Speech on Crown Heights and Race," *NYT*, November 26, 1992; James C. McKinley, "Dinkins, in TV Speech, Defends Handling of Crown Hts. Tension," *NYT*, November 26, 1992.

43. Alan Finder, "Crown Hts. Gets Offering from Mayor," *NYT*, Dec 18, 1992; Todd Purdum, "Crown Hts. Drives Contest for Mayor," *NYT*, December 7, 1992; Craig Horowitz, "The New Anti-Semitism," *New York*, January 11, 1993.

44. Shapiro, *Crown Heights*, 26–29; Joseph P. Fried, "19 1/2 –Year Term Set in Fatal Stabbing in Crown Heights," *NYT*, April 1, 1998.

45. "Metro Briefing New York: Crown Heights Figure Freed," *NYT*, June 3, 2004; Jennifer B. Lee, Marc Santora contributing, "City Settles with Family Of '91 Victim," *NYT*, June 18, 2005.

46. Joseph P. Fried, "19 1/2 –Year Term Set in Fatal Stabbing in Crown Heights," *NYT*, April 1, 1998; Joseph P. Fried, "Mayor Apologizes for City Response to Crown Heights," *NYT*, April 3, 1998; Martin Gottlieb, "Police in Crown Heights: 'A Holding Approach,'" *NYT*, November 19, 1992; Joseph P. Fried, "Following Up: Crown Hts. Defendant Is Set for Jail Release," *NYT*, May 9, 2004; Alan Finder, "Dinkins, in Testimony, Defends His Response on Crown Heights," *NYT*, August 25, 1993; Tina Kelley, "City and Crown Hts. Family Reach $400,000 Settlement," *NYT*, January 10, 2002.

47. James Barron, "Survey Places New York Police Last in Hiring of Black Officers," *NYT*, October 8, 1992.

48. Michael Winerip, "Kelly, A Savvy Insider, Remakes Police Force," *NYT*, May 22, 1993.

49. George James, "Commissioner Asks Black Clergy to Review Police Testing System," *NYT*, November 6, 1992.

50. Alan Finder, "Top Deputy Named New York Police Commissioner," *NYT*, October 17, 1992; Jonathan P. Hicks, "Minority Groups Call for Changes in Police Recruiting Methods," *NYT*, November 1, 1992; George James, "Commissioner Asks Black Clergy to Review Police Testing System," *NYT*, November 6, 1992.

51. Eric Pooley, "Bulldog," *New York*, February 22, 1992, 33–40; Michael Winerip, "Kelly, a Savvy Insider, Remakes Police Force," *NYT*, May 22, 1993.

52. Eric Pooley, "Bulldog," *New York*, February 22, 1992, 33–40; Michael Winerip, "Kelly, a Savvy Insider, Remakes Police Force," *NYT*, May 22, 1993.

53. Eric Pooley, "Bulldog," *New York*, February 22, 1992, 33–40.

54. *An Investigation into the Police Department's Conduct of the Dowd Case and an Assessment of the Police Department's Internal Investigation Capabilities*, November 1992, Raymond W. Kelly, Commissioner.

55. *An Investigation into the Police Department's Conduct of the Dowd Case and an Assessment of the Police Department's Internal Investigation Capabilities*, November 1992, Raymond W. Kelly, Commissioner; Robert D. McFadden, "Commissioner Orders an Overhaul in Fight against Police Corruption," *NYT*, November 17, 1992; Craig Wolff, "Kelly Report Stops Short, Lawyer Says," *NYT*, November 18, 1992; Eric Pooley, "Bulldog," *New York*, February 22, 1993, 33–40; Author's interview with Raymond D. Kelly, October 7, 2010.

56. Eric Pooley, "Bulldog," *New York*, February 22, 1993, 33–40; George James, "Foe of Corruption Named to No. 2 Police Dept. Job," *NYT*, December 4, 1992.

57. Selwyn Raab, "Mollen Panel to Recommend Permanent Corruption Body," *NYT*, December 28, 1993; Selwyn Raab, "New York's Police Allow Corruption, Mollen Panel Says," *NYT*, December 29, 1993; *Anatomy of Failure: A Path for Success, Report of the Commission to Investigate Allegations of Police Corruption and the Anti-Corruption Procedures of the Police Department*, July 7, 1994, Milton Mollen, Chairman.

58. Selwyn Raab, "Head of New York Police Offers Compromise on Outside Monitor," *NYT*, October 7, 1993; Eric Pooley, "The City Politic: Good Cop, Bad Cops," *New York*, October 11, 1993, 26–29.

59. George James, "Crime down in New York for 2nd Year in Row," *NYT*, March 19, 1993.

8

Defeat

Mayor Dinkins entered 1993 defiant. In his State of the City Address, he told an audience of some five hundred people, most of them political allies, "I come to you filled with both pride and determination. Proud that we have laid the foundation to insure that our city's economy remains world class and poised to take us into the next century, proud that New York is safer today than it was before, and proud, of course, that all the while we never lost our compassion and our commitment to make life better for all of our residents." Dinkins would defend his record, not run from it. Toward the end of the speech, the city's first African American mayor spoke from his heart in a highly personal way. "I stand before all of you, my friends and colleagues, ready to share again the dream that only New Yorkers can know, the dream of Manhattan's towers, and the bravery of firefighters, the dream of home-owners and barrio dwellers, the dream of a maid's son from Harlem who became Mayor of this greatest house ever built." In response, the audience stood and applauded without pause for several minutes. His advisors confirmed the mayor's reelection campaign would feature the themes of the speech.[1]

Just a few days earlier, in a year-end press conference, Dinkins responded to questions about his handling of the Crown Heights disturbance with similar brass. Reporters asked if the discontent surrounding the role he played while the riots raged would haunt his reelection campaign. He replied frostily that public reaction would depend on how the media treated the subject. "I know what I did and what I said and I am satisfied with my behavior," he declared. Analysts wondered if Jews, who cast more votes for Dinkins than other whites in his 1989 election, would view the mayor's actions as he did or how the Crown Heights' Lubavitch did.[2]

Predictably, Dinkins's challengers dismissed the mayor's State of the City rhetoric as the idle bragging of a man presiding over unacceptable levels of crime, racial disharmony, school board chaos, a weak economy, and perennial budget challenges. "His speech attempts to be everything to everybody instead of setting forth priorities and talking about the overall things that would be helpful, like how to get control of the government work force," Rudolph Giuliani said. He faulted the mayor for failing to offer a jobs program or a plan to cut the structural deficit or to improve the productivity of city employees. Andrew Stein also belittled the mayor's talk. "What the city needs is not some good rhetoric but sweeping change," he said.[3]

The *New York Times* editorial board seemed equally unimpressed. The very day the mayor delivered his State of the City Address, under the headline, "New Year's in the City," the editors wrote:

> New York's leaders remain set in old and wasteful ways. . . . Mayor David Dinkins has achieved some modest improvements, but the true innovations, like privatization and holding city workers more accountable, still elude New York. Can it reform wasteful civil service laws, write equitable property taxes, get sanitation workers to work a full day for a day's pay, revise rent control, revamp a petty, meddling Board of Education? Debating such issues would make for a lively and constructive mayoral contest. But continuing racial tension raises the specter of a polarizing campaign.[4]

A few months earlier, a prominent businessman had summarized David Dinkins's relationship with the people he served in succinct, if vulgar terms: "Here's the question none of us could answer," he told a reporter. "Is the guy fucked up, or has he run into a set of circumstances that would make *anyone* seem fucked up?" How New Yorkers responded to the question would affect the mayor's chance for reelection.[5]

I. An Incumbent's Unshakeable Base

New York's Democrats understood Dinkins's vulnerability. They also recognized his strength. Despite dissatisfaction and a lack of trust among significant blocs of white voters that prevented the mayor from expanding his political base, he was New York's first black mayor seeking his party's renomination. African American commitment to Dinkins remained unassailable, and analysts estimated the group would cast one-third of the votes in the Democratic primary. This made the mayor almost impossible to beat for his party's nomination. In a general election, with additional backing from those liberal whites and Latinos who remained loyal, the mayor had a base of support that seemed never to drop below 40 percent in citywide polls—a formidable starting point for any politician running for elective office. The Marist Institute for Public Opinion reported 53 percent of respondents gave the mayor a favorable rating in February 1993, compared with 39 percent unfavorable. As the incumbent, Dinkins retained the power to help or hurt anyone seeking city business. Manhattan's financial, real estate, and business elite—Edgar Bronfman, Jack Rudin, Felix Rohatyn, Jonathan Tisch, and others—supported his reelection, ensuring ample funding.[6]

David Dinkins also possessed considerable charm, never to be underestimated as an asset for a candidate campaigning for elective office. *New York Times* reporter Todd Purdum described the public man as someone "who speaks softly and smiles easily, whose gray-blue eyes exude charm, who greets every man he meets as 'buddy' and kisses women's hands." He won the hearts of some cynical City Hall denizens one day when a seven-year-old boy showed up asking for the mayor's autograph. The youngster declared he would wait as long as it took. After hours passed a detective in Dinkins's detail learned of the matter and escorted the boy to the mayor, who told him, "I'm sorry you had to wait so long. I would have seen you sooner if I'd known you were out there." He signed a photograph of himself and handed it to the child. "Do you know how to read?" he asked. "Yes," the boy answered proudly, and read out loud what the mayor had written. "To Jason, You are our future. David Dinkins." The mayor readily displayed photographs of his grandchildren to any who would look at them.[7]

The mayor spoke at an event honoring Muhammad Ali. "Today . . . [we] pay tribute to perhaps The Greatest Fighter ever to have stepped into the ring. Of all time? Yes, of all time. Just ask him," Dinkins said. After poking some fun at the boastful champion, he cheered him warmly, saying, "He used his fame to make others walk a little taller and feel a little prouder." At a tribute for Diana Ross, during which he praised the pop idol, who used her "God given musical talent . . . to get out of the ghetto," for inspiring others to do the same, he bragged that New York City had produced some songs as popular as the ones the glamorous star sang, citing "Endless Love," by Ed Koch and Jesse Jackson. When AIDS activists publicly handed him condoms, he passed them to a staff member known to be a lady's man, saying, "Here, you take care of these." The pleasure the mayor took in the ceremonial aspects of his job had put his appealing human warmth on display to many thousands of people over the years. People liked David Dinkins.[8]

Most Democrats who aspired to be mayor chose not to challenge the incumbent. They feared the wrath of African American Democrats, whose votes they might need one day to move up and who kept them in office in the meantime. Only city council president Andrew Stein, Herman Badillo, the elder statesman of New York's Puerto Rican leaders, and Roy Innis, the controversial neoconservative black chairman of the Congress of Racial Equality threatened to battle Dinkins for the Democratic nomination for the city's highest office.[9]

Dinkins's reelection campaign began, in effect, when the Democratic National Convention came to New York City in July 1992. Attracting the convention is itself an achievement for a mayor. It demonstrates political muscle and standing in the national party while bringing an influx of tourist dollars to town. Then the convention provides the city's top-elected official with a platform for demonstrating leadership, one Dinkins used to great effect in the days leading up to and during the event itself.

The mayor logged sixty-five radio and television appearances in the weeks surrounding the convention, according to an unofficial tally from his press office. He welcomed the delegates with a televised speech at Madison Square Garden. He addressed an AIDS rally at Times Square attended by tens of thousands, escorted Nelson Mandela to meet with Democratic presidential nominee Bill Clinton, and hosted a meeting at Gracie Mansion with ten big-city mayors. Three events produced for the convention—a fashion show, an open-air Broadway review in which the stars of dramatic plays introduced the casts of musicals who performed their hits, and a restaurant promotion that offered prix fixe lunches for the price of the year ($19.92 during the convention)—became annual events. Unconfirmed estimates reported a $300 million boost to the city's flagging economy. Praise rained down on the mayor. When a reporter asked how he felt about the city's reaction to the convention and his role in it, Dinkins responded with self-satisfied understatement. "It sure as hell is better than a jab in the eye with a sharp stick," the often-beleaguered mayor said. "This is all good for our city. It may also not be bad for me," he allowed.[10]

Shortly after the successful convention boosted the mayor's spirits and standing, Bill Lynch, instrumental in bringing the Democrats to town, left city government to serve as deputy director of operations for the Clinton-Gore campaign in New York State. "We will be using

Clinton's money to sign up our voters," one mayoral aide said about the move. In November 1992 Lynch transitioned seamlessly to Dinkins's reelection campaign. For the man who remained a community organizer at heart, the move meant a shift to what he loved most and did best. As deputy mayor, he had been forced to contend with the bureaucratic workings of government administration. He was not particularly good at it, and he never really liked it.[11]

Deputy Mayor Steisel assumed responsibility for Lynch's intergovernmental duties. The change resolved the tension that persisted while Steisel and Lynch served simultaneously as Dinkins's top deputies. The two pros respected each other and collaborated as necessary, but their overlapping responsibilities gave each a say in almost every policy. They pulled the mayor's senior team in somewhat different directions. Steisel, a budget hawk and numbers-based manager committed to more efficient service delivery, had one set of priorities. Lynch, more a relationship-based manager, cared more about higher wages and benefits for municipal workers and more services for disadvantaged communities than productivity improvements. The agendas were never aligned, and the mayor never reconciled them. Most senior staff got their daily marching orders from Steisel and Lynch, not Dinkins, so the different perspectives contributed to the confusion surrounding the mayor's priorities. Steisel's ascension promised greater clarity. And while the first deputy's style could offend unnecessarily—"more than once," council speaker Peter Vallone "warned the mayor that if Norman did not watch his mouth someone was going to pop him one"—few ever doubted his competence or his loyalty.[12]

With Lynch's departure, the role of the mayor's counsel, George B. Daniels, always important, became more pronounced. Daniels, like Dinkins, had a cautious, deliberate way about him. With no departments to run, he had no turf to defend. An easy personal chemistry caused a tight bond between the two African American men. They spoke several times a day on a broad range of issues, and the mayor came to trust Daniels as someone who could reflect his ideas and wishes accurately on any subject. "Talk with George. That's the same as talking to me," Dinkins had taken to telling people on a range of issues. The skilled attorney handled his tasks with quiet competence and discretion.[13]

No one in the administration, it seemed, could manage the same with the media. The mayor had long believed journalists and reporters overplayed the challenges his administration faced and failed to feature his achievements fairly. The urgency of gaining control over media communications grew as the reelection campaign approached. The typical courtly tone of Dinkins's public comments on media coverage, statements such as, "I believe many people are not aware or are not sufficiently aware of what we do," masked the bitterness he harbored about the way journalists reported on his administration. In moments of candor, he attributed the often negative tone of his press coverage to a double standard rooted in racism. Rather than leave the fate of his reelection bid to newspaper writers and television reporters he did not trust, Dinkins wanted his team to find ways to promote his administration's top initiatives directly with the public without the filter of New York's media professionals and editorial boards. He sought once again to hire media manager Randy Daniels to lead the effort, but past allegations of sexual harassment, although never proven, scuttled the appointment. Eventually, Dinkins appointed Joyce Brown, a vice chancellor at the City University of New York and the wife of H. Carl McCall, to the job.[14]

By the end of 1992, the mayor's office published a twenty-seven-page report titled *New York City ROARING BACK: Changing the City for Good*. It catalogued city government efforts to improve service delivery to residents. "From the first day I took office," Dinkins wrote in a letter to his "Dear Fellow New Yorkers," "I recognized that in order to address the daunting and unprecedented challenges facing the City . . . New York City government would have to change for good." In other cities, his letter continued, "hurdles such as closing multi-billion dollar budget gaps might have arrested any plans for City government other than cutting services." Yet in David Dinkins's New York, his talented commissioners and city workers "saw our difficult circumstances as an opportunity to make government work better." Dinkins concluded the introduction to the report on an optimistic note: "We enter the final year of my first term as Mayor with much accomplished, but still very much left to do. The achievements of our past permit us to look to our future with hope and encouragement for fashioning a better government for New Yorkers and the benefits it will advance."[15]

As Dinkins turned his attention toward reelection, he recognized that his promise to bring racial harmony to the city made the tone of public discourse on the topic critically important. So he dispatched intermediaries to meet with executives at local radio stations to encourage them to moderate the language of their talk show hosts and to rein in callers making bigoted comments. One strongly suspects Dinkins and his aides expected little from the initiative, other than reinforcement of the mayor's image as a man making a concerted effort to dial down the racially charged volume of the noise heard on the city's airwaves.[16]

Black activists responsible for their share of the nasty rhetoric often ridiculed and insulted David Dinkins. His conventional politics and formal manners offended their sense of urgency and anger. Alton Maddox once called Dinkins "an Ed Koch in black face." Over the years, Reverend Al Sharpton had called him an Uncle Tom and once referred to him as "that nigger whore turning tricks in City Hall." Others, resentful of Dinkins's consistent condemnation of African American anti-Semites, referred to him derisively as David Dinkinstein. To black militants, Dinkins no doubt fit the mold of what Cornel West called a "race-effacing managerial leader . . . trying to reach a large white constituency, and keep a loyal black one." The approach, in West's view, tended "to stunt progressive development and silence the prophetic voices in the black community by casting the practical mainstream as the only game in town." But such a candidate typically represented "the lesser of two evils . . . where the only other electoral choice is a conservative (usually white) politician." This was exactly the situation developing in New York City in 1993, and none of the militants wanted to be blamed for the defeat of New York's first African American mayor, so an uneasy truce settled in.[17]

Sharpton in particular had begun to adopt new tactics. In part, he realized his old ways were wearing thin. A *Daily News* poll published in 1990 had revealed 90 percent of whites and 73 percent of blacks believed he damaged race relations. But he experienced a more profound epiphany in January 1991 after a drunken twenty-seven-year-old named Michael Riccardi plunged a five-inch steak knife into Sharpton's chest while he led a march in Bensonhurst. He awoke in Coney Island Hospital after the stabbing to find David Dinkins standing by his bedside. "I thought I had died and went to hell," Sharpton joked about the episode. But the gesture made an impression. The activist, by then thirty-six with two children, had been thinking about his life and the role he played. "I wanted to be known for more than slogans and I wanted to be remembered for more than arguing with knuckleheads on television," he would write. He did not want the legacy of a man who preached peace but inspired violence. The stabbing helped convince him "[i]t was time to bring down the volume and bring up the program," he told a reporter. "I've called the Mayor names and I've called other people names. But now I've learned," he said.[18]

Throughout 1992 contract negotiations with many of the city's most important municipal unions had dragged on without resolution. By the middle of January 1993, the political imperative of a reelection campaign led to a settlement. It called for modest increases in wages and benefits retroactive to January 1992 when the last contract expired. The agreement covered 180,000 workers in nineteen organizations, including Barry Feinstein's Teamsters and Stanley Hill's District Council 37. The contract lacked clear productivity commitments that the mayor had promised to deliver. Instead, a clause established a three-member panel to negotiate efficiencies. Fiscal hawks expressed serious disappointment, but the accord ensured labor peace and secured important union support for Dinkins.[19]

The mayor submitted his election-year preliminary budget as required before the end of January 1993. It totaled nearly $32 billion, proposing an increase of nearly 5 percent over the prior year, despite continuing fiscal challenges. As usual, it included expectations of support from the state and federal governments unlikely to be met in full as a negotiating ploy. Analysts described the budget as reflecting "[Dinkins's] desire to sew together the coalition of labor, minorities and liberals that elected him four years ago by avoiding deep service cuts or layoffs." As the year progressed, a projected budget gap would grow and force the mayor to adopt changes that did little to strengthen his credibility or his political position.[20]

To secure the Latino component of his coalition, Dinkins agreed not to build a sludge-treatment plant in the heavily Puerto Rican neighborhood of Sunset Park, Brooklyn, after intense lobbying by Latino politicians. "I told him that it's very difficult for the Latino community to be supportive when we are being taken for granted," Congresswoman Nydia Velazquez explained to reporters. "He understood my message," she said. Bronx borough president Fernando Ferrer also weighed in. The proposed facility was one of three required to comply with federal rules to prevent dumping untreated sludge into the ocean. The others, one in Queens and one in Staten Island, communities offering Dinkins weak political support, would proceed.[21]

Publicly, Dinkins often acknowledged his debt to Latinos. "The Puerto Rican community is a cornerstone of the coalition of conscience that stood together in 1989 and put me in the Mayor's Office. I am deeply grateful for your support," he told the Bronx Puerto Rican Conference in one of many expressions of thanks. He was not shy telling Puerto Ricans about the extent of the payback they received. In remarks before the Puerto Rican Legal Defense and Education Fund, for example, he told the audience that he had named an unprecedented number of their ranks to high-level posts, and he also reported that his administration had been the first to hire a Latino-owned investment bank to manage a New York City bond issue. He traveled to Puerto Rico and to the Dominican Republic as well, honored the mayor of San Juan, hosted breakfasts on the mornings of the Puerto Rican Day Parade, and undertook any number of gestures, large and small, designed to show respect for a key element of his coalition.[22]

Despite these important measures, Dinkins's relationship with Latinos suffered from the same challenges as other elements of his coalition—perhaps a little more so. Puerto Rican and Dominican New Yorkers needed the same things from municipal government as African Americans. They relied disproportionately on the city for social services, public housing, health care, schools, and jobs. The severe budget constraints Dinkins faced limited his ability to deliver benefits and services for those who needed them most. Some Latino leaders worried that the African American mayor in City Hall would shortchange them. Persistent complaints from advocates—who viewed their job as demanding more for their people no matter how much they received—reinforced concerns. Mostly, they were unfounded. Some Latino leaders found the mayor distant and aloof, but so did many others who believed they had a claim on the man they helped elect. Among Latinos, the administration compensated in part by relying on Dinkins's all-purpose advance man, Arne Segarra, to maintain an informal, more accessible back channel.[23]

Bronx borough president Fernando Ferrer, the city's senior-elected Latino and de facto leader of the sometimes-fractious ethnic group, maintained a mutually supportive if at times testy personal relationship with the mayor. Ferrer's intuitive, street-smart decision-making style contrasted sharply with what he called Dinkins's "maddeningly slow" approach to making up his mind. The severe difference in temperaments had caused the two men to clash fiercely when they served together on the Board of Estimate, but they remained political allies. Ferrer's "shrewd approach" to politics applied to his posture toward Dinkins—"cautious in public, cutthroat behind the scenes," in the words of New York magazine journalist Eric Pooley, and it worked effectively. Ferrer always had access to the mayor, and his recommendations for high-level appointments received serious consideration. Policy recommendations, even if rejected, received detailed, respectful replies. [24]

A number of specific issues arose with Latinos that required careful management. Shortly before Nelson Mandela visited New York in 1990, in response to a reporter's question, Dinkins condemned three Puerto Rican nationalists who attacked the House of Representatives and shot five Congressmen in 1954 as "assassins." He rejected the notion that they should be among the guests meeting with Mandela. The comment outraged many Puerto Rican leaders. They considered the gunmen freedom fighters, cut from the same cloth as the South African hero, who, even as he negotiated peace with his nation's white rulers, declined to renounce the African National Congress and violent revolution. According to press secretary Albert Scardino, the ferocity of the reaction surprised Dinkins, who found himself issuing a carefully worded statement. "After speaking with many of my friends in the Puerto Rican community, I realize that my response to a question [about the nationalists] came too quickly. . . . I can identify with and appreciate their yearning for economic justice and political freedom." He went on to make clear that he did not condone their use of violence but declared that his comment did not adequately account for the emotions on the subject. He expressed regret if his words "offended my brothers and sisters in the Latino community."[25]

William Nieves, a community board activist Dinkins appointed to head the Office of Latino Affairs, resigned after just a few months in the job, implying when he did that the mayor's deputies lacked sensitivity to Latino history, culture, and politics. The resignation created mild controversy and gave advocates who liked to read their name in the newspaper a chance to declare that Dinkins kept the Latino community "remote from him," a charge Dinkins dismissed as "nonsense." Attention-fetching headlines reported growing tensions in the mayor's multiethnic coalition, but the Latinos who mattered most downplayed the issue. "David's heart is in the right place," Fernando Ferrer declared when asked to comment on the resignation, allowing only that it would help if the mayor were "a little more hands-on." Dennis Rivera, the powerful head of hospital workers' Local 1199, had at times expressed disappointment the mayor could not deliver more for Latinos. But after Nieves's resignation he explained away his own and other criticisms that ultimately stemmed from the city's fiscal constraints. "Some of us who got impatient with David failed to see the immense pressure he has. There are those in the financial community and those who didn't vote for him who really want him to fail," Rivera declared, in obvious sympathy with the mayor.[26]

Drawing the new city council districts required to expand it to fifty-one seats from thirty-five caused Dinkins some grief. When the federal government reviewed the first proposal for the new map, it declared it unfair to Latinos. Dinkins had appointed seven of the fifteen members on the redistricting commission who developed the plan, so Puerto Rican and Dominican politicians unhappy with the outcome accorded him ample blame, along with the disproportionately white city council that selected the other eight. "David's got to play to his strength by boldly reaching out to the constituencies that elected him," Bronx assemblyman and Democratic Party leader Roberto Ramirez said at the time of the council district controversy. "If he denies his key constituencies a sense they are part of his decision-making process, his political future is in danger," Ramirez warned. Dennis Rivera weighed in as well. "The only way he gets our respect," the union leader who supported Dinkins in 1989 said, "is to take care of us."[27]

After revisions, a three-judge panel approved new districts. The Puerto Rican Legal Defense and Education Fund continued to protest, but Latinos won nine seats in the next election, so their representation on the council more or less matched their proportion of the population. The new districts also allowed the election of the city's first Dominican council member, Guillermo Linares, in Washington Heights.[28]

Some friction with Latinos occurred when Dr. J. Emilio Carillo resigned as the president of the city's Health and Hospitals Corporation amid concern over poor standards of care and reports that the administrator had sought personal loans from subordinates. Carillo lashed out, calling his ouster a "targeted assassination" by City Hall officials on a "witch hunt." One journalist wrote that "Hispanic groups considered their support essential" to Dinkins's election, "but have been disappointed since, complaining the Mayor has failed to appoint large numbers of Hispanic officials to high-ranking jobs." As in other instances, the charges came from single-issue advocates, not Latinos with real clout who recognized Dinkins's solid record of inclusion. Still the episode made all involved look bad.[29]

Within weeks, Dinkins responded by naming Puerto Rican State welfare commissioner Cesar Perales deputy mayor for Health and Human Services. The appointment allowed the mayor to brag that Latino officials controlled over $10 billion of budget money—one-third of the city's total. "If that's not empowerment I don't know what is," Dinkins would tell Latino audiences. Naming Perales to so big a responsibility made clear Carillo's departure did not signal an anti-Latino bias, although the ethnically driven selection caused the mayor's credibility to suffer with others. The *New York Times* took note that Perales, "an experienced but unremarkable state official," would be the sixth deputy mayor in "an already crowded City Hall. Commissioners complain now that they have trouble getting the Mayor's attention," the editorial lamented, "and outsiders . . . don't know who is in charge. The last thing the administration needs is more splintering of authority."[30]

Despite Latino audience's disappointment with Dinkins's ability to respond to their disparate demands, as he approached reelection, politics ruled. Freshman state senator Pedro Espada captured the conflicting attitudes many Latino politicians and voters harbored toward the mayor in 1993. "There's always been an unspoken competition between the Latino and African American communities, and it was kept under wraps in 1989," he told a reporter. "We threw our hope into the hopper, backed Dinkins—and he has been a huge disappointment. He locked us out of the process," Espada complained. "He blew opportunity after opportunity. He delegated and relegated leadership to people like Norman Steisel, who stifled Latino progress," the Bronx politician charged, without offering details to substantiate the accusation against Dinkins's first deputy. And then he finished by saying, "Oh, by the way, I'm backing Dinkins" for reelection. Dinkins would have the support of the city's Latino politicians in his effort to hold onto his office, but the hard realities of governing had tempered their enthusiasm for the mayor.[31]

David Dinkins's standing among New York's considerable gay population remained strong. Exercising the power of the incumbent, early in 1993, Dinkins signed an executive order allowing gays and other unmarried couples living together to register with the city as domestic partners. They would receive many of the benefits afforded to spouses—unpaid leave to care for a new child, apartment residency status, hospital visitation rights, and others. Dinkins also pledged support for granting health insurance to city workers in domestic partnerships. Many conservative New Yorkers opposed the measure, of course, but they were unlikely to vote for Dinkins in any event. Andrew Stein tried to twist the mayor's support for gays into a negative. His campaign mailed an anonymous pamphlet in pink envelopes to three thousand gay activists, accusing the mayor of acting too little too late on matters important to homosexuals. But when it surfaced that the unsigned accusatory document came from Stein, the ruse backfired.

Dinkins dismissed the "sad and unfortunate" ploy as the desperate act of a candidate low in the polls.[32]

David Dinkins's support for gays had an impact on his standing with New Yorkers of Irish descent. He favored the right of a group of self-identified Irish American homosexuals to march in the St. Patrick's Day Parade, with a banner of their own. The Ancient Order of Hibernians, the parade's sponsors since 1836, objected. Gays were not banned per se—they could march as individuals—but the Hibernians did not want the celebration used for political posturing. They had declined the right to a separate banner to other groups in the past, notably the Irish Republican Army and an antiabortion group with whom many Irish Americans sympathized. One year the mayor walked with a group of gay marchers, and he sat it out in another when the Hibernians prevented the group from participating.[33]

Conservatives denounced the mayor's position on the parade as "enforced diversity," and they objected to efforts he made to transfer sponsorship of the celebration to a group that would let gays march. They accused him of trying to use his office to impose social values about which many people remained ambivalent, just as he had with the multicultural school curriculum. "The intent may be inclusion," one said, "but the result is division. The mayor thinks he is bringing people together, but in truth he is driving them apart." While some Irish New Yorkers obsessed about the mayor's views on gay rights, others focused on his staunch support for the cause of Joe Doherty. A soldier in the Irish Republican Army, Doherty was wanted for the murder of a British soldier in Northern Ireland. The man escaped to the United States, where he was captured and jailed while the British government sought his deportment. Irish nationalists sought political asylum for him instead. Dinkins visited the man in a federal prison and wrote to President Bush on his behalf, earning the loyalty of Doherty's defenders.[34]

II. Incumbents Take the Bad with the Good

The incumbent takes the bad with the good. During late 1992 and early 1993, a series of unsettling cases revealed serious gaps in the city's Child Welfare Administration, the unit responsible for protecting youngsters from abuse. Dinkins had dedicated his mayoralty to children in his inaugural address, yet on his watch the number of child-welfare caseworkers declined by 25 percent, the consequence of budget cuts, according to the unit's managers. The mayor's staff claimed the resources for caseworkers had been granted but had been allocated poorly, causing the shortage. Vulnerable children suffered, while all involved in the acrimonious public dispute looked bad.[35]

Advocates for the homeless sued the city for forcing New Yorkers with no place to sleep to spend nights in city administrative offices instead of beds. The practice violated an agreement signed years earlier establishing minimum levels of care. The judge in the case threatened to sentence senior city officials, including Deputy Mayor Norman Steisel, to spend nights in the offices with the homeless. The Human Resources Administration was supposed to remedy the problem, but a city audit reconfirmed that the illegal condition persisted. An exchange of testy memos between Steisel and Human Resources Administration commissioner Barbara Sabol spilled into the public domain. Long-standing tensions between the two senior members of Dinkins's administration made collaboration on important social services issues difficult. "The Mayor doesn't have one administration, he has at least two," one union official familiar with the conflict complained. "They spend so much time fighting each other, they don't know where they're going. There's never been a team." When the mayor announced a new plan to build more permanent housing for the homeless with money initially targeted for social service support for the destitute, the mixed message caused confusion and anger among advocates for the poor.[36]

In February the mayor led a twenty-five-member delegation on a trip to Tokyo and Osaka in a high-profile effort to encourage Japanese businesses to maintain their presence in New York City. A severe economic downturn in Japan had caused one automotive parts manufacturer to close its New York office. The action prompted fear among real estate developers and city tax authorities that others might follow and depress property values. Dinkins's political team viewed the trade mission as a way to portray the mayor as a world-class statesman protecting the city's economic interests. It seemed to be working—until eighteen minutes after noon on Friday, February 26, 1993, when a bomb exploded in the World Trade Center, shaking Lower Manhattan with the force of an earthquake.

Radical Islamic terrorists hid explosives in a rental truck and parked it in the garage beneath the World Trade Towers. It blew a hole seven stories high. One demented conspirator would later tell police he had hoped the bomb would kill 250,000 innocent civilians. Miraculously, just six people died. More than one thousand were injured. The blast destroyed the buildings' command center and emergency power system, rendering closed-circuit television monitors and the public-address system inoperable. Security officials who could not see what was happening had no means of directing people to safety or helping rescue workers find injured or stranded victims. Implementation of carefully designed evacuation plans proved impossible. In the first critical minutes following the explosion, the towers' occupants—an estimated fifty-five thousand office workers and an additional eighty thousand visitors on any given day, some trapped one hundred stories or more above the ground—were left to make their own way to safety through unlit stairwells thick with smoke.[37]

New York Times reporter Martin Gottlieb captured the scene in the streets outside the towers. " [I]t was clear that many trade center workers, their faces streaked with soot as they streamed from buildings only to slip on snow-slicked pavements, were furious at being left to guess their way out. . . . 'There was no information anywhere about anything,' said Karen Eggleston, who was attending a training seminar on the 87th floor when the lights went out. 'It was totally uncoordinated. You were on your own.'" Individual acts of courage and heroism abounded as New Yorkers demonstrated the grit and resilience they are known for in adversity. Despite the collapse of the evacuation plan, hundreds of police, fire, and emergency medical professionals arrived to help. As the day wore on, emergency workers could be seen in the streets beneath the towers, faces covered in soot, breathing in oxygen from tanks to replenish their strength so they could reenter the buildings again in search of others.[38]

The next day a horde of government officials spoke to reporters about the disaster. First Deputy Mayor Steisel, who had personally overseen coordination of rescue efforts on the scene, led the battery of speakers. A few days after the episode, the usually anonymous public servant and his wife entered a Manhattan restaurant for a quiet dinner. To their surprise, the patrons recognized the man and burst into spontaneous, grateful applause. Governor Cuomo, New Jersey governor Jim Florio, Stanley Brezenoff, the executive director of the Port Authority which owned the Towers, James Fox of the Federal Bureau of Investigation, and police commissioner Ray Kelly all spoke to reporters about the disaster. Mayor Dinkins, his absence obvious, was stuck on a plane. After communicating with his staff from Osaka, he took the long flight home from Japan, arriving in New York around 5:00 p.m. on February 27, more than twenty-four hours after the explosion. He immediately toured the site and later announced an award of $100,000, the largest ever offered, for information leading to the arrest and conviction of those responsible. Yet in the crucial first hours after the bomb struck the World Trade Towers, David Dinkins found himself half a world away.[39]

Within days FBI agents arrested Mohammed Salameh across the Hudson River in Jersey City. He had rented the truck that contained the bomb the day before the attack. He reported the vehicle stolen and sought to recover his $400 security deposit. When he arrived at the rental office to collect it, federal agents seized him. "I cannot believe that such devastation could be caused by someone so dumb," one detective said. Investigators rapidly arrested two more conspirators, who in turn led police to the Farouq Mosque in Brooklyn. There the "Blind Sheikh," Omar Abdel Rahman, preached that Muslims had a religious duty to attack the United States, which he called a worldwide oppressor of Islam. "If there's a center of wackos in the world, it's right here in New York," Kelly said at one point in the investigation. In June 1993 the FBI arrested Rahman and others for plotting to blow up several New York landmarks. The US attorney for the Southern District of New York eventually prosecuted them. One key conspirator, Khalid Sheikh Mohammed, remained at large overseas. Federal prosecutors issued a warrant for his arrest in 1995, but, apparently with help from a friendly government, Mohammed evaded capture. New York would hear from him again on September 11, 2001.[40]

Despite its spectacular nature, New Yorkers took the attack in stride. A few weeks later when the NYPD published statistics showing major crime had dropped meaningfully in 1992 for the second year in a row, Dinkins took credit for the downward direction while reasserting his commitment to reduce it further. "As promising and encouraging as these trends may be, I am not close to satisfied. . . . [T]here is still far too much crime on our streets," he said in a press release. Experts disagreed about how much of the decline to attribute to Dinkins's policing policies. Deputy Mayor Steisel asked the NYPD to connect the dots, but Commissioner Kelly demurred. Citing the large number of factors that can affect police statistics, he wrote, "While the coincidental timing [of implementation of community policing and the drop in reported crime] presents a tempting opportunity to link the two directly . . . I believe the most prudent posture . . . is to simply let the facts speak for themselves, allowing observers and commentators to draw their own conclusions." And they did. Thomas Reppetto of the Citizens Crime Commission offered this judgment: "While it is difficult, in a scientific sense, to link changes in police strength and operational methods to a decline in crime, the decreases of the past two years strongly suggest the [mayor's] . . . strategies are responsible." Dinkins hoped the city's voters would see it the same way. His opponents would dispute the claim.[41]

III. The Dissolution of Democratic Challengers

By the time he sought to challenge David Dinkins for the Democratic nomination for mayor in 1993, Andrew Stein had become a fixture in Manhattan politics. Trading on his father's connections and wealth, he became an assemblyman at age twenty-three in 1968. He launched an investigation of nursing home abuse and established a reputation as a crusading public official. Unfortunately, he also established himself as a brash a young man in a hurry. *New York Times* reporter Joyce Purnick described him as "the not-so-smart one with the not-so-subtle toupee who courted the press, loved the headlines and tended to be dismissed as a creation of a superb staff." The young politician openly expressed his desire to be the governor, or a US senator, or the first Jewish president. He made no effort to hide ambitions many dismissed as outsized in comparison to his intellect and talent.[42]

When Stein won the city council president's office, the post included the considerable power of two votes on the Board of Estimate. And the council president succeeded the mayor if the city's chief executive died in office or became incapacitated. During his third term, Mayor Koch suffered a stroke that his doctor termed trivial. "Trivial to him," Koch would quip. When the news broke, Stein rushed to the hospital, more quickly than decorum warranted in the view of some. The would-be successor told reporters that Koch seemed fine but spoke slowly, suggesting the episode left the mayor partially incapacitated. In private Koch ridiculed the comment. "I always speak slowly to Andrew," he said.[43]

Over the years Stein's reputation had evolved. Supporters insisted, and opponents conceded, that the man was not as dumb as detractors said. He knew urban issues, had a knack for directing publicity to the causes he chose to pursue, and earned his staff's loyalty by giving them the latitude capable professionals seek to produce good work. Insiders found him a shrewd judge of the city's politics and the behavior of its elected officials. "The political firmament is not filled with Albert Einsteins," Felix Rohatyn said of Stein. "When you see a politician who picks his issues sensibly, surrounds himself with good people and takes positions that are not always popular, you tip your hat to him." John E. Zuccotti, a real estate developer and former deputy mayor summed up Stein succinctly. "[He] probably has a better sense of how to get something done in city government than 90 percent of the people who call him a dummy."[44]

Charter revision, adopted in 1989, greatly diminished the role of the city council president when it eliminated the Board of Estimate. All of the office's responsibilities could easily and logically have been distributed to the council speaker. Peter Vallone thought little of the incumbent or the position, and he also objected strongly to the title, since New Yorkers often confused his role and Stein's. Dinkins and Vallone both wanted to eliminate the post altogether, but that would require a citywide referendum. So early in 1992, with Dinkins's support, Vallone had the council rename Stein's position "public advocate," adding at the time of the vote: "This is setting the stage for what I hope will be an intelligent debate as to whether or not you need the office at all." The name change would take effect January 1, 1994, amid clear signals from the city's two most powerful leaders that they would prefer to see the post disappear entirely.[45]

By the second year of Dinkins's term, in particular after the Crown Heights riots, Stein deemed the mayor's tenure disastrous and anointed himself the logical successor. He held citywide office, he had defeated Dinkins twice before in borough president races, and he had a strong fund-raising network. In August 1991 a reporter asked political consultant David Garth to assess Stein's chances to win a race for mayor. "He looks taller because the rest of the field has shrunk, and if things don't change, he could very well be the only real candidate against Dinkins." A poll soon after suggested Stein could beat the mayor in a Democratic primary. Some speculated that if Rudy Giuliani faltered, Stein could secure the Liberal Party endorsement from boss Ray Harding. Conceivably, even the Republican Party might nominate him since Stein kept cordial relations with leaders across the political spectrum, and conservative Jews and Catholics who made up the city's GOP did not find him objectionable.[46]

Stein used the platform of the city council president's office to court the press and Manhattan elites of all kinds. He made friends with actors and entertainers, sports figures, and celebrities. The man believed his famous contacts would allow him to attract more money than City Hall's wounded incumbent or other potential challengers, so he opted out of city election finance rules designed to level the electoral playing field. Extravagant fund-raisers followed, complete with appearances by stars like Frank Sinatra, Liza Minnelli, and Joan Rivers generating over $1.5 million in one evening. His success, criticized by good government groups and his opponents, meant he could outspend his rivals. To raise his profile he began attacking the Dinkins administration at nearly every turn, seeking political gain on a range of controversial issues. He portrayed himself as an untraditional Democrat, determined to promote more efficient government through privatization of city services, reorganization of the bureaucracy, and Civil Service reform while remaining a moderate liberal on social issues.[47]

To the council president's supporters, the plan sounded terrific, but not to the average New Yorker. By early 1993, despite Stein's successful press hounding and fund-raising, he had lost credibility with Democratic voters, not gained it. He found himself trailing Dinkins by about thirty percentage points. Even more important, the proportion of likely voters with a negative view of Stein had risen to just under half by February 1993, up from just over a quarter in September 1992. The more New Yorkers saw and heard Stein and read about him in the press, the more they viewed him as an unintelligent rich kid with bad hair, under the influence of his father—hardly a winning profile. Long-term supporters, surprised at how poorly Stein stood in the polls, sat on the sidelines.[48]

By the middle of May, Congressman Thomas J. Manton, Queens Democratic Party leader, endorsed Dinkins and called on Stein to quit the race. Manton had long been a friend and political ally of Stein. The local party he led, disproportionately white, working- and middle-class in comparison to the city's overall demographics, constituted Stein's strongest potential base of support. But Manton put shrewd politics ahead of personal loyalty. He simply did not see how any of Dinkins's opponents could defeat the mayor in a Democratic primary, so he played his smartest card. Within two weeks, a 6:30 a.m. call from Governor Cuomo sealed the outcome. Stein announced he would drop out of the mayor's race in the interest of party unity and seek reelection as city council president. Then, a month later, he decided to quit politics all together. The high-flying plans to ascend to the city's top political office that seemed so likely to Stein two years earlier had crashed to the ground with a thud.[49]

About the same time Andrew Stein's campaign dissolved, Herman Badillo transformed his. Born in Caguas, Puerto Rico in 1929, by the time he turned five both of Badillo's parents had died of tuberculosis, the consequence of the efforts of the two devoutly religious Protestants to help neighbors suffering from the disease. At the age of eleven, Badillo came to New York City, where an aunt raised him. While working odd jobs, including as a pinboy in a midtown bowling alley, the youngster channeled his formidable intellect and energy into his education. He graduated high school, then earned a bachelor's degree magna cum laude in business administration at City College of New York. He worked as an accountant and attended Brooklyn Law School at night, graduating the class valedictorian in 1954. He became a certified public accountant along the way.

In 1963 Mayor Robert F. Wagner chose Badillo to head the Department of Relocation, a city unit responsible for helping twenty thousand New Yorkers affected every year by slum-clearance projects to find new homes. The appointment made him the city's first Puerto Rican–born commissioner. In 1965 he became the first Puerto Rican elected to the Board of Estimate when he won the Bronx borough presidency. In 1973 he ran for mayor. In a four-way Democratic primary, Badillo came in second behind Abe Beame, who failed to win 40 percent of the vote, forcing a runoff. In the head-to-head contest, Badillo won strong majorities among Latino and African American voters, but not enough white votes to win. In 1974 Badillo won election to Congress, once again the first man born in Puerto Rico to do so, and in 1977 he ran for mayor once more, when seven candidates spanning the city's ethnic landscape slugged it out for the right to their party's nomination. Koch ultimately prevailed, and he appointed Badillo one of seven deputy mayors at the start of his first term in an effort to create a team representative of the city's people. In 1979 Koch reduced the number of deputies reporting to him to four, dispatching Badillo among others. "He thought he was mayor," Koch said later of the episode. The two outsized egos could not fit comfortably in a building the size of City Hall.[50]

In 1981 Badillo made noise about running for mayor, but Koch's popularity had soared. The city's political classes took no opposition seriously that year. By 1985 things changed. Koch had alienated African Americans and Latinos as well as liberals of many stripes during his second term. His behavior inspired a movement to deny him a third. After a strong showing by Jesse Jackson in New York during the 1984 Democratic presidential primary, forty prominent African American and Puerto Rican leaders created the Coalition for a Just New York in a bid to unite the opposition to Koch. Congressman Charles Rangel,

Assemblyman Denny Farrell, who was Manhattan Democratic Party leader, and Dinkins proposed Basil Paterson as the coalition's candidate. Badillo sought the nomination himself but pledged not to run without the coalition's backing and to support whomever it chose. After months of deliberation, Paterson elected not to run, citing ill health as the reason. Badillo rapidly became the leading contender. He lined up a majority of the coalition's votes, and it appeared he would run against his former boss with the support of the city's African American and Latino leaders lined up behind him.[51]

Harlem's African American politicians could not accept Badillo's candidacy. To do so would have ceded control of the coalition—and potentially City Hall to a Puerto Rican. It was a matter of ethnic pride and self-interest as well. They wanted Koch out, but they wanted themselves, not others, in. And on a personal basis, they did not trust Badillo, whose independence made him highly unpredictable. To break the support Badillo had cultivated among the coalition's black politicians, they had to offer an African American alternative. After a series of delaying maneuvers, on February 11, 1985, two days before the coalition met to choose its candidate, Denny Farrell finally agreed to run himself. He won the coalition's support amid charges that his candidacy was just a ploy to stop Badillo, who was outraged, but saw little point to running without support. As predicted, Farrell never did mount a serious campaign, and Koch won reelection again in a landslide.[52]

In the early 1980s Governor Hugh Carey appointed Badillo a trustee of City University of New York (CUNY). The position provided the man who had conquered adversity and succeeded by his own hard work with a platform for promoting his commitment to high educational standards. He held the view that government policies that allowed poor people of color to advance without true achievement, such as social promotion in public school systems or bilingual education that did not insist Spanish speakers learn English, actually crippled the people they intended to help. In 1986 Badillo ran for New York State comptroller. He took a majority of the votes cast in New York City but lost the statewide race. He continued as a CUNY trustee, reappointed by Governor Mario Cuomo, and he practiced law and remained a prominent figure in Democratic Party circles, always a persistent advocate for high standards for Latinos and blacks.[53]

In Badillo's own judgment, none could match his unique qualifications to be mayor, so as Dinkins faltered he explored his chances.

He raised $200,000, secured the endorsement of Ed Koch, despite the fallout between the two prickly personalities years earlier, and began campaigning. He presented himself as a candidate who could appeal to New Yorkers of disparate ethnic backgrounds but who would govern more effectively than the man in office. He got nowhere. Polls showed him stuck with single-digit support. Even many Latinos viewed him—at the age of sixty-three and out of elected office since 1977—as a man whose better days had passed. His quest for the mayor's office—at least his fourth—never caught on, and by May 1993 he prepared to end it. Yet conversations between Badillo and David Garth, by then Giuliani's key strategist, offered him another option.[54]

IV. Ethnic Arithmetic

The night David Dinkins defeated Giuliani by just two percentage points in 1989, the vanquished candidate sat in bed, lamenting to his wife, Donna Hanover, "Do they really hate me? Do they really think I'm mean?" he asked plaintively. Indeed, earlier in the evening as he sought to silence supporters who reacted to his gracious acknowledgment of Dinkins's victory with hoots and catcalls, he screamed from the podium, "No, no, no. . . . Quiet. Quiet!" over and over again in what television cameras projected as an emotional meltdown and a harsh and futile effort to control his supporters. It did nothing to soften his image. A city seeking law-and-order surely wanted a tough mayor, but a city seeking a leader who could calm nerves rubbed raw by racial disharmony just as surely did not want a man who screamed at the public, nor a man who represented only one of New York's feuding tribes.[55]

The ethnic politics of a head-to-head contest between Dinkins and Giuliani were simple and stark. Dinkins would win nearly all the African American votes. Giuliani would win the ballots of 80 percent or more of white Catholics. Of New York's major voting blocs, only Latinos and Jews could be drawn toward or pulled away from the two candidates. So when Badillo's campaign for the Democratic nomination for mayor fizzled, Giuliani's team cleverly invited him to join their campaign as the candidate for comptroller. The elder statesman of Puerto Rican politicians, highly qualified for the position, would give the Giuliani camp credibility with Latinos. More important, it demonstrated that Giuliani, if elected mayor, could work across ethnic boundaries. It took Badillo two weeks to sort through his options, as the wily politician engaged in a series of conversations with representatives of the mayor and the governor to see if he could secure their support for the Democratic nomination for comptroller. In the end Badillo joined Giuliani's team and entered the Democratic race for comptroller as well. On May 28, 1993, the tall, regal Puerto Rican stood with his new ally atop a flatbed truck at East 116th Street and Lexington Avenue in East Harlem, where Fiorello LaGuardia had once launched a fusion campaign for mayor. He announced that he was joining forces with Giuliani "to rebuild our great city, restoring it to a place where standards are applied and met." Susan D. Alter, their running mate for public advocate, joined them.[56]

Less than a week earlier, in another maneuver managed by Garth, Alter declared she would seek the public advocate's office on Giuliani's ticket—as well as pursue the Democratic Party's nomination for the spot. An Orthodox Jew and fourteen-year city council veteran from Brooklyn, who in 1991 had won reelection to a district reconfigured to include a majority of African Americans, Alter lent Giuliani's ticket credibility on a range of dimensions. Her gender softened the prosecutor's harsh image and her religion offered a gesture to Jews. Her ability to poll well with blacks also helped. The likelihood Giuliani would win many black votes remained remote, but, by associating himself with a candidate who black voters trusted, he signaled that as mayor he would select a team able to work with all segments of the city. And as a Democrat and early supporter of Dinkins who now publicly declared the mayor "a disappointment," Alter served as a role model for Democratic voters to follow at the polling booth. "You touch so many bases. If you didn't exist, we'd have to invent you," Garth told her.[57]

Alter criticized Dinkins as "conflicted as an African-American Mayor, about representing the black community." She referenced his handling of the Crown Heights riot and the Korean grocers boycott as episodes that revealed "a struggle within him to figure out how and where to act" on race-related issues. She implied he favored his own unfairly. In part, the view emerged from personal experience. Alter bore a grudge against Dinkins because he did not intervene on her behalf when realignment recast the boundaries of her council district to favor a minority candidate. Among other things, her alliance with Giuliani constituted payback.[58]

The two Democrats joined Giuliani on the Liberal as well as the Republican Party line. Ray Harding assured the former. The Liberal Party endorsement for Giuliani had never really been in doubt. After his near victory in 1989, political observers presumed he would run again and that the Liberals who backed him the first time would name him their candidate once more. The decision guaranteed Giuliani a ballot line and provided him with a modest but important dose of ideological immunization. Political insiders knew that the Liberals had long since lost any philosophical integrity and its boss, Ray Harding, cast the support of the party he controlled to the candidate most likely to provide him and his followers with the best jobs and most lucrative contracts. Yet the label, though no longer authentic, mattered a lot in a city where registered Democrats outnumbered Republicans by a ratio of five-to-one and where conservative opinions normally voiced by the GOP on a national level generated little echo. The line provided disaffected Democrats with a way to cast a ballot for a candidate they preferred without appearing to endorse Republican policies they found distasteful.[59]

To run as Republicans, Badillo and Alter needed the party committee's approval. To avoid a repeat of the corrosive $11 million primary battle Ronald Lauder waged against him in 1989, Giuliani had mended his relationship with Senator Alfonse D'Amato. There were Republican Party officials in Queens and Brooklyn who found Giuliani too liberal for their taste on social issues, and others had friends caught up in the former prosecutor's pursuit of Wall Street traders and believed him reckless with power. D'Amato shut down opposition to the candidate with whom he had made peace and secured the nomination for Guiliani's running mates as well. Giuliani's relations with Roy Goodman, leader of the party in Manhattan, had always been good. He also got on well with the two Guys—state senator Guy Velella, head of the Bronx Republican Party, and borough president Guy Molinari, Republican leader of Staten Island, a borough with intense interest in a local issue.[60]

When New Yorkers agreed to eliminate the Board of Estimate to comply with the United States Supreme Court decision ruling the city's long-standing governing body unconstitutional, Staten Islanders took offense. For nearly a century, New York's tiniest borough had held the same clout on the influential board as did the other four boroughs, whose populations dwarfed its own. Without the equal protection the board offered, Staten Islanders feared their nearly all-white, working- and upper-middle-class enclave would find itself subsumed by the greater metropolis. They worried decisions made by the rest of the city, whose demographics, economics, and ethnic and racial composition differed substantially from their own, would not reflect their interests. In response, Staten Islanders sought permission to secede from New York City and to establish themselves as a separate metropolis.

The initial step in the process involved a borough-wide referendum, which would occur in November along with the citywide election for mayor and other municipal offices. The ballot measure promised to bring a disproportionate number of Staten Islanders—a population heavily concentrated with Giuliani supporters—to the polls.[61]

So the Giuliani team successfully created a contemporary version of a balanced ticket and built momentum around a modern-day fusion campaign for mayor. For several decades Democrats and Republicans in New York had typically nominated one Irish candidate, one Italian, and one Jew for citywide office in an effort to appeal to the three voting blocs that once dominated the city's electoral politics. Demographic change and the decline of party discipline caused the practice to fade, but the logic remained sound. As an Italian candidate for mayor seeking the votes of Jews and Latinos, Giuliani teamed up with citywide candidates from those two groups. And in a town where registered Democrats outnumbered Republicans by five-to-one and where many voters considered themselves moderate to liberal, victory against a Democratic nominee required the fusion of multiple opposition parties and disaffected Democrats. Reformers from the late nineteenth century through the successful twentieth-century campaigns of Fiorello LaGuardia and John Lindsay had followed that strategy. The ticket Giuliani's team attracted provided a platform for the broad-based coalition he needed.

The campaign tried to add the Conservative Party nomination as well, ignoring the cognitive dissonance of a candidate's name appearing on both the Liberal and Conservative lines. The latter party balked at the prospect. Its leaders feared it would alienate their ideologically committed supporters and render them even less relevant than usual in a city election if they endorsed the Liberal Party choice. Their nomination went to a US Trust Company vice president named George Marlin. Concern about the multicultural school curriculum that taught young students to accept homosexuals inspired him to run. "I am not going to let anybody take away my ability to tell my kid what's right or wrong," Marlin said, curiously, since he had no children. The Right to Life Party also endorsed him.[62]

Mayoral master David Garth directed the sophisticated strategy unfolding as Giuliani's campaign took form. Ever since he directed John Lindsay to victory in 1965 and again in his stunning 1969 reelection, insiders considered Garth the most brilliant of New York's political advisors. He steered Koch to City Hall in 1977, and in two subsequent contests placing Garth on the winning team in five of New York's previous seven mayoral elections. In 1989 Giuliani had relied on Roger Ailes, the darling of right-wing Republicans at the national level, for media advice. Ray Harding thought the outcome a disaster, among other reasons because of Ailes's poor understanding of how New Yorkers attitudes on issues like abortion and race, gun control, and the death penalty differed from attitudes in other parts of the country. To the Liberal Party leader, Garth was not just the obvious choice but the only one. Giuliani and Garth did not get on well when they first met—two hard-driving personalities, each man highly confident in his own views. But in time, over several months, Harding persevered, and the two men developed a degree of mutual respect. By January 1993 Garth had signed on.[63]

Giuliani's standing on Memorial Day 1993 contrasted sharply with the state of his candidacy on Memorial Day 1989. He still had his long-time loyal aides at his side—notably Denny Young and Peter Powers—but he also had Garth and a more fully developed relationship with Ray Harding. His campaign war chest contained $3 million compared with $200,000 four years earlier, and Democratic politicians of stature from the two key voting blocs whose support he needed joined him on the Republican–Liberal ticket without intraparty opposition. He confronted an incumbent rather than an aspirant in 1993, but one with a mixed record. And the exceptional enthusiasm among Dinkins's base in 1989—when the chance of making history by electing a black man mayor of New York for the first time propelled African Americans to the polls—had tempered some.

Village Voice political columnist Michael Tomasky offered three reasons Giuliani stood a better chance in 1993 than four years earlier. "First, Giuliani has a better campaign and will probably be a better candidate," he reasoned. Second, "a small percentage of white voters, maybe 4 or 5 percent [voted] for an African American hoping that his ascent would reduce racial tensions. . . . [W]ith matters on the racial front no better than they were, that 4 or 5 percent might, to put it bluntly, go back to the white guy." And third, "The simplest and most race-neutral of reasons: The city's in bad shape and Dinkins hasn't been a leader."[64]

V. Giuliani Goes to School

Giuliani himself had evolved, at least in some respects. After his defeat, he returned to private practice, first as a partner with the prestigious law firm White & Case, and then later at another Manhattan firm, Anderson Kill. But he spent most of his time thinking about urban issues and developing his ideas about what it would take to govern New York City. Four years earlier, when he stepped down as federal prosecutor in January of a mayoral election year, he spent several months focused on policy study. But then the blizzard of activity required to mount a citywide campaign consumed him. Losing the election liberated him. It gave him the time to apply his considerable intellect to deepening his understanding of the complexities the city faced and the options open to a mayor willing to confront creatively New York's tough, seemingly intractable problems.[65]

Giuliani began with a city government tutorial from Bobby Wagner. The self-effacing, shy man had grown up in Gracie Mansion, the son of a three-term mayor. As Ed Koch's all-purpose advisor for a dozen years, he had held an unusually broad range of senior city government positions. It made him the closest thing to a know-it-all that could be found in New York's sprawling municipal bureaucracy. By 1992, Giuliani engaged in a series of sessions organized by Fred Siegel, a history professor at the Cooper Union for Science and Art and senior editor of *City Journal,* the publication of the Manhattan Institute. Topics ranged from homelessness to policing tactics, from tax policy to labor efficiency, from garbage collection to health care, and on and on. The Manhattan Institute was an urban-affairs center whose mission was to develop creative ideas to make government work better. It attracted scholars who had come to doubt the effectiveness of liberal policies, particularly as implemented in New York City. The teachers who schooled Giuliani left the sessions impressed with the student. By the time he started to campaign in earnest, Giuliani could offer a coherent message that went beyond a declaration that he was not David Dinkins.[66]

The candidate did not neglect his political education either. Giuliani and key advisors met with John Mollenkopf, political science professor at the City University of New York Graduate Center. Mollenkopf was the city's academic master of electoral district by electoral district voting patterns having created maps that recorded balloting by race, class, and other demographic factors. He had analyzed the coalitions that elected Koch and that later turned him from office, topics of keen interest to Giuliani and his aides.[67]

Fred Siegel had come to the Giuliani team's attention after he devoted the entire spring 1992 issue of *City Journal* to the quality of urban life. "Public space is both the glory and shame of New York,"

Siegel wrote. The vitality of the city's sidewalks and plazas contrasted with "[o]ur shame . . . that we've allowed fear and filth to subvert one of our most important assets." The degree of harassment drove people to lock themselves inside their apartments in despair, Siegel asserted. It converted what urban sociologist Jane Jacobs had called the "intricate ballet" of New York's streets, where busy pedestrians danced through urban life with unchoreographed license, into an in-your-face assault akin to "roller derby."[68]

The belief that social disorder causes lawlessness anchored Giuliani's newfound understanding of urban policy and what it would take to restore civility to New York's streets. Ten years earlier sociologist James Q. Wilson and Harvard professor George Kelling wrote an article for the *Atlantic Monthly,* setting out what came to be known as the broken-window theory. When a vandal breaks a window and goes unpunished and the window remains unrepaired, it invites others to do the same. Soon all the windows in the neighborhood get broken, and a sense of disorder emerges that encourages more antisocial behavior. Stopping the small indignities that affront people daily discourages the larger ones, they concluded.[69]

When he headed New York's transit police, William Bratton put the idea to the test and discovered it worked better than he imagined. His underground police force cracked down on fare-beaters who hopped the turnstile or sneaked into the subway through the exit gates, and they took on the token suckers—thieves who stuffed slugs into subway fare slots to jam tokens in place, which they then sucked out with their mouths like urban leeches. It turned out that the people committing these pettiest of violations included many criminals with outstanding arrest warrants for serious offenses. More than a few had illegal weapons when the police seized them. The obvious point that muggers thought nothing of cheating the Metropolitan Transit Authority for a dollar and change surprised no one, so it turned out that by focusing on the minor issue of fare beating the transit police reduced serious crime significantly. Eventually, Giuliani would link the concept holistically to the health of the city's economy, the state of its schools, and to the psychological well-being of New Yorkers as well as to a strategy for combating crime.[70]

Presenting his ideas to the public required some art from Giuliani. It suited him to portray New York as a city in crisis, suffering from unacceptable levels of violent crime with a government that no longer functioned. He wanted voters to believe the city desperately needed radical change of a kind no one should expect from a man with David Dinkins's heritage, a servant of the Democratic clubhouse, tied to the status quo and the city's unions, stale from steeping for decades in the warm beer of a bloated bureaucracy. Yet if he spoke too harshly, it provoked the image of the prosecutor out of control—a man who would drag suspects from their offices in handcuffs before trying or convicting them, who would scream at poorly behaved supporters, and who would hurl vulgar incitements to police protestors as they degenerated into a mob. Always skin-deep lurked the specter of race. Nasty words about New York's first black mayor risked offending in ways that would damage rational debate as well as Giuliani's cause. He had to choose his words with unaccustomed caution to avoid accusations that he sought to disparage his opponent with nasty stereotypes.[71]

The challenger got cover from an unexpected source when Senator Daniel Moynihan delivered a speech he called, "Toward a New Intolerance," in April 1993 at a gathering of the Association for a Better New York. The brainiest politician in Gotham had recently attended his fiftieth high school reunion and asked himself the question, "What is better today than it was then?" His disconcerting answer—nothing. One year in his youth, the imposing silver-haired intellect intoned, New York suffered 44 murders with handguns. Last year, he told his listeners, the number reached 1,499. In 1943, 73,000 people received welfare, and the illegitimacy rate hovered around 3 percent. A half century on, more than one million were on the dole, and 45 percent of babies were born of single mothers. The George Washington Bridge, built in the days of boss-ridden Tammany took forty-nine months to complete and opened ahead of schedule. Modern New York could not complete the Westway road project, or any other major undertaking.[72]

Moynihan quoted at length New York State Supreme Court Judge Edwin Torres, one of five Manhattan judges assigned specifically to homicides, violent felonies, and gun cases. The fifteen-year veteran of the judicial system lamented that the "slaughter of the innocent marches unabated: subway riders, bodega owners, cab drivers, babies; in laundromats, at cash machines, on elevators, in hallways." The city's reaction to all this, the judge likened to a "narcoleptic state of acceptance" similar to the way combat soldiers retreat into a protective emotional shell when surrounded by intolerable levels of violence. They would become so inured that they could eat their rations seated amid the dead bodies of fallen comrades. "A society that loses its sense of outrage is doomed to extinction," Torres concluded. Moynihan agreed, and he went on to reference a comment made by police commissioner Kelly. "No Radio" signs affixed to car windows in anonymous pleas to thieves not to break into the owners' automobiles constituted "urban flags of surrender" when indignation and outrage would serve society better. "We need to do *something,* or lose our freedom to crime and violence," Kelly told an FBI audience. "Acceptance leads people to pack up and leave, and the idea is to stay and fight," the former marine had said. "Defining Deviance Down," the title of an article the senator had penned for *American Scholar,* captured Moynihan's view of New York City in 1993. He decried the willingness of city dwellers to tolerate conditions that should have been unacceptable.[73]

David Dinkins sat in the audience alongside many of the city's most prominent businessmen and real estate developers steaming. He expected New York's senior US senator, chair of the powerful finance committee, reared on Manhattan's West Side, to tell his listeners how Washington, with a Democrat in the White House for the first time in twelve years, would treat his birthplace better. "In the 'good old days,'" the mayor acerbically told a reporter present, "I wore the uniform of a US Marine and had to sit in the back," suggesting the idyllic city described had never existed, certainly not for African Americans. The speech did not single out Dinkins, but a politician as shrewd as Moynihan surely understood his comments would scarcely help an incumbent mayor seeking reelection. "And because Moynihan is accorded a gravitas in the world of ideas that neither Rudy Giuliani nor Andy Stein can lay claim to," *Village Voice* columnist Michael Tomasky wrote, "an ounce of vinegar from [him] sprays more thoroughly than the bucketfuls of spit the unpolished Giuliani and the feckless Stein will rain on the incumbent." Giuliani headquarters considered the speech a gift.[74]

VI. The Battle Joins

Through April and into May, Dinkins and his team mostly ignored Giuliani. They adopted an urban "Rose Garden" strategy, emphasizing the mayor's responsibilities for running the city while organizing a campaign that would feature Dinkins's commitment to reducing crime and to improving education. After all, crime had begun to drop, and education statistics suggested progress on certain test scores and attendance levels.[75]

Michael Tomasky, by then writing about the emerging contest for mayor in just about every issue of the *Village Voice,* ridiculed the strategy. "These are big losers, as anyone who hasn't been living in Uzbekistan will tell you," he wrote of the mayor's campaign themes. He likened Dinkins relying on falling crime statistics as a reason for a second term to a fifteenth-century king asking for loyalty from his subjects because "the bubonic plague is subsiding somewhat." He pointed out that a lag occurs between statistical improvement in crime rates and public perception. "It is a dubious prospect indeed that people actually feel safer walking the streets these days than they did three years ago, and for Dinkins to rely on that assumption to lift him above a law-and-order type like Rudy Giuliani is ridiculous," he wrote. On education, Tomasky called the ouster of Chancellor Fernandez by "anti-Dinkins forces" at the Board of Education "the harshest whipping of his mayoralty." Other reports reinforced Tomasky's point about public perceptions of street violence. In "The Worst Crimes of '93 (So Far)," *New York* magazine catalogued multiple murders, an attack by a homeless man on a twenty-two-month-old boy, a running gun battle between police and bank robbers that left a hostage dead, and on and on. "The level of cruelty just keeps going up in the city," one detective said. "People set on fire, shot over nothing. It just doesn't stop."[76]

Soon the mayor's campaign team would take such criticisms seriously. A *New York Times*/CBS poll taken between May 10 and 14, 1993, showed the contest between Dinkins and Giuliani a virtual dead heat. Of registered voters, 45 percent favored the mayor and 44 percent supported his challenger. Race remained the swamp in which the two candidates swam. To no one's surprise, blacks overwhelmingly approved of how the mayor handled the city. Whites overwhelmingly disapproved, although even they gave Dinkins relatively strong ratings for his efforts to manage down racial tensions. And more New Yorkers thought race relations would sour if Giuliani won than thought they would improve. Yet crime topped the list of problems New Yorkers wanted the next mayor to fix—which favored the former prosecutor—followed by the economy, unemployment, and homelessness. The poll suggested the mayor's standing had improved slightly in Queens and that a strong majority of gays preferred him to his opponent. But it also showed that he had lost significant ground in Brooklyn, where the Crown Heights riots and the Korean grocers boycott had occurred and where protest marches took place in Bensonhurst and Canarsie. Most important perhaps, Latino voters divided evenly when asked if they approved of Mayor Dinkins, a sharp decline compared with the nearly 70 percent of Latinos who cast ballots for the mayor in 1989.[77]

New York Newsday reported some more ominous news. "Poll: Most Voters Feel the Mosaic Is Cracked; Race Relations Are Seen as Worsened," read a June 14, 1993, headline. Fifty-five percent of the city believed race relations deteriorated during Dinkins's term as mayor, while just 23 percent thought they had improved, according to a survey the newspaper conducted in conjunction with WABC TV. By a margin of 38 percent to 34 percent, a small plurality of blacks thought things had gotten better. So even among Dinkins's strongest defenders, the mayor did little better than break-even in delivering on the fundamental promise of his initial campaign. Nearly two-thirds of whites reported a sense of deterioration, four times more than thought they were better. And critically, twice as many Latinos thought race relations had declined rather than improved, 52 percent to 26. "What is very significant here—and what is damaging to the mayor—is that Hispanics feel race relations are worse and Hispanics are the swing vote in this election," historian Richard Wade said. "Dinkins campaigned in large part to promote racial harmony," he continued. "This is a very important part of the poll and a real problem for the mayor." A reporter asked Giuliani what he thought of the numbers. "It's a shame for the city that Dinkins' record has been such that it has undercut the premise of his administration—healing," the challenger said.[78]

Results from the two polls implied that the mayor's campaign had stalled, and polls from several recent elections around the country involving black and white candidates gave cause for more alarm. White voters, it seemed, did not always respond honestly when asked if they would vote for a black man they did not favor. They feared the answer would mark them as racist. The discrepancy in some instances amounted to 8 percent of respondents, more than enough to indicate Mayor Dinkins might actually be trailing.[79] So Dinkins went on the offensive. He accused his opponent of keeping his positions deliberately vague so he would not have to defend them, a luxury not available to the incumbent. The press, the mayor believed, had an obligation to scrutinize Giuliani's policies as closely as they did his, and he aimed to force them to do their job. At a midtown Manhattan breakfast sponsored by Crain's New York Business and the New York City Chamber of Commerce and Industry, Dinkins defended his administration's programs to create jobs and to keep businesses in New York. While he had been working on the full range of issues facing the city every day, he told his audience, his opponent "had done nothing—absolutely nothing." He referenced a Giuliani statement indicating he was developing a position paper on how the Board of Education should operate, and then ridiculed it. "It's O.K. if he doesn't have one, but he's had three and a half years," the mayor said. "Rudolph Giuliani has never run a government," he reminded his audience, and he also told them, "I truly do have a fashion of relating to people that is superior to his." This last comment played to the mayor's strength and subtly evoked the images of Giuliani as a man who could spin out of control. The mayor belittled the former prosecutor's record, pointing out that many of the high-profile cases he pursued had been overturned on appeals.[80]

Dinkins took a few days in early July 1993 to travel to Israel. He had gone there before in February 1991, shortly after the US forces landed in Kuwait to repel Iraqi dictator Saddam Hussein's invading army. Saddam retaliated against the US military action by firing Scud missiles at Tel Aviv in an effort to provoke a response from America's ally and rally Arab support to his side. The Machiavellian tactic failed, but the threat to Israeli civilians alarmed New York's Jews, and Dinkins's 1991 trip had mattered to them. Tel Aviv mayor Shlomo Lahat, a retired general known as Cheech, told Dinkins in front of reporters in July 1993, "We'll never forget that you were with us. People say you came for elections, or not for elections. I couldn't care less. The important thing is you came." Dinkins's antagonist, Riverdale rabbi Avi Weiss, tried to ruin the mayor's trip. He took out a large advertisement in the *Jerusalem Post* to tell his fellow Jews that the mayor's mishandling of the Crown Heights riots had fostered "bigotry, lawlessness and pogroms." Thousands of miles away, the Brooklyn disturbances that had occurred two years before cast a shadow over David Dinkins that would follow him home.[81]

Governor Cuomo's director of criminal justice, Richard Girgenti, released his report on the disturbances in Crown Heights and the ac-quittal of Lemrick Nelson shortly after Dinkins returned from Israel. It highlighted the severity of the violence, the ineffectiveness of police tactics, and the slowness of the mayor and his senior staff to respond. "The Mayor, as the City's Chief Executive, did not act in a timely and decisive manner . . . 'to protect the lives, safety and property of the residents of Crown Heights, and to quickly restore peace and order to the community,'" the report declared. To deflect the criticism, Dinkins invoked his leadership in the aftermath of the Rodney King verdict in Los Angeles. "We worked to control things here—using some of the things we had learned in Crown Heights, I would add—and things were so well in hand we had calm in the city. You in the media praised me editorially, and Ed Koch and Al D'Amato and Rudy Giuliani praised me at the time," he reminded reporters. Giuliani released a statement that said the Girgenti report would force New Yorkers to "decide whether this was an isolated instance of failed leadership by the Mayor or whether it was part of a pattern which has serious implications for the city." On a WABC radio interview, Giuliani responded more pointedly. "It's incomprehensible that a mayor of a major city would be as disengaged as this Mayor was during Crown Heights," he told listeners.[82]

Shortly before the report he commissioned appeared, Governor Cuomo entered the fray on behalf of his fellow Democrat in an effort to limit the damage. "David Dinkins is an authentic American hero," the state's chief executive told a church congregation in Bedford Stuyvesant. "I've said it before and . . . I will say it all over this city. . . . I will say it even louder and more frequently now that it's more necessary. . . . He is the essence of civility and he can show us how to live together as one city going forward." No doubt the mayor welcomed the ringing endorsement, but at the same time Dinkins and many of his supporters resented the governor's posture. During budget negotiations earlier in the year, Cuomo had shown the mayor no quarter. In his role as chair of the Financial Control Board, he had embarrassed Dinkins and held the city to a standard of financial discipline the governor failed to achieve for the state. The timing behind the release of the governor's Crown Heights report could scarcely help the man he praised so effusively in his reelection effort. The governor, who one longtime ally described as a "Queens district leader with the voice of Abraham Lincoln," proved himself a shrewd politician more than a loyal ally. He supported Dinkins when it suited him. He distanced himself when he found it expedient. One Dinkins supporter offered a crude summary of the relationship. "The Governor is peeing in our face . . . [and] wants us to believe it's rain."[83]

Toward the end of August, a federal judge ordered Mayor Dinkins to allow attorneys pursuing a civil suit filed by Yankel Rosenbaum's family and Lubavitch Hasidim from Crown Heights to depose him about his actions during the riots. She also ruled the litigation a matter of public interest and authorized a press pool to attend the sessions in Gracie Mansion, ensuring complete coverage of the drama. "On trial in his own house, the Mayor was by turns tight-lipped and combative, quietly sincere and sarcastic, as he endured five hours of harsh questioning by Franklyn Snitow," the New York Times reported. When asked if he ordered the police held back, Dinkins replied curtly, "[I]t never happened. It's just a lot of nonsense." He acknowledged tactical errors by the police and agreed that undoubtedly some lawbreakers escaped punishment, but that was because the police could not arrest them safely with the forces deployed. Other members of his administration confirmed his recollection. No one ordered police to ignore violence or lawlessness or withhold protection from the Hasidim to allow rioting blacks to "vent their rage," as the lawsuit claimed. Milton Mollen suggested that Lee Brown's "reserved" communication style and a general reluctance by the police to discuss their tactics left the mayor and his team less well-informed about important details than outsiders might have imagined. Dinkins summed up the episode that took place ten weeks before the general election bitterly. "They seek only to embarrass me and my administration," he said.[84]

The release of the Crown Heights report and headlines about the mayor's sworn testimony reopened deep wounds, but they revealed little new about an episode already thoroughly aired. One journalist wrote, "[U]ntil the report's release, Rudolph Giuliani had failed to offer a truly persuasive reason Dinkins should be turned out of office. Now Dinkins will have to convince voters that he should be reelected." But most analysts suggested the impact of the report would be minimal. People's minds had largely been made up on the issue long before.[85]

While Lubavitch lawyers interrogated the mayor on his role in Crown Heights, details of the Board of Education asbestos scandal and the implications for the start of the school year were unfolding. The episode played perfectly into Giuliani's campaign theme. The municipal bureaucracy—bloated, corrupt, inefficient—had reached the point that it endangered the city.

Then the ghost of the Parking Violations Bureau scandal that haunted Ed Koch his last term in office appeared in David Dinkins's City Hall. On August 18 the Department of Investigation released a report that accused Budget Director Philip Michael of overzealous behavior and bad judgment. It said he had showed "favoritism toward Lockheed while the City was considering the company's proposals to privatize New York City's parking management services, in violation of the Procurement Policy Board Rules." It also said that "Lockheed had greater access than other vendors to high-level City officials" in a position to influence the scope and award of the contract, and that the project's request for proposal (RFP) had been structured to favor Lockheed. The report criticized First Deputy Mayor Norman Steisel for violating policies designed to ensure fairness in awarding city contracts, and it declared that his chief of staff, Ellen Baer, had engaged in inappropriate employment conversations with Lockheed while helping oversee the project for the city. The report called into question the motivation behind the initiative, stating that none of the responsible parties actually "made the determination called for by the RFP that contracting out PVB's functions was 'in the best interests of the city.'"[86]

Philip Michael championed the idea of privatizing the Parking Violations Bureau (PVB) collection process as early as 1990 with First Deputy Steisel's strong support. Michael's experience as commissioner of finance during the Koch administration had taught him the city could generate much more revenue than it did from existing sources—with less pain than higher taxes or staffing cuts—if its departments would seize the initiative. Michael viewed the PVB privatization proposal as a prime project that could generate an additional $100 million per year at a time when the city desperately needed it. Department of Transportation commissioner Lucius Riccio agreed that the department's computer systems could be improved through outsourcing but wanted the project stopped there to limit the impact on his department. Lockheed, on the other hand, sought to take over virtually all of the transportation department's functions as First Deputy Steisel remembered it—parking violation collections, ticket issuance, vehicle towing, scofflaw enforcement, metering activities, and other tasks.[87]

Steisel brokered conversations with Michael and Riccio and set the project on a path to contract out responsibility for computer technology and the parking violation collection process, provided a company could demonstrate the capacity to handle both roles effectively. Before long, "[W]orking with Riccio became very difficult," Steisel recalled. The man did not fully support the project that would reduce the size of his department by some four hundred staff, and at one point, he shared his concerns with the press, even though administration policy had been set. So Steisel asked his top aide, Ellen Baer, to oversee the project and make sure it got done.[88]

Almost from the start, Commissioner Riccio and Budget Director Michael clashed. Progress on the project remained slow, and in several meetings the budget director and transportation commissioner exchanged unusually harsh words in front of others. Steisel met with the men and told them to stop what he would later call "unfortunate, unseemly public and private bickering." The city issued the RFP in February 1992, and in December of that year Commissioner Riccio and First Deputy Steisel accepted the recommendation of the evaluation committee that the city enter into contract negotiations with Lockheed. Michael had recused himself from a formal role in the decision to avoid any appearance of conflict of interest. The exact nature of the contract would depend in part on the company's ability to demonstrate in appropriate detail, beyond its answers to the RFP, that it could improve upon the city's own performance. In Steisel's mind, only then could the project team determine definitively if the move was "in the city's best interest."[89]

At the end of January 1993, the transportation department's deputy commissioner issued a memo to the PVB staff announcing the status of the project. It acknowledged, "Significant change always produces some anxiety," and went on to assure people that any action was months away. The memo reminded staff that the city and relevant unions had agreed to achieve privatization without layoffs, and that those who might wish to join a privatized PVB, should the project proceed, would have an opportunity to do so. Within days, Bill Lynch, then running Dinkins's reelection campaign, sent Steisel a memo. "It is my understanding that the privatization process at PVB is moving forward quickly," he wrote of the project first conceived in 1990. "I am concerned about the timing and implementation process for these changes because approximately 400 jobs will be affected that are currently held by members of DC37 and CWA Local 1180." The initials "CC: DND" appear at the bottom of the page.[90]

A month after that, DC 37 executive director Stanley Hill sent a two-page letter to the mayor expressing "strong opposition" to the PVB privatization plan. He wrote, "[P]ublic employee organizations have yet to receive any documentation," supporting the claim that the decision is in the best interest of the city, and it went on to accuse the city of "an obvious intent . . . to circumvent public employee unions, undermine collective bargaining law, and evade constitutional merit and fitness protections." A few months earlier the city had agreed to allow municipal unions to offer counterproposals in response to privatization plans. Steisel reportedly had told a working committee that since the PVB privatization RFP had been issued before the agreement, he did not think the agreement applied to the project.[91]

Shortly after Hill's letter of protest, the Department of Investigation launched its probe. The city's inquiry had barely begun when someone delivered extensive details on every aspect of the matter to Wayne Barrett, investigative reporter for the *Village Voice*, who proceeded to write a mind-numbingly dense exposé of the matter. The front-page headline read, "The City Scandal That Won't Go Away." Side by side pictures of Ed Koch and David Dinkins appeared underneath the dramatic banner, as if they were partners in contract crime. Their troubled faces scarily filled the photo frames, with an oversized caption that read, "The Dinkins Administration Is about to Sign a $200 Million Contract with the Same Firm Whose Corruption Helped Bring down Ed Koch." The article recounted the crimes the company had committed years earlier and implied it continued to operate with disregard for ethical standards.[92]

"The mayor who presides over this incestuous intertwine of influence peddlers and compromised officials," Barrett wrote, "was elected by a progressive constituency that wants a government dedicated to acting in the public interest, not in the interests of its pirating friends." He went on to cast the matter in the broadest and worst possible way. "David Dinkins has known for many, many months that there is a cancer of conflict at the very top of his government. This contract is merely one of its fleshy by-products." That day, Dinkins announced contract negotiations with Lockheed would halt until the investigation department completed its work. At Steisel's suggestion, the mayor created a three-person panel, including his private counsel, George Daniels, to review the report that might normally go to the first deputy for action. The next week, the *Voice* published another highly detailed, extremely harsh story on the episode with others to follow.[93]

Stanley Hill's letter of protest to the mayor took on a hot potato quality. The mayor's office referred it to Steisel for response. He in turn referred it to Riccio, who passed it off to labor commissioner James Hanley. Hanley prepared a response for the mayor's signature. Steisel sent it back to Hanley with instructions to send it out under the commissioner of labor's own signature. "As you know," Hanley wrote to Hill, "the Mayor has directed that all negotiations with Lockheed Information Management Services be suspended pending an . . . inquiry into this matter by Commissioner of Investigation Susan Shepard."[94]

The Department of Investigation's report—over two hundred pages long—revealed nothing criminal, and no charges were ever filed against any of the city officials accused of mishandling the project. But the appearance of impropriety oozed throughout. And because the company had been central to the scandals that so damaged the Koch administration, it allowed newspaper editors to write sensational headlines such

316

as, "80s Scandal Unraveled in Suicide," and link Dinkins's name back to the bribery and looting that occurred long before he took office.[95]

So the commissioner of investigation had issued a report accusing Budget Director Michael of favoritism and bad judgment, and in private she suggested more damaging headlines would occur if the man did not resign. Union leaders playing a central role in the mayor's reelection campaign wanted Michael out—they had wanted the administration's fiscal strong-arm out from the start. The mayor's media advisors said the budget director had to go to end the drama playing into Giuliani's campaign theme of an incompetent mayor. On top of that, Michael and Dinkins had tensions of their own. The mayor sought to undo budget cuts agreed upon earlier in the summer to forestall a bond-ratings downgrade. Michael thought the decision financially unwise, and according to one source, lacking in integrity since the mayor had made commitments to the rating agencies.[96]

The political pressure to dismiss Philip Michael proved irresistible. His strongest supporters among the mayor's senior staff chose not to fight a battle they did not believe they could win, something they would later remember with regret. Two days after the report appeared, Michael resigned. In it, he wrote, "While I recognize the difficulty that the recent Department of Investigation report posed for you, I also believe the report to be incomplete and subjective in its conclusions. It is clear I did nothing wrong, and I am glad that you agree that my only 'sin' was seeking greater City revenues." To balance future budgets facing a cumulative gap of $8 billion, "[Z]ealousness by the Budget Director becomes essential. For that zealousness, I make no apology," he continued. "I applied pressure and did a tough job—since that is what it takes to get anything done in this convoluted bureaucracy, but I never stepped over the line. There is no smoking gun here." He ended by thanking Dinkins for allowing him to cap his city government career as budget director and offered him best wishes in an effort to exit gracefully from a situation that lacked grace. Ellen Baer suffered a demotion. A number of public officials called for Steisel's resignation, but the mayor demurred.[97]

So the man the mayor had entrusted with the city's finances for nearly four years had to resign in what the press called a scandal. "You can use the word scandal, if you wish," the mayor protested to the city's press core, but "[i]t's not a corruption scandal. It is overzealousness on the part of persons in my administration who were working very hard to help the people of our city to see to it we did not have to raise taxes."

Just a few weeks later, the mayor's credibility as a financial manager suffered yet again. The Campaign Finance Board announced it had discovered "a clear violation" of law serious enough to cause them to levy a $320,000 fine against Dinkins's campaign. That disclosure came just a day after his reelection team announced it had agreed with the board to repay certain money improperly spent as a result of a different error.[98]

Giuliani tied together his opponent's troubles and presented them as a package of clubhouse cronyism and incompetence, a lack of accountability and poor management, the practices of a mayor too detached from the details of government to do his job effectively. He described New York as a city in trouble that required a strong leader to restore harmony, economic development, and happier days. *New York Times* reporter Todd Purdum described Giuliani as a Wonder Bread candidate—a throwback to earlier, simpler times, perhaps to an image of New York that existed only in the far reaches of nostalgic memories. Yet it seemed to be working. And Giuliani continued to hammer away at the decline in jobs that occurred while Dinkins served as mayor, the poor condition of the schools, and the lack of safety in the streets. "It is patently clear he can't manage a riot, he can't manage a boycott, he can't manage a budget, and he can't manage a campaign to keep it even vaguely in compliance with the law," Giuliani told Purdum.[99]

Convincing people David Dinkins did not know how to govern— casting the man as inept—became the overriding objective of Giuliani's campaign. In contrast to his somewhat clumsy and at times nasty run in 1989, Giuliani tried hard to steer clear of race as an explicit issue in 1993. Unlike Roger Ailes, who advised Giuliani during his first effort to become mayor of New York, David Garth understood that any hint his candidate planned to drive white voters to the polls by stoking the flames of racial fears would backfire. The vulgar and offensive tactic had often proved effective in contests around the country. But in 1993 New Yorkers—distressed by the racial animosity they lived with daily and their leaders' seeming inability to do anything about it—would punish a politician they perceived as making things worse. "I've got to get this city to stop thinking in terms of black and white and Hispanic, and gay and heterosexual, and get us to start thinking about people," Giuliani told a group of working-class Latinos in Sunset Park, Brooklyn, one day. When he did engage race, he tried to present himself as the candidate who would rise above it. "If I were mayor and some Italian-Americans were intimidating a black shopkeeper, I'd come down on them hard and fast," he told one audience, in obvious reference to Mayor Dinkins's behavior during the Korean grocers boycott. "People have to be able to feel confident that they'll be protected, whatever the mayor's color." He presented his quest as a high-minded goal, yet smart politics drove it. He needed to attack the mayor's record without allowing his opponent to tag him with the racist label. "From a cold political calculation, you take the issue of race out of this and I win by 15 to 20 points," Giuliani told a reporter. "You make this a normal American election between an incumbent and a challenger, and I win."[100]

Garth also sought to soften Giuliani's scary image. In a series of ads, the challenger appeared with his wife and children, seven-year-old Andrew and four-year-old Caroline. He wanted them to grow up in a city with safe parks, good schools, and places to play, Giuliani told New Yorkers in a transparent effort to project a warmth known to his friends but not to the public. "He'll fight as hard for you and your family as he does for his own," a silent tagline read. The clip sought to transform the candidate's harsh image as a nasty prosecutor into a picture of a strong father and husband, a defender of the vulnerable rather than a man who attacked the innocent. By late August, for the first time, a poll showed Giuliani with a meaningful lead over Dinkins. The mayor's team disputed the results that appeared in the *Daily News,* but some of the city's political leaders detected a shift in the public mood.[101]

VII. Democratic Landslide, Citywide Showdown

The Democratic primary arrived in mid-September. Roy Innis remained on the ballot, along with an obscure municipal employee named Eric Ruano Melendez who managed to qualify for the contest. Neither posed a threat to the mayor. Indeed, their presence suited Dinkins. For a candidate to receive matching funds and spend up to $4 million in the primary, the city's campaign finance law required a contest. The number of petitions Innis filed to qualify for the ballot seemed low enough that a challenge and audit to weed out ineligible signatures would likely have eliminated him. Bill Lynch declined to take the step, preferring the financial benefit Innis's involvement assured. On primary day Dinkins won nearly 70 percent of Democratic ballots cast for the party's candidate for mayor, more or less as expected. In what Innis and others viewed as a protest against the mayor, 25 percent of voters cast ballots for Innis, while Melendez registered 7 percent. In his victory speech, Dinkins called the faithful to arms. "Tonight, the fight begins for the soul and future of New York," he told his supporters. The battle, of course, had been underway for some time. "We know where we stand," he told the city from the steps of City Hall the next morning, surrounded by prominent local and national Democrats. "And we know where our Republican opponent stands. . . . This election is a choice between dividing our city and uniting it."[102]

Mark Green, who had been Dinkins's commissioner for consumer affairs, beat out Susan Alter and four others for the right to the Democratic line for public advocate. In the comptroller contest, to the surprise of many, Queens assemblyman Alan Hevesi placed first with 35 percent of the vote, ahead of incumbent Liz Holtzman and also Herman Badillo. Since no candidate passed the 40 percent threshold, Hevesi and Holtzman met two weeks later in a head-to-head runoff that Hevesi won handily. Suddenly Dinkins shared his ticket with two Jewish Democrats. "Maybe they will be popular in neighborhoods where I am not and I will be popular in neighborhoods where they are not," he said of his two allies. Badillo and Alter remained in their general election races on the Republican and Liberal lines.[103]

Dinkins's media managers, veteran campaign consultants David Doak and Robert Shrum, launched their candidate's general election television ads just after the comptroller primary runoff. Some contrasted Dinkins posture as a lifelong Democrat with his opponent's changing positions and Republican affiliation. Referring to comments Giuliani made in 1989 that the landmark US Supreme Court case on abortion, *Roe v. Wade*, should be overturned, a narrator in one commercial asked, "Can we elect a man who's fought against everything we stand for?" Giuliani had long since asserted he would support a woman's right to choose, but the question posed surely raised doubts about his conviction. Another commercial sought to reinforce the view Dinkins would do more to keep peace in the city. It featured a *New York Post* headline that appeared after the Rodney King episode: "Mayor praised for keeping calm as riots hit nation."[104]

Dinkins had invoked his reputation as a racial healer the night he won the Democratic primary and contrasted it to Giuliani's behavior. "While I walked the streets of Washington Heights with John Cardinal O'Connor, calming tensions between the community and the police, the Republican candidate played chief cheer leader and angry master of ceremonies at the first City Hall police riot in our city's history," he said. Dinkins refused to cede the crime-buster title to Giuliani. "In four years as Mayor, I was able to do what the Republican candidate failed to do in a lifetime as a prosecutor—reduce crime in the city," he declared. He called his opponent out of touch, "mired" in "the good old days that never were," temperamentally ill-suited to lead.[105]

Dinkins got some powerful help late in September from President Clinton. The mayor went to Washington to meet with the president to demonstrate he would have greater access to federal money and support than his opponent since Democrats controlled the White House. Then he returned to New York aboard *Air Force One* when the president came to the city for a day of fund-raising and politicking. That evening, Clinton addressed a crowd of supporters at a packed Manhattan fund-raiser, where, to the surprise of many, he spoke of race as an explicit issue in the mayor's reelection.

"I'm going to get into a lot of trouble," the skillful campaigner warned aloud as he prepared to confront the topic. Then he went on to tell the audience that on the flight from Washington he wondered why Dinkins, who had steered the city through tough fiscal times and who had hired more police and begun to force crime down should face a competitive race against a Republican in New York City where Democrats had a five-to-one advantage in registration. The conclusion he came to is that "too many of us are still too unwilling to vote for people who are different than we are. This is not as simple as overt racism," he continued. "That is not anything I would charge. . . . It's not that simple. It's this deep-seated reluctance we have, against all our better judgment, to reach out across these lines."

"You tell 'em, Bubba!" one enthusiastic listener shouted.

Knowing Jewish votes hung in the balance, the president drew an analogy to the efforts to secure peace between Israel and the Palestinian Liberation Organization, and he talked of the importance of reaching out to others to accomplish important things in a divided world. Then he issued a ringing endorsement. "[T]his man, who has a good record, who has a good plan, who has a good heart, has earned the right to your vote, and you ought to make sure he gets it and is returned to City Hall." The black mayor wrapped the southern president in a hug of gratitude and declared, "For me, it does not get better than this."[106]

Throughout September, Dinkins announced plans for improving a broad range of city government functions. He promised to combine the city's three police forces to fight crime more effectively and efficiently. He proposed dismantling the Board of Education and replacing it with local school councils. He announced plans to increase the number of health-care centers in neighborhoods around the city and to construct a new emergency medical services center. He gave an address on how he would stimulate the city's economy and outlined his vision for the future. City agencies released reports that presented old programs repackaged as new ideas. "It's part of a strategy to lay out the Mayor's plan for the next four years," Cesar Perales, deputy mayor for health and human services, told a reporter. "Obviously we are in an election, and the people want to know what the candidates are offering for the future."[107]

In a speech at the Metrotech Center in downtown Brooklyn, Dinkins unveiled a development plan he promised would create over one hundred thousand private-sector jobs in the next four years. For a mayor who had insisted for nearly four years that the city's job losses were beyond his control—a result of the weak national economy—the announcement seemed incongruous. The mayor claimed that early signs of economic recovery that would spur business activity made it the right time for the city to act. A $250 million economic development bank funded by the city capital budget anchored the plan, which proposed investments in computer software companies, biotechnology, fashion, and other industries. Deputy Mayor Barry Sullivan called the politics of the timing coincidental. The mayor's opponents, detractors, and others dismissed the proposal as so much political theater.[108]

By September the Giuliani campaign felt they had softened their candidate's harsh image and its media strategy moved to a new phase. Advertisements returned to the theme of law-and-order, nuanced to deflect concerns their candidate would harm race relations. Commercials aired showing Giuliani on the move, bending down to shake hands with an elderly woman and talking to a young man while walking under an elevated subway, projecting an image of engaged energy as he connected with the city's people. Then white, black, and Latino New Yorkers lamented the impact of crime on their lives. "Rudy Giuliani could bring this city together by first getting rid of the problems that separate us," one said. The clip ended with a silent, printed tagline: "Rudolph Giuliani—You know he'll be tough on crime."[109]

Giuliani's pledge to restore the quality of life resonated in neighborhoods around the city. As part of his commitment to bring order to the streets, he took on the squeegee men. At busy intersections, especially near the tunnel and bridge entrances to Manhattan, clusters of vagrants armed with spray bottles of window-washing fluid and windshield brushes rushed to clean car windows when motorists stopped at red lights. Some performed the service and then politely, even charmingly, asked for a tip for their troubles, engaging drivers in light-hearted banter or bowing dramatically. Others, many of them drug addicts and alcoholics, did little more than smear dirt across the windshields and expected a handout nonetheless. Others still, repeat-offending convicted criminals, wiped the windshields and menacingly demanded money. Motorists feared the unwanted welcoming committees and the threat of damage to their cars or themselves if they refused to pay. Attempts to discourage them became an aggravating urban game. Drivers braked well back from the intersection, hoping the squeegee men would not approach, and then drove forward past them if they did, and then turned on the windshield wipers if the men caught up and began to wipe the glass. The experience epitomized the city's inability to control its public space. Giuliani swore he would rid the streets of the scourge.[110]

Efforts by Mayor Koch and early on under Mayor Dinkins to eliminate the offensive behavior ran into legal challenges. Civil libertarians invoked freedom of speech laws protecting panhandlers to prevent the police from arresting the squeegee men for loitering. As a result, drivers suffered the indignity for years. Dinkins tried to defuse the matter as a campaign issue. "Killers and rapists are a city's real public enemies—not squeegee pests and homeless mothers," the mayor said in a ploy to trivialize the problem and portray Giuliani's policy prescriptions as picking on the vulnerable. But the matter had become a high-profile symbol of Dinkins's inability to establish order. Police commissioner Kelly hired Harvard professor George Kelling, one of the developers of the broken-window theory, to study the topic along with NYPD deputy chief Michael Julian. They determined that a city traffic ordnance, Regulation 4-04, specifically forbade pedestrians to approach a car to wash its windshield, so the police actually had the authority they needed. They also determined that some of the squeegee men could be chased away, but the recalcitrant in the group would ignore even a summons. These offenders, the most menacing ones, had to be arrested. So they arrested them all and made it a priority to sweep the most active intersections every two hours. In a matter of weeks, the squeegee men all but disappeared. The action, initiated in October 1993, occurred on Dinkins's watch, but too late in his term for the mayor to get credit for it.[111]

Giuliani's pledge to restore order to the city continued to resonate with voters. In an October 1993 article titled "How Bad Is It?" *New York* magazine journalist Craig Horowitz cited polls in which nine out of ten responded negatively to questions about safety on the streets. Forty-five percent said they were likely to move out of New York over the next three years, 40 percent because of crime. Horowitz traced the widespread dissatisfaction to

> the deterioration in the city's quality of life, the sense that the system has broken down and is spinning out of control. Shoplifting, token-sucking, vandalism, aggressive panhandlers, hostile squeegee people, homeless people, car break-ins, drunken or drug-induced disorderly behavior, peddlers, drag racing, noise, filthy streets . . . all contribute not only to a growing sense of social disorder—which many studies have shown leads to still more crime—but to a growing sense of hopelessness.[112]

In early October, with just a month to go before the election, the contest remained a dead heat. Over 90 percent of blacks planned to vote for David Dinkins, a base of support that never wavered. And the mayor had restored his position with women, who seemed to trust him more than they trusted Giuliani. But the numbers contained danger signals for the mayor. His support among Latinos sagged modestly behind where it had been in 1989. Most importantly, his support among Jewish voters had fallen to 23 percent, not much different than the 21 percent of all whites who hoped to reelect the mayor. This showed significant deterioration from May, when one-third of Jews had reported they would vote for Dinkins, closer to the proportion that actually cast ballots for him in 1989. The mayor scored higher than his opponent when pollsters asked people if the candidates cared about the needs of the average New Yorker, but the former prosecutor scored higher when interviewers asked who was tough enough to deal with crime. On most other factors, scores did not differ by much. "[T]his thing is going to go down to the wire," Bill Lynch recognized. "Turn-out is obviously going to be key, and we've got to have a big vote-pulling operation out there."[113]

The mayor's team secured the support of the New York City Central Labor Council and many of the major municipal unions that had helped him last time. But the teachers' union that broke with tradition four years earlier to endorse Dinkins in the primary took a pass in 1993. The large wage increase awarded the teachers during Dinkins's first year in office that created controversy and accusations that the mayor had used city money to reward his political supporters gave way to givebacks and more tortured negotiations in the years that followed.

"There were people working for the Mayor who cut the school system more than they did other areas," United Federation of Teachers president Sandra Feldman said, not necessarily accurately. "The Mayor trusted their judgments, but from our perspective they were out to hurt the schools. I wonder if they had the Mayor's interests at heart." The decision deprived the Dinkins campaign of the most potent field operation in the city as the union sat out the election.[114]

Even some unions that supported the mayor reported a slide in their members' commitment to the man. "There's no question the enthusiasm is not what it was the last time," Sonny Hall of the Transport Workers said. The head of Local 1180 of the Communications Workers of America, Arthur Cheliotes, told a reporter, "It's going to take some work to get people motivated." Lack of a better alternative was the main reason some unions expected to back the incumbent. "Giuliani is too conservative for the city's traditionally liberal and Democratic labor leaders," one journalist writing on the topic concluded. The mayor's field operation, anchored by labor support and Democratic Party loyalists, dwarfed what the Giuliani campaign could muster relying on Republican and Liberal Party followers, but it lacked the electric energy that surged through it four years before.[115]

In the weeks leading up to the election, the candidates campaigned constantly on streets and in churches, in synagogues and bodegas, at senior centers and community events. Jesse Jackson came to Harlem and Brooklyn to encourage blacks to vote in force. In interviews at radio stations popular with blacks, Dinkins called on his base to come to the polls. "If we can turn out the vote we need, we should succeed, but it's a very close election," he told followers over WLIB. Dinkins enjoined voters to cast ballots for him "not because of the color of my skin but because of the content of my heart." Yet in a clever formulation he introduced race as an issue by saying it should not be one. "To pretend that people in our city don't discuss [race] is silly," he told a Manhattan audience. "If you want to play the race card, then you should deal the whole deck. Lay out your plan on how to improve race relations in our city," he said.[116]

When asked about Dinkins's comments Giuliani responded, accurately, "It does illustrate the fact that it is the Mayor and his campaign that introduces this issue." The Italian American challenger also lashed out at Dinkins for allowing his supporters to accuse Giuliani of being a "crypto-fascist" surrounded by Ku Klux Klan sympathizers. "I have the sense that because they can't do the Mafia thing on me—because it would be ludicrous, because I put two to three hundred of them in prison—they do the fascist thing on me," he complained. He cited an editorial critical of him with references to Mussolini, calling it an ethnic smear. To fight back, the Giuliani campaign aired ads using the candidate's wife and Herman Badillo, so Giuliani could avoid political mudslinging.[117]

To deflect charges he shared a philosophy with unpopular national Republicans, Giuliani fired a double-barreled endorsement from Ed Koch and Bobby Wagner, two of the city's biggest Democratic guns. In an orchestrated day of announcements, the two longtime staples of city politics said New York's problems needed fresh ideas and forceful leadership of a kind Giuliani could provide, but Dinkins could not. Television ads featuring the respected Democrats—earlier in the year a poll showed Koch might have beat Dinkins had he chosen to challenge him—appeared in the final days of the campaign. Wagner cited Dinkins's handling of the Korean grocers boycott as a particularly troublesome event. The mayor's refusal to enforce the law "sent a terrible message about standards of fairness," he said.[118]

New York's liberals screamed betrayal, but the positions Wagner and Koch adopted should have surprised no one. In addition to the philosophical rationale Wagner offered, Dinkins had allowed his term as school board president to expire without renewal, so there was no personal loyalty between the two sometimes rivals. And over the years Koch had roundly criticized Dinkins. The former mayor responded to suggestions that New York would be better off had he continued in office by saying: "The people threw me out. Now they have to be punished." And he told interviewers, "Dinkins said his mere election would change race relations. He was right. They got worse." If the city did not change direction, he warned, "We become Detroit."[119]

The *New York Times* endorsed Dinkins for reelection, but its editorial criticized him roundly. "Either choice requires a leap of faith," they wrote, "faith that Mr. Dinkins can govern more effectively, faith that Mr. Giuliani can think more judiciously about the city's problems. . . . We fully understand why some former Dinkins supporters have drifted to Mr. Giuliani and why others are wavering." This election was so close, the piece contended, because voters were "warning [Dinkins] that they want to see more discipline and diligence from him . . . they want . . . a higher order of competence." Still they concluded Dinkins had more chance of governing better than Giuliani had of tempering his urge to excess.[120]

Newsday also endorsed the mayor. So did the *Jewish Forward*, the *Irish Voice*, and a dozen neighborhood newspapers, many of them with ethnic readerships. In Harlem the *Amsterdam News* denounced "two horrible years of the most intense, malicious and superbly orchestrated media assault on David Dinkins." The newspaper's editors encouraged its readers to "go out en masse and vote for David." *El Diario/La Prensa,* the city's largest Spanish-language daily endorsed Dinkins, causing Giuliani to dismiss the paper as "garbage." The newspaper responded to the insult by issuing a front-page editorial the day before the election demanding respect from Giuliani for the paper and its readers. Dinkins took pleasure in reciting the editorial in its entirety to reporters following him around the city.[121]

The *Daily News,* in language that echoed the ambivalence of the *Times*, endorsed Rudy Giuliani. While recognizing the "excruciatingly difficult circumstances Dinkins inherited" and acknowledging that "[u]rging voters to turn Dinkins out of office is not easily done" because he was a decent man with a heartfelt commitment to the city, they concluded that the story of the Dinkins administration was "one of unfulfilled promise." The incumbent, they wrote, had not "earned four more years." Giuliani, in their view, offered "fresh ideas" and "contagious energy and a capacity for leadership" that could "rally [the city's] spirit. . . . Sword flashing, he'd set out to slay the beasts of business as usual. . . . The intensity level [of leadership] would rise," they crowed. But they also issued a warning. "That same intensity could be dangerous if it were too often combined with Giuliani's tendency toward intemperate reactions. In the worst case, he could prove divisive. . . . But the greater danger is that the city's downhill slide will be allowed to continue." The *New York Post* backed Giuliani as well.[122]

By the last week of the campaign, Dinkins had secured endorsements from nineteen of twenty-one elected Latino officials holding seats in congress, city government, and the state legislature. Polls showed the mayor had recovered much of his lost ground with Latinos. And the Sunday before the election, the mayor had breakfast on Delancey Street with four Jewish US senators who urged their fellow Jews to look beyond the mistakes Dinkins made at Crown Heights and to focus instead on his lifelong support for Jewish causes.[123]

Late in the campaign, Dinkins's team released a negative ad that included footage of Giuliani from the prior fall provoking the police protesters at City Hall on the verge of a riot. An ominous voice cited the midday arrest of three Wall Street traders, two of whose charges were later dropped. Then it referred to the Bess Myerson bribery case, telling viewers, "[Giuliani] planted a microphone on a daughter and sent her to spy on her mother." The ad skillfully sought to present Dinkins's opponent at his worst in the final days before New Yorkers cast ballots. Giuliani denounced the spot as "one of the more disgusting things that any politician has done in New York City," and dismissed it as the sign of a desperate candidate. Dinkins relentlessly promoted the idea that Giuliani's personality made him unfit to lead. "We don't need an angry mayor. You don't have to be loud to be strong. You don't have to be mean to be tough," Dinkins told audiences around the city.[124]

The candidates debated debating and ultimately never did. The Giuliani campaign insisted on a one-on-one forum, just him and the mayor. Dinkins's team insisted Conservative candidate George Marlin participate. The mayor presented his position as a matter of principle—a commitment to inclusion of all legitimate political views in the conversation about the future of the city. A majority of New Yorkers agreed with him. At least as much as principle, a desire to divide the opposition motivated the mayor's posture. Marlin had become a relentless critic of Giuliani, whose mainstream views and pragmatic compromises on a range of social issues offended hard-core conservatives. The mayor's team sought to provide the smart and witty Marlin with a citywide audience for his denunciations of their opponent in the hope he would siphon away a few critical percentage points of votes.[125]

The cable channel New York 1 and WNBC-TV each invited all three candidates to debate. Giuliani did not show, and the sessions turned into "tag-team attacks" on him. Marlin got the biggest chuckle during the latter show when he threw a rubber chicken onto the place at the table where Giuliani should have been, accusing the absent man of being afraid to defend his beliefs. Moderator Gabe Pressman asked Marlin to say who he thought worse, Mayor Dinkins or Mr. Giuliani. "The lesser of two evils is just that; too evil," came the sardonic reply. A few days later CBS-TV invited just the mayor and Giuliani to debate. This time the mayor did not show, and Giuliani spent the evening answering questions from four panelists, essentially an uninterrupted hour of television time for him to present his case just days before the election. At one point, a questioner asked if David Garth had remade his image. In response, Giuliani pursed his lips in a snarl mimicking an unflattering image of him the Dinkins campaign used in a negative advertisement they had begun to air. "Even I get frightened," he said. He hoped the laughter he evoked would defuse the accusation that, despite more clever management of his image, his harsh temperament made him unfit to govern.[126]

Giuliani presented himself as a unifier and continued his relentless campaign to portray himself as likeable and the incumbent as inept. "I'm not mean," he told a reporter, matter-of-factly. "I'm really not. I love my wife and kids. I don't kick dogs. I'm a nice guy. This idea that I'm mean-hearted is a myth," he declared. Despite the transparency of the drive, it seemed to be working. "In person, Giuliani is surprisingly relaxed, unpretentious, intelligent, and funny," one reporter informed his readers. At appearances around the city, Giuliani told audiences, "We've spent too much time on the divisions. . . . Our problems unite us." Even as he criticized the mayor, he sought to keep the tone civil and, when circumstances allowed, even light-hearted. When radio icon Don Imus interviewed Giuliani shortly after George Marlin introduced his rubber chicken to the campaign, the man, seeking to soften his harsh image, joked, "Unfortunately in our polls, the chicken's doing pretty well."[127]

Two days before the election, cable channel New York 1 released the results of a poll. Dinkins had the support of 48 percent of New Yorkers and Giuliani 47 percent. The margin of error of 4 percent meant the race remained too close to call. It promised to be so close both sides feared even modest electoral irregularities could affect the outcome. Federal election monitors descended on New York at the mayor's request to ensure fair results, particularly in minority communities. Also at the request of the mayor, police commissioner Kelly took the unusual step of assigning more than fifty police captains to monitor polling stations, a response to fears that off-duty police, at the urging of the Patrolman's Benevolent Association, might try to intimidate voters in neighborhoods known to support Dinkins. In the event, few episodes of inappropriate polling behavior occurred.[128]

VIII. Defeat

On November 2, 1993, more than 1.8 million New Yorkers went to the polls. For some, the election had become a referendum on David Dinkins's ability to govern, for others, a referendum on Rudy Giuliani's temperament. By the barest of margins, Dinkins lost. The rematch ended nearly as close as the initial contest in 1989. Giuliani took 51 percent of the vote, and Dinkins 48 percent, with George Marlin winning just under 1 percent. In a winner-take-all contest so evenly matched, every issue mattered, every factor made a difference, every vote counted. Yet a close examination of the electoral results reveals that a surge in turnout on Staten Island and a spike among Giuliani voters in Brooklyn accounted for the reversal in fortunes more than anything else, combined with modest erosion in Dinkins's support from Jews and Latinos.

The ballot referendum to allow Staten Island to consider seceding from New York City and establish itself as a separate metropolis brought record numbers of residents from that borough to the polls. The proposition passed easily, and, in an unintended consequence, the small but sturdy Republican redoubt delivered twenty-five thousand additional votes to Giuliani, a meaningful windfall in so close a battle. On election night, Bill Lynch still thought David Dinkins would win until the returns from Staten Island started arriving.[129]

Brooklyn had been a battleground throughout Dinkins's four years in office. The Korean grocery drama played out in Flatbush; African American rioters battled Hasidic Jews in Crown Heights; the Yusuf Hawkins trials rocked Bensonhurst; and black protesters had marched in response to racially motivated violence in Canarsie. These local issues had an impact at the polls. Giuliani won twenty thousand more Brooklyn votes in 1993 than he had four years before, principally from Hasidic, conservative Jewish, and Italian neighborhoods, according to election result maps developed by CUNY Graduate Center political scientist John Mollenkopf. Dissatisfaction with David Dinkins's leadership caused a surge in the number of Giuliani supporters who went to Brooklyn's polls.

Mollenkopf's maps show that Giuliani won more support among Asians in Chinatown in 1993 than in 1989 and that he did better among Dominicans in Washington Heights as well. He polled modestly better in Jewish neighborhoods in Manhattan too. In Queens Giuliani polled stronger in Korean neighborhoods. In the Bronx, the only borough where Giuliani did not pick up appreciably more votes in 1993 than he had in 1989, he won some additional support in Rabbi Avi Weiss's Riverdale.[130]

In his second bid for the mayor's office, Giuliani proved more seasoned than during his first. He had spent the better part of four years developing his rationale for wanting to run the city, and he had also assembled a better campaign team to help him articulate it, in particular by hiring David Garth. He softened his reputation for meanness by avoiding race-baiting at a time when it would have backfired and by showing the city a more human side of himself. These changes made it easier for ambivalent voters to cast ballots for Giuliani.[131]

David Dinkins held his coalition together more than not in 1993, but it sagged and weakened enough to convert his 1989 victory into defeat. *New York Newsday's* exit poll showed Dinkins's support among African Americans at 95 percent in 1993 compared with 97 percent in 1989. In the rematch, the mayor won 60 percent of Latino votes—a strong majority—but down from 70 percent in 1989. Dinkins won 34 percent of the votes cast by Jews, down from 39 percent four years before. But in both years the percent of votes he won from Jewish New Yorkers exceeded what he achieved with other whites significantly. In 1993 he won 23 percent of white votes overall, compared with nearly 30 percent in 1989, and he won the support of just 13 percent of white Catholics in the rematch compared to 23 percent in the first contest.[132]

Since Jews made up nearly 20 percent of the electorate, the 5 percent decline in support from the group cost Dinkins 1 percent overall, damage that mattered in an election where every percentage point counted. Yet, considering the intensity of concern that the Crown Heights catastrophe would cause Dinkins's position among Jews to collapse, the erosion seems quite modest. Indeed, New York's first black mayor polled eleven points higher with Jews than with other whites in 1993 compared with 9 percent higher four years before. Dinkins retained substantial residual loyalty among Jewish New Yorkers, despite the tumultuous events that happened on his watch. Latinos constituted about 13 percent of votes, so the ten-point drop in that group's loyalty cost Dinkins another 1 percent he could not afford.[133]

The number of ballots cast for David Dinkins in 1993 declined by about 3 to 5 percent in every borough, slightly more in Staten Island, in comparison to his historic first bid for the mayoralty. Some of the mayor's supporters lost confidence, or at least enthusiasm, for their candidate. Yet, if Rudy Giuliani had won only the number of votes he won in 1989, Dinkins would have beat him by a few thousand ballots in 1993, despite weaker turnout among the incumbent's supporters. The windfall in Staten Island plus more intense opposition to the mayor, particularly in Brooklyn, coupled with modest erosion in the mayor's standing with Jews and Latinos, determined the outcome of the election much more than the decline in turnout among the mayor's supporters.

Giuliani won 75 percent of white votes—85 percent of Catholics, 65 percent of Jews—and he won 37 percent of Latino ballots in 1993. This compared with 66 percent of white votes—73 percent of Catholics, 60 percent of Jews—and 30 percent of Latinos in 1989. With modest improvement in all elements of his coalition, Giuliani secured City Hall. Of his 930,000 votes, Giuliani won 868,000 of them on the Republican ticket and 62,000 votes on the Liberal Party line, which provided his margin of victory. The invisible influence meter hovering over Ray Harding's head soared.[134]

Race dominated the 1993 electoral outcome as it had in 1989. Any analysis of the numbers demonstrates the impact of color on the count. Near unanimous commitment to Dinkins's cause among African Americans confronted overwhelming loyalty to Giuliani among whites, and especially Catholics. Since the electorate consisted of twice as many whites as blacks—56 percent versus 28 percent—Giuliani had the stronger base despite the less complete nature of the commitment. Yet it is hard to make the case that racism defeated New York City's first black mayor in his bid for reelection. Surely New York had its share of white bigots who distrusted David Dinkins because of his skin color. But there is no particular reason to think the city had more of them in 1993 than in 1989 when it had elected the same man by a slim margin. Ironically, the falloff in the white vote for Dinkins from 30 percent in victory to 23 percent in defeat supports the point. It strains credibility to argue that whites who cast ballots for a black man in 1989 refused to on the basis of skin color in 1993. Dinkins's stewardship of the city, policies that antagonized a largely white police force and the Catholic Church, decisions on racially charged events like the Korean grocery boycott, Crown Heights, with particular resonance among Jews, and the myriad points of contention that attend any incumbent provided the basis for the shift. These are the factors that in a close race caused a small but significant number of white voters who helped elect David Dinkins mayor in 1989 to decide that reelecting him was not in their view in the city's best interest.

While race colored the landscape in both 1989 and 1993, the tone of the two contests differed markedly. In the first one, Giuliani ran a vulgar campaign. He race-baited aggressively, seeking to scare white voters to the polls. In the rematch he steered clear of the tactic, having realized that a city in pain over the black-white animosity that plagued it would punish a candidate who touched the wound. Dinkins evoked black pride to draw out his voters and he sought to portray Giuliani as racist, but he did so with characteristically cautious language. In part, it simply suited his style to speak obliquely. As a practical matter, he needed to avoid alienating moderately progressive whites whose votes he needed and who were no more inclined to tolerate overt race-baiting from a black man than from a white one. The absence of extreme militants like Sonny Carson from Dinkins's campaign in 1993 eliminated another potential source of acrimony. Dinkins did allow some of his supporters to target Giuliani with harsh rhetoric, but in general the 1993 campaign, while hard fought to the end, lacked the nastiness of the 1989 contest.[135]

New York City Elections for Mayor Results by Borough 1989 and 1993[136]

Borough	1989		1993	
	Dinkins	Giuliani	Dinkins	Giuliani
Brooklyn	276,903	237,832	269,343	258,058
Queens	190,096	284,766	180,527	291,625
Manhattan	255,286	157,686	242,524	166,357
Bronx	172,271	99,800	162,995	98,780
Staten Island	22,988	90,380	21,507	115,416
Total	917,544	870,464	876,896	930,236

IX. A Graceful Exit

David Dinkins showed grace in defeat. A crowd of his supporters, crushed and dazed to hear their candidate acknowledge his loss, booed Giuliani's name. Dinkins would have none of it. "We must help him to be as good a mayor as he can be. . . . Mayors come and go but the life of the city must endure," he said. "Never forget this city is about dignity. It is about decency." And he reminded his followers of something, and perhaps himself as well. "My friends we have made history. Nothing can ever take that away from us," New York's first black mayor told the crowd. The next day, standing on the steps of City Hall with the man who had just defeated him, he repeated the message in a show of unity that put the interests of the city before his own.[137]

Still, the loss hurt. Dinkins's defeat was the first time any of America's major cities had cast out an African American mayor after a single term. Outcomes in the other citywide races added to the sting. Alan Hevesi won the election for comptroller, and Mark Green won the public advocate's office, both men white Democrats. Many wondered how a city where Democrats outnumbered Republicans five-to-one could throw an incumbent Democratic mayor out of office. Race seemed to many the sad, compelling answer. "Anyone who denies there was a strong racial component is living in a dream world," one black man told a reporter the day after the election. "People feel betrayed. People feel that we as black Democrats played by the rules, and the rules were changed," said another. However disappointed, Dinkins himself maintained his poise and composure. "Our city is in his hands," Mayor Dinkins said of Rudolph Giuliani on election night, a simple statement of the new fact of life of New York City politics. What that would mean for New York remained to be learned.[138]

****

Shortly after his defeat, Dinkins traveled to Puerto Rico for a vacation. While there he played tennis, sometimes three times a day, while coming to terms with what his life as a private citizen would be like after more than three decades of public service. Before leaving office, he savored one more official victory. After two years of negotiations, his administration agreed to an expansion plan for the National Tennis Center in Queens. The United States Tennis Association, host of the prestigious US Open, agreed to pay $172 million to improve the facilities. They also committed to keep the annual national tournament in New York for at least twenty-five years and potentially for ninety-nine. In return, the city agreed to lease the stadium to the association for the US Open, and it granted an additional forty-two acres of parkland to the project. For most of the year, the city would use the facility for public programs. With support from city council speaker Vallone who lived in Queens, Dinkins concluded the deal and signed it as mayor in December 1993. He did so despite objections from Mayor-Elect Giuliani, who wanted a chance to review the details before the city entered into such a long-term commitment. For Dinkins this event, which occurred just days before he left power, was the perfect culmination of his personal interests and his commitment to public service.[139]

In one of his final official acts, Dinkins blocked an effort by municipal unions to get the city council to pass a law that would make it harder for the new mayor to outsource jobs. Citing existing agreements that required the city to consult with unions and perform cost-benefit studies of proposals to contract out for services, the mayor refused to make his successor's job harder. "Given the protections already in place, I do not believe the legislative branch ought to assume responsibilities already borne by the executive," he said. His position caused Stanley Hill, executive director of District Council 37, to denounce him. "It's a lousy act on his part. It's a mega-disappointment. He forgot who helped him in the election." One imagines it was not the part of the mayor's job David Dinkins would miss.[140]

A few days before leaving office for the last time, Mayor Dinkins spoke to reporters. By then he had agreed to teach courses on public affairs as a professor at Columbia University. His long political career had ended at the age of sixty-six. He offered his own reflections on his legacy. "I would hope that I'd be remembered as somebody who genuinely cared about people, about all people, especially children. And that Crown Heights notwithstanding, that I did bring people in the city together. That I have provided some inspiration to children, particularly children from the minority community." And he expressed no regrets. "I'm glad I did it," he said of his time in the mayor's office. "It's the greatest job in the world. For those who like public service, it doesn't get better than being Mayor of the City of New York."[141]

Notes

1. Mayor David Dinkins, "State of the City Address," January 4, 1993; James C. McKinley, "Defending Record, Dinkins Sees City As a Safer Place," *NYT*, January 5, 1993.
2. James C. McKinley, "Political Notes; Dinkins May Have Regrets, but Not on Crown Hts.," *NYT*, January 3, 1993.
3. James C. McKinley, "Defending Record, Dinkins Sees City As a Safer Place," *NYT*, January 5, 1993.
4. Editorial, "New Year's in the City," *NYT*, January 4, 1993.
5. Eric Pooley, "Air Dinkins," *New York*, May 25, 1992, 32–35.
6. Marist Poll New York City Registered Voters, Dinkins Favorability, in the author's possession, courtesy of Lee Miringoff and the Marist Institute for Public Opinion; James C. McKinley, "Dinkins Retains Financing from Groups of 4 Years Ago," *NYT*, October 29, 1993.
7. Todd S. Purdum, "Buttoned Up," *The New York Times Sunday Magazine*, September 12, 1993, online version; Joe Klein, "The Mayor on the Town," *New York*, April 30, 1990, 48.
8. "Remarks by David N. Dinkins, Potamkin Humanitarian Award for Muhammad Ali, Hotel Pierre, 2 East 61st Street at 5th Avenue, Manhattan, April 20, 1992," and "Remarks by Mayor David N. Dinkins, Diana Ross Tribute," June 2, 1990," in New York City Municipal Archives, Office of the Mayor, 1990–1993, David N. Dinkins, Speeches, Roll #1; Calvin Sims, "This Man Whispers in Dinkins's Ear (a Lot)," *NYT*, July 14, 1992.
9. Sam Roberts, "Metro Matters; a Vote, but No Winner, Many in Electorate Say," *NYT*, May 24, 1993.
10. Alan Finder, "Convention Spotlight Has Warm Glow for the Mayor," *NYT*, July 18, 1992; Author's interview, Bill Lynch, October 29, 2010; "Mayor David Dinkins and the Hosting of the 1992 Democratic National Convention," personal files of Harvey Robins.
11. "Dinkins Aide to Join the Clinton Campaign," *NYT*, August 6, 1992.
12. Vallone, *Learning to Govern*, 196.

13.   Jonathan P. Hicks, "The Mayor's Quiet Counselor: at Dinkins's Side, George Daniels Has Power, Not Flash," *NYT*, May 8, 1993.

14.   Robert D. McFadden, "Dinkins Appointee Withdraws over Allegation of Harassment," *NYT*, October 27, 1992; Eric Pooley, "The City Politic: Randy Politics: Dinkinstein and the Flap," *New* York, November 9, 1992, 24–25; James C. McKinley Jr. "Dinkins Picks an Educator As a Deputy," *NYT*, December 11, 1992; Sam Roberts, "Metro Matters; A Look Back: Were Reporters Fair to Dinkins?" *NYT*, May 7, 1990; "Dinkins Aid to Join Clinton Campaign," *NYT*, August 6, 1992; James C. McKinley, "Dinkins's Tactic: Start Spreading the News," *NYT*, October 18, 1992.

15.   *New York City ROARING BACK: Changing the City, for Good*, December 1992.

16.   Mary B. W. Tabor, "Dinkins Urging Radio Stations to Curb Talk-Show Bigotry," *NYT*, January10, 1993.

17.   Shapiro, *Crown Heights*, 13; Craig Horowitz, "The New Anti-Semitism," *New York*, January 11, 1993, 25; West, *Race Matters*, 39.

18.   Catherine Manegold, "The Reformation of a Street Preacher," *The New York Times Magazine*, January 24, 1993, online version; Craig Horowitz, "The Sharpton Generation," *New York*, April 4, 1994, 36–45; Sharpton and Walton, *Go and Tell Pharaoh*, 189–90.

19.   James C. McKinley, "Municipal Unions and New York City Reach Pay Accord," *NYT*, January 12, 1993.

20.   James C. McKinley, "Dinkins Proposes a Financial Plan to Fill Budget Gap," *NYT*, January 30, 1993.

21.   James Bennet, "Hispanic Voters and the Politics of Sludge," *NYT*, March 5, 1993.

22.   "Remarks by Mayor David N. Dinkins, Bronx Puerto Rican Conference," May 18, 1991; Remarks by Mayor David N. Dinkins, Puerto Rican Legal Defense and Education Fund," October 11, 1990 and various other statements New York City Municipal Archives, Office of the Mayor, David N. Dinkins, Speeches, Roll #10.

23.   Author's interview, Fernando Ferrer, November 30, 2010; Author's interview, Bill Lynch, October 29, 2010; Michael Powell, "Dinkins Defends His Record As Hispanics Fume," *New York Newsday*, August 5, 1991.

24.   Author's interview, Fernando Ferrer, November 30, 2010; Letter from Fernando Ferrer to Mayor David N. Dinkins, August 6, 1990 in New York City Municipal Archives, Office of the Mayor 1990–1993, David N. Dinkins Departmental Correspondence, Roll #1; Author's interview, Bill Lynch, October 29, 2010; Eric Pooley, "Dave's Latin Test," *New York*, August 23, 1993, 14; Calvin Sims, "This Man Whispers in Dinkins's Ear (a Lot)," *NYT*, July 14, 1992.

25.   Todd. S. Purdum, "Praising Mandela, Dinkins Shakes Fragile Coalition," *NYT*, June 16, 1990; Author's interview, Albert Scardino, December 10, 2010; Press Release, June 15, 1990, "Statement By Mayor David N. Dinkins Regarding Puerto Rican Nationalists,"

26.   James Barron, "Dinkins's Latino Chief, Feeling Stymied, Quits," *NYT*, October 18, 1990; Todd S. Purdum, "Political Notes: Man behind the Scenes Tries to Step into Spotlight," *NYT*, September 27, 1992; David Gonzalez, "Hispanic Aide's Departure Signals Growing Tensions," *NYT*, October 21, 1990.

27. Sam Roberts, "Metro Matters: Return of Badillo As Council Girds for Redistricting," *NYT*, April 15, 1991; Robert Pear, "Council Map Makers Argue It Mirrors New York 'Mosaic,'" *NYT*, July 19, 1991; Metro Datelines; Puerto Rican Group Sues to Halt Election," *NYT*, June 9, 1991; Felicia R. Lee, "Judges Clear Way for New Council Election," *NYT*, July 31, 1991; Michael Powell, "Dinkins Defends His Record As Hispanics Fume," *New York Newsday*, August 5, 1991.

28. Sam Roberts, "Metro Matters: Return of Badillo As Council Girds for Redistricting," *NYT*, April 15, 1991; Robert Pear, "Council Map Makers Argue It Mirrors New York 'Mosaic,'" *NYT*, July 19, 1991; Metro Datelines; Puerto Rican Group Sues to Halt Election," *NYT*, June 9, 1991; Felicia R. Lee, "Judges Clear Way for New Council Election," *NYT*, July 31, 1991; Eric Pooley, "The City Politic: Dave's Latin Test," *New York*, August 23, 1993, 14.

29. James Barron, "Ousted New York Hospitals Chief Says He's a 'Witch Hunt' Victim," *NYT*, October 25, 1991.

30. Editorial, "Ethnic Politics at City Hall," NYT, November 16, 1991; "Remarks by Mayor David N. Dinkins at Welcoming Reception, San Juan Airport, San Juan, Puerto Rico, September 24, 1992," New York City Municipal Archives, Office of the Mayor, David N. Dinkins, Speeches, Roll #10.

31. Eric Pooley, "The City Politic: Dave's Latin Test," *New York*, August 23, 1993, 14.

32. Alan Finder, "Rights of 'Domestic Partners' Broadened by Dinkins Order," *NYT*, January 8, 1993; James C. McKinley, "Dinkins Criticizes Stein over Campaign Mailing," *NYT*, February 10, 1993.

33. Alan Finder, "Rights of 'Domestic Partners' Broadened by Dinkins Order," *NYT*, January 8, 1993; James C. McKinley, "Dinkins Criticizes Stein over Campaign Mailing," *NYT*, February 10, 1993; James Barron, "Beer Shower and Boos for Dinkins at Irish Parade," *NYT*, March 17, 1991; John Taylor, "The City Politic: P.C. Marches On," *New York*, January 25, 1993, 12–13.

34. "Dinkins Meets with Former I.R.A. Member," *NYT*, February 10, 1992; John Taylor, "The City Politic: P.C. Marches On," *New York*, January 25, 1993, 12–13.

35. Celia W. Dugger, "Dinkins to Step up Hiring to Monitor Child Abuse Cases," *NYT*, January13, 1993.

36. Celia W. Dugger, "Feud between Top Dinkins Aides Is Seen Hurting Social Programs," *NYT*, January 1, 1993; Celia W. Dugger, "Dinkins Plans Shift in Funds for Homeless," *NYT*, January 8, 1993.

37. The 9/11 Commission, *Final Report of the National Commission on Terrorist Attacks upon the United States* (New York: W.W. Norton & Company, authorized edition); Martin Gottlieb, "Explosion at the Twin Towers: The Response; Size of Blast 'Destroyed' Rescue Plan," *NYT*, February 27, 1993.

38. Martin Gottlieb, "Explosion at the Twin Towers: The Response; Size of Blast 'Destroyed' Rescue Plan," *NYT*, February 27, 1993; Lynette Holloway, "Explosion at the Twin Towers: The Heroes; Many Dramas, One Story: Only the Details Differ," *NYT*, February 28, 1993; Robert D. McFadden, "Explosion at the Twin Towers: The Overview; Blast Hits Trade Center, Bomb Suspected; 5 Killed, Thousands Flee Smoke in Towers," *NYT*, February 27, 1993.

39. Martin Gottlieb, "Explosion at the Twin Towers: The Response; Size of Blast 'Destroyed' Rescue Plan," *NYT*, February 27, 1993; Lynette Holloway, "Explosion at the Twin Towers: The Heroes; Many Dramas, One Story: Only

the Details Differ," *NYT*, February 28, 1993; Robert D. McFadden, "Explosion at the Twin Towers: the Overview; Blast Hits Trade Center, Bomb Suspected; 5 Killed, Thousands Flee Smoke in Towers," *NYT*, February 27, 1993; Author's interview, Norman Steisel, August 29, 2011.

40. *9/11 Commission Report*; Alison Mitchell, "Specter of Terror; Egyptian Was Informer, Officials Say," *NYT*, June 26, 1993; Eric Pooley, "The Arab Connection: Breaking the World Trade Center Bombing Case," *New York*, March 15, 1993, 31–33.

41. George James, "Crime down in New York for 2nd Year in Row," *NYT*, March 19, 1993; Memorandum To: Raymond Kelly, From: Norman Steisel, Date: March 3, 1993, Subject: December 1992 Monthly Report and Police Department, City of New York, Monthly Report—February/March 1993, in New York City Municipal Archives, Office of the Mayor 1990–1993, D.M. Steisel, Roll #128.

42. Joyce Purnick, "Stein, Once Politics' Bad Boy, Is Putting on a New Face," *NYT*, June 28, 1988; Todd S. Purdum, "Stein, Trailing Badly in the Polls, Quits New York Race for Mayor," *NYT*, May 28, 1993.

43. Edward I. Koch, conversation with author.

44. Sam Roberts, "Ever Unabashed, Stein Emerges Again," *NYT*, August 27, 1991.

45. James C. McKinley, "A New Job for Stein, Without a Race?" *NYT*, February 23, 1993.

46. Sam Roberts, "Ever Unabashed, Stein Emerges Again," *NYT*, August 27, 1991; Sam Roberts, "Stein Starts Mayoral Bid with a Bash," *NYT*, January 22, 1992; Sam Roberts, "Political Memo: Sign of Mayoral Race: Stein's Emerging Bid," *NYT*, February 16, 1993.

47. Alison Mitchell, "In Barrage of Ads, Stein Strives for Surge in Polls," *NYT*, March 3, 1993; Jeanie Kasindorf, "The City Politic: Before the Revolution," *New York*, February 5, 1992, 12–13.

48. Todd S. Purdum, "TV Commercials for Stein Are First in Race for Mayor," *NYT*, April 9, 1993.

49. Alan Finder, "Queens Party Leader Urges Stein to Quit Mayoral Race," *NYT*, May 15, 1993; Sam Roberts, "Stein Pulls out of Advocate Race, Saying His Political Career Is Over," *NYT*, June 30, 1993.

50. Hope MacLeod, "Closeup: Young Man on the Rise," *New York Post*, September 1, 1965; McNickle, *To Be Mayor of New York*, 226–28, 244–59, 266, 274–77, 285.

51. McNickle, *To Be Mayor of New York*, 285–86.

52. McNickle, *To Be Mayor of New York*, 285–86.

53. Karen W. Arensen, "Critic of CUNY, Badillo, Chosen to Head Board," *NYT*, May 31, 1999.

54. Todd S. Purdum, "Badillo Joins Race on Giuliani Ticket to Oppose Dinkins," *NYT*, May 29, 1993; Eric Pooley, "Rudy's Secret Weapon: Can David Garth Steer Giuliani through the Race Race?" *New York*, July 12, 1993, 30.

55. Barrett with Fifield, *Rudy*, 240.

56. Todd S. Purdum, "Badillo Joins Race on Giuliani Ticket to Oppose Dinkins," *NYT*, May 29, 1993; Eric Pooley, "Rudy's Secret Weapon: Can David Garth Steer Giuliani through the Race Race?" *New York*, July 12 1993, 30.

57. Catherine S. Manegold, "Alter Crosses Party Lines to Back Giuliani for Mayor," *NYT*, May 22, 1993. Catherine S. Manegold, "Balance-Beam

Politics: Giuliani's Second Try," *NYT*, May 23, 1993; Eric Pooley, "Rudy's Secret Weapon: Can David Garth Steer Giuliani through the Race Race?" *New York*, July 12, 1993, 30.

58. Catherine S. Manegold, "Alter Crosses Party Lines to Back Giuliani for Mayor," *NYT*, May 22, 1993. Catherine S. Manegold, "Balance-Beam Politics: Giuliani's Second Try," *NYT*, May 23, 1993.

59. Catherine S. Manegold, "Balance-Beam Politics: Giuliani's Second Try," *NYT*, May 23, 1993.

60. Catherine S. Manegold, "Alter Crosses Party Lines to Back Giuliani for Mayor," *NYT*, May 22, 1993; Barrett with Fifield, *Rudy!* 253–54.

61. Kirtzman, *Rudy Giuliani*, 36–38.

62. James McKinley Jr., "Conservative Foe Challenges Giuliani," *NYT*, March 4, 1993; James McKinley Jr., "Political Notes; Fire on the Right: Giuliani Spurned," *NYT*, May 30, 1993; Peter Hellman, "The Marlin Factor," *New York*, July 26, 1993, 35–37.

63. Todd S. Purdum, "Giuliani's Man: On Winning Side in 5 Mayoral Elections," *NYT*, May 27, 1993; Author's conversation with Bobby Wagner, 1993; Eric Pooley, "Rudy's Secret Weapon: Can David Garth Steer Giuliani through the Race Race," *New York*, July 12, 1993, 27–30.

64. Michael Tomasky, "Public Enemies: Will It Be Rudy's Tuesday," *The Village Voice*, June 1, 1993.

65. Barrett assisted by Fifield, *Rudy!* 241–45.

66. Kirtzman, *Rudy Giuliani*, 38–40.

67. Author's interview, John Mollnekopf, November 29, 2010.

68. Fred Siegel, "Reclaiming Our Public Spaces," *City Journal* (Spring 1992) online version; Kirtzman, *Rudy Giuliani*, 38–40.

69. James Q. Wilson and George L. Kelling, "Broken Windows: The Police and Neighborhood Safety," *Atlantic Monthly* (March 1982) online version.

70. Kirtzman, *Rudy Giuliani*, 39–40; William Bratton with Peter Knobler, *Turnaround: How America's Top Cop Reversed the Crime Epidemic* (New York: Random House, 1998), 152–54; Siegel, *Prince of the City*, 74–75.

71. Todd S. Purdum, "Giuliani and the Color of Politics," *NYT*, July 25, 1993; Eric Pooley, "Rudy's Secret Weapon: Can David Garth Steer Giuliani through the Race Race," *New York*, July 12, 1993, 28.

72. Siegel, *Prince of the City*, 74, Kirtzman, *Rudy Giuliani*, 38.

73. Linda Wolfe, "The Toughest Judges: A New Panel to Mete out Rigorous Justice," *New York*, January 14, 1991, 41–44; Daniel Patrick Moynihan, "Defining Deviancy Down," *American Scholar Magazine* (Winter 1993) online version; Craig Horowitz, "How Bad Is It?" *New York*, October 18, 1993, 63.

74. Siegel, *Prince of the City*, 74, Kirtzman, *Rudy Giuliani*, 38, Michael Tomasky, "Public Enemies: Our Jobs and the Mayor's," *The Village Voice*, April 27, 1993.

75. Michael Tomasky, "Public Enemies: A Slogan in the Making," *The Village Voice*, April 20, 1993.

76. Michael Tomasky, "Public Enemies: A Slogan in the Making," *The Village Voice*, April 20, 1993; Chris Smith, "The Worst Crimes of '93 (So Far)," *New York*, July 19, 1993, 20–24.

77. Todd S. Purdum, "New York's Blacks Back Dinkins but Whites Don't, Poll Indicates," *NYT*, May 19, 1993.

78. Michael H. Cottman, "Poll: Most Voters Feel the Mosaic Is Cracked; Race Relations Are Seen As Worsened," *New York Newsday*, June 14, 1993.

79. Todd S. Purdum, "Dinkins or Giuliani? Voters Equally Unimpressed," *NYT*, October 5, 1993; Editorial, "Clinton Hits a Nerve on Race," *NYT*, September 30, 1993.

80. Catherine S. Manegold, "Political Memo; Giuliani's Strategy: Don't Give Dinkins a Target," *NYT*, July 3, 1993; Todd S. Purdum, "Dinkins Fires Sharp Jabs at Giuliani," *NYT*, July 16, 1993.

81. Felicia R. Lee, "Dinkins's Trip to Israel Upsets Some Blacks," *NYT*, February 2, 1991; Clyde Haberman,"Specter of Crown Heights Clings to Dinkins, Even in Israel," *NYT*, July 7, 1993.

82. Alan Finder, "Dinkins Counterattacks; Giuliani Hammers Away," *NYT*, July 23, 1993.

83. Todd S. Purdum, "Dinkins Fires Sharp Jabs at Giuliani," *NYT*, July 16, 1993; Author's interview, Norman Steisel, October 28, 2010; Author's interview, Bill Lynch, October 29, 2010; Joe Klein, "Mario the Magician," *New York*, February 5, 1990, 34; Daughtry, *No Monopoly on Suffering*, 266.

84. Joseph P. Fried, "Officials Testify on Crown Heights Response," *NYT*, August 22, 1993; Alison Mitchell, "Reliving Crown Heights Violence; Under Oath, Dinkins Is to Describe Handling of 1991 Clash," *NYT*, August 24, 1993; Alan Finder, "Dinkins, in Testimony, Defends His Response on Crown Heights," *NYT*, August 25, 1993; Todd S. Purdum, "Playing Tug-of-War in Gracie Dining Room," *NYT*, August 25, 1993.

85. John Taylor, "The Program Papers," *New York*, August 2, 1993, 24–26; Eric Pooley, "The City Politic: Heaven Sent," *New York*, August 9, 1993, 22–23.

86. Alan Finder, "Company Resurrected Itself with the Arrival of Dinkins," *NYT*, August 20, 1993; *Report to the Mayor: The Recommended Award of the PVB Privatization Contract to Lockheed I.M.S.* August 1993, The City of New York Department of Investigation, Susan E. Shepard, Commissioner; Richard C. Daddario, First Deputy Commissioner, 5–7.

87. Author's interview, Philip Michael, November 6, 2010; Author's interview, Norman Steisel, October 28, 2010; Norman Steisel, "In Parking Violations Uproar, Good Intentions Weren't Enough," Letter to the Editor, *NYT*, September 20, 1993.

98. Author's interview, Norman Steisel, October 28, 2010; Norman Steisel, "In Parking Violations Uproar, Good Intentions Weren't Enough," Letter to the Editor, *NYT*, September 20, 1993.

99. Author's interview, Norman Steisel, October 28, 2010; Author's interview, Philip Michael, November 6, 2010; Steisel,"In Parking Violations Uproar, Good Intentions Weren't Enough, *NYT*, September 20, 1993.

90. Memorandum To: Norman Steisel, From: Bill Lynch, Date: February 3, 1993, RE: PVB Privatization, in New York City Municipal Archives, Office of the Mayor, David N. Dinkins, D.M. Norman Steisel, Roll #128.

91. New York City Department of Transportation Parking Violations Bureau, Memorandum To: PVB Staff From: Joseph A. Spencer, Deputy Commissioner/Director Re: PVB Privatization Date: January 28, 1993; American Federation of State, County & Municipal Employees, AFL-CIO DC 37, letter dated March 16, 1993 to Hon. David N. Dinkins from Stanley Hill. Both documents are in New York City Municipal Archives, Office of the Mayor, David N. Dinkins, D.M. Norman Steisel, Roll #128.

92. Wayne Barrett, "The City Scandal That Won't Go Away," *Village Voice,* April 13, 1993.

93. Wayne Barrett, "The City Scandal That Won't Go Away," *Village Voice,* April 13, 1993; Wayne Barrett, special reporting by Kristen King, "A Bidder Battle: Inside the PVB Contract Scandal," *Village Voice,* April 20, 1993; Wayne Barrett, "The Mayor's Baer Headache," *Village Voice,* May 11, 1993.

94. The City of New York Office of Labor Relations, letter dated April 30, 1993, addressed to Stanley Hill, Executive Director, District Council 37, AFSCME From James F. Hanley, Commissioner, in Steisel, Roll #128.

95. *Report to the Mayor: The Recommended Award of the PVB Privatization Contract,* 47; Seth Faison, "80s Scandal Unraveled in a Suicide," *NYT,* August 19, 1993.

96. Author's interview, Off the Record.

97. City of New York Office of Management and Budget, Letter dated August 20, 1993 To Honorable David N. Dinkins From Philip Michael, Director in D.M. Steisel, Roll #128.

98. James C. McKinley, "Dinkins Blames 'Overzealousness' for Parking-Bureau Furor," *NYT,* August 21, 1993; William Bunch and Nick Chiles, "Dinkins Camp Is Fined $320G," *New York Newsday,* October 21, 1993; Kevin Flynn, "Funny Money: Rogues Give Campaigns $100,000," *Daily News,* October 21, 1993.

99. Todd S. Purdum, "Rudy Giuliani and the Color of Politics," *NYT,* July 25, 1993; Todd S. Purdum, "Giuliani Campaign Theme: Dinkins Isn't up to the Job," *NYT,* October 24, 1993.

100. Todd S. Purdum, "Giuliani's Man: On Winning Side in 5 Mayoral Elections," *NYT,* May 27, 1993; Todd S. Purdum, "Rudy Giuliani and the Color of Politics," *NYT,* July 25, 1993; Jim Sleeper, "The End of the Rainbow," *The New Republic,* November 1, 1993; Eric Pooley, "Rudy's Secret Weapon: Can David Garth Steer Giuliani through the Race, Race?" *New York* July 12, 1993, 28; John Taylor, "The City Politic: Defining Moments," *New York,* August 30, 1993, 24; John Taylor, "What's at Stake?" *New York,* November 1, 1993, 38–41.

101. Todd S. Purdum, "Giuliani Begins Taking Message to the Airwaves," *NYT,* August 6, 1993; Catherine S. Manegold, "Parking Bureau Issue Gives Giuliani What He Sought," *NYT,* August 22, 1993; Todd S. Purdum, "Political Memo; Troubled Mayor Seeks to Shift Campaign's Focus to Giuliani," *NYT, August* 22, 1993; Larry Olmstead, "Dinkins's Vision for City Unveiled in 'Future-Print,'" *NYT,* September 14, 1993.

102. Todd S. Purdum, "Rivals Sound Themes in New York Mayoral Battle," *NYT,* September 16, 1993.

103. Alison Mitchell, "The 1993 Primary: The Overview; Hevesi Outpolls Holtzman, Forcing a Runoff Vote," *NYT,* September 15, 1993; Larry Olmstead, "The 1993 Primary: Mayor; Dinkins Defeats 2 Opponents By 2-to-1 Margin in Primary," *NYT,* September 15, 1993.

104. Larry Olmstead, "Dinkins Vision for City Unveiled in 'Future-Print,'" *NYT,* September 14, 1993; Todd S. Purdum, "Dinkins Goes on Offensive over Giuliani's Views," *NYT,* September 30, 1993.

105. Larry Olmstead, "Dinkins Vision for City Unveiled in 'Future-Print,'" *NYT,* September 14, 1993; Todd S. Purdum, "Dinkins Goes on Offensive over Giuliani's Views," *NYT,* September 30, 1993.

106. Todd S. Purdum, "Supporting Dinkins, Clinton Worries about Role of Race," *NYT,* September 27, 1993.

107. Jonathan P. Hicks, "Dinkins to Propose Health Plans," *NYT,* September 27, 1993.
108. Alan Finder, "Dinkins Outlines Plan for Future Economic Growth," *NYT*, September 22, 1993.
109. James Dao, "The Ad Campaign; Giuliani: Burnishing the Crime-Fighting Image," *NYT*, September 24, 1993.
110. Michael Gross, "The Village under Siege: The Struggle to Save a Neighborhood," *New York*, August 16, 1993, 31–37; Francis X. Clines, "Candidates Attack the Squeegee Men," *NYT,* September 26, 1993; George L. Kelling, Deputy Chief Michael Julian, Sergeant Stephen Miller, "Managing 'Squeegeeing;'A Problem Solving Exercise," undated report received at the New York City Municipal Reference and Research Center February 14, 1994.
111. Alison Mitchell, "Giuliani Zeroing in on Crime Issue; New Commercials Are Focusing on Fears of New Yorkers," *NYT*, September 20, 1993; Francis X. Clines, "Candidates Attack the Squeegee Men," *NYT*, September 26, 1993; John Taylor, "Rudy's Shot: Are New Yorkers Ready for Giuliani's Tough Love," *New* York, October 11, 1993; Bratton with Knobler, *Turnaround*, 214; Leonard Levitt, *NYPD Confidential*, (Thomas Dunne Books, 2010 electronic version), location 1657–75; George L. Kelling, Deputy Chief Michael Julian, Sergeant Stephen Miller, "Managing 'Squeegeeing'; A Problem Solving Exercise," undated report received at the New York City Municipal Reference and Research Center February 14, 1994.
112. Craig Horowitz, "How Bad Is It?" *New York*, October 18, 1993, 60.
113. Todd S. Purdum, "Dinkins or Giuliani? Voters Equally Unimpressed," *NYT,* October 5, 1993.
114. Alan Finder, "Group by Group, Dinkins Seeks to Unite Support," *NYT,* October 6, 1993.
115. William Murphy, "Who Will Wear the Union Label?" *New York Newsday*, July 4, 1993.
116. Alan Finder, "Group by Group, Dinkins Seeks to Unite Support," *NYT,* October 6, 1993; Todd S. Purdum, "Challenging Giuliani, Dinkins Spells out His Politics of Race," *NYT*, October 15, 1993; John Taylor, "The City Politic: Racial Circus," *New York*, October 18, 1993, 24; Joel Siegel, "Dinkins Targets Blacks, Jews, Dems," *Daily* News, November 1, 1993; Bob Liff, "Mayor Urges Black Voters to Turn Out," *New York Newsday*, October 27, 1993.
117. Catherine S. Manegold, "Giuliani Says Dinkins Aides Conduct a Smear Campaign," *NYT*, October 8, 1993; John Taylor, "The City Politic: Defining Moments," *New York*, August 30, 1993, 24; John Taylor, "The City Politic: Racial Circus," *New York*, October 18, 1993, 24.
118. Paul Schwartzman, "In Last Leg, Rudy Armed with Dems," *Daily News*, November 1, 1993; Eric Pooley, "How Bad Is It?" *New York*, October 18, 1993, 61; John Taylor, "What's at Stake," *New York*, November 1, 1993, 41.
119. Paul Schwartzman, "In Last Leg, Rudy Armed with Dems," *Daily News*, November 1, 1993; Eric Pooley, "How Bad Is It?" *New York*, October 18, 1993, 61; John Taylor, "What's at Stake," *New York*, November 1, 1993, 41.
120. Editorial, "A Second Term for Mayor Dinkins," *NYT*, October 24, 1993.
121. *New York Newsday*, November 1, 1993.
122. *Daily News*, October 27, 1993; *New York Newsday*, October 30, 1993.

123. Mireya Navarro, "Dinkins Seeks Hispanic Forgiveness," *NYT*, October 28, 1993; Alan Finder, "The 1993 Campaign: The Incumbent; Dinkins and Giuliani Grapple for Voters—Mayor Aims Efforts at Reinvigorating Vote Coalition," *NYT*, November 1, 1993; Jonathan P. Hicks, "The 1993 Campaign: The Incumbent; Dinkins Focuses on Groups He Sees as Crucial," *NYT*, November 2, 1993.

124. Todd S. Purdum, "Conservative Candidate Seen as Spoiler and Foil," *NYT*, October 18, 1993; Alison Mitchell, "Giuliani Gets Free TV Time But It's a One-Man Debate," *NYT*, October 29, 1993; Ellen Tumposky, "Dinkins' Nice-Guy Spiel," *Daily News*, November 2, 1993; "The New York Newsday Interview with David N. Dinkins," *New York Newsday*, October 29, 1993; Harry Berkowitz, "Ad Shows Rudy at His Worst," *New York Newsday*, October 30, 1993.

125. Todd Purdum, "Conservative Candidate Seen as Spoiler and Foil," *NYT*, October 18, 1993; Peter Hellman, "The Marlin Factor," *New York*, July 26, 1993, 35–37.

126. Alison Mitchell, "Giuliani Gets Free TV Time but It's a One-Man Debate," *NYT*, October 29, 1993.

127. Todd S. Purdum, "Giuliani Campaign Theme: Dinkins Isn't up to the Job," *NYT*, October 24, 1993; Francis X. Clines, "Giuliani, Striving to Be Liked, Tries to Elude Shadow of '89," *NYT*, October 25, 1993; John Taylor, "Rudy's Shot: Are New Yorkers Ready for Rudy's Tough Love?" *New York*, October 11, 1993, 40–45; Denene Miller, "Ranting Rudy Turns into Gentle Giuliani," *Daily News*, October 27, 1993.

128. Alan Finder, "The 1993 Campaign: The Incumbent; Dinkins and Giuliani Grapple for Voters—Mayor Aims Efforts at Reinvigorating Vote Coalition," *NYT*, November 1, 1993; Jonathan P. Hicks, "The 1993 Campaign: The Incumbent; Dinkins Focuses on Groups He Sees As Crucial," *NYT*, November 2, 1993; Alice McQuinlan, "Top Cop: Brass Join Poll Patrol," *Daily News*, November 1, 1993; William Murphy, "Dirty but Done," *New York Newsday*, November 3, 1993.

129. *General Election, City of New York, Statement and Return of the Votes for the Office of Mayor of the City of New York*, 1989 and 1993, New York City Board of Elections; Author's interview, Bill Lynch, November 10, 2010; Sam Roberts, "The 1993 Elections: News Analysis; The Tide Turns on Voter Turnout," *NYT*, November 4, 1993; Todd S. Purdum, "The 1993 Elections: Mayor; Giuliani Ousts Dinkins by a Thin Margin; Whitman Is an Upset Winner over Florio," *NYT*, November 3, 1993.

130. *General Election, City of New York, Statement and Return of the Votes for the Office of Mayor of the City of New York*, 1989 and 1993, New York City Board of Elections; Electoral Map, Change in Dinkins Margin 1989 to 1993 by Election District; Change in Dinkins Vote, Change in Giuliani Vote, in possession of the author. I am grateful to John Mollenkopf for his generous collaboration on this analysis.

131. *General Election, City of New York, Statement and Return of the Votes for the Office of Mayor of the City of New York*, 1989 and 1993, New York City Board of Elections.

132. *New York Newsday*, "Sources of Support," November 9, 1989 based on the result of 2,362 voters interviewed by the NBC polling unit as they left the

polls between 10 a.m. and 9 p.m. The margin of error is 3 percent. *New York Newsday*, "Picking a Candidate," November 3, 1993 based on the results of 1,746 voters interviewed as they left the polls by Voter Research and Surveys, a cooperative of ABC, CBS, CNN and NBC. The margin of error is plus or minus 3 percent.

133. *New York Newsday*, "Sources of Support," November 9, 1989 based on the result of 2,362 voters interviewed by the NBC polling unit as they left the polls between 10 a.m. and 9 p.m. The margin of error is 3 percent. *New York Newsday*, "Picking a Candidate," November 3, 1993 based on the results of 1,746 voters interviewed as they left the polls by Voter Research and Surveys, a cooperative of ABC, CBS, CNN, and NBC. The margin of error is plus or minus 3 percent.

134. *New York Newsday*, "Sources of Support," November 9, 1989 based on the result of 2,362 voters interviewed by the NBC polling unit as they left the polls between 10 a.m. and 9 p.m. The margin of error is 3 percent. *New York Newsday*, "Picking a Candidate," November 3, 1993 based on the results of 1,746 voters interviewed as they left the polls by Voter Research and Surveys, a cooperative of ABC, CBS, CNN, and NBC. The margin of error is plus or minus 3 percent. *General Election, City of New York, Statement and Return of the Votes for the Office of Mayor of the City of New York*, 1989 and 1993, New York City Board of Elections.

135. Alan Finder, "Group by Group, Dinkins Seeks to Unite Support," *NYT*, October 6, 1993; Todd S. Purdum, "Challenging Giuliani, Dinkins Spells out His Politics of Race," *NYT*, October 15, 1993; John Taylor, "The City Politic: Racial Circus," *New York*, October 18, 1993, 24; Joel Siegel, "Dinkins Targets Blacks, Jews, Dems," *Daily News*, November 1, 1993; Bob Liff, "Mayor Urges Black Voters to Turn Out," *New York Newsday*, October 27, 1993; Author's interview, Bill Lynch, November 10, 2010; Catherine S. Manegold, "Giuliani Says Dinkins Aides Conduct a Smear Campaign," *NYT*, October 8, 1993.

136. *General Election, City of New York, Statement and Return of the Votes for the Office of Mayor of the City of New York*, 1989 and 1993, New York City Board of Elections.

137. Francis X. Clines, "The 1993 Elections: The Incumbent; Dinkins Ends the Campaign on Note of Gratitude," *NYT*, November 3, 1993; Alison Mitchell, "The 1993 Elections: The Transition; Dinkins and Giuliani Join in a Call for Healing and Unity," *NYT*, November 4, 1993.

138. Felicia R. Lee, "The 1993 Elections: Voices; For Blacks, Loss by Dinkins Undermines Hopes of Change," *NYT*, November 4, 1993; Francis X. Clines, "The 1993 Elections: The Incumbent; Dinkins Ends the Campaign on Note of Gratitude," *NYT*, November 3, 1993.

139. Alan Finder, "Game, Set, Match to Dinkins on Tennis Center," *NYT*, December 14, 1993; "Lease in Tennis Deal Is Signed by Dinkins," *NYT*, December 23, 1993.

140. James C. McKinley, Jr., "Dinkins, in Labor Rebuff, Blocks Council Bill as a Curb on Giuliani," *NYT*, December 21, 1993.

141. Alan Finder, "Ever Wary, Dinkins Clears His Desk," *NYT*, December 29, 1993.

9

Measuring Mayor
Dinkins's Mettle

Mayor Dinkins grappled with the extraordinary challenges New York City faced between 1990 and 1993 with grace and dignity, with poise and compassion. He brought to his task ample intellect, keen understanding of municipal issues, and a history of reaching across the boundaries of race and religion with unusual skill. Yet he proved the wrong man for the times.

Suffering from a fiscal crisis, a crime wave, and a broken school system, New York needed an aggressive reformer—a mayor who would restructure city government and its costs, who would restore a sense of law-and-order to its streets, and who would revamp an educational system that crippled the city's ability to teach its children. Faced as well with serious racial tensions that threatened the civic peace, New York needed someone to heal its black-and-white wounds. The emotions surrounding race relations in 1989, particularly after Yusuf Hawkins's killing, caused the desire for harmony to trump all other considerations in that year's election for mayor. That made David Dinkins, with his fierce civility and his promise to craft New York's feuding tribes into a gorgeous mosaic, seem a fitting choice.

In the process of selecting a man they hoped would heal the city, New Yorkers elected a Tammany-clubhouse politician with a liberal philosophy of government. He had African American sensibilities toward law enforcement and other issues and a cautious, dispassionate decision-making temperament. David Dinkins had little interest in government reform, he harbored a deep suspicion of the NYPD and its use of force, and he maintained an abiding commitment to community control of schools at a time when that system had failed.

Tragically, Mayor Dinkins mishandled the Korean grocers boycott, the Crown Heights riots, and the Washington Heights disturbances, and he pursued policies that contributed to cultural collision at the school board. As a consequence of these decisions and others, his fundamental promise to heal racial wounds, the basis for his election, went unfulfilled. When asked in June 1993 if race relations had deteriorated or improved while Dinkins governed, a majority of New Yorkers declared them worse—whites and Latinos by very large margins. Blacks surveyed said race relations had improved rather than deteriorated by a measure of 38 percent to 34, the barest of margins even among the mayor's most sympathetic supporters. In a 2001 essay, "David Dinkins and the Politics of Race in New York City," Roger Biles called Dinkins's 1989 electoral victory a "political coming of age," while his "failure to convince voters of his ability to deal fairly and evenhandedly with all ethnic groups and races . . . proved a lethal shortcoming," in 1993.[1]

The narrowness of Mayor Dinkins's 1993 defeat belies the softness of his support. His policies lost him key backers, like the United Federation of Teachers. Unions that stayed with him complained that inspiring enthusiasm for the candidate had become very hard. A majority of Puerto Rican community leaders polled rated the mayor's leadership as poor. Felix Rohatyn, a committed Democrat, backed his party's candidate even though in October 1993 he told a journalist that New York's spirit was lower than during the 1970s when the city flirted with bankruptcy. A black weekly in Brooklyn, the *City Sun*, in a front-page editorial, encouraged the mayor to shake off his reserve. "Frankly, you are beginning to look like a wimp," it wrote. Herbert Daughtry, among Dinkins's more militant African American allies, backed him in 1993, even though "Mayor Dinkins has not been able to ameliorate the pain, despair, and anger" many New Yorkers suffered, despite gallant efforts. Many of the ballots cast for David Dinkins in 1993 were not votes of confidence, but rejections of his opponent that overpowered disappointment with the incumbent. Such is often the way in America's two-party system.[2]

New York's successful leaders inspire confidence across the diverse population of the city. David Dinkins did not. A large majority of white New Yorkers doubted his capacity to govern when the city first elected him. In significant measure, his rise to power and his promotion of all the groups in New York's gorgeous mosaic upended a status quo dominated by white men for decades. Faced with their displacement, many were bound to find themselves uncomfortable with their new mayor. It is easy to argue that nothing New York's first African American mayor did would have attracted more whites to his cause—that the sliver he won in victory and defeat was all he could hope for in a racially petrified city. Yet the more convincing case is that Dinkins's decisions destroyed whatever chance he had to improve his standing with whites of good faith. Different choices could have diminished white discomfort. Instead, his policies intensified white anxieties, and white support for him drifted down. Latinos cut their vote for Dinkins in 1993 by 10 percent—to 60 percent from 70 percent. Support among Asian New Yorkers fell too. African American voters cast almost all their ballots for Dinkins in 1993, just as they had in 1989, but fewer bothered to go the polls. Dinkins's coalition never collapsed, but it sagged and weakened as a result of his poor leadership.

The two ethnic coalitions in play during the 1989 and 1993 mayoralty campaigns had been wrangling for power in New York City since the 1960s. The liberal one consisted of African Americans, a majority of Latinos, and a crucial element of liberal white voters, mostly Jews. The conservative one consisted of Catholics, not-so-liberal Jews, and a significant minority of Latinos. By the time Dinkins ran for mayor, demographic shifts left the two groups nearly evenly matched in the numbers of voters each could command. This explains how David Dinkins could win one election and lose the next by such narrow margins. Modest changes in turnout were sufficient to affect the outcome, along with modest shifts in voting patterns by Latinos and Jews, the two groups with significant standing in both camps.

Successful New York mayors elected with narrow mandates adopted policies and postures that expanded their popularity. Fiorello LaGuardia won only a plurality in 1933. In 1937, he won by a landslide. Robert F. Wagner won less than a majority in a three-way race for mayor in 1953 but secured the greatest margin of victory of any mayor up until his time in 1957. Ed Koch went from a bare majority in 1977 to huge wins in 1981 and 1985. Rudy Giuliani would expand his slim margin of victory in 1993 into much broader support in 1997. The shrinkage in Dinkins's coalition stands out by contrast.

The composition and narrowness of David Dinkins's 1989 victory should have made solidifying his base and expanding it within the constraints of the city's ethnic realities a fundamental goal. His administration's actions suggest a strategy based on the mayor's clubhouse heritage and his liberal political philosophy. In Tammany's heyday, Democratic party bosses controlled the municipal workforce, and they conspired with the mayors they helped to elect, or bullied them, to secure as many jobs as they could for party workers at taxpayer expense. The bosses cared not at all about efficient government. By the time Dinkins came to power, municipal labor leaders had secured control of the city's workers and in significant measure played the role party officials once had. The public unions that provided the mayor with crucial support in his bid for office expected the spoils that go to the victors. The mayor sought to accommodate them, and he also wanted to expand delivery of the social services that he believed in and that his base relied upon disproportionately. Since municipal union membership and its leadership were heavily black, Latino, and liberal, and since expanding city social services would create more union jobs, in theory the pieces fit nicely together. But the dire budget environment and the risk of a fiscal takeover by the Financial Control Board placed such limits on the approach that it proved untenable.

Dinkins's political philosophy exacerbated his disconnect with his times. As a classic urban liberal, he believed government had a compelling obligation to help the poor, the disadvantaged, and the vulnerable to balance the inherent unfairness of life in a capitalist society. This philosophy dominated public discourse in New York City between the days of the Great Depression—when economic collapse left many destitute for reasons perceived as beyond their control—and the 1970s. New York City's near bankruptcy in 1975 and all that followed had caused many New Yorkers to reconsider the limits of local government in the decade and a half prior to Dinkins's election. During the 1980s President Ronald Reagan recast in decidedly limited terms the proper role of government in social policy. New Yorkers never adopted the views wholesale, but they were not deaf to the sounds of a newly engaged debate over the philosophy of government in America. The emergence of the Manhattan Institute as New York's preeminent urban policy think tank makes this evident. Dinkins's liberal outlook, a consensus position in New York when he formed it as a young man, reflected the thinking of less of the city than it once had by the time he became mayor. No less than his clubhouse heritage, his political philosophy conflicted with the distressed budget realities he faced.

The tension between greater efficiency and more expansive services roiled David Dinkins's government inside and out. His administration's efficiency experts and its social service advocates sparred with each other continuously, allowing their competing visions and priorities to spill unhelpfully into the press at times. The confusion that followed demonstrated that David Dinkins—displaying a Tammany leader's reluctance to commit—never established a clear statement of the policies he wanted his senior staff to pursue within the constraints he faced. He also never established an effective decision-making process for sorting through the extraordinary range of options between more efficient and more expansive government, and reconciling the many inherent conflicts between the two. Without clearly articulated priorities and without a strong decision-making process to control a bureaucracy as large and unwieldy as New York's, David Dinkins's vision for the city ended up reduced to reactive rhetoric that seemed to ascribe comparable importance to every worthy idea, providing little sense of direction. He became a mayor perceived as responding to events rather than controlling them. Fiscal monitors lacked confidence in his budget management. Liberals and social service advocates accused him of betraying his promises and his commitment to their causes.

The lack of a clear decision-making process translated into a sense that the mayor did not truly command the government. "Certainly, David conveys a picture of decency and concern, but not of leadership," Robert F. Wagner Jr. said, speaking about the incumbent toward the end of the 1993 campaign. Manhattan borough president Ruth Messinger, a reliable Dinkins ally, offered a sympathetic interpretation that still recognized the mayor's approach to decision making harmed his standing with the city. "This is an administration that because of tough options and the Mayor's style, has made a commitment to being deliberative. Very often that doesn't please anyone," she acknowledged. *New York Times* journalist Todd Purdum came to the same conclusion. "He strives so hard to offend no one, that he often offends nearly everyone. At worst, he presents himself as a toothless sap," the journalist wrote, even as he hastened to add that the image was "something that the many aides who have been excoriated for falling short of his exacting standards will tell you he distinctly is not."[3]

J. Phillip Thompson, III, in *Double Trouble: Black Mayors, Black Communities and the Call for a Deep Democracy*, writes, "Dinkins had no framework to guide him" in the process of engaging with adversaries to "fight for [his] own concept of justice." Thompson, who worked in the Dinkins administration, observed firsthand the conflict between social service advocates and budget hawks that "repeatedly played out . . . with frequent feuding and occasional undermining of the mayor by his deputy mayors." Eventually, the fiscal crisis gave the money men the upper hand, and they pursued a series of "policies that

Dinkins's union and minority constituents opposed." Weaker union support meant Dinkins needed exceptional support from black civic organizations and from black activists to win reelection, particularly in Brooklyn, but he had to secure it without alienating white voters. According to Thompson, this presented Dinkins with the "impossible choice" to "go black" or "go white" in his reelection campaign, since his media strategy could not simultaneously appeal to the competing priorities of the two groups. The media strategy went white, and Dinkins lost, Thompson concludes.[4]

Dinkins complained about his treatment in the media and in moments of candor accused journalists of holding him to a higher standard than white politicians. In his mind, his administration's mistakes received prominent headlines and his successes scant attention. In *David Dinkins and New York City Politics: Race, Images and the Media,* Wilbur C. Rich asserts that deeply rooted national stereotypes make it "permissible for the public to hold reservations" about the intelligence of blacks and "their work ethic" and to cast them as more interested in the trappings of power than the substance. When Dinkins's actions could be cast in that light, for many whites these actions took on a self-validating quality, carrying greater currency than if a white leader did the same. Consciously or unconsciously, Rich believes journalists often wrote of Dinkins in unflattering "pre-packaged images" pertaining to his African American heritage and to his clubhouse background. Dinkins "may have been aware" that the media "was deflating his image, but he lacked the rhetorical skills to reframe the questions," Rich writes. "Dinkins's political socialization as a clubhouse politician did not prepare him to take control and impose his will on political events . . . politicians like Dinkins . . . do get to the top, but their personalities prevent them from dominating their environment." He describes Dinkins as a politician "careful not [to] offend any powerful group leaders or coalitions," ultimately undermining his own authority with indecisiveness.[5]

Whatever prejudices laced Dinkins's media coverage, the fundamental flaw in his communications with the city stemmed from inconsistent management of the government rooted in an effort to please irreconcilable constituencies. When policies lack coherence, so do messages about them. Priorities announced at one moment too often fell victim to budget realities or a change of focus shortly afterward, creating confusion and damaging credibility. Dinkins's overly deliberate and detached management style—his unwillingness to commit to policies and stick to them—prevented him from providing his administration with clear direction, which ensured inconsistent and confused communications with the press and the public.

David Dinkins's unyielding civility and graceful dignity often served as great sources of strength. Cautious language and polite manners had helped him to succeed in a world where angry African Americans tended to scare whites, and the traits had become an integral aspect of his personal style. But the man's highly self-conscious, fetish-like commitment to projecting a courtly demeanor and to personal elegance at times left the people he led feeling distant from their leader. It contributed to the impression that he was too aloof to govern effectively. His demeanor became more than just a matter of style. When the mayor declined to express outrage on behalf of a city frightened and furious about violent crime, he let the public down. He sometimes behaved as if he believed it beneath the dignity of a city's leader to busy himself with the tedious details of day-to-day operations in an often-messy metropolis. At critical moments, this trait left him detached from events too important to ignore. And the man could be unhelpfully stubborn, like when he refused to accelerate the release of his comprehensive crime program, even though the city's tabloids had launched a press riot in search of one. Stubborn pursuit of controversial policies at the Board of Education cost him control of the board. It is easy to imagine that a successful black man with a marine's steel in his spine, who grew up in a nation that bullied African Americans as a matter of law and custom, had learned to stand his ground. But Dinkins lacked the emotional agility to overcome this instinct when circumstances demanded.

David Dinkins's Tammany training, liberal political philosophy, and overly deliberate decision-making style are all apparent in his handling, and mishandling, of his budgets. The weak economy that endured for most of his term and the fiscal challenges that followed called for decisive management, a commitment to efficiency, and a willingness to impose austerity on city workers and programs. Dinkins's instincts were at odds with all three imperatives. As mayor, he delivered balanced budgets each year as required by law, and he prevented the surrender of the city's finances to the unelected Financial Control Board. Accomplishing these goals at a time when the city suffered from severe revenue shortfalls was worthy of praise. But the chaotic way the Dinkins administration achieved them left the mayor's reputation as the city's fiscal steward diminished. All in all, the outcomes of

David Dinkins's budget and financing decisions were unremarkable. They left the city in about the same condition as he found it, perhaps modestly worse off owing primarily to the weakness of the economy that prevailed during most of the time he governed. And like mayors before and since, Dinkins had to contend with highly irresponsible budget incompetence on the part of New York State, whose decisions play such an important role in city finances.

Spending grew a little over 4 percent per year from Dinkins's first budget to his last, modestly more than inflation. City headcount shrunk by nearly 5 percent, so some improvement in efficiency seems to have occurred. For all the rhetoric surrounding additional funding for police, the percent of the budget allocated to the NYPD changed little over four years, and the Board of Education budget also remained nearly the same proportion of the total. By filing a lawsuit against the state in 1993 to change the allocation formula used to apportion education money, Dinkins set in motion a long battle to fix a structural flaw in state financing that discriminated against New York City schoolchildren and cost them hundreds of millions of dollars a year in resources. Social services expenditures rose, driven by higher payments to impoverished New Yorkers suffering the effects of a hurting economy. Since recipients of social services money in New York are disproportionately black and Latino, this pattern suggests relatively greater economic support for Dinkins's political base. Property taxes rose from just over 40 percent of total tax revenue to close to 45 percent, and income taxes rose 2 percent, while sales tax receipts fell as a proportion of city financing. This shifted the burden of paying for city services from renters and poorer New Yorkers to coop and condominium owners, home owners, commercial real estate firms, and the businesses that rent from them. It also raised the burden on higher-income residents in general. The shift increased the responsibility of New Yorkers least supportive of the mayor to pay for services. Politically, this approach may have helped him maintain his base, but it did nothing to expand it.[6]

Total debt levels grew while David Dinkins governed, as they have for every modern mayor. General obligations and Municipal Assistance Corporation debt grew to over $26 billion at the end of fiscal year 1993, nearly $7.5 billion of additional borrowings, a rise of more than 35 percent during David Dinkins's four-year term. Debt constituted over 13 percent of the city's total personal income the year Dinkins left office, compared with less than 11.5 percent the year he won election. Yet the levels were well within normal ranges for the city. Mayor Dinkins's election-year budget left his successor with a looming gap, similar to the one he received from his predecessor. Mayors seeking to hold onto their jobs offer rich election-year budgets, and damn the consequences.[7]

Public safety is a tangible event—murders occur or they do not, crime rates rise or fall, people and their property are secure or at risk— but safety is also an emotion. It is the absence of fear. The mayor must make clear he understands that the primordial purpose of government is to protect its citizens. David Dinkins fared poorly on this aspect of the job. His overly deliberate decision-making process and aloof management style damaged his credibility with a public desperate for decisive law-enforcement leadership. He projected discomfort with the police department's use of force, even when objective conditions demanded it. His mistakes in handling the Korean grocers boycott, the Crown Heights riot, and Washington Heights disturbances caused whites and Asians to believe the city's first African American mayor would not enforce the law fairly against blacks and Latinos, even when they engaged in or threatened violence. More than anything else, David Dinkins's decisions during these three crucial events destroyed his credibility as an honest broker among the races and prevented him from fulfilling his promise to restore harmony to the city. And his actions projected the image of a mayor soft on crime. As a consequence, other defensible policy positions, like the mayor's unwillingness to support increased police firepower, his desire for a civilian complaint review board, or the decision to name a commission to investigate corruption could be cast as part of a pattern that diminished confidence he would keep the city safe.

Mayor Dinkins's public safety decisions emanated from his liberal political outlook and experiences as an African American, and they took place against the backdrop of New York City's tense racial landscape in the early 1990s. Among his reference points was the long history of overly aggressive police behavior in poor black and Latino neighborhoods. He was determined to curtail that injustice while he governed, and in his mind his decisions on crucial events constituted efforts to reduce the risk of civil unrest. Yet he overcompensated, alienating large segments of the city in the process. His management style worked against him in the Korean grocers controversy and in Crown Heights. In both, he overdelegated responsibility and waited too long to act. He compensated for those errors during unrest in Washington

Heights by acting with uncharacteristic swiftness before all the facts were known. In all three instances, his timing was tragically off. The police riot that followed the Washington Heights disturbance was a particularly unsettling moment in modern New York City history. Ten thousand police officers stopped traffic on the Brooklyn Bridge, trampled over cars, yelled racial curses at the mayor, and ignored their superiors' orders to cease and desist. Blame for the ugly event rests squarely on the renegade cops and the leaders who incited them. But the riot makes clear that rank-and-file police confidence in Mayor Dinkins's leadership had collapsed.

David Dinkins's impressive success defusing the potential for racially charged violence during the trials of Yusuf Hawkins's killers and after the acquittal of the Los Angeles police who beat Rodney King stand in contrast to his failures in other instances. The evolution of the Hawkins and King cases afforded the chance to reach out to angry citizens before rising furor metastasized into serious civil unrest. Dinkins's heartfelt, rational arguments against antisocial behavior worked with people willing to listen to reason. When circumstances called for such an approach, the man's instincts for conciliation served him and the city well. When events called for more decisive or tougher action, his playbook often seemed empty. Despite serious mistakes, most people never doubted David Dinkins's decency or the sincerity of his desire to reduce friction between feuding races, even at the end of his term. What people questioned was his competence and the objectivity of his judgment.

While David Dinkins served as mayor, crime in New York City crested and began a long, steady descent. A table of the number of murders and major crimes that occurred in the four years before Dinkins took office, the four years he sat in City Hall, and the four years after strongly suggest that the spike on his watch constituted the deadly momentum of policies and events that preceded him. Murder and crime peaked between 1988, when Ed Koch ruled, and 1990, when Dinkins first governed. The crime wave coincided with the crack epidemic that came and went when it did, for reasons criminologists struggle to explain convincingly. New York crime numbers mirror national movements during the period, although they began to fall somewhat sooner and somewhat more intensely than elsewhere.[8]

How much of the decline in crime during Dinkins's term and afterward resulted from policing practices and how much came from complex social forces is a question that has spawned a cottage industry

Murder and Major Crimes during Mayor Koch's Final Four Years in Office	Murders	Major Crimes
1986	1,582	635,199
1987	1,672	656,505
1988	1,896	718,483
1989	1,905	712,419
Murder and Major Crimes during Mayor Dinkins's Four Years in Office	Murders	Major Crimes
1990	2,245	710,221
1991	2,154	678,855
1992	2,035	656,572
1993	1,970	609,124
Murder and Major Crimes during Mayor Giuliani's First Four Years in Office	Murders	Major Crimes
1994	1,561	530,121
1995	1,177	444,758
1996	983	382,555
1997	770	355,893

of academic study and political debate. Ray Kelly, who oversaw development of "Safe Streets, Safe City" as first deputy and its implementation as police commissioner declined to draw a direct link between the program and the diminishment of mayhem that began on his watch. The most convincing argument is that a broad range of factors, police policy among them, caused both the spike and the crash.[9]

"[E]very one of the causal factors known to affect crime rates moved in the desired manner" in 1990s New York, according to criminologist Andrew Karmen. "No force or condition was out of step." Recovery in the local economy toward the end of Dinkins's term in office provided employment alternatives to selling drugs. It also renewed the attractiveness of New York City as a destination for a stabilizing population of law-abiding, hard-working immigrants. The number of prison cells available in New York State expanded during the 1990s and filled with career criminals responsible for disproportionate numbers of violent assaults on citizens. Improved policing worked in stages. Enforcing the law in the most blatant, open-air drug bazaars chased the dealers inside. Illegal activity continued, but indoors, so the number of violent, neighborhood-terrorizing turf wars and the unintended victims that accompanied them declined. The spread of AIDS among intravenous drug users had a cruelly effective Darwinian impact by killing off addicts prone to commit crimes to feed their habits. The city's demographics changed as the number of young men in the age range most prone to engage in criminal activity diminished. The cumulative effect of these trends, coupled with increased adult realization of the extraordinary danger drugs posed to their teenage children and the parental intervention that followed, caused the number of new recruits into the drug trade to decline.[10]

It seems safe to say that the increase in the number of police on patrol and the more effective deployment of them that the Dinkins administration initiated were significant factors in forcing down the upward arc of violent misery plaguing the city when David Dinkins took office. The meaningful success—a 14 percent drop in major crimes and a decline of more than 12 percent in the number of murders—came too little, too late for Dinkins to benefit politically from the thoughtful plan developed while he served as mayor. And the absolute levels of crime that endured throughout his term remained intolerable. Ultimately, however, New Yorkers would feel a real impact on their lives as a consequence of "Safe Streets, Safe City." Mayor Giuliani's first police commissioner, William Bratton, reaped the benefits of the thousands of additional officers hired under the program and credits the surge in resources as one of the factors that contributed to his success during his early months in office.[11]

Commissioner Bratton and Commissioner Kelly have both expressed the view that if Dinkins had accelerated implementation of "Safe Streets, Safe City" by just six months and sent a large, blue wave of freshly hired and trained police on patrol in the months leading up to the 1993 election, it would have changed the outcome of the close contest. It is an assertion impossible to prove, and not particularly convincing, but an interesting perspective from two highly respected NYPD chiefs attuned to the city's politics and the impact of crime on it.[12]

The work of the Mollen Commission revealed a police department that had lost the will to confront corruption. The seriousness of the crimes committed by multiple bands of rogue cops in the 1980s and 1990s, and the unwillingness of supervisors to shut them down, created a clear and present danger in some of New York's toughest, most disadvantaged neighborhoods. No civilized city could tolerate such a condition. David Dinkins refused to retreat from the menace. When he set in motion steps to end the police corruption and to prevent its return, he demonstrated wisdom and courage, even as it intensified his very damaging conflict with the city's police.

Like other New York City mayors forced to manage the school system under the 1970 school-decentralization law, David Dinkins discovered himself in an untenable position. Parents held him responsible for the quality of the education their children received from New York's schools, even though he had limited authority over them. Control over the size of the school budget and partial control over the central board, coupled with other formal and informal powers of the mayor, were the tools at his disposal. They proved insufficient for Dinkins, just as they had for others before him and others who followed him.

Interpreting the statistical evidence regarding reading and math levels in New York's school system is an uncertain science. Changes in testing methods and inconsistencies across years make simple comparisons suspect. Still the available data suggest things remained more the same than not between 1990 and 1993. The percent of students performing at grade level on standardized math tests surged in 1991 and plummeted in 1993. Both swings are too large to be credible, but even the highest score showed only 60 percent of students achieving the goal. The low score fell short of half. The Dinkins/Fernandez term began with 47 percent of students reading at grade level and ended there as well. High school class sizes did not shrink, the money budgeted per student remained about the same, and pupil attendance persisted where it had been according to the *Mayors Management Reports 1990–1993*.

Mayor Dinkins's posture toward the community school boards and the way he managed his relationship with the central Board of Education proved feckless. The man's outlook on city government included deep respect for neighborhood involvement in decision making. Yet in the context of the empirical facts available in 1990 about New York City's community school boards, it is hard to see how anyone would not conclude that the structure had failed. With the education of a million schoolchildren at stake, the mayor, who in his inaugural address dedicated his administration to children, had an obligation to take bold action to repair the system or to replace it. Dinkins remained captive to his own aversion to radical change and to his deep ideological belief in community involvement in schools, noble in the abstract, but harming the city's schoolchildren every day as practiced in the city he led. Dinkins's misguided support for the community-based structure is unsurprising. The racial venom injected into the controversy when the decentralization movement occurred and that so intensified the pain of the city's deepening racial wounds in the late 1960s left a lasting legacy. In the aftermath of the school strike, support for decentralization had become a litmus test for African American leaders in New York City, just as respect for workplace protections for teachers became something the city's white politicians, Jewish ones in particular, had to support.

At the central Board of Education, the mayor participated in policy and politics. Since the people held him responsible for the system the board manages, the mayor needed to manage the board—admittedly no easy task, but that was the job. With two appointments out of seven, to hold sway the mayor needed two allies at all times among the five members the borough presidents chose. Dinkins failed to maintain this crucial level of support on the all-important vote for renewal of Joseph Fernandez's contract and on other significant matters. He even struggled to maintain control over his own appointments. He did share in a few important victories, particularly when Fernandez, with Dinkins's support, succeeded in ending building tenure for principals and in eliminating the Board of Examiners. Yet these were tactical battles won while the educational war suffered neglect.

The polemical posturing pertaining to prophylactics and sex education, gay lifestyles, and the definition of tolerance distracted from the board's main task of setting educational standards to ensure adequate primary and secondary education. Dinkins played an active role in the controversial culture clashes that so tore apart the easily divided board. The acrimony contributed greatly to the decision not to renew Fernandez's contract as chancellor and to the mayor's loss of influence over the system, his compelling failure with respect to education.

Credit Mayor Dinkins with standing by his beliefs. He sought condoms for teens engaging in sex whether their parents liked it or not because the AIDS epidemic risked killing them if they copulated without protection. He sought to include acceptance of gay life in a program designed to teach the importance of tolerance, a position consistent with his lifelong commitment to promoting harmony amid human diversity. Whether the benefits of the battles exceeded the cost would seem to depend entirely on one's philosophical outlook. Even so, some of the tactics invite challenge. Introducing homosexuality as a topic of discussion to children as young as six caused sincere concern, even among supporters of the *Children of the Rainbow* curriculum. And the mayor's inability to introduce his policies and to maintain control of the board constituted a political failure of significant import. Whether his policies were right or wrong, a more effective leader would have pursued them with tactics that would have preserved his ability to influence management of the school system. The unhappy outcome caused Dinkins to renew his demand for authority to appoint a majority of school board members, but the posture meant little. The mayor had no strategy for securing the votes he would need from the state legislature, particularly the Republican-dominated state senate.

Mayor Dinkins modified Mayor Koch's far-reaching housing policy to suit his greater concern for poorer New Yorkers and saw it through to completion. His administration separated out from the Human Resources Administration the department responsible for managing the complex problem of homelessness, and created a new mayoral agency with a clear mission to respond to the compelling human needs of the deeply troubled homeless population. While he governed, the city also restructured, for the better, aspects of how it delivered and paid for medical services for impoverished New Yorkers.

Mayor Dinkins launched inspiring events. In 1991 New York City greeted the soldiers, airmen, sailors, and marines who fought in Operation Desert Storm in an extraordinary celebration. In 1992 Dinkins brought the Democratic National Convention to New York, a demonstration of political clout that promoted the city to the country and boosted its tourist economy at a time of particular need. The convention left a lasting legacy of three cultural events that continue to this day—Broadway Show Week, Restaurant Week, and Fashion Week. The agreement Dinkins struck at the very end of his term with the United States Tennis Association to keep the US Open in New York has served the city and tennis fans everywhere to this day, bringing prestige, national television coverage, and tourist dollars to the city every fall.

Nelson Mandela toured New York City in triumph in 1990. His presence constituted a celebration of the power of a courageous man to conquer brutal, racially motivated oppression through the force of human dignity and an unshakeable commitment to freedom. Hundreds of thousands saw him personally, while millions of New Yorkers and Americans watched him on television. The symbolic significance for Dinkins—himself a leader who wielded dignity as a weapon against racism—cannot be overestimated. He hoped the event would inspire a younger generation of African Americans and others to seek racial peace in years to come.

David Dinkins traveled an extraordinary personal journey. He was born in 1927 into an America that cruelly constrained choices for African Americans. In 1989, he won election to the highest office in the most important city in the most powerful nation in the world. His greatest legacy is the one he himself cited on the night of his victory. As the first African American to win the mayor's office in New York, he added another link to freedom's chain, and he brought the nation's premier metropolis, and therefore the country itself, one step closer to fulfilling the promise of American democracy.

Notes

1. Michael H. Cottman, "Poll: Most Voters Feel the Mosaic Is Cracked: Race Relations Are Seen As Worsened," *New York Newsday*, June 14, 1993; Biles, "David Dinkins," 135, 148–49.
2. Daughtry, *No Monopoly on Suffering*, 192.
3. Todd S. Purdum, "Buttoned Up," *The New York Times*, September 22, 1993; Todd S. Purdum, "Giuliani Campaign Theme: Dinkins Isn't up to the Job," *NYT*, October 24, 1993.
4. J. Phillip Thompson, III, *Double Trouble: Black Mayors, Black Communities, and the Call for a Deep Democracy* (New York: Oxford University Press, 2006), 199–200, 234–39. Thompson reports Bill Lynch attributed the lack of mobilization in Brooklyn as a key reason for Dinkins's loss in a 1999 interview. When the author interviewed him in 2010, Lynch emphasized the higher white turnout in Staten Island as the critical factor.
5. Wilbur C. Rich, *David Dinkins and New York City Politics*, 1, 15–16, 194.
6. The City of New York, *Executive Budget as Modified, Summary of the Expense Budget and the Revenue Budget*, Fiscal Years 1990–1994.
7. Independent Budget Office, "Debt Affordability Ratio Analysis," 1980–2006, spreadsheet in the possession of author, courtesy of Independent Budget Office and Douglas Turetsky.
8. *Statistical Report, Complaints and Arrests*, New York City Police Department, Office of Management Analysis and Planning, Crime Analysis Unit, 1986–1997.
9. Memorandum To: Raymond Kelly, From: Norman Steisel, Date: March 3, 1993, Subject: December 1992 Monthly Report and Police Department, City of New York, Monthly Report—February/March 1993, in New York City Municipal Archives, Office of the Mayor 1990–1993, D.M. Steisel, Departmental Correspondence Roll #128.
10. Karmen, *New York Murder Mystery*, 257–58.
11. Bratton with Knobler, *Turnaround*, 198.
12. Author's interview, Raymond D. Kelly, October 7, 2010; Bratton with Knobler, *Turnaround*, 1998.

Bibliography

Archives and Manuscripts

New York City Mayoral Archives, Mayors Papers: David N. Dinkins Papers (DND Papers).

New York City Politics Vertical Files, various years. The Municipal Reference and Research Library of New York City (MRRL).

New York City Municipal Archives, Board of Education, Chancellor Joseph Fernandez Papers, and Irene Impellizzeri Papers.

Author's Interviews

Fernando Ferrer, November 30, 2010.
Raymond D. Kelly, October 7, 2010.
Stanley Litow, September 30, 2010.
Bill Lynch, October 29 and November 10, 2010.
Philip Michael, November 6, 2010.
Milton Mollen, November 5 and November 10, 2010.
John Mollenkopf, November 29, 2010.
Sam Roberts, December 1, 2010.
Harvey Robins, December 1 and December 17, 2010.
Albert Scardino, December 10, 2010.
Joel Seigel, December 20, 2010.
Norman Steisel, October 28, 2010

Government Reports

Anatomy of Failure: A Path for Success. July 7, 1994. Report of the Commission to Investigate Allegations of Police Corruption and the Anti-Corruption Procedures of the Police Department. Milton Mollen, Chairman.

Annual Report on Social Indicators 1994. New York City Department of City Planning.

Census of the Population. U. S. Census Office. Vol. I, 85.

The City of New York Budget. Fiscal Years 1990–1994.

The City of New York Financial Plan. Fiscal Year Five-Year Plans 1990–1994.

Civil Rights Issues Facing Asian Americans in the 1990s. February 1992. A Report of the United States Commission on Civil Rights.

"Debt Affordability Ratio Analysis, 1980–2006." Independent Budget Office Tables.

The Disturbance at the Rikers Island Otis Bantum Correctional Center, August 14, 1990: Its Causes and Department of Corrections Response. Office of the Inspector General, Department of Correction, Michael Caruso, Inspector General.

Entrepreneurial Government: A New York City Approach. December 1, 1992. Mayor's Office of Operations, Harvey Robins, Director with New York City Partnership.

Entrepreneurial Government: New York City's Approach. May 1993. Mayor's Office of Operations, Harvey Robins, Director, Allan Dobring, Deputy Director, Janet Lindner, Assistant Director.

Failed Promises: Child Welfare in New York City: A Look at the Past, A Vision for the Future. July 1989. Report of the Manhattan Borough President's Advisory Council on Child Welfare.

A Failure of Responsibility: Report to Mayor David N. Dinkins on the December 21, 1991 Tragedy at City College of New York. January 1992. Office of Deputy Mayor Milton Mollen.

Financial Plan Modification Fiscal Years 1992–1996: Economic and Tax Revenue Forecasts. November 1991. Office of Management and Budget, Philip R. Michael, Director.

Financial Planning in the Nineties: Building on New York's Pioneering Efforts in the Seventies. June 1992. New York State Financial Control Board. p. ii.

Findings and Recommendations of the Joint Commission on Integrity in the Public Schools. April 1990. James F. Gill, Chairman.

A Futureprint for New York City's Youth: Building Our Future, Preserving Our Present. October 27, 1993. Office of Deputy Mayor Cesar A. Perales.

Governing for Results: Decentralization with Accountability. April 1991. Report of the Temporary State Commission on New York City School Governance, John S. Marchi, Chairman.

Improving the Odds: Making Decentralization Work for Children, for Schools, and for Communities. December 1987. Report to Manhattan Borough President, David N. Dinkins.

Investigating the Investigator: Interim Report of the Joint Commission on Integrity in the Public Schools. James F. Gill, Chairman.

An Investigation into the Police Department's Conduct of the Dowd Case and an Assessment of the Police Department's Internal Investigation Capabilities. November 1992. Raymond W. Kelly, Police Commissioner.

Management Initiative Highlights: The Dinkins Administration: The First Two Years. December 1991. Mayor's Office of Operations, Harvey Robins, Director.

Management Initiative Highlights: The Dinkins Administration: The First Three Years. December 1992. Mayor's Office of Operations, Harvey Robins, Director.

Managing "Squeegeeing:" A Problem-Solving Exercise. Undated. Received at Municipal Reference and Research Center February 14, 1994. Dr. George L. Kelling, Deputy Chief Michael Julian, Sergeant Steven Miller.

Maximizing Resources: Managing in a Time of Retrenchment: Commitment to Neighborhood Services 1990–1992. December 1992. Mayor's Office of Operations, Harvey Robins, Director.

Mayor's Management Report. 1990–1994.

Medicaid Managed Care Plan: Year One. November 1992. Cesar A. Perales, Deputy Mayor Health and Human Services, Florence H. Frucher, Director, Office of Medicaid Managed Care.

Memorandum "From: David N. Dinkins To: Deputy Mayor Norman Steisel, Deputy Mayor Cesar A. Perales, Deputy Mayor Bill Lynch, Date: May 15, 1992, Subject: Plan for Implementation of [Cuomo] Commission Recommendations."

The Newest New Yorkers 1990–1994: An Analysis of Immigration to NYC in the Early 1990s. New York City Department of City Planning.

New York City Five-Year Plan for Housing and Assisting Homeless Adults. October 1991. Report to Mayor David N. Dinkins. Felice Michetti, Commissioner Department of Housing, Preservation, and Development; Barbara Sobol, Commissioner Human Resources Administration; Nancy Wackstein, Director, Mayor's Office on Homelessness and SRO Housing.

New York City Human Resources Administration, Office of Health Services and Financial Planning, Medicaid Managed Care. Report A-5-92. August 19, 1992. Office of the State Deputy Comptroller for the City of New York.

New York City Revised and Updated Plan for Housing and Assisting Homeless Single Adults and Families. March 1993. Report to the Mayor. Marsha A. Martin, DSW, Director Mayor's Office on Homelessness and SRO Housing; Sally Hernandez Pinero, Chairwoman, NYCHA; Luis R. Marcos, MD, Commissioner Department of Mental Health, Mental Retardation, and Alcoholism Services; Felice Michetti, Commissioner, Department of Housing Preservation and Development; Charles V. Raymond, Director, Mayor's Office for Homeless Facilities and Service Development; Barbara Sabol, Commissioner, Human Resources Administration.

New York City Roaring Back: Changing the City, for Good. December 1992. Office of the Mayor.

New York State Department of Labor Employment Data. Online, 1990–1993.

Policing New York City in the 1990s: The Strategy for Community Policing. January 1991. Lee P. Brown, Police Commissioner.

Preliminary Strategic Policy Statement for the City of New York. January 14, 1991. Office of the Mayor.

Report of the Special Deputy Commissioner Concerning the Transfer of Inner City Broadcasting Corporation Stock by David Dinkins. January 10, 1991. Transmitted by Elkan Abramowitz, Special Deputy Commissioner to Susan E. Shepard, Esq., Commissioner, Department of Investigation.

A Report to the Governor on the Disturbances in Crown Heights: An Assessment of the City's Preparedness and Response to Civil Disorder, Volume I. July 1993. Richard H. Girgenti, Director of Criminal Justice.

A Report to the Governor on the Disturbances in Crown Heights: A Review of the Investigation into the Death of Yankel Rosenbaum and the Resulting Prosecution, Volume II. July 1993. Richard H. Girgenti, Director of Criminal Justice.

Report to the Mayor: Staffing Needs of the New York City Police Department. October 1, 1990. Lee P. Brown, Police Commissioner.

Report to the Mayor: The Recommended Award of the PVB Privatization Contract to Lockheed I.M.S. August 1993. The City of New York Department of

Investigation, Susan E. Shepard, Commissioner; Richard C. Daddarios, First Deputy Commissioner.

Reshaping New York City's Policies and Programs for Homeless Individuals and Families: A Comprehensive Strategy for Implementing the Recommendations of the New York City Commission on Homelessness. May 1992. Office of the Mayor.

Safe Streets, Safe City: An Omnibus Criminal Justice Program for the City of New York. October 2, 1990. New York City Office of the Mayor.

Safe Streets, Safe City II: A Futureprint for Success. September 1993. New York City Office of the Mayor.

A Shelter Is Not a Home. March 1987. Report of the Manhattan Borough President's Task Force on Housing for Homeless Families. Dr. James R. Dumpson, Chairman.

Statement by Mayor David N. Dinkins: Meeting of the State Financial Control Board. July 2, 1991.

State of the City Address Presented by Mayor David N. Dinkins in the City Council Chamber—City Hall. January 8, 1991; January 2, 1992; January 4, 1993.

Statistical Report, Complaints and Arrests. 1986–1997. New York City Police Department, Office of Management Analysis and Planning, Crime Analysis Unit.

The Structure of the FYs 1993–1996 Financial Plan. July 29, 1992. New York State Financial Control Board.

A System Like No Other: Fraud and Misconduct by New York City School Custodians. November 1992. Edward Stancyk, Inspector General of School Systems.

The Way Home: A New Direction in Social Policy. February 21, 1992. Report of the New York City Commission on the Homeless, Andrew M. Cuomo, Chairman.

Newspapers and Periodicals

Amsterdam News
New York
New York Times
New York Post
New York Newsday
Staten Island Advance
Time
Newsweek

Books, Articles, and Miscellaneous Publications

Abbott, David W., Louis H. Gold, and Edward T. Rogowsky. *Police, Politics and Race: The New York City Referendum on Civilian Review.* New York: American Jewish Committee and the Joint Center for Urban Studies of the Massachusetts Institute of Technology and Harvard University, 1969.

Barrett, Wayne, assisted by Adam Fifield. *Rudy! An Investigative Biography of Rudolph Giuliani.* New York: Basic Books, 2000.

Bratton, William with Peter Knobler. *Turnaround: How America's Top Cop Reversed the Crime Epidemic.* New York: Random House, 1998.

Browne, Arthur, Dan Collins, & Michael Goodwin. *I, Koch: A Decidedly Unauthorized Biography of the Mayor of New York City, Edward I. Koch.* New York: Dodd, Mead & Company, 1985.

Cannato, Vincent J. *The Ungovernable City: John Lindsay and His Struggle to Save New York.* New York: Basic Books, 2001.

Colburn, David R. and Jeffrey S. Adler, eds. *African-American Mayors: Race, Politics and the American City.* Urbana and Chicago: University of Illinois Press, 2001.

Daughtry, Herbert D., Sr. *No Monopoly on Suffering: Blacks and Jews in Crown Heights (and Elsewhere).* Trenton, NJ: Africa World Press, Inc., 1997.

Fernandez, Joseph A. with John Underwood. *Tales out of School: Joseph Fernandez's Crusade to Rescue American Education.* Boston, MA: Little Brown & Company, 1993.

Fitch, Robert. *The Assassination of New York.* New York: Verso, 1993.

Foner, Nancy, ed. *New Immigrants in New York.* New York: Columbia University Press, 1987.

Freeman, Joshua B., *Working Class New York.* New York: The New Press, 2000.

Fuchs, Ester. *Mayors and Money: Fiscal Policy in New York and Chicago.* Chicago: University of Chicago Press, 1992.

Gittell, Marilyn, "Education: the Decentralization-Community Control Controversy," in Jewel Bellush and Stephen M. David, eds. *Race and Politics in New York City.* New York: Praeger, 1971.

Gordon, John Steele. *An Empire of Wealth: The Epic History of American Economic Power.* New York: Harper Collins, 2004.

Hacker, Andrew. *Two Nations: Black and White, Separate, Hostile, Unequal.* New York: Charles Scribner's Sons, 1992.

Harris, Louis and Bert E. Swanson. *Black–Jewish Relations in New York City.* New York: Praeger, 1970.

Jacobson, Matthew Frye. *Whiteness of a Different Color: European Immigrants and the Alchemy of Race.* Cambridge, MA: Harvard University Press, 1998.

Kagann, Stephen. "New York's Vanishing Supply Side," *City Journal* (Autumn 1992).

Karmen, Andrew. *New York Murder Mystery: The True Story behind the Crime Wave of the 1990s.* New York: New York University Press, 2000.

Kessner, Thomas and Betty Boyd Caroli. *Today's Immigrants: Their Stories.* New York: Oxford University Press, 1982.

Kirtzman, Andrew. *Rudy Giuliani: Emperor of the City.* New York: Harper Collins, 2001.

Koch, Edward I. *Mayor: An Autobiography.* New York: Warner Books, 1985.

Kroessler, Jeffrey A. *New York Year by Year: A Chronology of the Great Metropolis.* New York: New York University Press, 2002.

Lachman, Seymour P. and Robert Polner. *The Man Who Saved New York: Hugh Carey and the Great Fiscal Crisis of 1975.* Albany: State University of New York Press, 2010.

Levine, Naomi. *Ocean Hill–Brownsville: A Case History of Schools in Crisis.* New York: Popular Library, 1969.

Lewinson, Edwin R. *Black Politics in New York City.* New York: Twayne Publishers, Inc., 1974.

Litow, Stanley, "Problems of Managing a Big City School System," In *Brookings Papers on Education Policy 1999,* edited by Diane Ratvitch, 185–217. Washington, DC: Brookings Institution Press, 1999.

Mayer, Martin. *The Teachers Strike: New York 1968.* New York: Harper, 1968.

McFadden, Robert D. et al. *Outrage: The Story behind the Tawana Brawley Hoax.* New York: Bantam Books, 1990.

McNickle, Chris. *To Be Mayor of New York: Ethnic Politics in the City.* New York: Columbia University Press, 1993.

Morsell, John Albert. "The Political Behavior of Negroes in New York City." PhD diss., Columbia University, 1950.

Mollenkopf, John Hull. *A Phoenix in the Ashes: The Rise and Fall of the Koch Coalition in New York City Politics.* Princeton, NJ: Princeton University Press, 1992.

Mollenkopf, John Hull and Manuel Castells, eds. *Dual City: Restructuring New York.* New York: Russell Sage Foundation, 1991.

Moynihan, Daniel Patrick, "Defining Deviancy Down," *American Scholar Magazine* (Winter 1993).

Newfield, Jack and Wayne Barrett. *City for Sale: Ed Koch and the Betrayal of New York.* New York: Harper & Row, 1988.

Osofsky, Gilbert. *Harlem: The Making of a Ghetto,* 2nd ed. New York: Harper & Row, 1971.

Piatt, Bill. *Black and Brown in America.* New York: New York University Press, 1997.

Podair, Jerald E. *The Strike That Changed New York: Blacks, Whites and the Ocean Hill–Brownsville Crisis.* New Haven: Yale University Press, 2002.

Pritchett, Wendell. *Brownsville, Brooklyn.* Chicago: University of Chicago Press, 2002.

Rangel, Charles B. with Leon Wynter. *And I Haven't Had a Bad Day Since: From the Streets of Harlem to the Halls of Congress.* New York: Thomas Dunne Books/St. Martin's Press, 2007.

Ravitch, Diane. *The Great School Wars: New York City 1805–1973.* New York: Basic Books, 1974.

Rich, Wilbur C. *David Dinkins and New York City Politics: Race, Images and the Media.* Albany, NY: State University of New York Press, 2007.

Rieder, Jonathan. *Canarsie: The Jews and Italians of Brooklyn against Liberalism.* Cambridge, MA: Harvard University Press, 1985.

Riordan, William L. *Plunkitt of Tammany Hall.* New York: E.P. Dutton, 1963. Introduction by Arthur Mann.

Shapiro, Edward S. *Crown Heights: Blacks, Jews and the 1991 Brooklyn Riot.* Waltham, MA: Brandeis University Press, 2006.

Sharpton, Al and Anthony Walton. *Go and Tell Pharaoh: The Autobiography of the Reverend Al Sharpton.* New York: Doubleday, 1996.

Shefter, Martin. *Political Crisis/Fiscal Crisis: The Collapse and Revival of New York City.* New York: Basic Books, 1985.

Siegel, Fred. "Reclaiming Our Public Spaces," *City Journal* (Spring 1992).

Siegel, Fred. *The Future Once Happened Here: New York, D.C., L.A. and the Fate of America's Big Cities.* New York: The Free Press, 1997.

Siegel, Fred. *The Prince of the City: Giuliani, New York and the Genius of American Life.* San Francisco: Encounter Books, 2005.

Silverman, Eli B. *NYPD Battles Crime: Innovative Strategies in Policing.* Boston: Northeastern University Press, 2001.

Sleeper, Jim. *The Closest of Strangers: Liberalism and the Politics of Race in New York.* New York: W.W. Norton & Company, 1990.

Soffer, Jonathan. *Ed Koch and the Rebuilding of New York.* New York: Columbia University Press, 2010.

Spinrad, William. "New Yorkers Cast Their Ballots." PhD diss., Columbia University, 1955.

Thompson, J. Phillip, III. *Double Trouble: Black Mayors, Black Communities and the Call for Deep Democracy.* New York: Oxford University Press, 2006.

Vallone, Peter, F. *Learning to Govern: My Life in New York Politics, From Hell Gate to City Hall.* New York: Chaucer Press, 2005.

Walter, John C. *The Harlem Fox: J. Raymond Jones and Tammany, 1920–1970.* Albany, NY: State University of New York Press, 1989.

Weikart, Lynne A. *Follow the Money: Who Controls New York City Mayors.* Albany, NY: State University of New York Press, 2009.

Weiss, Avaraham. "Confronting David Dinkins," unpublished manuscript in possession of the author, courtesy of Rabbi Avraham Weiss.

Weiss, Nancy J. *Farewell to the Party of Lincoln: Black Politics in the Age of FDR.* Princeton, NJ: Princeton University Press, 1983.

West, Cornel. *Race Matters.* Boston: Beacon Press, 1993.

Wilson, James Q. and George L. Kelling. "Broken Windows: The Police and Neighborhood Safety," *The Atlantic Monthly* (March 1982).

Index

Koch and, xiii, 35
lack of trust in Dinkins, xi
media control by, 18
perceptions on race relations, 310
political party affiliations, 36
progressives/liberals, 23, 50n71, 281
relations with blacks, 159
support for Dinkins, 35, 309, 331, 347
support for Giuliani, 331–32
union leaders, 30–31
white-superiority doctrines, 225
Wicks Law, 156
Will Rogers Follies, The, 125
Wilson, James Q., 306
Winley, Diane Lacey, 22
Witmire, Kathryn J., 60

women's support for Dinkins, 324
World Trade Center bombing (1993), 131, 292–94
World War I, 12
"Worst Crimes of '93," 309
Wriston, Walter, 78

Y
Young, Denny, 36–37, 304

Z
zedakah, 107
Zionism, 39, 43
Zodiac killer, 202
Zuccotti, John E., 296
Zucker, Donald, 255

MY OWN PRIVATE GERMANY

MY OWN PRIVATE GERMANY

DANIEL PAUL SCHREBER'S
SECRET HISTORY OF MODERNITY

Eric L. Santner

PRINCETON UNIVERSITY PRESS

PRINCETON, NEW JERSEY

COPYRIGHT © 1996 BY PRINCETON UNIVERSITY PRESS
PUBLISHED BY PRINCETON UNIVERSITY PRESS, 41 WILLIAM STREET,
PRINCETON, NEW JERSEY 08540
IN THE UNITED KINGDOM: PRINCETON UNIVERSITY PRESS,
CHICHESTER, WEST SUSSEX

LIBRARY OF CONGRESS CATALOGING-IN-PUBLICATION DATA

SANTNER, ERIC L. 1955–

MY OWN PRIVATE GERMANY : DANIEL PAUL SCHREBER'S
SECRET HISTORY OF MODERNITY / ERIC L. SANTNER.

P. CM.

INCLUDES BIBLIOGRAPHICAL REFERENCES AND INDEX.

ISBN 0-691-02628-9 (ALK. PAPER)

1. SCHREBER, DANIEL PAUL, 1842–1911—MENTAL HEALTH.

2. SCHREBER, DANIEL PAUL, 1842–1911—INFLUENCE.

3. GERMANY—INTELLECTUAL LIFE—19TH CENTURY.

4. GERMANY—INTELLECTUAL LIFE—20TH CENTURY.

5. NATIONAL SOCIALISM—PSYCHOLOGICAL ASPECTS.

6. MODERNISM (ART)   7. MODERNISM (LITERATURE)   I. TITLE.

RC520.S33S26   1996

616.89′7′0092—dc20   95-43738   CIP

THIS BOOK HAS BEEN COMPOSED IN PALATINO

COVER ART BY ANSELM KIEFER, GERMAN, B. 1945, *PATHS OF THE WISDOM
OF THE WORLD: HERMAN'S BATTLE*, WOODCUT, ADDITIONS IN ACRYLIC AND
SHELLAC, 1980, 344.8 × 528.3 CM. THE ART INSTITUTE OF CHICAGO. RESTRICTED GIFT
OF MR. AND MRS. NOEL ROTHMAN, MR. AND MRS. DOUGLAS COHEN, MR. AND
MRS. THOMAS DITTMER, MR. AND MRS. RALPH GOLDENBERG, MR. AND MRS. LEWIS
MANILOW, AND MR. AND MRS. JOSEPH R. SHAPIRO; WIRT D. WALKER FUND,
1986.112. PHOTOGRAPH BY COURTESY OF THE ARTIST.

PRINCETON UNIVERSITY PRESS BOOKS ARE PRINTED
ON ACID-FREE PAPER AND MEET THE GUIDELINES
FOR PERMANENCE AND DURABILITY OF THE COMMITTEE
ON PRODUCTION GUIDELINES FOR BOOK LONGEVITY
OF THE COUNCIL ON LIBRARY RESOURCES

PRINTED IN THE UNITED STATES OF AMERICA
BY PRINCETON ACADEMIC PRESS

1   3   5   7   9   10   8   6   4   2

To Pamela Pascoe

WITH LOVE

CONTENTS

PREFACE

M Y INTEREST in Daniel Paul Schreber, whose autobiographical account of mental illness and psychiatric confinement has become, since its publication in 1903, the locus classicus for the study of paranoia in the psychiatric and psychoanalytic literature, began in earnest when my research turned to the history and prehistory of National Socialism. It was obvious that paranoia had played a crucial role in the ideology of National Socialism, that it had enjoyed the status of a quasi-official state ideology, even religion. It struck me that a proper understanding of the successes of the Nazis in mobilizing the population could only be achieved by a detailed study of the nature and structure of paranoid mechanisms as they functioned individually and collectively. Daniel Paul Schreber's *Denkwürdigkeiten eines Nervenkranken* (Memoirs of my nervous illness), a work drawing on the very phantasms that would, after the traumas of war, revolution, and the end of empire, coalesce into the core elements of National Socialist ideology, offered itself as a unique textual archive and "laboratory" for just such a study.[1]

Connections between the Schreber case and the paranoid core of National Socialist ideology had already been noted, albeit in broad and idiosyncratic strokes, by Elias Canetti in his remarkable treatise on mass psychology, published in 1960.[2] The final two chapters of that monumental work are dedicated to Schreber, whose *Memoirs* Canetti reads as nothing short of a precursor text to that more famous paranoid autobiography composed in confinement, Hitler's *Mein Kampf*. As Canetti puts it apropos of the political references and allusions in Schreber's text, "his political system had within a few decades been accorded high honor: though in a rather cruder and less literate form it became the creed of a great nation, leading . . . to the conquest of Europe and coming within a hair's breadth of the conquest of the world." For Canetti, the crucial link between paranoia and totalitarian leadership was not so much a matter of the historical content of the conspiratorial "plots" against which the paranoid and the totalitarian leader struggle—both Schreber and Hitler saw their fates profoundly bound to that of all sorts of historically specific dangers, including the danger of Jewish contamination and corruption. For Canetti, the link between paranoia and Hitlerite leadership was of a more formal nature. The paranoid and the dictator both suffer from a *disease of power*, which involves a pathological will to sole survivorship and a concomitant willingness, even drivenness, to sacrifice the rest of the world

in the name of that survivorship. Apropos of Schreber's apocalyptic delusions in which the end of the world is staged in numerous ways, Canetti writes:

> We do not get the impression that these disasters came upon mankind against Schreber's will. On the contrary, he appears to feel a certain satisfaction in the fact that the persecution he was exposed to . . . should have had such appalling consequences. The whole of mankind suffers and is exterminated because Schreber thinks there is someone who is against him. . . . Schreber is left as the sole survivor because this is what he himself wants. He wants to be the only man left alive, standing in an immense field of corpses; and he wants this field of corpses to contain all men but himself. It is not only as a paranoiac that he reveals himself here. To be the last man to remain alive is the deepest urge of every seeker after power. . . . Once he feels himself threatened his passionate desire to see *everyone* lying dead before him can scarcely be mastered by his reason.

Because of this shared psychic disposition, because the paranoid and the totalitarian leader are both caught up in the same drive for power—and for Canetti, power is the ultimate object of the drives—he concludes that a "madman, helpless, outcast and despised, who drags out a twilight existence in some asylum, may, through the insights he procures us, prove more important than Hitler or Napoleon, illuminating for mankind its [i.e., power's] curse and its masters."[3]

Although far more sympathetic to the ambiguously transgressive dimensions of Schreber's delusions, Gilles Deleuze and Félix Guattari ultimately second Canetti's reading of Schreber's text as a storehouse of protofascist fantasies and fantasy structures. Referring to Canetti's work, they characterize the paranoid type as someone who "engineers masses," as the "artist of the large molar aggregates . . . the phenomena of organized crowds." And regarding the 1902 decision of the Saxon Supreme Court—the very court on which Schreber had served as presiding judge—to rescind his incompetency ruling, they suggest that the decision might have gone differently for the former colleague "if in his delirium he had not displayed a taste for the socius of an already fascisizing libidinal investment" or, as they put it, "if he had taken himself for a black or Jew rather than a pure Aryan."[4] There will be much to say about Schreber's imaginary identifications, one of which happens to be with the Wandering Jew; for now, suffice it to say that these commentators on Schreber establish a powerful link between the *Memoirs* and some of the core features and obsessions of National Socialism.

A somewhat different approach to the larger political implications of the Schreber material and its ultimate relevance for the study of Ger-

man fascism was broached by the American psychoanalyst William Niederland who, beginning in the 1950s, focused on the importance of Schreber's father, Daniel Moritz Schreber, in his son's mental illness. According to Niederland, Moritz Schreber, an ambitious physician, author, and promoter of exercise and physical fitness, chronically traumatized his son by a series of aggressive orthopedic and pedagogical interventions and controls. Schreber's paranoia was, Niederland suggested, the monstrous product of a monstrous medicopedagogical project, the delusional elaboration of years of real and systematic child abuse experienced at the hands of a domineering and medically trained paterfamilias.[5] These views were amplified and popularized in the early 1970s by Morton Schatzman, who, combining Niederland's findings and Canetti's speculations on power, proposed a direct link between the "micro-social despotism in the Schreber family and the macro-social despotism of Nazi Germany." Schatzman claimed that "Hitler and his peers were raised when Dr. Schreber's books, preaching household totalitarianism, were popular," and added that "anyone who wishes to understand German 'character structure' in the Nazi era could profitably study Dr. Schreber's books."[6]

Although my interpretation of the Schreber case differs in a number of crucial ways from the particular views proposed by these writers, I remain indebted to their intuition as to the profound connections between the Schreber material and the social and political fantasies at work in Nazism, fantasies endowing Nazism with the status of a perverse political religion. The wager of this book is that the series of crises precipitating Schreber's breakdown, which he attempted to master within the delusional medium of what I call his "own private Germany," were largely the same crises of modernity for which the Nazis would elaborate their own series of radical and ostensibly "final" solutions. I am, in a word, convinced that Schreber's breakdown and efforts at self-healing introduced him into the deepest structural layers of the historical impasses and conflicts that would provisionally culminate in the Nazi catastrophe. In contrast to Canetti, however, my question will ultimately be not how Schreber's delusional system prefigured the totalitarian solution to the crises already afflicting the bourgeois-liberal order at the turn of the century, but rather how Schreber, who no doubt experienced the hollowing out of that order in a profound way, managed to avoid, by way of his own series of aberrant identifications, the totalitarian temptation.

My hypothesis is that these impasses and conflicts pertain to shifts in the fundamental matrix of the individual's relation to social and institutional authority, to the ways he or she is addressed by and re-

sponds to the calls of "official" power and authority. These calls are largely calls to order, rites and procedures of *symbolic investiture* whereby an individual is endowed with a new social status, is filled with a symbolic mandate that henceforth informs his or her identity in the community. The social and political stability of a society as well as the psychological "health" of its members would appear to be correlated to the efficacy of these symbolic operations—to what we might call their *performative magic*—whereby individuals "become who they are," assume the social essence assigned to them by way of names, titles, degrees, posts, honors, and the like. We cross the threshold of modernity when the attenuation of these performatively effectuated social bonds becomes chronic, when they are no longer capable of seizing the subject in his or her self-understanding. The surprise offered by the analysis of paranoia—which, as shall become clear, bears important structural relations to *hysteria*, the proliferation of which in fin-de-siècle Europe has been much researched—is that an "investiture crisis" has the potential to generate not only feelings of extreme alienation, anomie, and profound emptiness, anxieties associated with *absence*; one of the central theoretical lessons of the Schreber case is precisely that a generalized attenuation of symbolic power and authority can be experienced as the collapse of social space and the rites of institution into the most intimate core of one's being. The feelings generated thereby are, as we shall see, anxieties not of absence and loss but of overproximity, loss of distance to some obscene and malevolent presence that appears to have a direct hold on one's inner parts. It is, I think, only by way of understanding the nature of this unexpected, historical form of anxiety that one has a chance at understanding the libidinal economy of Nazism, and perhaps of modern and postmodern forms of totalitarian rule more generally.[7]

Toward the end of his *Memoirs*, Schreber writes that his aim is to show the reader that his discoveries about, among other things, the profound connections between the nature of God, the soul, and sexuality "are the fruit of many years' hard thinking and based on experiences of a very special kind not known to other human beings." He adds that "these may not contain the complete truth in all its aspects, but will be incomparably nearer the truth than all that has been thought and written about the subject in the course of thousands of years" (185).[8] In a manner of speaking, I take Schreber seriously when he makes such albeit megalomanaical claims. I believe that he has indeed made genuine discoveries about a variety of important matters, above all about matters pertaining to the theological dimension of political and social authority, to what Clifford Geertz has called the "inherent sacredness of sovereign power." Geertz writes:

At the political center of any complexly organized society . . . there is both a governing elite and a set of symbolic forms expressing the fact that it is in truth governing. No matter how democratically the members of an elite are chosen . . . or how deeply divided among themselves they may be . . . they justify their existence and order their actions in terms of a collection of stories, ceremonies, insignia, formalities, and appurtenances that they have either inherited or, in more revolutionary situations, invented. It is these—crowns and coronations, limousines and conferences—that mark the center as center and give what goes on there *its aura of being not merely important but in some odd fashion connected with the way the world is built.*[9]

Schreber made his discoveries at the very moment he entered, by way of a symbolic investiture, one of the key centers of power and authority in Wilhelmine Germany, the Saxon Supreme Court. His discoveries were grounded in an intuition that his symptoms were, so to speak, symptomatic, that they were a form of knowledge concerning profound malfunctions in those politicotheological procedures that otherwise sustain the very ontological consistency of what we call the "world." It is my purpose in this essay to unpack and evaluate this knowledge and to indicate the difficult pathways by which Schreber came to possess it.

My work on Schreber has coincided with a disturbing rise of expressions of paranoia in the United States and elsewhere just as new geopolitical arrangements, ideological investments, and shifts of populations and capital come to fill the vacancy left by the end of the cold war. To use Walter Benjamin's phrase, with regard to the question of paranoia and its critical analysis, we find ourselves at a "moment of danger."[10] One of the central fixations of recent paranoid anxieties, at least in the United States, has been the notion of the "new world order." When George Bush invoked that term it signified, first and foremost, the new geopolitical mappings that were to follow from the dissolution of socialist states at the end of the 1980s. It signified, in other words, the end of an era of the extreme paranoia that had dominated the years of the cold war. Paranoia about the "new world order" thus represents something of a paradox; it emerges at precisely that moment when one would expect an easing of paranoid anxieties about dangers emanating from the "evil empire" and its satellites. It now appears that cold war paranoia may have actually played the role of a collective psychological defense mechanism against a far more disturbing pathology that is only now beginning to find public avenues of expression. Nostalgia for the more ordered world of cold war anxieties would appear to be a nostalgia for a paranoia in which the persecutor had a more or less recognizable face and a clear geographical location. Although I make

no efforts to forge explicit links between Schreber's "prefascist" paranoia and our own "postfascist" variety, my work is informed by a concern that where there is a culture of paranoia, fascism of one kind or
another may not be far behind.[11]

My understanding of Schreber's paranoid universe as well as of the
current crises of social, political, and cultural meaning is greatly indebted to Slavoj Žižek's dialectical revisions of the fundamental concepts of psychoanalysis. Few contemporary thinkers have done more
to clarify the connections between the "private" domain of psycho-
pathological disturbances and the "public" domain of ideological and
political forces and realities. I also owe a large debt of gratitude to a
number of other friends, colleagues, students, and institutions. I would
like to thank the Cornell University Society for the Humanities for allowing me to try out my ideas about Schreber early on in the project; I
am grateful to Jonathan Culler, Dominick LaCapra, and the wonderful
staff at the society for making my stay there possible, productive, and
thoroughly enjoyable. I would especially like to thank the students
who took part in my seminar there. Their contributions to my thinking
about a number of issues have been substantial. I would also like to
thank the members of my seminar on the Schreber material at Princeton University who came in on the project at a much later date. Their
involvement in the final formulations of my thoughts on Schreber has
been significant. As always, colleagues and friends have helped with
criticisms, suggestions, and the inspiration of their own work; special
thanks to Diana Fuss, Eduardo Cadava, Stanley Corngold, Barbara
Hahn, Hal Foster, Dominick LaCapra, Andreas Huyssen, Steven Beller,
Biddy Martin, Mandy Merck, David Bathrick, and especially to fellow
"Schreberians" Sander Gilman, Jay Geller, Philippe Despoix, Daniel
Boyarin, and Louis Sass. I am particularly grateful to Zvi Lothane for
his enormous generosity as the de facto dean of contemporary Schreber
studies. I want to thank Mary Murrell for her energy, vision, and
humor. My ongoing dialogue with David Schwarz on psychoanalysis,
culture, and life in general has, as always, provided sustained intellectual, moral, and emotional nourishment. Finally, thanks to Pamela
Pascoe whose love, good cheer, and jargon-free brilliance were crucial
to the project and my general sense of psychic equilibrium as I made
my way through Daniel Paul Schreber's "own private Germany."

MY OWN PRIVATE GERMANY

INTRODUCTION

I

D ANIEL PAUL SCHREBER was born in Leipzig on July 25, 1842, the third of five children born to Daniel Gottlob Moritz Schreber and Pauline Schreber née Haase. The Schreber name is now known in Germany primarily for the small garden plots—*Schrebergärten*—that dot the perimeters of German cities and which were named after Moritz Schreber, whose numerous writings on public health, child rearing, and the benefits of fresh air and exercise inspired the institution of these gardens in the late nineteenth century. More recently, Moritz Schreber has become demonized as the sadistic paterfamilias whose pedagogic practices and orthopedic devices allegedly produced his son's psychotic predisposition. Schreber's older brother committed suicide in 1877; his three sisters all outlived him, though only the oldest, Anna Jung, had any children.

Schreber began to study law in 1860, one year prior to his father's death. After passing the state bar exam, he worked in various legal capacities, which included service in the civil administration of Alsace-Lorraine during the Franco-Prussian War as well as on the federal commission charged with producing the new Civil Code for the Reich. After his marriage to Sabine Behr in 1878, Schreber was appointed *Landgerichtsdirektor* (administrative director) of the District Court in Chemnitz.[1] During the Reichstag elections of 1884, he ran as a candidate of the National Liberal Party (with the support of the Conservative Party). His loss to the socialist Bruno Geiser triggered his first nervous breakdown, which culminated in a six-month stay at the Psychiatric Hospital of Leipzig University under the care of its director, Paul Emil Flechsig. His primary symptom at this time was severe hypochondria, which passed, as Schreber notes in his *Memoirs*, "without any occurrences bordering on the supernatural" (62). After his release from Flechsig's clinic, Schreber occupied various district judgeships in Saxony and appeared to enjoy good health and relative contentment. As he puts it himself, "After recovering from my first illness I spent eight years with my wife, on the whole quite happy ones, rich also in outward honours and marred only from time to time by the repeated disappointment of our hopes of being blessed with children" (63). Schreber is referring here to a series of miscarriages his wife suffered. But things were to take a turn for the worse with his nomination, in June 1893, to the position of *Senatspräsident* or presiding

judge of the third chamber of the Supreme Court of Appeals. Under the shadow of this impending appointment, Schreber begins to develop new symptoms, one of which he singles out for its special significance:

> During this time I had several dreams to which I did not then attribute any particular significance, and which I would even today disregard ... had my experience in the meantime not made me think of the *possibility* at least of their being connected with the contact which had been made with me by divine nerves. I dreamt several times that my former nervous illness had returned.... Furthermore, one morning while still in bed (whether still half asleep or already awake I cannot remember), I had a feeling which, thinking about it later when fully awake, struck me as highly peculiar. It was the idea that it really must be rather pleasant to be a woman succumbing to intercourse. (63)

Schreber assumed his post as *Senatspräsident* in October 1893. After an initial and stressful period of adjustment, he begins to experience more severe symptoms of anxiety, above all insomnia: "I started to sleep badly at the very moment when I was able to feel that I had largely mastered the difficulties of settling down in my new office and in my new residence, etc." (64). During his first extreme bout with sleeplessness he experienced "an extraordinary event": "when I could not get to sleep, a recurrent crackling noise in the wall of our bedroom became noticeable at shorter or longer intervals; time and again it woke me as I was about to go to sleep." At the time, Schreber assumed that the noises were caused by a mouse. "But having heard similar noises innumerable times since then, and still hearing them around me every day in daytime and at night, I have come to recognize them as undoubted divine miracles" (64). This was, in a word, the first act in what Schreber would experience as an elaborate and divine conspiracy: *"right from the beginning the more or less definite intention existed to prevent my sleep and later my recovery from the illness resulting from the insomnia for a purpose which cannot at this stage be further specified"* (64; emphasis in original). By November 9—the day before the anniversary of his father's death—his level of anxiety was severe enough to lead to suicide attempts. He consulted Flechsig and was admitted, once again, to the University Clinic where the continuation of his insomnia left him feeling shattered: "I was completely ruled by the idea that there was nothing left for a human being for whom sleep could no longer be procured by all the means of medical art, but to take his life" (66). Several months into this second hospitalization Schreber experienced a further decline in his condition triggered by his wife's four-day visit to her father in Berlin:

> My condition deteriorated so much in these four days that after her return
> I saw her only once more, and then declared that I could not wish my wife
> to see me again in the low state into which I had fallen. From then on my
> wife's visits ceased; when after a long time I did see her again at the win-
> dow of a room opposite mine, such important changes had meanwhile
> occurred in my environment and in myself that I no longer considered
> her a living being, but only thought I saw in her a human form produced
> by miracle in the manner of the "fleeting-improvised-men" [*flüchtig hinge-*
> *machte Männer*]. (68)

Schreber notes here the sexual dimension of this turn for the worse:
"Decisive for my mental collapse was one particular night; during that
night I had a quite unusual number of pollutions (perhaps half a
dozen)" (68). It was also at this time that the structure of his paranoia
began to take its definitive shape with his psychiatrist at the center of
a vast and ultimately divine conspiracy: "From then on appeared the
first signs of communication with supernatural powers, particularly
that of nerve-contact which Professor Flechsig kept up with me in such
a way that he spoke to my nerves without being present in person.
From then on I also gained the impression that Professor Flechsig had
secret designs against me" (68).

After a brief stay in a private clinic, Schreber was transferred on June
29, 1894, to the Royal Public Asylum at Sonnenstein, where he remained under the care of its director, Guido Weber, until December 20,
1902. In the meanwhile he had been officially declared incompetent, a
ruling rescinded only after Schreber had filed his own writ of appeal to
the Supreme Court. Among the documents submitted to the court was
the text of the *Memoirs*, which Schreber had more or less completed
by 1900 based on notes he had kept since 1897. After his release from
Sonnenstein, Schreber published his *Memoirs* with the Leipzig publishing house Oswald Mutze, known for its promotion of occult and theo-
sophical works.[2]

Upon his release, Schreber lived briefly with his mother and one of
his sisters but soon moved with his wife into a newly built house in
Dresden above whose entrance they had inscribed the Siegfried motif
from Wagner's *Siegfried*. In 1906 the couple adopted a teenage daughter, Fridoline, who later reported that her adoptive father was "more of
a mother to me than my mother."[3] He did legal work for the family,
including the administration of his mother's bequests upon her death
in 1907, took long walks with his daughter, played chess and piano,
and continued to be an avid reader (he was comfortably fluent in Latin,
Greek, French, English, and Italian). His general well-being was spo-
radically interrupted by short fits of bellowing, and, though he did not

speak much about his illness, his sister reported that the voices that had tormented him for so many years had become a constant, unintelligible noise.[4] Sabine Schreber suffered a stroke in November 1907. Within weeks Schreber was hospitalized for the third and last time, now at the new state asylum in the village of Dösen outside of Leipzig. He remained there until his death on April 14—Good Friday—1911. Among the symptoms reported in his chart are outbursts of laughter and screaming, periods of depressive stupor, suicidal gestures, poor sleep, and delusional ideas of his own decomposition and rotting.[5]

II

Schreber's preoccupation with decomposition is a recurrent, even obsessive theme in the *Memoirs*. At one point, Schreber cites Hamlet's words that *"there is something rotten in Denmark"* (164; emphasis in original) to indicate the extent of the corruption of the normal relationship between God and himself as well as the physical states of decomposition that were among the by-products of that disordered relation. The metaphors Schreber uses to evoke this literal and figurative rottenness strongly resonate with the terms with which a general sense of decay, degeneration, and enervation were registered in fin-de-siècle social and cultural criticism. Max Nordau's famous treatise on decadence in the arts and culture, *Degeneration* [*Entartung*] (1892) helped to establish that term as the central metaphor for the diagnosis of cultural decline up to its fateful appropriation by National Socialist ideologues.[6] Though Nordau, a physician and writer who would become one of Herzl's key allies in the Zionist movement, himself remained committed to a bourgeois faith in progress through knowledge, science, discipline, and strength of will, he was acutely attuned to the signs of that faith's dissolution among his contemporaries, particularly among artists, writers, and intellectuals.

Nordau characterizes the fin-de-siècle mood as "a compound of feverish restlessness and blunted discouragement" culminating in feelings of "imminent perdition and extinction," a sense of the "Dusk of Nations, in which all suns and all stars are gradually waning, and mankind with all its institutions and creations is perishing in the midst of a dying world" (2). Central to Nordau's diagnosis of degeneration is what he characterizes as a condition of perpetual liminality or *interregnum* by which he means a state of cultural fatigue in which symbolic forms, values, titles, and identities have lost their credibility, their capacity to elicit belief, and so structure the life-worlds of individuals and communities:

There is a sound of rending in every tradition, and it is as though the morrow would not link itself with today. Things as they are totter and plunge, and they are suffered to reel and fall, because man is weary, and there is no faith that it is worth an effort to uphold them. Views that have hitherto governed minds are dead or driven hence like disenthroned kings. . . . Meanwhile interregnum in all its terrors prevails. (5–6)[7]

This general sense of ideological fatigue, which Nordau specifically links to that most famous of fin-de-siècle maladies, hysteria, is, he argues, fostered by the jarring rhythms of technological innovations and their socioeconomic consequences:

All its [civilized humanity] conditions of life have, in this period of time, experienced a revolution unexampled in the history of the world. Humanity can point to no century in which the inventions which penetrate so deeply, so tyrannically, into the life of every individual are crowded so thick as in ours. . . . In our times . . . steam and electricity have turned the customs of life of every member of the civilized nations upside down. (37)

Because of innovations in information technologies and transport— Nordau is thinking above all of the proliferation of newspapers and the expansion of railway and postal networks—"the humblest village inhabitant has today a wider geographical horizon, more numerous and complex intellectual interests, than the prime minister of a petty, or even a second-rate state a century ago" (39). By reading even a provincial newspaper, "he takes part . . . by a continuous and receptive curiosity, in the thousand events which take place in all parts of the globe" (39). Nordau's conclusions from these observations are representative of a widespread nineteenth-century tendency to transpose the terms pertaining to social and cultural crisis into a scientific and medical idiom: "All these activities, however, even the simplest, involve an effort of the nervous system and a wearing of tissue" (39). Equally typical of the late nineteenth century are Nordau's fears that the demands placed on the human organism by the accelerated rates of social change, the chronic shocks of urban life, and the labor requirements of a rapidly industrializing society will deplete its reserves of energy: "This enormous increase in organic expenditure has not, and cannot have, a corresponding increase in supply" (39).[8]

Anson Rabinbach has analyzed the nineteenth-century preoccupation with fatigue and enervation in light of the discovery, in the middle of the nineteenth century, of the second law of thermodynamics—the law of entropy—which drastically undermined the optimism inspired by the first law, that of the conservation of energy elaborated by Hermann von Helmholtz in 1847. The prospect of the wasting away of

human energy and labor power generated not only anxieties of decline and even cosmic death, but also a new social ethic of energy conservation and a proliferation of research programs geared to maximize the productivity of the "human motor" and to minimize "the body's stubborn subversion of modernity."[9] Most important, the localization of the social dislocations that characterize modernity in the *body* and its relative states of vitality or degeneration opened the prospect of a scientific and medical analysis and, possibly, mastery of otherwise diffuse social, political, and cultural disorientations. Recalling Nordau's emphasis on the dissolution of symbolic identities, it was as if scientific and medical knowledge could become the source of a renewed sense of social and cultural location, a sense of certainty as to one's place in a symbolic network.

The lack of such certainty and strength of will and purpose that flows from it is seen by Nordau as part and parcel of a sort of generalized attention deficit disorder, for, as he puts it, "culture and command over the powers of nature are solely the result of attention" (55). The attenuation of mental focus and attention results in an overexposure of the mind to stimulation from *within*, from the forces of the unconscious: "Untended and unrestrained by attention, the brain activity of the degenerate and hysterical is capricious, and without aim or purpose. Through the unrestricted play of association representations are called into consciousness, and are free to run riot there" (56). Such morbid overstimulation can in turn produce an intense "feeling of voluptuousness," a state of bliss mixed with pain which Nordau links to "extraordinary decompositions in a nerve-cell" (63).

In the nineteenth century, jouissance and the decomposition of cell tissue were, of course, already strongly linked through widespread fears about venereal disease, especially syphilis. In the fin-de-siècle imagination, the venereal peril, which was linked above all to the practice of prostitution, called forth a veritable phantasmagoria of bodies in various states of decay and rot, as well as the prospect of dementia and enfeebled progeny.[10] But as with all sexual ailments, syphilis was a highly overdetermined disease formation, absorbing a wide array of social anxieties and cultural meanings. In an article on "Nervousness and Neurasthenic States" (1895), the leading German sexologist, Richard von Krafft-Ebing, evokes syphilitic contamination as the culmination and condensation of nearly all the social, cultural, and physiological deformations thought under the term "degeneration" at the fin de siècle:

> Countless modern human beings spend their lives not in fresh air, but in gloomy workshops, factories, and offices, etc., others in stressful duties which have been imposed on them by steam and electricity, the means

of transport as well as the driving forces of modern times. However, increased work creates the demand for more of the pleasures of life. The progress of civilization has created a life style with greater needs, and the brain has to pay for the gratification of such needs. . . . One can see them [the human beings in their struggle for existence] in continuous feverish excitement hunting for money, using all their physical and mental powers in the form of railway, post and telegraph. However, such strained nervous systems develop an increased need for consumption and excitement (coffee, tea, alcohol, tobacco). Hand-in-hand with the improved living-conditions of the modern era it has become increasingly difficult to establish a home of one's own: the man of upper social classes might be able to feed a woman but not to clothe her. The consequences are extramarital sexual intercourse—specially in the big cities—, remaining single and late marriages. When such a modern man of business and work eventually gets married at an advanced age, he is decrepit, debauched and often syphilitic; with the modest remains of his virility, in the midst of the haste and exhaustion of his professional life, he fathers only sickly, weakly and nervous children.[11]

In a certain sense, Schreber's *Memoirs* could be seen as an attempt to answer the question implicit in this list of pathologies: *What remains of virility* at the end of the nineteenth and beginning of the twentieth century? No doubt because of Schreber's position as a jurist, his efforts to provide an answer to this question led him beyond the syphilophobia and ergonomic preoccupations of his era to a source of rot much closer to his professional home.

III

In 1921, three years after he found a copy of Schreber's "famous *Denkwürdigkeiten eines Nervenkranken*" in a secondhand bookstore, Walter Benjamin wrote an essay that, although addressing issues seemingly far afield from what he would later recall as the salient features of Schreber's text, nonetheless takes us into the heart of the latter's preoccupations with decay.[12] The essay, "Zur Kritik der Gewalt" (Critique of violence), has remained, because of its ominous ambiguities regarding "divine" force and violence, one of the more problematic texts in Benjamin's corpus.[13]

At the center of Benjamin's reflections is a meditation on a certain self-referentiality of law and legal institutions, which, Benjamin suggest, manifests itself most forcefully in the death penalty. He writes that "in the exercise of violence over life and death more than in any other legal act, *law reaffirms itself*. But in this very violence *something*

rotten in law [*etwas Morsches im Recht*] is revealed."[14] What manifests itself as the law's inner decay is the fact that rule of law is, in the final analysis, without ultimate justification or legitimation, that the very space of juridical reason within which the rule of law obtains is established and sustained by a dimension of force and violence that, as it were, holds the place of those missing foundations. At its foundation, the rule of law is sustained not by reason alone but also by the force/violence of a tautologous enunciation—"The law is the law!"—which is for Benjamin the source of a chronic institutional disequilibrium and degeneration.[15]

Benjamin distinguishes two aspects of this "outlaw" dimension of law: law-making violence (*rechtsetzende Gewalt*) and law-preserving violence (*rechtserhaltende Gewalt*). The former refers to the series of acts that first posits the boundary between what will count as lawful and unlawful, the latter to those acts which serve to maintain and regulate the borders between lawful and unlawful acts once they have been established. Benjamin devotes some remarkable passages to the role of the police in the modern state because they, not unlike the institution of the death penalty, represent a "kind of spectral mixture" of these two forms of violence and thus mark "the point at which the state, whether from impotence or because of the immanent connections within any legal system, *can no longer guarantee through the legal system* the empirical ends that it desires at any price to attain." The police is for Benjamin the site where the extralegal violence on which the rule of law is structurally dependent is most clearly manifest. In his evocation of the quasi-demonic aspect of the police, Benjamin does not shy away from a rhetoric one would be tempted to call paranoid: "Its power is formless, like its nowhere tangible, all-pervasive, ghostly presence in the life of civilized states." He concludes by suggesting that in democratic societies, where the constitutive role of law-making and law-preserving violence is most fervently disavowed, the open secret of sanctioned police violence can be especially unnerving:

> And though the police may, in particulars, everywhere appear the same, it cannot finally be denied that their spirit is less devastating where they represent, in absolute monarchy, the power of a ruler in which legislative and executive supremacy are united, than in democracies where their existence, elevated by no such relation, bears witness to the greatest conceivable degeneration of violence.[16]

As Jacques Derrida has emphasized in a fine commentary on Benjamin's essay, the extralegal dimension of force that it was Benjamin's concern to lay bare to postwar and postrevolution Weimar parliamentarians can be subsumed under a more general notion of the performa-

tive structure of speech acts.[17] A performative utterance is one that brings about its own propositional content, that establishes a new social fact in the world by virtue of its being enunciated in a specific social context, as when, for example, a judge or priest pronounces a couple "husband and wife." Performative utterances are, as a rule, enchained or nested in sets of relations with "lower" levels of performatives that set the stage for their felicitous functioning. Before a judge can perform a marriage ceremony, for example, his effectivity as a social agent must first be established, his symbolic power and authority must first be transferred to him by other performatives that pronounce him "judge." Benjamin's claim is that at a certain point this chain of transferences bottoms out, encounters a missing link at the origin of the symbolic capital circulating through it.[18] To those of a "finer sensibility," this missing link is, however, *everywhere* present as, precisely, "something rotten in law."[19] It is, Benjamin suggests, this missing link pertaining to the emergence of institutions that *drives* the symbolic machinery of the law—for Benjamin, the paradigmatic institution—and infuses it with an element of violence and compulsion. Although he does not evoke the psychoanalytic theory of the drives, Derrida's particular contribution to our understanding of Benjamin's "Critique of Violence," and the "mystical foundation of authority" more generally, is his insistence on the link between performativity and the compulsion to repeat:

> It belongs to the structure of fundamental violence that it calls for the repetition of itself and founds what ought to be conserved, conservable, promised to heritage and tradition. . . . A foundation is a promise. Every position . . . permits and promises. . . . And even if a promise is not kept in fact, iterability inscribes the promise as guard in the most irruptive instant of foundation. Thus it inscribes the possibility of repetition at the heart of the originary. . . . Position is already iterability, a call for self-conserving repetition.[20]

When, in other words, one is "pronounced" husband, wife, professor, *Senatspräsident*, one is invested with a symbolic mandate, which in turn compels a regulated series of social performances, rituals, behaviors that corresponds to that symbolic position in the community, that "iterates" and thereby certifies the originary performative establishing the change in one's status.

This peculiar combination of performativity, repetition, and force intrinsic not only to the efficacy of law, which it was Benjamin's concern to reveal, but to the "magical" operation of all rites of institution and their procedures of symbolic investiture has been explored in great detail by the noted sociologist of symbolic power, Pierre Bourdieu. Bourdieu has emphasized the imperative and, indeed, coercive, nature

of acts of symbolic investiture, acts such as of the call issued by the Ministry of Justice to Daniel Paul Schreber in 1893 nominating him to the position of *Senatspräsident*. Official acts of interpellation, which, as Bourdieu notes, must be undergirded by "incessant calls to order" once the new social identity has been assumed, function in the manner of an act of fate:

> "Become what you are": that is the principle behind the performative magic of all acts of institution. The essence assigned through naming and investiture is, literally, a *fatum*. . . . All social destinies, positive or negative, by consecration or stigma, are equally *fatal*—by which I mean mortal—because they enclose those whom they characterize within the limits that are assigned to them and that they are made to recognize.[21]

The (repetitive) demand to live in conformity with the social essence with which one has been invested, and thus *to stay on the proper side of a socially consecrated boundary*, is one that is addressed not only or even primarily to the mind or intellect, but to the body. The naturalization of a symbolic identity, its incorporation in the form of a habitus, is, as Bourdieu emphasizes, a process involving ascetic practices, training, even physical suffering: "All groups entrust the body, treated like a kind of memory, with their most precious possessions."[22] In light of this dimension of corporeal mnemotechnics pertaining to symbolic identity and function, it may then be in a more than metaphorical sense that, as Bourdieu puts it, "elites are destined to '*waste away*' when they cease to believe in themselves, when they . . . begin to cross the line in the wrong direction."[23] It might, of course, be said that the crucial lesson of Benjamin's "Critique of Violence" is that this process of internal decomposition afflicting elites in crisis is, in fact, the *normal* state of things, which is then only more or less successfully disavowed, more or less successfully repressed into the unconscious. It will be my argument in this book that Schreber's *Memoirs* tells the unnerving story of a massive return of this repressed knowledge.

IV

Although Benjamin's passionate engagement with the work of Franz Kafka was to begin later, his reflections on what is rotten in law suggests why he would come to feel such a powerful affinity for the work of the Prague writer. Kafka's prose is largely a meditation on communities in chronic states of crisis, communities in which the force of social laws no longer stands in any relation to the meaningfulness of their content and the traditions from which they derive. No doubt the most explicit statement of this disproportion in Kafka's oeuvre is the inter-

pretation offered by the priest apropos of the famous parable of the law in *The Trial*. At the end of their long exchange about the possible meanings of the relation between the doorkeeper and the man from the country seeking access to the Law, Josef K. expresses perplexed disagreement with the priest's point of view:

> "for if one accepts it, one must accept as true everything the doorkeeper says. But you yourself have sufficiently proved how impossible it is to do that." "No," said the priest, "it is not necessary to accept everything as true, one must only accept it as necessary." "A melancholy conclusion," said K. "It turns lying into a universal principle."[24]

Among the paradoxical features of Kafka's universe is that this surplus of necessity over truth endowing institutional authority (and its various representatives) with a dimension of obscene inscrutability is, in Kafka's texts, often linked to impotence, inconsistency, and debility on the part of that very authority. In his remarkable politicotheological allegory, "The Great Wall of China," for example, Kafka's narrator, a participant in the great national project as well as amateur historian and political theorist, produces the following surprising assessment of the empire: "Now one of the most obscure of our institutions is that of the empire itself. In Peking, naturally, at the imperial court, there is some clarity to be found on this subject, though even that is more illusive than real." At the lower levels of the educational hierarchy, what remains are "a few precepts which, though they have lost nothing of their eternal truth, remain eternally invisible in this fog of confusion."[25] Correlative to this confusion is the precarious status of the emperor himself whose very existence is shrouded in uncertainty and who, when he is imagined at all, is on his deathbed sending final missives that can never arrive at their destination.

This same admixture of inconsistency, weakness, and "law-making violence" also informs the narrative of one of Kafka's most famous short prose texts, "In the Penal Colony," where the letter of every law that has been transgressed is inscribed on the body of the transgressor, radicalizing and literalizing with grotesque brutality the mnemotechnics alluded to by Bourdieu. The debility of authority is here indicated by numerous details, from the displacement of the previous Commandant by one unfriendly to the penal apparatus, to the unreadability of the old Commandant's notations, to the impossible complexity and ultimate breakdown of the apparatus itself. We will return to Kafka in the course of this study; indeed, we will be approaching Schreber's universe as if it were the obverse of Kafka's. It is a world equally exposed to something rotten in law, but that exposure takes place from the opposite side—from the side of the judge rather than that of the supplicant to the law.

V

Before closing this series of literary historical digressions, we must briefly recall the figure whose writings about symbolic authority and power no doubt strongly influenced both Kafka and Benjamin: Schreber's Saxon contemporary, Friedrich Nietzsche.[26] In this context, one need only glance at a few key passages from *On the Genealogy of Morals*, published in 1887, to get a sense of the literary "genealogy" of Kafka's and Benjamin's thought regarding what is rotten in law. Consider the following remarks on what Benjamin later termed "law-making violence":

> The most decisive act, however, that the supreme power performs . . . is the institution of *law*, the imperative declaration of what in general counts as permitted, as just, in its eyes, and what counts as forbidden, as unjust: once it has instituted the law, it treats violence and capricious acts on the part of individuals or entire groups as offenses against the law, as rebellion against the supreme power itself. . . . "Just" and "unjust" exist, accordingly, only after the institution of the law. . . . To speak of just or unjust *in itself* is quite senseless.[27]

Indeed, Nietzsche goes on to make the paradoxical claim that true states of emergency or exception (*Ausnahme-Zustände*) are inaugurated by the legal order itself rather than by any criminal act committed against it.[28] For Nietzsche, the state of emergency is where the performative magic that animates all rites of institution is at its highest potency: at the moment of *emergence* of a new order of institutional conditions or interpretations. Nietzsche's name for this performativity was, of course, *will to power*, and his radical conclusion from the omnipresence of its effects was a view of history as a nonteleological series of ruptures and usurpations:

> there is for historiography of any kind no more important proposition than the one it took such effort to establish but which really *ought to be* established now: the cause of the origin of a thing and its eventual utility, its actual employment and place in a system of purposes, lie worlds apart, whatever exists, having somehow come into being, is again and again reinterpreted to new ends, taken over, transformed, and redirected by some power superior to it; all events in the organic world are . . . *becoming master*, and all . . . becoming master involves fresh interpretation. . . . [P]urposes and utilities are only *signs* that a will to power has become master of something less powerful and imposed upon it the character of a function; and the entire history of a "thing," an organ, a custom can in

this way be a continuous sign-chain of ever new interpretations and adaptations. . . . The "evolution" of a thing, a custom, an organ is thus by no means its *progressus* toward a goal, even less a logical *progressus* by the shortest route and with the least expenditure of force—but a succession of more or less profound, more or less mutually independent processes of subduing, plus the resistances they encounter, the attempts at transformation for the purposes of defense and reaction, and the results of successful counteractions. The form is fluid, but the "meaning" is even more so.[29]

Nietzsche's work has long been recognized as a radical and potent critique of the faith in progress that formed such an essential part of the Enlightenment legacy and bourgeois ideology in the late nineteenth century, particularly in Wilhelmine Germany during the postunification boom years. What has been less appreciated, with regard to the *Genealogy* in particular, is its relation to debates concerning the legal culture of the new Reich. When read against the background of the debates surrounding the unification and codification of law in the new state, Nietzsche's work takes on an added dimension of historical urgency.

The debates about legal codification in Germany, which extended from the beginning of work on the new Civil Code in 1874 to its completion in 1896, was one of the key sites where German society confronted the radical social changes associated with modernization and state formation as well as the shifting meanings of national identity in a period of cultural turbulence and contestation. The codification of a unified law of the Reich would have to come to terms not only with strong differences and conflicts between the heterogeneous legal codes and interests of the various German states and regions, but also with the needs and interests of new social constituencies whose contours were taking shape in the waves of industrialization and urbanization that dominated the last decades of the nineteenth century. Of considerable importance in the debates about codification was the question of the social and political neutrality of the law, one of the basic tenets of the reigning Pandectist School, whose logical and systematic approach to legal questions was termed "conceptual jurisprudence" (*Begriffsjurisprudenz*).

Following Savigny's idealization of Roman law, the adherents to this positivist approach concerned themselves above all with highly technical aspects of legal interpretation and systematization in ostensible abstraction from questions of moral, social, or political justification. In the context of the debates on the Civil Code, they sought to restrict the degree of legislative "creativity" to be allowed the code; those who favored more creativity hoped that the code might thereby be adapted

to the needs of a rapidly changing society. The effect of these debates concerning the role of legislative will in the codification of law was to force into the open the moral, social, and political commitments behind the supposed neutrality of the legal positivists; they exposed, so to speak, the degree of "law-making violence" behind the neutral face of conceptual jurisprudence. As Michael John has put it, "the fundamental norms from which conceptual jurisprudence attempted to deduce the details of the legal system involved value judgments with an obvious social and political relevance. To Savigny and his followers, the private legal order was composed of individual legal subjects whose wills operated within spheres of private autonomy."[30] Legal positivism's blend of principles, derived from Roman law and Kant, produced a legal philosophy that emphasized, in the realms of contract and property law, the free exercise of individual choice by autonomous legal subjects, a philosophy suited above all to property owners and entrepreneurs. Thus, as John notes, the "pursuit of legal certainty on the basis of individual freedoms came to seem a defence of the class interests of a narrow band of property-owners at the expense of the broader interests of the nation as a whole," and notes that "once the draft code was published in 1888 and subjected to public criticism, the social and political neutrality of conceptual jurisprudence could no longer be sustained."[31] The debate between the positivists and their various critics from the right and the left was thus not one between a "pure" and fundamentally "conceptual" jurisprudence, on the one hand, and one stained by sectional interests, on the other, but rather a debate between different conceptions of the society; it was, in a word, a *social* antagonism and not merely a legal-philosophical one.[32] And it was, I think, one of Nietzsche's fundamental insights that such social antagonisms bring out into the open what is normally repressed, namely that the texture of social reality is always at least in part constituted by a play of wills and forces whose outcome has a great deal more to do with compulsion and necessity than with truth. We might say, then, that at moments of heightened social antagonism, what is "rotten in law" begins to leak through from its normally circumscribed spaces. It was at such a moment that Daniel Paul Schreber underwent his symbolic investiture as *Senatspräsident* of the Supreme Court of Saxony.

The following chapters take up different aspects of the crisis inaugurated by this investiture and different features of the delusional world it "opened" for Schreber. I call this world Schreber's "own private Germany" because of his profound attunement to the exemplarity of the crisis he was undergoing, its resonances with the larger social and cultural crises of his era. The first chapter introduces the basic structure

of Schreber's fantasy space by way of a commentary on Freud's famous interpretation of the material. The decision to begin with Freud is motivated by several considerations. First, because of the interpretive force and strong canonical nature of Freud's case study, Schreber is always, at some level, still *Freud's* Schreber; after Freud, one cannot read Schreber except in some sort of dialogue with Freud, however agonistic that dialogue might be. (As we shall see, the question of influence anxiety powerfully informs Freud's own reading of Schreber's anxieties about overexposure to malevolent influences.) Furthermore, Freud's interpretation of Schreber's breakdown as an instance of homosexual panic has become newly resonant in the field of gay and lesbian studies, thereby increasing the importance of Freud's reading of Schreber for a more general understanding of the cultural meanings of "aberrant" sexualities.[33] Finally, Freud's study of the Schreber material was conducted at a moment in the history of psychoanalysis when the symbolic authority of that new institution was being strongly contested from within the ranks as well as from without—at a moment of institutional stress that, I will argue, made Freud particularly sensitive to the nature of Schreber's investiture crisis even though Freud never explicitly addressed it. This chapter thus raises in a provisional way the question of the relation between a crisis in the domain of symbolic authority and the production of "deviant" sexualities and gender identities.

The second chapter turns to the historical background of Schreber's apparent predisposition to experience his crisis in the culturally resonant terms we find in his *Memoirs*. What was it about Schreber's biography that allowed him to enter so deeply into this "private Germany" and to tell, from the perspective of this fantasy space, a kind of secret history of modernity? In the course of this chapter, I will enter into the debates broached by the work of Niederland and others whose researches raise the question of the role played by Moritz Schreber in his son's psychosis and thus the whole question of childhood abuse and trauma. This will lead to a dialogue with the work of Michel Foucault, whose writings on institutional power and the history of sexuality will help to situate the discussion of Moritz Schreber's role (as well as of the pathogenic influences of Schreber's psychiatrists) within a larger history of post-Enlightenment transformations of symbolic power and authority.

The final chapter addresses in detail the cultural meanings of two of Schreber's core delusions: his slow metamorphosis into a woman—a process he was compelled to support through transvestitism—and his merging with the figure of the Wandering Jew. What was the historical background of this nexus of identificatory mutations? What cultural

landscape did Schreber have to traverse to arrive at his perverse destination of unmanned Wandering Jew? All of these questions are motivated by a hope that by, so to speak, taking after him along his path, by
traversing with him the space of his own private Germany, one has
also, if only in the most modest and provisional of ways, entered into
the process of working through the very totalitarian temptation that so
many Germans after Schreber were unable to resist.

ONE

FREUD, SCHREBER, AND THE PASSIONS

OF PSYCHOANALYSIS

I

PSYCHOANALYSTS have long known about the transferential dimension of literary production, about the ways in which texts provide opportunities for their writers to act out or, ideally, work through, some of the very issues animating the subject matter of the text. This insight applies as much to the texts produced by psychoanalysts as by any other group of writers. And, indeed, Sigmund Freud, who founded psychoanalysis to a large extent on the basis of his own self-analysis, was profoundly aware of this transferential dimension of his own literary production. As it turns out, with regard to the text of concern to us here, his study of Daniel Paul Schreber—"Psychoanalytic Notes on an Autobiographical Account of a Case of Paranoia (Dementia Paranoides)"[1]—Freud left a detailed record of the transferential dynamic informing its composition. A brief look at this record will allow us to appreciate better what we might call the passions of psychoanalysis, namely, the deeper motives and motivations animating its choices of subjects. Among the things that made Schreber matter to Freud, that made his *Memoirs* a subject matter worthy of a major study based exclusively on a reading of that text, was, it appears, Freud's own defensive struggles with what he would come to see as Schreber's core issue: homosexuality.

According to letters written around the composition of the Schreber essay, Freud was still very much engaged with bringing to emotional closure his homosexually charged relation with Wilhelm Fliess, who, it seems, was able to find new and troubling incarnations in various members of Freud's inner circle. On October 6, 1910, for example, Freud wrote to Ferenczi, who had accompanied him to Italy the previous summer while he was at work on the Schreber material, that this work had helped him to overcome much of his own homosexual inclinations: "since the case of Fliess, with whose overcoming you just saw me occupied, this need has died out in me. A piece of homosexual charge has been withdrawn and utilized for the enlargement of my own ego. I have succeeded where the paranoiac fails." Several months

later, in another letter to Ferenczi, Freud widens the circle, as it were, of the paranoid queers with whom he saw himself struggling: "Fliess— you were so curious about that—I have overcome. . . . Adler is a little Fliess redivivus, just as paranoid. Stekel, as appendix to him, is at least named Wilhelm." In an earlier letter to Jung, Freud had already written, "My erstwhile friend Fliess developed a beautiful paranoia after he had disposed of his inclination, certainly not slight, toward me." Finally, in another letter to Jung written during the Italian journey with Ferenczi (and in the midst of the Schreber project), Freud characterized his traveling companion as being excessively passive and receptive toward him: "He has let everything be done for him like a woman, and my homosexuality after all does not go far enough to accept him as one."[2] Peter Gay's conclusion from this series of confessional remarks on Freud's part is fairly typical in the literature on Freud's Schreber essay; it opens up a kind of allegorical reading, one sensitive to traces of Freud's mimetic relation to Schreber, to his own struggle with Schreberian demons:

> Freud's rather manic preoccupation with Schreber hints at some hidden interest driving him on: Fliess. But Freud was not just at the mercy of his memories; he was working well and derived much comic relief from Schreber. . . . Still, Freud's work on Schreber was not untouched by anxiety. He was in the midst of his bruising battle with Adler, which, he told Jung, was taking such a toll "because it has torn open the wounds of the Fliess affair." . . . He blamed his memories of Fliess for interfering with his work on Schreber, but they were also a reason for his intense concentration on the case. To study Schreber was to remember Fliess, but to remember Fliess was also to understand Schreber. . . . Freud used the Schreber case to replay and work through what he called (in friendly deference to Jung, who had invented the term) his "complexes."[3]

Although this provisional reading of Freud's "allegorical" presence in his own text is persuasive, there are a number of details in Freud's essay suggesting a different set of emphases, suggesting that if indeed Freud was struggling with Schreberian demons, we may have to rethink their nature, reimagine the "closet" from which they emerged. I am thinking, for example, of Freud's surprising protestation, enunciated toward the end of his essay, concerning the originality of the views presented there. Freud remarks that certain details of Schreber's delusions "sound almost like endopsychic perceptions of the processes whose existence I have assumed in these pages as the basis of our explanation of paranoia." Apparently concerned by Schreber's analytic prescience, he goes on to reassure the reader that he has at least one witness who can testify "that I had developed my theory of paranoia

before I became acquainted with the contents of Schreber's book" (*SE* 12:79; my emphasis).[4]

What are we to make of this "masculine protest"—to use the Adlerian term Freud will himself employ in his reading of Schreber—pertaining to possible doubts about the originality of his insights? To anticipate Freud's reading further, we might say that this protest translates a proposition, or rather the negation of one; it is *not* the case, Freud is claiming, that "I, a scientist, plagiarized a dement." Against the backdrop of this protest, the anxious irony of Freud's further remark becomes more palpable; he writes that it "remains for the future to decide whether there is more delusion in my theory than I should like to admit, or whether there is more truth in Schreber's delusion than other people are as yet prepared to believe" (*SE* 12:79). What is particularly striking about Freud's somewhat anxious claim not to be, as it were, one of Schreber's epigones—indeed, very early in his essay Freud remarks that one could almost suspect Schreber of being a disciple of the psychoanalytic school[5]—is that this anxiety is uncannily reminiscent of one of the central themes of Schreber's psychotic fantasies, namely a confusion about and concern with the originality of his own thoughts, thought processes, and language. Freud appears, in other words, to exhibit apprehensions about Schreber not unlike those which Schreber had experienced with regard to the maleficent forces assaulting his soul and body, the theological systematization of which makes up the bulk of his *Memoirs*. Both Schreber and Freud, it would appear, are, albeit with quite different degrees of intensity, concerned that they might only be repeating, might only be parroting back, thoughts, words, and phrases originating elsewhere. If there is indeed a transferential dimension to Freud's passionate involvement with the Schreber material, then it concerns not only matters of same-sex passion but also questions of originality and influence, questions pertaining to the transfer of knowledge and authority in the very domain that Freud was staking out as his own.[6]

II

The extent and intensity of Freud's influence anxieties during his work on Schreber become increasingly evident over the course of his essay. I have already noted that Freud explicitly and uneasily refers to parallels between Schreber's mystical visions and the theory of libido, which at this time formed the centerpiece of Freud's conception of psychic functioning. Alluding to Schreber's notion of nerves and rays as those substantial emanations making possible not only contact between the

living and the dead, God and mortals, but also the phenomenon of "soul murder," which, as we shall see, suggests a traumatic experience of interpersonal influence at the hands of a powerful and trusted figure of authority, Freud remarks, "Schreber's 'rays of God,' which are made up of a condensation of the sun's rays, of nerve-fibers, and of spermatozoa, are in reality nothing else than a concrete representation and projection outwards of libidinal cathexes; and they thus lend his delusions a striking conformity with our theory" (*SE* 12:78).[7] In the course of his interpretation of Schreber's unwitting contribution to psychoanalytic theory, a contribution that produced for Freud no small degree of what I have called, following Bloom, anxiety of influence, Freud alludes to the work of colleagues who have helped him to come to the views presented in the text.[8] He notes, for example, at the beginning of the second part of his essay, that C. G. Jung had already made a pathbreaking contribution to the study of dementia praecox.[9] In the context of Schreber's preoccupation with rays and emanations as the materializations of potentially excessive and dangerous influences, it is interesting to note Freud's language in referring to Jung's priority in the study of the psychoses. He speaks of Jung's "brilliant example" (*SE* 12:35)— "das glänzende Beispiel"—of interpretation performed several years earlier on what Freud characterizes as a far more severe case of dementia than Schreber's. What Freud, however, does not mention is the fact that Jung also discusses Schreber in the book praised by Freud. It is also very likely that it was Jung who first brought Schreber to Freud's attention.[10]

Immediately after his reference to Jung's "brilliant" or "dazzling" example of interpretation, Freud goes on to discuss a hermeneutic principle intrinsic to psychoanalytic modes of interpretation according to which the usual hierarchical relation of principle and example is reversed. In psychoanalysis, Freud suggests, the example enjoys a paradoxical priority over the principle it would only seem to serve as illustration, and this reversal of priority extends to citations, glosses, and footnotes, which, as any reader of Schreber knows, play a rather large role in his text. Regarding the excess of such only apparently ancillary material in the Schreber memoir, Freud advises that "we have only to follow our usual psycho-analytic technique . . . to take his example as being the actual thing, or his quotation or gloss as being the original source—and we find ourselves in possession of what we are looking for, namely a translation of the paranoic mode of expression into the normal one" (*SE* 12:35).[11] Not surprisingly then, Freud's own footnotes turn out to be a key locus of what I have characterized as the allegorical dimension of the essay—a site where Freud stages some of his own

defensive maneuvers against influences that would compromise the originality and integrity of his own authorial voice.

Toward the end of his essay, Freud remarks in a footnote that Karl Abraham's short paper, "Die psychosexuellen Differenzen der Hysterie und der Dementia praecox," published in 1908, "contains almost all the essential views put forward in the present study of the case of Schreber" (*SE* 12:70).[12] Freud had, in fact, already noted his debt to Abraham's exemplary paper earlier, upon first introducing the notion of transference into his account. This earlier footnote effects, however, a curious reversal of priority and indebtedness with regard to Abraham: "In the course of this paper its author, referring to a correspondence between us, scrupulously attributes to myself an influence upon the development of his views" (*SE* 12:41). Influence anxiety on Freud's part is made unnecessary by Abraham's deference to him; if, indeed, the essential views put forward by Freud in his Schreber essay were prefigured in Abraham's earlier work, this turns out to be the result of Freud's own seminal influence on Abraham. An intellectual debt is, thanks to a citation of thanks, converted into more authorial capital.

Freud's admiration for such a scrupulous attribution of influence did not prevent curious lapses in his own practice of paying intellectual debts. I have already noted that despite his homage to Jung's exemplary work in the analysis of the psychoses he failed to indicate that it was Jung who alerted him to the Schreber memoir in the first place. In the final section of his essay, Freud thanks Jung (and Ferenczi) yet again for providing crucial case material to support his hunch that paranoia is as a rule generated by a quasi-natural homophobia: "we [Freud, Jung, and Ferenczi] were astonished to find that in all of these cases a defence against a homosexual wish was clearly recognizable at the very centre of the conflict which underlay the disease, and that it was in an attempt to master an unconsciously reinforced current of homosexuality that they had all of them come to grief" (*SE* 12:59). At this point, Freud adds a footnote in which he refers the reader to Alphonse Maeder's analysis of a paranoid patient, "Psychologische Untersuchungen an Dementia praecox–Kranken," published in August 1910 in the *Jahrbuch für psychoanalytische und psychopathologische Forschungen*, in which, as it happens, an article of Freud's had also appeared.[13] In his citation of the paper, Freud expresses regret that his Schreber essay "was completed before I had the opportunity of reading Maeder's work" (*SE* 12:162). However, as Lothane has pointed out, Freud admitted to Ferenczi in a letter of October 10, 1910, that he had indeed read Maeder's report.[14]

Yet another instance in which Freud's own contemporary struggle with issues of priority, authority, and influence comes to haunt his essay from the "preconscious" space of the footnotes comes after proposing his crucial thesis that Schreber's second illness was precipitated by a homosexually charged longing for reunion with his psychiatrist, Paul Flechsig. There Freud notes that "This feminine phantasy, which was still kept impersonal, was met at once by an indignant repudiation—a true 'masculine protest,' to use Adler's expression," but, Freud is quick to add, "in a sense different from his" (*SE* 12:42). Freud provides a footnote to this, his own "masculine protest" against Adler, in which he elaborates that "According to Adler the masculine protest has a share in the production of the symptom, whereas in the present instance the patient is protesting against a symptom that is already fully fledged" (*SE* 12:42). In this context, one should recall that when Adler presented his views in detail to the members of the Psychoanalytic Society in January and February 1911, Freud had responded quite critically, suggesting that some of Adler's key ideas, including that of "masculine protest," were, in essence, misguided appropriations of his own prior insights and ideas—were examples of, to use Gay's phrase, "spurious, manufactured originality."[15]

This apparent obsession with issues of originality and influence around the composition of the Schreber essay had a particular historical context. These were crucial years in the consolidation of the psychoanalytic movement in the face of increasingly profound internal divisions—the final break with Adler would come in 1911, with Jung two years later—which, of course, only intensified and complicated the ongoing struggle for recognition from the larger scientific and intellectual community. The institution of psychoanalysis was, one could say, in a state of emergency, meaning a state of *emergence*, of coming-into-being, as well as one of *crisis* and endangerment. This was a period during which the founding words and concepts—what we might call, with Schreber, the *Grundsprache* or "basic language" of psychoanalysis—that would establish the shape and intellectual direction of this new and strange science, when the boundaries that would determine the inside and outside of psychoanalytic thought proper, were being hotly and bitterly contested. As I have indicated, these are conditions in which there is, so to speak, maximum exposure to the dimension of "performative magic," which under normal circumstances—or, as Schreber puts it, under conditions consonant with the Order of the World—provides a necessary though unconscious support to symbolic authority of all kinds. It will be my argument in this book that the crucial features of Daniel Paul Schreber's "nervous illness," including the central fantasy of feminization, only become intelligible when seen

against the background of the issues and questions generated by such institutional and political states of emergency. Freud's passion for the Schreber material takes on an added dimension of internal "necessity" when set in relation to the anxieties of influence made urgent by the crisis in which the institution of psychoanalysis found itself in the years in which Freud was occupied with the case. Freud's preoccupation with originality indicates, in other words, his profound—and defensive—attunement to the performative force of his colleagues' utterances at a moment of heightened contestation of the fundamental concepts of psychoanalysis.[16]

Now it could be argued that psychoanalysis exhibits an especially strong dependence on the performative magic that contributes to the symbolic authority of institutional speech in general, that allows that speech to effectuate changes in social reality. With the notion of transference, psychoanalysis has, in essence, formally inscribed the dependence on performativity into its very foundations. An analysis or therapy will be effective only if the analysand at some level believes that it will, only if he or she believes that the analyst enjoys a privileged access to the true meaning of his or her words, stories, and symptoms. This transfer of faith and credit to the analyst and his or her power to decode, appreciate, and ultimately to participate in the analysand's message, is crucial to the production of that power in the analyst.[17] To put it somewhat differently, the analyst, like the classical monarch, has two bodies; the analyst's second, call it "sublime" body, is produced—and produces, in turn, analytical and therapeutic effects—to the extent that the analysand posits the analyst as a subject with special knowledge of one's deepest desires and secrets.[18]

The authorization of the analyst's power, his or her accreditation as a privileged subject of the transference in the preceding sense, comes, at least in part, by way of a prior transfer of credit and authority, namely the "consecration" or "investiture" of the analyst by the institution of psychoanalysis itself. As Bourdieu has put it, the efficacy of speech acts performed by delegates of an institution, specifically the ability of these speech acts to effect changes in reality—in this case, in the psychic states of the analysand—depends on the delegate's access to something on the order of a *skeptron*, some embodiment of institutional power that marks its bearer as an authentic representative of the institution:

> It is the access to the legitimate instruments of expression, and therefore the participation in the authority of the institution, which makes *all* the difference—irreducible to discourse as such—between the straightforward imposture of masqueraders, who disguise a performative utter-

ance as a descriptive or constative statement, and the authorized imposture of those who do the same thing with the authorization of an institution. The spokesperson is an impostor endowed with the *skeptron*.[19]

Whether one is performing the role of psychoanalyst or judge, one's performance must, in other words, be authorized. One cannot invest oneself with the authority to act as analyst or judge, one cannot produce one's own private *skeptron*; it must be transmitted and the transmission must follow a particular and quasi-public procedure.[20] Around the time that Freud was at work on the Schreber case he was himself embroiled in a series of "fiduciary" failures, challenges to his role as the one who passes the *skeptron*, who authorizes the speech of others as that of legitimate representatives of psychoanalysis.

The importance of these reflections becomes obvious when one recalls the specific occasions that triggered Schreber's two breakdowns. Each one involved an experience of a *crisis of symbolic investiture*. The first, still relatively mild breakdown occurred in conjunction with Schreber's failure, in 1884, to win a seat in the Reichstag; the second breakdown, the one that initiated the full-fledged psychosis with its strangely sexualized delusions of wasting away, occurred in the wake of his appointment, in 1893, to one of the highest positions of judicial authority in Saxony. What I have been suggesting in these pages is that Freud's attraction to and passion for the Schreber material was above all a function of his own deep involvement with the "rites of institution" at a moment of significant crisis—one might even say at a moment of "signification crisis"—within the institution of psychoanalysis. With these parallels in mind, I turn now to a detailed commentary on Freud's "Psychoanalytic Notes on an Autobiographical Account of a Case of Paranoia (Dementia Paranoides)."[21]

III

Freud's essay is divided into three sections, framed on one side by a brief preface, in which he admits his limited experience with the treatment of the psychoses and justifies his use of a text as the basis of a case study, and on the other by a postscript, in which he briefly suggests possibilities of coordinating his findings in the Schreber case with anthropological studies of myth, ritual, and the religious imagination. The first section offers a presentation of the case history, in which Freud lays out the chronology of Schreber's various illnesses and treatments, discusses salient features of his delusional system, and sketches out some preliminary aspects of an interpretation. In the sec-

ond section, "Attempts at Interpretation," Freud presents his central thesis regarding the etiology of paranoia as a defense against a sudden and overstimulating influx of homosexual libido. In the third and final part of the essay addressing the "mechanism of paranoia," Freud touches on, among other things, the role of projection in the formation of paranoid symptoms, the radical nature of repression in psychotic disorders and the metapsychological category of narcissism. In the final pages of the essay, Freud also begins to explore, in a preliminary and tentative fashion, the frontiers between libido theory and what would become the psychology of the ego. This final section also enters into debates on nosology, suggesting his own revisions of current diagnostic terminology.

Already in his initial presentation of the case material, culled in large measure from the judgment of the Saxon Supreme Court rescinding Schreber's tutelage and the reports of Dr. Guido Weber, director of the Sonnenstein Asylum where Schreber was confined from June 1894 to December 1902,[22] the general direction of Freud's interpretation begins to take shape. From these documents Freud concludes that the two salient features of Schreber's delusional system are, first, the fantasy of messianic calling, of being chosen by God and the so-called Order of the World to redeem mankind from a condition of cosmic disequilibrium generated in large measure as a consequence of his own nervous agitation; and, second, the imperative to undergo, by way of divine miracles, a process of gender transformation for the purpose of repopulating the world with the issue of his divinely inseminated body. Freud hypothesizes, however, that the fantasy of feminization, which Schreber for the most part refers to as *Entmannung* or "unmanning," is the real core and primary symptom of the psychosis and that the soteriological fantasy arrives only after the fact to endow retroactively a condition of abjection and degradation with sublime meaning and purpose:

> It is natural to follow the medical report in assuming that the motive force of this delusional complex was the patient's ambition to play the part of Redeemer, and that his *emasculation* [*Entmannung*] was only entitled to be regarded as a means for achieving that end. Even though this may appear to be true of his delusion in its final form, a study of the *Denkwürdigkeiten* compels us to take a very different view of the matter. For we learn that the idea of being transformed into a woman (that is, of being emasculated) was the primary delusion, that he began by regarding that act as constituting a serious injury and persecution, and that it only became related to his playing the part of Redeemer in a secondary way. There can be no doubt, moreover, that originally he believed that the transformation was to be effected for the purpose of sexual abuse and not so as to serve

higher designs. The position may be formulated by saying that a sexual delusion of persecution was later on converted in the patient's mind into a religious delusion of grandeur. The part of persecutor was at first assigned to Professor Flechsig, the physician in whose charge he was; later, his place was taken by God Himself. (*SE* 12:18)[23]

Freud bases this view on the numerous allusions in Schreber's text to the humiliations and abuses to which his transformation into a woman left him exposed. Freud refers, for example, to Schreber's account of Flechsig's machinations in this regard:

> Professor Flechsig had found a way of raising himself up to heaven . . . and so making himself a leader of rays, without prior death and without undergoing the process of purification. In this way a plot was laid against me (perhaps March or April 1894), the purpose of which was to hand me over to another human being after my nervous illness had been recognized as, or assumed to be, incurable, in such a way that my soul was handed to him, but my body—transformed into a female body . . . was then left to that human being for sexual misuse and simply "forsaken," in other words left to rot. (75; cf. *SE* 12:19)

To support his thesis of the priority and initial autonomy of the feminization fantasy further, Freud emphasizes that something on the order of a feminine identification had already surfaced during what he calls the "incubation period" of the second illness. Freud is thinking, of course, of Schreber's remarkable prodromal premonition, experienced just prior to assuming his post at the Saxon Supreme Court, of feminine jouissance: "one morning while still in bed (whether still half asleep or already awake I cannot remember), I had a feeling which, thinking about it later when fully awake, struck me as highly peculiar. It was the idea that it really must be rather pleasant to be a woman succumbing to intercourse" (63; cf. *SE* 12:20). Schreber adds that he "cannot exclude the possibility that some external influences were at work to implant this idea in me" (63), suggesting, in a way, that Freud was more right than he knew when he called this the "incubation period" of the illness: this was Schreber's first encounter with his "incubus." How this incubus was called into being, what forces it figured, by what processes of condensation and displacement it was produced—these are the questions Freud proposes to answer in the course of his case study.

After establishing to his satisfaction the centrality of the feminization fantasy,[24] Freud goes on to characterize the peculiarities of Schreber's relation to God as presented in the *Memoirs*. Absolutely central to this

relation is the fact, emphasized by Schreber over and over again, that under conditions consonant with the Order of the World—Schreber's term for something like a cosmological *rule of law*—God does not generally enjoy intimate knowledge of or sustain prolonged contact with living human beings and their affairs. Freud cites a series of passages attesting to this crucial feature of Schreber's universe:

> *A fundamental misunderstanding* obtained however, which has since run like a red thread through my entire life. It is based upon the fact *that, within the Order of the World, God did not really understand the living human being* and had no need to understand him, because, according to the Order of the World, He dealt only with corpses. (75; cf. *SE* 12:25)

In a later passage describing some of the torments he underwent in the course of his illness, Schreber suggests that the apparent purposelessness of much of the suffering he had to endure in his relation to God "must be connected . . . with God not knowing how to treat a living human being, as He was accustomed to dealing only with corpses or at best with human beings lying asleep (dreaming)" (127; cf. *SE* 12:25). And finally, with regard to further episodes of physical and mental suffering, Schreber writes:

> *Incredibile scriptu* I would like to add, and yet everything is really true, however difficult it must be for other people to reconcile themselves to the idea that God is totally incapable of judging a living human being correctly; even I myself became accustomed to this idea only gradually after innumerable observations. (188; cf. *SE* 12:25)

Freud concludes from these passages that "as a result of God's misunderstanding of living men it was possible for Him Himself to become the instigator of the plot against Schreber, to take him for an idiot, and to subject him to these severe ordeals" (*SE* 12:25). Among the ordeals of special interest to Freud were the divine interventions in Schreber's bowel movements, descriptions of which Freud quotes at length, and the so-called *Denkzwang*, Schreber's compulsion to keep his thoughts in a kind of incessant motion so that God would not consider him to be demented and thus worthy of abandonment. For Freud, these characterizations of God's peculiarly flawed omniscience and authority along with Schreber's equally adamant defense of God as a worthy object of worship and reverence, places in the foreground of the analysis Schreber's deep ambivalence with regard to the deity and whatever other agencies or domains of authority he might eventually be seen to represent: "No attempt at explaining Schreber's case will have any chance of being correct which does not take into account these peculiarities in his

conception of God, this mixture of reverence and rebelliousness in his attitude towards Him" (*SE* 12:28–29). Before going on to provide a more or less comprehensive explanation of these peculiarities, Freud dwells on a feature of Schreber's relation to God that struck Schreber as being especially paradoxical.

IV

In Schreber's cosmology there obtains a deep affinity or near identity between the state of blessedness or *Seligkeit* that, after a period of purification, awaits the soul after death as it becomes assimilated to the "forecourts of Heaven," and the state of feminine jouissance or female sexual pleasure called by Schreber *weibliche Wollust* and produced in him by overexposure to supernatural influences, ultimately identified as God's penetrating rays. As Freud has noted, at a certain point in his illness, Schreber not only reconciles himself to the process of feminization at first experienced as insulting and injurious, but endows it with soteriological purpose and significance. Part and parcel of this shift in perspective so crucial to Schreber's views on the possibility of his and the world's redemption is a transformation in the moral dimension of his relation to sexual pleasure.[25]

As Freud emphasizes in his presentation of the case material, Schreber considered himself to be a man of distinctly sober if not puritanical and even ascetic habits and attitudes with regard to sensual pleasures of all kinds. At a certain point in the progress of his illness, however, the moral pressure to abstain from such pleasures is transmuted into *a moral duty to enjoy*:

> Few people have been brought up according to such strict moral principles as I, and have throughout life practised such moderation especially in matters of sex, as I venture to claim for myself. Mere low sensuousness can therefore not be considered a motive in my case. . . . But as soon as I am alone with God, if I may so express myself, I must continually or at least at certain times, strive to give divine rays the impression of a woman in the height of sexual delight; to achieve this I have to employ all possible means, and have to strain all my intellectual powers and foremost my imagination. . . . Voluptuous enjoyment or Blessedness is granted *to souls* in perpetuity and as an end in itself, but to *human beings* and other living creatures *solely as a means for the preservation of the species*. Herein lie the moral limitations of voluptuousness for human beings. An excess of voluptuousness would render man unfit to fulfil his other obligations; it would prevent him from ever rising to higher mental and

moral perfection; indeed experience teaches that not only single individuals but also whole nations have perished through voluptuous excess. *For me such moral limits to voluptuousness no longer exist, indeed in a certain sense the reverse applies.* (208)

And further, attempting to explain his exceptional status as a man compelled by moral duty to "imagine myself as man and woman in one person having intercourse with myself," Schreber writes,

This behaviour has been forced on me through God having placed Himself into a relationship with me which is contrary to the Order of the World; although it may sound paradoxical, it is justifiable to apply the saying of the Crusaders in the First Crusade to myself: *Dieu le veut* (God wishes it). God is inseparably tied to my person through my nerves' power of attraction which for some time past has become inescapable; there is no possibility of God freeing Himself from my nerves for the rest of my life—although His policy is aimed at this—except perhaps in case my unmanning were to become a fact. On the other hand God demands *constant enjoyment*, as the normal mode of existence for souls within the Order of the World. It is my duty to provide Him with it in the form of highly developed soul-voluptuousness, as far as this is possible in the circumstances contrary to the Order of the World. (208–9)

Finally, Schreber summarizes this peculiar reversal in the moral universe by noting that in "my relation to God . . . voluptuousness has become 'God-fearing' [*gottesfürchtig*], that is to say it is the likeliest satisfactory solution for the clash of interests arising out of circumstances contrary to the Order of the World" (210).

Passages such as these were so crucial to Freud's reading of the Schreber case because they seem to underline the connection between mental illness and disturbances in the domain of sexuality, the connection that, as we have seen, Freud was so hard at work defending against doubts raised by Jung, Adler, and others at the time of his work on the essay. As Freud notes,

we psychoanalysts have hitherto supported the view that the roots of every nervous and mental disorder are chiefly to be found in the patient's sexual life. . . . The samples of Schreber's delusions that have already been given enable us without more ado to dismiss the suspicion that it might be precisely this paranoid disorder which would turn out to be the "negative case" which has so long been sought for—a case in which sexuality plays only a very minor part. Schreber himself speaks again and again as though he shared our prejudice. He is constantly talking in the same breath of "nervous disorder" and erotic lapses, as though the two things were inseparable. (*SE* 12:30–31)

Freud's recruitment of Schreber as a disciple *avant la lettre* was, as we have seen, a gesture not without certain disturbing resonances for Freud. More important, his own struggles within what I have called the state of emergency of the *institution* of psychoanalysis kept him from seeing in the paradoxes of Schreber's sexualized relation to God the breakdown products of what I have referred to as an investiture crisis—a crisis pertaining to the *transfer* of symbolic power and authority. Schreber's paradoxical experience that the Order of the World—Schreber's term for cosmic rule of law and regulation of individual boundaries—became the locus of a carnevalesque command to transgress all boundaries and proprieties would seem to point beyond the "repressive hypothesis" that shapes Freud's view of the conflictual relations between psychic systems and agencies and which would become the object of Michel Foucault's powerful critique in the first volume of his *History of Sexuality*. Schreber discovers that power not only prohibits, moderates, says "no," but may also work to intensify and amplify the body and its sensations. Put somewhat differently, Schreber discovers that symbolic authority in a state of emergency *is* transgressive, that it exhibits an obscene overproximity to the subject: that it, as Schreber puts it, *demands enjoyment*. Schreber's experience of his body and mind as the site of violent and transgressive interventions and manipulations, which produce, as a residue or waste product, a kind of surplus enjoyment, is, I am suggesting, an index of a crisis afflicting his relation to the exemplary domain of symbolic authority to which his life was intimately bound, namely the law.[26]

V

Freud, we recall, begins the second section of his essay with an homage to Jung's "dazzling example" followed by a methodological reflection on the privileged status of examples in psychoanalytic interpretation. He then goes on to apply his method to the example of the talking birds in Schreber's text. These miraculous birds are introduced in chapter 15 of the *Memoirs* and rehearse a number of themes and motifs played out in other, equally striking incarnations in earlier chapters. Schreber notes early in the chapter that although, since the end of 1895 and the beginning of 1896, he "could no longer doubt that a real race of human beings . . . did in fact exist," it was "still perfectly clear . . . that, in Hamlet's words, *there is something rotten in the state of Denmark*—that is to say in the relationship between God and mankind" (163–64). Despite his restored confidence in the existence of the world, he thus continues to experience his body, mind, and environment as the site of divine inter-

ventions and manipulations. Perhaps the most striking feature of Schreber's illness is that his manipulation by divine rays—in Schreber's system "rays" are God's nerves—occurs above all in a *linguistic* register. As Schreber puts it, "it seems to lie in the nature of rays that they must *speak* as soon as they are set in motion; the relevant law was expressed in the phrase 'do not forget that rays must speak,' and this was spoken into my nerves innumerable times" (121). Here one should add that the rays speak a sort of dialect—the *Grundsprache* or "basic language," which is "a somewhat antiquated but nevertheless powerful German, characterized particularly by a wealth of euphemisms" (50). Schreber's experience of voices and fragments of speech being projected into his body by way of a kind of miraculous ventriloquism is among the torments that most directly endangers his capacity to experience himself as a source of individual agency and initiative. Schreber's initial definition of the "nerve-language" at the beginning of chapter 5 forms the basis of all later characterizations of this unnerving experience of divine ventriloquism:

> Apart from normal human language there is also a kind of *nerve-language* of which, as a rule, the healthy human being is not aware. In my opinion this is best understood when one thinks of the processes by which a person tries to imprint certain words in his memory in a definite order, as for instance a child learning a poem by heart which he is going to recite at school, or a priest a sermon he is going to deliver in Church. The words are *repeated silently* . . . that is to say a human being causes his nerves to vibrate in the way which corresponds to the use of the words concerned, but the real organs of speech . . . are either not set in motion at all or only coincidentally. . . . Naturally under normal (in consonance with the Order of the World) conditions, use of this *nerve-language* depends only on the will of the person whose nerves are concerned; no human being as such can force another to use this nerve-language. In my case, however . . . my nerves have been set in motion *from without* incessantly and without respite. (69)

Schreber situates this peculiar ventriloquism within the framework of a more global anxiety of influence:

> Divine rays above all have the power of influencing the nerves of a human being in this manner; by this means God has always been able to infuse dreams into a sleeping human being. I myself first felt this influence as emanating from Professor Flechsig. The only possible explanation I can think of is that Professor Flechsig in some way knew how to put divine rays to his own use; later, apart from Professor Flechsig's nerves, direct divine rays also entered into contact with my nerves. This influence has

in the course of years assumed forms more and more contrary to the Order of the World and to man's natural right to be master of his own nerves, and I might say become increasingly grotesque. (69–70)

The miracle of the talking birds that so intrigued Freud is but one example of a divine violation that reduces Schreber's body to a condition of abjection and putrescence ("One probably . . . believed that at least one could choke me through the mass of poison of corpses [*Leichengift*] which in this manner was daily heaped upon my body"). The link between the birds and dead matter is secured by Schreber's view that "*the nerves which are inside these birds are remnants . . . of souls of human beings who had become blessed*" (167). Schreber then makes the association of the birds with language, and more precisely, with a language produced under conditions of *mechanical reproduction*:

> I recognize the individual nerves exactly by the tone of their voices from years of hearing them; I know exactly which of the senseless phrases learnt by rote I can expect of each one of them. . . . Their property as erstwhile human nerves is evidenced by the fact that *all* the miraculously produced birds *without exception*, whenever they have completely unloaded the poison of corpses which they carry, that is to say when they have reeled off the phrases drummed into them, then express *in human sounds* the *genuine* feeling of well-being in the soul-voluptuousness of my body which they share, with the words "Damned fellow" or "Somehow damned," *the only words in which they are still capable of giving expression to genuine feeling.* (167)

Schreber extends these metalinguistic reflections by noting the unexpected affinity between these privileged moments of genuine feeling, and the poetic dimension of language:

> It has already been mentioned that the miraculously created birds do not understand the *meaning* of the words they speak; but apparently they have a natural sensitivity for the *similarity of sounds*. Therefore if, while reeling off the automatic phrases, they perceive *either* in the vibrations of my own nerves (my thoughts) *or* in speech of people around me, words which *sound* the same or similar to their own phrases, they apparently experience surprise and in a way fall for the similarity in sound; in other words the surprise makes them forget the rest of their mechanical phrases and they suddenly pass over into *genuine* feeling. (168–69)[27]

After noting these peculiarities of the "miracled birds"—Schreber's phrase is "gewunderte Vögel"—Freud draws a stunning conclusion: "As we read this description, we cannot avoid the idea [*kann man sich des Einfalles nicht erwehren*; my emphasis] that what it really refers to

must be young girls" (*SE* 12:36). I call this conclusion stunning not in view of the peculiar blend of patriarchal complacency and rhetorical virtuosity with which Freud supports his claim.[28] Rather, what is striking here is the way in which Freud's deduction repeats the crucial structural features of the object under investigation: the experience is one of an irresistible linguistic or ideational "implantation." With Freud's reading of the miracled birds we have encountered, once more, his allegorical presence in the text, the point at which his own analytic language mimes the processes being analyzed. To be seized by an "Einfall" against which one cannot defend, is, at a formal level, not unlike the situation described by Schreber as a kind of intoxication—having toxic matter, the "poison of corpses," unloaded into one's body. Schreber, for his part, is very clear about the nature of these toxins: they are bits of linguistic matter, phrases learned by rote and repeated mechanically *without concern for meaning*. These toxins materialize what I will call the *drive dimension of signification*; they link to abjection that aspect of signification that is purely "dictatorial" in that it positions its bearer as a kind of bird-brained stenographer taking dictation. Although Freud clearly senses that the "feminine" aspect of the miracled birds— Freud notes that Schreber eventually makes this association explicit[29]— is tied to a particular relation to and experience of the signifier, he seems at this point to want to quarantine the example from the larger consequences to be drawn from such a connection. But if "femininity" is in some sense linked to this drive dimension of signification, then Freud's own experience of ideational implantation—of being dictated to by foreign thoughts and linguistic associations—might indeed be viewed as an instance of feminization not unlike that experienced by Schreber under the overwhelming influence of the voices and language particles entering his body.[30]

VI

Freud continues his reading by noting the constraints placed upon any attempt to interpret the *Memoirs* by the fact that the crucial third chapter, in which Schreber ostensibly discussed details of his family history, was withheld from publication.[31] Although Freud could have made inquiries at the Sonnenstein asylum and possibly even tracked down an extant copy of the missing chapter in the asylum's records, he chose instead to "be satisfied . . . in tracing back . . . the nucleus of the delusional structure . . . to familiar human motives" (*SE* 12:37). According to Freud, one is thereby led to the centrality in Schreber's delusional system of his first psychiatrist, Dr. Paul Emil Flechsig. As

Freud notes, "the first author of all . . . acts of persecution was Flechsig, and he remains their instigator throughout the whole course of the illness" (*SE* 12:38).

Freud emphasizes the vagueness and obscurity of the charges leveled against Flechsig, a prominent neuroscientist and forensic psychiatrist known above all for his work on the myelination of nerve fibers.[32] Given Freud's decision to perform a close reading of Schreber's text rather than engage in more extratextual, historical research,[33] it is, perhaps, not quite so surprising that he should have failed to consider the possibility that Schreber's fixation on Flechsig could have derived at least in part from the actual interpersonal dynamics between patient and doctor. But it is a surprise nonetheless. For in his open letter to Flechsig appended to the beginning of the *Memoirs*, Schreber makes an explicit connection between soul murder and medical malpractice.

In the letter, Schreber confesses to Flechsig that "the *first impetus* to what my doctors always considered mere 'hallucinations' but which to me signified communications with supernatural powers, consisted of *influences on my nervous system emanating from your nervous system*" (34). Schreber admits the possibility, and even likelihood, that such an influence, understood on the model of hypnotic suggestion, was originally initiated for strictly therapeutic purposes. He suggests, however, that once realizing the uniqueness of the case, Flechsig was unable to resist the temptation to maintain a telepathic connection with him "out of scientific interest" (34). Schreber surmises that in the midst of this already transgressive contact with the patient—transgressive because no longer constrained by the demands of the therapy—"it is possible that . . . part of your own nerves—probably unknown to yourself—was removed from your body . . . and ascended to heaven as a 'tested soul' and there achieved some supernatural power" (34). Once cut off from Flechsig and, as it were, the law of healing, this outlaw soul "simply allowed itself to be driven by the impulse of ruthless self-determination and lust for power, without any restraint by something comparable to the moral will power of man" (34). Given such a scenario, Schreber is willing to consider that "all those things which in earlier years I erroneously thought I had to blame you for—particularly the definite damaging effects on my body—are to be blamed only on that 'tested soul'" (34). The gist of this scenario is, according to Schreber, that

> there would then be no need to cast any shadow upon your person and only the mild reproach would perhaps remain that you, like so many doctors, could not completely resist the temptation of using a patient in

your care *as an object for scientific experiments* apart from the real purpose of the cure, when by chance matters of the highest scientific interest arose. One might even raise the question whether perhaps all the talk of voices about somebody having committed soul murder can be explained by the souls (rays) deeming it impermissible [*als etwas Unstatthaftes*] that a person's nervous system should be influenced by another's to the extent of imprisoning his will power, such as occurs during hypnosis; in order to stress forcefully that this was a malpractice [*Unstatthaftigkeit*] it was called "soul murder." (34–35)

It is clear, I think, that Schreber's purpose here and throughout his *Memoirs* is to tell the story of the catastrophic effects that ensue when a trusted figure of authority exercises a surplus of power exceeding the symbolic pact on which that authority is based.[34] Schreber's *Memoirs* attempt to bring into a narrative and theological system the crisis of authority—the *rottenness* in the state of Denmark, the breach in the Order of the World—which manifests itself at least in part as a demonic imbalance in the "professional" relationships imposed on him by his illness. Much of the difficulty faced by the reader of Schreber to make sense of this "system," which very quickly takes on Wagnerian proportions, is a function of Schreber's own difficulty in isolating and identifying this transgressive surplus, locating its origin and articulating its patterns of expansion and proliferation into what ends up as a generalized state of emergency of human relations and of relations between humans and God. The energies for this global expansion derive from structural homologies between the collapse of symbolic exchange (with Flechsig) into direct, "experimental" power over body and soul, on the one hand, and Schreber's investiture crisis, on the other (the fact that his symbolic investiture did not "take hold," was unable to seize him in his self-understanding). What becomes manifest in Flechsig-qua-"tested soul" is the inner "rottenness" of every symbolic investiture insofar as it remains dependent on a dimension of performative force, compulsion, drive. Schreber's fixation on Flechsig indicates that he materializes for him the emergence of this normally secret dependence—a dependence normally "secreted" in the unconscious—into the field of conscious experience. The "directness" of Flechsig's alleged influence and manipulations is thus correlative to Schreber's relation of exteriority to the symbolic operations governing his own investiture.[35]

Freud, for his part, is confident that he has discovered the true and, ultimately, erotic, origins of this "extrajuridical" surplus of power/influence that disturbs Schreber's relations first with Flechsig and then

with God. He prepares his discovery by introducing the formula he and other researchers and clinicians have found to be key to deciphering persecutory anxieties in general:

> It appears that the person to whom the delusion ascribes so much power and influence, in whose hands all the threads of the conspiracy converge, is, if he is definitely named, either identical with some one [sic] who played an equally important part in the patient's emotional life before his illness, or is easily recognizable as a substitute for him. The intensity of the emotion is projected in the shape of external power, while its quality is changed into the opposite. The person who is now hated and feared for being a persecutor was at one time loved and honoured. The main purpose of the persecution asserted by the patient's delusion is to justify the change in his emotional attitude. (SE 12:41)

Noting that Schreber seemed to have had a quite positive impression of Flechsig at the time of his first illness, Freud's application of this formula suggests that Schreber's anxiety dreams of a recurrence of his illness along with the prodromal fantasy of feminine jouissance— "that it really must be rather pleasant to be a woman succumbing to intercourse"—which occur after being named to his new post as *Senatspräsident*, are to be understood as signs of a profound, though unconscious, *longing* for Flechsig. This longing, combining infantile dependency and homosexual desire, generates what Freud calls "the feminine phantasy": "The exciting cause of his illness, then, was an outburst of homosexual libido; the object of this libido was probably from the very first his doctor, Flechsig; and his struggles against the libidinal impulse produced the conflict which gave rise to the symptoms" (SE 12:43). According to Freud, the strange surplus of power/influence that precipates the unmaking of Schreber's world is nothing other than an outburst of homosexual libido on Schreber's part, originally felt for his psychiatrist, Flechsig. Flechsig's ostensible transgression of the law of the cure regulating the "boundaries" between patient and doctor is, in other words, a projection of Schreber's own "perverse" desires. Freud stresses that his admittedly speculative claims concerning Schreber's homosexuality must be understood in the context of a theory of the unconscious, a theory implied by Schreber's own formulations.[36] Freud is thinking here of Schreber's distinction between Flechsig the real person and Flechsig-as-tested-soul; only the latter is of interest to Freud as the placeholder of the surplus value assigned to Flechsig in the unconscious. That this surplus value is produced by homosexual libido is indicated, for Freud, by several details in the *Memoirs*.

First, Freud argues that in the numerous passages linking feminiza-

tion to sexual exploitation, there is little question that Flechsig is the intended beneficiary of this perverse enjoyment: "It is unnecessary to remark that no other individual is ever named who could be put in Flechsig's place" (*SE* 12:44). Furthermore, in one of his attempts to explain the meaning of "soul murder," which is, of course, the main charge brought against Flechsig in the *Memoirs*, Schreber refers to folkloric and literary examples of what appears to be at stake in this strange crime of taking "possession of another person's soul in order to prolong one's life at another soul's expense, or to secure some other advantages which outlast death." He adds that "one has only to think . . . of Goethe's Faust, Lord Byron's Manfred, Weber's Freischütz, etc." (55). The special importance of Byron's *Manfred* is indicated, for Freud, by an earlier reference to that dramatic poem in a footnote apropos of Schreber's use of the Persian Gods Ariman and Ormuzd to refer to the lower and upper Gods, respectively, who in Schreber's theological system together constitute the so-called posterior realms of God: "The name Ariman occurs by the way also in Lord Byron's Manfred in connection with a soul murder" (53). Regarding Byron's play, Freud suggests that "the essence and secret of the whole work lies in—an incestuous relation between a brother and a sister" (*SE* 12:44).[37] Freud's crucial point here is that soul murder is connected with incest; Flechsig-as-soul-murderer becomes a figure of *incestuous enjoyment*. The surplus of power/influence that Schreber sees as emanating first from Flechsig and then from God is thereby linked to that most powerful and primordial of transgressive stains on the "lawful" structure of kinship relations.

Freud appeals, finally, to another detail of Schreber's story to support his thesis that an outburst of homosexual libido was the basis of Schreber's illness. One will recall that Schreber's illness took a turn for the worse in February 1894, when Sabine Schreber went to Berlin for four days to visit her father, interrupting for the first time her routine of daily visits to her husband. After this interruption, Schreber's condition deteriorated so rapidly that he no longer accepted visits from her and indeed came to see her as one of those phantom beings produced by miracle in the manner of the "fleeting-improvised-men" [*flüchtig hingemachte Männer*]. It was, according to Schreber, at this turning point that the structure of the plot against him, with all its supernatural manifestations, took on its definitive shape. One will also recall the sexual dimension of this peripeteia: "Decisive for my mental collapse was one particular night; during that night I had a quite unusual number of pollutions (perhaps half a dozen)" (68). Freud concludes from this concatenation of events

that the mere presence of his wife must have acted as a protection against the attractive power of the men about him; and if we are prepared to admit that an emission cannot occur in an adult without some mental concomitant, we shall be able to supplement the patient's emissions that night by assuming that they were accompanied by homosexual phantasies which remained unconscious. (*SE* 12:145)[38]

VII

Citing a lack of sufficient historical and biographical information, which, as I have indicated, he might have been able to acquire, Freud acknowledges an uncertainty pertaining to his hypothesis that Schreber's breakdown was triggered by homosexual panic following his appointment to the position of *Senatspräsident*: "The question of why this outburst of homosexual libido overtook the patient precisely at this period (that is, between the dates of his appointment and of his move to Dresden) cannot be answered in the absence of more precise knowledge of the story of his life" (*SE* 12:45–46). Curiously, Freud never seems to consider the possibility of a connection between Schreber's "perversion" and this important change in his symbolic status. In a sense, Schreber undergoes *two* changes in his symbolic status, which taken together constitute the full extent of what I have characterized as his investiture crisis: *Ernennung* or nomination to a powerful position of juridical authority—the *Senatspräsident* of the highest court in Saxony—and *Entmannung* or unmanning, which Freud reads as an outburst of homosexual libido. A connection between these two symbolic mutations is made plausible not simply by the obvious temporal contiguity, suggesting a causal sequence, but also by the fact that Schreber's gender transformation is at a crucial moment itself associated with an act of naming or nomination, that is, with a performative utterance endowing the subject with a new symbolic status.

The performative utterance I have in mind here is of a very particular kind; it is an *insult*, and indeed one issued by no less an authority than God Himself in a scene of high operatic drama:

> I believe I may say that at that time and at that time *only*, I saw God's omnipotence in its complete purity. During the night . . . the lower God (Ariman) appeared. The radiant picture of his rays became visible to my inner eye . . . that is to say he was reflected on my inner nervous system. Simultaneously I heard his voice; but it was not a soft whisper—as the talk of the voices always was before and after that time—it resounded in a mighty bass as if directly in front of my bedroom window. The impres-

sion was intense, so that anybody not hardened to terrifying miraculous impressions as I was, would have been shaken to the core. Also *what* was spoken did not sound friendly by any means: everything seemed calculated to instil fright and terror into me and the word "wretch" [*Luder*] was frequently heard—an expression quite common in the basic language to denote a human being destined to be destroyed by God and to feel God's power and wrath. (124)

In spite of the insulting content of this quasi-operatic epiphany of divine power, the effects produced by its form, or more precisely by the performative force of its enunciation, turn out to be, as Schreber insists, strangely beneficial:

> Yet everything that was spoken was *genuine*, not phrases learnt by rote as they later were, but the immediate expression of true feeling. . . . For this reason my impression was not one of alarm or fear, but largely one of admiration for the magnificent and the sublime; the effect on my nerves was therefore beneficial despite the insults contained in some of the *words*. (124–25)

The most important of these words, "Luder," has especially rich connotations in the context of Schreber's torments. It can indeed mean wretch, in the sense of a lost and pathetic figure, but can also signify a cunning swindler or scoundrel; whore, tart, or slut; and, finally, the dead, rotting flesh of an animal, especially in the sense of carrion used as bait in hunting. The last two significations capture Schreber's fear of being turned over to others for the purposes of sexual exploitation as well as his anxieties, which would seem to flow from such abuse, about putrefaction, being left to rot. The latter anxieties merge at times with fantasies of being sick with the plague, leprosy, or syphilis.[39] I would like to suggest that this insulting nomination issued by the lower God Ariman stands in a direct relation to the crisis precipitated by that other nomination or official *Ernennung* that—inexplicably for Freud[40]—appears to "secrete" the unexpected by-product of feminine jouissance, itself bearing associations with abjection.

In a first approach, one can point to the structural similarities of the two speech acts. An official interpellation of the kind issued by the Ministry of Justice functions in much the same way as an insult issued in a quasi-public setting. Both share what Bourdieu has called the "performative or magical intention," both indicate to someone—often in the name of a group—that he "possesses such and such a property, and indicates to him at the time *that he must conduct himself in accordance with the social essence which is thereby assigned to him.*"[41] But there is more at stake here than a formal symmetry or homology between the perfor-

mative magic whereby one becomes a *Senatspräsident* (i.e., because the Saxon Ministry of Justice has declared it to be the case) and the effectivity of a divine interpellation. Indeed, I would like to make the stronger claim that in the second assignation Schreber experiences the *secret* of the first, that in the second performative utterance Schreber experiences what the first nomination begins to *secrete* when the institutional authority behind it is in crisis, no longer consonant with the Order of the World, as Schreber would say. With Ariman's epiphany, we are, in a word, in the midst of that dimension of symbolic function that Benjamin characterized as an internal, structural rottenness.[42]

Michel de Certeau's brief reflections on Schreber's text address precisely this "secret" relation between Schreber's two crucial encounters with the force of the performative or magical intention. Certeau translates, in effect, Benjamin's notion of "law-making violence" into the Lacanian notion of the *master signifier*:[43]

> In addition the name imposed by the other is authorized by nothing, and that is its special trait. . . . The name is not authorized by any meaning; on the contrary, it authorizes signification, like a poem that is preceded by nothing and creates unlimited possibilities for meaning. But this occurs because the word *Luder* plays the role of that which cannot deceive. It compels belief more than it is believed. . . . Naming does in effect assign him a place. It is a calling to be what it dictates: your name is *Luder*. The name performs.[44]

The privileged performativity of this name—what distinguishes it from an ordinary insult—is the fact that "in circumscribing the object of belief, it also articulates the *operation* of believing. . . . The signified of the word, which oscillates between decomposition and slut, designates the overall functioning of the signifier, or Schreber's effective relation to the law of the signifier."[45] Certeau's crucial point, which goes a long way in explaining why Schreber has continued to attract readers, is that this "madness is not a particular madness. It is *general*. It is a part of any institution that assures a language of meaning, right or truth. The only odd thing about Schreber, the jurist, is that he knows its hard and 'insulting' secret. He is not someone who can go on knowing nothing about it."[46]

As Certeau has emphasized, torture has much the same function in political contexts as the lower God's transformation of Schreber into a *Luder*, a process that, as the reader of Schreber well knows, makes ample use of a rich and varied technology of mental and physical torture: the production in the subject of a heightened experience of *abjection*. Torture is the way an institution simultaneously confesses and represses its deepest secret: that its consistency, its enjoyment of recog-

nition as *a really existing social fact*, ultimately depends on the magic of performative utterances, on the force of their own immanent process of enunciation. The abjection produced in the torture victim, his betrayal of everything that matters and is dear to him, his confession of his own putrescence, is, as it were, the "substance" that stands in for the lack of substantial foundations to which the institution might appeal for final and ultimate legitimation. The torture victim's abject body is the "privileged" site of a politicotheological epiphany, for it is there that the reality of institutions and the social facts they sponsor—contracts, titles, money, property, marriages, and the like—bottoms out, touches on a dimension of vicious circularity that cannot be avowed if these social facts are to continue to enjoy credibility, if the social field structured by them is to remain consistent for the subject.[47] One could say, then, that the practice of torture serves to keep localized and off-scene the chronic state of emergency that, in effect, haunts all institutions insofar as they are dependent on the reality effects of performative utterances—utterances that bring about the propositional content of the social facts they pretend merely to certify. The torture victim's body is one of the places where, as it were, the knowledge is secreted that crucial constative utterances on which any social ontology depends really mask a performative, the form of which is, ultimately, that of a tautology—for example, "the law is *the law*."[48]

The Kafkan dimension of these reflections immediately strikes the eye. One could say that Josef K. encounters, but fails to comprehend, this insulting secret of the law, as the exemplary locus of symbolic power and authority, when, in the fifth chapter of *The Trial*, he stumbles upon the strangely sexualized—indeed, homosexualized—scene of sadomasochistic torture in the storage room hidden among the offices of the bank where he works. At such moments, it is as if the taint of tautological nonsense, the performative force that pertains, at some level, to all institutions and the social facts they sponsor, has begun to leak beyond its "normally" circumscribed space and to dissolve the institution's capacity to provide a credible context of meaningful reality. At such moments we are at the threshold of a psychotic universe where the subject has become unable to forget, unable (primordially) to repress, the drive dimension of symbolic function, which expands into a general state of rottenness and decay. The sense of surreal corruption in Kafka's texts would appear to derive from getting *too close* to this dimension of social reality.[49]

When one considers Kafka's own struggles with his sexuality, another, perhaps more obvious reading of this scene—and one in the spirit of Freud's reading of Schreber—suggests itself: Josef K., this typical Kafkan bachelor, has simply stumbled upon his own—and his

society's—*closet*, the social space where homosexuality is constituted as a refused yet insistent possibility. Josef K.'s entire story becomes thereby the unfolding of a kind of litigious paranoia generated by homosexual panic. The curious fact that everyone K. encounters knows about his trial would serve to underline the dimension of open secrecy constitutive of the "epistemology of the closet."[50] Josef K.'s guilt could then be read as an indication that he ceded his homosexual desire and naively presupposed the unproblematic efficacy and stability of the closet. My argument about Schreber would, however, serve as a critique of this otherwise cogent reading of Kafka as well. By too quickly specifying the ideological content of the "closet" before sufficiently analyzing the closet as *form*, as a place where such ideological meanings can be inscribed, such a reading remains at the level of the cultural discourses, in this case homophobic ones, it sets out to undermine (a similar critique could be made of Freud's always disappointing specification of the *contents* of the unconscious). As a fantasy frame in which various ideological meanings can be inscribed and command a maximum of fascination, the closet is, I am suggesting, first and foremost a site where the drive dimension of symbolic functioning becomes manifest. Every ideological content borrows the "stuff" secreted within or, perhaps better, *as* this fantasy frame. When, in other words, an ideology captures the imagination, comes to matter for an individual or collective in a profound way, its "matter" has a share in, is animated by, this drive dimension of symbolic function. The importance of the Schreber material for the analysis of ideology is that it offers a glimpse of this "matter" of ideological fascination in a quasi-pure state, that is, at the moment of its inscription within a field of cultural values.[51]

VIII

These remarks on what we might call Schreber's *Ludertum*, his elaboration of a kind of abject femininity, were evoked by an impasse in Freud's argument. He was, we recall, unable to understand why an overstimulating outburst of homosexual libido should occur in conjunction with Schreber's nomination to the position of *Senatspräsident* of the Supreme Court of Saxony. After briefly alluding to the lifelong oscillation on the part of most adults between heterosexual and homosexual desire and the possibility of biological causation—a disturbance in sexual function as a consequence of male menopause—Freud returns to the main thread of his argument, which focuses on the role of Flechsig in Schreber's illness. What needs to be explained is, as Freud puts it, "that a man's friendly feeling towards his doctor can suddenly

break out in an intensified form after a lapse of eight years and become the occasion of such a severe mental disorder" (*SE* 12:46). To put it in the terms I have been suggesting here, Freud's question is this: What was the nature of this dangerous surplus of power/influence that threatened Schreber's sanity and bodily integrity and how did it come to attach itself to Flechsig? Freud's answer to the question of the origin and dissemination of this dangerous "surplus value" leads him to the crucial notion of the *transference*:

> But for the benefit of those who . . . regard our hypothesis as altogether untenable, it is easy to suggest a possibility which would rob it of its bewildering character. The patient's friendly feeling towards his doctor may very well have been due to a process of "transference," by means of which an emotional cathexis became transposed from some person who was important to him on to the doctor who was in reality indifferent to him; so that the doctor will have been chosen as a deputy or surrogate for some one much closer to him. To put the matter in a more concrete form: the patient was reminded of his brother or father by the figure of the doctor, he rediscovered them in him; there will then be nothing to wonder at if, in certain circumstances, a longing for the surrogate figure reappeared in him and operated with a violence that is only to be explained in the light of its origin and primary significance. (*SE* 12:46–47)

The place that Flechsig came to occupy in Schreber's imagination and psychic economy was, in other words, already carved out in the course of his earlier relationships with significant male others. Although Freud alludes to the importance of an older brother, he identifies the father as the original locus of the disturbing surplus that only later gets transferred to Flechsig.[52] Wherever Schreber encounters this surplus he finds himself, as if by miracle, subject to a process of feminization, of unmanning, which Freud characterizes as homosexualization—the stimulation of a "feminine (that is, a passive homosexual) wishful phantasy" (*SE* 12:47). According to Freud, this surplus is a surplus of desire, of a primitive and overpowering longing for the father, against which Schreber defends by means of a paranoid delusion: "The person he longed for now became his persecutor, and the content of his wishful phantasy became the content of his persecution" (*SE* 12:47).

Freud supports his thesis of the paternal origins of the surplus that, once transferred to him, transfigures Flechsig into a demonic persecutor, by following the path whereby Flechsig comes to be displaced by God as the main focus of Schreber's persecutory anxieties. As Freud already noted, the latter displacement prepares the way for a triumphant reconciliation with what had at first appeared as a humiliation,

his feminization: "Emasculation was now no longer a disgrace; it became 'consonant with the Order of Things,' it took its place in a great cosmic chain of events, and was instrumental in the re-creation of humanity after its extinction" (*SE* 12:48); Schreber would give birth to a new race of human beings by divine insemination. At a formal level, this displacement of Flechsig by God is made possible by the natural tendency of paranoia to split and divide up identifications into constituent parts, which may then, in turn, engage in struggles for predominance:

> the persecutor is divided into Flechsig and God; in just the same way Flechsig himself subsequently splits up into two personalities, the "upper" and the "middle" Flechsig, and God into the "lower" and the "upper" God. . . . A process of decomposition of this kind is very characteristic of paranoia. Paranoia decomposes just as hysteria condenses. Or rather, paranoia resolves . . . into their elements the products of the condensations and identifications which are effected in the unconscious. The constant repetition of the decomposing process in Schreber's case would . . . be an expression of the importance which the person in question possessed for him. All of this dividing up of Flechsig and God . . . had the same meaning as the splitting of the persecutor into Flechsig and God. They would all be the duplications of one and the same important relationship. (49–50)[53]

That this "same important relationship" (i.e., Schreber's relationship with his father) should have been able to generate such an opulent array of phantasmagorical duplications and splittings, was, according to Freud, a function not simply of the senior Schreber's "normal" status as a figure of paternal authority, but rather of a certain surplus authority attributable to his professional status as a physician and, as Freud seems to suggest, to the particular kinds of professional activities in which he engaged. "Now the father of Senatspräsident Dr. Schreber was no insignificant person," Freud notes. "He was the Dr. Daniel Gottlob Moritz Schreber whose memory is kept green to this day by the numerous Schreber Associations which flourish especially in Saxony; and, moreover, he was a *physician*." Such a father, whose "activities in favour of promoting the harmonious upbringing of the young, of securing co-ordination between education in the home and in the school, of introducing physical culture and manual work with a view to raising the standards of health . . . exerted a lasting influence upon his contemporaries"; such a father, whose "great reputation as the founder of therapeutic gymnastics is still shown by the wide circulation of his *Ärztliche Zimmergymnastik* [*Medical Indoor Gymnastics*] . . ."; such a father, Freud finally insists, "was by no means unsuitable for transfigura-

tion into a God in the affectionate memory of the son from whom he had been so early separated by death" (*SE* 12:51). That is, Schreber senior was not simply an average bourgeois father toward whom the typical "infantile attitude of boys," composed as it is—or at least as Freud understood it—of a "mixture of reverent submission and mutinous insubordination," would suffice to explain the peculiarities of Schreber's relation with his God; by virtue of his status as a physician, someone who, like God, "performs miracles ... effects miraculous cures" (*SE* 12:52), Moritz Schreber was, in a sense, *more father* than the typical father: he embodied a surplus of paternal power, influence, and authority that predisposed him for the transfiguration effected in his son's deranged imagination.

A feature of this transfiguration of particular interest to Freud is Schreber's appropriation of various elements of solar myth to symbolize the complex terrain of paternity on which he apparently faltered. That for Schreber the sun should be associated or even identified with God is already implied in the characterization of God's nerves as *rays*, which, according to Schreber, "have ... the faculty of transforming themselves into all things of the created world." Schreber adds that the "light and warmth-giving power of the sun, which makes her the origin of all organic life on earth, is only to be regarded as an indirect manifestation of the living god," and notes that the "veneration of the sun as divine by so many peoples since antiquity contains a highly important core of truth" (46).[54] And later, after introducing a more detailed account of the heavenly architecture, Schreber notes that at a certain point early on in his stay at *Sonnenstein*—literally Sun-Stone— "the sending forth of the sun's rays was taken over directly by God, and in particular by the lower God (Ariman); the voices that talk to me now (since July 1894) identify him with the sun" (95). Freud concludes from these passages that the sun "is nothing but another sublimated symbol for the father" (*SE* 12:54). He develops this point more fully in the postscript to his essay in which he briefly enters the domain of comparative religion and mythology that would occupy him more fully in *Totem and Taboo*. Noting that in one of his footnotes Schreber claims that the sun pales before him if he addresses it in a loud voice and that he is furthermore able to stare into the sun without being blinded by its brilliance (cf. 126), Freud remarks that it is "to this delusional privilege of being able to gaze at the sun without being dazzled that the mythological interest attaches":[55]

the natural historians of antiquity attributed this power to the eagle alone, who, as a dweller in the highest regions of the air, was brought into especially intimate relation with the heavens, with the sun, and with

lightning. We learn from the same sources, moreover, that the eagle puts his young to a test before recognizing them as his legitimate offspring. Unless they can succeed in looking into the sun without blinking they are thrown out of the eyrie. (*SE* 12:81)

Freud concludes that "this is merely ascribing to animals something that is a hallowed custom among men. The procedure gone through by the eagle with his young is an *ordeal*, a test of lineage, such as is reported of the most various races of antiquity" (*SE* 12:81).[56] This ordeal or test of lineage is one of the ways in which a culture frames or encodes what Kierkegaard proposed as the fundamental question of social existence: "*How does the single individual reassure himself that he is legitimate?*"[57] Given the rigidly partriarchal society in which Schreber lived and in which Freud developed his own theoretical elaborations of the codes of social and existential legitimation and the ways in which they can be "jammed," it is no surprise that Freud concludes that "in the case of Schreber we find ourselves once again on the familiar ground of the father-complex" (*SE* 12:55). For reasons that Freud is unable to fathom but which he assumes more biographical and historical research would reveal, Schreber is unable to make "normal" use of, to inherit in an unimpeded way, the paternal resources that would have allowed him to reassure himself that he was, indeed, "legitimate."

That it was, indeed, the resources of legitimation and the paths and modalities of their transmission that were in crisis in Schreber's case, is underlined by Schreber's preoccupation with names, titles, and lineage. We read, for example, that "Both the Flechsigs and the Schrebers belonged, it was said, to 'the highest nobility of heaven'; the Schrebers had the particular title 'Margraves of Tuscany and Tasmania,' according to the souls' habit of adorning themselves with high-sounding worldly titles from a kind of personal vanity" (55). Indeed, Schreber himself seems to suggest that the crisis afflicting the Order of the World, beginning with the transgression which he calls "soul murder," may be understood as a disturbance first and foremost within the domains of symbolic power represented and transmitted by *names*; his very first formulation of the crisis, which his text frenetically, though never quite successfully, tries to endow with a narrative structure, points in this direction:

This "miraculous structure" has recently suffered a rent, intimately connected with my personal fate. . . . I want to say by way of introduction that the leading roles in the genesis of this development, the first beginnings of which go back perhaps as far as the eighteenth century, were

played on the one hand by the names of Flechsig and Schreber (probably not specifying any individual member of these families), and on the other by the concept of *soul murder*. (54)[58]

Earlier, in his open letter to Flechsig, Schreber writes:

> I have no doubt that your name plays an essential role in the genetic development of the circumstances in question, in that certain nerves taken from your nervous system became "tested souls" . . . and in this capacity achieved supernatural power by means of which they have for years exerted a damaging influence on me and still do to this day. . . . I still feel daily and hourly the damaging influence of the miracles of those "tested souls"; the voices that speak to me even now shout your name again and again at me hundreds of times every day in this context. (33)

Freud, for his part, draws Schreber's preoccupation with names and titles into the domain of issues pertaining to homosexuality:

> His marriage, which he describes as being in other respects a happy one, brought him no children; and in particular it brought him no son who might have consoled him for the loss of his father and brother and upon whom he might have drained off his unsatisfied homosexual affections. His family line threatened to die out, and it seems that he felt no little pride in his birth and lineage. (*SE* 12:57–58)

The first clause of the last sentence of this passage is one of the more remarkable and telling formulations in Freud's essay. In German it reads: "Sein Geschlecht drohte auszusterben. . . ."[59] Schreber's *Geschlecht*, that which threatens to exhaust itself, waste away, can, of course, signify not only lineage, family line, stock, or race, but also gender as well as sex. If we take the pun seriously—more seriously than Freud apparently did—it suggests that Schreber discovered, no doubt unwittingly and unwillingly, something quite remarkable about the relationship between symbolic function and sexuality: a crisis of symbolic function—one's inscription within a symbolic network by means of names and titles—can manifest itself in the realm of, or, to put it in more Foucauldian terms, *as sexuality*. It is almost as if Schreber himself were half-aware that his florid sexual fantasies were elaborations of the breakdown products of those symbolic resources which might have reassured him that he was legitimate in the "eyes" of the symbolic community, or what Lacan refers to as the "big Other."

A good example of Freud's failure to appreciate Schreber's "marvelous" discovery that symbolic power in distress "secretes" a kind of sexuality occurs just prior to the passage cited earlier dealing with

Schreber's endangered *Geschlecht*. Here we find Freud luxuriating in a sort of intellectual homecoming to the "familiar ground of the father-complex":

> None of the material which in other cases of the sort is brought to light by analysis is absent in the present one: every element is hinted at in one way or another. In infantile experiences such as this the father appears as an interferer with the satisfaction which the child is trying to obtain; this is usually of an auto-erotic character, though at a later date it is often replaced in phantasy by some other satisfaction of a less inglorious kind. In the final stage of Schreber's delusion a magnificent victory was scored by the infantile sexual urge; for voluptuousness became God-fearing, and God Himself (his father) never tired of demanding it from him. His father's most dreaded threat, castration, actually provided the material for his wishful phantasy (at first resisted but later accepted) of being transformed into a woman. (*SE* 12:55–56)

With this reading of God-the-Father's paradoxical demand that Schreber cultivate feminine jouissance, we have encountered once again the limits of the "repressive hypothesis" guiding Freud's analysis. The fact that voluptuousness had become, as Schreber put it, God-fearing—*gottesfürchtig*—leads us not to the masturbator's triumph, as Freud would have it, but rather, I would suggest, to the domain of symbolic power in distress and the secret of names revealed therein.

Fear-(of)-God—*Fürchtegott*—is, as we know, an important name for Schreber.[60] Immediately after noting the "souls' habit of adorning themselves with high-sounding worldly titles," Schreber continues his genealogy of the rupture in the miraculous structure of the world by listing the names of Flechsig family members implicated in the crisis:

> Several names of both families are concerned: of the Flechsigs particularly Abraham Fürchtegott Flechsig, Professor Paul Theodor Flechsig, and a Daniel Fürchtegott Flechsig; the latter lived towards the end of the eighteenth century and was said to have been an "Assistant Devil" because of something that had happened in the nature of a soul murder. . . . The only knowledge I possess of the Flechsig family tree comes from what was said by the voices that talk to me; it would therefore be interesting to find out whether there had actually been a Daniel Fürchtegott Flechsig and an Abraham Fürchtegott Flechsig among the forbears of the present Professor Flechsig. (55–56)

The resonances of this genealogy with Schreber's later claim that jouissance had become *gottesfürchtig* suggest that the middle names of these delusional forbears of Schreber's psychiatrist need to be understood not so much as indications of Schreber's deification of Flechsig—such

a reading still remains within the orbit of Freud's analysis of the case—but rather as placeholders of the surplus of power/influence that Schreber experienced in his encounters with Flechsig's institutional authority. Schreber's own text indicates that he experienced this surplus as a kind of sexual transgression, as an obscene, even incestuous, indifference to his well-being culminating in a global condition of corruption and decadence. The middle name of (at least two of) Flechsig's imagined ancestors is thus both more and less than a name; it is the exceptional name that holds the place of a kind of state secret, which marks the place where the symbolic power and authority normally represented by the name secrete a kind of obscene, though *gottesfürchtig*, enjoyment.[61]

I would certainly agree with Freud that Schreber's extreme response to Flechsig—his perhaps excessive sensitivity to this other dimension of power, which "stains" Flechsig's institutional authority as a man of medicine—must have been in part the result of a transferential dynamic, the origins of which need to be sought in Schreber's relation to his own *Geschlecht* and above all to his father, Dr. Daniel *Gottlob* Moritz Schreber.[62] Schreber's uncertainty as to the identity of the original "soul murderer," his inability *to isolate* the original trauma and to provide a linear narrative of its sequelae, leads him to the vague supposition "that at one time something had happened between perhaps earlier generations of the Flechsig and Schreber families which amounted to soul murder" (55). My own conclusion from these difficulties in isolating the originary traumatic encounter is that the obscene dimension of power, which seemed to migrate, as a kind of transferential *daimon*, from Moritz Schreber to Paul Flechsig, enjoyed wide circulation throughout Schreber's *Gründerjahre* society, leaking, as it were, beyond the boundaries of either the Schreber family home or the psychiatric institutions in which Schreber lived, although these particular locations were no doubt sites of especially high "toxicity," of especially high concentrations of this other form or dimension of power.

Schreber tends to characterize the maddening fact that agencies and institutions entrusted with the care of individual and social well-being exert a sexualizing pressure in the language that dominated cultural analyses of late nineteenth-century bourgeois society. In one of Schreber's many attempts to explain the nature of the cosmic trauma to which his individual illness was tied, he cites topoi familiar from critiques of decadence and degeneration:

> The realms of God may always have known that the Order of the World however great and magnificent, was yet not without its Achilles' heel, inasmuch as the human nerves' power of attracting God's nerves consti-

tuted some danger for the realms of God. These dangers were likely to become more acute when somewhere on earth or on any other star nervousness or moral depravity gained the upper hand. (140)

Schreber adds that such "a general spread of nervous overexcitement" might be understood as a "consequence of over-civilization" (140). Earlier, Schreber had offered a similar view in language underlining his deep affinity with Wagner:

> Not even God Himself is or was a being of such *absolute perfection* as most religions attribute to Him. The power of attraction, this even to me unfathomable law, according to which rays and nerves mutually attract one another, harbours a kernel of danger for the realms of God; this forms perhaps the basis of the Germanic saga of the Twilight of the Gods [*Götterdämmerung*]. Growing nervousness among mankind could and can increase these dangers considerably. (59)

What distinguishes Schreber's delusional "analysis" of decadence from the work of other bourgeois theorists of cultural decline is that Schreber was unable to maintain a safe distance from the "symptoms" of degeneration. Indeed, the force of Schreber's neurotheological analysis is inseparable from his "perverse" capacity for identifying with, acting out, and, so to speak, enjoying these symptoms.

IX

Toward the beginning of the final section of his essay, "On the Mechanism of Paranoia," Freud introduces what could be understood as his own theory of decadence. He claims, in effect, that Schreber's psychosis compels him to experience in direct fashion the real "glue" of social relations in nineteenth-century bourgeois society: sublimated homoerotic desire. On this reading, "decadence" or "degeneration" would be that condition in which the social glue assumes the properties of a solvent, a condition in which the homosexual component of social relations and fellow feeling begins to separate out from its place within a system of "higher" cultural purposes and becomes autonomous and purposeless. Summarizing his conclusion that Schreber, like other paranoids, had come to grief in an attempt "to master an unconsciously reinforced current of homosexuality" (*SE* 12:59), Freud writes:

> So long as the individual is functioning normally and it is consequently impossible to see into the depths of his mental life, we may doubt whether his emotional relations to his neighbours in society have anything to do with sexuality, either actually or in their genesis. But delusions never

fail to uncover these relations and to trace back the social feelings to their roots in a directly sensual erotic wish. So long as he was healthy, Dr. Schreber, too, whose delusions culminated in a wishful phantasy of an unmistakably homosexual nature, had, by all accounts, shown no signs of homosexuality in the ordinary sense of the word [*im vulgären Sinne*]. (*SE* 12:60)

Freud goes on to situate this claim within a developmental theory according to which the human subject's sense of inherent relatedness to a world of objects is *constituted* across a series of differentiated stages of psychosexual organization. In this developmental model, one's sense of, to use Heidegger's phrase, Being-in-the-World, of involvement in a spatially, temporally, and symbolically complex network of social facts and relations, is *made real* (i.e., into a matter of profound existential care and concern) by way of an incremental and conflictual process of maturation in which the human child finds him- or herself increasingly implicated and interested in the affairs of other human subjects and the world more generally. At this point in his thinking about such matters, Freud proposes that this complex process of initiation into the world of "object relations" passes through a stage of extreme, even absolute, narcissism. This is a mode of libido organization in which the incipient self "unifies his sexual instincts (which have hitherto been engaged in auto-erotic activities) in order to obtain a love-object; and he begins by taking himself, his own body, as his love-object, and only subsequently proceeds from this to the choice of some person other than himself as his object" (*SE* 12:60–61). Narcissism is in this view a kind of psychosexual holding pattern in which the human subject gathers its energies and prepares, as it were, to make the inevitable choice of throwing its lot with the world of other subjects, which in a certain sense is *created* in and through that forced choice. That is, only by *positing* the world himself does the human subject begin effectively to take up positions, assume symbolic mandates, within the complex organization of social space, and it is Freud's view that this act of positing—of repeating the forced choice of being-in-the-world—has its own proper time or moment within an ontogenetic sequence.[63] Furthermore, Freud suggests, the path from a narcissistic libido organization to one allowing for a passionate engagement with the dimension of otherness, often, if not always, traverses a stage of homosexual object-love. Homosexuality functions in this schema as a kind of transitional compromise formation between narcissism and libidinal cathexis of otherness: I love an other, but one who is (anatomically) not too other—too "hetero"— from me (Freud's allusion to his idea that infants "theorize" that all people have the same genitals suggests that a pre-oedipal boy's love for

his mother must in some sense be considered *homoerotic*). Freud concludes his brief summary of psychosexual development by returning to his thesis of the homoerotic nature of the social glue holding together human society:

> After the stage of heterosexual object-choice has been reached, the homosexual tendencies are not, as might be supposed, done away with or brought to a stop; they are merely deflected from their sexual aim and applied to fresh uses. They now combine with portions of the ego-instincts and, as "attached" components, help to constitute the social instincts, thus contributing an erotic factor to friendship and comradeship, to *esprit de corps* and to the love of mankind in general. (*SE* 12:61)

Appealing to the notion of "fixation" points put forth in his earlier *Three Essays on the Theory of Sexuality*, Freud now suggests that Schreber, and paranoids more generally, have never fully succeeded in negotiating the passage beyond a narcissistically tinged homosexuality. The residues of this unfinished process mark the subject as one "exposed to the danger that some unusually intense wave of libido . . . may lead to a sexualization of their social instincts and so undo the sublimations which they had achieved in the course of their development" (*SE* 12:62). Freud then famously suggests that the various kinds of paranoid responses whereby an individual whose development has been arrested in this fashion defends against libidinal intensities "can all be represented as contradictions of the single proposition: 'I (a man) *love him* (a man)'. . ." (*SE* 12:63). According to this remarkable transformational grammar of symptom formation, delusions of persecution are generated by negating the *verb*: "'I do not *love* him—I *hate* him, because HE PERSECUTES ME.'" The final clause is necessary because "the mechanism of symptom-formation in paranoia requires that internal perceptions—feelings—shall be replaced by external perceptions" (*SE* 12:63). Feelings are thus not only negated; the homophobic law of this disorder demands that they also be disavowed and *projected* onto external reality.[64]

Eve Sedgwick has translated Freud's formula into terms much closer to my own emphasis on Schreber's crisis of initiatory investiture. She writes that "the usefulness of Freud's formulation, in the case of Dr. Schreber, that paranoia in men results from the repression of their homosexual desire" has primarily "to do with the foregrounding . . . of intense male homosocial desire as at once the most compulsory and the most prohibited of social bonds."[65] Expanding upon Freud's thesis, she argues that in nineteenth-century bourgeois society the normal patterns and procedures of male entitlement *demand* from men a high degree of homosocial desire that can only be distinguished from homosexuality *im vulgären Sinne* by means of arbitrary and inconsistent

cultural mappings. As a result, the very procedures of investiture that inserted Judge Schreber into a powerful homosocial elite would have exposed him to the chronic threat of homosexual panic (which can in turn function only when *homosexual desire* signifies *dysfunctional masculinity*):

> If such compulsory relationships as male friendship, mentorship, admiring identification, bureaucratic subordination, and heterosexual rivalry all involve forms of investment that force men into the arbitrarily mapped, self-contradictory, and anathema-riddled quicksands of the middle distance of male homosocial desire, then it appears that men enter into adult masculine entitlement only through acceding to the permanent threat that the small space they have cleared for themselves on this terrain may always, just as arbitrarily and with just as much justification, be foreclosed.[66]

My claim here, as in my earlier discussion of Freud's struggle with the homosociality pervading the inner circle of psychoanalytic pioneers, is that homosexual panic was only one of the chronic breakdown products of symbolic power and authority in Schreber's Germany. But as any reader of the *Memoirs* knows—and as the following chapters will develop in more detail—Schreber experienced what threatened his rights/rites of institution under a number of different "ideological" signs: as a feminization not always reducible to homosexualization; as the threat of contamination by machine-like, depersonalized linguistic operations; as the prospect of "Jewification" (metamorphosis into the Wandering Jew). What I call Schreber's "own private Germany" consists of his attempts, using the available repertoire of cultural values and valences, to interpret and to assign meaning to a maddening blockage in meaning that prevented him from assuming his place as a master of juridical hermeneutics and judgment. The gesture of ideological specification—of historical and cultural content analysis—that reads Schreber's breakdown as homosexual panic may in fact serve to occlude the more primary question as to the nature of the semiotic blockage at the core of Schreber's troubles. And it is to Freud's credit, I think, that his attention to this more primary matter compelled him to question his own previous "queer" reading.

X

After presenting his remarkable grammar of homophobic negation, Freud turns to the mechanism of repression (a promise to address the "more general psychological problems . . . involved in the question of the nature of projection" [*SE* 12:66] is never honored). After a brief

presentation of the dynamic structure of repression as it functions in the sorts of neurotic disorders that had been the main focus of Freud's work up to this time, he proposes to explore the particular profile of this pathogenic mechanism as it functions in the more extreme case of paranoia. This path of investigation leads him to a consideration of one of Schreber's central delusions, namely the conviction that the world as he knew it had come to a catastrophic end.

In the sixth chapter of the *Memoirs*, Schreber writes of the period in the spring of 1894 while still a patient in Flechsig's clinic, which, though "the most gruesome time of my life . . . was also the *holy* time of my life, when my soul was immensely inspired by supernatural things, which came over me in ever increasing numbers amidst the rough treatment which I suffered from the outside" (79–80). During these months, Schreber came to believe that the whole of mankind had perished or that an end of the world was imminent:

> It was repeatedly mentioned in visions that the work of the past fourteen thousand years had been lost . . . and that approximately only another two hundred years were allotted to the earth. . . . During the latter part of my stay at Flechsig's Asylum I thought this period had already expired and therefore thought I was the last real human being left, and that the few human shapes whom I saw apart from myself—Professor Flechsig, some attendants, occasional more or less strange-looking patients—were only "fleeting-improvised-men" created by miracle. (85)

Schreber associates these phenomena with various political and religious conflicts, in particular with Protestant Germany's struggle against Catholic, Slavic, and Jewish forces arrayed against it and seeking to convert it.[67]

In the next chapter of the *Memoirs*, Schreber develops more fully the fantasy of the end of the world:

> Varying with the suggestions I received I formed different opinions about the manner in which it might have come about. In the first place I always thought of a decrease in the warmth of the sun through her moving further away, and consequently a more or less generalized glaciation. In the second place I thought of an earthquake or suchlike. . . . I further thought it possible that news had spread that in the modern world something in the nature of a wizard had suddenly appeared in the person of Professor Flechsig and that I myself, after all a person known in wider circles, had suddenly disappeared; this had spread terror and fear amongst the people, destroying the bases of religion and causing general nervousness and immorality. In its train devastating epidemics had broken upon mankind. (97)

Among the diseases contributing to the apocalyptic demise of mankind, the abject signs of which had already become visible on his own body, Schreber mentions the plague along with several varieties of leprosy: "*Lepra orientalis, Lepra indica, Lepra hebraica*, and *Lepra aegyptica*" (97).

Freud takes his cue for interpreting these eschatological fantasies from Schreber's belief, expressed after he had reassured himself that the world had in fact not come to an end, that "*a very profound inner change has taken place nevertheless*" (93). On the basis of his theory of libido, Freud writes, "we shall not find it difficult to explain these catastrophes":

> The patient has withdrawn from the people in his environment and from the external world generally the libidinal cathexis which he has hitherto directed on to them. Thus everything has become indifferent and irrelevant to him, and has to be explained by means of a secondary rationalization as being "miracled up, cursorily improvised." The end of the world is the projection of this internal catastrophe; his subjective world has come to an end since his withdrawal of his love from it. (*SE* 12:70)[68]

Freud's reading of this delusion culminates in a remarkable claim that gives the psychic mechanisms of paranoia a nearly kabbalistic cast; if Freud is right, it is as if Schreber had recreated, in debased form, the Lurianic "procedure" of *tikkun*, the recollection of divine sparks scattered into earthly exile through the cosmic trauma of the "breaking of the vessels":

> And the paranoiac builds [the world] again, not more splendid, it is true, but at least so that he can once more live in it. He builds it up by the work of his delusions. *The delusion-formation, which we take to be the pathological product, is in reality an attempt at recovery, a process of reconstruction.* Such a reconstruction after the catastrophe is successful to a greater or lesser extent, but never wholly so. . . . But the human subject has recaptured a relation, and often a very intense one, to the people and things in the world, even though the relation is a hostile one now, where formerly it was hopefully affectionate. We may say, then, that the process of repression proper consists in a detachment of the libido from people—and things—that were previously loved. It happened silently; we received no intelligence of it, but can only infer it from subsequent events. (*SE* 12:70–71)

As I've already indicated, Freud's reading of Schreber's "internal catastrophe" initiates a revision of his previous claim regarding homophobic negation/projection:

What forces itself so noisily upon our attention is the process of recovery, which undoes the work of repression and brings back the libido again on to the people it had abandoned. In paranoia this process is carried out by the method of projection. It was incorrect of us to say that the perception which was suppressed internally is projected outwards; the truth is rather, as we now see, that what was abolished internally returns from without. (*SE* 12:71)

Like a tiny thread that, once pulled, unravels an entire garment, this seemingly modest revision inaugurates a long series of reservations, doubts, confessions of confusion and ignorance, speculations on (possibly) related issues, and calls for further research. The crux of Freud's dissatisfaction is the fit between his interpretations of what he sees as the two central delusions described by Schreber, the one dealing explicitly with sexuality and the sexed body, the other with the unmaking and making of the world as a space of meaningful social facts and relations. Freud reads the delusion of unmanning as a wishful fantasy to occupy a feminine position vis-à-vis key male figures of authority and power and the delusion of cosmic disaster as a generalized withdrawal of libidinal cathexes from the world, which serves as a defense against the intensity of the "homosexual" fantasy.

After noting that only a more thorough examination of the process of projection "will clear up our remaining doubts on this subject" (*SE* 12:71), Freud admits that his analysis of paranoid mechanisms do not sufficiently delimit them from other psychic disturbances in which libido is withdrawn from the world, such as occurs, for example, in mourning. His own answer to this difficulty, however, defines paranoia in language that almost exactly matches the way in which he would soon characterize melancholia in his famous essay on the subject. In paranoia, thanks to a fixation point at the stage of narcissism, the free-floating libido withdrawn from the world becomes the source of a pathologically heightened secondary narcissism: "we can assert that the length of *the step back from sublimated homosexuality to narcissism* is a measure of the amount of *regression* characteristic of paranoia" (*SE* 12:72).[69]

Another problem raised by Freud's dependence on libido theory concerns what appears to be the paradoxical temporality of the relation between the two central delusional complexes, for, as Freud notes, "it can be urged that the delusions of persecution . . . made their appearance at an earlier date than the fantasy of the end of the world; so that what is supposed to have been a return of the repressed actually preceded the repression itself—and this is patent nonsense" (*SE* 12:72–73). Freud's answer to this more serious objection is also far more equivo-

cal; for the ear attuned to Schreber's diction, it has all the markings of one of Schreber's speculations on the mechanisms of soul murder or one of the many miraculous "systems" by which he was tormented:

> We must admit the possibility that a detachment of the libido such as we are discussing might just as easily be a partial one. . . . The process may then stop at the stage of a partial detachment or it may spread to a general one, which will loudly proclaim its presence in the symptoms of megalomania. Thus the detachment of the libido from the figure of Flechsig may nevertheless have been what was primary in the case of Schreber; it was immediately followed by the appearance of the delusion, which brought back the libido on to Flechsig again (though with a negative sign to mark the fact that repression had taken place) and thus annulled the work of repression. And now the battle of repression broke out anew, but this time with more powerful weapons. (SE 12:73)

The third and final objection that Freud entertains apropos of his insistence on the primacy of libido theory proves to be the most far-reaching and in fact returns us to some of the issues raised at the very beginning of our discussion. For this final objection concerns the on-going conflict between Freud and the dissident members of the psycho-analytic circle—above all Adler and Jung—who were pushing beyond the limits of Freud's conception of libidinal cathexis. This final objection was anticipated in a footnote that Freud appended to his initial reading of the delusion of the end of the world. Freud writes there: "He has perhaps withdrawn from [the world] not only his libidinal cathexis, but his *interest in general*—that is, the cathexes that proceed from his ego as well" (SE 12:70; my emphasis). What is at stake here is nothing less than the question of the primacy of the domain of sexuality for understanding the emergence and nature of the self's cognitive, moral, and existential involvement with the social world. How does the human subject come to have a rapport with other subjects and the world more generally, how does the human subject come to inhabit a world of institutions and social facts (money, marriage, laws, governments, etc.) that profoundly matter, that are experienced as real, vital, and meaningful, and how does such a rapport come to be shattered? These questions, it would seem, push beyond the limits of the theory of libidinal cathexis that had guided Freud throughout his reading of the Schreber case. Indeed, given Freud's ultimate dependence on this theory and his sense that the very identity and integrity of the institution of psychoanalysis stands or falls with it, one can only agree with Robert Jay Lifton's astute remark that "Freud's views on imagery of the end of the world [in Schreber's text] were in some measure a defense of—or at least a warding off of a beginning attack on—his own ideological

world."[70] With the questions raised by Schreber's apocalyptic visions we have, in other words, encountered once again what I earlier characterized as Freud's allegorical presence in the text. The rhythm of equivocation and doubt that informs these final pages of Freud's essay registers the degree of "seismic" unrest provoked by the task of applying libido theory, and the "repressive hypothesis" to which it is committed, to the sort of radical disturbance in one's sense of (one's right to) being-in-the-world manifest in the delusion of world destruction. Confessing his helplessness in the face of such matters, Freud summarizes the central theoretical questions in the following terms:

> We can no more dismiss the possibility that disturbances of the libido may react upon the ego-cathexes than we can overlook the converse possibility—namely, that a secondary or induced disturbance of the libidinal processes may result from abnormal changes in the ego. Indeed, it is probable that processes of this kind constitute the distinctive characteristic of psychoses. (*SE* 12:75)

Following a series of speculative interventions into current debates concerning diagnostic categories and the remarkable confession, noted previously, of a structural homology between libido theory and Schreber's delusional cosmology, Freud concludes by giving the final word of the essay not to the libido but rather to the ego, the *Ich*. It is the developmental history of the ego and, ultimately, of that more amorphous locus of agency, *the self*, which, Freud seems to suggest, holds the key to understanding the sort of profound disturbance registered in Schreber's apocalyptic delusions. This disturbance is, I would suggest, best understood not in the context of the ego psychology that was to emerge from these final reflections,[71] but rather in one attuned to the operations and crises of symbolic power and authority.

XI

Freud shows his greatest sensitivity to these crises in the postscript to the case study, published a year after the original essay. In these reflections on Schreber's deep affinities with totemistic patterns of thought and on what Lifton has aptly termed the "disquieting border area of theology and psychopathology,"[72] Freud demonstrates a keen awareness of the problems pertaining to the historical transmission of legacies of social and existential legitimation. If Freud is right about Schreber's obsessions with names, titles, and lineage (i.e., the dimension of legitimacy ultimately transmitted by way of the patronymic—the Name-of-the-Father, as Jacques Lacan puts it), then it behooves us

to attend more closely to the clues Schreber gives as to what has gone awry in the transmission of those symbolic resources with which he might have reassured himself that he was, in a deep and dependable sense, legitimate. Schreber himself indicates that the disturbance or blockage in question and the various aberrations in the psychic and cosmic order that follow from it, are the results not so much of an absence or lack of access to sites and resources of legitimation as of a kind of uncanny surplus of power and influence secreted by them. If Lacan is right about Schreber—that his psychosis is the result of a "foreclosure" of the paternal metaphor, the Name-of-the-Father, in short, what I have been referring to as the *symbolic* resources allowing for a deep and dependable sense of existential legitimacy—then this default would seem to be a function not of a "too little" but rather of a "too much," not of an excessive distance from the attentions of a solicitous authority but rather of an excessive proximity. Nowhere is Schreber clearer about this than in his repeated references to the fact that God normally remains distant from and ignorant of living human beings.

Freud's reading of Schreber's conception of God's *lack* of omnipotence as a critique or attack and thus as a sign of rebellion, hostility, and aggression vis-à-vis God and the paternal agency Freud sees him as representing, has become the standard reading of this peculiar element of Schreber's theological system. And yet we should recall Schreber's quite emphatic insistence that this lack is precisely what is demanded by, or better, what constitutes the so-called Order of the World, that reign of cosmic law the transgression of which is figured as excessive and prolonged "nerve contact" between God and Schreber. "As a rule," Schreber writes, "God did not interfere directly in the fate of peoples or individuals—I call this the state of affairs in accordance with the Order of the World" (48). This rule served, it seemed, to protect not only mortals from the overwhelming force of divine immediacy but also God Himself from the dangers of too much nerve contact, "because for reasons which cannot be further elucidated, the nerves of *living* human beings particularly when in a state of *high-grade excitation*, have such power of attraction for the nerves of God that He would not be able to free Himself from them again, and would thus endanger his own existence" (48). For these reasons, God entered into nerve contact with living human beings only in exceptional circumstances, for example, in dream states, states of poetic inspiration, or in moments of political and social crisis of entire nation-states, such as in war. The law regulating distances and proximities between the sacred and the profane—the Order of the World—deemed that "regular contact between God and human souls occurred . . . only after death" (48). Schre-

ber notes that, from the perspective he is presenting, "'the Order of the World' may appear as something impersonal and higher, more powerful than God or even as ruling God." "In fact," he continues, "there is no obscurity. *'The Order of the World'* is the lawful relation which, *resting on God's nature and attributes, exists between God and the creation called to life by Him*" (79).[73] Schreber admits that such a view implies the paradox that

> God, whose power of rays is essentially constructive in nature, and creative, came into conflict with Himself when he attempted the irregular policy against me, aimed solely at destroying my bodily integrity and reason. . . . Or perhaps, using an oxymoron, God Himself was on my side in His fight against me, that is to say I was able to bring His attributes and powers into battle as an effective weapon in my self-defence. (79)

If Freud is right, that God stands in for the father, then Schreber has discovered a remarkable feature of this figure, a feature absolutely central to the emergence of Schreber's paranoid universe. Indeed, with his insight into God's internal division, Schreber may have discovered the key to that aspect of paranoia that, according to Freud, was typical for the illness, namely a certain tendency toward splitting (the father into God and Flechsig; God into the upper and lower God; Flechsig into multiple Flechsig-souls, etc.).[74] The father figure, it seems, undergoes a kind of self-division into two distinct paternal agencies: the one distant and marked by a peculiar ignorance about living human beings and their bodily functions—an ignorance that, as Schreber takes pains to emphasize, *accords with the law*—and the other, once lured by the right bait, the right *Luder*, obscenely involved in the affairs of sentient human beings: their sexual pleasures, their most private thoughts and dreams, even their bowel movements. One might say that the entire "plot" of the *Memoirs* revolves around Schreber's attempt to integrate these two fathers, to find a way to reconcile the "outlaw" or extralegal paternal presence—this "surplus father"—with the father identified with the Order of the World and the law of proper distances. In the following chapters, we will be concerned with what might be called the historical truth of this surplus father: the specific historical conditions under which such a figure comes to exercise his power.

TWO

THE FATHER WHO KNEW TOO MUCH

I

S INCE the publication of Freud's essay, much of the literature on Schreber has focused on efforts to flesh out the historical and biographical details surrounding Schreber's breakdown, to establish the referential dimension of the "surplus father" whose intrusive presence Schreber most often names "Flechsig" and which he ultimately makes responsible for the degeneration of the Order of the World. These efforts begin, in a sense, with Freud's own disclaimer regarding such concrete historical knowledge. Toward the end of the second part of his essay, just at the moment when he announces triumphantly that his analysis has found its way to "the familiar ground of the father-complex," Freud alludes to the missing historical dimension of his analysis: "The patient's struggle with Flechsig became revealed to him as a conflict with God, and we must therefore construe it as an infantile conflict with the father whom he loved; the details of that conflict (*of which we know nothing*) are what determined the content of his delusions" (*SE* 12:55; my emphasis). He later adds the following remark:

> Any one who was more daring than I am in making interpretations, or who was in touch with Schreber's family and consequently better acquainted with the society in which he moved and the small events of his life, would find it an easy matter to trace back innumerable details of his delusions to their sources and so discover their meaning, and this in spite of the censorship to which the *Denkwürdigkeiten* have been subjected. (*SE* 12:57)

Such disclaimers notwithstanding, Freud did, as we have seen, make a number of assumptions about Schreber's biography in general and the personality of his father, Daniel Gottlob Moritz Schreber, in particular (to avoid confusion, I will refer to the father as Moritz Schreber; the name Schreber will be reserved for the son, Daniel Paul). One will recall Freud's remarks about Moritz Schreber's significance as a doctor, public figure, and author of a popular exercise book, *Ärztliche Zimmergymnastik*. This is, of course, the one book among Mortiz Schreber's numerous publications on health, calisthenics, orthopedics, and child rearing that his son refers to in his *Memoirs*.[1] Freud acknowledges, also,

the existence of numerous "Schreber Associations" in Germany (and in Saxony, in particular), which testify to Moritz Schreber's lasting influence (it was these organizations, formed after Moritz Schreber's death for the purpose of carrying forth his spiritual and cultural legacy, that first introduced "Schreber Gardens" in Germany). Finally, Freud also acknowledges the help of a Dresden psychiatrist, Dr. Arnold Georg Stegmann, in obtaining certain biographical data about Schreber and his family; there is no evidence as to what information Stegmann passed on to Freud.

The real breakthrough in efforts to situate Schreber more firmly within his historical and biographical context occurred in the 1950s with a series of publications by the American psychoanalyst, William Niederland. Niederland was the first "professional" reader of Schreber to submit the father's publications to systematic study. As he puts it in the introduction to his collection of essays on Schreber, the careful study of Moritz Schreber's theories and practices of health, fitness, and child rearing makes it "possible to correlate the bizarre mental formations in Schreber's delusional system (including florid fantasies, distorted images, hallucinatory experiences) to specific events in the early father-son relationship and thus to demonstrate *the nucleus of truth* in the son's paranoid productions."[2]

The symptoms whose referential truth is of most concern to Niederland are those affecting the body. Here is Schreber's own list of some of the body parts and organs that were subject to manipulation by supernatural forces:

> The miracles enacted against the organs of the thoracic and abdominal cavities were very multifarious. . . . I . . . remember that I once had a different heart. . . . On the other hand my *lungs* were for a long time the object of violent and very threatening attacks. . . . At about the same time some of my *ribs* were sometimes temporarily smashed, always with the result that what had been destroyed was re-formed after a time. One of the most horrifying miracles was the so-called *compression-of-the-chest-miracle*, which I endured at least several dozen times; it consisted in the whole chest wall being compressed, so that the state of compression caused by the lack of breath was transmitted to my whole body. . . . I existed frequently without a stomach. . . . Of other internal organs I will only mention the *gullet* and the *intestines*, which were torn out or vanished repeatedly, further the *pharynx*, which I partly ate up several times, finally the *seminal cord*, against which very painful miracles were directed. . . . Those miracles always appeared most threatening to me which were in one way or another directed against my reason. These concerned firstly my head; *secondly* . . . also the *spinal cord*, which next to the head was considered as

the seat of reason. One therefore attempted to pump the spinal cord out, which was done by so-called "little men" placed in my feet. . . . All my *muscles* were (and still are) the object of miracles for the purpose of preventing all movements and every occupation I am about to undertake. . . . My *eyes* and the *muscles of the lids* which serve to open and close them were an almost uninterrupted target for miracles. . . . Some of the "little devils" participated in a miracle which was often enacted against my head. . . . This was perhaps the most abominable of all miracles—next to the compression-of-the-chest-miracle; the expression used for it if I remember correctly was "the head-compressing-machine." In consequence of the many flights of rays, etc., there had appeared in my skull a deep cleft or rent roughly along the middle, which probably was not visible from outside but was from inside. The "little devils" stood on both sides of this cleft and compressed my head as though in a vice by turning a kind of screw, causing my head temporarily to assume an elongated almost pear-shaped form. . . . Manifold miracles were also directed against my *skeleton*, apart from those against my ribs and skull. . . . In the foot bones particularly in the region of the heel, *caries* was often caused by miracle, causing me considerable pain. . . . A similar miracle was the so-called *coccyx miracle*. This was an extremely painful, caries-like state of the lowest vertebrae. Its purpose was to make sitting and even lying down impossible. (132–39)

According to Niederland, many of these examples of a radically distorted bodily ego can be traced to the father's *actual handling* of his son during childhood. Others, Niederland allows, may have their source in the father's books, many of which were copiously illustrated and which detail a wide spectrum of medical and parental interventions into the physical and mental life of children. Still others might be traced to Schreber's encounter with the deformed bodies of his father's young orthopedic patients who, as a rule, lived in the Schreber home and took meals with the family. "One can assume," Niederland concludes, "that by the time the child Schreber entered his third or fourth year of life, he had already undergone a notable degree of traumatization." Schreber's delusional theological system is, in Niederland's view, a byproduct of this traumatization by the father's peculiar system of health and fitness: "He brought to bear on the child a whole system of medical gymnastics, calisthenic exercises, orthopedic appliances, and other regulatory practices which he had invented." In Niederland's view, then, each of Schreber's bodily symptoms has a kernel of referential truth to be found in the father's system. The "coccyx miracle" refers, for example, "to the strict rules for sitting down enforced by the father," while the miracles directed against the eyes and eyelids allude to fact that the "prescriptions of Schreber's father included a whole

system of eye-washing, eye-sponging, lid-cleansing procedures and that this system was put into action several times a day beginning in the postnatal period." The two miracles that Schreber characterizes as among the most painful, the "head-compressing-machine," and the "compression-of-the-chest-miracle," are traced to the father's orthopedic inventions designed to improve the posture of children, the *Kopfhalter* and the *Geradehalter*, as well as to a system of straps pulled across the child's chest in bed to make sure that he or she remained supine during sleep. Schreber's sensations of bodily fragmentation refer, according to Niederland, to unconscious memories of illustrations of dissected bodies and body parts observed in his father's medical books, while the miracle whereby Schreber is himself addressed (by the souls in contact with him) as having several heads is to be traced to illustrations of exercises in Moritz Schreber's books on gymnastics. Schreber's characterization of the Order of the World as a "miraculous structure" or *wundervoller Aufbau*—Schreber himself notes that this expression was "suggested to me from outside" (54)—is seen by Niederland as an allusion to one of the father's books: *Anthropos: Der Wunderbau des menschlichen Organismus.*[3]

In summary, Niederland argues that although Schreber's symptoms at times resemble the manifestations of the "influencing machines" found in the persecutory delusions of many schizophrenics, "there is a realistic core in this [Schreber's] delusional material," the historical truth of which is to be found in the father's medical, orthopedic, and pedagogical theories and practices. These theories and practices provide the program, as it were, of that obscene paternal agency that I have referred to as the "surplus father." As Niederland puts it,

> With respect to the father, one might reason he was the type of "symbiotic father," whose all-pervasive presence, usurpation of the maternal role, and other domineering features (overtly sadistic as well as paternalistically benevolent, punitive as well as seductive) lent themselves to their fusion with the bizarre God hierarchy characteristic of the son's delusional system.

In Niederland's view, the *overproximity* of such a father to a son created an environment in which, as he puts it, "there was always castration in the air":

> The father's aggressive and coercive actions; the orthopedic contraptions; the disrupted, dismembered, and dissected aspects of the human body; the violence and authoritarian impetus of the injunctions; the sequence masturbation-plague-sterility-insanity (castration)—all belong in this setting.[4]

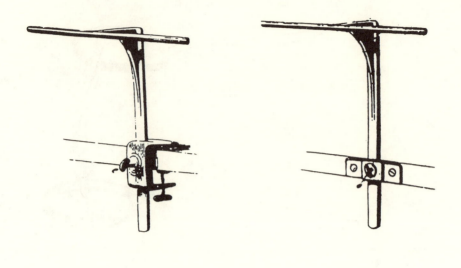

The "Geradehalter." (Drawings from Moritz Schreber's writings)

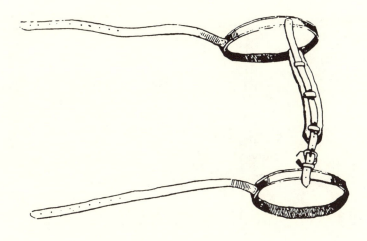

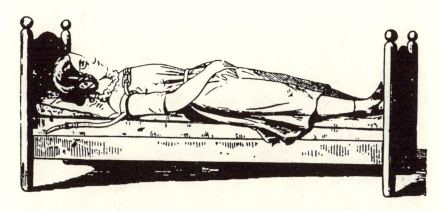

Straps to insure proper posture during sleep. (Drawings from
Moritz Schreber's writings)

Recalling Niederland's remarks on Moritz Schreber's preoccupation
with eyes, this reading of the pathogenic effects of the father on the son
exhibits strong parallels with Freud's reading of E. T. A. Hoffmann's
"The Sandman" in his essay on "The Uncanny."[5] In his interpretation
of the story, Freud posits a splitting of the father into two distinct paternal agencies, the one nurturing and caring, the other demonic and cas-

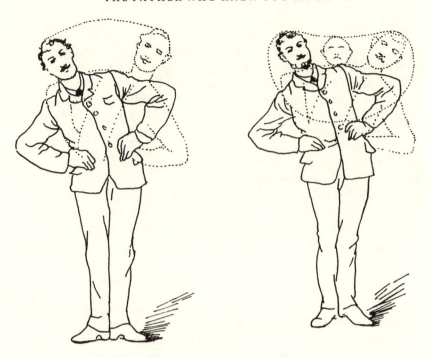

Recommended exercises. (Drawings from Moritz Schreber's writings)

trating. In the story, this second, obscene father splits, in turn, into two figures, Coppelius and Coppola, thereby allowing for the repetition of the encounter with this "second" father (one will recall that in his reading of Schreber, Freud stresses the splitting of Flechsig and God into multiple agencies). The crucial difference between Niederland's approach and Freud's is, of course, that for Niederland this second, castrating father *really existed* and is not, as for Freud, largely the product of the son's delusional elaboration of an inevitable and universal ambivalence vis-à-vis the father. Although he never puts it quite in these terms, for Niederland, it would appear, it is only the actual encounter with such a "demonic" father that *converts normal ambivalence into delusional splitting*.

As evidence of the historical truth of the "Coppelius" aspect of Moritz Schreber, Niederland refers not only to the latter's orthopedic and pedagogical theories and practices but to indications of a kind of psychic, even psychotic, doubling on the father's part.[6] Niederland notes, for example, that the last years of Moritz Schreber's life were marked by recurrent depressions, the likely sequelae of a concussion caused by a falling ladder in 1851 when he was forty-three years old.[7]

Niederland also refers to a curious notation in Schreber's medical records about Schreber *père* stating that "The father . . . suffered from obsessional ruminations with homicidal impulses."[8] Niederland connects this notation to a strange bit of text found in one of Moritz Schreber's early works, *The Book of Health*, which he published in 1839 at the age of thirty-one. In that work, he cites a case history of a man whom he had ostensibly met by chance while traveling through southern Germany and who as a youth had suffered from what would appear to be an extreme manic-depressive illness. He inserts this case material in the form of a first-person narrative, "Confessions of a Former Melancholic."[9] In effect, Niederland reads this remarkable text as the confessions of Moritz Schreber's mentally unstable, castrating *Doppelgänger* who, over the course of his last ten years of life, elaborated his aggressive-destructive impulses in the form of a pedagogical system.[10]

II

More recent efforts to flesh out the "historical truth" behind Schreber's delusions of persecution have taken Schreber at his word that the real persecutory figure in his life was not his father, whom he mentions only four times in the course of the *Memoirs*, but rather his psychiatrist, Paul Emil Flechsig, who treated Schreber twice at his Leipzig clinic, and whose "tested soul" Schreber repeatedly characterizes as the real demonic force in the plot against him. Although it is no doubt true that Flechsig's name would have largely been forgotten were it not for his immortalization by his most famous patient, Daniel Paul Schreber, he was, at the end of the nineteenth century, a neuroanatomist of considerable renown. Because of his groundbreaking work on the myelination of nerve fibers and the localization of nervous diseases, he was appointed professor of psychiatry at Leipzig University, a position that in 1882 would include the directorship of the new Psychiatric Clinic of the University Hospital. As Lothane has noted, the appointment of a brain anatomist with no real psychiatric experience to the directorship of a psychiatric clinic signaled a historical shift of paradigms in the discipline of psychiatry toward extreme medicalization: "in one fell swoop, through Flechsig's nomination, the tradition of the soul ended and the reign of the brain began."[11]

Flechsig's interest in the localization and mapping of brain functions and the purely physical causes of mental illness had immediate consequences for the administration of the clinic of which he was in charge. In order to guarantee a steady stream of fresh cases to study, he took an active role in the admission and discharge of patients. If a patient

proved to be of little research interest—chronic patients, for example, whose disorders would offer nothing new to observe—they could be quickly transferred to state hospitals like the Sonnenstein asylum. As a neuroanatomist, Flechsig was particularly interested in patients who were near death, for brain dissection was, as he put it, "the most direct way to penetrate to the knowledge of the lawful relations between mental illnesses and brain anomalies."[12] In his perhaps most famous work, a lecture delivered in 1894 and published two years later as a monograph with the title "Brain and Soul" (*Gehirn und Seele*), Flechsig brings his biological approach to psychopathology to a point: "Diseases of the association centers are the foremost cause of mental illness; they form the proper object of psychiatry."[13] Toward the end of his life, Flechsig would finally characterize his contribution to the understanding of the mind as the localization of the crucial categories of Kant's transcendental idealism in the frontal lobe of the brain.[14]

Recent readers of Schreber have tried to discern in the *Memoirs* specific references and allusions to Flechsig's theories and practices, to discover in the latter's approach to mental illness the key to his demonization by Schreber. Flechsig's advocacy of castration, for example, even though this term was reserved for the surgical removal of the ovaries and uterus of women diagnosed with hysteria, has been cited as one of the sources of Schreber's anxieties about unmanning.[15] Similarly, Flechsig's dependency on corpses for his neuroanatomical researches has been offered as the historical truth behind Schreber's "thesis" that God dealt only with corpses and knew nothing about living human beings.[16] Indeed, Friedrich Kittler has suggested that an overemphasis on Moritz Schreber's role in his son's psychosis amounts to a failure to appreciate the historical rupture signaled by Flechsig's "psychophysics," which along with Schreber's delusional text, is seen as the elaboration of a new paradigm of social and psychic organization—of nothing short of a second industrial revolution. For Kittler, Schreber's language, the language "spoken" by his overexcited nerves, is "the language of the experimental neurologist Flechsig": "Flechsig's message of the death of man, more hidden than Nietzsche's, has not reached the exegetes. Again and again the attempt is made to explain the second industrial revolution by the first. . . . Beyond mechanical head bandages, Schreber's paranoia followed the lead of an insane neurologist."[17]

Flechsig's neuroanatomical paradigm, which, according to Kittler, ultimately figures the brain as a network of channels and relays in which—Flechsig's residual Kantianism notwithstanding—*personhood* is dissolved into systems of *information* transfer, marks the advent of a far more radical and efficient intervention of power into the body of its "object" than Moritz Schreber's merely *mechanical* manipulations of

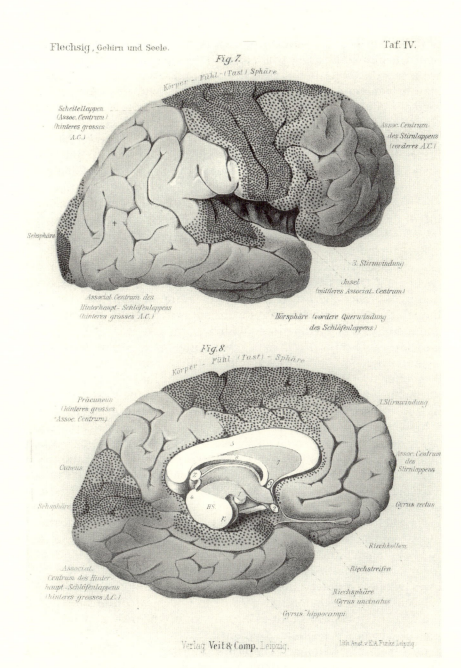

Illustrations from Flechsig's monograph, *Gehirn und Seele*.
(Leipzig: Veit and Co., 1896)

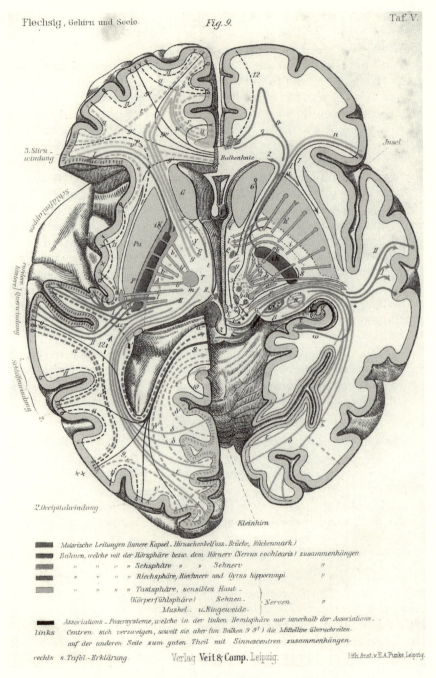

Illustration from Flechsig's monograph, *Gehirn und Seele*.
(Leipzig: Veit and Co., 1896)

children's muscles and activities: "nothing allows us to equate the classical pedagogical power of Schreber senior with the incomparably more efficient disposition of power in 1900."[18] In Kittler's view, the "second industrial revolution" is not only capable of producing soul murder, it is conceived from the start *as* soul murder—as the annihilation of the very horizon of intelligibility in which words like soul, psyche, or spirit would make any sense. In essence, Kittler takes Schreber *literally* when, in the open letter to Flechsig published in the *Memoirs*, Schreber writes: "I have not the least doubt that the *first impetus* to what my doctors always considered mere 'hallucinations' but which to me signified communication with supernatural powers, consisted of *influences on my nervous system emanating from your nervous system*" (34). Flechsig's "nervous system," understood as the radical medicalization of all disturbances of the "soul," their ultimate reduction to anomalies in the hard wiring of the brain, finishes off the subject already moribund at the end of the nineteenth century as a result of excessive handling by the likes of Moritz Schreber. A clinical environment organized under the sign of Flechsig's psychophysical research paradigm would be, in this view, *inherently traumatizing*. Or to return to Niederland's formulation, in such an environment "castration" would have been in the air.[19]

The delusion offering the clearest picture of the new "episteme" from whose torments Schreber struggles to free himself—in part, as we shall see, by miming the enemy—is that of the *Aufschreibesystem* or writing-down-system described in the ninth chapter of the *Memoirs*:[20]

> *Books or other notes* are kept in which for years have been *written-down* all my thoughts, all my phrases, all my necessaries, all the articles in my possession or around me, all persons with whom I come into contact, etc. I cannot say with certainty who does the writing down. As I cannot imagine God's omnipotence lacks all intelligence, I presume that the writing down is done by creatures given human shape on distant celestial bodies after the manner of the fleeting-improvised-men, but lacking all intelligence; their hands are led automatically, as it were, by passing rays for the purpose of making them write down, so that later rays can again look at what has been written. (119)

For Kittler, the crucial feature of this registration system is its purely *mechanical and automatic* nature, specifically the absence of any animating soul or spirit: "If the recording occurs mechanically and without any *Geist*, the probability of its being a purely technical procedure is greater."[21] Kittler's important insight is that a radical despiritualization of language production (and reproduction) is structurally inscribed in Flechsig's neuroanatomical understanding of the mind.

To put it somewhat differently, Flechsig's biologistic approach to "brain and soul" is unable to account for—and, indeed, ultimately eliminates—the *heterogeneity* of organic, bodily *causes*, on the one hand, and *effects* of signification, on the other. Within Flechsig's paradigm, effects of symbolic meaning are produced *directly* by biochemical processes; no gap separates them. This is also, of course, one of the central features of Schreber's psychotic universe: Schreber experiences his own language production as a series of mechanical vibrations of nerve fibers set in motion by external physical causes. Kittler's thesis is that both Flechsig and Schreber elaborate in their writing a universe in which the symbolic-spiritual dimension—*Geist*—in its radical heterogeneity with regard to organic processes has been nullified. As Schreber's text amply demonstrates, once the symbolic dimension collapses into the domain of bodily causes, we are in a universe of extreme *literalization*, where words are assimilated to things that in turn produce immediate alterations in the body. Influence anxiety becomes the fear of real bodily violation. Kittler's point is that such fears were warranted; the new paradigms of brain science participated in this "psychotic" tendency to eliminate the gap separating the domain of bodily causes from that of meaning, to see signification as a series of *direct* effects of purely mechanical, physical causes. We might say that Flechsig's brain science is the *theory* and Schreber's delusions are the *practice* of the same traumatic collapse of the symbolic dimension of subjectivity, of the gap separating bodily cause and symbolic effect. Schreber's point would seem to be that the elimination of that gap—the attempt to fill it with neuroanatomical knowledge—is nothing short of soul murder.

The notion of a purely mechanical reproduction or registration of signifiers calls to mind those remnants of the erstwhile "forecourts of heaven" that appeared to Schreber in the form of talking birds. We have already learned that it was the nature of those birds to reel off automatically phrases drummed into them by rote, a process Schreber experiences as the unloading into his body of putrescent matter. These birds materialize the nature of the "nerve-language" more generally—language viewed under the aspect of the mechanical repetition and memorization of signifiers without regard to meaning or, as Schreber sometimes puts it, "genuine feeling." In one of his postscripts to the *Memoirs*, Schreber links the talking birds to Flechsig's "tested soul"; together they provide those "intermediary instances" [*Mittelinstanzen*] responsible for the writing-down system (235). These strange intermediaries offer one of the most compelling links between Schreber's mad cosmos and the Kafkan world of semihuman copyists, secretaries, and assorted servants. Such figures, partaking in characteristics of animal and machine, occupy an uncanny ontological domain—call it the *subal-*

tern sublime. They serve to mediate the transfer, the conversion of the materiality of meaningless, physical causes—the rote repetition of dead letters—into ideal, symbolic effects. They inhabit a space comparable with that impossible frontier that Freud identified as the locus of the drives, the site where blind nature begins to exceed itself—where the merely *sinnlich* becomes *über-sinnlich*—and is thereby converted into culture.[22] That these peculiar mediators—these "drive representatives"—appear at all, let alone command the stage of psychic and literary attention, indicates that something has gone profoundly awry with this conversion.[23]

At this point, we should pause to consider a peculiar paradox apropos of Schreber's methods of defense against the assault by the forces of mechanical repetition, of which the writing-down system is only one, more fully elaborated, instance. All such "systems" are species of that larger genus of torture, which Schreber calls *compulsive thinking* or *Denkzwang*. "Compulsive thinking," as Schreber defines it immediately after his discussion of the talking birds,

> contravenes man's natural right of mental relaxation, of temporary rest from mental activity through thinking nothing, or as the expression goes in the basic language, it disturbs the "basis" [*Untergrund*] of a human being. My nerves are influenced by the rays to vibrate corresponding to certain human words; their choice therefore is not subject to my own will, but is due to an influence exerted on me from without. (171–72)[24]

Schreber adds that what he directly feels is "that the talking voices (lately in particular the voices of the talking birds) as *inner voices* move like long threads" into his head and "there cause a painful feeling of tension through the poison of corpses which they deposit" (174), once more linking a linguistic repetition compulsion to death and abjection. It is here that Schreber introduces his paradoxical strategy of defense, which amounts to an attempt to appropriate for himself the abject site of this compulsion and, as it were, beat the psychophysical repetition machine at its own game:

> In earlier years my nerves simply had to think on, to answer questions, to complete broken-off sentences etc. Only later was I gradually able to accustom my nerves (my "basis") to ignoring the stimulation which forced them to think on, *by simply repeating the words and phrases and thus turning them into not-thinking-of-anything-thoughts*. I have done that for a long time now with conjunctions and adverbs which would need a full clause for their completion. If I hear for instance "Why, because I," or "Be it," *I repeat these words for as long as possible without attempting to complete the sense by trying to connect them with what I thought before*. (174; my emphasis)

Later in the same chapter, elaborating on his inventiveness in developing methods of defense, Schreber suggests that in addition to playing the piano and reading, he "usually found committing poems to memory a successful remedy"(176). The remedy against rote repetition, in other words, turns out to be a self-inflicted dose of rote repetition in which the content of the material mechanically committed to memory is of little or no importance:

> I learnt a great number of poems by heart particularly Schiller's ballads, long sections of Schiller's and Goethe's dramas, as well as arias from operas and humorous poems, amongst others from Max and Moritz, Struwelpeter and Spekter's fables, which I then recite in silence . . . verbatim. *Their value as poetry naturally does not matter*; however insignificant the rhymes, even obscene verses are worth their weight in gold as mental nourishment compared with the terrible nonsense my nerves are otherwise forced to listen to. (176; my emphasis)

Schreber adds to this catalog of defenses "counting aloud up to a large figure" and notes that when "severe bodily pain sets in or persistent bellowing occurs, the last remaining remedy is swearing aloud" (176).

III

Our interpretive dilemma has been, not unlike Schreber's own, to locate and identify the forces and entities producing his suffering without, however, falling back into Schreberian demonology or other, less fantastic, ideological habits of mind. We are, in other words, still very much within the Freudian project of accounting for the "demonic" in human affairs in a post-Enlightenment framework. What links Niederland's approach to Moritz Schreber and Kittler's approach to Paul Flechsig is an intuition that Schreber was traumatized not, as Freud had argued, by a close encounter with purely intrapsychic demons (i.e., previously repressed libidinal *desires*), but rather by exposure to particular forms of intersubjective *power*, in the one case, of a more paternal and pedagogical nature, in the other, of a more "scientific" and institutional kind. The advantage of Kittler's approach lies not so much in his appreciation of the differences, neglected by Niederland and others, between pedagogical and "psychophysical" power, between Moritz Schreber's child-rearing practices and Paul Flechsig's brain science, as in his insight that the possession and elaboration of certain kinds of *knowledge*—in this case, knowledge about the body, its development, and its functions—is already a form of power that can produce traumatic effects in those positioned as objects of such knowledge. Indeed,

Kittler's crucial insight about Flechsig's neuroanatomical paradigm was that the attempt to account for Schreber's demons within such a paradigm can, by way of a "dialectic of Enlightenment," actually generate more demons.

Perhaps the best characterization of the traumatizing effects of a mode of expert knowledge is offered by Schreber himself in his open letter to Flechsig inserted at the beginning of his *Memoirs*. There, as we have already seen, Schreber suggests that the aspect of Flechsig responsible for his torments—Schreber refers to this dark, Coppelius-like side of Flechsig as the latter's "tested soul"—might be correlated with Flechsig's transgression of his clinical mandate for the purposes of scientific experimentation, and that "in order to stress forcefully that this was a malpractice it was called 'soul murder'" (34–35).

In a legal essay appended to the *Memoirs*, Schreber revisits the question of the limits of psychiatric expertise and power from another direction. In this "brief," Schreber considers the question: "In what circumstances can a person considered insane be detained in an asylum against his will?" (255). Here Schreber is concerned with a transgression of the clinical mandate not into the field of *scientific* knowledge but rather into that of *forensic* knowledge; he is concerned with the participation of medical practitioners in the domain of legal questions and concerns pertaining to the rights of patients. Certainly one of the most significant contributions of Lothane's work has been to profile the role played by the new discipline of forensic psychiatry, embodied in the persons of Schreber's two psychiatrists, Paul Flechsig and Guido Weber, in Schreber's symptomatology.[25]

The establishment of forensic psychiatry as a proper domain of medical expertise and authority accompanied the rise of institutional psychiatry in Germany since the mid-nineteenth century. Of particular importance for the consolidation of the forensic dimension of psychiatric expertise was the emergence of the first antipsychiatry movement in modern Europe, a public outcry over abuses of psychiatric practices culminating in Reichstag debates in the late 1890s on insanity laws, commitment procedures, living conditions within psychiatric institutions, and the state supervision of psychiatrists. It is likely that Flechsig's extreme ideological commitment to a medical-materialist conception of mind was in some measure motivated by the political need to repair the damaged image of psychiatry by endowing it with the status of a true science.

The antipsychiatry movement in Wilhelmine Germany crystallized around a series of prominent cases, including Schreber's, in which individuals had been declared incompetent and committed to psychiatric institutions against their will. The cases became known to the public in

part through the publication of pamphlets and books in which the patients detailed their struggles with the medical and legal systems. In a speech delivered in 1896, the year he became a legal medical officer of the county court, Flechsig admitted to errors on the part of the psychiatric establishment but ultimately defended the integrity of the discipline in its scientific *and* forensic capacities:

> Among the alleged victims of the psychiatrist, who in the last years have mightily stirred public opinion, there is one group of persons occupying a prominent place, who live in a continuous state of war with the courts and the authorities. . . . These individuals, upon whose mental equilibrium state order and valid laws in many ways act as a poison, are commonly qualified as litigious . . . [or as sufferers from] *litigious paranoia* [*Querulantenwahnsinn*] . . . this question is of a predominantly practical importance also in the political sense. . . . Even if I know of no case in which a mentally healthy person has been declared mentally incompetent [*entmündigt*] on the basis of litigious paranoia . . . the psychiatrists are guilty of the error . . . of unjustifiably generalizing single observations. The so-called querulants are in no way uniformly afflicted by *psychosis* [*Wahnsinn*], they are not all of them driven by delusional *ideas*!

Flechsig concludes by insisting on the authority of the *"biologico-pathological* method of investigation" as the surest way of avoiding the errors to which an insufficiently scientific psychiatry had been heretofore susceptible.[26]

In the context of the public and parliamentary debates concerning the status of forensic psychiatry and the potential for conflicts of interest in this hybrid form of medicojuridical expertise, Flechsig actually proved to be more sensitive to the concerns of patients than many of his colleagues in the profession.[27] Schreber's expectations would have been shaped by Flechsig's reputation as a relatively propatient forensic expert. Against this background, Flechsig's decision to transfer Schreber to the public asylum at Sonnenstein would have been experienced as a particularly traumatic betrayal.[28]

Once at Sonnenstein, Schreber came under the care of Guido Weber, a psychiatrist firmly committed to the new and growing forensic authority of institutional psychiatry.[29] It was on the basis of Weber's various reports to the courts, which diagnosed Schreber as suffering from a dementia due to chronic neurological disorders, that Schreber was declared mentally incompetent and permanently retired from the bench. Beginning in 1897, Schreber undertook to have his incompetency ruling repealed; he lost these appeals in the county and district courts. In each instance, Weber's reports to the court provided the decisive forensic evidence against release. Interestingly, one of Weber's

central arguments against Schreber's efforts to have his tutelage rescinded was the latter's desire to have his *Memoirs* published. I would
like to quote at length from Weber's second report, dated November
28, 1900:

> The most important moment in judging the capacity of the patient to look
> after his own affairs is and remains the fact that he lacks insight into the
> pathological nature of the hallucinations and ideas which influence him;
> what objectively are delusions and hallucinations are to him unassailable
> truth and adequate motive for action. It follows from this that the patient's
> decisions at a given moment are quite unpredictable; he may follow and
> turn into action what his relatively intact mental powers dictate or he may
> act under the compulsion of his pathological mental processes. In this
> connection I wish to draw particular attention to a very pregnant example
> and for this reason also I enclose the patient's "Memoirs." It is understand-
> able that the patient felt the urge to describe the history of his latter years,
> to lay down his observations and sufferings in writing and to put them
> before those who have in this or that matter a lawful interest in the shape
> of his fate. But the patient harbours the urgent desire to have his "Mem-
> oirs" (as presented here) printed and made available to the widest circles
> and he is therefore negotiating with a publisher—until now of course
> without success. When one looks at the content of his writings, and takes
> into consideration the abundance of indiscretions relating to himself and
> others contained in them, the unembarrassed detailing of the most doubt-
> ful and aesthetically impossible situations and events, the use of the most
> offensive vulgar words, etc., one finds it quite incomprehensible that a
> man otherwise tactful and of fine feeling could propose an action which
> would compromise him so severely in the eyes of the public, were not his
> whole attitude to life pathological, and he unable to see things in their
> proper perspective, and if the tremendous overvaluation of his own per-
> son caused by lack of insight into his illness had not clouded his apprecia-
> tion of the limitations imposed on man by society.[30]

On July 23, 1901, having fired his lawyer, Schreber filed his own writ of
appeal with the Saxon Supreme Court, the very court of whose Third
Chamber he had been president. One year later, the Sixth Chamber of
the court rescinded Schreber's incompetency ruling; five months later,
Schreber left Sonnenstein.

Schreber's formal appeal as well as his brief forensic essay concerning the general principles of his case are, in essence, attempts to delimit
the boundaries of medical and juridical realms of power and authority.
Schreber argues that in entire classes of cases—he is thinking primarily
of patients who do not present an immediate danger to society or themselves—institutionalization represents a transgression of medical com-

petence and authority into a realm that, one might say, is in principle ignorant of the internal workings of the body or brain. In his essay, Schreber formulates this thesis as a distinction between medical and police powers: "Towards harmless mental patients the Director of a Public Asylum is after all not an organ of the security police with authoritative power, but essentially only a medical advisor; *on the question of deprivation of liberty* his relation to his patients is in no way different from that of any private practitioner towards his patients" (260). He further argues that liberty must be granted to patients even if the medical evidence speaks for institutionalization: "Should the administration [of an asylum] force this opinion on the patient (capable of managing his affairs) himself or on his legal representatives, whether persons or bodies, they would transgress the limits of their competence" (261). In effect, Schreber is arguing that the state has no mandate pertaining to the physical or mental *health* of its citizens. The only concern should be, as Schreber paraphrases the relevant legal principle in his writ of appeal, *"whether I possess the capacity for reasonable action in practical life"* (290). If the state can be confident that a citizen can manage his personal affairs, there can be no *medical* ground for the deprivation of liberty. To take the example of his compulsive bellowing, Schreber argues that it should be treated as a normal case of a disturbance of the peace—a strictly police matter. Although Schreber explains that his attacks of bellowing are not willful but rather generated by miraculous processes, his crucial point is that *medical* knowledge of his bodily or mental state would in this instance be irrelevant and, indeed, inadmissible. We might say that in conditions in accordance with the Order of the World, the *law* is ignorant of living human beings; it deals only with juridical subjects and brackets out the individual's "life substance."

In an attempt to further clarify the boundaries of medical and psychiatric competence, Schreber addresses the status of the religious beliefs and practices he had, over the course of his illness, come to maintain, above all those pertaining to his feminization: "The *only thing* which could be counted as somewhat unreasonable in the eyes of other persons is, as mentioned by the medical expert, that at times I was seen standing in front of the mirror or elsewhere with some female adornments (ribbons, trumpery necklaces, and suchlike), with the upper half of my body exposed" (300). Schreber defends this practice on several fronts. He argues first that he is very careful to engage in cross-dressing only when he is alone. He further notes that since his female adornments are for the most part rather cheap, his transvestitism cannot be cited as an example of poor judgment in the management of his financial affairs. As additional evidence of his capacity for judgment he adds that the "danger of catching cold which the medical expert considers

possible, certainly does not arise at usual room temperatures, as the example of ladies in *décolleté* sufficiently shows" (301). His final and most forceful argument in defense of cross-dressing is, however, that it is for him a religious practice, one necessitated by the special relation he has come to have with God. Regarding his delusional system in general, Schreber maintains, "I could even say with Jesus Christ: 'My Kingdom is not of this world'; my so-called delusions are concerned solely with God and the beyond; they *can* therefore *never in any way influence my behaviour* in any worldly matter" (301). He then adds: "apart from the whim already mentioned [i.e., cross-dressing], *which is also meant to impress God*" (301–2; my emphasis).

Although Schreber expresses the desire to have his body examined by scientists to verify his feminization, it is, finally, not to medical science but rather to theology and philosophy that he addresses his *Memoirs*. His response to Weber's argument that the very desire to have the *Memoirs* published be construed as a further symptom of psychopathology is to appeal precisely to those disciplines for which the radical heterogeneity of organic, bodily causes and symbolic-spiritual effects continues to be of crucial importance:

> The medical expert acknowledges . . . that the "emanations of my pathologically altered psychic state" are not, as commonly in similar cases, meagre and monotonous, but show a fantastically formed intricate structure of ideas very different from the usual way of thinking. Pursuing this remark, I plan to submit my Memoirs for examination to specialists from other fields of experience, particularly theologians and philosophers. This would serve a double purpose, firstly to prove to the judges that my "Memoirs," however strange much of their content may be, could yet form an appreciable stimulus to wider scientific circles for research in a most obscure subject and make understandable how lively my wish must be to have them published. Secondly, I would then welcome the expert opinion of men of science in the mentioned fields, so as to ascertain whether it is probable, even psychologically possible, that a human being of cool and sober mind as I used to be in the eyes of all who knew me in my earlier life, and besides a human being who . . . did *not have a firm belief in God and the immortality of the soul* before his illness, should have *sucked from his fingers* so to speak the whole complicated structure of ideas with its enormous mass of factual detail. . . . Does not rather the thought impose itself that a human being who is able to write on such matters and attain such singular ideas about the nature of God and the continued existence of the soul after death, must in fact have had some particular experiences and particular impressions from which other human beings are excluded? (296)

In the context of his more general effort to circumscribe the proper domains of medical and juridical power, Schreber's appeal to theologians and philosophers suggests an awareness that the real causes and significance of his illness are not only inaccessible to the neuroanatomical/forensic gaze embodied by Flechsig and Weber, but that exposure to that very gaze may have contributed to his derangement in the first place.[31]

IV

It is, of course, in the work of Michel Foucault that we find the most sustained analysis of just such professional gazes and the will to knowledge embodied by them.[32] Foucault's radical depsychologization of this will to knowledge is anticipated by Schreber's remarkable willingness to abstract the demonic aspect of the professional gazes disturbing his psychic equilibrium from the person of their bearers. As he puts it in his open letter to Flechsig,

> you might have continued contact with me for a time out of scientific interest, until you yourself felt as it were uneasy about it, and therefore decided to break it off. But it is possible that in this process a part of your own nerves—probably unknown to yourself—was removed from your body, a process explicable only in a supernatural manner, and ascended to heaven as a "tested soul" and there achieved some supernatural power. (34)

Schreber returns to these ideas in his writ of appeal:

> I dare not state definitely that the supernatural events with which his name [i.e., Flechsig] is connected and during which his name was *and is still daily given to me* by the voices, ever reached his awareness. It is of course a possibility that in his role as a human being he was and remains removed from these events. *The question how it is possible to speak of the soul of a still living person as different from him and existing outside his body naturally remains mysterious.* (311; my emphasis)

Freud's answer to this mystery was, as we know, that what Schreber refers to as Flechsig's "tested soul" corresponds to the *libidinal value* assigned to Flechsig in Schreber's unconscious. "Flechsig" was, thus, first and foremost the name of that upsurge of homosexual desire against which Schreber defended himself by a psychotic act of world destruction—radical withdrawal of libidinal cathexes from all objects. That inner "end of history" was, in Freud's reading, followed by an effort at self-healing, an attempt, as it were, to repopulate the world.

But because this effort took place under the sign of (homophobic) repression, this new world order had a distinctly paranoid coloration and was populated by persecutors.

Foucault's analyses of power allow us, I think, to follow Schreber much more closely and precisely in his awareness that certain kinds of expert knowledge and research paradigms—Flechsig's form of brain science, for example—may *in themselves* produce an array of maddening effects in the mind and body of a person positioned as an object of such knowledge. The particular bearer of such knowledge need *not*, in other words, have been a tyrant, a sadist, or even especially unempathic. Flechsig's *"tested* soul" becomes, in Foucault's terms, the locus of a will to knowledge that exercises power precisely by testing and examining. Indeed, it is Foucault's thesis in the first volume of his *History of Sexuality* that the domain of functions, sensations, pleasures, and perversions known as human sexuality—the primary locus of Schreber's symptoms—was largely a by-product of an institutionalized will to knowledge whose regimen of tests and examinations became, in the nineteenth century, obsessively focused on the body.[33]

The History of Sexuality, whose introductory volume was originally entitled the *La volonté de savoir* or "the will to knowledge," develops and augments analyses begun in Foucault's earlier work on the will to punish and imprison, which contains, as far as I can tell, the only direct reference to Schreber in Foucault's oeuvre.[34] Schreber appears there as a signifier for a general tendency that became dominant in the nineteenth century toward that form of individuation that allows the human life to be understood as a "case," the life story as a "case history." It was, Foucault argues, only against the background of ever expanding regimes of expert knowledge or "disciplines"—criminology, psychiatry, pedagogy, among others—that something like the "Schreber case" could first emerge and become the "classic" text that it is today. Of special interest to Foucault were the procedures of examination elaborated by the disciplines that served to interpellate the "individual as a describable, analysable object" (*Discipline*, 190):

> The examination as the fixing, at once ritual and "scientific," of individual differences, as the pinning down of each individual in his own particularity (in contrast with the ceremony in which status, birth, privilege, function are manifested with all the spectacle of their marks) clearly indicates the appearance of a new modality of power in which each individual receives as his status his own individuality, and in which he is linked by his status to the features, the measurements, the gaps, the "marks" that characterize him and make him a "case." (*Discipline*, 192)

In Foucault's view, the crucial model of the procedures of observation, examination, and registration that characterize the disciplines and therewith "constitute the individual as effect and object of power, as effect and object of knowledge" (*Discipline*, 192), was provided by Jeremy Bentham's *Panopticon*. Not simply an ingenious architectural design for an ideal prison in which the inmate would learn to internalize the agency of observation, it was, for Foucault a crucial metaphor for the technical rationality that emerged in the Enlightenment, "a figure of political technology that may and must be detached from any specific use" (*Discipline*, 205).[35]

In the context of Schreber's efforts to defend his juridical personhood against what he experienced as a transgressive expansion of psychiatric powers, Foucault's characterization of this new political technology as a kind of "counter-law" becomes especially compelling. Foucault describes the kind of power exercised within the disciplines as a kind of chronic, institutional violence that both supports and undermines the rights and liberties of the juridical subject normally seen as the primary legacy of the Enlightenment project:

> Historically, the process by which the bourgeoisie became in the course of the eighteenth century the politically dominant class was masked by the establishment of an explicit, coded and formally egalitarian juridical framework, made possible by the organization of a parliamentary, representative regime. But the development and generalization of disciplinary mechanisms constituted the other, dark side of these processes. The general juridical form that guaranteed a system of rights that were egalitarian in principle was supported by these tiny, everyday, physical mechanisms, by all those systems of micro-power that are essentially non-egalitarian and asymmetrical that we call the disciplines. And although, in a formal way, the representative regime makes it possible . . . for the will of all to form the fundamental authority of sovereignty, the disciplines provide, at the base, a guarantee of the submission of forces and bodies. . . . The contract may have been regarded as the ideal foundation of law and political power; panopticism constituted the technique, universally widespread, of coercion. . . . The "Enlightenment," which discovered the liberties, also invented the disciplines. (*Discipline*, 222)

Foucault's analysis of panoptical discipline makes it plausible to read Schreber's struggle with what I have characterized as the "obscene father" as an *agon* between these conflicting legacies of the Enlightenment: the *liberties* and the *disciplines*. This struggle must have been especially poignant for Schreber whose father's orthopedic and pediatric treatments, pedagogical theories and practices, and public health and

fitness programs offer a near caricature of those "systems of micro-power" that Foucault associates with the disciplines. Schreber's own legal philosophy and political loyalties placed him, by contrast, squarely on the side of a "formally egalitarian juridical framework," exemplified by the ideology of liberal individualism promoted by the National Liberal Party, on whose ticket Schreber ran for Parliament in 1884.[36] Schreber's struggle with the obscene, surplus father—with the demonic, "Coppelius" aspect of paternal and institutional authority—becomes legible as one between the law and a transgressive infra- or counter-law, which Foucault characterizes as an "unassimilable residue of 'delinquency'" (*Discipline*, 282) pertaining to the very functioning of the law:

> In appearance, the disciplines constitute nothing more than an infra-law. They seem to extend the general forms defined by law to the infinitesimal level of individual lives; or they appear as methods of training that enable individuals to become integrated into these general demands. They seem to constitute the same type of law on a different scale, thereby making it more meticulous and more indulgent. The disciplines should be regarded as a sort of counter-law. They have the precise role of introducing insuperable asymmetries and excluding reciprocities. . . . Moreover, whereas the juridical systems define juridical subjects according to universal norms, the disciplines characterize, classify, specialize; they distribute along a scale, around a norm, hierarchize individuals in relation to one another and, if necessary, disqualify and invalidate. In any case, in the space and during the time in which they exercise their control and bring into play the asymmetries of their power, they effect a suspension of the law that is never total, but is never annulled either. (*Discipline*, 222–23)

The characterization of disciplinary power as a counter-law secreted by and within the law—Foucault's version of the violence or force internal to law that preoccupied Benjamin in his "Critique of Violence"—exactly parallels Schreber's efforts to elucidate what he calls conditions contrary to the Order of the World, conditions under which, as we have seen, God takes an exceptional interest in and comes to have knowledge of *living human beings*. One might say, then, that the chronic state of emergency generating the bizarre array of symptoms and delusions described in the *Memoirs* was inaugurated by that partial suspension of the law effectuated by the disciplinary power to which Schreber had been exposed since early childhood and to which he was exposed again, though in a different form, in the psychiatric institutions of Flechsig and Weber; Schreber's soul murder becomes, from this perspective, a sustained traumatization induced by exposure to, as it were, *fathers who knew too much* about living human beings. Cer-

tainly Foucault's most "Schreberian" insight is that exposure to this excess of knowledge that characterizes the disciplines produces a new kind of "intensified" body, one that, in a certain sense, recollects and travesties the sublime body of the king.[37] And for Schreber as well as for Foucault, such an intensification of the body is first and foremost a *sexualization*.

Foucault's central thesis in *The History of Sexuality* is that sexuality, understood in its modern sense as a defining and essential feature of human existence, as the locus of one's core identity, the expression of which comes to be seen as a form of *self*-expression considered to be crucial for one's mental and physical well-being—that sexuality in this sense is largely a product of a panoptical attentiveness focused on the body and its sensations. This attentiveness is, for Foucault, manifest above all in the proliferation of medical, psychiatric, pedagogical, and other "professional" discourses addressed to questions of human sexuality that achieved a critical density in the nineteenth century, culminating in the formation of a "science of sexuality." It is easy to recognize in Foucault's description of this discursive production of sexuality the precise pattern of Schreber's struggle first with Flechsig's "tested soul" and then with the "rays of God," a struggle that, as we know, produced ever greater degrees of sexual excitation, culminating in Schreber's mutation into a woman completely saturated with sexuality:

> More than the old taboos, this form of power demanded constant, attentive, and curious presences for its exercise; it presupposed proximities; it proceeded through examination and insistent observation. . . . It implied a physical proximity and an interplay of intense sensations. . . . The power which . . . took charge of sexuality set about contacting bodies, caressing them with its eyes, intensifying areas, electrifying surfaces, dramatizing troubled moments. It wrapped the sexual body in its embrace. There was undoubtedly an increase in effectiveness and an extension of the domain controlled; but also a sensualization of power and a gain of pleasure. . . . Power operated as a mechanism of attraction; it drew out those peculiarities over which it kept watch. Pleasure spread to the power that harried it; power anchored the pleasure it uncovered. (*History*, 44–45)

Foucault's characterization of the *"perpetual spirals of power and pleasure"* (*History*, 45), generated within the overproximities of medical examinations, psychiatric investigations, pedagogical reports, and family controls, accords exactly with Schreber's encounter with a God who demands from him the perpetual cultivation of jouissance.[38] Indeed, Schreber's repeated requests that he be examined by scientists to confirm the spread of nerves of "feminine voluptuousness" throughout his body might be understood as a distorted confirmation of Foucault's

thesis that the sexual agitation he experiences is in large measure produced by such "scientific" examinations.

This sexual agitation was, as we now know, experienced by Schreber
as a transgression of the laws normally regulating relations between
God and living human beings, laws that normally impose on the former *ignorance* of somatic depths and sensations, of, in a word, the life
substance. What Schreber characterizes as conditions contrary to the
Order of the World corresponds, then, quite closely with what Foucault
refers to as the "juridical regression" (*History*, 144) which obtains when
law becomes entangled in the management of *life*, a state of affairs
which is for Foucault and, I would suggest, for Schreber, a defining
feature of modernity:

> For the first time in history, no doubt, biological existence was reflected
> in political existence; the fact of living was no longer an inaccessible
> substrate that only emerged from time to time . . . ; part of it passed into
> knowledge's field of control and power's sphere of intervention. Power
> would no longer be dealing simply with legal subjects over whom the
> ultimate dominion was death, but with living beings, and the mastery it
> would be able to exercise over them would have to be applied at the level
> of life itself; it was the taking charge of life, more than the threat of death,
> that gave power its access even to the body. If one can apply the term
> *bio-history* to the pressures through which the movements of life and the
> processes of history interfere with one another, one would have to speak
> of *bio-power* to designate what brought life and its mechanisms into the
> realm of explicit calculations and made knowledge-power an agent of
> transformation of human life. (*History*, 142–43)

When God's legitimate involvement with the *dead* as well as ignorance
of *living human beings* is, so to speak, perverted by knowledge of the life
substance, society has reached, as Foucault puts it, its "threshold of
modernity" (*History*, 143).

Foucault further characterizes this tension between competing forms
of power as one between a "deployment of alliance" (i.e., a "system of
marriage, of fixation and development of kinship ties, of *transmission of
names and possessions*"), on the one hand, and a "deployment of sexuality," on the other, which in its turn "has been linked from the outset
with an *intensification of the body*—with its exploitation as an object of
knowledge and an element in relations of power" (*History*, 106–7; my
emphasis). The two systems provide the matrix of Schreber's struggle
with the sexualizing and soul-murdering power that, as he puts it, created a rent in the miraculous structure of the world and threw into
disarray the symbolic ordering of names and titles regulating relations

within and between (Schreber and Flechsig) family lines and generations. The "case" of Daniel Paul Schreber no doubt owes much of its
fascination to the fact that it brings into such sharp relief a moment of
crisis in this history of tension between different forms and systems of
power and authority.[39]

V

According to Foucault, the techniques elaborated by the institutions of
disciplinary knowledge function as methods of training that serve, as
he puts it, to "extend the general forms defined by law to the infinitesi-
mal level of individual lives" and thereby to "enable individuals to
become integrated into these general demands" (*Discipline*, 222). Such
methods of training are the subject of Moritz Schreber's important
book on child rearing, *Kallipädie*, published in 1858 as a practical guide
for parents, educators, and teachers.[40]

Moritz Schreber's book, which represents a grand synthesis of his
medical and pedagogical thought, is in essence a detailed pediatric,
hygienic, and educational program for fostering in children the central
values of Enlightenment ideology and culture, above all a sense of individual moral agency and autonomy.[41] The book is divided into four
main parts, each dedicated to a phase in the life of the child: the first
year ("infancy"); two to seven ("age of play"); eight to sixteen ("age of
learning"); seventeen to twenty ("coming of age: transition to independence"). Each section is in turn divided into two subsections addressing the physical and mental sides of life, respectively, which are in turn
subdivided into discussions of behaviors and activities appropriate to
each phase of life and the things parents and teachers can do to control
and regulate them. Among the topics covered are nutrition, movement
and exercise, sleeping habits and positions, posture, hygienic practices,
and forms of play. The entire program is organized around rituals and
procedures of repetition and habituation. These rituals are designed
not only to instill certain behaviors in the child; they aim also to convert
these behaviors elicited in *heteronomous* fashion (i.e., by means of external commands and pressures) into behaviors willed by the child *auton-
omously*, of its own free volition. The goal is, in other words, that habits inculcated by the sheer (and repetitious) force of parental authority
and the child's absolute obedience to that authority be "sublimated," as
he puts it, "to an act of free will," and "that obedience become self-
conscious." "The child," he continues, "should not become the slave
of another will, but rather be educated toward a noble independence

and the full strength of his own will." "This transition," as is claimed repeatedly in the book, *"is made much easier by the prior habituation"* (*Kallipädie*, 135; my emphasis).[42]

That Moritz Schreber's program is designed to produce proper Enlightenment subjects capable of thinking (the right things) for themselves is most evident in his remarks on religious education. As a Lutheran and a Kantian, Moritz Schreber associates true religiosity with a person's capacity to experience and to heed the inner voice of reason and conscience. For that reason, he insists that a child be protected from coercive impositions of religious practices and that regular visits to church first begin at the age of twelve. Otherwise the child is in danger of forever confusing the dead letter of religious doctrine—one can't help but think of Schreber's phrase for rote repetition: "poison of corpses"—with the voice of authentic spiritual authority:

> *This spirit, which stands in the most intimate, God-given relationship with the kernel of our selfhood [dem Kernpunkte unseres Ichs], with the freedom of conscience, thought, and will—this we do not allow to be robbed from us, which occurs when it is subordinated to the letter. The compulsion to believe that comes from the outside is the death of true religiosity. Thousands of people are thereby driven to (open or dissimulated) irreligiousness, or among the more impressionable souls some even to religious insanity.* (*Kallipädie*, 255; emphasis in original)

Here he adds a footnote in which he acknowledges, close to forty years before the outbreak of his own son's "religious insanity," that *"in recent years observations of alienists have established a significant increase of such cases . . . especially among the female sex"* (*Kallipädie*, 255; italics in original). True faith, he continues, presupposes that the object of faith be *"thought through or felt through, spiritually digested, appropriated, transformed into the blood of spirit [Geistesblut]"* (*Kallipädie*, 255; emphasis in original).

We might say, then, that Moritz Schreber's program offers a practical guide for fostering the proper metabolization—conversion into second "nature"—of the principles and values of enlightened Christian culture. It is, in short, a systematic training program for the Enlightenment, a kind of instruction manual for parents to supplement Kant's philosophical formulation of Enlightenment values. Foucault's analyses of power suggest, however, that just such a disciplinary supplement may ultimately serve to undermine the values they are intended to promote. One of the lessons of Foucault's work is that the disciplinary side of Enlightenment culture represents a chronic endangerment to its ethical, political, and juridical project. Rather than fostering a capacity for independent thought and volition, rather than attuning the body to the inner voice of reason and conscience, programs such as

those of Moritz Schreber for the regulation of a child's physical, mental, and spiritual development, well meaning though they may be, may end up producing what, from the perspective of Enlightenment culture, can only be called monstrosities. Foucault's studies of the disciplines and the emergence of what he calls "bio-power" are, in effect, elaborations of a fundamental paradox at the heart of the Enlightenment project, a paradox related to what Adorno and Horkheimer famously theorized as that project's dialectical undoing: the "scientific" knowledge that accompanies and puts into practice the principles of Enlightenment culture, that seeks to foster, in the terms of technical rationality, the cultivation—the *Bildung*—of Enlightenment subjects, is marked by a kind of aberrant and "perverse" productivity.

To put these matters in somewhat different terms, we might say that the *conversion of heteronomy into autonomy* so crucial to Moritz Schreber's medicopedagogical system leaves a residue of heteronomy—of *Leichengift* ("poison of corpses"), as Schreber would say—that not only resists metabolization (transmutation into *Geistesblut*) but returns to haunt and derange the subject whose physical, moral, and aesthetic cultivation that system was designed to achieve. It was, I would suggest, Schreber's overexposure to this nonmetabolizable remainder of the rituals of Enlightenment *assujetissement*—the social processes whereby one is interpellated as an autonomous subject—that predisposed him to experience that sexualized wretchedness that would later constitute his "secret" status as *Luder*.[43] What Foucault calls disciplinary power is potentially so damaging not because it opposes the principles of Enlightenment or the liberal values of Schreber's National Liberal Party—rule of law, universal rights of property and contract—from some exterior cultural domain, but rather because it in effect *literalizes* the "performative magic" sustaining the authority of those values and the institutions built upon them. The disciplines transform the performative dimension of *symbolic* authority into regulations for the *material* control and administration of bodies and populations. Such a literalization has the effect of reversing the most fundamental processes whereby humans are initiated into a world of symbolic form and function.[44] For Schreber, as we know, signification is repeatedly drawn back into the bodily depths, symbolic function repeatedly experienced in a register of purely biomechanical causation (e.g., vibration of nerve fibers, deposits of putrid matter).

Although never stated as such, Foucault's fundamental insight about psychosis would seem to be that the psychotic's entanglement in "the real" of his intensified body, his repeated failure to convert soma into signification—this blockage seems to be the crux of what Schreber means by *conditions contrary to the Order of the World*—is at least in part

brought about by exposure to the literalizing tendencies of disciplinary power, specifically forms of power conceived as direct interventions in and manipulations of somatic existence. What Foucault associates with juridical power and the "deployment of alliance" are, by contrast, eminently *symbolic functions*: marriage systems, kinship ties, transmission of names, titles, and possessions. Put somewhat differently, the domain of juridical power in the broad sense used by Foucault is structured around laws of *symbolic causation* (e.g., one's becoming a *Senatspräsident* is "caused" by an official act of nomination). When this symbolic or pseudocausality, on which all acts of symbolic investiture depend, becomes chronically dysfunctional, we have crossed the threshold into a psychotic realm of extreme literalization. Foucault's Schreberian point would seem to be that disciplinary power fosters this chronic dysfunction. Schreber's struggle with Flechsig, Weber, and, no doubt, with his own father, to limit the reach of the disciplines and to clear a space for the rule of law, which, as Schreber insists, must remain ignorant of living human beings and their bodies, might thus be conceived against the backdrop of a Foucauldian variation of Freud's famous maxim: *Wo Es war, soll Ich werden*. In Foucauldian terms, this imperative would run something like: Where It, the proliferation of disciplinary power, is, there the juridical subject, the subject of *symbolic* power and authority, must (re)emerge.

VI

It would, however, be a mistake to see in such an imperative the essence of Foucault's intellectual or political position regarding the proliferation of disciplinary power in the modern period. Foucault's apparent nostalgia for all that he associates with the "deployment of alliance" is not his last word on these matters. Indeed, Foucault's ambivalent position with regard to psychoanalysis is tied to his understanding of Freud's innovation as a failure to come to terms with the radical transformations brought about by the new techniques of power, a failure caused by just such a nostalgia. According to Foucault, psychoanalysis attempts "to reinscribe the thematic of sexuality in the system of law, the symbolic order, and sovereignty" (*History*, 150). He suggests that it was the great surge of racism and the proliferation of racial theories of degeneration that led Freud "to ground sexuality in the law—the law of alliance, tabooed consanguinity, and the Sovereign-Father, in short, to surround desire with all the trappings of the old order of power" (*History*, 150). Although this allegiance to "system of law, the symbolic order, and sovereignty" guaranteed that psychoanal-

ysis was "in theoretical and practical opposition to fascism," Foucault insists on the fundamental blindness of psychoanalysis to the crucial features of its own historical moment. For "to conceive the category of the sexual in terms of the law, death, blood, and sovereignty . . . is in the last analysis a historical 'retro-version.'" Psychoanalysis fails, in other words, in the essential historical task of conceiving "the deployment of sexuality on the basis of the techniques of power that are contemporary with it" (History, 150).[45]

Foucault's ambivalence concerning psychoanalysis and its attempt to theorize sexuality around issues of law, taboo, and desire—in a word, around oedipal relations—has a close parallel in Schreber's Memoirs.[46] Earlier in this chapter, we noted a paradox apropos of one of Schreber's strategies of defense against the tortures suffered under conditions contrary to the Order of the World, conditions marked by the collapse of symbolic function into the symptoms of an "intensified" body. We saw that Schreber found relief from the torments of rote repetition not only by struggling to recuperate meaning from these mechanically reproduced signifiers, but also by the reverse strategy of beating the repetition machine at its own game. Rather than simply trying to restore the lawful syntax and semantics of his "prelapsarian" symbolic order, Schreber finds a way to meet his symptoms on their own terms and thereby gain a modicum of mastery over them. Kittler has characterized this strategy as a prefiguration of avant-garde artistic practices. Like so many modernist experimenters, Schreber deploys a parodically mimetic mode of defense: he mimes the mechanical and the mechanistic in order not to be reduced to the status of a psychophysical machine: "In the Sonnenstein asylum high above the Elbe, a solitary and unrecognized experimenter practiced the apotropaic techniques that twelve years later would win fame and a public for the Zurich Dadaists in the Café Voltaire."[47] Schreber discovers what might be called the paradox of modernist masochism. Engulfed by a meaningless chatter of voices and inarticulate noise, Schreber survives, at least in part, by momentarily refusing to make sense of it all and by himself becoming a player in the ruination of meaning. Rather than trying to restore his symbolic identity by repressing the drive dimension underlying it, he finds a kind of relief by entering more deeply into its patterns of repetition and acting them out.[48] Whether this strategy could be called "modernist," "avant-garde," or already "postmodernist," it was surely linked, for Schreber, to his feminization. Schreber experiences exposure to the dimension of nonsensical drivenness at the core of his own identity as an elite and powerful heterosexual male—a dimension he finds "doubled" in the uncanny, Coppelius-like aspect of Flechsig—as the beginnings of his unmanning.[49]

VII

We might clarify some of these implications by way of reference to recent theoretical work on gender identity. Schreber's "perverse" strategy of identifying with his *Ludertum,* an eroticized condition of abjection produced at least in part through excessive and chronic proximity to the normative pressures of disciplinary power, is consistent with much of what Judith Butler has argued in her groundbreaking study, *Gender Trouble.*[50] Butler claims, in essence, that gender identities are constituted in and through socially regulated *performances,* that gender is a *social fact* produced, and not simply expressed, through the performances one is *compelled to repeat* as a member of the social group. When, in other words, a doctor or parent establishes the fact of a newborn's gender, the speech act enunciating that fact—"it's a girl"—is, in other words, not simply a constative speech act; it is also, in part, a performative one. In human culture, gender is *established* not simply in the sense of ascertaining and certifying, but also in the sense of constituting and setting up what must then be (performatively) elaborated.[51] One of the central tasks of disciplinary power, as Butler glosses that Foucauldian notion, is to regulate particular gender performances, to compel their rule-governed repetitions and thereby to guarantee the social intelligibility of the sexed body. But because no performative gesture or utterance can be completely predicted or controlled—an insight that Schreber invokes apropos of the writing-down-system's failure to exhaust his inventory of possible utterances and thoughts—the social laws and institutions regulating gender performances can never achieve full consistency. Rather, such laws will always exhibit an inadvertent and aberrant productivity, the possibility, namely, of deviant, "queer" performances. Butler suggests that such queer performances do not exist in a space or time "before" or "outside" of the law they appear to transgress but are rather secretions *of* the law, points at which the secret of the law's performative "ground"—its ultimate dependence on the compulsion to repeat—is, so to speak, leaked to the public. At such moments, the compulsion to repeat that otherwise serves to stabilize gender identities can become the pulsive force whereby such identities are disrupted and shattered. Butler's political project strives to enlist that pulsive force—what I have called the drive dimension of symbolic function—in the service of a new conception of moral and political *agency;* indeed, her project might even be characterized as an *ethicopolitics of the drive*:

> As a process, signification harbors within itself what the epistemological discourse refers to as "agency." The rules that govern intelligible identity,

i.e., that enable and restrict the intelligible assertion of an "I," rules that are partially structured along matrices of gender hierarchy and compulsory heterosexuality, operate through *repetition*. . . . The subject is not *determined* by the rules through which it is generated because signification is *not a founding act, but rather a regulated process of repetition* that both conceals itself and enforces its rules precisely through the production of substantializing effects. In a sense, all signification takes place within the orbit of the compulsion to repeat; "agency," then, is to be located within the possibility of a variation on that repetition. If the rules governing signification not only restrict, but enable the assertion of alternative domains of cultural intelligibility, i.e., new possibilities for gender that contest the rigid codes of hierarchical binarisms, then it is only *within* the practices of repetitive signifying that a subversion of identity becomes possible. The injunction *to be* a given gender produces necessary failures, a variety of incoherent configurations that in their multiplicity exceed and defy the injunction by which they are generated.[52]

Particularly these last remarks could be read as a commentary on Schreber's discovery of a kind of "Dadaist" agency in his strategy of repeating back in parodic form the phrases mechanically repeated by the voices—his way, in other words, of transforming abjection, the "poison of corpses," into cure.

In subsequent work, Butler has revisited questions of gender and sexuality from the perspective of a new conception of *matter* understood "not as site or surface, but as *a process of materialization that stabilizes over time to produce the effect of boundary, fixity, and surface we call matter.*"[53] In this later work, Butler shows a far greater sensitivity than previously to the kinds of "gender trouble" suffered by a Schreber, to the enormous pain and psychic disequilibrium that can follow when one finds oneself at the place of the law's "perverse" productivity. In a word, she attends to the link between "gender trouble" and trauma: "The normative force of performativity—its power to establish what qualifies as 'being'—works not only through reiteration, but through exclusion as well. And in the case of bodies, those exclusions haunt signification as its abject borders or as that which is strictly foreclosed: the unlivable, the nonnarrativizable, the traumatic."[54] If Schreber has anything to teach us about these matters, it is surely that the bodies which find themselves at the place of *abjection*—of that sexualized wretchedness denoted by the title *Luder*—are those which have been positioned in closest proximity to the drive dimension of symbolic function, bodies in which a society "deposits" its knowledge of what Schreber repeatedly refers to as *enjoyment*. And if Foucault is right that disciplinary power "intensifies" the body, produces rather than represses sexuality, then it is because such power *literalizes* the scandal-

ous dependence of socially established ontologies on performativity-as-repetition-compulsion—on what Schreber has characterized as a certain (normally repressed, normally secret) *rottenness* internal to every symbolic identity.

VIII

Finally, Schreber's own language suggests that this perverse dependence is intimately connected to that most problematic of Freudian agencies, the *superego*. In a sense, Schreber defines the superego as a *super ego*, that is, as the ego-drives of the "big Other": God's instincts of self-preservation manifest in the miracles to which he subjects Schreber to defend against the latter's forces of attraction. "I have no doubt," he writes in his last postscript to the *Memoirs*,

> that God, in His relation to me, is ruled by egoism. . . . Egoism, particularly in the form of the instinct of self-preservation, which at times demands the sacrifice of other beings for one's own existence, *is a necessary quality of all living beings*; individuals cannot do without it, if they are not themselves to perish. . . . *God is a living Being* and would Himself have to be ruled by egoistic motives, if other living beings existed who could endanger Him or in some way be detrimental to His interests. *In circumstances in accordance with the Order of the World there could not be, nor indeed were there, such beings next to God*; this *is the only reason* why the question of God's egoism could not arise as long as these circumstances remained in unadulterated purity. But in my case different circumstances have set in as an exception; since God by tolerating tested souls—probably in connection with occurrences of a soul-murder-like character—had tied Himself to a single human being by whom He had to let Himself be attracted, albeit unwillingly, the conditions for egoistic actions were given. These egoistic actions have been practiced against me for years with the utmost cruelty and disregard as only a beast deals with its prey. (251–52)

Conditions contrary to the Order of the World are, in a word, conditions in which the superego, which Schreber, like Freud, associates with law and morality, takes on a cruel and obscene aspect. One of Schreber's most persistent symptoms, the so-called bellowing miracle or *Brüllwunder*, might indeed be understood as Schreber's horrified response to the torments of this punishing superego. But as we have seen, his most effective and fully worked out response to this divine superego pressure is to provide that "agency" with enjoyment, more precisely, with feminine enjoyment. Schreber actually identifies the period—November 1895—when he began to embrace and to elaborate,

by means of, among other "perverse" procedures, cross-dressing, the damage caused by exposure to this superego:[55]

> I remember the period distinctly; it coincided with a number of beautiful autumn days when there was a heavy morning mist on the Elbe. During that time the signs of a transformation into a woman became so marked on my body, that I could no longer ignore the imminent goal at which the whole development was aiming. In the immediately preceding nights my male sexual organs might actually have been retracted had I not resolutely set my will against it, still following the stirring of my sense of manly honour. . . . Soul-voluptuousness had become so strong that I myself received the impression of a female body, first on my arms and hands, later on my legs, bosom, buttocks and other parts of my body. . . . Several days' observations of these events sufficed to change the direction of my will completely. Until then I still considered it possible that . . . it would eventually be necessary for me to end [my life] by suicide. . . . But now I could see beyond doubt that the Order of the World imperiously demanded my unmanning, whether I personally liked it or not, and that therefore . . . nothing was left to me but reconcile myself to the thought of being transformed into a woman. Nothing of course could be envisaged as a further consequence of unmanning but fertilization by divine rays for the purpose of creating new human beings. (148)

Schreber notes that this change of will was facilitated by his belief that all of mankind had already perished. He also adds that there existed rays that worked to hinder his unmanning by appealing to his sense of manly honor with phrases such as "Are you not ashamed in front of your wife?" or "Fancy a person who was a *Senatspräsident* allowing himself to be f . . . d" (148). He did not, however, allow himself to be diverted from that behavior which, as he puts it, "I had come to recognize as essential and curative for all parties—myself and the rays" (148). He even proclaims a kind of manifesto of femininity: "Since then I have wholeheartedly inscribed the cultivation of femininity on my banner, and I will continue to do so as far as consideration of my environment allows, whatever other people who are ignorant of the supernatural reasons may think of me" (149). Schreber acknowledges that his yielding of the phallic prerogative and cultivation of femininity is really a forced choice: "I would like to meet the man who, faced with the choice of either becoming a demented human being in male habitus or a spirited woman, would not prefer the latter. Such and *only such* is the issue for me" (149).[56]

Though Schreber did indeed find a way to enjoy and to cultivate his unmanning, a certain ambiguity attaches to this enjoyment. Schreber's own formulations indicate that his cultivation of femininity is intended

Family portrait of the Schrebers, 1851. (Courtesy of Zvi Lothane)

above all *for the enjoyment of God*. It is God who, as Schreber puts it, "demands *constant enjoyment*" and it is Schreber's duty "to provide Him with it in the form of highly developed soul-voluptuousness" (209), a duty he is able to fulfill only by means of various perverse procedures. These include imagining himself as "man and woman in one person having intercourse" with himself or standing in front of a mirror with bared upper body, adorned only with ribbons and jewelry (208, 207). "I believe," Schreber writes, "that God would never attempt to withdraw (which always impairs my bodily well-being considerably) . . . if only I could *always* be playing the woman's part in sexual embrace with myself, *always* rest my gaze on female beings, *always* look at female pictures, etc." (210). To emphasize that these various perverse behaviors are cultivated above all for the enjoyment of God, Schreber adds: "If I can get a little sensuous pleasure in this process, I feel I am entitled to it as a small compensation for the excess of suffering and privation that has been mine for many years past" (209).[57]

The point not to be missed, however, is that Schreber's relation to the divine ego/superego does *not* work to deny the scandal of what he

repeatedly refers to as God's lack of omnipotence and omniscience. On the contrary, his cultivation of femininity must be understood as a means of keeping this unnerving secret well in the foreground of his—and the reader's—awareness. Schreber's elaboration of his *Ludertum* is, in other words, the exact opposite of a fetishistic disavowal. It is rather a way of structuring a relation to *God's desire*, to the revelation that this ultimate master's knowledge and powers are *lacking*. Schreber's perversion is, I am suggesting, precisely his way of *refusing* the "normal" path of the fetish, the "normal" process of disavowing a master's lack.[58] If, as Freud insisted, God occupies the place of the father formerly occupied by Moritz Schreber and then Paul Flechsig, Schreber's delusional system is not, in the end, designed to repair the imperfections and inconsistencies of these paternal masters but rather to elaborate a *modus vivendi* with the lack manifest in them. Indeed, by publishing his *Memoirs*, Schreber performs an eminently *democratic* gesture: he insists on sharing his crisis, on disseminating its significance as a general state of emergency of symbolic authority that touches everyone, but above all those who occupy elite positions of institutional power.[59] In Wilhelmine Germany and late nineteenth-century Europe more generally, that meant of course not only *men* of a certain class but of a certain religious confession as well, which, at the fin de siècle, came to be understood in *racial* terms. In the following chapter we will explore the ways in which Schreber's text not only registers these other social and cultural dimensions but becomes legible as a forceful intervention in the European debates on the "Jewish question."

Moritz Schreber, ca. 1855.
(Courtesy of Zvi Lothane)

Pauline Schreber, ca. 1855.
(Courtesy of Zvi Lothane)

Daniel Paul Schreber.
(Courtesy of Zvi Lothane)

Sabine Schreber. (Courtesy of Zvi Lothane)

Daniel Paul Schreber and his adopted daughter, Fridoline, ca. 1906.
(Courtesy of Zvi Lothane)

Paul Emil Flechsig, 1906. (Photograph by Nichola Perscheid;
courtesy of Zvi Lothane)

THREE

SCHREBER'S JEWISH QUESTION

I

IN THE PAGES of Schreber's *Memoirs* one finds numerous references and allusions to historical events, circumstances, and figures in Wilhelmine Germany and in European culture and society more generally. One cluster of references to contemporary political life that attracted the early notice of commentators attentive to the historical context of Schreber's delusions centers on Bismarck's struggles with the Catholic Church in the 1870s, the so-called Kulturkampf. Bismarck's antipapal campaign, aggressively supported by the liberal parties and designed, in large measure, to limit the power of the (Catholic) Centrist Party, resulted in, among other things, the institution of civil marriage in Prussia, the extension of state authority over ordinations of priests and ministers, and restrictions of church supervision of schools. The most aggressive governmental measures to emerge from the Kulturkampf, measures suggesting a paranoid core to this entire campaign against transmontanism, were reserved for the Jesuits whose institutions were systematically dismantled. To indicate the extent of the Kulturkampf and its effects, Gordon Craig notes that by 1876, due to the imprisonment and expulsion of clerics refusing to comply with the new state regulations of religious institutions, some 1,400 parishes were left without incumbents.[1]

In the fifth chapter of his *Memoirs*, immediately after introducing the notion of the "nerve-language" as the medium through which, among other "miracles," the painful practice of "compulsive thinking" was maintained, Schreber begins to connect his personal struggle to larger politicotheological motifs largely derived from the Kulturkampf. Recalling the period during which the influence emanating from Flechsig's nerves was supplemented by a series of "departed souls," Schreber writes,

> In this connection I could mention hundreds if not thousands of names, many of which I learnt later, when some contact with the outside world was restored to me through newspapers and letters, were still among the living; whereas at the time, when as souls they were in contact with my nerves, I could only think they had long since departed this life. Many of the bearers of these names were particularly interested in religion, many

were Catholics who expected a furtherance of Catholicism from the way I was expected to behave, particularly the Catholicizing of Saxony and Leipzig; amongst them were the Priest S. in Leipzig, "14 Leipzig Catholics" (of whom only the name of the Consul General D. was indicated to me, presumably a Catholic Club or its board). The Jesuit Father S. in Dresden, the Ordinary Archbishop in Prague, the Cathedral Dean Moufang, the Cardinals Rampolla, Galimberti and Casati, the Pope himself who was the leader of a peculiar "scorching ray," finally numerous monks and nuns; on one occasion 240 Benedictine Monks under the leadership of a Father whose name sounded like Starkiewicz, suddenly moved into my head to perish therein. (70–71)

In the next chapter, Schreber recalls that various political and religious events had played an important part in his visions. He notes, for example, that "a widespread Catholicizing was said to have taken place; my own mother was to have been converted, I myself was continually the object of attempts at conversion by Catholics" (85). Schreber later offers a quasi-physiological, neuroanatomical metaphor for such efforts at conversion: "'Jesuits,' that is to say departed souls of former Jesuits, repeatedly tried to put into my head a different 'determinant nerve' [*Bestimmungsnerven*], which was to change my awareness of my own identity" (99). Finally, attempting to elucidate the period in early April 1894 that he calls the "time of the first Divine Judgment," Schreber writes that this particularly concentrated series of religious and political epiphanies was based on "one common basic *general idea*":

> This was the idea that after a crisis dangerous for the existence of the realms of God which had arisen in the circles of the German people through the conflict between Professor Flechsig and myself, the German people, particularly Protestant Germany, could no longer be left with the leadership as God's chosen people, had perhaps even to be excluded altogether when other "globes" ("inhabited planets?") were occupied, unless a champion appeared for the German people to prove their continued worth. At one time I myself was to be that champion, at another a person chosen by me. (92)[2]

It may not be surprising that a man who failed to win a seat in the Reichstag on a National Liberal ticket, a party counting among the most aggressive anti-Catholic forces during the Kulturkampf, should, in paranoid hindsight, see himself as a victim of a transmontane conspiracy. There was, as I have noted, already a rather strong dose of paranoia in the initial and ultimately ill-fated antipapal campaign initiated by Bismarck and his supporters.[3] But when one reads further in those passages of the *Memoirs* concerned with the threats emanating

from Catholics and Jesuits, one discovers that the focus of Schreber's fantasies about political and religious conspiracies periodically shifts from the Catholics to the Jews. This shift of focus within Schreber's fantasy space was, in many ways, prefigured by the course of events in Germany in the decade prior to his first mental collapse, namely the deepening discontent with and eventual abandonment of the policies instituted against the Catholics and, more important, the widespread revival and increasing social acceptability of anti-Semitic discourses and sentiments, particularly in the wake of the stock market crash of 1873. To return to Schreber, one might say that at certain points in the *Memoirs* his Kulturkampf fantasies begin to secrete a deeper level of preoccupation with the "Jewish question." The mediating or transitional term between these clusters of motifs would appear to be "Slavism," a signifier allowing Schreber to shift the focus of his politico-religious preoccupations from Polish Catholics—a crucial target in the Kulturkampf—to Eastern European Jews.

The previously cited passage in which Schreber recalls the 240 Benedictine Monks who, under the leadership of a priest whose name sounded like Starkiewicz, perished in his head, continues as follows:

> In the case of other souls, religious interests were mixed with national motives; amongst these was a Viennese nerve specialist whose name by coincidence was identical with that of the above mentioned Benedictine Father, a baptised Jew and Slavophile, who wanted to make Germany Slavic through me and at the same time wanted to institute there the rule of Judaism; like Professor Flechsig for Germany, England and America (that is mainly Germanic States), he appeared to be in his capacity as nerve specialist a kind of administrator of God's interests in another of God's provinces (the Slavic parts of Austria). (71)

And in a later chapter, in the midst of an inventory of miraculous bodily transformations undergone since his contact with divine rays began, Schreber reports that "already during my stay in Flechsig's Asylum the Viennese nerve specialist named in chapter 5 miraculously produced in place of my healthy natural stomach a very inferior so-called 'Jew's stomach'" (133).

But certainly the most remarkable reference to Jews in Schreber's text occurs where Schreber addresses the phenomenon by means of which the Order of the World is able to weather extremes of decadence and moral decay among mortals:

> When on some star moral decay ("voluptuous excesses") or perhaps nervousness has seized the whole of mankind to such an extent that the forecourts of heaven . . . could not be expected to be adequately replen-

ished . . . or there was reason to fear a dangerous increase of attraction on God's nerves, then the destruction of the human race could occur either spontaneously (through annihilating epidemics, etc.) or, being decided on by God, be put into effect by means of earthquakes, deluges, etc. . . . In such an event, in order to maintain the species, one single human being was spared—perhaps the relatively most moral—called by the voices that talk to me the *"Eternal Jew."* (73)[4]

Given the salvific role assigned to this Eternal or Wandering Jew and the fact that a non-Jew is to assume his place, Schreber suggests that this "appellation has . . . a somewhat different sense from that underlying the legend of the same name of the Jew Ahasver" and goes on to link him to a series of other mythical "survivor" figures such as Noah, Deucalion and Pyrrha, and Romulus and Remus. In the context of Schreber's *Memoirs*, however, the most salient feature of the Wandering Jew is his status as a feminized (i.e., unmanned) survivor and savior:

The Eternal Jew . . . had to be *unmanned* (transformed into a woman) to be able to bear children. This process of unmanning consisted in the (external) male genitals (scrotum and penis) being retracted into the body and the internal sexual organs being at the same time transformed into the corresponding female sexual organs, a process which might have been completed in a sleep lasting hundreds of years. (73–74)

After noting that this process was prevented from occurring in its purity and in accordance with the Order of the World due to the interference of Flechsig's impure rays and those of other "tested souls," Schreber continues his characterization of the Eternal Jew:

The Eternal Jew was maintained and provided with the necessary means of life by the "fleeting-improvised-men" . . . that is to say souls were for this purpose transitorily put into human shape by miracles, probably not only for the lifetime of the Eternal Jew himself but for many generations, until his offspring were sufficiently numerous to be able to maintain themselves. This seems to be the main purpose of the institution of "fleeting-improvised-men" in the Order of the World. (74)

Schreber adds in a footnote that "perhaps in some vastly dim and distant period of the past and on other stars, there might even have been a number of Eternal Jews," and that "amongst them occurred, if I am not mistaken, something like the name of a Polish Count Czartorisky" (74).

Commentators on Schreber have pursued the thread of the Jewish question in the *Memoirs* by, in effect, applying Freud's approach to dreams and parapraxes to the vast array of proper names that populate

Schreber's text. As I have already suggested, the more one digs into the names linked with the Kulturkampf, the more one discovers traces of a deeper preoccupation with the Jews. While exploring the passage cited here in which Schreber's anxieties about Catholics are first registered, Niederland, for example, discovered that there was a crucial anomaly in the list of cardinals provided by Schreber ("the Cardinals Rampolla, Galimberti and Casati"). Casati, it turns out, was not a church dignitary but rather an Italian major and explorer who participated in African expeditions led by Emin Pasha and, after a break with Pasha, by Stanley. He became known in Germany through the translation, in 1891, of his account of his adventures with Pasha (*Dieci Anni in Equatoria*). Niederland has suggested that some of Schreber's delusions of catastrophic epidemics and strange journeys might have been appropriated from Casati's memoir. In the present context, however, it is Casati's link to Pasha that is of interest. Emin Pasha, alias Eduard Schnitzer, was a (baptized) Jewish physician from Silesia who eventually became governor of the Sudan and agent of the German government in its quest for colonies in Africa. Niederland's reconfiguration of these associations, supported in part by certain biographical parallels between Pasha and Moritz Schreber, suggests that a fusion of these two figures might stand behind Schreber's delusions of persecution by Jews and Slavophiles.[5]

Though ultimately calling into question Niederland's essentially oedipal reading of the associations generated by the name Casati, Lothane suggests that Niederland stopped too short in his analysis of the Jewish dimension of this remarkable chain of signifiers. Lothane's research has shown that a certain Carl Paasch, author of numerous anti-Semitic pamphlets during the 1890s, was a patient at Flechsig's clinic in 1894, during the period of Schreber's second residence there. Among Paasch's anti-Semitic writings was an "Open Letter to His Excellency the Reichskanzler von Caprivi" (1891), in which Major Casati is mentioned as an ally of Stanley against the Jew Emin Pasha who is in turn accused of various crimes and transgressions that resonate with popular anti-Semitic fantasies about the Jewish role in the spread of alcoholism and syphilis.[6]

And in a recent postscript to his book on Schreber, Lothane has attempted to follow the thread of Schreber's speculation linking the unmanned Wandering Jew to a Polish aristocrat named Czartorisky. In this instance too, Lothane suggests, the name of a (Polish) Catholic serves as a metonymy for a chain of associations that ultimately widen the range of Schreber's Jewish preoccupations. For as Lothane reports, Prince Adam Jerzy Czartoyski, who died the same year as Moritz Schreber, was a Polish statesman whose sympathies with occult doc-

trines and mystical philosophies involved him in circles of Polish thinkers, poets, and mystics who made extensive use of the Jewish Kabbalah
in their elaboration of a distinctly Polish Messianism.[7] Among these
figures, Lothane mentions the poet Adam Mickiewicz who in his turn
"came under the spell of Martinism, the Kabbalah, and the Frankists,
the eighteenth-century Jewish sect in Poland formed by Jacob Frank,
reviving the messianism of the seventeenth-century false messiah
Sabbatai Zevi."[8] Lothane suggests that Mickiewicz might be the figure
behind the Jewish alienist mentioned by Schreber whose name, like
that of the Benedictine father who perished in his head, sounded like
Starkiewicz, and whose aim was to Slavicize Germany and institute
there the rule of Judaism.[9]

II

Certainly the boldest attempt at articulating the depth of Schreber's
preoccupation with the Jewish question has been argued by Sander
Gilman in a recent study of Freud.[10] Gilman has been at the forefront of
new historicist efforts to provide "thick descriptions" of the cultural
milieu out of which the fundamental concepts of psychoanalytic
thought emerged in the European fin de siècle. In particular, Gilman's
research aims at demonstrating the extent to which these fundamental
concepts were formed in the crucible of a virulent and racially—rather
than theologically—understood anti-Semitism. The basic tenets of
Freudian thought, particularly those pertaining to female sexuality, become legible, in Gilman's view, as a series of phobic gestures designed
to clear Freud himself of the charges that were being systematically
lodged against Jews as being predisposed to those pathologies that sex-
ological discourses had been busily inventorying in the late nineteenth
century under the general heading of *degeneration*. The degeneration of
the male Jew in particular, as Gilman's research has amply docu-
mented, was, in scientific and popular literatures, obsessively figured
as correlative to his feminization—that is, to his status as a man never
quite at home in masculinity. The male Jew's ostensible predisposition
to an array of behavioral and physical aberrations and pathologies was
to a large extent understood as a by-product of a masculinity variously
conceived as congenitally damaged, underdeveloped, or pathetically
conflictual.

The locus classicus of the fin-de-siècle obsession with Jewish effeminacy is, of course, Otto Weininger's hugely influential treatise, *Sex and
Character*, published in 1903, the year in which Schreber's *Memoirs* ap-

peared. In this book, whose popularity among European intellectuals was perhaps as much a function of Weininger's spectacular suicide in the house where Beethoven had died as of its radical and deeply misogynist theses about the psychological, intellectual, and moral limitations of women, Weininger proposes that femininity and Jewishness are profoundly linked. He argues that Jews and Jewishness are saturated with a femininity itself conceived as an abject sensuality impeding the (Kantian) faculties of theoretical and practical reason from attaining the levels of sublime abstraction proper to them. For Weininger, femininity and Jewishness are in essence the names for the metaphysical guilt man brings upon himself by commingling the purity of his theoretical, moral, and aesthetic callings with the base needs and desires of material, embodied existence. I will return to Weininger's work later in this chapter; for now suffice it to say that Gilman's reading of Schreber is largely a demonstration that the latter's symptomatology was generated out of the same misogynist and anti-Semitic cultural archive as was Weininger's metaphysical phantasmagoria and, more important, that Freud's reading of the case was structured around a radical disavowal of his own implication in that cultural archive.

Gilman thus places the link between feminization and Jewishness, a link suggested by the image of the unmanned Wandering Jew, at the very center of his reading of Schreber. As he programmatically puts it: "Daniel Paul Schreber was afraid he was turning into an effeminate Jew, a true composite of Weininger's images of the Jew and the woman" (142). He traces, one by one, the fundamental features of Schreber's delusional system to cultural images and discourses, culled primarily from nineteenth-century medical and popular literature, of the "diseased Jew." The nineteenth-century medical literature that formed the backdrop of Schreber's diagnosis and treatment was, Gilman argues, so steeped in racialist biology and anti-Semitic ideology that Schreber had little choice but to experience his nervous agitation as indicative of a metamorphosis of Kafkan proportions—a metamorphosis into an object of sublime monstrosity: the unmanned Wandering Jew. "Schreber's paranoid system," Gilman writes, "uses the vocabulary of fin-de-siècle scientific anti-Semitism as a rhetorical structure to represent his anxiety about his own body. Schreber senses himself being transmuted from a 'beautiful,' masculine Aryan to an 'ugly,' feminized Jew" (147).

In the framework of such an interpretation, certain curious details from Schreber's *Memoirs* take on added weight. One thinks, for example, of the racial coding of the Zoroastrian gods, Ormuzd and Ariman,

who together constitute what Schreber refers to as the posterior realms of heaven. Schreber notes, for example that "the lower God (Ariman) seems to have felt attracted to nations of originally brunette race (the Semites) and the upper God to nations of originally blond race (the Aryan peoples)" (53). Furthermore, given the notoriety of Nietzsche's *Also sprach Zarathustra*, one can readily assume Schreber's knowledge that in Zoroastrian theology Ariman represented the evil principle. If one adds to this the fact that in Schreber's system the lower god is intimately connected with the miracle of unmanning—"The rays of the lower God (Ariman) have the power of producing the miracle of unmanning; the rays of the upper God (Ormuzd) have the power of restoring manliness when necessary" (74)—then we are indeed faced, once more, with the link between femininity and Jewishness.[11] As Gilman sees it, Schreber's central fantasy about unmanning was primarily an expression of anxiety "about acquiring the Jew's circumcised penis, the sign of the feminization of the Jew" (155). Against this background and given the sensitivity of the voices that speak to Schreber to the similarities of sounds, one begins to hear in the word *Luder*, that insulting nomination at the center of Ariman's solar revelation, another, equally problematic nomination: *Jude*.

Gilman's work presupposes the predominance, in the nineteenth-century European imagination, of a connection between circumcision, feminization, and anti-Semitism. Perhaps the clearest formulation of such a connection was provided by Freud himself in a now famous footnote to the case of "Little Hans." Once more, it is Weininger who figures as the exemplary representative of these cultural fantasies:

> The castration complex is the deepest root of anti-Semitism; for even in the nursery little boys hear that a Jew has something cut off his penis—a piece of his penis, they think—and this gives them a right to despise Jews. And there is no stronger unconscious root for the sense of superiority over women. Weininger (the young philosopher who, highly gifted but sexually deranged, committed suicide after producing his remarkable book, *Geschlecht und Charakter*), in a chapter that attracted much attention, treated Jews and women with equal hostility and overwhelmed them with the same insults. Being neurotic, Weininger was completely under the sway of his infantile complexes; and from that standpoint what is common to Jews and women is their relation to the castration complex. (*SE* 10:36; cf. Gilman, 77)

According to Gilman, florid fantasies about the consequences of circumcision abounded in nineteenth-century European culture in general and in medical discourse in particular:

In the medical discourse of the nineteenth century, circumcision was as evil as it was inescapable for the Jew because it led to specific diseases that corrupted the individual and eventually the body politic. . . . The linked dangers of sexuality, syphilis, and madness were constantly associated with the figure of the male Jew. The Jew, who had become identified with his circumcised state, came to personify this threat. Central to the definition of the Jew was the image of the male Jew's circumcised penis as impaired, damaged, or incomplete, and therefore threatening to the wholeness and health of the male Aryan. The damaged penis represented the potential ravages of sexually transmitted disease. (60–61)

Against the backdrop of this chain of associations (within the context of a widespread syphilophobia in the nineteenth century) and Schreber's own reference to a syphilitic epidemic in one of his more elaborate fantasies of cosmic disaster, Schreber's other references and allusions to plagues and various forms of leprosy—including *"Lepra orientalis, Lepra indica, Lepra hebraica* and *Lepra aegyptica"* (97)—might be read as further expressions and ramifications of Schreber's troubled identification with the image of the diseased, feminized Jew: "But being Jewish means . . . suffering from a disease, and Schreber suffered from a disease of the body that was at the same time a disease of the mind. . . . The disease of the Jews alters the Jew's skin, the shape of the Jew's nose. . . . It is syphilis, the plague associated by Schreber with the Jews and leprosy" (157).[12] The fantasy that Jewish sexuality was particularly prone to degeneration allowed for the further association of Jews and "the relatively newly medicalized 'disease' of homosexuality" (159).

Gilman argues that other details of Schreber's delusions, particularly delusions associated with the body, need to be understood as outgrowths of a core identification with the diseased/feminized body of the Jew as it was "constructed" in the medical discourses and popular anti-Semitic literature of the nineteenth century. For example, apropos of Schreber's delusions of miracles affecting his bowels as well as his repeated allusions to the smell of particular souls and putrescence more generally, Gilman writes:

Even the act of defecation was associated with an anti-Semitic image of the Jew. In contemporary culture, the Jew stank of the *foetor judaicus.* The smell, like the smell of the sewers of the nineteenth century, which epitomized the source of decay for nineteenth-century public health, was the smell of shit. Within the scatological culture of Germany, Jews had a special role in the German fantasy about defecation. Beginning with Luther, there had been a powerful association between the act of defecation and being Jewish. (155)

Finally, Gilman suggests that the contributions of Niederland and other commentators who have emphasized the role of Moritz Schreber's orthopedic manipulations in the etiology of his son's psychosis should be reread in light of the Jewish dimension of Schreber's phantasmatic world: "The machines have another level of meaning. They are machines for the restructuring of the body, they are machines that feminize Schreber's body by unmanning him with magical rays. These machines also make the body into a Jew" (160).

Many of these arguments can be found in somewhat different form and with somewhat different emphasis in a series of articles by Jay Geller.[13] Geller's more Foucauldian reading suggests that the social and economic crises that plagued Germany in the 1870s played a key role in strengthening the hand of disciplinary forms of power, that when "the Great Depression revealed the inadequacy of liberalism, the administrative rule of expertise and welfare mechanisms embodied by public health policy came to the fore." Once crises of political economy were translated into anxieties about degeneration, the future health of the body politic could become a matter for doctors and psychiatrists. Geller, however, makes the more radical claim that, in the context of the nineteenth-century "sciences" of degeneration, "to be the object of the psychiatrist's gaze . . . is also to be the Jew."[14] He supports this claim, which is also central to Gilman's work, by referring to, among other things, Charcot's well-known hypothesis that "Jewish families furnish us with the finest subjects for the study of hereditary disease" and that among Jews "nervous symptoms of all sorts . . . are incomparably more frequent than elsewhere."[15] Geller also cites the work of one of Charcot's pupils, Henri Meige, who wrote a brief monograph on the Jewish predisposition to nervous illness in 1893 with the telling title *Le Juif-errant à la Salpêtrière: Études sur certains nevropathes.*[16]

Meige begins his remarkable essay by citing one of Charcot's case presentations from 1889, that of a Hungarian Jew named Klein who was apparently subject to compulsive wanderings and migrations: "I introduce him to you," Charcot reported, "as *a true descendant of Ahasverus or Cartophilus*, as you would say. The fact is that, like the compulsive (neurotic) travelers of whom I have already spoken, he is constantly driven by an irresistible need to move on, to travel, without being able to settle down anywhere. That is why he has been crisscrossing Europe for three years in search of the fortune which he has not yet encountered."[17] Meige's typical Wandering Jew is not so much a man in search of fortune as one driven to wander in search of a cure for the compulsion to wander:

They are constantly obsessed by the need to travel, to go from city to city, from hospital to hospital, in search of a new treatment, an unfindable remedy. They try all the recommended medications, avid for novelty, but they soon reject them, inventing a frivolous pretext for not continuing, and, with the reappearing impulse, they flee one fine day, drawn by a new mirage of a distant cure.

Meige adds to this description the following *racial* diagnosis:

Let us not forget that they are Jews, and that it is a characteristic of their race to move with extreme ease. At home nowhere, and at home everywhere, the Israelites never hesitate to leave their homes for an important business affair and, particularly if they are ill, to go in search of an effective remedy.

In Meige's view, what is ultimately pathological about these modern Wandering Jews, whose trajectory is not surprisingly from an impoverished Eastern to a more affluent Western Europe, is their *drivenness*, the intensity of their compulsion "to be always seeking *something else and somewhere else*. What is pathological is not to be able to resist this need to keep moving, which nothing justifies and which may even be detrimental."[18] At least one of the results of such views was indeed that maladies that had been typically associated with women—above all hysteria—came to be seen as diseases to which Jewish men in particular were also prone.[19]

In their efforts to establish the predominance of the anti-Semitic discourses under whose auspices Schreber ostensibly elaborated his mutation into the unmanned Wandering Jew, both Gilman and Geller make extensive use of another curious cultural document, a bizarre prose text entitled "Der operierte Jude" written by the psychiatrist, author, and eventual psychiatric patient, Oskar Panizza.[20] Published in 1893, "The Operated Jew" tells the ghastly story of a Jewish medical student, Itzig Faitel Stern—a stock character of nineteenth-century anti-Semitic literature—who undergoes a series of surgical and orthopedic procedures in his efforts to transform himself, body and soul, into a true German. As Geller notes, in this quasi-pornographic narration of a pathetically literal attempt at assimilation, Panizza "drew on virtually the entire repertoire of anti-Semitic stereotype."[21]

And indeed he did. Panizza's narrator describes Faitel Stern as a physically deformed and "dreadful piece of human flesh" (52) whom Christian tailors are unable to fit properly; his speech is characterized as a "mixture of Palatinate Semitic babble, French nasal noises, and some high German vocalic sounds that he had fortuitously overheard"

(50); his aggressive gesticulations are portrayed as a grotesque theater of bestial expressiveness:

> But when he became zealous and had a good opportunity to wage an argument, then he reared up, raised a hand, pulled back his fleshy, volatile upper lip like a piece of leather so that the upper row of teeth became exposed, spread open both his hands like fans pointing upward with his upper body leaning backward, bobbed his head up and down against his breast a few times, and rhythmically uttered sounds like a trumpet. (50)

And of course Stern is enormously wealthy. But perhaps the most curious detail of all is a peculiar linguistic repetition compulsion attributed to Stern, a habit of peppering his speech with a series of meaningless phrases or "speech particles":

> Faitel Stern said something like this when I questioned him about the immense luxury of his wardrobe and toilet articles: "Why shoodn't I buy for me a new coat, a bootiful hat—menerá, fine wanished boots—menerá, me, too, I shood bicome a fine gentilman after this Deradáng! Deradáng!" His upper body rocked back and forth. At the same time, there was a spreading of the hands at shoulder height in a slightly squat position; an ecstatic look with a glossy reflection; an exposure of both rows of teeth; a rich amount of saliva. (51)

As disturbing as these passages may be, Panizza reserves his most grotesque descriptions for Faitel's surgical metamorphosis the goal of which, as Faitel puts it, is "'to become such a fine gentilman just like a goymenera and to geeve up all fizonomie of Jewishness'"(55). He enters the care of a Heidelberg anatomist named Professor Klotz, who strikes the reader familiar with the Schreber material as a kind of monstrous parody of Moritz Schreber. Klotz has Faitel strapped into a series of orthopedic apparatuses designed to "Aryanize" his physique; his bones are broken and reset; he is subjected to a series of violent and "neck-breaking exercises"(55); to prevent his body from bobbing up and down "a barbed wire belt similar to a collar was placed around his hips on his bare skin (as they do with dogs) so that he was immediately spiked when he tended to move up and down or from side to side" (56); he relearns high German "like a totally new, foreign language"(56); he takes a mysterious drug to change the color of his skin so that it would "yield to a fine, pastel lead tint" (57); and finally, in order to be sure that his soul, too, was German, he receives blood transfusions from seven robust women from the Black Forest, "since it was possible to assert to a certain degree that the abode of the soul could be located in the blood"(60).

The story culminates in the scene of Faitel's wedding banquet when, under the influence of alcohol and, it is suggested, anxieties about exposing his circumcised penis to his Christian bride, Othilia Schnack, Faitel's body and soul regress back to their preoperative Jewish condition. The advent of the breakdown is signaled by the return of the repressed linguistic repetition compulsion: "Those people who had a good ear could already hear now a few 'Deradángs! Deradángs!'"(71). Eventually Faitel's entire "assimilation" comes undone:

> Those people who remained behind watched with horror as Faitel's blond strands of hair began to curl during the last few scenes. Then the curly locks turned from red to dirty brown to blue-black.... His arms and legs, which had been stretched and bent in numerous operations, could no longer perform the recently learned movements, nor the old ones.... Everyone looked with dread at the crazy circular movements of the Jew.... Klotz's work of art lay before him crumpled and quivering, a convoluted Asiatic image in wedding dress, a counterfeit of human flesh, Itzig Faitel Stern. (74)

Both Gilman and Geller suggest that Schreber's transformation into an unmanned Wandering Jew needs to be understood as a kind of mirror image of the process undergone by Faitel Stern. To repeat Gilman's earlier thesis, "Schreber senses himself being transmuted from a 'beautiful,' masculine Aryan to an 'ugly,' feminized Jew." The claim is that when, at the end of the nineteenth century, a German man belonging to an elite (such as the judiciary) comes, for whatever reasons, to feel his identification with his status disturbed, he will automatically find himself in the symbolic position of the marginal figures of that culture—in this instance women and Jews—and begin, unconsciously and conflictually, to elaborate the consequences of his new set of identifications using whatever images and fantasies are ready to hand in the cultural "archive." Here one might recall Bourdieu's remarks on the "wasting away" of elites:

> That is ... the function of all magical boundaries (whether the boundary between masculine and feminine, or between those selected and those rejected by the educational system): to stop those who are inside, on the right side of the line, from leaving, demeaning or down-grading themselves. Pareto used to say that elites are destined to "waste away" when they cease to believe in themselves ... and begin to cross the line in the wrong direction. This is also one of the functions of the act of institution: to discourage permanently any attempt to cross the line, to transgress, desert, or *quit*.[22]

It would appear, then, that once Schreber's investiture as *Senats-präsident* began wasting away, Schreber crossed the lines that had heretofore separated him from his "others," namely women and Jews. Once one admits the cogency and force of this reading, Freud's own failure so much as to mention the Jewish dimension of Schreber's delusions—what we might refer to as Schreber's *Jewish transvestitism*—itself takes on the status of a symptom. Both Gilman and Geller maintain that this failure was a result of Freud's profound—and historically quite understandable—anxiety about being caught on the wrong side of both of these lines. Each critic argues that Freud strategically misread (i.e., ignored) the Jewish dimension of Schreber's psychotic universe and that such a misreading was part of a larger defensive formation that determined the shape and intellectual direction of psychoanalysis for years to come. Offered as a partial answer to the difficult question of the "Jewishness" of psychoanalysis, the thesis is that the founding concepts and terms of this peculiar institution were in large part determined by a kind of extended "masculine protest"—by the struggle of a male, Jewish scientist-physician with a scientific and medical culture for which Jews embodied a condition of effeminate degeneration and abjection. Freud's paradoxical situation was, in a word, this: How could someone who occupied the structural position of the symptom offer authoritative knowledge about the cure? Gilman and Geller argue that in the context of the Schreber study, the pressures of this paradox prevented Freud from acknowledging the Jewish question in the Schreber material:

> The Jew within had to be repressed in the now neutralized discourse of science. This was achieved through a creative repression of the overt link between mental illness and Schreber's internalization of his anxiety about becoming a Jew. As with Freud's reading of the life histories of his hysterics, Schreber came to represent his own anxieties about his identity as a physician and male Jew in the culture of fin-de-siècle Vienna.[23]

III

This reading of Schreber—and of Freud on Schreber—has been taken up by a number of scholars within what might be called the new Jewish cultural studies, scholarly efforts to bring recent innovations in the study of gender and sexuality to bear on readings of canonical Jewish texts. In a series of essays on Jewish culture at the margins of empire—both Roman and Hapsburg—Daniel Boyarin has, for example, persuasively argued that the "representation of the . . . male Jew as female . . .

was not only an external one, one that originated in the fantasies of anti-Semites, but also an internal one that represented a genuine Jewish cultural difference."[24] What Boyarin has in mind here is above all the image of the pale, studious, and sedentary *Yeshiva Bokhur*—an ideal of manhood in Eastern European Jewish culture—whose attributes in many ways corresponded to common descriptions of the male hysteric in nineteenth-century medical literature. Freud's failure to read Schreber's hybrid identity as unmanned Wandering Jew, Boyarin insists, was a failure or refusal to recognize himself, a former *Ostjude* like so many Viennese Jews, in that figure; it was thus of a piece with Freud's more general strategy of self-fashioning, elaborated within the terms of an aggressively heterosexual psychoanalytic theory, as a man fully at home in his German (i.e., Occidental) masculinity. Freud's compulsive elaboration, in the Schreber essay and elsewhere, of the so-called positive Oedipus complex as the model of psychic health and maturity thus comes to resemble the ordeal undergone by Faitel Stern to transform himself into "the equivalent of an Occidental human being."[25] The goal was to demonstrate to oneself and to others that one had, as it were, purified oneself of any traces of the Eastern Jew whose perverse, effeminate carnality would most certainly have disqualified him from the world of Western science and *Bildung*. Boyarin's crucial point is that, like Faitel Stern, Freud engaged in a sort of colonial mimicry that not only distorted the theoretical edifice he was in the midst of constructing; it furthermore prevented him from embracing the resources of *alternative models of gender and sexual organization* that might have become available to him within Jewish culture. For Boyarin, then, the "Jewishness" of psychoanalysis is legible only as so many traces of refusals and disavowals. Freud's failure to hear Schreber's Jewish question has, in this reading, the status of an eminently phobic gesture generated by a culturally overdetermined counter-transference: *"I'm not that!"*

Boyarin's readings of rabbinic literature indeed suggest that Schreber gets something right about masculinity as constructed within traditional Jewish culture, that he discovers the theological resources of an alternative masculinity authorized by canonical Jewish texts. Commenting, for example, on a midrashic text on Song of Songs in which the (circumcised) men of Israel are addressed as the Daughters of Zion,[26] Boyarin suggests that the text enacts a blurring of gender familiar from mystical texts in which the adept is figured as the female partner in an encounter with the divine: "Circumcision is understood by the midrash as feminizing the male, thus making him open to receive the divine speech and vision of God." And apropos of the verse of Ezekiel (16:6) in which Israel is figured as a female child along with

other rabbinic interpretations suggesting that the Torah feminizes its devotees, Boyarin concludes that in Judaism

> circumcision was understood somehow as rendering the male somewhat feminine, thus making it possible for the male Israelite to have communion with a male deity. In direct contrast to Roman accusations that circumcision was a mutilation of the body that made men ugly, the Rabbinic texts emphasize over and over that the operation removes something ugly from the male body.[27]

According to Boyarin, then, in the context of rabbinic Judaism a man comes to have a body that matters, a body whose "matter" is holy, a body inscribed by the divine Word, *by way of feminization*.[28]

In an essay on Jewish (male) masochism, Boyarin has amplified this claim by suggesting that in rabbinic Judaism a man comes to have a body that matters precisely through a kind of couvade, a mimesis of the feminine prerogative of childbirth.[29] Citing talmudic narratives in which rabbis undergo Schreber-like mortifications of the body, mortifications that involve, as with Schreber, a mimesis of femininity, Boyarin concludes:

> In the Greco-Roman world, the deeds that would render a man a suitable erotic object would have been phallic deeds par excellence, deeds of valor of one sort or another, while for the Rabbi these deeds are precisely anti-phallic, masochistic challenges to the coherence and impermeability of the male body. Paradoxically, it is the penetrated, violated, bleeding body that constructs the penile ideal. Where the "Roman" had to show that he had a phallus to win a woman, the Rabbi has to show he has none. . . . This male subject . . . is called upon and learns to recognize himself . . . not through an image of "unimpaired masculinity," rather through an image of masculinity as impairment, as what would be interpreted in another culture as castration.[30]

The affirmation of phallic ruination—not castration—is mobilized through a series of mimetic performances of childbirth. What distinguishes this rabbinic masculinity from the masculinity of Christian saints is, Boyarin finally claims, the paradox that for the rabbis the destruction or wasting away of the "phallus" performed in talmudic couvade narratives is understood as passage toward procreative manhood rather than sexual asceticism.[31]

If I might rephrase Boyarin's point in Winnicottian terms, we might say that Jewish masculinity is, at least on a certain reading of rabbinic literature, *good enough masculinity*. It is a masculinity that has undergone a destruction and survival via a symbolic ordeal resembling couvade, a masculinity that has, so to speak, allowed its (phantasmatic)

phallus to waste away in order to survive with a penis. To be a man, in Judaism, means, according to this reading, to know, in a profound and *embodied* way, that one's being is defined by a lack that only subordination to God and his commandments—a subordination itself imagined as feminizing—can ever "make good." To bring these views to a point, we might say that traditional Jewish masculinity is defined by a fundamental paradox: *that men be initiated into manhood through a mimesis of femininity.*

A number of these arguments have been articulated apropos of biblical literature by Howard Eilberg-Schwartz.[32] Eilberg-Schwartz, too, associates Jewish masculinity with the fundamental paradox he sees Schreber struggling with: "Whatever the cause of Schreber's fantasies of being unmanned and sexually desired by God, his writings took him to the heart of . . . the dilemma of monotheism" (137). According to Eilberg-Schwartz, masculinity in ancient Israelite religion is effectively traversed by the same double bind that Sedgwick has located at the heart of male elites in modern Western cultures, namely of homosocial desire "as at once the most compulsory and the most prohibited of social bonds."[33] Jewish men, who are otherwise enjoined to maintain strictly heterosexual unions, are expected to strive for intimacy with a God figured as masculine and, even more radically, as bridegroom to his people. According to Eilberg-Schwartz, the primary strategies for circumventing the homoerotic implications of such intimacy was, first, "a prohibition against depicting God (veiling the body of God)" and, second, "the feminization of men" (3). In this way, a male-male relation could become "intelligible" as a variation of a heterosexual union. Circumcision is one of the key elements in this difficult cultural and theological negotiation:

> Circumcision was for the ancient Israelites a symbol of male submission. Because it is partially emasculating, it was a recognition of a power greater than man. The symbolism of submission to God is obviously related to the images of feminization of Israelite men in the Hebrew Bible. Both were symptoms of the same phenomenon. God was acknowledged as the ultimate male and in his presence human masculinity was seen to be compromised and put at risk. (161–62)

No doubt the figure in the Hebrew scriptures who was most forcefully exposed to these double binds of Jewish masculinity was Moses. Eilberg-Schwartz discusses several biblical passages suggesting a partial gender reversal or at least a mode of transvestitism on Moses' part. One such passage, Exodus 34:29–35, describes the transfiguration of Moses' skin when he comes down from Mount Sinai. Because of an ambiguity of the verb used to signify this transfiguration, the passage

became the basis of the tradition picturing Moses with horns. Whatever the exact meaning of the passage, the change in Moses' face was disturbing enough that he had to wear a veil, which in turn suggests a degree of feminization:

> Veils do carry associations of femininity. Although the veil was not standard attire of women in ancient Israel, it is viewed as feminine attire. . . . Moses is the only Israelite male to be described as covering his face. . . . In addition to hiding his transfiguration, the veiling of Moses partially feminizes him. It points to his transformation into the intimate of God. (144)

Eilberg-Schwartz suggests that the tradition endowing Moses with horns could be understood as a sort of "masculine protest" evoked by the feminizing implications of the events described: "Moses is imagined with his face covered like a woman, but with horns like a proud bull. He is caught between genders—a man as a leader of Israel, a woman as the wife of God" (145). Finally, Eilberg-Schwartz suggests that the inevitable tensions generated by a masculinity constructed under these inconsistent, even contradictory demands, came to be displaced onto women and figured as *female impurity*.[34]

To return to Freud, Eilberg-Schwartz makes the now familiar argument that under the social and political pressures of his historical moment, Freud was unable to acknowledge any proximity to femininity, and especially to a Judaism "stained" by effeminacy. He then follows the trace of this inability or, perhaps, more accurately, this refusal, from Freud's essay on Schreber, in which the Jewish dimension of Schreber's unmanning is, as it were, made inert, to Freud's "historical novel" about the nature and origins of the Jewish national character, *Moses and Monotheism*. Eilberg-Schwartz sees both texts as structured around the avoidance of a femininity that within Jewish culture is the implicit risk of proximity to the divine; what Freud fails to understand is, in a word, the *theological necessity* of Jewish transvestitism.

Moses and Monotheism does indeed construct an image of Judaism as a sort of hypermasculine, neo-Kantian religion of reason, as if Freud were arguing, in the spirit of Jewish rationalist philosophers such as Hermann Cohen, against the specter of Weininger's claim that the (masculine/Christian) point of view of Kantian critical philosophy was as foreign to the (feminized) Jewish psychic and moral constitution as was Wagner's *Parsifal* to the Jewish aesthetic sensibility.[35] The conception of Jewish spirituality and intellectuality proffered by Freud suggests a posture of severe self-control grounded in an endless series of instinctual renunciations. For Eilberg-Schwartz, Freud's insistence on instinctual renunciation and a concomitant privileging of intellectual and moral reasoning—all of which are figured as masculine in Freud's

culture and text—as the core tendencies of Judaism must be understood as elements of a defensive, even phobic gesture. By locating the essence of Jewish spiritual and moral development in a triumphant transcendence of sensuousness and sensuality, Freud avoids the homoerotic and potentially feminizing implications of a man's intimacy with God-the-Father, that is, of a theological version of the *negative* Oedipus complex. That is why, Eilberg-Schwartz suggests, Freud's entire conception of Jewish spirituality comes to be centered on the prohibition on images, i.e., on representing the *body of God*, why *that* renunciation becomes Freud's model for all further acts of renunciation/sublimation of instinctual urges.

In his own reading of *Moses and Monotheism*, Boyarin has taken a step beyond this interpretation. Not only was the avoidance of homoeroticism a dynamic cause of Freud's transformation of a God who, at privileged moments in the Hebrew scriptures, is indeed figured as visible and present to his people into a sublime abstraction;[36] rather, Freud's own argument is riddled by a fundamental inconsistency: "Renunciation of the fulfillment of desire, which is encoded in Freud's text as masculine, is occasioned by a submissiveness vis-à-vis a male other, whether it be the 'great man' Moses or the deity. But that very submissiveness, the mark of the religious person, *is itself feminizing* in the terms of nineteenth-century culture."[37]

Although I think that Boyarin is quite right about this inconsistency, I think he misses an important dimension of its significance. His misreading, if I might call it that, is, I believe, based on an error he shares with all readings that locate that which is "abjected" from a symbolic identity—in this instance "queerness" and "femininity"—at *the same ontological level* as the identity that is thereby constructed. A closer look at *Moses and Monotheism* will suggest, however, how we might think the ontological *asymmetry* of a symbolic identity and its abject "others," those who figure the "submissiveness" internal to that symbolic identity.

IV

Several years before beginning his work on *Moses*, Freud wrote in a new preface prepared for the Hebrew edition of *Totem and Taboo*—the edition appeared years later, in 1939—that although he is "completely estranged from the religion of his fathers . . . and . . . cannot take a share in nationalist ideals," he nevertheless feels that "he is in his essential nature a Jew." He added that "he could not now express that essence in words; but some day, no doubt, it will become accessible to the scien-

tific mind."[38] *Moses and Monotheism* is at least in part Freud's effort to make this, his own "essential nature" as a Jew, an essence that somehow persists despite his alienation from all embodied, ritual practices—from what we might call the "carnality" of Judaism—accessible to the "science" of psychoanalysis. But beyond that, this curious book was also Freud's most extended response to and analysis of anti-Semitism. In effect, Freud will attempt to explain anti-Semitism as a refusal to mourn the losses and dislocations that found modern subjectivity and that had, in a sense, been rehearsed over the course of the mournful history of Jewish monotheism.

In a series of highly speculative gestures, Freud links the core *structural* features of Jewish monotheism, imposed on the Jews, according to Freud's story, by an Egyptian Moses, and the *historical* condition of diaspora, which begins with the destruction of the Temple and the subsequent reorganization of communal life around the study of Torah in dispersed centers of learning and worship. For Freud, the ethically oriented monotheism of the Jews and the historical condition of diaspora are linked by a series of traumatic cuts: of the deity from plastic representation; of spirituality from magic, animism, and sexual excess; of the passions from their violent enactments; of the people from a territory conceived as proper to them. These various modalities of loss, separation, and departure, which Freud views as so many forms of the instinctual renunciation (*Triebverzicht*) that undergirds the rule of law in the most general sense, procure for the Jews what he calls "their secret treasure," namely a sense of self-confidence and superiority with regard to pagan cultures whose spirituality has remained, as he puts it, "under the spell of sensuality" (*SE* 23:115). It is no doubt this "secret treasure" that Freud was thinking of when he spoke of his essential nature as a Jew that persists as a core identity despite estrangement from all cultic and cultural practices.

However, in the midst of his reconstruction of Jewish cultural identity, Freud encounters the impasse of the utter illegitimacy of what he has characterized as the "secret treasure" of the Jews. "It is not obvious and not immediately understandable," he writes, "why an advance in intellectuality [*Geistigkeit*], a set-back to sensuality, should raise the self-regard both of an individual and of a people. It seems to presuppose the existence of a definite standard of value and of some other person or agency which maintains it" (*SE* 23:116). After some brief reflections on the superego, Freud returns to this impasse:

> Moreover, in the case of some advances in intellectuality . . . we cannot point to the authority which lays down the standard which is to be regarded as higher. . . . Thus we are faced by the phenomenon that in the

course of the development of humanity sensuality is gradually overpowered by intellectuality and that men feel proud and exalted by every such
advance. *But we are unable to say why this should be so.* (*SE* 23:118; my
emphasis)

In Freud's reading of Jewish spiritual development, this unnerving gap
in knowledge apropos of what Nietzsche referred to as the *value of values*, is filled, in the end, by the infamous myth of the primal father and
murder whose archetypal pattern is, Freud maintains, played out once
more on the person of Moses. This myth helps Freud to account for
what might be called *Jewish transference*, the unconscious transmission
of the cultural patterns and values—of *essence*—that make a Jew a Jew.
By transference I mean here the condition of finding oneself obsessively engaged in the effort to interpret, to translate into the language
of reason, valuational speech acts whose ultimate authority remains
grounded in the performative force of their enunciation. What is ultimately untranslatable—we might even say nonmetabolizable—about
such utterances, is this dimension of pure performativity that coconsti-
tutes their authority. To be in transference in the sense I am using the
term here means, in other words, to be caught up in an interminable
translation project. Freud's myth of the primal father is in the last resort
an attempt to put a human face on the dimension of symbolic authority
that is *nonsymbolizable*, or, as he puts it, "in a mystical fashion, so self-
evident." It is, in short, the myth of the emergence of the superego
dimension of ethical thought and feeling:

> Going back to ethics, we may say in conclusion that a part of its precepts
> are justified rationally by the necessity for delimiting the rights of society
> as against the individual, the rights of the individual as against society
> and those of individuals as against one another. But what seems to us so
> grandiose about ethics, so mysterious and, in a mystical fashion, so self-
> evident, owes these characteristics to its connection with religion, its ori-
> gin from the will of the father. (*SE* 23:122)[39]

Earlier, Freud had linked this superego dimension of ethical feeling
to a peculiar form of pleasure: "But whereas instinctual renunciation,
when it is for external reasons, is *only* unpleasurable, when it is for
internal reasons, in obedience to the super-ego, it has a different economic effect. In addition to the inevitable unpleasurable consequences
it also brings the ego a yield of pleasure—a substitutive satisfaction, as
it were" (*SE* 23:116–17). But it is in the final pages of the book that
Freud really lays his cards on the table and suggests that the ethical
genius of the Jews derives from a kind of perverse capacity for this
sublime pleasure-in-pain: "In a fresh rapture of moral asceticism [*In*

einem neuen Rausch moralischer Askese] they imposed more and more instinctual renunciations on themselves and in that way reached—in doctrine and precept, at least—ethical heights which had remained inaccessible to the other peoples of antiquity" (*SE* 23:134). The word Freud uses here, "rapture" or *Rausch*, bears distinctly Dionysian connotations of sensual excess and intoxication. The path of Jewish spiritual development traced by Freud turns out to have been shaped like a Moebius band: in their attempt to structure a relationship to the mystically self-evident, nonsymbolizable dimension of their ethical commandments the Jews rediscover, *on a different level of experience and imagination*, the "pagan" excesses which Judaism had ostensibly evacuated from the religious experience. The "secret treasure" of the Jews turns out to be dependent on an uncanny secretion of jouissance within the precincts of the moral law. It is this "pagan" intoxication, this "carnal" excess at the very core of what Freud characterizes as Jewish *Geistigkeit*—the spiritual/intellectual genius built around loss, instinctual renunciation, deterritorialization—that represents, I think, the deeper layer of what Boyarin has identified as a crucial inconsistency in Freud's argument. What Freud discovers as a paradoxical kernel of jouissance within the domain of an otherwise austere, Kantian moral universe is, as Boyarin has rightly noted, occasioned, *in Freud's narrative*, by submissiveness to a "great man." But that narrative construction was itself generated by an impasse in his argument apropos of the Jewish valuation of *Geistigkeit*. Freud was unable to imagine a resolution of that impasse—the impossibility of accounting for the value of this value—outside the terms of the "father complex." Freud's "great man" fills a gap, a missing link in his argumentation about the emergence of a new cultural value. But to follow Freud here, as I think Boyarin does, is to miss, once more, the encounter with this missing link. To interpret Freud's failure as the avoidance of a homoeroticism implied by his own narrative domesticates the impasse on which Freud's interpretation founders, the impasse that called his narrative into being in the first place. And it repeats the error Freud made in his reading of Schreber.

Schreber's crisis was a crisis of investiture. He discovered that his own symbolic power and authority as judge—and German man—was founded, at least in part, by the performative magic of the rites of institution, that his symbolic function was sustained by an imperative to produce a regulated series of repeat performances. It was this idiotic repetition compulsion at the heart of his symbolic function that Schreber experienced as profoundly sexualizing, as a demand to cultivate jouissance. That he experienced this sexualization as feminizing and

"Jewifying" suggests that at the advent of European modernity, "knowledge" of jouissance was ascribed to women and Jews, meaning that women and Jews were *cursed* with the task of holding the place of that which could not be directly acknowledged: that symbolic identities, are, in the final analysis, sustained by *drive*, by performativity-as-repetition-compulsion. I would like to elaborate these points further by returning, briefly, to Panizza's "Operated Jew." I will then turn to another famous case of bodily transformation and mutation, that of Kafka's Gregor Samsa. In each instance we shall see that abjection, the experience of something rotten within, signifies a cursed knowledge of jouissance, which only by way of a kind of secondary revision becomes legible as "homosexuality," "femininity," or "Jewishness"—what Schreber condenses by means of the name *Luder*.

V

A hint on how we might revise our initial impression of Panizza's text as little more than a grotesque, anti-Semitic story of an impossible Jewish assimilation, comes from an unexpected source. In a 1930 essay written for the radio, Walter Benjamin suggested that one might rehabilitate the work of Panizza by placing him alongside another master of the fantastic: E.T.A. Hoffmann. Benjamin asserts that Panizza shared Hoffmann's profound enmity toward the good burgher or *Alltagsmensch* who comes to appear, in all of his virtues and positive attributes, "as the product of a nefarious artificial mechanism whose inner parts were ruled by Satan."[40] Noting the profound connections between paranoia and theology—Benjamin was, we recall, himself well versed in Schreber's writings[41]—Benjamin suggests that it was above all Panizza's theological disposition that made him so sensitive to the contaminations of human life and spirit by mechanical and mechanistic forces.

It is, of course, Hoffmann's "The Sandman," a text to which we have already referred, that most famously and poignantly addresses the complications of such contaminations. The doomed protagonist of that story, Nathanael, falls in love with Olympia, a mechanical doll constructed with the aid of his demonic nemesis, Coppola/Coppelius. A fellow student of Nathanael's tells his friend that because of her stiff and mechanical comportment Olympia makes an impression of utter soullessness: "Her step is peculiarly measured; all of her movements seem to stem from some kind of clockwork. . . . We found Olympia to be rather uncanny [*unheimlich*], and we wanted to have nothing to do with her. She seems to us to be playing the part of a human being."[42]

Nathanael, for his part, suffers his major breakdown when he can no longer deny Olympia's true status as automaton. This occurs when he stumbles upon Coppola and Spalanzani struggling for possession of her lifeless body:

> The professor was grasping a female figure by the shoulders, the Italian Coppola had her by the feet, and they were twisting and tugging her this way and that. . . . Coppola threw the figure over his shoulder and with a horrible, shrill laugh, ran quickly down the stairs, the figure's grotesquely dangling feet bumping and rattling woodenly on every step. Nathanael stood transfixed; he had only too clearly seen that in the deathly pale waxen face of Olympia there were no eyes, but merely black holes. She was a lifeless doll.

Spalanzani picks up the missing eyes from the ground and flings them at Nathanael, pushing him into an abyss of insanity: "Then madness racked Nathanael with scorching claws, ripping to shreds his mind and senses."[43]

Freud's own notoriously complex reading of the story begins with a critique of a previous study of the "Psychology of the Uncanny" written by E. Jentsch in 1906. Jentsch had argued that the effect of uncanniness is produced, as in Hoffmann's story, whenever uncertainty is created as to a thing's life or lifelessness: "one of the most successful devices for easily creating uncanny effects is to leave the reader in uncertainty whether a particular figure . . . is a human being or an automaton."[44] Freud criticizes this view in favor of one attuned to the castration imagery repeatedly evoked in conjunction with the figure of Coppelius/Coppola. What Freud failed to see was the connection between Jentsch's notion of intellectual uncertainty and his own conception of repetition compulsion, which at a formal level is the distinguishing feature of the uncanny effect. Repetition compulsion is at work when one's actions appear to be controlled by a demonic force, lending those actions a mechanical, automatic quality.[45] One will recall that Olympia's "expressivity"—what lured Nathanael into believing in her depth of feeling and soulfulness—was more or less confined to the repeated production of the interjection "Ach, Ach!" What Freud failed to notice was, in other words, that in the story Olympia herself serves as a primary figuration of repetition compulsion. Nathanael falls into madness not over the grotesque deidealization of his beloved but rather because she is suddenly no longer there to protect him from his own "knowledge" of repetition, from his own subjection to the demonic/mechanistic forces embodied by Coppelius/Coppola. Once Olympia collapses into a grotesque assemblage of lifeless parts, the

knowledge of repetition *falls into him*, a knowledge figured by the eyes Spalanzani throws at him.[46]

Panizza's "Operated Jew" would remain a purely anti-Semitic text if it did not include or imply a comparable moment when the forces materialized by the repulsive, though doubtlessly fascinating, presence of Faitel Stern did not, as it were, fall into the non-Jew, who is in this case not another figure in the story but rather an implied non-Jewish reader. The failed transformation of Faitel Stern into a specimen of ideal masculine *Germanentum* functions as a narrative lure; along the way, the non-Jewish German reader is confronted with the knowledge that he, too, has doubtlessly failed at being fully "assimilated" to the Germanness that is ostensibly his natural element. What is at stake here, then, is not simply Panizza's ridicule of German vulgarity and stupidity, which is no doubt also present in the text, but rather his suggestion that, in a sense, "the German" does not exist.

Panizza indicates the imposture of the German at several points in his text. When, for example, Faitel decides to obtain a German soul—"the chaste, undefined Germanic soul, which shrouded the possessor like an aroma"—he is advised to go to England, "where the purest effusion of this Germanic soul was to be found" (59).[47] This plan is abandoned due to language difficulties. After his next plan, infusion with German blood, fails to obtain the desired results, Faitel, who had by now changed his name to Siegfried Freudenstern, makes a Pascalian wager: "he began reciting pathetic and sentimental passages by poets, especially in the social gatherings of the ladies' salons, and he astutely observed the position of the mouths, breath, twinkle of the eyes, gestures, and certain sighs that emanated so passionately and strenuously from German breasts satiated with feelings" (61). In time he had "learned to inhale and exhale superbly. And one time he had the satisfaction of hearing from a student in the ladies' salons that Siegfried Freudenstern was a man with soul through and through" (62).

Before the story culminates in Faitel's disastrous wedding night, the narrator addresses the reader directly with a curious series of remarks suggesting the difficulty, even impossibility, of attaining complete certainty as to the state of another person's or even one's own soul.[48] Invoking a "trivial" metaphor of coats trimmed with fur to suggest the presence of more luxuriant inner linings hidden from view, the narrator admonishes his *male* readers to resist such dissimulation: "Do you also wear a coat like this? Oh, then throw it away if you're a man" (67). He then goes on to elucidate his own metaphor's hidden lining:

Still, haven't you seen people, my dear reader, who wear such furs around their souls in order to conceal their porous and shabby constitution? And then they act as though they had a noble soul clad in the finest of fabrics. . . . Perhaps you yourself, my reader, possess such wrappings for your soul? Oh, then throw this book in a corner if you're a man and spew everything out! This is not for you. Only a woman may lie and cloak herself in false wrappings. (67)

The narrator concludes this curious digression with a retelling of the myth of Prometheus, who receives permission from God to make human beings only on the condition that they be cursed by a quality which makes them morally inferior to animals whose communications are unclouded by dissimulation:

It was the lie. Oh, base contract that allowed us all to be born under the same sign of the lie! And were you perhaps the cause for that lying tower of Babel forcing people to separate because they no longer understand each other in spite of the coughing and gesticulating? And, even if the German nations were the last to be created, received the least repercussions from all this because so much of the lying substance [*Lügensubstanz*] had already been used up by the previous Asiatic and Latin races, there is still enough there.—Oh, reader, if you can, spit out this dirt like rotten slime, and show your lips, your tongue, and your teeth just as they are! (68)[49]

Although Faitel is described as a man who secretes unusual amounts of this slime, the narrator's crucial point is that no one, not even the purest exemplar of Germanic masculinity, will ever be able to purify himself of this *Lügensubstanz*. This abject substance would seem to be a form of that putrescent matter that Schreber refers to as *Leichengift* or the "poison of corpses" and which figured, in the context of the *Memoirs*, the repetition compulsion at the heart of symbolic function.

When, at the end of the story, Faitel's "true" Jewish condition returns—a return signaled by a linguistic repetition compulsion: "Deradáng! Deradáng!"—the reader may no longer be as firmly at home in the social fantasy he has traversed over the course of this story, namely, that it is the Jew who embodies the contamination of the human soul by *Lügensubstanz*. He may still try to respond to the "counterfeit of human flesh" to which Faitel Stern is reduced at the end of the story with the phobic gesture: "That's not me!" He has, however, been informed that such a gesture can never fully succeed, that there will always be a residue of this strange substance that he can never quite spit out and that marks him, too, as counterfeit, as a subject driven by the imperatives of performativity-as-repetition-compulsion.

VI

Much like Schreber's *Memoirs* and Panizza's "Operated Jew," the story of Gregor Samsa is an initiation into a universe of abjection.[50] Not only is Gregor transformed into a species of repulsive vermin, not only is he fed garbage, but his family gradually turns his room into a dumping grounds for all sorts of refuse—for what is refused from the family. Gregor's desiccated body is also finally expelled as so much trash, as if he had come to embody the waste products of the very family he had previously nourished with care and dedication. Although Kafka does not offer the reader anything like a causal account of Gregor's transformation, he does suggest a number of possible systemic or structural features that help make sense of it. In other words, Gregor's fall into abjection can be approached as a *symptom* whose fascinating presence serves as a displaced condensation of larger and more diffuse disturbances within the social field marked out by the text.

The story begins with a community—the Samsa family—in disarray. A strange, even miraculous, physical transformation, and indeed one not unlike Schreber's mutation into a *Luder*, has made it impossible for Gregor to perform the duties that had heretofore been the lifeblood of the family. The reader first encounters the members of this microcommunity as a series of *voices* recalling Gregor to his "official" responsibilities. Among the voices imploring Gregor to do his duty, the father's voice doubtlessly distinguishes itself as the most urgent and insistent one. This quasi-operatic mise-en-scène, whereby characters are introduced as voices with distinctive vocal registers, may be, on Kafka's part, an allusion not merely to the world of opera in general but rather to a particular work whose cultural significance would not have escaped him: Wagner's final opera, *Parsifal*.

In *Parsifal*, too, we find a community—the Grail Society—in disarray; there too the communal state of emergency is called forth by a son's inability to perform his official duties because of a bodily mutation or mutilation. Amfortas, the Fisher King, is unable to officiate over the Grail miracle. Seduced by Kundry—embodiment of Woman and Wandering Jew—and wounded by the evil wizard Klingsor, Amfortas now longs only for the death that would put an end to his suffering. The gaping wound in his thigh materializes his liminal state between symbolic death—he is unable to assume his symbolic identity as king of the Grail Society—and the real death he so powerfully desires.[51] Finally, as in the early pages of *Metamorphosis*, the paternal voice—here, the voice of Titurel—assumes a special status and urgency. Žižek has noted a more general analogy between *Parsifal* and the world of Kafka's fiction:

At first sight, Wagner and Kafka are as far apart as they can be: on one hand, we have the late-Romantic revival of a medieval legend; on the other, the description of the fate of the individual in contemporary totalitarian bureaucracy . . . but if we look closely we perceive that the fundamental problem of *Parsifal* is eminently a *bureaucratic* one: the incapacity, the incompetence of Amfortas in performing his ritual-bureaucratic duty. The terrifying voice of Amfortas's father Titurel, this superego-injunction of the living dead, addresses his impotent son in the first act with the words: "Mein Sohn Amfortas, bist du am Amt?", to which we have to give all bureaucratic weight: Are you at your post? Are you ready to officiate?[52]

In *Metamorphosis*, the paternal injunction recalling the son to his post is, however, marked by a peculiar ambiguity. In Kafka's story, we are never quite certain about the status of the father as a source of social power and authority, never sure of the degree of *imposture* informing that authority. Already in the short prose text "The Judgment," written months before *Metamorphosis*, Kafka had already placed this uncertainty apropos of the father's potency in the foreground of his fictional universe. No doubt the most breathtaking scene of that story involves the father's sudden mutation from frail and childlike dependent to death-bringing tyrant. With regard to that metamorphosis, Stanley Corngold has remarked that its surreality "suggests the loss of even fictional coherence; we are entering a world of sheer hypothesis."[53] A careful reading of *Metamorphosis* suggests that the hypothesis in question refers to a change in the nature of patriarchal authority that infects its stability, dependability, and consistency with radical uncertainty.

The first indication of this uncertainty concerns not the father but the other paternal master in Gregor's life, his boss. Reminding himself that were it not for the family's outstanding, though curiously unspecified, debt to his boss, he would have long given notice, Gregor muses about this master's ultimate imposture: "He would have fallen off the desk! It is funny, too, the way he sits on the desk and talks down from the heights to the employees, especially when they have to come right up close on account of the boss's being hard of hearing" (4). This curious uncertainty about the force of institutional power and authority is, so to speak, transferred to Gregor's father several pages later, in a single sentence: "But their little exchange had made the rest of the family aware that, contrary to expectations, Gregor was still in the house, and already his father was knocking on one of the side doors, *feebly but with his fist*" (6; my emphasis). In each instance a male figure of authority seems to reveal a double aspect: a master's force and power are shown

to contain an impotent, even laughable dimension. One of the most uncanny features of Kafka's literary universe is the way in which such impotence can suddenly reverse itself into awesome power or, better, the way in which impotence reveals itself to be one of the most disturbing attributes of power.

The inconsistencies and uncertainties informing patriarchal power get played out in *Metamorphosis* above all through the apparent and otherwise inexplicable reinvigoration of the father in the wake of Gregor's transformation. For the previous five years, since the collapse of the father's business, Gregor had lived a life of sacrifice and self-denial, becoming the sole means of support for his family and even securing its present lodgings. In the course of his early morning musings made possible by the forced interruption of normal activities, Gregor makes abundantly clear just how much he has suffered under the burdens of this sacrificial existence, burdens that have been, as noted earlier, aggravated by the parents' debt:

> "Oh God," he thought, "what a grueling job I've picked! Day in, day out—on the road. . . . I've got the torture of traveling, worrying about changing trains, eating miserable food at all hours, constantly seeing new faces, no relationships that last or get more intimate. . . . If I didn't hold back for my parents' sake, I would have quit long ago." (4)

This sacrificial logic is reiterated and given a turn of the screw in the direction of middle-class sentimentality in the second part of the story:

> In those days Gregor's sole concern had been to do everything in his power to make the family forget as quickly as possible the business disaster which had plunged everyone into a state of total despair. And so he had begun to work with special ardor and had risen almost overnight from stock clerk to traveling salesman. (27)

Soon it is only Grete, Gregor's sister, who seems not to take Gregor's sacrifices completely for granted: "Only his sister had remained close to Gregor, and it was his secret plan that she, who, unlike him, loved music and could play the violin movingly, should be sent next year to the Conservatory, regardless of the great expense involved" (27).

After his transformation, however, Gregor quickly learns that his family's financial situation was not nearly as grave as he had previously assumed. On the very first day of his new condition, he overhears his father opening a strongbox containing monies rescued from the failed business: "He had always believed that his father had not been able to save a penny from the business, at least his father had never told him anything to the contrary, and Gregor, for his part, had

never asked him any questions" (27). Although Gregor seems to be pleasantly surprised by this discovery, noting that his father had even managed to stash away some of Gregor's own salary, he also realizes that his father's "unexpected foresight and thrift" has also postponed the day on which the family debt could be paid off and he, Gregor, could quit his job and be free. But now, he concludes, "things were undoubtedly better the way his father had arranged them"(28).

Just as Gregor has been mistaken about the state of his family's financial health, he appears to be equally deluded about his sister's warm and seemingly nonexploitative regard for him. It is hardly possible, for example, to take at face value Gregor's assumptions about his sister's motives when she locks the door behind her after bringing Gregor an assortment of half-rotten leftovers: "And out of a sense of delicacy, since she knew that Gregor would not eat in front of her, she left hurriedly and turned the key, just so that Gregor should know that he might make himself as comfortable as he wanted" (24). How, then, are we to make sense of Gregor's apparent confusion and ignorance as to how things really stand in the family? And how is Gregor's original "innocence" and progressive initiation into the family's secrets related to his physical transformation and the father's (and family's) renewal and regeneration upon his death and decay?

It would seem that Gregor's new knowledge about the family is related to the rupture in the sacrificial logic by which he had previously organized his life. No longer able to live the life of the long-suffering son, he is compelled to perform what might be called the *sacrifice of sacrifice*. This radical act of sacrifice, of the very sacrificial logic that had given his life its doubtlessly bleak consistency, makes possible Gregor's discovery that the necessity of his former life, its apparent fatefulness, had been an artificial construction. His life of self-abnegation had been, it now appears, a kind of social game he had actively worked to perpetuate through a kind of self-inflicted "law-preserving violence" (one will recall that Gregor never asked about the father's finances, never asked what was in the strongbox). In this light, Gregor's condition anticipates that of the man from the country in the parable from *The Trial* who, after a lifetime of waiting at the gates of the Law, learns that its entrance had been designed for him all along and that his exclusion had been staged with his own complicitous participation. Gregor's metamorphosis might thus be understood as a sign of his abjuration of just such complicity, in this case with the "plot" imposing on him a life of self-sacrifice. His abjection would indicate his new position outside that plot—outside the narrative frame that had given his life meaning and value. This reading is, it turns out, supported by the

etymological resonances of the words Kafka uses—*ungeheuere(s)*
Ungeziefer ("monstrous vermin")—to introduce Gregor's transformation in the famous first sentence of the story. "*'Ungeheuer'*," as Stanley
Corngold has emphasized, "connotes the creature who has no place in
the family; *'Ungeziefer,'* the unclean animal unsuited for sacrifice, the
creature without a place in God's order" (xix).[54]

To bring these findings to a point, I am arguing that Gregor's fall into
abjection be understood as a by-product of his encounter with the ultimate *uncertainty* as to his place in the community of which his father is
the nominal master. Gregor's mutation into an *Ungeziefer*, a creature
without a place in God's order, points, in other words, not to Gregor's
unsuitability for sacrifice due to some positive, pathological attribute
but rather to a disturbance *within the divine order itself*. Gregor discovers
one of the central paradoxes of modern experience: uncertainty as to
what, to use Lacan's term, the "big Other" of the symbolic order really
wants from us can be far more disturbing than subordination to an
agency or structure whose demands—even for self-sacrifice—are experienced as stable and consistent. The failure to live up to such demands
still guarantees a sense of place, meaning, and recognition; but the subject who is uncertain as to the very existence of an Other whose demands might or might not be placated loses the ground from under his
feet.[55] The mythic order of fate where one's lot is determined behind
one's back—in Kafka's story, as in ancient tragedy, the force of fate
corresponds to a familial debt or guilt—is displaced by a postmythic
order in which the individual can no longer find his place in the texture
of fate. This distance from the mythic force of fate, this interruption of
the transference of a debt from generation to generation, introduces
into the world a new and more radical kind of guilt.[56] In *Metamorphosis*,
the interruption of those entanglements we call fate opens up a space
within which monstrosities can appear. This interruption is figured in
the story by means of a series of ambiguities pertaining to patriarchal
power and authority.

Significantly, as in *Parsifal*, a crisis in the domain of patriarchal authority is registered at the level of voice and staging. At the end of the
first part of the story, Gregor's father chases his son back into his room,
producing a strange and disturbing hissing noise: "Pitilessly his father
came on, hissing like a wild man" (19). Gregor struggles to comply but
is distracted and unnerved by this curious vocalization: "If only his
father did not keep making this intolerable hissing sound! It made
Gregor lose his head completely. He had almost finished the turn
when—his mind continually on this hissing—he made a mistake and
even started turning back around to his original position" (19). During

the final moments of this ordeal, the father's hissing achieves an intensity such that *"the voice behind Gregor did not sound like that of only a single father;* now this was really no joke anymore" (19; my emphasis). It is as if the father's voice had assumed the quality of an uncanny chorus, signaling the dimension of an implacable and horrific paternal force exceeding that of any single individual. Our perplexity about this weird amplification and distortion of the father's voice is heightened in the third and final part of the story. At a moment when the family's rejuvenation is well underway, Kafka indicates that the father's reinvigoration may be nothing more than a pathetic imposture: "Sometimes his father woke up, and as if he had absolutely no idea that he had been asleep, said to his mother, 'Look how long you're sewing again today!' and went right back to sleep, while mother and sister smiled wearily at each other" (41). In the next sentence the question of imposture is placed directly into the foreground: "With a kind of perverse obstinacy his father refused to take off his official uniform even in the house; and while his robe hung uselessly on the clothes hook, his father dozed, completely dressed, in his chair, as if he were always ready for duty and were waiting even here for the voice of his superior" (41). The ambiguity of Kafka's diction makes possible the reading that the father has refused to remove his uniform not just at home but in public as well; his recent "investiture" with a kind of official status and authority, low though it is, might, in other words, be a sham. Be that as it may, the father's clinging to the outward appearance—to the vestments—of institutional authority suggests just how precarious and uncertain this authority really is. Gregor's father achieves his new patriarchal authority, restores his damaged masculinity, by means of a kind of cross-dressing.

In a diary entry of September 23, 1912, Kafka registered the miraculous composition of "The Judgment" in the course of a single night's labor, one he would, the following year, characterize as a kind of couvade in which his story emerged covered with the "filth and mucus" of birth. In the entry of September 23, he recollects various associations that passed through his mind during the composition of the story and notes, "naturally, thoughts of Freud."[57] The year before the composition of "The Judgment" and *Metamorphosis*, Freud had, of course, published his study of Schreber. There is no direct evidence that Kafka read Freud's essay on Schreber or Schreber's own text; the parallels between Kafka's story of bodily metamorphosis and Schreber's are, however, quite stunning.[58] As with Gregor, Schreber's demise is correlated with a form of vocational failure: an inability to heed an official call, to assume a symbolic mandate, in this case as presiding judge in the Saxon Court of Appeals. After his mental collapse

and forced withdrawal from his position in the courts, Schreber begins to suffer from what eventually becomes one of his core symptoms: the hearing of voices. These voices, which torment Schreber for most of the rest of his life, embody the excess of demands that made the administration of his office insupportable. In a sense, they represent these demands purified of any instrumental value or meaning-content, a kind of pure and nonsensical "You must!" abstracted from the use value of any particular activity. At this zero level of meaning, the voices eventually come to be heard by Schreber as a steady hissing sound, the sound which for Gregor was that of a kind of wild and perverse paternal chorus: "But the slowing down has recently become still more marked and the voices . . . degenerated into an indistinct hissing" (226). The vocalizations tormenting Schreber became, as we know, particularly concentrated one day, manifesting themselves in the form of a singular, revelatory enunciation, the meaning and force of which effectuated Schreber's "conversion" to *Ludertum*. But how might we correlate the particular connotations of Schreber's status as *Luder*— whore, rottenness, Jew—with the details of Gregor Samsa's "conversion" to verminousness?

Amid the wealth of striking details that have preoccupied readers of Kafka's *Metamorphosis*, the one that situates Kafka's text most firmly within fin-de-siècle obsessions with gender and sexuality is the brief indication of Gregor's erotic life suggested by a bit of interior decorating he had engaged in shortly before his verminous transformation: "Over the table . . . hung the picture which he had recently cut out of a glossy magazine and lodged in a pretty gilt frame. It showed a lady done up in a fur hat and a fur boa, sitting upright and raising up against the viewer a heavy fur muff in which her whole forearm had disappeared" (3). The importance of this peculiar detail, alluding, very likely, to Leopold von Sacher-Masoch's infamous novella, *Venus in Furs* (1870),[59] is underlined by its placement in the text: it appears in the second paragraph following immediately upon the famous inaugural sentences announcing Gregor's metamorphosis and is introduced as if in answer to the question with which the paragraph begins: "What's happened to me?" The picture, most likely part of an advertisement, figures once more, in the second part of the story, when Gregor is struggling to save some piece of his former life from the efforts of his mother and sister to clear his room:

> And so he broke out—the women were just leaning against the desk in the next room to catch their breath for a minute—changed his course four times, he really didn't know what to salvage first, then he saw hanging conspicuously on the wall, which was otherwise bare already, the picture

of the lady all dressed in furs, hurriedly crawled up on it and pressed himself against the glass, which gave a good surface to stick to and soothed his hot belly. At least no one would take away this picture, while Gregor completely covered it up. (35)

The importance of this possession is further emphasized by Gregor's willingness to attack his otherwise beloved sister rather than part with his picture: "He squatted on his picture and would not give it up. He would rather fly in Grete's face" (36).

Gregor's peculiar attachment to this piece of pornographic kitsch is obviously central to the text. Indeed, the entire story seems to crystallize around it as an elaborate punishment scenario called forth by guilt-ridden sexual obsessions. The indications of putrescence that proliferate in the course of the story suggest fantasies of the consequences of a young man's autoerotic activities. In this perspective, many hitherto unintelligible details take on importance. When, for example, the maid announces at the end of the story that she has removed the insect's corpse from Gregor's room, the word she uses—*das Zeug* ("the stuff")—evokes what is allegedly cut short by compulsive autoeroticism, namely the capacity for *Zeugen*, the generation of offspring. The final sentences of the story, which circle around Grete's sexual coming-of-age and prospects of imminent union with "a good husband," constitute the closure made possible by the elimination of the perverse (i.e., nonreproductive) sexuality embodied in Gregor's abject, putrescent condition.

This reading is supported by a wide array of medical treatises and popular literature concerning the dangers of masturbation circulating in fin-de-siècle Europe; it presupposes, however, that the woman in furs must be understood as an object of heterosexual desire. But if we are to take the comparison with Schreber seriously, a different, more "perverse," reading becomes possible, namely, one in which the woman in furs is not an object of desire but rather one of (unconscious) *identification*. In other words, Gregor's picture of the woman in furs represents the unconscious "truth" of the other picture described in the story, the photograph of Gregor from his "army days, in a lieutenant's uniform, his hand on his sword, a carefree smile on his lips, demanding respect for his bearing and his rank" (15). Gregor's metamorphosis now becomes legible as a kind of feminization; his verminous state suggests the mode of appearance of a femininity disavowed under the pressures of a misogynist and homophobic cultural imperative shared by Kafka's Austria-Hungary and Schreber's Germany.[60]

This reading is supported by a detail pertaining, once again, to the voice. After missing the train on the first morning of his new condition,

Gregor's mother calls to him from the other side of his locked door to remind him of the time. After noting the softness of his mother's voice, he notices a new quality in his own voice:

Gregor was shocked to hear his own voice answering, unmistakably his own voice, true, but in which, as if from below, an insistent distressed chirping [*ein nicht zu unterdrückendes, schmerzliches Piepsen*] intruded, which left the clarity of his words intact only for a moment really, before so badly garbling them as they carried that no one could be sure if he had heard right. (5)

Gregor's *Piepsen* suggests the mutation of the male voice in the direction of the feminine. The importance of this birdlike vocalization could be confirmed, once more, by an important detail from Schreber's text we have already encountered. At various moments, the voices that tormented Schreber miraculously took the form of little birds—*gewunderte Vögel*—who were understood by Schreber to be made up of residues of departed human souls that had, in his delusional cosmology, previously made up the so-called forecourts of heaven. Schreber characterizes their chirpings as a series of mechanically repeated turns of phrase. As we know, thanks to their purely repetitive and meaningless nature—their *deadness*—Schreber associates these vocalizations with putrescence or what he calls *Leichengift*, the poison of corpses. Freud, one will recall, heard them as the voices of young girls: "In a carping mood people often compare them to geese, ungallantly accuse them of having 'the brains of a bird' and declare that they can say nothing but phrases learnt by rote and they betray their lack of education by confusing foreign words that sound alike" (*SE* 12:36).

But Gregor's *Piepsen* points also in the direction indicated by Schreber's other pole of identification: that of the Wandering Jew. Central to the preoccupations of fin-de-siècle culture with the peculiarities of Jewish physical and mental constitution was, as became stunningly clear in Panizza's text, an obsession with the Jewish voice and Jewish language production. This obsession, already important in premodern Europe, was recoded in the nineteenth century in the idiom of racial biology and conjoined with fantasies about Jewish sexuality and the impaired masculinity of Jewish men, in particular. At the end of the nineteenth century, the faulty command of discourse attributed to Jews and condensed in the term *mauscheln*, meaning to speak (German) like Moses, was thus coupled with femininity and, hence, homosexuality. To return to *Metamorphosis*, we might say that the Jew's *Mauscheln* was recoded as a kind of feminized, queer *Piepsen*.[61]

Kafka's text, however, is more than a literary version of a kind of Jewish self-hatred, more than the narrative and poetic elaboration of a

series of internalized anti-Semitic prejudices. For though Kafka is a writer whose work is at times burdened by negative conceptions about Jews, Judaism, and Jewishness, *Metamorphosis* is a text that indicates Kafka's profound awareness of the ideological role such conceptions played within the larger culture. In *Metamorphosis*, the cultural fantasies positioning the Jew, along with everything feminine, at the place of abjection, are led back to the deeper cultural crises and anxieties fueling them. These anxieties arise, as we have seen, from a fundamental crisis or dysfunctionality at the core of patriarchal power and authority. Kafka's story suggests, in other words, that at least in the modern period the domain of the abject and monstrous, or, to use the term that would prove so fateful and fatal during the Nazi period, the "degenerate," is linked to a chronic uncertainty haunting the institutions of power. The "redemption" of the Samsa family at the conclusion of Kafka's story thus represents the ultimate ideological fantasy, not unlike the conclusion of Wagner's *Parsifal*, where the restoration of the Grail Society is linked to Kundry's demise. With the destruction of Gregor *qua* feminized Wandering Jew, the family can thrive, perhaps now for the very first time.[62]

VII

These reflections compel us to revise the perspective apropos of the Jewish question in Freud and Schreber proposed by Gilman, Geller, Boyarin, and Eilberg-Schwartz. These scholars all argue that Freud's reading of the Schreber case was produced under pressures to disavow those "feminine" tendencies, strivings, and desires that in the cultural climate of fin-de-siècle Central Europe had increasingly come to be associated by racialist anti-Semitism with an ostensibly Jewish pathological disposition. It was, according to this reading, this unique historical formation that led Freud to miss a crucial interpretive possibility opened by the Schreber case, namely that homophobia, rather than homosexuality per se, produces paranoia.[63] As evidence of Freud's own defensive posturings with regard to femininity and homosexuality, one cites Freud's correspondence with members of his circle—above all Jung and Ferenczi—around the time of his work on Schreber. I have argued that the references to homosexuality and its "overcoming" (by way of the work on Schreber) found in these documents should be read against a backdrop of issues concerning originality and influence anxiety. I suggested that these issues were particularly acute for Freud and his circle because of the tenuous status of psychoanalysis as a science and institution, a tenuousness that has never ceased to haunt

psychoanalysis. I have furthermore proposed that Freud's attraction to the Schreber material was ultimately a function of his identification not with Schreber's ostensible homosexuality, but rather with the latter's struggle with a crisis of investiture, a breakdown in the *transfer* of symbolic capital that would have allowed him to assume his mandate within the institution of the courts. It was *this breakdown and its hallucinatory repair* that Freud misread as Schreber's homosexual longings for paternal substitutes, figures bearing phallic attributes and prerogatives.

My point, once again, is not that homosexual desire and its repression (under the pressures of a compulsory and compulsive heterosexuality) played no role in Schreber's delusional system or in Freud's relations with Fliess and various members of his inner circle; I have focused rather on the paths whereby a crisis of symbolic power and its transfer comes to be sexualized, or perhaps better, comes to be experienced *as sexuality*, as the very "matter" of sexuality.[64] In any case, Schreber's *Memoirs* makes quite clear that where there is such a crisis, the irreducible dependency of symbolic function—the production of credible symbolic identities—on the performative magic of (repeated) rites of institution becomes impossible to repress. Once it emerges from the individual and "political" unconscious, this dependency is experienced as *decadence*, as a chronic *wasting away* of one's symbolic power and authority. The decay and rottenness produced thereby are figured by the work of individual and social fantasy as *contaminations*, as a leakage of toxins—and transgressive intoxications—emanating always from the *other* side of a social boundary. Within the terms of Schreber's "own private Germany," a fantasy space shared, to a large extent, by Freud, Panizza, Kafka, and a host of others, the "other side" was above all the side of women, Jews, homosexuals (and to some extent Catholics), the key representatives of Schreber's *Ludertum*.[65] At this point I would like to return, briefly, to the influential work of Otto Weininger whose *Geschlecht und Charakter* is doubtlessly the single most important "philosophical" elaboration of this fantasy space.

In Weininger's neo-Kantian "theory" of gender, sexuality, and race, dependency on the rites of institution and all that they imply is denoted by the term *heteronomy*. From the perspective of Kant's conception of practical reason—a perspective that, as we have seen, was crucial for Moritz Schreber—heteronomy signifies a merely mimetic relation to morality resulting from a failure to be oneself the legislator of the moral law. The capacity for self-legislation, or rather for speaking from the place of the moral law, is achieved by way of purifying oneself of all external, and so "pathological," influences and determinations.[66] Heteronomy results, in other words, from the subject's failure to iden-

tify fully and without remainder with the transcendental locus of the moral law beyond all empirical, social, even human, benefits and considerations, from the failure to assume, to put it in Freudian terms, an ethical position *beyond the pleasure principle*. And for Weininger, femininity and Jewishness are ultimately the names for this condition of failing to (cor)respond to the moral law, they are the names for the residues, the "refuse," of heteronomy that endangers the (Enlightenment) project of Kantian ethics, the conception of which Weininger characterized as the most sublime event of world history.

Put somewhat differently, Weininger proposes an ideal of masculinity that would be immune to that psychic disorder—and for Weininger, that ultimately means an *ethical* and *logical* disorder—produced by heteronomy and that, in the view of a great deal of nineteenth-century medicine, typically plagued women and Jews: hysteria. For Weininger, hysteria is ultimately the condition of being unable *to void* oneself of— or, to use Panizza's terms, to spit out—all "pathological" determinations of the will in the name of the moral law. The avoidance of this void that is the Kantian moral subject, the expectation that someone else—some master—will tell me who I am and what I ought to value and desire, *is* hysteria, in Weininger's view. The inability to occupy this place of the subject conceived as the void of all heteronomous determinations, left women and Jews in a condition of dispersal, adrift amid flows of impressions, empirical causations and influences, but without the pure ego-centering force of self-legislation. At best, women and Jews could *mime* ethical action, but the moral law would always be experienced as an external imposition occupying the place of simply another cause or influence within the domain of *phenomenal experience* to which one had to *assimilate*, but never as a call, a categorical imperative issued from, or better, *as* the noumenal dimension of one's own subjectivity: "Man becomes free only when he himself becomes the law: only in this way does he escape heteronomy, determination through outside forces or persons, which is ineluctably tied to [the other's] caprice" (246).[67]

For Weininger, one of the "faces" of heteronomy is the particular way in which *value* is determined in capitalist social relations—the mediation of desire in accordance with the law of exchange value. In a discussion of feminine vanity, Weininger argues, in effect, that women lack an inborn—an *urwüchsigen*—standard of value, that they feel no absolute value in themselves, "which scorns everything but itself" (263). From Weininger's "Kantian" perspective, woman's allegedly extreme dependence on others for the mediation of her own value—in essence, her *market value*—"is equivalent with the lack of a transcendental ego [*intelligibles Ich*], that which is always and absolutely posited as having value; it derives from the lack of a proper value [*Eigenwert*].

Since they lack a proper value for themselves and before themselves, they strive to become an object of value for others" (260). For Weininger, a (Protestant) man is by definition that being who is absolutely sure of his value, a being who is in no way dependent on others for the mediation of his proper value. Paradoxically, the religious formation that Max Weber would characterize as being deeply compatible with capitalist social relations is for Weininger the one that lays claim to a kind of immunity to the social and psychic imbalances generated by one of capitalism's most fundamental laws, that of the transmutation of all value into exchange value. For Weininger, it is precisely this immunity to the derangements of capitalism—above all, to the forces of commodification—that determines whether one has a soul and so *exists* in an emphatic sense; in Weininger's view, women have no soul—defined as the capacity for a radical disidentification with the community and its modalities of valuation—and so *do not exist*: "Women have neither existence nor essence; they *are* not, they are *nothing*" (383).[68] Heteronomy would seem to be, then, Weininger's name for social mediation of any kind, for the subject's dependency on tradition in the widest possible sense, on the transmission of symbolic power from the outside—from institutions, authorities, and ancestors—in a word, the subject's irreducible dependency on procedures of *investiture*. It is this dependency, along with the multiple layers of *transference* that it implies, that psychoanalysis has theorized under the sign of symbolic castration and that Weininger—and here he is exemplary for fin-de-siècle "theorists" of gender and sexuality—wants to exclude from the domain of masculinity proper. This (phantasmatic) construction of masculinity as a mode of subjectivity beyond all heteronomy (and the transferential relations generated thereby) breaks down, however, in a number of different ways in Weininger's text. Perhaps the most telling example of such a breakdown occurs in Weininger's discussion of a topic that was also an object of some concern to Schreber: the status of proper names and the relation one has to one's name.

After arguing that women in general have no sense for property or property rights,[69] Weininger broaches the subject of proper names [*Eigennamen*]: "Even more than property, the name, and a heartfelt relation to one's name, is a necessary dimension of human personhood" (267). About women's relation to names, he says the following:

> Women . . . have no real bonds with their names. Telling in this regard is already the fact that they give up their names and take on [the name] of the man they marry, and that they don't even experience this name change as significant or as a loss to be mourned. . . . The name, however, is conceived as a symbol of individuality; only among the most primitive races of the earth . . . is there apparently no such thing as proper names because of

insufficient development of the natural need among human beings to
make distinctions among themselves. Woman is essentially nameless and
is so because she, by definition [*seiner Idee nach*], lacks personhood. (267)[70]

However, in a discussion of the family in the chapter on Judaism,
Weininger writes of the rage [*Zorn*] that every real man consciously or
unconsciously feels toward his father "who, without asking him,
forced him into life and at birth gave him the name that seemed appropriate [to the father]" (416). Because one is *forced* to choose life, *forced*
into a relation with one's name, the autonomy of even the most masculine of men is stained by heteronomy, realizes itself as a purely formal
affirmation of an already given state of affairs. By virtue of being
named, through "subjection" to this minimal procedure of initiatory
investiture—which, one might add, places the son in a passive-recep-
tive relation to his progenitor—no man, apparently, completely escapes from transference. The rage Weininger associates with the residues of heteronomy that resist conversion into autonomy—the feat
that both Weininger and Moritz Schreber associate with authentic,
"Kantian" masculinity—becomes, within the cultural codes of the fin
de siècle, a rage against women and Jews and *one's own transgressions*
into their domains. It is, in a word, a rage against the fact that one has
always already crossed the line in the wrong direction, that one has
secretly "converted" to *Ludertum* and its disturbing jouissance.[71] It is
the knowledge of such crossings, of this transgressive traffic, that
Schreber elaborates in his *Memoirs*.

VIII

Weininger's most important precursor text apropos of the "problem"
of Jewish creativity was, as I have indicated, Wagner's notorious essay
"Das Judentum in der Musik." That essay, which at one point associates Jewish productivity in the arts with worms consuming the flesh of
a corpse—an image that calls to mind Schreber's neologism for what is
rotten in the order of the law: *Leichengift*—concludes with a call for the
overcoming/destruction, the *Untergang*, of Ahasver. That destruction
is most powerfully figured in Wagner's last opera, *Parsifal*, as the death
of Kundry, whom we might characterize as Wagner's pendant to
Schreber's unmanned Wandering Jew.[72]

I have already noted that Schreber was quite "fluent" in the idiom of
Wagnerian opera and that the text of his *Memoirs* contains numerous
references and allusions to Wagner's work.[73] Although there is no evidence of any direct knowledge on Schreber's part of *Parsifal*, which
premiered in Bayreuth in 1882, there are numerous structural similari-

ties between Wagner's last opera and Schreber's theological system. The state of emergency in which Schreber's universe finds itself is not unlike that of the Grail Society in which the blessings of eternal life provided by the Grail miracle have been suspended. Indeed, what Schreber says apropos of his own cosmic circumstances could equally apply to the crisis with which *Parsifal* begins: "the state of *Blessedness* is so to speak suspended and all human beings who have since died or will die *can for the time being not attain to it*" (60–61). In Schreber's case, that cosmic disturbance was, as we know, the ultimate consequence of a prior and more mundane one, one I have characterized as an *investiture crisis*, namely, the breakdown of Schreber's capacity to assume his mandate as *Senatspräsident* of the Saxon Supreme Court. Schreber's incapacity to fulfill his duties in the administration of the law and his subsequent condition of chronic, though largely phantasmatic, woundedness, closely parallel the condition of the Fisher King, Amfortas, whose own wounded body attests to his inability to officiate over the Grail Society and whom we have already compared with another failed bureaucrat/employee, Gregor Samsa.

In *Parsifal*, the institutional domain in crisis—the Grail Society—is redeemed when a pure and innocent fool heals Amfortas by touching his wound with the reclaimed spear of Longinus. As Parsifal declaims: "Nur eine Waffe taugt: / die Wunde schliesst / der Speer nur, der sie schlug" ("One weapon alone can do it: / the wound is healed / solely by the spear that made it"). Parsifal comes into possession of the spear and, eventually, the throne of the Grail Society, after rejecting the lures of Kundry, an action that prefigures her final overcoming/destruction in and through the restitution of the Grail miracle. Parsifal's rejection of Kundry at the moment of her kiss is mediated in its turn by his recollection of Amfortas's suffering. It is, perhaps, in this "primal scene" of compassion or *Mitleid* that the difference between Wagner and Schreber becomes most palpable. The two universes are, we might say, structured around fundamentally different readings of this woundedness, different renderings of the "institutional" and, ultimately, political knowledge secreted therein. In the opera, Parsifal's initiatory investiture as king of the Grail Society makes use of Amfortas's suffering and, indeed, depends upon it. In the end, Parsifal interprets Amfortas's wound as a coded message, blesses his suffering as that which has taught him, Parsifal, that he must assume his place as administrator of the Grail miracle. The wound merely confirms what he was already chosen to be and thereby becomes the means for the restitution of the collectivity, but one, of course, which has eliminated all traces of the feminine (and the Jewish).

Schreber's chosenness is of a completely different order and, indeed, nothing could be further from the pattern of repair, restitution, and

healing exhibited in Schreber's *Memoirs* than Parsifal's final act as, we might say, *Senatspräsident* of the Grail Society. Rather than reclaiming the phallic emblem and the symbolic authority attached to it, Schreber reiterates its "miraculous" ruination. By becoming the unmanned Wandering Jew, Schreber, in effect, *identifies with the symptom* that for Wagner—and for German culture more generally—materialized the blockage in the smooth functioning of the social body. The lure of Wagner's opera—one resisted in the Schreberian fantasy scenario—is to see in Amfortas's wound, this embodiment of social crisis, of a chronic malfunction in the administration of symbolic power and authority, the work of Kundry, Woman and Wandering Jew. One of the many reasons for Schreber's appeal—for his remarkable "attractiveness," as he would put it—and his belated canonization as a compelling modernist writer, is that he offers the prospect of new strategies of sapping the force of social fantasies that might otherwise lend support to the totalitarian temptation. To traverse, with Schreber, the fantasy space of *his* own private Germany (rather than, say, Wagner's) is to encounter European modernity from the perspective of those figures in whom modern European society "secreted" its disavowed knowledge of chronic structural crisis and disequilibrium. Schreberian compassion or *Mitleid*, in contrast to the Wagnerian variety, is a way of refusing to refuse the knowledge of the impasses and dilemmas of symbolic power and authority. At some level, Schreber was saying, indeed screaming, to those figures who were, whether they were fully conscious of it or not, cursed with the role of embodying these impasses: "That is me!" "I am Kundry!" Of course, Schreber's fate as a psychotic suggests that one should not, as they say, try this at home; it is, in other words, genuinely maddening to find oneself occupying the place of abjection in the absence of some minimal form of human solidarity. What ultimately saved Schreber from psychological death, at least for a short while, was no doubt his residual need and capacity to *communicate and transfer* his "discoveries," to inaugurate a new *tradition* constructed out of and upon the inconsistencies and impasses of the one he had known and which he had been called upon to represent. (The proliferation of books, articles, conferences, and seminars dedicated to Schreber, which shows no signs of abating, testifies to the revelatory force and productivity of his transmission.)

Schreber's legacy concerns the crucial value of fantasy, the passions, and even the so-called perversions as sources of knowledge about the state of those symbolic resources that human societies depend upon to assure their members that they are "legitimate." The rites and procedures of investiture whereby an individual is endowed with a socially

intelligible status and filled with symbolic mandates corresponding to that status function not only as compelling reassurances for those individuals but for the society as well. The smooth functioning of these procedures reassures the community that it, too, *exists*, that there is something "real" about the social facts and values—names, titles, currency, genders, and the like—that it consecrates and produces. Schreber's delusions figure a crisis pertaining to these rites and procedures, a fundamental and disorienting shift in the subject's relation to them. His "secret history of modernity" suggests that we cross the threshold of that era where and when those symbolic resources no longer address the subject where he or she most profoundly "lives," which is, beginning at least with the European Enlightenment, the negative space hollowed out by the will to autonomy and self-reflexivity. Once those values have established their hegemony, individuals are, so to speak, chronically out of joint, called to order by a community whose very existence as a meaning-giving, symbolic whole can no longer—and perhaps never again—be experienced as fully trustworthy or of ultimate value. (At this point, the symbolic causation on which all acts of symbolic investiture depend undergoes a kind of literalization into a more mechanical, more "disciplinary" mode of causation.) Schreber's cultivation of an ensemble of "perverse" practices, identifications, and fantasies allows him not only to *act out*, but also to *work through* what may very well be the central paradox of modernity: that the subject is solicited by a will to autonomy in the name of the very community that is thereby undermined, whose very substance thereby passes over into the subject. Schreber's phantasmatic elaboration of that paradox allows him to find his way back into a context of human solidarity without having to disavow this fundamental breach of trust, without having to heal it with a "final" and definitively redemptive solution.

NOTES

PREFACE

1. I cite the reprint of the 1955 English translation of Schreber's text prepared by Ida Macalpine and Richard A. Hunter (Cambridge, Mass.: Harvard University Press, 1988). References to the German text are taken from a recent reprint edited by Peter Heiligenthal and Reinhard Volk (Frankfurt: Syndikat, 1985). References to the English edition will be given parenthetically in the text. Regarding other sources, translations are my own unless otherwise noted.

2. Elias Canetti, *Crowds and Power*, trans. Carol Stewart (New York: Seabury Press, 1978).

3. Ibid., 447, 443, 448.

4. Gilles Deleuze and Félix Guatarri, *Anti-Oedipus: Capitalism and Schizophrenia*, trans. Robert Hurley, Mark Seem, and Helen Lane (Minneapolis: University of Minnesota Press, 1983), 279, 364.

5. See William Niederland, *The Schreber Case: Psychoanalytic Profile of a Paranoid Personality* (Hillsdale, N.J.: Analytic Press, 1984).

6. Morton Schatzman, *Soul Murder: Persecution in the Family* (New York: Random House, 1973), 170, 171. Building on Schatzman's work, Alice Miller offers a psychobiography of Hitler in which the "poisonous pedagogy" codified in Moritz Schreber's writings is made largely responsible for Hitler's own paranoid hatred of Jews and other "enemies." See Miller, *For Your Own Good: Hidden Cruelty in Child-Rearing and the Roots of Violence* (New York: Farrar, Straus, Giroux, 1984).

7. It is perhaps no accident that Max Weber "became who he was," i.e., the father of modern sociology in Germany and great theorist of historical forms of symbolic authority and leadership, only in the course of recovering from a psychotic breakdown not unlike Schreber's. Weber's recovery is usually dated with the year 1903, the year Schreber published his *Memoirs*.

8. Schreber is not always so modest. He later asserts, for example, that he had become "for God the only human being, or simply the human being around whom everything turns" (197), and at the end of his *Memoirs* he writes that "the spread of my religious ideas and the weight of proof of their truth will lead to a fundamental revolution in mankind's religious views unequalled in history" (215).

9. Clifford Geertz, "Centers, Kings, and Charisma: Reflections on the Symbolics of Power," in *Local Knoweldge: Further Essays in Interpretive Anthropology* (New York: Basic Books, 1983), 123, 124; my emphasis.

10. As to the transferential short-circuit between a contemporary "moment of danger" and an object of scholarly/historical interest, see Walter Benjamin, "Theses on the Philosophy of History," in *Illuminations*, trans. Harry Zohn (New York: Schocken, 1969), 255.

11. See Umberto Eco's provocative reflections on the contemporaneity of the fascist danger in "Ur-Fascism," *New York Review of Books*, June 22, 1995, 12–15.

INTRODUCTION

1. The *Landgericht* or District Court occupies the middle level of jurisdiction between the *Amtsgericht* or County Court and the *Oberlandesgericht*, the highest or Supreme Court of Appeals in Saxony.

2. The blurb on the original 1903 edition included these words: "The work includes a great many stimulating ideas and will therefore be found worthwhile by *theologians, philosophers, physicians, jurists*, particularly *psychiatrists*, and in general all *educated persons interested in questions relating to the hereafter*" (cited in Zvi Lothane, *In Defense of Schreber: Soul Murder and Psychiatry* [Hillsdale, N.J.: Analytic Press, 1992], 319).

3. This according to Niederland who interviewed her in 1972. See William Niederland, *The Schreber Case: Psychoanalytic Profile of a Paranoid Personality* (Hillsdale, N.J.: Analytic Press, 1984), 31.

4. Cited in Schreber's hospital chart from the Leipzig-Dösen Asylum discovered by Franz Baumeyer and published as part of an essay, "Der Fall Schreber," which has been reprinted in the German edition of Schreber, *Denkwürdigkeiten*, 341–63. See also Lothane, *In Defense of Schreber*, for a translation of the chart.

5. On December 1, 1907, he mumbled about the "odor of corpses" and "rotting" (*Leichengeruch, Verwesung*); shortly thereafter he is reported to have claimed that his body had begun to rot while his head continued to live (cited in Baumeyer, "Der Fall Schreber," 347).

6. The 1895 English translation of Nordau's work has been reissued by the University of Nebraska Press (Lincoln, 1993). In his use of the term, Nordau was following the French psychiatrist B. A. Morel for whom it meant *"a morbid deviation from an original type"* (cited in Nordau, *Degeneration*, 16). References will be given parenthetically in the text.

7. This language recalls Marx and Engel's description in *The Communist Manifesto* (1848) of the negative energies released by capitalist modes of production. See Marshall Berman's fine discussion of that "definitive vision of the modern environment" in his *All That Is Solid Melts into Air: The Experience of Modernity* (New York: Simon and Schuster, 1982).

8. The prospect of a sort of ergonomic bankruptcy is opened, for Nordau, above all by the traumatic speed of social change in modern society: "We know that our organs acquire by exercise an ever greater functional capacity, that they develop by their own activity, and can respond to nearly every demand made upon them; but only under one condition—that this occurs gradually, that time be allowed them. It they are obliged to fulfil, without transition, a multiple of their usual task, they soon give out entirely. No time was left to our fathers. Between one day and the next, as it were, without preparation, with murderous suddenness, they were obliged to change the comfortable creeping gait of their former existence for the stormy stride of modern life, and their heart and lungs could not bear it" (*Degeneration*, 40). Nordau adds that the resulting fatigue and exhaustion "showed themselves in the first generation, under the form of acquired hysteria; in the second, as hereditary hysteria" (40).

9. Anson Rabinbach, *The Human Motor: Energy, Fatigue and the Origins of Modernity* (Berkeley: University of California Press, 1992), 6. Mindful of the specific national inflections of these anxieties, Rabinbach notes that in Wilhelminne Germany the "fatigue mania . . . grew out of a society less fearful of imminent disintegration than of its dizzying ascent to industrialization and economic triumph" (22).

10. In her study, *Sexual Anarchy: Gender and Culture at the Fin de Siècle* (New York: Viking, 1990), Elaine Showalter discusses the primarily masculine iconography of syphilis in the Victorian imagination: "With its dramatic inscriptions on the male body, the hideous ravages of syphilis, from an enormous and Miltonic list of skin disorders—macules, papules, tubercules, pustules, blebs, tumors, lesions, scales, crusts, ulcers, chancres, gummas, fissures, and scars—to cardiovascular disturbances, locomotor ataxia, tabes, blindness, and dementia, made the disease a powerful deterrent in theological and moral reform campaigns to control male sexuality, seen as one of the main causes of degeneration" (192–93).

11. Cited in Andreas Hill, "'May the Doctor Advise Extramarital Intercourse?': Medical Debates on Sexual Abstinence in Germany, c. 1900," in *Sexual Knowledge, Sexual Science: The History of Attitudes to Sexuality*, ed. Roy Porter and Mikulás Teich (Cambridge: Cambridge University Press, 1994), 287–88.

12. Benjamin writes briefly about Schreber's text in "Bücher von Geisteskranken. Aus meiner Sammlung," in *Gesammelte Schriften*, ed. Rolf Tiedemann, Hermann Schweppenhäuser, and Tillman Rexroth, vol. 11 (Frankfurt: Suhrkamp, 1980), 615–16. In his biography of Benjamin, Gershom Scholem recalls his friend's participation in a seminar on Freud during his years in Bern for which Benjamin read Schreber's *Memoirs* and wrote a paper about Freud's theory of drives. Scholem remembers that Schreber's book made a more powerful impression on Benjamin than Freud's case study. Benjamin also managed to persuade Scholem to read the *Memoirs*. See Gershom Scholem, *Walter Benjamin. Die Geschichte einer Freundschaft* (Frankfurt: Suhrkamp, 1976), 75.

13. Benjamin, "Zur Kritik der Gewalt," in *Gesammelte Schriften*, 4:179–203. The essay appears in English as "The Critique of Violence" in *Reflections. Essays, Aphorisms, Autobiographical Writings*, ed. Peter Demetz, trans. Edmund Jephcott (New York: Schocken, 1986), 277–300. *Gewalt* denotes not only violence but also the more ambiguous concept of force. The work on this essay also likely began in Bern when in 1919 Benjamin was introduced to Georges Sorel's *Réflexions sur la violence* through conversations with Hugo Ball and Ernst Bloch. See Scholem, *Walter Benjamin*, 109.

14. Benjamin, "Critique," 286; my emphasis.

15. Much of Slavoj Žižek's work has been dedicated to the elaboration of this dimension of tautology or vicious circularity normally subject to what Freud called "primordial repression." Compare, for example, the following formulation from *For They Know Not What They Do: Enjoyment as a Political Factor* (London: Verso, 1991): "'At the beginning' of the law, there is a certain 'outlaw', a certain Real of violence which coincides with the act itself of the establishment of the reign of law: the ultimate truth about the reign of law is that of an usurpation, and all classical politico-philosophical thought rests on

the disavowal of this violent act of foundation. The illegitimate violence by which the law sustains itself must be concealed at any price, because this concealment is the positive condition of the functioning of law: it functions in so far as its subjects are deceived, in so far as they experience the authority of law as 'authentic and eternal' and overlook 'the truth about the usurpation'" (204). For a highly nuanced discussion of the political dangers of an overvaluation of this "truth about the usurpation," see Dominick LaCapra's discussion of Benjamin's essay in "Violence, Justice, and the Force of Law," *Cardozo Law Review* 11 (July–August 1990): 1065–78.

16. Benjamin, "Critique," 286–87 (my emphasis), 287, 287. For a study of the police function as the "open secret" of modern societies and its characteristic literary form, the novel, see D. A. Miller, *The Novel and the Police* (Berkeley: University of California Press, 1988).

17. Jacques Derrida, "Force of Law: The 'Mystical Foundation of Authority,'" in *Deconstruction and the Possibility of Justice*, ed. Drucilla Cornell, Michel Rosenfeld, and David Gray Carlson (New York: Routledge, 1992), 3–67.

18. Much of what Benjamin argues in extremely compact and hermetic prose has been elaborated in a more experience-near idiom by Elaine Scarry in her book *The Body in Pain: The Making and Unmaking of the World* (New York: Oxford University Press, 1985). Scarry's book explores the ways in which, above all in the practices of torture and war, human pain, the "obscenely . . . alive tissue" (31) of the human body, is enlisted as a source of verification and substantiation of the symbolic authority of institutions and the social facts they sponsor. This bottoming out of symbolic function on the body in pain becomes urgent, Scarry argues, when there is a crisis of belief or legitimation in a society: "at particular moments when there is within society a crisis of belief—that is, when some central idea or ideology or cultural construct has ceased to elicit a population's belief either because it is manifestly fictitious or because it has for some reason been divested of ordinary forms of substantiation—the sheer material factualness of the human body will be borrowed to lend that cultural construct the aura of 'realness' and 'certainty'" (14). One might say that the wounded body is where a society "secretes" what is rotten in law. Speaking more specifically of the structure of war, Scarry argues that "injuring is relied on as a form of legitimation because, though it lacks interior connections to the issues, wounding is able to open up a source of reality that can give the issue force and holding power. That is, the outcome of war has its substantiation not in an absolute inability of the defeated to contest the outcome but in a process of perception that allows extreme attributes of the body to be translated into another language, to be broken away from the body and relocated elsewhere at the very moment that the body itself is disowned"(124). This conception of the injured body as an unspeakable piece of the real that provides the ultimate support of a symbolic order, that (unconsciously) helps to make social facts—governments, money, marriage, social titles, etc.—feel real rather than fictional, allows Scarry, in effect, to recast the psychoanalytic concept of *transference* in more social and political terms. It comes to signify, for Scarry, the "intricacies of the process of transfer that make it possible for the *incontestable reality of the physical body to now become an attribute of an issue that at that moment has no*

independent reality of its own" (124–25). What becomes painfully manifest in both war and torture "is the process by which a made world of culture acquires the characteristics of 'reality,' the process of perception that allows invented ideas, beliefs, and made objects to be accepted and entered into as though they had the same ontological status as the naturally given world" (125). We might add that the often spectacular, even theatrical quality of both torture and war underlines the connection to performativity.

19. Benjamin, "Critique," 286.

20. Derrida, "Force," 38.

21. Pierre Bourdieu, *Language and Symbolic Power*, trans. Gino Raymond and Matthew Adamson (Cambridge, Mass.: Harvard University Press, 1991), 122. This characterization of the rites of institution might be read as a commentary on Benjamin's otherwise enigmatic use of the terms "fate" and "mythic violence" in his "Critique of Violence." In his difficult essay on "The Economic Problem of Masochism," Freud links the "dark power of fate" to the series of symbolic and ethical mandates individuals are called upon to introject and naturalize, beginning with the demands structuring the oedipal pact. He suggests that masochism is one of the ways in which a subject comes to terms with the surplus of force or violence that compels—one might say *drives*—this labor of naturalization. Freud links this surplus to what he calls the *decomposition* of the drives. He furthermore suggests that this surplus of drive force is borne by the superego: "this super-ego is as much a representative of the id as of the external world. It came into being through the introjection into the ego of the first objects of the id's libidinal impulses—namely, the two parents. In this process the relation to those objects was desexualized. . . . Only in this way was it possible for the Oedipus complex to be surmounted. The super-ego retained essential features of the introjected persons—their strength, their severity, their inclination to supervise and to punish. . . . [I]t is easily conceivable that, thanks to the drive-decomposition which occurs along with this introduction into the ego [*durch die Triebentmischung, welche mit einer solchen Einführung ins Ich einhergeht*], the severity was increased. The super-ego—the conscience at work in the ego—may then become harsh, cruel and inexorable against the ego which is in its charge" (*The Standard Edition of the Complete Psychological Works of Sigmund Freud*, 24 vols., ed. and trans. James Strachey [London: Hogarth, 1953–74], 19:167; I have slightly modified the translation). Alluding to the work that no doubt forms a crucial point of reference for Benjamin's "Critique," Freud adds that "Kant's Categorical Imperative is thus the direct heir of the Oedipus complex" (167). Regarding this conception of the superego as the bearer of an ultimately unjustifiable call to order, see Žižek, *The Sublime Object of Ideology* (London: Verso, 1989), 37–38: " 'External' obedience to the Law is . . . not submission to external pressure, to so-called non-ideological 'brute force,' but obedience to the Command in so far as it is 'incomprehensible,' not understood; in so far as it retains a 'traumatic,' 'irrational' character: far from hiding its full authority, this traumatic, non-integrated character of the Law is *a positive condition of it*. This is the fundamental feature of the psychoanalytic concept of the *superego*: an injunction which is experienced as traumatic, 'senseless'—that is, which cannot be integrated into the symbolic universe of the subject. But for

the Law to function 'normally,' this traumatic fact that 'custom is the whole of equity for the sole reason that it is accepted'—the dependence of the Law on its process of enunciation . . . must be repressed into the unconscious, through the ideological, imaginary experience of the 'meaning' of the Law, of its foundation in Justice, Truth. . . ."

22. Bourdieu, *Language*, 123.

23. Ibid., 122. Bourdieu adds that it is "the function of all magical boundaries (whether the boundary between masculine and feminine, or between those selected and those rejected by the educational system) . . . to stop those who are inside, on the right side of the line, from leaving, demeaning or down-grading themselves" (122).

24. Franz Kafka, *The Trial*, trans. Willa Muir and Edwin Muir (New York: Schocken, 1984), 220.

25. Franz Kafka, "The Great Wall of China," trans. Willa Muir and Edwin Muir, in *The Complete Stories*, ed. Nahum N. Glatzer (New York: Schocken, 1971), 242.

26. Nietzsche was born in 1844, two years after Schreber. His own mental breakdown occurred in 1889, four years before Schreber's second illness; he died in 1900, the year Schreber finished the composition of his *Memoirs*. Max Nordau devotes an entire chapter to Nietzsche in *Degeneration*, arguing that his writings exhibit "a series of constantly reiterated delirious ideas, having their source in illusions of sense and diseased organic processes," and indeed compares his work with the manuscripts of the mentally ill which the psychiatrist must read "not for his pleasure, but that he may prescribe the confinement of the author in an asylum" (416, 417).

27. Friedrich Nietzsche, *On the Genealogy of Morals*, trans. Walter Kaufmann (New York: Vintage, 1969), 76.

28. Ibid. These reflections inform Carl Schmitt's theory of sovereignty which in turn exerted a powerful influence on Benjamin. On the Schmitt-Benjamin connection, see, for example, Sam Weber, "Taking Exception to Decision: Walter Benjamin and Carl Schmitt," *Diacritics* (Fall–Winter 1992): 5–18.

29. Nietzsche, *Genealogy*, 77–78. Nietzsche, of course, had a great deal to say about the body as a repository of cultural memory. Much of the second essay in the *Genealogy* addresses the often cruel mnemotechnics devised by man to insure that he would not forget his promises, contractual agreements, and social position.

30. Michael John, *Politics and the Law in Late Nineteenth-Century Germany: The Origins of the Civil Code* (Oxford: Clarendon Press, 1989), 86.

31. Ibid., 104. See also Konrad Zweigert and Hein Kötz, *Introduction to Comparative Law*, trans. Tony Weir (Oxford: Clarendon Press, 1987): "the draftsmen of the BGB [Bürgerliches Gesetzbuch or Civil Code] seem to have taken no notice of the great social change which was occuring in Germany during the final decades of the nineteenth century; commerce and industry were becoming much more important economically than farming, and urban populations were expanding rapidly, especially with industrial workers. Yet for the BGB the typical citizen is not the small artisan or the factory worker but rather the moneyed entrepreneur, the landed proprietor, and the official, people who can

be expected to have business experience and sound judgment, capable of succeeding in a bourgeois society with freedom of contract, freedom of establishment, and freedom of competition, and able to take steps to protect themselves from harm" (150).

32. It was above all this social antagonism that led, after Bismarck's resignation, to what Hans-Ulrich Wehler has referred to as a "permanent state crisis." See Hans-Ulrich Wehler, *Das Deutsche Kaiserreich: 1871–1918* (Göttingen: Vandenhoeck and Ruprecht, 1988), 63–72.

33. See, for example, Eve Kosofsky Sedgwick's use of Freud's essay for the analysis of what she refers to as the "paranoid Gothic," in her *Epistemology of the Closet* (Berkeley: University of California Press, 1990), 186–87.

CHAPTER ONE
FREUD, SCHREBER, AND THE PASSIONS
OF PSYCHOANALYSIS

1. Citations of Freud's work in English will be taken from *The Standard Edition of the Complete Psychological Works of Sigmund Freud*, 24 vols., ed and trans. James Strachey (London: Hogarth Press, 1953–74). References to this edition will be made parenthetically in the text (*SE* with volume and page). Citations of the German text of Freud's works will be taken from the *Studienausgabe*, 12 vols., ed. Alexander Mitscherlich et al. (Frankfurt: Fischer, 1982).

2. Cited in Peter Gay, *Freud: A Life for Our Time* (New York: Norton, 1988), 275, 274, 275. In his monumental study of the Schreber case, Zvi Lothane suggests that Freud had wanted Ferenczi to collaborate on the Schreber essay and that the latter politely refused when it became clear that Freud really wanted him to serve as a kind of personal secretary. See Zvi Lothane, *In Defense of Schreber: Soul Murder and Psychiatry* (Hillsdale, N.J.: Analytic Press, 1992), 362.

3. Gay, *Freud*, 279. Zvi Lothane suggests more radically that Freud's focus on homosexuality in his reading of Schreber was entirely a product of a transferential dynamic on Freud's part and without a counterpart in Schreber's life or text: "scientific formulations about paranoia aside, latent homosexuality played a role in Freud and in the relations among the pioneers [of psychoanalysis] themselves: it was both an overt and a covert current in the early days of the history of the psychoanalytic movement, when it was an exclusively male club and a mutual admiration—and interpretation—society. The earliest personal linkage between paranoia and homosexuality was made by Freud himself in relation to Fliess. . . . In addition, homosexual concerns repeatedly came up as countertransference in the psychotherapy of male patients. Thus, Freud's attribution of homosexuality to Schreber is, among other motives, a projection onto Schreber of his own sexual conflicts and emotions" (Lothane, *In Defense of Schreber*, 338–39).

4. Freud's witness is Sandor Ferenczi.

5. Freud notes in the first section of his essay that Schreber associates mental illness with disturbances in the domain of sexual function "as though he shared our prejudice" (*SE* 12:31). Even earlier, in the preface to his essay, Freud explicitly cites Schreber's justification of publishing what might appear to the reader

as indiscretions or even libelous speech about his first psychiatrist, Dr. Paul Flechsig, as a moral cover for his own publication of the case study: "He urges upon Dr. Flechsig . . . the same considerations that I am now urging upon him" (*SE* 12:10).

6. Freud's relationship with Fliess was, of course, in its own way overdetermined by a preoccupation with influence and originality with regard to theoretical insights about the nature of human sexuality. The correspondence between Freud and Fliess ended in a dispute over Fliess's claim that Freud had passed along his own unpublished theories on bisexuality to Otto Weininger (perhaps by way of Hermann Swoboda, a patient of Freud's and friend of Weininger), who then published them in his notorious volume *Sex and Character* in 1903. In his discussion of this affair, Gay defends Freud's forthrightness in matters of intellectual property: "Intellectual robbery is after all easily done, but, he [Freud] protested, he had always acknowledged the work of others, never appropriated anything that belonged to anyone else. This was not the best place or time for Freud to assert his innocence in the contentious arena of ideas competing for priority. But to forestall further disputes, he offered Fliess a look at the manuscript of his still-unfinished *Three Essays on the Theory of Sexuality*, so that Fliess might study the passages on bisexuality and have any offending ones revised. Freud even offered to postpone publishing the *Three Essays* until Fliess had brought out his own book. These were decent gestures, but Fliess chose not to take them up. . . . This was the end of the Freud-Fliess correspondence" (Gay, *Freud*, 155). For a brilliant reading of yet another chapter in Freud's intense preoccupation with questions of originality and influence, see Neil Hertz, "Freud and the Sandman," in his *The End of the Line: Essays on Psychoanalysis and the Sublime* (New York: Columbia University Press, 1985), 97–121.

7. Lothane has noted even more striking parallels between Schreber's delusional sexology and Freud's earlier *Project for a Scientific Psychology*. See Lothane, *In Defense of Schreber*, 366 n. 32.

8. My understanding of "influence anxiety" has been enriched not only through Harold Bloom's programmatic presentation of that notion in *The Anxiety of Influence: A Theory of Poetry* (London: Oxford University Press, 1973), but also through his extensions and elaborations of the concept in *Kabbalah and Criticism* (New York: Continuum, 1983) and *Ruin the Sacred Truths: Poetry and Belief from the Bible to the Present* (Cambridge, Mass.: Harvard University Press, 1987). The classic text in the psychoanalytic literature on influence anxiety and mental illness is, of course, Victor Tausk's famous essay on the influence machines of schizophrenics, "Über die Entstehung des 'Beeinflussungsapparates' in der Schizophrenie," first published in the *Internationale Zeitschrift für Ärztliche Psychoanalyse* 5 (1919): 1–33.

9. See C. G. Jung, *The Psychology of Dementia Praecox* (1907), in *The Psychogenesis of Mental Illness*, trans. R.F.C. Hull (Princeton: Princeton University Press, 1989).

10. In his postscript to the Schreber case in which Freud ventures on the Jungian terrain that would occupy him more centrally in *Totem and Taboo*, Freud refers in a footnote to another work of Jung's as well as an essay by

Sabina Spielrein, both of which deal to some extent with Schreber and both of which appeared, thanks to a "freundlicher Zufall," a "happy coincidence," as Freud put it, in the same issue of the *Jahrbuch für psychoanalytische und psychopathologische Forschungen* (3, no. 1 [1911]) as Freud's Schreber text.

11. In an earlier footnote, Freud anticipates this larger hermeneutic claim concerning the proper interpretation of footnotes and other such material: "It not infrequently happens in the *Denkwürdigkeiten* that an incidental note upon some piece of delusional theory gives us the desired indication of the genesis of the delusion and so of its meaning" (*SE* 12:22).

12. In a letter to Abraham, Freud even joked that "I have of course to plagiarise you very extensively in this paper" (cited in Lothane, *In Defense of Schreber*, 337).

13. Maeder, a close associate of Jung's, is known for his racialist interpretation of the break between the Viennese and Swiss schools, which he expressed in a letter to Ferenczi in 1913. Freud's advice to Ferenczi on how to respond to Maeder's insistence on fundamental differences between the Jewish and Aryan spirit is particularly interesting when seen against the background of Schreber's preoccupations with these very racial differences, a matter that Freud left unaddressed in his Schreber study: "Certainly there are great differences between the Jewish and the Aryan spirit. We can observe that every day. Hence there would be here and there differences in outlook on life and art. But there should not be such a thing as Aryan or Jewish science. Results in science must be identical, though the presentation of them may vary. If these differences mirror themselves in the apprehension of objective relationships in science there must be something wrong." Cited in Ernest Jones, *The Life and Work of Sigmund Freud*, ed. Lionel Trilling and Steven Marcus (New York: Basic Books, 1961), 325.

14. Lothane sees this lapse as part of a larger failure on Freud's part to integrate research that shifted the analytic focus from sexual etiologies to other dynamic factors such as rage, frustration, and contemporary conflicts. See Lothane, *In Defense of Schreber*, 341–42.

15. See Gay, *Freud*, 221–22. Jacques Le Rider turns Adler's phrase into a central organizing metaphor of his recent study of crises of gender, national, and ethnic identity in fin-de-siècle Austrian literature: *Modernity and Crises of Identity: Culture and Society in Fin-de-Siècle Vienna*, trans. Rosemary Morris (New York: Continuum, 1993). There Le Rider characterizes Schreber's *Memoirs* as a "disturbing parody of the literary presentations of depersonalization and mystic or narcissistic reconstruction of the deeper self," which he analyzes in the works of Hofmannsthal, Rilke, and Lou Andreas-Salomé (81). Friedrich Kittler reverses this relation of original and parody when he claims, for example, that Rilke's *Notebooks of Malte Laurids Brigge* might be profitably reexamined under the heading *Memoirs of My Simulations of Nervous Illness*. See Kittler, *Discourse Networks. 1800/1900*, trans. Michael Metteer and Chris Cullens (Stanford, Calif.: Stanford University Press, 1990), 329.

16. The existence of Jungian and Adlerian schools of psychoanalysis testifies to the success of these contestations. That these schools bear the name of their founders suggests the continued efficacy of the founding utterances. The

"truth" of the Jungian, Adlerian, or Freudian position continues, in other words, to be at least in part dependent on the force of the master's speech and the pupil's transferential relation to it.

17. What Pierre Bourdieu has argued apropos of the "political capital" of institutions applies, in other words, in an emphatic way to psychoanalysis. It is, he suggests, "a form of symbolic capital, *credit* founded on *credence* or belief and *recognition* or, more precisely, on the innumerable operations of credit by which agents confer on a person (or on an object) the very powers that they recognize in him (or it). This is the ambiguity of the *fides* . . . : an objective power which can be objectified in things (and in particular in everything that constitutes the symbolic nature of power—thrones, sceptres and crowns), it is the product of subjective acts of recognition and, in so far as it is credit and credibility, exists only in and through representation, in and through trust, belief and obedience. Symbolic power is a power which the person submitting to *grants* to the person who exercises it, a credit with which he credits him, a *fides*, and *auctoritas*, with which he entrusts him by placing his trust in him. It is a power which exists because the person who submits to it believes that it exists. *Credo*, says Benveniste, 'is *literally* "to place one's *kred*," that is "magical powers," in a person from whom one expects protection thanks to "believing" in him.' The *kred*, the credit, the charisma, that '*je ne sais quoi*' with which one keeps hold over those from whom one holds it, is this product of the *credo*, of belief, of obedience, which seems to produce the *credo*, the belief, the obedience" (*Language and Symbolic Power*, trans. Gino Raymond and Matthew Adamson [Cambridge, Mass.: Harvard University Press, 1991], 192).

18. Regarding the transferential mechanism that supports the symbolic authority of the "classical master," Žižek writes: "The transubstantiated body of the classical Master is an effect of the performative mechanism already described by la Boétie, Pascal and Marx: we, the subjects, think that we treat the king as a king because he is in himself a king, but in reality a king is a king because we treat him like one. And this fact that the charismatic power of a king is an effect of the symbolic ritual performed by his subjects must remain hidden: as subjects, we are necessarily victims of the illusion that the king is already in himself a king. That is why the classical Master must legitimize his rule with a reference to some non-social, external authority (God, nature, some mythical past event . . .)—as soon as the performative mechanism which gives him his charismatic authority is demasked, the Master loses his power" (*The Sublime Object of Ideology* [London: Verso, 1989], 146). Adam Phillips has offered a rather more straightforward account of the problematic—and exemplary—nature of psychoanalytic authority: "Psychoanalysis began . . . as a kind of virtuoso improvisation within the science of medicine; and free association—the heart of psychoanalytic treatment—is itself ritualized improvisation. But Freud was determined to keep psychoanalysis officially in the realm of scientific rigour, partly, I think, because improvisation is difficult to legitimate—and to sell—outside of a cult of genius. With the invention of psychoanalysis . . . Freud glimpsed a daunting prospect: a profession of improvisers." But precisely because of this problematic status of psychoanalytic knowledge and authority, Phillips adds that "psychoanalysis can be good at showing the ways in which

certain points of view become invested with authority" (*On Kissing, Tickling and Being Bored: Psychoanalytic Essays on the Unexamined Life* [London: Faber and Faber, 1993], xv, xvi).

19. Bourdieu, *Language*, 109.

20. "An *investiture* . . . consists of sanctioning and sanctifying a difference . . . by making it *known* and *recognized*; it consists of making it exist as a social difference, known and recognized as such by the agent invested and everyone else" (Ibid., 119).

21. That Lacan was, in the end, more aware than Freud of these parallels between Schreber's psychosis and problems internal to the rites of institution of psychoanalysis itself is indicated by a persistent emphasis in his work on the problem of investiture. In his seminar on the psychoses, noting the importance of Schreber's nomination/election as *Senatspräsident*, he writes: "But where the psychoses are concerned, things are different. It's not a question of the subject's relation to a link signified within existing signifying structures, but of his encounter *under elective conditions* with the signifier as such, which marks the onset of psychosis" (Jacques Lacan, *The Seminar of Jacques Lacan. Book III: The Psychoses, 1955–1956*, trans. Russell Grigg [New York: Norton, 1993], 320). We might compare this remark with a much later pronouncement of Lacan's apropos of the "magical" procedure instituted by the Lacanian School—*la passe*—marking the symbolic election of the analyst: "Now that I think about it, psychoanalysis is untransmittable. What a nuisance that each analyst is forced . . . to reinvent psychoanalysis. . . . I must say that in the 'pass' nothing attests to the subject's [that is, the candidate-analyst's] knowing how to cure a neurosis. I am still waiting for someone to enlighten me on this. I would really love to know, from someone who would testify in the 'pass,' that a subject . . . is capable of doing more than what I would call plain old chattering. . . . How does it happen that, through the workings of the signifier, there are people who can cure? Despite everything I may have said on the topic, I know nothing about it. It's a question of trickery [*truquage*]" (cited in Mikkel Borch-Jakobsen, *Lacan: The Absolute Master*, trans. Douglas Brick [Stanford, Calif.: Stanford University Press, 1991], 158).

22. These reports were submitted as documents to the courts adjudicating the question of Schreber's guardianship and confinement. Schreber included them as appendixes to his memoirs, adding the following note: "The comparison with the corresponding accounts in the Memoirs and in my grounds for appeal will show immediately that the reports contain some *factual* mistakes, inexactitudes and misconceptions. But I have no doubt that the reason lies to some extent in unreliable reports furnished by third persons (attendants, etc.)" (267).

23. In the German, the temporal structure of reinterpretation described by Freud takes on an added dimension. In the penultimate sentence of the quoted passage where we read "later on," we find, in the original, the word "nachträglich," which carries with it the association not only of "Nachtrag," meaning addendum, addition, or supplementary revision, but also of the verb "nachtragen," which means to bear a grudge against someone for a past injury.

24. This aspect of Freud's reading has, as might be expected, come under attack from a number of different quarters. Perhaps the most controversial aspect of Freud's claims thus far is his equation of feminization with emasculation, i.e., castration, an equation that forces Freud to marginalize those aspects of Schreber's feminine identification which do not accord with the sense of radical loss and mutilation one associates with castration. See, for example, Ida Macalpine and Richard A. Hunter's analysis of the case in the appendix to their translation of Schreber's *Memoirs* and, more recently, Lothane, *In Defense of Schreber*, as well as Jay Geller, "Freud v. Freud: Freud's Reading of Daniel Paul Schreber's *Denkwürdigkeiten eines Nervenkranken*," in *Reading Freud's Reading*, ed. Sander Gilman, Jutta Birmele, Jay Geller, and Valerie Greenberg (New York: New York University Press, 1994), 180–210.

25. For Schreber as for Otto Weininger, who was developing his notorious theories of sexuality, gender, and race more or less contemporaneously with Schreber, sexual pleasure that escapes genital localization is *by definition* feminine. Schreber notes his willingness to offer his body to medical examination "for ascertaining whether my assertion is correct, that my whole body is filled with nerves of voluptuousness from the top of my head to the soles of my feet, such as is the case only in the adult female body, whereas in the case of a man, as far as I know, nerves of voluptuousness are only found in and immediately around the sexual organs" (204). See also Otto Weininger, *Geschlecht und Charakter. Eine prinzipielle Untersuchung* (Munich: Matthes & Seitz, 1980).

26. "It is my duty to provide Him with it [enjoyment] in the form of highly developed soul-voluptuousness, as far as this is possible in the circumstances contrary to the Order of the World. If I can get a little sensuous pleasure in the process, I feel I am entitled to it as a small compensation for the excess of suffering and privation that has been mine for many years past" (209). The original German endows this surplus enjoyment with the status of refuse or waste product: "soweit dabei für mich etwas von sinnlichem Genusse *abfällt . . .*" (*Denkwürdigkeiten*, 194).

27. Schreber gives a brief list of examples of the birds' susceptibility to homophony: "It has already been said that the sounds need not be completely identical; a similarity suffices, as in any case the birds do not understand the *sense* of the words; therefore it matters little to them—in order to give some examples—whether one speaks of

'Santiago' or 'Cathargo'
'Chinesentum' or 'Jesum Christum'
'Abendroth' or 'Athemnoth'
'Ariman' or 'Ackermann'
'Briefbeschwerer' or 'Herr Prüfer schwört' " (168–69).

28. He notes, for example, that "in a carping mood people often compare them [young girls] to geese, ungallantly accuse them of having 'the brains of a bird' and declare that they can say nothing but phrases learnt by rote and they betray their lack of education by confusing foreign words that sound alike" (36).

29. Schreber writes that "To a large number of the other bird-souls I jokingly gave girls' names in order to distinguish them, because all of them can best be compared to little girls in their curiosity, their inclination to voluptuousness, etc. These girls' names were then taken up by God's rays and used for the respective bird-souls concerned" (171; cf. *SE* 12:36).

30. One will recall that in a later metapsychological study, Freud posits *moral masochism*, the analysis of which follows an account of *feminine masochism*, as one of the typical products of the drive-decomposition that normally accompanies the introduction into the ego of foreign matter, i.e., the symbolic and ethical mandates of parents and other social authorities (see "The Economic Problem of Masochism," *SE* 19:159–70). It is not out of the question that Schreber's experience of the talking birds was suggested to him by his knowledge, attested to at several points in the *Memoirs*, of Wagnerian opera. One will recall that in the third opera of the *Ring*, Siegfried, upon slaying Fafner, is able to understand the language of birds. We recall that after attaining his release from the Sonnenstein asylum, Schreber had the *Siegfried*-motif inscribed above the entrance to his new home in Dresden. A more noxious Wagnerian association, one to which we will return later, is the one the composer made in his essay on "Judaism in Music" between the meaningless repetitions of parrots and Jewish discourse.

31. Based on interviews with a descendant of the Jung family into which Schreber's sister Anna had married, Lothane reports that it might have been Carl Jung, Anna's husband, who was responsible for the deletion of the third chapter from the *Memoirs* and for the efforts to buy up and destroy the printed copies of the text. See Lothane, *In Defense of Schreber*, 26.

32. Lothane writes that Flechsig turned his discovery of myelination, made in 1872 while dissecting the brain of a five-week old boy named Martin Luther, "into the foundation of his research methodology and his entire neuroanatomical as well as psychiatric system. Flechsig was able to demonstrate that myelination of nerve fibers was a lawful and sequential process in the development of the nervous system of man, reflecting the maturation of various neural systems" (*In Defense of Schreber*, 203). Freud's neurological writings contain numerous references to Flechsig's work and in a letter to his bride, Martha, he even refers to Flechsig as his "competitor" (cf. ibid., 241).

33. Freud seems to want to turn this self-imposed methodological asceticism into a boast about his hermeneutic prowess when he brags that apart from some biographical information about Schreber passed on to him by the Dresden psychiatrist Dr. Arnold Georg Stegmann, "I have made use of no material in this paper that is not derived from the actual text of the *Denkwürdigkeiten*" (*SE* 12:46). Included in the material that Stegmann passed along was the October 1908 issue of *Der Freund der Schrebervereine* (Friend of the Schreber Associations), the offical organ of the Schreber Associations, which, as we shall see, Freud uses to piece together an ultimately positive appraisal of the role of Schreber's father in the life of his psychotic son.

34. In a certain sense, Freud begins his own case study with a kind of confession that is the mirror image of Schreber's accusation against Flechsig. Freud begins his opening remarks by noting that because he is not attached to a public

institution and because paranoia rarely offers the prospect of therapeutic success, it is, Freud admits, "only in exceptional circumstances . . . that I succeed in getting more than a superficial view of the structure of paranoia—when, for instance, the diagnosis . . . is uncertain enough to justify an attempt at influencing the patient, or when, in spite of an assured diagnosis, I yield to the entreaties of the patient's relatives and undertake to treat him for a time" (*SE* 12:9). It is, of course, uncertain whether this sort of "transgression" of the purely therapeutic mandate would count for Schreber as an instance of malpractice.

35. Žižek has described this correlation in terms of a Lacanian understanding of the superego: "It is this very exteriority which, according to Lacan, defines the status of the superego: the superego is a Law in so far as it is not integrated into the subject's symbolic universe, in so far as it functions as an incomprehensible, nonsensical, traumatic injunction . . . bearing witness to a kind of 'malevalent neutrality' directed towards the subject, indifferent to his empathies and fears. At this precise point, as the subject confronts the 'agency of the letter' in its original and radical *exteriority*, the signifier's nonsense at its purest, he encounter's the superego command 'Enjoy!' which addresses the most *intimate* kernel of his being" (*The Metastases of Enjoyment: Six Essays on Woman and Causality* [London: Verso, 1994], 20).

36. Freud's equation of the delusion of being transformed into a woman with male homosexuality is, of course, problematic and has been challenged by critical readers, most notably by the English translators of Schreber's *Memoirs*. See Ida Macalpine and Richard Hunter, "Translators' Analysis of the Case," in Daniel Paul Schreber, *Memoirs*, 369–411.

37. Freud uses the word "Geschwisterinzest" which could also signify an instance of homosexual incest.

38. In one sense, Freud is teasing out an ambiguity in Schreber's own language. Schreber's phrase for "communication with supernatural forces" (*Memoirs*, 68) is "Verkehr mit übersinnlichen Kräften." "Verkehr" could be translated as "commerce," "traffic," or "intercourse," and, given a certain literalizing tendency typical of psychotic disorders, "übersinnlich" might suggest not so much the dimension of the supersensible as an excess or surplus of the "sinnlich," of the sensuous and sensual. These ambiguities are familiar to anyone who has struggled with the translation and interpretation of the final lines of Kafka's short prose text, "The Judgment," in which a similarly overdetermined "Verkehr" figures in a crucial way.

39. Dr. Weber's report of December 9, 1899, cited by Freud, recalls Schreber's main symptoms during his stay in Flechsig's asylum. Weber notes that among the central delusions, Schreber "thought he was dead and rotten, suffering from the plague" (appendix to *Memoirs*, 267). One also recalls in this context Schreber's own characterization of the conspiracy against him: "in this way a plot was laid against me (perhaps March or April 1894), the purpose of which was to hand me over to another human being after my nervous illness had been recognized as, or assumed to be, incurable, in such a way that my soul was handed to him, but my body—transformed into a female body . . . was then left to that human being for sexual misuse and simply 'forsaken,' in other words left to rot" (*Memoirs*, 75).

40. One really begins to appreciate Freud's confusion upon reading his quite unexpected appeal to a biological contingency—the possibility that Schreber was experiencing the effects of male menopause—to explain the timing of the outburst of homosexual libido (cf. *SE* 12:46).

41. Bourdieu, *Language*, 105–6; my emphasis.

42. Apropos of this epiphany, Lacan notes that "Insults are very frequent in the divine partner's relations with Schreber, as in an erotic relationship that one initially refuses to take part in and resists. This is the other face, the counterpart, of the imaginary world. The annihilating insult is a culminating point, it is one of the peaks of the speech act. . . . Around this peak all the mountain chains of the verbal field are laid out . . . in a masterly perspective by Schreber. Everything that a linguist could imagine as decompositions of the function of language is encountered in what Schreber experiences, which he differentiates with a lightness of touch, in nuances that leave nothing to be desired as to their information" (*Seminar. Book III*, 100). Taking Lacan's reading as his point of departure, Philippe Despoix has noted not only the importance of insults in the Israelite God's relation to the prophets—as in, for example, Hos. 1:8—but also the fact that it was Max Weber who, in his *Sociology of Religion*, written in the years of great productivity following his own psychotic breakdown and recovery, underlined this feature of Old Testament rhetoric. See Despoix, "Buch und Wahn: Die sprachliche Struktur im 'Psychotischen' Diskurs—Schreber mit Lacan," in *Die Spur des Unbewußten in der Psychiatrie*, ed. Stefan Priebe, Martin Heinze, and Gerhard Danzer (Würzburg: Königshausen & Neumann, 1995), 45–69.

43. Lacan introduced the notion of the master signifier as *point de capiton* or "quilting point" in his seminar on the psychoses. There, perhaps playing on the crucial role in Schreber's *Memoirs* of the signifiers *Fürchtegott* and *gottesfürchtig*, Lacan writes apropos of Jehoiada's pronouncement, in Racine's *Athalie*, that the fear of God is his only fear: "The fear of God isn't a signifier that is found everywhere. Someone had to invent it and propose it to men, as the remedy for a world made up of manifold terrors, that they fear a being who is, after all, only able to exercise his cruelty through the evils that are there, multifariously present in human life. To have replaced these innumerable fears by the fear of a unique being who has no other means of manifesting his power than through what is feared behind these innumerable fears, is quite an accomplishment. . . . To invent a thing like this you have to be a poet or a prophet, and it's precisely insofar as this Jehoiada is one to some extent . . . that he can use as he does this major and primordial signifier. . . . This famous fear of God completes the sleight of hand that transforms, from one minute to the next, all fears into perfect courage. All fears . . . are exchanged for what is called the fear of God, which, however constraining it may be, is the opposite of fear. . . . The power of the signifier, the effectiveness of this word *fear*, has been to transform the *zeal* at the beginning . . . into the *faithfulness* of the end. The transmutation is of the order of the signifier as such. No accumulation, no superimposition, no summation of meanings, is sufficient to justify it. . . . The quilting point is the word *fear*. . . . Everything radiates out from and is organized around this signifier, similar to these little lines of force that an upholstery button forms on the sur-

face of material. It's the point of convergence that enables everything that happens in this discourse to be situated retroactively and prospectively" (*Seminar. Book III*, 266–68). See also Lacan's more condensed essay on Schreber, "On a Question Preliminary to Any Possible Treatment of Psychosis," in Lacan's *Écrits: A Selection*, trans. Alan Sheridan (New York: Norton, 1977), 179–225.

44. Michel de Certeau, "The Institution of Rot," in *Psychosis and Sexual Identity: Toward a Post-Analytic View of the Schreber Case*, ed. David Allison, Prado de Oliveira, Mark Roberts, and Allen Weiss (Albany: SUNY Press, 1988), 91–92.

45. Ibid., 92.

46. Ibid. As we have already noted, Friedrich Nietzsche, whose own breakdown occurred almost simultaneously with Schreber's, dedicated much of his life to the philosophical elaboration of precisely this insulting secret.

47. As Certeau puts it, the "goal of torture, in effect, is to produce acceptance of a State discourse, through the confession of putrescence. What the torturer in the end wants to extort from the victim he tortures is to reduce him to being no more than *that* [*ça*], rottenness, which is what the torturer himself is and knows that he is, but without avowing it. The victim must be the *voice* of the filth, everywhere denied, that everywhere supports the *representation* of the regime's 'omnipotence,' in other words, the 'glorious image' of themselves the regime provides for its adherents through its recognition of them. The victim must therefore assume the position of the subject upon whom the theater of identifying power is performed" (Ibid., 93). In this context, see once more Elaine Scarry's lucid reflections on torture and symbolic power in *The Body in Pain: The Making and Unmaking of the World* (New York: Oxford University Press, 1985). The ethical and political dimension of Scarry's project lies in her efforts to demonstrate "that it is part of the original and ongoing project of civilization to diminish the reliance on (and to find substitutes for) this process of substantiation, and that this project comes in the west to be associated with an increased pressure toward material culture, or material self-expression" (14).

48. One might note a further cluster of meanings evoked by the divine nomination *Luder*. Schreber may well have known that Martin Luther's family name had been "Luder" before he himself changed it to "Luther" in 1517, the year of his famous ninety-five theses. Before settling on "Luther," he also used a Hellenized form, "Eleutherius," meaning "one who is free." While early enemies of the Reformation made use, in their polemics, of the connotations of putrescence in the name *Luder*, Luther's supporters produced etymologies according to which his name signified "Herr" of the "Leute" ("the people's master") or was derived from the adjective *lauter*, meaning pure, undefiled, genuine. (For a comprehensive discussion of Luther's names, see Bernd Moeller and Karl Stackmann, "Luder—Luther—Eleutherius. Erwägungen zu Luthers Namen," *Nachrichten der Akademie der Wissenschaften in Göttingen. Philologisch-Historische Klasse* 11 [1981]: 171–203; I am grateful to Peter Schöttler for this reference and to Werner Hamacher for alerting me to the possible significance of Luther's names in the first place.) An unconscious identification with the great theological reformer, whose own change of name dotted the "i," so to speak, on his radical reshaping of the Christian subject's relation to religious and secular authority, might thus have been operative in Schreber's own expe-

rience of spiritual chosenness. In this context one will also recall the bizarre coincidence that the patient on whom Flechsig made some of his first neuroanatomical discoveries was a baby named Martin Luther, thereby offering another layer to the overdeterminations of Schreber's "wretched" nomination; to identify with Luther/Luder in this sense would mean to be the "privileged" object of Flechsig's direct and intrusive powers.

49. Cf. Žižek's perspicacious remarks on this experience of overproximity in Kafka's work in *Looking Awry: An Introduction to Jacques Lacan through Popular Culture* (Cambridge, Mass.: MIT Press, 1991), 146.

50. I am following here Sedgwick's discussion of homosexual panic in *Epistemology of the Closet* (Berkeley: University of California Press, 1990).

51. One might recall, in this context, Freud's remarks on the decomposition of drives that serves to amplify the force of the superego to the level of "moral masochism." Freud seems to suggest that the interest of Kant's formalist ethics for psychoanalysis is that the categorical imperative, too, offers a glimpse of this drive dimension purified of empirical, ideological contents ("The Economic Problem of Masochism," in *SE* 19:167).

52. Schreber's older brother Gustav, whose own story has yet to be told, committed suicide in 1877 shortly after his own appointment as appeals judge of the District Court in Bautzen.

53. On this tendency of paranoia to divide the persecutor into constituent "demons," see Angus Fletcher's psychoanalytically informed analysis of this tendency in allegorical works of fiction, *Allegory: The Theory of a Symbolic Mode* (Ithaca, N.Y.: Cornell University Press, 1964). Fletcher suggests that an "almost analytic purpose, pseudoscientific if not protoscientific, follows from the very idea of daemon itself. Coming from the term that means 'to divide,' *daemon* implies an endless series of divisions of all important aspects of the world into separate elements for study and control. The daemon of a man is his fate, his Moira, his fortune, his lot, whatever is specifically divided up and allotted to *him*. Through the working of destiny he is narrowed to the function represented by his daemon. It follows that if nature is a composite system all parts and aspects of which are daemonically controlled, and if man acts only within such a system, the allegorical agent—whose paradigm is daemonic man—is always a division of some larger power" (59–60).

54. The English translators of Schreber have retained the grammatical gender of *Sonne* in the English.

55. To return to the matter of Freud's preoccupation with priority and originality, we might note that in this postscript Freud has entered a domain already staked out by Jung whose own "dazzling" work in the study of the psychoses Freud set out to supersede in his own study of Schreber. Freud both acknowledges and denies Jung's priority in the direction of thought sketched out in the postscript: "This short postscript to my analysis of a paranoid patient may serve to show that Jung had excellent grounds for his assertion that the mythopoeic forces of mankind are not extinct, but that to this very day they give rise in the neuroses to the same psychological products as in the remotest past ages. I should like to take up a suggestion *that I myself made some time ago*, and add that the same holds good of the forces that construct religions" (*SE*

12:82; my emphasis). Freud's preoccupation with originality stands here in stark contrast with the *theme* of these reflections, namely rites of initiatory investiture that by definition *devalue* originality. In this context, see Jean-Joseph Goux's fine discussion of the problem of initiatory investiture in the discourse of philosophy and psychoanalysis, *Oedipus, Philosopher*, trans. Catherine Porter (Stanford, Calif.: Stanford University Press, 1993).

56. Many of these motifs are found in the work of another key figure from German cultural history whose struggle for a position of existential and social legitimacy pushed him to the edge of mental breakdown: Friedrich Hölderlin. Indeed, the breakdown is prefigured in the fragmentary poem that most directly and consistently deploys the metaphorics of ordeal discussed by Freud, "Wie wenn am Feiertage . . ." (As on a holiday . . .). The poem seems to collapse under the weight of uncertainty apropos of the mythic lineage it sets out to celebrate:

> . . . So once, the poets tell, when she desired to see
> The god in person, visible, did his lightning fall
> On Semele's house, and the divinely struck gave birth to
> The thunderstorm's fruit, to holy Bacchus.
>
> And hence it is that without danger now
> The sons of Earth drink heavenly fire.
> Yet, fellow poets, us it behoves to stand
> Bare-headed beneath God's thunderstorms,
> To grasp the Father's ray, no less, with our own two hands
> And, wrapping in song the heavenly gift,
> To offer it to the people.
> For if only we are pure in heart,
> Like children, and our hands are guiltless,
> The Father's ray, the pure, will not sear our hearts
> And, deeply convulsed, and sharing his sufferings
> Who is stronger than we are, yet in the far-flung down-rushing
> storms of
> The God, when he draws near, will the heart stand fast.
> But, oh, my shame! when of
>
> My shame!
>
> That I approached to see the Heavenly,
> And they themselves cast me down, deep down
> Below the living, into the dark cast down
> The false priest that I am, to sing,
> For those who have ears to hear, the warning song.
> There

In *Friedrich Hölderlin: "Hyperion" and Selected Poems*, ed. Eric L. Santner, trans. Michael Hamburger (New York: Continuum, 1990), 195–97). Although this poem was written some hundred years before Schreber's *Memoirs*, a certain "contemporaneity" of Hölderlin and Schreber is suggested, first, by the fact that Schreber dates the beginnings of the disturbance in the Order of the

World associated with the phenomenon of "soul murder" in the eighteenth century and, second, by the great renaissance of interest in Hölderlin in the first decades of the twentieth century. It might also be noted that the most fully developed psychoanalytic study of Hölderlin's life and writings, Jean Laplanche's *Hölderlin et la question du père* (Paris: Presses Universitaires de France, 1961), is grounded in Jacques Lacan's theoretical reflections apropos of the Schreber case.

57. Søren Kierkegaard, *Fear and Trembling*, ed. and trans. Howard V. Hong and Edna H. Hong (Princeton: Princeton University Press, 1983), 62; my emphasis.

58. The "presence" of Moritz Schreber is indicated not only by the family name whose quasi-autonomous power Schreber emphasizes, but also by the phrase "miraculous structure" which Schreber glosses in a footnote: "Again an expression which I did not invent. I had spoken—in the thought—or nerve-language . . . of *miraculous organization* whereupon the expression 'miraculous structure' was suggested to me from outside" (54). This phrase—*wundervoller Aufbau*—is, as William Niederland has pointed out, very likely an allusion to the title of one of Moritz Schreber's books: *Anthropos: Der Wunderbau des menschlichen Organismus* (see Niederland, *The Schreber Case: Psychoanalytic Profile of a Paranoid Personality* [Hillsdale, N.J.: Analytic Press, 1984], 99).

59. *Studienausgabe*, 7:182.

60. See once more Lacan's introduction of the concept of the master signifier as "quilting point" apropos of the notion of "fear of God" in Racine's *Athalie* in his *Seminar. Book III.*

61. In his analysis of symbolic power, Bourdieu provides an interesting example of a crisis of liturgical discourse and authority which suggests how a state of emergency of symbolic power can manifest itself as sexual transgression (his example is interesting in part because of its seeming triviality at a historical moment when news of sexual transgressions on the part of priests has become a staple of the media). "For ritual to function and operate," Bourdieu argues, "it must first of all present itself and be perceived as legitimate, with stereotyped symbols serving precisely to show that the agent does not act in his own name and on his own authority, but in his capacity as a delegate." Bourdieu cites an anonymous text attesting to a breach of this law of delegation: " 'Two years ago an old lady who was a neighbor of mine lay dying, and asked me to fetch the priest. He arrived but without being able to give communion, and, after administering the last rites, kissed her. If, in my last moments on earth, I ask for a priest, it isn't so that he can kiss me, but so that he can bring me what I need to make the journey to eternity. That kiss was an act of paternalism and not of the sacred Ministry.' " Bourdieu summarizes the larger implications of such a transgression in terms which resonate strongly with the Schreber material: "The crisis over the liturgy points to the crisis in the priesthood . . . which itself points to a general crisis of religious belief. It reveals, through a kind of quasi-experimental dismantling, the 'conditions of felicity' which allow a set of agents engaged in a rite to accomplish it *felicitously*; it also shows retrospectively that this objective and subjective felicity is based on a total lack of awareness of these conditions, a lack of awareness which, in

so far as it defines the doxic relation to social rituals, constitutes the most indispensable condition for their effective accomplishment. The performative magic of ritual functions fully only as long as the religious official who is responsible for carrying it out in the name of the group acts as a kind of *medium* between the group and itself: it is the group which, through its intermediary, exercises on itself the magical efficacy contained in the performative utterance" (*Language*, 115–16).

62. Schreber's paternal great grandfather was named Daniel *Gottfried* Schreber, and was a jurist and economics professor; his grandfather, a lawyer, was named Johann *Gotthilf* Daniel Schreber. It was doubtlessly important to Daniel Paul Schreber that he lacked a reference to God in his middle name.

63. It was, of course, D. W. Winnicott who, with his theory of the intermediate area and transitional objects, did more than any other post-Freudian thinker to articulate the kinds of preparations and psychic labors a child must accomplish in order to "posit" the world, and the ways in which the responses of the child's immediate environment to these labors affect the ultimate success or failure of this process by which the child discovers/makes the world. See especially *Playing and Reality* (London: Tavistock, 1971).

64. Freud summarizes his transformational grammar of paranoia as follows: "Delusions of jealousy contradict the subject, delusions of persecution contradict the verb, and erotomania contradicts the object." A fourth possibility, that of contradicting the entire proposition, generates megalomania, the "psychological equivalent of the proposition: 'I love only myself'" (*SE* 12:64–65).

65. Sedgwick, *Epistemology*, 187.

66. Ibid., 186.

67. See, for example, Schreber, *Memoirs*, 49, 71, 85, 92. I will address these matters, especially Schreber's delusions concerning Catholics and Jews, in Chapter 3.

68. Recalling that Schreber had already alluded to the Wagnerian motif of a *Götterdämmerung* to characterize the end of the world, it is interesting to note that Freud reads Schreber's inner catastrophe as a variation of another Wagnerian scene of destruction and demise: "An 'end of the world' based upon other motives is to be found at the climax of the ecstasy of love (cf. Wagner's *Tristan and Isolde*); in this case it is not the ego but the single love-object which absorbs all the cathexes directed upon the external world" (*SE* 12:69).

69. Compare Freud's formulation concerning the regression characteristic of melancholia: "Melancholia . . . borrows some of its features from mourning, and the others from the process of regression from narcissistic object-choice to narcissism" (*SE* 14:250).

70. Robert Jay Lifton, "The Image of the 'End of the World': A Psychohistorical View," in *Visions of Apocalypse: End or Rebirth?*, ed. Saul Friedländer, Gerald Holton, Leo Marx, and Eugene Skolnikoff (New York: Holmes and Meier, 1985), 157.

71. As Lothane puts it, "it is on the very pages of the Schreber case, as already noted by Strachey, that a major theoretical revision is taking shape: the revolution called ego psychology is blowing in the wind. It was Freud himself who showed the first cracks in the edifice of the libido theory." And regarding

the crucial role played by pressures exerted by Jung in this revolution, Lothane notes that in Jung's 1913 monograph, *The Theory of Psychoanalysis*, Jung continued the "challenge to Freud's libido theory and his formulations of Schreber. In the second section of his 1912 work ["Wandlungen und Symbole der Libido"], Jung had quoted an entire passage from the section 'The Mechanism of Paranoia' in Freud's essay on Schreber, to argue that Freud had himself broadened the concept of libido to mean interest in general . . . a harbinger of ego psychology" (*In Defense of Schreber*, 339, 346).

72. Lifton, "The Image of 'The End of the World,'" 163.

73. Žižek has compared Schreber's theology with that of Alfred Hitchcock. Apropos of the use of a "God's-view" perspective in *Psycho*, Žižek writes that "Hitchcock's explanation according to which the function of 'God's view' was to keep us, viewers, in ignorance . . . without arousing suspicion that the director is trying to hide something from us . . . imposes an unexpected yet unavoidable conclusion: if we are kept in ignorance by assuming God's view, then *a certain radical ignorance must pertain to the status of God Himself*, who clearly comes to epitomize a blind run of the symbolic machine. Hitchcock's God goes His own way, indifferent to our petty human affairs—-more precisely, He is *totally unable to understand us, living humans*, since His realm is that of the dead (i.e., since symbol is the murder of thing). On that account, he is like God from the memoirs of Daniel Paul Schreber." Žižek goes on to define Schreber's Order of the World as "the symbolic order which mortifies the living body and evacuates from it the substance of Enjoyment. That is to say, God as Name-of-the-Father, reduced to a figure of symbolic authority, is 'dead' (also) in the sense that *He does not know anything about enjoyment*, about life-substance: the symbolic order (the big Other) and enjoyment are radically incompatible" ("'In His Bold Gaze My Ruin Is Writ Large,'" in *Everything You Always Wanted to Know about Lacan But Were Afraid to Ask Hitchcock*, ed. Slavoj Žižek, [London: Verso, 1992], 250).

74. Melanie Klein's remarks on the Schreber case also focus on the role of splitting in the *Memoirs*. See the appendix to "Notes on Some Schizoid Mechanisms," in *The Selected Melanie Klein*, ed. Juliet Mitchell (New York: Free Press, 1986), 198–200. In contrast to Klein, I am suggesting that it is the father figure that splits.

CHAPTER TWO
THE FATHER WHO KNEW TOO MUCH

1. For a complete bibliography of Moritz Schreber's works addressing questions of orthopedics, pediatrics, physical education, and the importance of body culture for the health of the nation, see Zvi Lothane, *In Defense of Schreber: Soul Murder and Psychiatry* (Hillsdale, N.J.: Analytic Press, 1992), 513–15.

2. William Niederland, *The Schreber Case: Psychoanalytic Profile of a Paranoid Personality* (Hillsdale, N.J. Analytic Press, 1984), xvi; my emphasis.

3. Ibid., 72, 82, 77–78, 94, 99. Niederland reserves special scorn for Mortiz Schreber's ostensible participation in the campaign against masturbation, which became so virulent in the nineteenth century: "To the analytically

trained observer, it is obvious that Dr. Schreber's energetic crusade was really directed against masturbation and other 'dangerous, hidden aberrations,' which in his thinking led to physical and mental 'softness' in children. Indeed, at the time, this belief caused virtually all physicians and parents to dread masturbatory practices in their offspring. An arsenal of anti-masturbatory devices was therefore invented and applied not only by Dr. Schreber in Germany but also by others in various countries. That Dr. Schreber's use of violent, sadistically tinged methods in this fight prevented at least one of his children from establishing an identity for himself, particularly a sexual identity, is recorded throughout the *Memoirs*" (57). Lothane has criticized Niederland on this point, noting that Moritz Schreber's writings say nothing about antimasturbatory devices (see Lothane, *In Defense of Schreber*, 190).

4. Niederland, *The Schreber Case*, 74, 82.

5. See Freud, in *SE* 17:219–56.

6. With regard to the structural relation between Hoffmann's Coppelius and Moritz Schreber, one will recall that in Hoffmann's story, Coppelius's actions toward Nathanael are characterized in part as a sort of fantastic "orthopedic" intervention. Once discovered by Nathanael, Coppelius yields to the father's entreaties to spare the boy's eyes. " 'Let the child keep his eyes and do his share of the world's weeping,' Coppelius shrieked with a shrill laugh, 'but now we must observe the mechanism of the hands and feet.' He thereupon seized me so violently that my joints cracked, unscrewed my hands and feet, then put them back, now this way, then another way" (*Tales of E. T. A. Hoffmann*, trans. Leonard J. Kent and Elizabeth C. Knight [Chicago: University of Chicago Press, 1969], 98).

7. Niederland mistakenly dates the trauma in 1858 or 1859. As C. H. Schildbach, Moritz Schreber's friend and associate, put it in a biographical supplement to the obituary he wrote in 1862: "The brain congestions that filled the last ten years of life with bitterness, were supposedly due to an external wound, caused by a heavy object that fell on his head, half a year prior to the beginning of the illness" (cited in Lothane, *In Defense of Schreber*, 127). Lothane notes that "Although it resulted in a curtailment of his professional, familial, and social activities, the illness ushered in the most prolific period of writing on the subject of education" (127).

8. "Der Vater . . . litt an Zwangsvorstellungen mit Mordtrieb" (cited in appendix to Schreber, *Denkwürdigkeiten*, 343; cf. Niederland, *The Schreber Case*, 57–58).

9. This is Lothane's translation of *Geständniss eines wahnsinnig Gewesenen* (Lothane cites the entire text in his translation). Lothane rejects Niederland's more obvious translation—"Confessions of One Who Had Been Insane"—because of the clinical facts of the case: "the patient in the story was neither diagnosed as psychotic nor committed to an asylum; the clinical picture was predominantly melancholia, with an admixture of tormenting idées fixes, that is, obsessive-compulsive behaviour in the form of ruminations and horrific temptations, not delusions. . . . The patient had insight concerning the absurdity of his ruminations but fluctuated in his capacity to oppose them or master them or extinguish them completely" (*In Defense of Schreber*, 139).

10. For an interesting critique of Niederland, see Han Israëls, *Schreber: Father and Son* (New York: International Universities Press, 1989). Israëls focuses on Niederland's considerable influence anxiety vis-à-vis Freud, which prevents Niederland from appreciating the extent of his own critical distance from Freud's purely intrapsychic reading of Schreber. Morton Schatzman's contribution to the debates on Moritz Schreber's role, *Soul Murder*, is largely a radicalization and popularization of Niederland's work. Schatzman makes the important observation that Moritz Schreber's program of child rearing was organized around techniques that would secure, through *repetition*, the transmutation of (parental) *heteronomy* into (the child's) *autonomy*. I will return to these techniques later in this chapter.

11. Lothane, *In Defense of Schreber*, 205. Lothane cites one of Flechsig's supporters as claiming: "The psychiatrists know nothing about the psyche—at least Flechsig knew something about the brain!" (ibid., 242). Among Flechsig's competitors for the job were August Forel, who would become the director of the Burghölzli clinic in Zürich, and Bernhard von Gudden, Forel's teacher in Munich. Von Gudden became famous by drowning with his patient, King Ludwig II of Bavaria, in Lake Starnberg in 1886. As noted earlier, Flechsig's important first discovery of the sequential process by which nerve fibers acquired a myelin sheath was made in 1872 during the dissection of the brain of a five-week old boy with the name Martin Luther. In his autobiography, *Meine myelogenetische Hirnlehre mit biographischer Einleitung* (Berlin: Springer, 1927), Flechsig endows this infant Luther with the status of a great reformer in the field of neuroscience. The surgical procedure used by Flechsig came to be referred to, by Charcot and others, as the "Coup de Flechsig."

12. Paul Emil Flechsig, *Die körperlichen Grundlagen der Geistesstörungen* (The physical bases of mental disturbances, inaugural lecture at the Leipzig University, March 4, 1882), cited in Martin Stingelin, "Die Seele als Funktion des Körpers. Zur Seelenpolitik der Leipziger Universitätspsychiatrie unter Paul Emil Flechsig," in *Diskursanalysen 2. Institution Universität*, ed. Friedrich A. Kittler, Manfred Schneider and Samuel Weber (Opladen: Westdeutscher Verlag, 1990), 105.

13. Paul Flechsig, *Gehirn und Seele* (Leipzig: Veit & Comp., 1896), 24. Here is Lothane's commentary on this passage: "In the association centers the impressions of the senses, the images of memory, and imagination were transformed into reason and understanding. Thus, a thoroughgoing and exact parallelism was postulated between the functioning of the brain and the functioning of the mind. The very term *association centers* harks back to the notion of association of ideas. The faculties of the psychologists and the metaphors of the metaphysicians have been neatly and concretely converted into myelinated fibers. . . . Correspondingly, disease in the sensory and association centers, that is, the functions of sense perception and judgment, leads to disorders of identity, and a variety of illusions, hallucinations, and delusions. . . . The point in all this is not, of course, to deny the fact that lesions in the brain cortex will cause disturbances in performance: this is a basic clinical fact; the correlation of structure and function is also a fact, although some localizations are more controversial than the effects of lesions. The point here is that Flechsig converted the facts

concerning lesions and localizations into an overriding philosophy that applied to *all* disorders of behavior and performance, including those he himself classified as functional, that is, disorders in which no focal, that is, specific, lesion could be demonstrated" (*In Defense of Schreber*, 216).

14. "Man is capable of entertaining the idea of the I, and in this he is *infinitely* above all the creatures upon the earth. . . . This I-ness . . . this faculty (that is, to think) is reason . . . the brain part to which the 'I'-idea is attached is *the one most developed in man* . . . one cannot imagine a more perfect agreement than that between introspective observation and biology. . . . I must say that of all my discoveries none has given me more joy than this apotheosis of our Kant . . . the frontal lobe is the seat of logic and the totality of all ideas" (cited in Lothane, *In Defense of Schreber*, 229).

15. Niederland, who otherwise placed his emphasis on the pathogenic role of Moritz Schreber, was the first to suggest this connection. See *The Schreber Case*, 104.

16. See, for example, Friedrich Kittler, *Discourse Networks. 1800/1900*, trans. Michael Metteer and Chris Cullens (Stanford, Calif.: Stanford University Press, 1990), especially 295–98. Kittler cites Flechsig's paper on the organic bases of mental illness (1882) in which the latter notes that the chemical and mechanical brain anomalies responsible for mental illness "can be detected in *the living* only through more or less composite inferences" (cited in Kittler, 295). Lothane has noted that in his admission policies, which we might call, with Schreber, his "Soul politics," Flechsig showed a special preference for sufferers from paresis, since such cases were most easily explained in terms of somatic anomalies. Once patients were admitted, Flechsig's therapeutic procedures included, as already noted, surgical interventions, but also a variety of less aggressive procedures: bed rest, tepid baths, moderate use of physical restraints, narcotic drugs. Apropos of the use of drugs, Lothane describes Flechsig's preferred treatment of epilepsy with opium and bromides as a kind of "chemical shock, which helped some patients but caused death in others." He concludes: "The striking fact in all this is that there is neither awareness nor interest on the part of Flechsig in anything remotely related to psychotherapy, that is, treatment of mental disorders by psychological means. In this regard Flechsig remained an organicist to the very end" (Lothane, *In Defense of Schreber*, 212–13).

17. Kittler, *Discourse Networks*, 296–97.

18. Ibid., 297 (I have changed the translation, which unfortunately negated the meaning of Kittler's sentence).

19. Following Kittler's lead, Martin Stingelin has put together an impressive concordance of passages from Schreber's *Memoirs* and Flechsig's monograph, "Brain and Soul," suggesting that Schreber's text could be read as kind of mad commentary on an already mad, death-driven science. See Stingelin, "Paul Emil Flechsig. Die Berechnung der menschlichen Seele," in *Wunderblock. Eine Geschichte der modernen Seele*, ed. J. Clair, C. Pichler, and W. Pichler (Vienna: Löcker, 1989), 297–307. For an intriguing novelistic treatment of the Flechsig-Schreber relation and the Schreber material more generally, see Roberto Calasso's *L'impuro folle* (Milan: Adelphi, 1974; the novel has been translated into French and German).

20. The German title of Kittler's study—*Aufschreibesysteme*—is an allusion to this Schreberism.

21. Kittler, *Discourse Networks*, 298. To support his contention that Schreber's "neurotheological" notation system is linked to new technologies of writing and communication, Kittler refers to a passage from one of the postscripts to the *Memoirs* in which Schreber compares the linguistic production of the divine rays with telephones: "It is presumably a phenomenon like telephoning; the filaments of rays spun out towards my head act like telephone wires; the weak sound . . . coming from an apparently vast distance is received *only by me* in the same way as telephonic communication can only be heard by a person who is on the telephone" (229). In this context, one should consider Avital Ronell's work on the relations between technology, psychopathology, and philosophy in *The Telephone Book: Technology, Schizophrenia, Electric Speech* (Lincoln: University of Nebraska Press, 1989).

22. In the Schreber essay Freud admits, as he does in a number of other writings, that analytic interpretation continues to be hampered by the lack of a well-grounded theory of the drives or instincts: "we have nothing of the kind at our disposal." He adds that "We regard instinct as being the concept on the frontier-line between the somatic and the mental, and see in it the psychical representative of organic forces" (*SE* 12:74). Freud's major breakthrough apropos of the drives will come with the theorization of repetition compulsion, a phenomenon that quite clearly dominates Schreber's universe.

23. The novels and short prose texts of Robert Walser are largely populated by figures whose proper domain is this sublime subaltern realm, which no doubt accounts for their strong appeal to a writer like Kafka.

24. In chapter 18 of the *Memoirs*, Schreber offers several examples of the productive side of compulsive thinking, i.e., how this sort of mental torture has forced him to assume a philosophical frame of mind, to contemplate the reasons for things being what and how they are. The main example he offers returns us to Schreber's preoccupation with names and titles: "I meet a person I know by the name of Schneider. Seeing him the thought automatically arises 'This man's name is Schneider' or 'This is Mr. Schneider.' With it 'But why' or 'Why because' also resounds in my nerves. In ordinary human contact the answer would probably be: 'Why! What a silly question, the man's name is simply Schneider.' But my nerves were unable or almost unable to behave like this. Their peace is disturbed once the question is put why this man should be Mr. Schneider or why he is called Mr. Schneider. This very peculiar question 'why' occupies my nerves automatically—particularly if the question is repeated several times—until their thinking is diverted in another direction. My nerves perhaps answer first: Well, the man's name is Schneider because his father was also called Schneider. But this trivial answer does not really pacify my nerves. Another chain of thought starts about why giving names was introduced at all among people, its various forms among different peoples at different times, and the various circumstances . . . which gave rise to them. Thus an extremely simple observation under the pressure of compulsive thinking becomes the starting point of a very considerable mental task, usually not without bearing fruit" (180). The potential for despair in the face of such mental tasks calls to

mind Kant's famous formulation of the hopelessness generated by the antinomies of pure reason: the *"euthanasia* of reason." Schreber's example of tracing a lineage across generations in search of an unconditioned origin of the chain is also one of Kant's examples of a mathematical antinomy. See *The Critique of Pure Reason*, trans. Norman Kemp Smith (New York: St. Martin's Press, 1965), 452–53 [B541]). Schreber's reflections on Mr. Schneider might also have been inspired by an unconscious identification with Martin Luther, the possibility of which, mediated by the insulting nomination "Luder," was addressed earlier. In a *Tischgespräch* or table talk from 1539, Luther cites the case of a man named *Schneider* who changed his name to *Schnitter* (harvester or reaper) because he wanted his name to have agricultural connotations (cited in Bernd Moeller and Karl Stackmann, "Luder—Luther—Eleutherius. Erwägungen zu Luthers Namen," *Nachrichten der Akademie der Wissenschaften in Göttingen, Philologisch-Historische Klasse* 11 [1981]: 184–85). See, finally, Samuel Weber's Lacanian intepretation of this passage in his introductory essay on Schreber in the English edition of the *Memoirs*.

25. The following discussion of forensic psychiatry is indebted to Lothane's work. See *In Defense of Schreber*, especially chaps. 5 and 6.

26. Cited in ibid., 222–23.

27. Lothane discusses at length the case of Johann Andreas Rodig, a Leipzig shoemaker and contemporary of Schreber's who fought his incompetency ruling up to the very court in which Schreber had been a judge. In one of the two pamphelets Rodig published, *Without Rights in a Constitutional State: A Faithful Representation of the Legal Injustices and Errors by a Victim Thereof J.A.R. or How to Declare Someone Crazy Made Easy as ABC* (1897), he expressly thanks Flechsig for his empathic treatment: "Upon his return to Leipzig, Herr Professor Flechsig and Herr Dr. Teuscher continued to treat me for my nerves, and I have to thank these gentlemen for still having my wits with me" (cited in Lothane, *In Defense of Schreber*, 234).

28. Lothane suggests that Flechsig's initial diagnosis of Schreber—"sleeplessness"—might have been designed to protect his patient from the consequences of the stigmatization of the diagnosis "psychosis." Lothane offers a number of possible motivations for Flechsig's ultimate abandonment of Schreber including the rather sobering thought that a "patient who gets worse does not thereby endear himself to his doctor." Particularly traumatizing for Schreber must have been the alliance formed between his wife, Sabine, and Flechsig. As Lothane notes, "In Sabine, Flechsig had an ally with whom he could share his frustration over this difficult patient; moreover, as a patient in her own right, she proved herself to be responsive to Flechsig's therapeutic interventions, quite unlike the intractable husband." Lothane notes that Schreber had to some extent forced his wife's hand by denying her direct access to his salary while he was hospitalized. "Sabine was driven to consider her options, and among those options the determination of incompetency naturally loomed largest. The option would allow her to receive the funds she needed to maintain herself and the household without any further need for continuing negotiations with her difficult, manifestly ill husband, who was at that time finding fresh avenues for distancing himself and for violating the terms of their hitherto

shared sensibility. Necessarily, Sabine would have discussed the issue of incompetency with Flechsig, just as he would have discussed with her his plan to have Schreber transferred" (Lothane, *In Defense of Schreber*, 237–38). Sabine Schreber's request for a temporary incompetency ruling was granted in November 1894 after Schreber had already been transferred to Sonnenstein; a permanent incompetency ruling was issued the following year.

29. Lothane notes that Weber "made no original contribution to clinical psychiatry. However, as dean of the Saxon institutional psychiatrists, he achieved fame as a forensic expert whose opinion was frequently sought by the courts. His interests remained limited to psychiatric paradigms hardened into habit and dogma and to the interface between psychiatry and law. He also acted for the preservation of the power of the psychiatrist vis-à-vis other professionals, physicians and lawyers" (ibid., 271).

30. Cited in Schreber, *Memoirs*, 282–83. Schreber published the three reports submitted by Guido Weber to the County, District, and Supreme Courts, respectively, in the appendixes to the *Memoirs*.

31. Given the fact that Schreber had to struggle so long and so hard with his second psychiatrist, Guido Weber, one wonders why Weber never figures in any important way in the "plot" of the *Memoirs*. Lothane's speculations on this matter are persuasive: "It is . . . another striking fact that Schreber never accused Weber of being his persecutor, even as he never stopped railing at Flechsig. The paradox can be read of course as evidence for the fantastic nature of the charges against Flechsig, but it might be more illuminating to consider the difference in terms of the different relationships the two physicians established with Schreber. Confronting a frank, unequivocal adversary in the person of Weber, Schreber found a way to mobilize his resources and deal with the man both face to face and in the courts. But faced with Flechsig, who presented himself in the guise of medical rescuer and protector only to ultimately betray Schreber's interests, Schreber reacted quite differently" (*In Defense of Schreber*, 295–96).

32. Because of the rather striking affinities between Foucault's analyses of this will to knowledge and the rhetoric of Schreber's delusions, I will be quoting Foucault at some length. Indeed, Foucault's language is at times so thoroughly Schreberian that one is tempted to apply Freud's ironic statement at the conclusion of his study of Schreber to Foucault's work on institutions and power: "It remains for the future to decide whether there is more delusion in my theory than I should like to admit, or whether there is more truth in Schreber's delusion than other people are as yet prepared to believe" (*SE* 12:79).

33. Michel Foucault, *The History of Sexuality. Volume 1: An Introduction*, trans. Robert Hurley (New York: Vintage, 1990). Further references will be made parenthetically in the text.

34. Michel Foucault, *Discipline and Punish: The Birth of the Prison*, trans. Alan Sheridan (New York: Vintage, 1977), 194. Further references will be made parenthetically in the text.

35. Louis Sass has appropriated Foucault's notion of the panoptical regime to characterize Schreber's particular form of hyperconsciousness. He interprets Schreber's "rays of God" not as libidinal cathexes but rather as "symbolic rep-

resentations of aspects of Schreber's own consciousness, a consciousness both rent and joined by an inner panopticism. Whereas the nerves represent the part of the mind that is observed—self-as-object—the rays represent the part of the mind that *does* the observing—self-as-subject. Further, the God who lies behind the rays (for rays . . . are the nerves of God) corresponds to that invisible, potentially omniscient, only half-internalized Other who is the source and grounding of Schreber's particular kind of introversion" (*Madness and Modernism. Insanity in the Light of Modern Art, Literature, and Thought* [New York: Basic Books, 1992], 253–54). Sass has pursued his primarily phenomenological account of Schreber's delusions as a product of an internalized panopticism in his *The Paradoxes of Delusion: Wittgenstein, Schreber, and the Schizophrenic Mind* (Ithaca, N.Y.: Cornell University Press, 1994). Here the impasses of inner panopticism are reinterpreted through Wittgenstein's analysis of metaphysical solipsism.

36. One will recall that in 1878–79, while working for the Reichsjustizamt in Berlin, Schreber was involved in the early phases of the codification of German laws that resulted, in 1900, in the Bürgerliches Gesetzbuch or Civil Code of the empire. In the long and heated debates and controversies about codification, the National Liberal Party was among the staunchest promoters of a legal philosophy emphasizing the rights (of contract and property) of autonomous legal subjects.

37. "The body of the king, with its strange material and physical presence, with the force that he himself deploys or transmits to some few others, is at the opposite extreme of this new physics of power represented by panopticism; the domain of panopticism is, on the contrary, that whole lower region, that region of irregular bodies, with their details, their multiple movements, their heterogeneous forces, their spatial relations; what are required are mechanisms that analyse distributions, gaps, series, combinations, and which use instruments that render visible, record, differentiate and compare: a physics of a relational and multiple power, which has its maximum intensity not in the person of the king, but in the bodies that can be individualized by these relations" (*Discipline*, 208).

38. One need only recall Schreber's insistence that the cultivation of voluptuousness "has been forced on me through God having placed Himself into a relationship with me which is contrary to the Order of the World" (209).

39. Both Schreber and Foucault locate the beginnings of this agonistic history in the eighteenth century: "Particularly from the eighteenth century onward, Western societies created and deployed a new apparatus which was superimposed on the previous one, and which, without completely supplanting the latter, helped to reduce its importance. I am speaking of the *deployment of sexuality*: like the *deployment of alliance*, it connects up with the circuit of sexual partners, but in a completely different way. The two systems can be contrasted term by term. The deployment of alliance is built around a system of rules defining the permitted and the forbidden, the licit and the illicit, whereas the deployment of sexuality operates according to mobile, polymorphous, and contingent techniques of power. The deployment of alliance has as one of its chief objectives to reproduce the interplay of relations and maintain the law that governs them; the deployment of sexuality, on the other hand, engenders

a continual extension of areas and forms of control. For the first, what is pertinent is the link between partners and definite statutes; the second is concerned with the sensations of the body, the quality of pleasures, and the nature of impressions, however tenuous or imperceptible these may be. Lastly, if the deployment of alliance is firmly tied to the economy due to the role it can play in the transmission or circulation of wealth, the deployment of sexuality is linked to the economy through numerous and subtle relays, the main one of which, however, is the body—the body that produces and consumes. In a word, the deployment of alliance is attuned to a homeostasis of the social body, which it has the function of maintaining; whence its privileged link with the law; whence too the fact that the important phase for it is 'reproduction.' The deployment of sexuality has its reason for being, not in reproducing itsef, but in proliferating, innovating, annexing, creating, and penetrating bodies in an increasingly detailed way, and in controlling populations in an increasingly comprehensive way" (*History*, 106–7). One will recall that at the beginning of the second chapter of the *Memoirs*, Schreber writes that the "leading role in the genesis of this development [i.e., the rent in the miraculous structure of the world], the first beginnings of which go back perhaps as far as the eighteenth century, were played on the one hand by the names of Flechsig and Schreber (probably not specifying any individual members of these families), and on the other by the concept of *soul murder*" (54).

40. *Kallipädie oder Erziehung zur Schönheit* (Leipzig: Friedrich Fleischer, 1858). Further references will be made parenthetically in the text. Lothane translates the full title of the book as *Callipedia, or Education towards Beauty by Means of the Natural and Even Promotion of Normal Body Growth, Life-Sustaining Health and Spiritual Cultivation and in Particular through the Optimal Use of Special Educational Aids: For Parents, Educators, and Teachers.*

41. Lothane situates Moritz Schreber in a lineage of Kantian and post-Kantian ethics, "dietetics," and psychiatry whose key representatives include Christoph Wilhelm Hufeland, Philipp Carl Hartmann, and J.C.A. Heinroth. (See *In Defense of Schreber*, 147–64.) In his most successful book, *Medical Indoor Gymnastics*, Moritz Schreber cites Horace's famous dictum, *sapere aude!* (Dare to be wise) as the central commandment of his "ethical life-philosophy" (*Ärztliche Zimmergymnastik* [Leipzig: Friedrich Fleischer, 1899], 32). That dictum had, of course, already been appropriated by Kant in 1784 in his famous response to the question, "What Is Enlightenment?" published in the *Berlinische Monatsschrift*.

42. For Moritz Schreber, habituation, or more accurately, the gradual naturalization of "good" habits through regulated repetition, is the key to proper development in both physical and mental realms. His recommended procedure for the correction of a snub-nose—repeated manual manipulation—closely parallels his recommendations for more spiritual forms of "corrections" (see *Kallipädie*, 110).

43. At one point in the *Memoirs*, Schreber actually characterizes Flechsig's malevolent influence as a bulky mass that can't be metabolized: "about that time I had Professor Flechsig's soul and most probably his *whole* soul temporarily in my body. It was a fairly bulky ball or bundle which I can perhaps best

compare with a corresponding volume of wadding or cobweb, which had been thrown into my belly by way of miracle. . . . In view of its size it would in any case probably have been impossible to retain this soul in my belly, *to digest it so to speak*" (91–92; my emphasis).

44. As indicated earlier, the most famous literary example of such a literalization is the writing/punishing machine in Kafka's "In the Penal Colony."

45. Mikkel Borch-Jacobsen's essay on the "The Oedipus Problem in Freud and Lacan" (*Critical Inquiry* 20 [Winter 1994]: 267–82) echoes in many ways Foucault's critique of psychoanalysis. Borch-Jacobsen's language suggests that the modern dissolution of what Foucault refers to as "deployment of alliance" almost necessarily produces men like Schreber: "What I really want to do is recall what Lacan himself emphasized in *Family Complexes*; that is, the '*complex* kinship structures' that define modern societies are accompanied by a 'deficiency' and a 'narcissistic bastardization' of the paternal figure. So how is it possible to prevent the identification with the symbolic father-phallus from being confounded with the rivalrous and homosexualizing imaginary father-phallus? How is it possible to prevent that outcome *in fact*? For it does absolutely no good whatsoever to invoke the *rightful* difference between the two identifications, since that difference, far from being a fundamental, a priori structure of every society, turns out actually to be bound solely to the '*elementary* structures of kinship.' Our societies, on the other hand, are defined by a general crisis of symbolic identifications—'deficiency' of the paternal function, 'foreclosure of the name-of-the-father,' perpetual questioning of the symbolic Law and pact, confusion of lineage and general competition of generations, battle of the sexes, and loss of family landmarks. . . . Let us not be fooled by Lacan's invocation of the symbolic Law: What he described as an a priori law of human desire is nothing but a convenient hypothesis of the 'elementary structures of kinship' in Lévi-Strauss's sense, and it cannot be applied to modern societies, where it simply does not apply *as a law*. . . . How is it possible to separate good from bad oedipal identification if the law that guarantees that difference is slowly being eroded in our societies?" (282). It is in this context that Jürgen Habermas's efforts, begun in the 1970s, to flesh out paradigms of "post-conventional" moral education, to adjust Enlightenment paradigms of subject formation to the complex conditions of industrial and postindustrial societies, again become interesting. See, for example, the two chapters on "Identity" in *Zur Rekonstruktion des Historischen Materialismus* (Frankfurt: Surhkamp, 1976).

46. Foucault's critique of psychoanalysis's fixation on oedipal relations is, of course, unambivalently prefigured in Deleuze and Guattari's *Anti-Oedipus*, a work which makes some interesting use of Schreber as a resource of anti-oedipal productivity.

47. Kittler, *Discourse*, 301–2. What Kittler apparently did not know was that there may have been a more direct connection between Schreber's mimesis of the drive dimension of signification and the practices of the Zurich Dadaists. One of the first references to Schreber in the psychiatric literature appears in an essay by Otto Gross, "Über Bewusstseinszerfall" (On the disintegration of consciousness), published in 1904 (*Monatsschrift für Psychiatrie und Neurologie* 15,

no. 1: 45–51; I am grateful to Zvi Lothane for drawing my attention to this essay), the year, according to Ernest Jones, of Gross's first meeting with Freud. Gross, a remarkable figure in his own right and one whose life and thought exhibit certain parallels with those of Schreber, was a crucial mediator of psychoanalytic thought for the circle of artists, musicians, dancers, and writers who habituated the famous artists' colony in Ascona in the Tessine Alps, among them the Zurich Dadaists. Certainly one of the central preoccupations of members of this alternative community was the elaboration of a new physical culture, indeed a kind of *countercultural body* that could be viewed as an alternative to the body whose cultivation was the object of Moritz Schreber's life work. For a discussion of Gross, including interesting comparisons with the Schreber case, see Jacques Le Rider, *Modernity and Crises of Identity: Culture and Society in Fin-de-Siècle Vienna*, trans. Rosemary Morris (New York: Continuum, 1993). There Le Rider remarks, for example, that "Otto Gross's vision of the 'revolution of matriarchy' are strongly reminiscent of Schreber. In his last work, 'Three Studies of Mental Conflict,' Gross talks of the inner wealth of bisexuality in men and says that men should foster their latent homosexuality, rediscover and cultivate the buried feminine in themselves. We might say that Gross's theories are a 'ratiocinated' form of the message contained in the madness of Dr. Schreber" (137). See also Martin Green's study of the Ascona community, *The Mountain of Truth: The Counterculture Begins: Ascona, 1900–1920* (Hanover, N.H.: University Press of New England, 1986), as well as Peter Wollen's historical study of the countercultural body, "Tales of Total Art and Dreams of the Total Museum," in *Visual Display: Culture beyond Appearances*, ed. Peter Wollen and Lynne Cooke (Seattle: Bay Press, 1995), 155–77.

48. Compare Žižek's reading of a scene of mad mimesis from Terry Gilliam's film *Brazil*; the scene portrays a mode of defense nearly identical with Schreber's strategy of circumventing the torture of compulsive thinking: "Throughout the film, it seems that the idiotic, intrusive rhythm of 'Brazil' serves as a support for totalitarian enjoyment, i.e., that it condenses the fantasy frame of the 'crazy' totalitarian social order that the film depicts. But at the very end, when his resistance is apparently broken by the savage torture to which he has been subjected, the hero escapes his torturers by beginning to whistle 'Brazil!' Although functioning as a support for the totalitarian order, fantasy is then at the same time the leftover of the real that enables us to 'pull ourselves out,' to preserve a kind of distance from the socio-symbolic network. When we become crazed in our obsession with idiotic enjoyment, even totalitarian manipulation cannot reach us" (*Looking Awry: An Introduction to Jacques Lacan through Popular Culture* [Cambridge, Mass.: MIT Press, 1991], 128).

49. For a study of the surrealists' preoccupation with drive, repetition compulsion, and a phantasmatic femininity, see Hal Foster's *Compulsive Beauty* (Cambridge, Mass.: MIT Press, 1993). There Foster emphasizes that women were seen or used within the historical avant-gardes to figure not only anxieties about machines and mechanization but also dread pertaining to the socioeconomic forces of *commodification*. Both series of anxieties could obviously meet in the figure of the prostitute, who no doubt also belongs within the semantic field of the word *Luder*.

50. *Gender Trouble: Feminism and the Subversion of Identity* (New York: Routledge, 1990).

51. Butler's arguments are anticipated by Bourdieu's remarks on the rites of institution: "How is what I would call the 'magical' consecration of a difference achieved, and what are its technical effects? Does the fact of socially instituting, through an act of *constitution*, a pre-existing difference—like the one separating the sexes—have only symbolic effects, in the sense that we give to this term when we speak of the symbolic gift, in other words, no effects at all?" His answer to these questions is very much in the spirit of Butler's work: "There is a Latin expression that means 'you're teaching fish to swim.' That is exactly what the ritual of institution does. It says: this man is a man—implying that he is a real man, which is not always immediately obvious. . . . To institute, in this case, is to consecrate, that is, to sanction and sanctify a particular state of things. . . . An *investiture* (of a knight, Deputy, President of the Republic, etc.) consists of sanctioning and sanctifying a difference (pre-existent or not) by making it *known* and *recognized*; it consists of making it exist as a social difference" (Pierre Bourdieu, *Language and Symbolic Power*, trans. Gino Raymond and Matthew Adamson [Cambridge, Mass.: Harvard University Press, 1991], 119). Butler's important point is related to the one stressed by Derrida in his reading of Benjamin, namely that symbolic mandates, including those pertaining to gender identities, do not accomplish their performative magic once and for all. Rather they function as *mandates for being* that demand a *repetitive* labor of culturally coded performances.

52. Butler, *Gender Trouble*, 145.

53. *Bodies That Matter: On the Discursive Limits of "Sex"* (New York: Routledge, 1993), 9.

54. Ibid., 188.

55. November 1895 was no doubt an overdetermined period for Schreber. Moritz Schreber died at the age of fifty-three on November 10, 1861. Schreber turned fifty-three in July of 1895.

56. That Schreber experiences masculinity as an insupportable habitus or even as a kind of masquerade is underlined by other formulations. He notes, for example, that "a distinction between masculine and feminine with respect to articles of clothing (the 'armamentarium' [*Rüstzeug*] as it was called in the basic language) is almost self-evident; boots appeared to the souls an especial symbol characteristic of manliness. To the souls, 'to take off boots' meant much the same as unmanning" (142).

57. As noted earlier, Schreber's language reiterates his association of femininity and abjection, an association canonized, as it were, by the title *Luder*. The sensuous pleasure he receives as compensation is characterized, namely, as a bit of surplus enjoyment that "falls off"—*abfällt*—in the manner of a *waste product*.

58. Schreber's awareness of this lack is expressed in countless ways. He notes, for example, that God is subject to "states of anxiety" (196), which is connected to a certain helplessness on God's part. In the later stages of his illness, Schreber notes that "God appears in almost everything that happens to me ridiculous or even childish. I am consequently often forced in self-defence

to *mock God* with a loud voice" (238). According to Schreber's medical reports, he would mock God with pronouncements such as: "The sun is a whore!" and "God is a whore!" (cited by Franz Baumayer in appendix to *Denkwürdigkeiten*, 345). Finally, Schreber notes that one of the phrases in the basic language used to signify the crisis in the Order of the World was, "O damn, it is extremely hard to say that God allows himself to be f . . . .'" (159). Louise Kaplan has stressed that for Schreber the cultivation of feminine strivings by way of trans-vestitism—his "perverse strategy"—allows him to gain a minimal distance from a cruel and punishing superegoic agency: "A perversion is a strategy for placating God, lawgiving father, protecting mother, or conscience, that inner voice of authority that represents the power of the gods." She goes on to note the counterintuitive, paradoxical nature of the perverse strategy: "It is fairly easy to understand that a perversion provides a way to express all variety of forbidden and shameful desires and that it should have the power to bring relief to a tormented soul. What is much harder to appreciate is *that a perversion, as act that seems so directly to violate the laws of conscience, could also serve the function of appeasing, even pleasing, one's conscience*" (my emphasis). Her explana-tion of this paradox is that the pervert is ultimately working not for his own, but rather for another's enjoyment: "Judge Schreber figured out that his most sacred duty was to satisfy God's need for constant sexual enjoyment. If he could satisfy God in this way, he could rest assured that God would never abandon him or mutilate his body." The pervert's attempt to become the instru-ment of the other's enjoyment ultimately attests to the other's lack: "When he arrived at a state of feminine voluptuousness, Schreber could give to God every proof of *His* virility. . . . With madness, the almighty is inflicting on one's body and soul the full extent of his wrath. And the soul is constantly tormented with not being able to figure out what He wants. With perversion the person has found the ecstasy He desires" (Louise J. Kaplan, *Female Perversions: The Tempta-tions of Emma Bovary* [New York: Doubleday, 1991], 481–83). I would only add to these astute remarks that Schreber's perversion lacks the dimension of fetish-istic disavowal suggested by some of Kaplan's formulations.

59. For this reason I think that Canetti's reading of Schreber as the prototype of the totalitarian leader is deeply flawed.

CHAPTER THREE
SCHREBER'S JEWISH QUESTION

1. See Gordon A. Craig, *Germany: 1866–1945* (New York: Oxford University Press, 1978), 75.

2. Apropos of the chosenness of the Germans, Schreber had already noted in conjunction with his claim that God's "basic language" consisted of a "some-what antiquated but nevertheless powerful German" (50), that "the Germans were in modern times (possibly since the Reformation, perhaps ever since the migration of nations) *God's chosen people* whose language God preferred to use. In this sense God's chosen peoples in history—as the most moral at a given time—were in order the old Jews, the old Persians . . . the 'Greco-Romans' (perhaps in ancient Greece and Rome, perhaps also as the 'Franks' at

the time of the Crusades) and lastly the Germans" (50). In the context framed by these passages, an identification with Martin Luther/*Luder* certainly becomes more plausible.

3. Speaking of Treitschke's "superstitious abhorrence of Rome," Craig notes that the former "always saw the Church of Rome as a vampire draining the vital energies of *Deutschtum*" (Craig, *Germany*, 70–71).

4. The shift of focus from Jesuits to Jews, and in particular to the legendary figure of the Eternal or Wandering Jew, was perhaps in part mediated by the popularity of Eugène Sue's novel *Le juif errant* (1844–45) in which the Wandering Jew actually helps to uncover a Jesuit conspiracy. Han Israëls has noted that a play based on Sue's novel premiered in Leipzig in 1845.

5. William Niederland, *The Schreber Case: Psychoanalytic Profile of a Paranoid Personality* (Hillsdale, N.J.: Analytic Press, 1984), 88. In his effort to establish a parallel with Pasha, Niederland dates Moritz Schreber's head injury incorrectly.

6. Zvi Lothane, *In Defense of Schreber: Soul Murder and Psychiatry* (Hillsdale, N.J.: Analytic Press, 1992), 101, 235. Lothane notes that the Paasch case became important to the antipsychiatry movement of the late 1890s and that the case was cited as an example of psychiatric abuse in Reichstag debates on mental hygiene laws during the 1897 session.

7. Zvi Lothane, "In Defense of Schreber: Postscript 1993," unpublished paper. I am grateful to Zvi Lothane for making this paper available to me. There is, of course, a long history of Christian appropriations of Jewish mystical doctrine.

8. Ibid., 26.

9. Ibid., 25–26. In his book, Lothane notes the two other possible referents of this allusion. The first, L. O. Darkschewitsch, was a Russian pupil of Flechsig's who became a close friend of Freud's and even coauthored a paper with him in 1886. Another possible referent was the Polish-Jewish neurologist Albert Adamkiewicz who opposed Flechsig's theories of myelogenesis in scientific journals. See Lothane, *In Defense of Schreber*, 247.

10. Sander L. Gilman, *Freud, Race, and Gender* (Princeton: Princeton University Press, 1993). Further references will be made parenthetically in the text.

11. In Weininger's *Sex and Character*, Ariman figures as the evil principle opposed to true genius (the prerogative of Aryan males). See *Geschlecht und Charakter. Eine prinzipielle Untersuchung* (Munich: Matthes & Seitz, 1980), 236.

12. Although Schreber was, during his first stay at Flechsig's clinic, treated with potassium iodide, a drug prescribed for syphilis, there were, as Lothane notes, no traces of the disease found at Schreber's autopsy. Lothane's assessment of the role of syphilophobia in Schreber's mental life makes no mention of a Jewish dimension of this piece of Schreber's decaying universe. He notes, however, that Schreber's description of the plague affecting his nerves "does not apply to either leprosy or bubonic plauge, because central nervous system disease is not a classical manifestation of either disease. It does . . . apply to syphilis, especially the mental disorders of tertiary syphilis, presumably the dual disease of his older brother and many other prominent persons of that

period. . . . Schreber is undoubtedly alluding to syphilis, or lues, when he says, 'the inner table of my skull was lined with a different membrane in order to extinguish the memory of my own ego.' Luetic meningitis, inflammation of the membranes (meninges) of the brain and spinal cord was a common complication of syphilis, while swings of depression and elation, with delusions and hallucinations, were the common mental manifestations." Lothane notes that "Luetic meningitis was also the topic of Flechsig's (1870) doctoral dissertation" (*In Defense of Schreber*, 55).

13. See above all, Geller, "The Unmanning of the Wandering Jew," *American Imago* 49 (Summer 1992): 227–62; "Freud v. Freud: Freud's Readings of Daniel Paul Schreber's *Denkwürdigkeiten eines Nervenkranken*," in *Reading Freud's Reading*, ed. Sander Gilman, Jutta Birmele, Jay Geller and Valerie Greenberg (New York: New York University Press, 1994), 180–211.

14. Geller, "Unmanning," 230, 244.

15. Cited in ibid., 231. An important source for Geller's work is Jan Goldstein's "The Wandering Jew and the Problem of Psychiatric Anti-Semitism in Fin-de-Siècle France," *Journal of Contemporary History* 20 (1985): 521–51. See also Gilman, *Freud*, 117.

16. This short monograph has been published in English as "The Wandering Jew in the Clinic: A Study of Neurotic Pathology," in a collection of essays on the figure of the Wandering Jew in history, *The Wandering Jew: Essays in the Interpretation of a Christian Legend*, ed. Galit Hasan-Rokem and Alan Dundes (Bloomington: Indiana University Press, 1986), 190–94.

17. Cited in Meige, "The Wandering Jew," 191.

18. Ibid., 192, 194.

19. Jews were not the only group that had been associated with nervous illness. In *Degeneration* (1892; Lincoln: University of Nebraska Press, 1993), Max Nordau argued that it was the French who suffered from hysteria in disproportionate numbers. Nordau offers a variety of reasons: excessive loss of blood during the Napoleonic wars; the violent moral upheavals of the French Revolution; the loss to Germany in 1870. Prior to this defeat, Nordau writes, France "had, with a self-satisfaction which almost attained to megalomania, believed itself the first nation in the world; it now saw itself suddenly humiliated and crushed. All its convictions abruptly crumbled to pieces. Every single Frenchman suffered reverses of fortune, lost some members of his family, and felt himself personally robbed of his dearest conceptions, nay, even of his honor. . . . Thousands lost their reason. In Paris a veritable epidemic of mental diseases was observed. . . . And even those who did not at once succumb to mental derangement, suffered lasting injury to their nervous system. This explains why hysteria and neurasthenia are much more frequent in France, and appear under such a greater variety of forms, and why they can be studied far more closely in this country than anywhere else" (*Degeneration*, 42–43). As noted earlier, Nordau's more general argument apropos of the etiology of hysteria and degeneration concerned the mental fatigue caused by the dislocations associated with modernization, which included residence in urban centers, railroad travel, proliferation of print media, etc. For further variations of the national, gender, and cultural codings of nervous illness, see Tom Lutz,

American Nervousness, 1903: An Anecdotal History (Ithaca, N.Y.: Cornell University Press, 1991).

20. Panizza left a short-lived medical practice in the 1880s to devote himself to writing poetry, fiction, and drama. In 1895, he was sentenced to a year in prison for blasphemy for a play—*Das Liebeskonzil* (The council of love)—that linked the origins of syphilis, which he had contracted some fifteen years earlier, to God and Maria. Panizza lived in Paris and Zurich before returning to Bavaria because of increasingly severe mental illness including auditory hallucinations. He was institutionalized in 1905 in an asylum near Bayreuth where he lived until his death in 1921. See Jack Zipes's essay on Panizza accompanying his translation of "The Operated Jew" as well as of Mynona's (Salomo Friedlaender) literary response, "The Operated Goy," in *The Operated Jew: Two Tales of Anti-Semitism*, trans. Jack Zipes (New York: Routledge, 1991). Further references will be made parenthetically in the text. Gilman discusses Panizza in both *Freud, Race, and Gender* as well *The Case of Sigmund Freud: Medicine and Identity at the Fin de Siècle* (Baltimore: Johns Hopkins University Press, 1993).

21. Geller, "Unmanning," 240.

22. Pierre Bourdieu, *Language and Symbolic Power*, trans. Gino Raymond and Matthew Adamson (Cambridge, Mass.: Harvard University Press, 1991), 122.

23. Gilman, *Freud*, 167.

24. Daniel Boyarin, "Freud's Baby, Fliess's Maybe: Homophobia, Anti-Semitism, and the Invention of Oedipus," *GLQ* 2 (1995): 131. In this essay, Boyarin argues more generally that Freud's formulation of the so-called "positive" oedipal scenario for male children—the exemplary Oedipus on whose rock Schreber foundered—was essentially a product of Freud's panic in the face of a particularly toxic "discursive configuration imposed on him by three deeply intertwined cultural events: the racialization/gendering of anti-Semitism, the fin-de-siècle production of sexualities, including the 'homosexual,' and the sharp increase in contemporary Christian homophobic discourse" (129). Freud needed a normative and rigidly heterosexualizing Oedipus because contemporary anti-Semitic discourses had come to associate hysteria and homosexuality—two "tendencies" which Freud had, as it were, admitted to in his relationship with Fliess—with Jewishness. "These discourses," Boyarin continues, "produced a perfect and synergistic match between homophobia and anti-Semitism. By identifying himself as hysterical and as Fliess's *eromenos*, Freud had been putting himself in the very categories that the anti-Semitic discourse of the nineteenth century would put him in: feminized, pathic, queer—Jewish" (129). I agree with Boyarin's suggestion that the ultimate danger for Freud in both hysteria and homosexuality was that each condition positioned him in what was perceived, within his culture, as a *passive*, and thus *feminine*, attitude. Noting that even among homosexuals in Germany there was a tendency to ascribe effeminacy to Jewish homosexuals in particular, Boyarin writes that "it would not be entirely wrong to suggest that it was passivity and effeminacy that were more problematic at this period than homoeroticism itself—i.e. homophobia is, *at this time*, almost subsumed under misogyny, to which anti-Semitism bears then a strong family connection as well" (142). Finally, in his own reformulation of Gilman and Geller's central thesis about Schreber,

Boyarin writes that "for Freud, recognition of the positive attraction that fe-maleness and being transformed into a female held for Daniel Schreber would have involved the psychological necessity for him of facing again his own unre-solved desires for femaleness, which in his own culturally conditioned eyes was equivalent to homosexuality. Both of these, feminization and homosexual-ity, were 'Jewish diseases' that Freud was anxious to overcome" (136). As was the case for Gilman and Geller, one of the keys, for Boyarin, to the fantasy of the male Jew's feminization was his circumcision: "the topos of Jewish men as a sort of women is a venerable one going back at least to the thirteenth century in Europe, where it was ubiquitously maintained that Jewish men menstruate. . . . As the fourteenth-century Italian astrologer Cecco d'Ascoli writes: 'After the death of Christ all Jewish men, like women, suffer menstruation.' . . . The expla-nation of this myth is to be found in the consistent representation of Jews as female in European culture, largely because of their being circumcised, which was interpreted as feminizing"(130).

25. Panizza, "Operated Jew," 57.

26. "The word *Zion* [Hebrew *Tsiyyon*] is taken as a noun derived from the root *ts/y/n* [to be marked], and accordingly the Daughters of Tsiyyon are read as the circumcised men of Israel" (Daniel Boyarin, "'This We Know to Be the Carnal Israel': Circumcision and the Erotic Life of God and Israel," *Critical Inquiry* 18 [Spring 1992]: 495).

27. Ibid., 495, 496–97.

28. In his essay, "Freud and Beyond," in *Ruin the Sacred Truths: Poetry and Belief from the Bible to the Present* (Cambridge, Mass.: Harvard University Press, 1989), Harold Bloom analyzes the relation between divine word and embodi-ment under the sign of the "bodily ego": "The difficult concept of the bodily ego, in which an imaginary object is introjected as though it were real, is uncan-nily similar to the prophetic concept of the placing of the Law in our inward parts" (165). Boyarin's reading of rabbinic literature suggests that the bodily ego is first and foremost a feminine one.

29. Daniel Boyarin, "Jewish Masochism: Couvade, Castration, and Rabbis in Pain," *American Imago* 51 (Spring 1994) 3–36.

30. Ibid., 10.

31. "Two things that ought not to be combinable have conjoined in the figures of these rabbis; on the one hand a male subjectivity that refuses the dominant fiction, if you will, that refuses to be a representation of wholeness, coherence, and impenetrability; on the other, sexual and procreative compe-tence. These men have no phallus, but their penises remain intact. It is this structure that I am referring to as Jewish masochism" (ibid., 22). Boyarin's terms are indebted to Kaja Silverman's *Male Subjectivity at the Margins* (New York: Routledge, 1992). Silverman's book addresses a variety of literary and cinematic performances of masculinity that masochistically chasten the phallic ideal, which in her view is maintained by a phantasmatic equation of phallus and penis. Such an equation is, she suggests, tantamount to conflating the differential structure of language, with which every human subject must (mournfully) come to terms, with a particular form of kinship structure. Such a conflation allows men to disavow the psychic traumas imposed by the "Law

of Language": "It is imperative that we understand that when the Name-of-the-Father organizes the rules determining marriage, reproduction, lineality, abode, and inheritance, the Law of Kinship Structure exists in a contradictory relationship to the Law of Language. The Law of Language dictates universal castration, whereas our Law of Kinship Structure equates the father with the Law, and hence exempts him from it. Our dominant fiction effects an imaginary resolution of this contradiction by radically reconceiving what it means to be castrated. . . . Our dominant fiction calls upon the male subject to see himself, and the female subject to recognize and desire him, only through the mediation of images of an unimpaired masculinity. It urges both the male and the female subject, that is, to deny all knowledge of male castration by believing in the commensurability of penis and phallus, actual and symbolic father" (42). Silverman's book is energized by the perhaps utopian cultural project of a more equitable distribution of the burdens of the sociosymbolic condition. Such a redistribution of psychosemiotic labor "would require that we collectively acknowledge, at the deepest levels of our psyches, that our desires and our identity come to us from the outside, and that they are founded upon a void. It would involve, as Julia Kristeva suggests, interiorizing '*the founding separation of the socio-symbolic contract*'—introducing 'its cutting edge into the very interior of every identity.' Renegotiating our relation to the Law of Language would thus seem to hinge first and foremost upon the confrontation of the male subject with the defining conditions of all subjectivity, conditions which the female subject is obliged compulsively to reenact, but upon the denial of which traditional masculinity is predicated: lack, specularity, and alterity. It would seem to necessitate, in other words, dismantling the images and undoing the projections and disavowals through which phallic identification is enabled" (50–51). Much of the book addresses the ways in which traumatic events such as war periodically shatter male patterns of fetishistic disavowal and serve, as it were, to refeminize the conditions of male subject formation, to make it impossible for men to project, thanks to fantasy scenarios of phallic mastery and entitlement, the impasses of subjectivity onto the "other," female, Jewish, or otherwise: "By 'historical trauma' . . . I mean any historical event . . . which brings a large group of male subjects into such an intimate relation with lack that they are at least for the moment unable to sustain an imaginary relation with the phallus, and so withdraw their belief from the dominant fiction. Suddenly the latter is radically de-realized, and the social formation finds itself without a mechanism for achieving consensus" (55). Boyarin's thesis is, in essence, that Jewish masculinity has never deeply participated in this consensus (his ultimate political claim is that Zionism represents Judaism's attempt to break with its traditional distance from this "dominant fiction"). Here I should note that for Silverman, too, a key exemplar of what could be called a masculinity beyond phallus is Daniel Paul Schreber.

32. Howard Eilberg-Schwartz, *God's Phallus: And Other Problems for Men and Monotheism* (Boston: Beacon Press, 1994). Further references will be made parenthetically in the text.

33. Eve Kosofsky Sedgwick, *Epistemology of the Closet* (Berkeley: University of California Press, 1990), 187.

34. "[O]n a heterosexual model of desire, an intimate of a male God should be female, so Moses can only insert himself into this equation through his own partial feminization and the exclusion of women. A hint of these tensions is evident in the myth of the Sinai revelation, the first revelation to the children of Israel after their departure from Egypt. This is the first time the impurity of women is referred to in the Hebrew Bible, and this myth may be one of the oldest sources of Israelite religion to refer to women's impurity" (146). And as he notes elsewhere: "The insistence on female impurity excluded women from competition with men for divine affections. Women's impurity, in other words, arose in part from attempts to shore up men's access to the sacred. If the conventional theory explains women's cultic impurity as a result of her otherness from God, we can also see it as motivated in part by her natural complementarity to a male deity and her symbolic threat to men's place in the religious system. Women's otherness from God is precisely what made them his expected partners. They had to be excluded from the cult because they challenged the male connection with God" (142).

35. Weininger, for whom Kant's *Critique of Practical Reason* was the "most sublime book on earth," argues that women and Jews lack transcendental subjectivity, the moral dimension of personhood necessary for true religious faith and genuine ethical and political responsibility. He argues that Zionism is doomed to failure because the idea of the state is foreign to Jews (as it is to women): "The state as a rational enterprise is the totality of all ends, which can only be realized through a union of rational beings. It is, however, this Kantian rationality, this Spirit, which above all appears to be lacking in the Jew and the woman" (*Geschlecht*, 196, 411).

36. See, for example, Daniel Boyarin, "The Eye in the Torah: Ocular Desire in Midrashic Hermeneutic," *Critical Inquiry* 16 (Spring 1990): 532–50.

37. Daniel Boyarin, "Bisexuality, Psychoanalysis, Zionism: Or, the Ambivalence of the Jewish Phallus," forthcoming in *Queer Diasporas*, ed. Cindy Patton (Durham, N.C.: Duke University Press).

38. *SE* 13:xv. Though he never addresses the issues of gender and sexuality we have been discussing here, Yosef Yerushalmi's book, *Freud's Moses: Judaism Terminable and Interminable* (New Haven, Conn.: Yale Univerity Press, 1991), remains one of the best studies of Freud's relation to Judaism to date.

39. Jean Laplanche's gloss on the Jewish ethical imagination is quite interesting in the present context: "In the context of an extreme form of religion, namely the Judaic religion to which Levinas refers, God hands down the Law, and the Law does not have to be justified. Freud too raises the issue of the categorical aspect of moral imperatives by pointing out that the orders given by the super-ego are tyrannical and unjustifiable. Because of his mania for phylogenesis, Freud traces this arbitrariness back to the first two tenets of the Father of the Horde: he was himself invulnerable and his possession of women must not be challenged. . . . These are good grounds for looking very seriously into the notion that categorical imperative is born of the super-ego, and for dwelling on one specific aspect of it: categorical imperatives cannot be justified; they are certainly enigmatic the same way that other adult messages are enigmatic; but not only are they unjustified, it is possible that they are unjustifiable, or in other

words non-metabolizable. This means that they cannot be diluted, and cannot be replaced by anything else. They exist, and they are immutable and cannot be symbolized" (*New Foundations for Psychoanalysis*, trans. David Macey [Cambridge: Basil Blackwell, 1989], 138–39).

40. Walter Benjamin, "E.T.A. Hoffmann und Oskar Panizza," in *Gesammelte Schriften* ed. Rolf Tiedemann and Hermann Schweppenhäuser, vol. 5 (II/2) (Frankfurt: Suhrkamp, 1980), 643–44.

41. See my introduction.

42. *Tales of E.T.A. Hoffmann*, trans. Leonard J. Kent and Elizabeth C. Knight (Chicago: University of Chicago Press, 1969), 117 (I have changed the translation of *unheimlich* from "weird" to "uncanny").

43. Hoffmann, "The Sandman," 119, 120.

44. Cited in Freud, "The 'Uncanny,'" in *SE* 17:227.

45. As Freud puts it, "For it is possible to recognize the dominance in the unconscious mind of a 'compulsion to repeat' proceeding from the instinctual impulses and probably inherent in the very nature of the instincts—a compulsion powerful enough to overrule the pleasure principle, lending to certain aspects of the mind their daemonic character, and still very clearly expressed in the impulses of small children; a compulsion, too, which is responsible for a part of the course taken by the analyses of neurotic patients. All these considerations prepare us for the discovery *that whatever reminds us of this inner 'compulsion to repeat' is perceived as uncanny*" (*SE* 17:238; my emphasis). In his reading of "The Sandman," Freud downplays the formal dimension of repetition in favor of the return/repetition of a particular set of contents and images, namely those associated with castration.

46. That Nathanael's madness is triggered by his awareness that he suddenly occupies the place of Olympia is also indicated by the fact that Nathanael's limbs had previously been subjected to the twisting and tugging that he sees being performed on Olympia. Once pushed over the edge, Nathanael's speech becomes, at the level of form and content, dominated by repetition compulsion: "'Whirl, whirl whirl! Circle of fire! Circle of fire! Whirl round, circle of fire! Merrily, merrily! Aha, lovely wooden doll, whirl round!'" ("The Sandman," 120).

47. In this context, one might recall that Weininger, citing Wagner's own authority, suggests that of all Europeans the English have the most similarities to the Jews (see *Geschlecht*, 426).

48. One might compare this direct address with the narrator's address to the reader in "The Sandman." There, too, what is at stake is the impossibility of communicating in any direct or immediate fashion the ostensible contents of one's soul to another human being. The most penetrating reading of Hoffmann's story as well as of Freud's essay—including some very lucid remarks on Hoffmann's narrator—remains Neil Hertz's "Freud and the Sandman," in his *The End of the Line: Essays on Psychoanalysis and the Sublime* (New York: Columbia University Press, 1985), 97–121. In his reading of these texts, Hertz addresses some of the major preoccupations of my reading of Schreber: questions of priority and influence anxiety; relations between (rhetorical) performativity, symbolic authority, and drive. At the end of his essay, Hertz

suggests that Freud's obsession with originality indicates a deeper level of pre-occupation and distress: "Whatever anxiety Freud may be imagined to have felt about his own originality . . . may not be exactly illusory, but displaced. . . . [M]ore fundamental 'doubts' and 'uncertainties' . . . may be at work generating the anxiety that is then acted out in the register of literary priority. The specificity of that range of wishes and fears—the wish to be original, the fear of plagiarizing or of being plagiarized—would act to structure and render more manageable, in however melodramatic fashion, the more indeterminate affect associated with repetition, marking or coloring it, conferring 'visibility' on the forces of repetition and at the same time disguising the activity of those forces from the subject himself" (120).

49. I am grateful to Eric Patton who, in an inspiring seminar presentation, underlined the importance of these sentences.

50. Among the definitions of "abjection" offered by the Oxford English Dictionary are the condition or estate of one cast down; abasement, humiliation, degradation; rejection; that which is cast off or away; refuse, scum, dregs.

51. We should recall that Gregor, too, becomes the bearer of a wound that refuses to heal, the product of an apple thrown by his father.

52. Slavoj Žižek, *The Sublime Object of Ideology* (London: Verso, 1989), 76–77.

53. Stanley Corngold, "Introduction," in *The Metamorphosis by Franz Kafka*, trans. and ed. Stanley Corngold (New York: Bantam, 1986), xv. References to this edition of the story will be made parenthetically in the text.

54. I am arguing, in effect, that we may observe two orders of abjection at work in Kafka's story. Abjection of the first order refers to Gregor's history prior to his metamorphosis, i.e., to his status as a sacrificial object *within* the family structure, and is thus linked to the introjection of the family debt or guilt. Abjection of the second order, a turn of the screw of the first, is the state of the metamorphosis: it signals precisely a radical separation from that family structure and the assumption of a position outside the texture of fate. From the perspective of this new position, what was concealed by the life of self-sacrifice, i.e., by the first order of abjection, becomes visible: the lack of a consistent and dependable master from whom one could expect a determination of one's identity, whose gaze could guarantee one's recognition, even as *an object worthy of sacrifice* (the metamorphosis might thus be conceived as indicating a transition from obsessional neurosis to psychosis). From a structural point of view, Gregor's verminousness *is* the becoming-visible of this very lack and that is why he provokes attempts not so much to sacrifice him as to *destroy* him. What must be destroyed is the object in which the inconsistency of the "master's discourse"—and so of the sacrificial order itself—has become visible. The inconsistency of Gregor's own physical attributes, which makes it impossible to form a coherent image of the insect, is no doubt a crucial aspect of his monstrousness, i.e., what makes it possible for him to embody the dysfunction of the master and his institutions. Kafka converted this impossibility into a prohibition when he stipulated to his publisher, Kurt Wolff, that no illustration of the insect adorn the title page of the 1916 edition of the story.

55. Thus the office manager's negative evaluation of Gregor's performance as a salesman represents the lure of a consistent Other whose demands one can

still struggle to satisfy. The failure to meet those demands does not yet produce the extreme form of abjection which marks Gregor's new condition.

56. As Žižek has elsewhere argued, "Therein consists the constitutive, fundamental guilt attested to by the neurotic symptoms which pertain to the very being of what we call 'the modern man': the fact that, ultimately, there is no agency in the eyes of which he can be guilty weighs upon him as a redoubled guilt. The 'death of God'—another name for this retreat of fate—makes our guilt absolute (Slavoj Žižek, *Enjoy Your Symptom! Jacques Lacan in Hollywood and Out* [New York: Routledge, 1992], 167). Žižek summarizes these two levels of guilt and sacrifice in terms that help to elucidate the experience of Gregor Samsa: "The first level is the symbolic pact: the subject identifies the kernel of his being with a symbolic feature to which he is prepared to subordinate his entire life, for the sake of which he is prepared to sacrifice everything—in short, alienation in the symbolic mandate. The second level consists in sacrificing this sacrifice itself: in a most radical sense, we 'break the word,' we renounce the symbolic alliance which defines the very kernel of our being—the abyss, the void in which we find ourselves thereby, is what we call 'modern-age subjectivity'" (167).

57. Franz Kafka, *Tagebücher. 1910–1923* (Frankfurt: Fischer, 1990), 217, 215.

58. A possible source of knowledge about Schreber on Kafka's part was Otto Gross's essay, "Über Bewusstseinszerfall" (On the disintegration of consciousness), published in 1904 and which, as noted earlier, includes one of the first discussions of Schreber in the psychiatric literature. Kafka met Gross for the first time only in 1917, but he may have had some familiarity with his work prior to that. Kafka had studied criminology with Gross's father, Hans Gross, at the University of Prague; the latter's tyrannical treatment of his son would eventually become a cause célèbre in intellectual circles in Central Europe.

59. One will recall that in Sacher-Masoch's story, the protagonist, Severin, receives a new name once he enters into his contract with his dominatrix Wanda: *Gregor*. See Leopold von Sacher-Masoch, *Venus im Pelz und andere Erzählungen*, ed. Helmut Struzmann (Vienna: Edition Christian Brandstätter, 1985).

60. Gregor expresses his envy vis-à-vis his colleagues at work by noting that they get to live like "harem women" (4).

61. Freud's characterization of the language of young girls matches, word for word, Wagner's characterization of *Jewish* discourse as a kind of parrotlike chatter in his notorious essay, "Judaism in Music" (1850), which Freud surely knew and which was the source of many of Weininger's positions on the Jewish relation to music and language (see *Richard Wagner: Stories and Essays*, ed. C. Osborne [London: Peter Owen, 1973]). For a compelling reading of Kafka's last story, "Josephine the Singer, or the Mouse Volk," through the prism of these cultural associations, see Mark Anderson's *Kafka's Clothes: Ornament and Aestheticism in the Habsburg* Fin de Siècle (Oxford: Clarendon Press, 1992), 194–215.

62. The "redemptive" closure of story and family around the death and removal of Gregor is given a Christological coloration when the Samsas are first brought by the cleaning woman to Gregor's corpse: "'Well,' said Mr. Samsa,

'now we can thank God!' He crossed himself, and the three women followed his example" (55). This passage reads as a conversion scenario, as if with Gregor's self-nullification the Samsas can enter into a new covenant free of the obligations of the old.

63. For discussions of this displacement, see, once more, Eve Kosofsky Sedgwick's work, especially *Between Men: English Literature and Male Homosocial Desire* (New York: Columbia University Press, 1985), as well as Kendall Thomas, "Corpus Juris (Hetero)Sexualis. Doctrine, Discourse, and Desire in *Bowers v. Hardwick*," *GLQ* 1 (1993): 34.

64. This thesis might be compared with Leo Bersani's claim that "sexuality would not be originally an exchange of intensities between individuals, but rather a condition of broken negotiations with the world, a condition in which others merely set off the self-shattering mechanisms of masochistic *jouissance*" (*The Freudian Body: Psychoanalysis and Art* [New York: Columbia University Press, 1986], 41). What makes Schreber so interesting is that he stages the production of sexuality in a kind of slow motion, which allows us to perceive connections and lines of derivation normally invisible.

65. If Schreber's identity as *Luder* is sustained in part by an identification with Martin Luther/Luder, his fantasies of contamination by the forces of Catholicism indicate, perhaps, that the confessional boundaries are, at least for Schreber, porous. Given Schreber's preoccupation with issues of power and authority, might it be that his anxieties vis-à-vis Catholics were triggered not merely at the level of historically specific social and political conflicts of interest—between, say, Saxony's mostly Lutheran population and its Catholic royal family—but at the level of *political theology*, i.e., the theological dimension of political and social authority? One of the key conflicts in the Kulturkampf concerned the doctrine of papal infallibility issued by Pope Pius IX in 1870. Perhaps no other doctrine so explicitly, literally, and even cynically affirms the performative dimension—and vicious circle—of symbolic authority as this decree, which means, in effect, that the truth is the truth not because it can be proved by a sufficient accumulation of evidence, but rather because the person occupying the place of authority says it. The papal infallibility doctrine concentrates into a formula a radical speech act theory of symbolic authority according to which the force of enunciation of a speech act, produced, of course, by the one vested with the appropriate emblems of power, grounds its own propositional content. The papal infallibility doctrine might thus be understood as a cynical absolutization of the performative magic on which all symbolic authority is to some extent dependent, a performativity that, in other words, also "stains" the Lutheran break with Catholicism.

66. Weininger refers to the decalogue as the paradigmatic example of a heteronomous ethics. See *Geschlecht*, 420. Further references will be made parenthetically in the text.

67. A major part of Weininger's book is a critique of Ernst Mach's highly influential conception of the ego as a concentrated bundle of sense impressions. Weininger views Mach's "empiricist" approach to psychology, which he associates with impressionism in the arts, as a kind of soul murder, for it ignores the "center of apperception," the transcendental ego that was the centerpiece

of the Kantian revolution in epistemology, moral philosophy, and aesthetics. For Weininger, this revolution, forgotten in the Machian dissolution of the ego—in effect a return to the precritical position of Hume—implies a fundamental unity of logic and ethics, since both demand that the subject obey absolute laws in the name of a singular will to truth: "Logic and ethics . . . are fundamentally one and the same thing—duty to oneself. They celebrate their unity in truth as the highest value, which in the one case is opposed by error and in the other by lie; truth itself is however always singular. All ethics is only possible through the laws of logic, all logic is also ethical law" (207). Some of Weininger's formulations suggest that the ego-centering force found in Kant's critical-transcendental philosophy, which he opposes to the dispersive tendencies of Mach's psychology (and the decadent aesthetic practices he associates with it), is ultimately that of an implacable superego, a kind of ruthless judge in the court of the subject's thought processes: "The question is whether someone recognizes the logical axioms as criteria of the validity of his thinking, *as judge* over what he says. . . . A man feels guilty if he has neglected to provide grounds for a thought, whether he has expressed it or not, because he feels the obligation to follow the norms of logic which he has, for once and for all, posited as his law [*über sich gesetzt hat*]" (192). Or later: "It is, of course, possible for someone to maintain the external form of judgment without doing justice to its inner condition. This inner condition is the sincere recognition of the idea of truth as the highest judge over all statements, and the heartfelt desire to stand the test before this judge with every pronouncement one makes" (249). Weininger's claim is, ultimately, that women and Jews have no intimate relation to this *inner judge*, a relation which serves to endow the subject with an awesome sublimity and grandeur: "Man [*Der Mensch*] is alone in the universe, in eternal, horrible loneliness. . . . He has no goal outside himself, nothing else for which he lives—he has flown far beyond all will to be a slave, capacity to be a slave, need to be a slave: far below him all human community has disappeared, as has all social morality; he is alone, *alone*" (210). Weininger calls this, the subject's will to identify fully with the pure "ought" of the moral law, the cruel greatness [*das Grauenvoll-Große*] of his vocation and suggests that one see in this absolute subjection to and affirmation of the categorical imperative the *Dionysian* element of Kant's philosophy (211). For Weininger, those who, as it were, lack this capacity for Kantian-Dionysian loneliness, are ideal subjects of hypnosis, which he characterizes as an extreme case of *heteronomy*, of influence by another will at the level of phenomenal causation. Indeed, Weininger goes so far as to characterize hypnosis as an "experimental confirmation of Kantian ethics" (364).

68. Weininger constructs a myth to correspond to this "philosophical" perspective on sexual difference: "Perhaps during the formation of the human race, through a metaphysical, atemporal act, man kept the soul, that which is godlike in humans, for himself alone. . . . Because he feels guilty for having robbed her of a soul, man now atones for this injustice against woman through the sufferings of love, in and through which he tries to give the soul he stole back to woman, to endow her with a soul. For it is precisely before the beloved woman . . . that man is most weighed down by a guilty conscience. The hope-

lessness of such reparation efforts through which man tries to expiate his guilt could well explain why a happy love does not exist" (341). These views anticipate in remarkable ways Lacan's notorious pronouncements apropos of the "nonexistence" of woman and the impossibility of the sexual relationship. What both thinkers share, of course, is the view that gender and sexuality are discursive formations arising out of structural dilemmas and crises introduced into organic existence through the intervention of "the signifier." On the connections between Weininger and Lacan, cf. Žižek, *The Metastases of Enjoyment: Six Essays on Women and Causality* (London: Verso, 1994), as well as *Enjoy Your Symptom*.

69. Among the "evidence" Weininger cites is the claim that cleptomania is a primarily feminine pathology and the observation that even women who could afford to own their own books often make use of public libraries! This latter "fact" suggests to Weininger that women lack an intimate and profound relation to objects of value and importance.

70. Weininger's "Platonism" is apparent here. "Woman," "Man," "Jew," etc. are for Weininger ideal types indicating structures or modes of existence, ultimately particular subject positions one assumes vis-à-vis the demands of logic and ethics. From each of these positions, Weininger maintains, flow a number of dispositions with regard to aesthetics, erotic relations, politics, etc. According to Weininger, these "types" are unevenly distributed in empirical human beings. It is clear, however, that Weininger wants to anchor his Platonism in a kind of biologism such that the distribution of dispositions is, as it were, passed along in the blood. Real Jews are thus biologically destined to manifest the idea of the Jew even though a Christian Aryan might not be completely free of "Jewishness," meaning a congeries of attitudes and inclinations about morality, beauty, commerce, marriage, etc. (see, for example, *Geschlecht*, 406).

71. In light of these remarks, we might say that circumcision becomes an object of such intense fascination and revulsion not because it mutilates the organ of procreation, but rather because it is a site of jouissance in the sense I have been elaborating in these pages. Circumcision is a rite of initiatory investiture that establishes, through the performative magic of the bodily inscription, the child's symbolic identity. What would have appalled Weininger, of course, is that this ritual leaves the mark of heteronomy on the body, "stains" the body with the mark of the forced choice that can never be converted into pure autonomy.

72. About Kundry, Weininger writes: "above [Wagner's] Kundry, the most profound female figure in art, hangs unmistakably the shadow of Ahasver" (429). Wagner is also the thinker who, according to Weininger, has most thoroughly thought through the problem of Judaism (428–29). We might also note the historical irony apropos of Weininger's claim that not only *Parsifal* but also the "Pilgerchor" and "Romfahrt" of *Tannhäuser* would always remain completely foreign to Jewish ears (*Geschlecht*, 408). It is well known that regular visits to the Paris production of *Tannhäuser* formed the "aesthetic" backdrop to Theodor Herzl's composition of the crucial manifesto of Zionism, *Der Judenstaat*, and that Herzl used portions of the opera, including the "Pilgerchor," as part of the musical mise-en-scène of the second Zionist Congress.

73. Let me briefly summarize the most obvious examples of the Wagnerian "intertext" in the *Memoirs*. In his initial presentation of his cosmology, Schreber refers to *Tannhäuser* to characterize the state of "Blessedness" reserved for souls: "Richard Wagner . . . as if with some insight into these things, makes Tannhäuser say in the ecstasy of love: 'Alas your love overwhelms me: *perpetual enjoyment is only for Gods*, I as a mortal am subject to change.'" (52). Schreber returns to *Tannhäuser* later in the *Memoirs* to describe his feelings upon playing the piano for the first time after an extended period in which he was denied access to music (143). A further Wagnerian motif particularly important in *Tannhäuser*, that of the redemption of man through a woman's sacrifice, is found in the following passage regarding Schreber's wife: "I repeatedly had the nerves belonging to my wife's soul in my body or felt them approaching my body from outside. . . . These soul parts were filled with the devoted love which my wife has always shown me; they were the only souls who showed willingness to renounce their own further existence and find their end in my body, expressing it in the basic language as 'let me.'" To this Schreber appends the note: "This expression could be rendered grammatically complete in the following words: 'Let me—you rays that are trying to pull me back—do let me follow the power of attraction of my husband's nerves: I am prepared to dissolve in my husband's body'" (116). Schreber's language apropos of the rent in the miraculous structure of the world (54) suggests an allusion to the Norns's cry "Es riß!" in *Götterdämmerung*, an allusion confirmed several pages later by a direct reference to the title of Wagner's opera: "The power of attraction, this even to me unfathomable law, according to which rays and nerves mutually attract one another, harbours a kernel of danger for the realms of God; this forms perhaps the basis of the Germanic saga of the Twilight of the Gods" (59). Schreber's father-in-law, Heinrich Behr, was an opera singer and successful producer of Wagner's works.

INDEX

Daniel Paul Schreber will be referred to in the index as Schreber; his father will be referred to as Moritz Schreber. Page numbers in boldface type refer to illustrations.

About the Author

ERIC L. SANTNER is Professor of German at Princeton University. He is the author of *Stranded Objects: Mourning, Memory, and Film in Postwar Germany*.